MW01091920

*Posterity! You will never know, how
much it cost the present Generation,
to preserve your Freedom!
I hope you will make a good Use of it.*

JOHN ADAMS
APRIL 26, 1777

FREEDOM

THE ENDURING IMPORTANCE OF THE AMERICAN REVOLUTION

His Excellency Gen.l Washington

George Washington, commander in chief of the Continental Army and first president of the United States, dedicated much of his life to establishing the United States as an independent republic. The freedoms we enjoy rest on the public service and sacrifices of Washington and thousands of others. Charles Willson Peale engraved this portrait—the first published image of Washington drawn from life—in 1778 (The Society of the Cincinnati).

FREEDOM

THE ENDURING IMPORTANCE OF THE AMERICAN REVOLUTION

JACK D. WARREN, JR.

**THE AMERICAN REVOLUTION INSTITUTE
OF THE SOCIETY OF THE CINCINNATI**

Essex, Connecticut

An imprint of Globe Pequot, the trade division of
The Rowman & Littlefield Publishing Group, Inc.
4501 Forbes Blvd., Ste. 200
Lanham, MD 20706
www.rowman.com

Distributed by NATIONAL BOOK NETWORK

Copyright © 2023 by The American Revolution Institute of The Society of the Cincinnati, Inc.

All rights reserved. No part of this book may be reproduced in any form or by any electronic or mechanical means, including information storage and retrieval systems, without written permission from the publisher, except by a reviewer who may quote passages in a review.

British Library Cataloguing in Publication Information available

Library of Congress Cataloging-in-Publication Data

Names: Warren, Jack D., Jr., 1962– author.
Title: Freedom : the enduring importance of the American Revolution / Jack D. Warren, Jr.
Other titles: Enduring importance of the American Revolution
Description: Essex, Connecticut : Lyons Press, [2023] | Includes bibliographical references and index.
Identifiers: LCCN 2022046829 (print) | LCCN 2022046830 (ebook) | ISBN 9781493071708 (cloth) |
     ISBN 9781493071715 (epub)
Subjects: LCSH: United States—History—Revolution, 1775–1783. | United States—Politics and
     government—1775–1783. | United States—Politics and government—To 1775. | United States—
     History—Colonial period, ca. 1600–1775. | Great Britain—Colonies—America—Administration. |
     Liberty. | National characteristics, American.
Classification: LCC E208 .W27 2023 (print) | LCC E208 (ebook) | DDC 973.3—dc23/eng/20220928
LC record available at https://lccn.loc.gov/2022046829
LC ebook record available at https://lccn.loc.gov/2022046830

Printed in India

On the cover: In this detail from *Washington Crossing the Delaware* (1851) by Emanuel Leutze, Continental soldiers fight their way across an icy river to carry out a daring attack on the Hessians at Trenton. The American Revolution was sustained by men like these, who risked their lives—and gave their lives—so America could be free (Metropolitan Museum of Art).

Contents

CONTENTS

CONTENTS

CONTENTS

CONTENTS

Twenty-four-year-old William Henry Bruce of Charles County, Maryland, enlisted in the Maryland Continental Line in 1776 as a private and rose to captain by the end of Revolutionary War. "As he had been a brave soldier," the *Maryland Gazette* reported after his death in 1825, "so he became an excellent citizen . . . as husband and father he was affectionate and indulgent; as a neighbor, urbane and friendly; as a citizen, frank and patriotic, and as a man, strictly and sternly honest." America is free because young men like William Bruce risked their lives to make it free (The Society of the Cincinnati).

Prologue   Why Is America Free?

America is free because nearly 250 years ago brave people fought a war to establish the independence of the United States and create a system of government to protect the freedom of its citizens. This book tells the story of how Americans came to fight for their freedom, how they won their independence in the Revolutionary War, established a republican system of government, and became a united people, with a shared history and national identity. It is a story in which all Americans, whatever their background, can take pride. It is a great story, full of courageous men and women who risked their lives to create a new nation based on the idea that government should serve people and protect their freedom.

The story of the American Revolution begins in our colonial past, when freedom as we understand it was not yet imagined. The people of colonial British America lived in a society characterized by deep and pervasive inequalities. Women were subordinated to men, their talents stifled, their natural rights ignored, and their civil rights denied. Indentured servitude was common and enslavement was practiced throughout the colonies, as it was through much of the Atlantic world.

Some British Americans—men who published newspaper essays and pamphlets and left their papers for us to read—were proud to claim "the rights of Englishmen," not understanding the limited, tenuous, and fragile nature of those rights. They were subjects of a king, not citizens of a republic. The wealthy and privileged among them had few opportunities to participate in government. Women, the poor, and the enslaved had none at all. Colonial British Americans enjoyed few of the rights we take for granted, including freedom of expression and of religion. They lived in a world of grotesque injustice, darkness, and oppression.

The American Revolution laid the foundation of free society. It did not destroy all existing inequalities, but it opened new opportunities for millions of Americans, including unprecedented opportunities to participate in public life. The Revolution made the injustice of slavery a subject of national debate that did not end until slavery was extinguished. No sooner had the Revolutionaries declared that all men are created equal than women began to assert that same equality and to demand the same inalienable rights so proudly asserted as the rights of men. The Revolutionaries framed constitutions for their governments based on the idea of natural rights, which were defined and protected by constitutional law. They created a nation dedicated, not to the interests of kings and aristocrats, but to the interests of ordinary people. Nothing like it had ever existed.

The causes of the Revolution defy easy analysis. The Revolution was *shaped* by high principles and low ones, by imperial politics, dynastic rivalries, ambition, greed, personal loyalties, patriotism, demographic growth, social and economic changes, cultural developments, British stubbornness, and American anxieties. It was shaped by conflicting interests between Britain and America, between regions within America, between families, and between individuals. It was shaped by religion, ethnicity, and race, as well as by tensions between rich and poor. It was shaped, perhaps above all else, by the aspirations of ordinary people to make fulfilling lives for themselves and their families, to be secure in their possessions, safe in their homes, free to worship as they wished, and to improve their lives by taking advantage of opportunities that seemed to lie within their grasp. No one of these factors, nor any specific combination of them, can properly be said to have *caused* the Revolution. An event so vast is simply too complex to assign it neatly to particular causes.

Although we can never know the *causes* of the American Revolution with precision, we can see very clearly the most important *consequences* of the Revolution. They are simply too large and important to miss, and so clearly related to the Revolution that they cannot be traced to any other sequence of events. Every educated American should understand and appreciate them.

First, the American Revolution secured the **independence** of the United States from the dominion of Great Britain and separated it from the British Empire. While it is altogether possible that the thirteen colonies would have become independent during the nineteenth or twentieth century, as other British colonies did, the resulting nation would certainly have been very different than the one that emerged, independent, from the Revolutionary War. The United States was the first nation in modern times to achieve its independence in a national war of liberation and the first to explain its reasons and its aims in a declaration of independence, a model adopted by national liberation movements in dozens of countries over the last 250 years.

Second, the American Revolution established a **republic**, with a government dedicated to the interests of ordinary people rather than the interests of kings and aristocrats. The United States was the first large republic since ancient times and the first one to emerge from the revolutions that rocked the Atlantic world, from South America to Eastern Europe, through the middle of the nineteenth century. The American Revolution influenced, to varying degrees, all of the subsequent Atlantic revolutions, most of which led to the establishment of republican governments, though some of those republics did not endure. The American republic has endured, due in part to the resilience of the Federal Constitution, which was the product of more than a decade of debate about the fundamental principles of republican government. Today most of the world's nations are at least nominal republics, due in no small way to the success of the American republic.

Third, the American Revolution created American **national identity**, a sense of community based on shared history and culture, mutual experience, and belief in a common destiny. The Revolution drew together the thirteen colonies, each with its own history and individual identity, first in resistance to new imperial regulations and taxes, then in rebellion, and finally in a shared struggle for independence. Americans inevitably reduced the complex, chaotic and violent experiences of the Revolution into a narrative of national origins, a story with heroes and villains, of epic struggles and personal sacrifices. This narrative is not properly described as a national myth, because the characters and events in it, unlike the mythic figures and imaginary events celebrated by older cultures, were mostly real. Some of the deeds attributed to those characters were exaggerated and others were fabricated, usually to illustrate some very real quality for which the subject was admired and held up for emulation. The Revolutionaries themselves, mindful of their role as founders of the nation, helped create this common narrative as well as symbols to represent national ideals and aspirations.

American national identity has been expanded and enriched by the shared experiences of two centuries of national life, but those experiences were shaped by the legacy of the Revolution and are mostly incomprehensible without reference to the Revolution. The unprecedented movement of people, money, and information in the modern world has created a global marketplace of goods, services, and ideas that has diluted the hold of national identity on many people, but no global identity has yet emerged to replace it, nor does this seem likely to happen any time in the foreseeable future.

Fourth, the American Revolution committed the new nation to **ideals of liberty, equality, natural and civil rights, and responsible citizenship** and made them the basis of a new political order. None of these ideals was new or originated with Americans. They were all rooted in the philosophy of ancient Greece and Rome, and had been discussed, debated, and enlarged by creative political thinkers beginning with the Renaissance. The political writers and philosophers of the eighteenth-century Enlightenment disagreed about many things, but all of them imagined that a just political order would be based on these ideals. What those writers and philosophers imagined, the American Revolution created—a nation in which ideals of liberty, equality, natural and civil rights, and responsible citizenship are the basis of law and the foundation of a free society.

The Revolutionary generation did not complete the work of creating a truly free society, which requires overcoming layers of social injustice, exploitation and other forms of institutionalized oppression that have accumulated over many centuries, as well as eliminating the ignorance, bigotry, and greed that support them. One of the fundamental challenges of a political order based on principles of universal right is that it empowers ignorant, bigoted, callous, selfish, and greedy people in the same way it empowers the wise and virtuous. For this reason, political progress in free societies can be painfully, frustratingly slow, with periods of energetic change interspersed with periods of inaction or even retreat. The wisest of our Revolutionaries understood this, and anticipated that creating a truly free society would take many generations. The flaw lies not in our Revolutionary beginnings or our Revolutionary ideals, but in human nature. Perseverance alone is the answer.

Our independence, our republic, our national identity, and our commitment to the high ideals that form the basis of our public life are not simply the consequences of the Revolution, to be embalmed in our history books. They are living legacies of the Revolution, more important now, as we face the challenges of a world demanding change, than ever before. Without understanding them, we find our history incomprehensible, our present confused, and our future dark. Understanding them, we recognize our common origins, appreciate our present challenges, and can advocate successfully for the Revolutionary ideals that are the only foundation for the future happiness of the world.

Numerous as the people are in the
several old provinces, they cost you nothing
in forts, citadels, garrisons or armies,
to keep them in subjection. They were
governed by this country at the expence
only of a little pen, ink, and paper.
They were led by a thread.

BENJAMIN FRANKLIN
FEBRUARY 13, 1766

BRITISH AMERICA

Migrants fleeing poverty, religious refugees, indentured servants, transported convicts, enslaved Africans, and American Indians created a society in British America unlike any in the world (Yale Center for British Art).

Chapter 1 The People of British America

The story of the American Revolution begins in the sixteenth and seventeenth centuries, when the major powers of western Europe established overseas empires through much of the world. Dramatic improvements in sailing ships and advances in navigation made it possible for European vessels to reach ports many thousands of miles from home and return with goods to sell as well as gold and silver from distant lands. Spain, Portugal, Holland, France, and England each established settlements and trading outposts wherever their ships could sail. They became global powers. Overseas trade made them rich.

The English began building an overseas empire later than the others. They settled on islands in the Caribbean the other powers had overlooked and on the coast of North America, which attracted little interest from other imperial powers. Their first settlement on the North American mainland was on Roanoke Island, in the coastal waters of what became North Carolina. An initial effort to establish a colony there in 1585 failed and the colonists were evacuated. A second party, including men, women, and children, arrived in 1587. They occupied a small fort, built simple wooden houses, and cleared land to grow food. Their ship went back to England. When another ship arrived with supplies in 1590, the settlement was empty. The people had all left. To this day no one knows what happened to them.

The mysterious fate of the Roanoke settlers should not surprise us. Crossing the Atlantic Ocean in a sailing ship took two months or more. When the first settlers arrived, they found what looked to them like endless forests, interrupted here and there by broad rivers, wetlands, and little streams. When the ship that brought them departed the settlers were left in a strange land they did not understand, a very long way from home.

The English and the Indians

They were not alone. There were people living in North America, but they were unlike any people the English had ever seen. The English called them all Indians, though they belonged to many different tribes, spoke many Indian languages, and lived in different ways. The Eastern Woodland Indians the English encountered lived in small villages and spent their time in simple farming, gathering wild food, hunting wild game, and fishing. They had done so for many thousands of years and their way of life was well adapted to the natural world. They knew when and where to gather oysters and clams, when the fish were abundant and how to catch them, where to hunt for deer, and how to grow corn, beans, pumpkins, and other foods that were native to North America. They made their simple clothing from animal skins and their tools and weapons from wood, stone, shell, and bone.

The English were not sure what to make of these Indians. They had chiefs, who the English imagined were like their kings, though in truth the Indians were much more loosely organized than Europeans and their chiefs were not much like kings at all. Traditions, much more than the authority of any chief, governed Indian life.

This was only one of many ways the Indians were strange to the English who landed at Roanoke, and that was strange to the thousands of European migrants who came to America later. Indians, the English learned, had no written language and no written law. Their ideas about property and trade were very different than those of the English. Indians owned things and would give them to the English and take things from the English in trade, but the Indians had no traditional understanding of money—the idea that a thing or a service can have a value defined using numbers

Artist John White accompanied the Roanoke colonists and painted a series of watercolors of the Algonquian people they encountered. His paintings, including this one of the village of Pomeiooc, are the only visual record of the sophisticated people who met the first British migrants to North America (©The Trustees of the British Museum).

and that this value can be traded using something like gold or silver.

This idea was the basis of commerce, which was common to European people but was strange to the Indians. The Indians would give things they owned to get things they needed, but if they needed something else they might expect the English to give it to them without giving the English anything in trade. They might, if the English needed something, give it without taking anything in return. Buying and selling, in the way Europeans did it, was unknown among the Indians. The Indians engaged in trade, but in ways

Europeans did not understand.

Cultural traditions and not law or European ideas about ownership and buying and selling shaped the way Indians thought about the land they occupied. The Indians did not imagine land as something to trade. They occupied land, in many cases in regions their tribes had lived in for centuries. To the English as to other Europeans most of eastern North America looked like an unoccupied wilderness, but the land and water was essential to the Indians, whose way of life required a lot of both.

The English, like other Europeans, occupied the land in a completely different manner than the

Indians. They grew wheat or some other grain on farms devoted to little else, and they raised cows, pigs, sheep, chickens, and other domesticated animals for food. This way of living did not always work well. When the weather was bad or crops failed for some other reason, people in Europe sometimes starved. But when it did work well European agriculture produced more food per acre than the people could eat.

The extra food, or surplus, was stored or sold, and the money it generated supported a life that included all kinds of activities the Indians could not even imagine. The surplus supported craftsmen who made things out of metal, which the Eastern Woodland Indians could not make, and it supported people who made cloth, which the Indians could only make in very small amounts by much simpler methods. The way the English and other European people raised food made it possible for them to build towns and cities out of brick and stone, to use metal tools and to invent and make things like clocks, guns, sailing ships, and printing presses.

Eastern Woodland Indian farming produced much less food per acre, and the Indians did not generally raise animals for food. They relied on gathering and hunting the food they did not grow. To Europeans, the vast woods of eastern North America looked like empty land waiting to be cleared for farms. The same woods were essential to the Indian way of life.

Because they occupied land in different ways and used it very differently, and because as a result their cultures were so different, the European and the Indian ways of life could not coexist, at least not peacefully. The Indians naturally resisted the English occupation of the land they needed to live, and the English could never accept that what looked like unoccupied land was essential to Indians who rarely seemed to occupy it. Despite the fact that some on each side tried to get along and learn from the other, their natural attitude toward each other was one of deep distrust.

That distrust frequently led to violence and often to war, which added anger and hatred to the distrust each felt toward the other. Both sides made war in brutal ways. It was not enough for warriors to kill one another. The Indians and the Europeans took turns slaughtering the families and burning the homes of their enemies. As long as the two

sides remained in contact with one another, wars between them were common.

In between, in times of cautious, distrustful peace, the two sides traded with one another. The Indians, who were master hunters, traded the hides of beavers, deer, and other woodland animals. The Europeans traded cloth, metal tools, and guns, all of which the Indians wanted but could not make for themselves. The English learned from the Indians how to grow native plants like corn, beans, squash, and pumpkins. The Indians learned how to shoot guns and use European tools. Some even built houses like the Europeans and farmed in European ways. A few Indians adopted the Christian religion of the English. A few English migrants learned to live among the Indians, and there were occasional marriages among them. But these were unusual.

The normal state of relations between the Indians and the English was one of conflict. This conflict continued through the American Revolution and beyond. War and peace alternated for more than a hundred years after the Revolution, until the Indians were driven out of every place the Europeans and their descendants wanted to occupy.

Despite this tragic conflict, there was much about the Indians that the Europeans who migrated to North America admired. The English envied the easy way the Indians managed to live in what seemed like a wilderness. The Indians were often fearless. They lived simply and faced life with courage. They had, by English standards, very few things, but they did not seem to need more. They seemed to embody personal independence, an idea many of the European migrants cherished. In time, despite the frequent wars, the Indian became a symbol of America.

The Disorderly Empire

The best guess anyone has about the English settlers who disappeared from Roanoke Island is that they went to live with the Indians, and that they may have been adopted by the Indians and lived the rest of their lives with them. The English gave up the idea of settling there and did not return for many years.

A new group of English settlers arrived in America in 1607. They landed on the James River

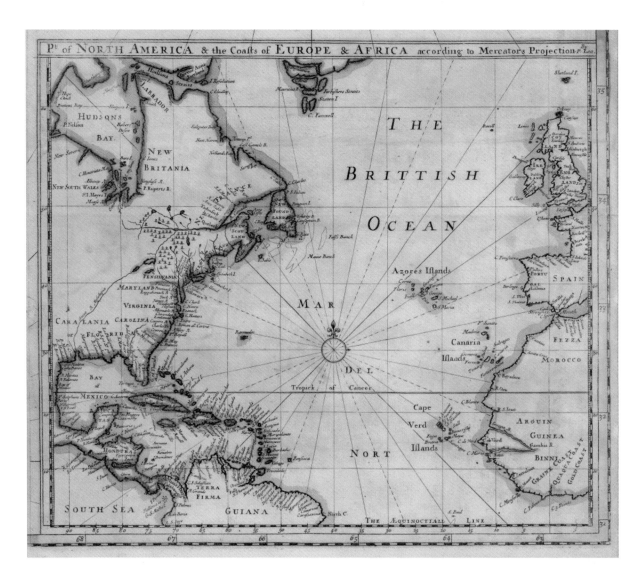

On this map published in London around 1695, the "Brittish Ocean" connects Britain and her American colonies. By the end of the seventeenth century, trade in colonial products, the sale of enslaved Africans, and the resale of colonial goods in Europe had become important sources of British wealth (Image courtesy of Barry Lawrence Ruderman Antique Maps, Inc.).

in what they called Virginia. Like the Roanoke settlers, they built a simple fort and small wooden houses. Conditions were hard. They had trouble growing enough food. Many died from illness. After a few years of uneasy peace the Indians in the region attacked their settlements in an effort to wipe them out. But their settlements survived and grew.

Virginia was the first enduring colony in England's overseas empire, which expanded slowly, over more than a hundred years, to include fourteen colonies spread along the Atlantic coast of North America from Nova Scotia to Georgia, in addition to several islands in the Caribbean, from the Bahamas in the north to Barbados, which is near the coast of South America. The English

also had trading posts on Hudson Bay in what is now Canada—though much of what we now call Canada was under the control of France—as well as trading posts in India, southeast Asia and west Africa, and isolated colonies in Bermuda and Honduras. From the early eighteenth century, when the once independent kingdoms of England and Scotland were unified as Great Britain, these far-flung possessions were known as the British Empire.

It was a disorderly empire, created without a plan. Virginia was established by a private company, the Virginia Company of London, that received a charter from the king. It began as a business venture, aiming at profit for the company's investors. Neighboring Maryland was established by an English aristocrat, Lord Baltimore, who secured it as a grant from the king and tried to manage the colony like a vast private estate. The Carolinas were granted to a group of eight English aristocrats who sought to enrich themselves by selling the land to migrants. New York, originally settled by the Dutch, was taken by the English during a war. The English took over the small Dutch colony that became Delaware at the same time. Georgia was established on land granted to a British general, James Oglethorpe, who wanted the colony to become a refuge for the poor and a defensive boundary between the Carolinas and the Spanish province of Florida.

As business ventures these North American colonies were, in general, disappointments. Granting land to settlers rarely produced the profits their wealthy promoters hoped for, and their efforts to control and profit from colonial trade nearly all failed. By the middle of the eighteenth century, management of most of the colonies had shifted to the British government, which did its best to oversee its distant possessions without ever investing the time and energy that would have been required to do it well. Responsibility for the colonies fell to a confusing bureaucracy of committees, boards, and officials, few of whom ever saw the colonies they were supposed to administer.

Migrants

Despite the confusing way Britain's North American colonies were managed and the disappointing returns they provided to their wealthy investors and proprietors, the colonies attracted settlers. Today we would call them migrants, because the most striking thing about them was that they left Britain and other European countries and risked their lives to move thousands of miles across a dangerous ocean to make a new life in a completely unfamiliar place. Migrants came to America by the thousands and ultimately to the United States by the millions, each with his or her own story, in individual acts of desperation and daring. Most were fleeing oppression, whether it was religious discrimination or simply the oppression of poverty, unemployment, hunger, and hopelessness. They looked to the American colonies—as millions

of later migrants from every part of the world have looked to the United States—as a New World, where with hard work and luck they might make a better life for themselves and their families.

The men and women who came to Britain's North American colonies in the seventeenth and eighteenth century did not understand freedom as we do. They had little voice in the decisions of government, and few of them expected to share in making those decisions. They were all the subjects of a king, and before they migrated to America they accepted that many of the decisions that shaped their lives would be made for them by the king, aristocrats, or the wealthy landowners who dominated life in every part of Europe.

Ordinary people were nowhere free to speak their minds—least of all to criticize the government or to challenge the teachings of the official church. The idea that governments exist to serve the interests of the people as a whole—a basic principle of government in free societies—was unknown. Governments existed to serve the interests of monarchs and their aristocratic supporters, and in England, the country gentlemen and city merchants on whom the monarchs relied for tax revenue, political support, and service in time of war.

Most of the migrants who came to the colonies had an idea of rights, but that idea was limited. If arrested and put on trial by the government for some alleged crime, for example, they expected to have a trial before a jury, but they might be tortured or suffer cruel punishments. Torture was commonly employed in seventeenth-century Britain and remained common in most of Europe in the eighteenth century. Its decline in Britain was widely considered a sign of advanced thinking, but people convicted of petty crimes still faced severe corporal punishment or even death. Ordinary British subjects who owned land—most did not—were usually secure in their right to their land. Tenants were less secure in their rights, and wealthy landowners who wanted to convert farm land to grazing land could usually manage to drive their tenants off.

Freedom of movement was limited. Displaced tenants and the poor could not simply move where they wished. The labor market was limited and employment usually scarce. Parishes and counties often drove the wandering poor away to avoid

FREEDOM

adding to the burdens of relieving even their most basic needs. Homeless people able to work— "sturdy beggars" as they were called—were unwelcome everywhere. Some drifted into crime, living on the margins of society as robbers or vagrants, poaching game from private woods. Many drained off into the larger towns, especially London, which grew quickly, its slums expanding despite waves of epidemic disease that made it a death trap for those who lived there.

Eighteenth-century Britons—at least the wealthy and the middling sort—boasted that Britain was a free country, and were proud to call themselves "freeborn Englishmen." But their boasted freedom was hardly what any of us would call free. Britain's freedom rested on its long tradition, not always honored, of the rule of law— though that law could be harsh—and on its relative prosperity. Though seasons of hunger and want stalked Britain in the seventeenth and eighteenth centuries, it was mostly spared the famines that wracked many Continental nations.

Britain's boasted freedom rested ultimately on geography. Britain is an island nation, separated from the European mainland. The chief powers on the Continent maintained large standing armies to engage in frequent and expensive wars with one another and taxed their people mercilessly to pay the costs of the military. France—Britain's chief rival in the century before the American Revolution and for a generation thereafter—was a vast military state with an aristocracy dedicated to military service and aristocrats hungry to distinguish themselves in war. The British distrusted large standing armies and avoided the expense of paying for them by relying on their navy to fend off invaders. With a long coast and an abundance of ports, the British were a seafaring people. In wartime merchant seamen could be recruited—or forced into service by press gangs—to man the king's warships, which they did remarkably well. The Atlantic coast of France, by contrast, offers few useful harbors and had a much smaller merchant marine. Its sailors were no rivals for the British.

Britain's success in defending itself at sea spared its people the confiscatory taxation imposed elsewhere. The money that was absorbed by the state in most of Europe was, in Britain, invested in trade, which in time made British merchants fab-

ulously rich. That wealth, reinvested in banks that loaned money to the government, gave the British government the means to create an empire that by the late nineteenth century covered a very large part of the Earth. But wealth and freedom are not the same thing and national wealth is no guarantee of a people's freedom. The British Empire of the nineteenth century demonstrated little regard for the rights of the many people it ruled.

Religious Refugees

Many of the early colonists were refugees from religious oppression. Britain, like other European countries, had an official religion. Everyone was required by law to attend the Church of England and accept its teachings, which included unquestioned loyalty to the king, who was the head of the church. People who disagreed with the teachings of the established church or who questioned the authority of its ministers, bishops, or the king, were harassed and punished for their beliefs. Many of them formed churches of their own and were persecuted for not accepting the authority of the established church. Others practiced their religion in secret to avoid punishment. All of them wanted to worship in their own way without interference by the government.

Some of these groups left Britain and migrated to North America, where the government would not harass them. The first were the Pilgrims. In 1620 they settled in Plymouth in what later became Massachusetts. A few years later much larger groups of English Puritans settled what became the towns of Boston, Salem, Gloucester, Marblehead, and other towns along the shores of Massachusetts Bay. They were called Puritans because they wanted to *purify* all the churches in England by creating a society in which the people were devoted to their religion and practiced it faithfully. They hoped the Church of England would follow their example— a hope in which they were disappointed. Massachusetts Puritans later settled what became Rhode Island, Connecticut, and New Hampshire, which became separate colonies.

At about the same time, Roman Catholics settled Maryland. Practicing the Roman Catholic religion was illegal in Britain, in part because Catholics

By the late seventeenth century, Puritan refugees from religious oppression had established stable communities in America. In this portrait painted in 1671, Elizabeth Freake of Boston wears finery that identifies her as a prosperous woman. The artist added baby Mary to the portrait in about 1674 (Worcester Art Museum).

regarded the pope, rather than the king, as the head of their church. Catholics were never the majority in Maryland, but many of the wealthiest landowners were Catholic. From the start, Maryland had a policy of religious toleration, which means that people were permitted to practice their religion without interference from the government as long as they conformed to certain rules.

Toward the end of the seventeenth century, Pennsylvania was founded by Quakers, an unusual religious sect established in Britain in the middle of the seventeenth century. Quakers believed that all people possess an "Inner Light" of goodness. They believed in the equality of all people before God, refused to swear oaths and refused to participate in war. Massachusetts Puritans, even though they had come to America to practice their religion as they wished, refused to allow Quakers to remain in Massachusetts. They were welcomed in nearby Rhode Island and settled in small groups elsewhere, but most of the Quaker refugees settled in Pennsylvania, where Quakers controlled the colonial government for many years. People of all faiths were welcomed in Pennsylvania, and the religious refugees from other parts of Europe settled there.

All of the religious refugees who fled to America from Britain did so to establish their personal independence from the tyranny of the Church of England. Few of them favored universal religious freedom. The Puritans of New England established their own faith as the official religion in Massachusetts, New Hampshire, and Connecticut and for many years imposed penalties and punishments on those who refused to accept the authority of their churches. Such efforts to impose religious orthodoxy gradually cooled in the late seventeenth and early eighteenth century, but a passion for independence from the Church of England and devotion to the their own churches characterized New England through the eighteenth century.

Most of the religious refugees came to the colonies from Britain, but many came from other countries in western Europe in the late seventeenth and eighteenth centuries. Among them were Lutherans and other German Protestants fleeing persecution and unrest in central Europe. French Protestants, called Huguenots, fled France in the late seventeenth century after the French king made the practice of their religion a crime and ordered their church schools closed and their churches destroyed. They included merchants or tradesmen who settled in or near the larger towns of several colonies. Many settled in Boston, New York, and Charleston. Among them was a thirteen year-old boy named Apollos Rivoire, who came to America alone. He settled in Boston and became a silversmith, a trade he passed on to his son, who was named after his father, but given a more English-sounding name: Paul Revere. A Huguenot in his early twenties named Benjamin Marion fled France and settled in South Carolina. His grandson Francis Marion became one of the great heroes of the American Revolution. A Huguenot named Antoine Bénézet migrated to Pennsylvania with his family at eighteen. As Anthony Benezet he became one of the most outspoken opponents of slavery in the English-speaking world.

By the middle of the eighteenth century, British America was home to people from more religious traditions than any other place in the Atlantic world. Nearly all were Christians, but there were Jewish colonists in some of the larger port cities from Newport, Rhode Island, to Savannah, Georgia. Many of them were descended from persecuted Spanish and Portuguese Jews who had fled first to London before settling in British America. Others had fled from parts of Germany. Among them were Benjamin and Perla Sheftall, who arrived in Savannah in 1733. Their son Mordecai Sheftall, born two years later, became a colonel in the Continental Army and fought for American independence.

Servants and Freeholders

Regardless of where they settled, most migrants came to Britain's North American colonies in a daring or desperate bid for a better life. Many were poor working people who did not own land and had no hope of acquiring a farm of their own in Britain or whatever other European country they left behind. In America, they believed, land was abundant and could be acquired for little money. Their first problem was getting to America. Passage on a ship crossing the Atlantic to the colonies was expensive.

To earn their passage, many poor people agreed to work as servants without pay for several

The population of British America was overwhelmingly rural. By modern standards, the largest cities—Philadelphia, New York, Boston, and Charleston—were modest towns. Baltimore, which would grow to become one of the most populous cities in the United States, was little more than a village in 1752 when John Moale drew the sketch on which this print was based (Enoch Pratt Free Library).

years after they reached America: three or four years if they had a useful skill, but often five to seven years if they did not. The contract between the master and servant was called an indenture, and such servants were known as indentured servants. Over half of the European migrants who came to Britain's North American colonies arrived as indentured servants.

Masters had to provide their indentured servants with food, clothing, and shelter during their years of service, but the masters did not have to pay them. Indentured servants were bought and sold, passed from one master to another. Most indentured servants worked in the fields, growing and harvesting crops. The death rate in colonies was very high, particularly in the first decades, and most people who arrived as servants died as servants, and never acquired a farm of their own.

John Harrower, who wrote a diary of his experiences, was among them. Harrower seems to have been nearing forty when he left his wife and children behind in Scotland to secure work

in London. There he found "many Hundreds are sterving for want of employment, and many good people are begging." The little money he had ran out before he could find a job. In desperation, he indentured himself for four years to a ship's captain bound for Virginia. When the ship reached Virginia, the captain sold Harrower's contract to a planter near Fredericksburg, who employed Harrower as a teacher to his four children. The planter treated Harrower well and helped him secure more students. From what he earned from teaching them, Harrower hoped to save enough to bring his wife and children over from Scotland, but he died in April 1777. His experience differed from that of most indentured servants, who worked as farm laborers, but like many of them he died far from home, separated from his family.

More fortunate migrants were able to pay their passage and arrived in the colonies without any obligation to serve someone else. But even for them, life was usually hard. If they arrived with enough money they could acquire a farm, but

15

By 1755, when Joseph Blackburn painted this portrait of Boston's Isaac Winslow and his family, the colonial gentry regarded themselves as peers of the British gentry, and proudly displayed the fine clothes and handsome property their wealth afforded them (Photograph © 2023 Museum of Fine Arts, Boston).

many had to work as hired laborers for someone else to save the money to acquire their own land. Some never did and lived out their lives as farm laborers or tenant farmers.

Those who became freeholders achieved a kind of personal independence that was rare in Europe, but their path was usually hard. A freeholder often had to clear his land of trees in order to start farming. He also had to build a house—or hire a housewright to build one—and a barn or shed to store his harvest, keep his tools, and protect his animals. If he could afford it, a new landowner bought an indentured servant or two to help do this difficult work. If he had enough money, a settler acquired land on a river or a large creek that

could be used to carry his harvest downstream to a market town or a waiting ship. Land beside a navigable stream was far more valuable than other land. Landlocked farmers had to move their crops to river landings on small dirt roads using wagons or by rolling his harvest along the road in large barrels. It was back breaking work.

Not all colonists were farmers, but nearly every colonist was tied to the farming economy in some way. Some ran ferries across rivers, collecting small fees for carrying people, animals, and crops to the other side. Some operated taverns in towns and country crossroads. Still others ran sawmills to make lumber for building and gristmills to grind grain. Others kept stores where colonists could buy tools, cloth, kitchen implements, metal buttons, and other goods, mostly brought from Britain. In port towns, many became sailors and worked on merchant ships. Elsewhere along the coast, fishermen made their living catching and selling fish, which was usually salted and dried so that it would keep for months.

In towns, men worked in dozens of different crafts. Blacksmiths made things from iron. Coopers made wooden barrels and buckets. Wheelwrights made wheels for wagons and carts. Whitesmiths made things out of tin. Larger towns had silversmiths and craftsmen who made fine furniture. The largest towns also had printers, who printed forms, pamphlets, newspapers, and even a few books, although most books were imported from Britain.

This pattern of small farms and towns, of farmers, craftsmen, and shopkeepers repeated itself, with regional and local differences, in every colony from Nova Scotia to Georgia. By 1750 there were about 1.5 million colonists living in British North America in a band of colonies along the Atlantic Ocean. Most of them lived near the coast, but the colonists were pushing west, settling as far as the foothills of the Appalachian Mountains. Most of the Indians had been pushed into the mountains and the valleys to the west, though a few remained east of the mountains, closer to the colonists.

These colonies had much in common. They all owed their allegiance to the king of England. They each had a local government, with a governor, an elected legislature, and a legal system based on the laws of England. The main businesses everywhere were farming, raising livestock, cutting wood for lumber, and fishing. Each colony had its ports, where merchants bought goods and shipped them to Britain or to other British colonies, and sold goods from Britain and elsewhere to the colonists. Each colony had wealthy and influential families, middling ones with farms and businesses, and working people who labored hard simply to survive.

The Gentry

The colonies had something else in common. They had no titled aristocracy. Few British aristocrats—the wealthy lords who dominated the social and political life of Britain—ever visited America, and even fewer stayed. Life in a land of hard labor without great cities or luxuries had no appeal for them. British aristocrats lived on inherited wealth and the rents collected from tenant farmers who occupied their vast estates. The dukes and earls of eighteenth-century Britain did not work, at least in the way we understand work. Hired agents collected their rents. They spent their times socializing with one another and serving in public offices or in the military, not always for the pay but because this was expected of aristocrats and because success in office or in war would add to their family's reputation and standing in society. Aristocrats were careful to make sure that their children married the children of other aristocrats, so the land that they all depended upon remained within their social class, or that their daughters married wealthy merchants and brought some of the new money being made in trade and commerce into their families.

This way of life was impossible in the American colonies, where unoccupied land was so abundant that few people rented the land they farmed. The wealthiest American landowners were farmers who owned large estates, but their income came mostly from the sale of what they grew, not from rents paid by tenants. They had laborers who did the hard work of plowing, planting, and harvesting, but they had to manage that work very carefully in order to make a profit and maintain their wealth and social standing. They socialized with their wealthy neighbors, held public offices, served as militia officers, and worked to make sure their sons and daughters married into the families of other wealthy Americans, but their status depended, in the end, on their success or failure as farmers.

They were not aristocrats. They were mostly the sons, grandsons, or great-grandsons of men who had arrived in the colonies with little money but who had succeeded in establishing productive plantations or large farms or who had succeeded as merchants, and then passed on their wealth to their children. The most successful of these gentry families, like the Lees, Carters, and Randolphs of Virginia; Carrolls of Maryland; Schuylers, Livingstons and DeLanceys of New York; Middletons and Pinckneys of South Carolina; or Shippens and Biddles of Pennsylvania, sustained their wealth and social prominence through several generations.

Members of this American gentry lived in gracious country homes or elegant townhouses, luxurious by American standards, but very small compared to the vast country houses of Britain. Since their wealth depended on their success as farmers and businessmen, members of the American gentry could lose their fortunes and their social standing through wastefulness, mismanagement, or bad luck. At the same time, farmers and merchants who managed their affairs wisely and who enjoyed good luck might secure places for themselves and their families in the first ranks of American society, taking advantage of a degree of social mobility that was unthinkable in Britain.

Without an aristocracy, American colonists experienced a much greater degree of social equality than people in Britain. The difference between the gentry and ordinary Americans, while great, was much less than the difference between an English lord and his tenants. The colonial gentry interacted with ordinary colonists, in taverns, courts, and churches, in the marketplace and at militia musters, in ways that demonstrated their higher social status, but that also drew them together in ways that rarely happened between British aristocrats and ordinary people in Britain. The American Revolution, when it came, was led by members of the gentry. The greater degree of social equality in America, and the awareness that their wealth was recently made and depended heavily on their own efforts, made it far easier for them to accept the idea that "all men are created equal" than would have been possible in Britain, or anywhere else in Europe.

The Enslaved

On the opposite end of the social scale from the gentry were enslaved Africans, mostly purchased from native slave traders operating on the west coast of Africa. Slavery had existed in various forms for thousands of years, most often as the fate of captives taken in war. In the fifteenth century, Portuguese explorers and traders brought thousands of captive Africans to southern Europe. Enslaved Africans were a common sight in southern Europe and the Mediterranean in the sixteenth century. In the New World the Spanish tried to enslave Indians, but their success was limited. Indi-

ans lacked immunity to diseases common to Europeans and died at appalling rates when forced to work beside them. If they escaped captivity, Indians often evaded capture by disappearing into the familiar forests. Most were poorly suited to agricultural labor, which was largely unfamiliar to them. Enslaved Africans were the answer to the chronic labor shortage of the Spanish Empire in America. Many were captives taken in wars between African peoples and sold to European traders like any other commodity. Enslaved Africans were a fixture in Spanish and Portuguese colonies in the New World by 1550.

The first Africans were brought to Virginia in 1619, when there was a shortage of labor needed to clear new ground and plant, tend, and harvest tobacco—miserable, back-breaking labor for which there were never enough white indentured servants. Evidence of how that first group was treated is sketchy, and it is not clear that they were bound to perpetual servitude and that the colonists expected to enslave their children from birth, treatments that came to distinguish the enslaved from indentured servants. Surviving evidence suggests that some of the first Africans brought in bondage to early Virginia and Maryland were bound to service for a period of years and then released. Free African Americans appear in the records as early as 1635. But it is plain that slavery in its fully developed form—enslavement of Africans for life and the enslavement of their children from birth—was practiced by 1639.

Enslavement did not take off quickly in Britain's mainland colonies immediately after 1619, probably because the cost of purchasing a person enslaved for life was greater than the cost of purchasing an indentured servant bound for five years, and both were likely to die within five years. In the brutal mathematics of colonial labor, the indentured servant was a better deal. In 1649 there were probably no more than three hundred Africans in Virginia, which then had a white population of about fifteen thousand.

Enslavement grew quickly in Britain's mainland colonies in the last years of the seventeenth century, as indentured servants became more expensive and the life expectancy of servants and enslaved people increased. In 1700 there were some 28,000 enslaved people in Britain's main-

Enslaved African Americans are marginalized in the surviving visual record of the colonial era, like the enslaved boy in the background of this drawing from about 1760 of South Carolina planter Peter Manigault entertaining his friends (Winterthur Museum, Garden and Library).

land colonies and many more in Britain's sugar islands in the West Indies. The number of enslaved people in the mainland grew steadily. By 1740 there were over 150,000 enslaved people in British North America. In New England they were used as household servants. They also worked on farms, cut timber, loaded and unloaded ships, moved goods to market, built roads, houses, shops, and storehouses, and were involved in nearly every productive enterprise. The same was true in the middle colonies, where they were more numerous. Some were skilled artisans whose creativity enriched their owners.

The majority of enslaved people lived in the southern colonies, where most were forced to work growing tobacco, rice, and other crops that required heavy manual labor to plant, cultivate, harvest, and prepare for market. Many came from predominantly agricultural societies in Africa and were used to hard agricultural labor, but the conditions under which they were forced to live and work in British America were degrading. Most enslaved people lived on large plantations and worked in gangs under constant threat of brutal punishments. Neither indentured servants nor slaves had a natural incentive to work hard, but a stubborn, unproductive servant could be punished by having his term of service extended. People enslaved for life could not be punished with longer terms of service. Avoiding severe corporal punishment was the only incentive many of them knew.

The enslaved people of colonial British America were all unwilling migrants, enslaved by force and held against their will, and denied even a small degree of personal independence or individual liberty. In a world where freedom as we know it was barely imagined, the enslaved enjoyed no freedom at all.

The people of British America lived in a rigidly hierarchical society in which power extended from the monarch—in 1744, when this portrait was painted, he was King George II—through the hereditary aristocracy to the local gentry. The farmers, tradesmen, laborers, and servants of the British Empire were the king's subjects; they enjoyed few of the privileges of those above them in the social hierarchy, and had few secure rights. The increasing number of enslaved people in the empire had no rights at all (© National Portrait Gallery, London).

Chapter 2 The Limits of Freedom

No one in colonial British America was free, at least not in the sense that we use the word free. Our idea of freedom was shaped by the American Revolution. It involves personal *independence, liberty, equality, natural and civil rights,* and the opportunities and responsibilities of *citizenship*. These principles were little understood or applied in very limited ways before the American Revolution. The Revolutionaries embraced and applied them in new and expansive ways and in the process dedicated their new nation to principles of freedom that have defined our history for nearly 250 years.

The people of colonial British Americans were all subjects. None were citizens. The idea of *citizenship*, involving opportunities for ordinary people to participate in public life, was unfamiliar to most Europeans. So were the obligations of citizenship, including the obligation to set aside selfish interests and serve the nation, especially in war and times of crisis. Military service was regarded as a duty subjects owed their king, not service given by one citizen to all. The idea of citizenship was an ancient one, derived from the political philosophy of ancient Greece and Rome and reimagined by political thinkers and writers beginning with the Renaissance in the fifteenth century, but in the centuries before the American Revolution it had been applied only in very limited ways in a few isolated places.

The idea that all people naturally possess certain rights, which we know as *natural rights* or *human rights*, was no more than a theory discussed by philosophers. No government acknowledged the existence of such rights. What we call *civil rights*—rights to vote, to hold public office, to trial by jury, and other rights that define our relationship to government—were extremely limited. People in Britain and her American colonies enjoyed more such rights than most people in the world, but they were far fewer than the civil rights we enjoy. As for *equality*, Christianity taught that all souls were equal before God. Beyond the realm of faith, profound inequalities were fundamental to the organization of earthly society, which was ordered by

ranks and degrees of privilege and subordination.

Liberty—freedom from restraints imposed by government or by others on the exercise of natural and civil rights—was limited and insecure. Ultimate authority, or sovereignty, rested with the state, either literally in the person of the sovereign king or more broadly in the king's government. That sovereign government was not restrained by a written constitution that defined and limited its powers, and thus protected liberty by limiting what government can do. Britain had no written constitution. Government operated on the basis of custom and tradition, and was subject to changes in policy and practice at the discretion of the Crown—the king and his ministers—and Parliament. In the eighteenth century the British were very proud of the "liberties" they had won from their kings and boasted loudly about "the rights of Englishmen," but their liberty was very limited compared to the liberty defined by the American Revolution.

Colonial British Americans enjoyed more personal *independence*—the opportunity to make choices for themselves about their lives—than most people in their world, but little of the personal independence we take for granted today. For most of the eighteenth century the colonists also enjoyed an unusual degree of political independence. Although they were subjects of the king and subject to laws passed by Parliament, the British government demonstrated little interest in the internal affairs of its North American colonies. As a result the colonists enjoyed a period of relative independence within the British Empire.

King and Parliament

In the middle of the eighteenth century, Britain was admired by political thinkers and writers as the most enlightened, rationally governed country in Europe and the British people were widely regarded as a free people. But the enlightened rationality of the British government was impressive only in comparison to the despotic monarchies on the Continent, and the British people were free only in relation to the unfortunate people those despots ruled. Observers attributed British prosperity to the rational organization of its government and the wisdom of its policies, not considering that Britain's prosperity was enjoyed very unevenly across British society, that few Britons had a voice in public life, and that liberty and personal independence were severely limited.

The people of Britain and its colonies were all subjects of the British king. In 1750 he was George II, King of Great Britain and Ireland. Kings ruled by hereditary right and were not accountable to their people. In theory, the king was expected to act like a royal father, the head of a great family. He was supposed to care for his subjects like a father cares for his children. In practice, kings did whatever suited their interests and ambitions and rarely put the welfare of their subjects ahead of their own. George II was born in northern Germany and concerned himself deeply in the affairs of the Duchy of Brunswick and Lüneburg, of which he was hereditary ruler. English was his third language (he learned French before he learned German) and he was more interested in the dynastic struggles of Continental Europe than in the welfare of his British subjects.

The king shared power with Parliament, which passed the laws. Parliament was divided between the House of Lords and the House of Commons. Men were not elected to the House of Lords. The lords, or peers as they were known, claimed their places in the Lords by hereditary right, as the senior members of aristocratic families. The House of Lords represented the interests of the wealthiest people in Britain.

The House of Commons, reputedly the more popular house of Parliament, had existed for hundreds of years. It had increased in power and influence in the seventeenth century, when its leaders had struggled with the king for power. This conflict led to a civil war in England in the 1640s, in which the Commons had imposed its will and limited the power of the king. The power of this elected part of the British government distinguished Britain from the other countries of the time, in which royal power was almost unlimited.

The House of Commons was widely admired by European thinkers and writers as a representative of the popular interest, but it did not, in fact, represent the common people. A less representative elected legislature would be hard to imagine. In the middle of the eighteenth century about one in five members of the House of Commons were close relatives of peers. Some were knights—a title passed down in their families. Most members of the Commons were local gentry—men distinguished for wealth and important in the towns and counties where they lived. Those who represented towns were sometimes merchants or lawyers. Others were placemen, chosen by aristocrats to represent their political interests.

Through most of the eighteenth century, the House of Commons had 558 members representing 314 constituencies, including 486 members from England, 27 from Wales, and 45 from Scotland. Each county in England and Wales elected two members, regardless of the population of the county. Each county in Scotland elected one member. There were 122 county seats in the House of Commons and 432 seats representing 230 towns or boroughs, as they were called, which had been granted charters by a king. The universities at Oxford and Cambridge each chose two members.

There was nothing remotely democratic about the distribution of the seats or the way elections were conducted. Most boroughs elected two members, regardless of their population. Some boroughs that were important towns in the Middle Ages had withered to nothing by the middle of the eighteenth century, but continued to be represented by two members. The most famous was "Old Sarum," near Salisbury, which had almost no resident population at all. The aristocrat who owned the land where the town had once stood chose the two members to represent Old Sarum in the House of Commons. At the same time, the people of Leeds, Birmingham, and Manchester—rapidly growing industrial towns with thousands of residents—did not choose a single member of the House of Commons. On the eve of the American Revolution, the merchants of Leeds were responsible for a third of Britain's woolen cloth exports; Birmingham was emerging as the center of British iron and steel manufacturing; and Manchester was a becoming a center of the cotton industry. Important as they were, they had no voice in the House of Commons.

The eighteenth-century House of Commons, depicted in this 1746 engraving, represented the interests of the British aristocracy and landed gentry who controlled most elections. The distribution of seats bore little relation to the distribution of population in Britain. The people of British America chose no representatives at all (©The Trustees of the British Museum).

Aristocrats and other wealthy landowners, like the men portrayed by Gawen Hamilton in *The Brothers Clarke with Other Gentlemen Taking Wine,* dominated eighteenth-century British society and monopolized political institutions for their benefit (Yale Center for British Art).

In those places that were represented, the right to vote for members of the House of Commons was extremely limited. Only adult men were allowed to vote, and property qualifications excluded eighty percent or more of them. In many towns, the right to vote was limited to men who occupied particular pieces of property. But none of this mattered much, because in most places elections often went uncontested. Spirited contest for seats in the House of Commons took place in London and some of the larger towns and the counties close to the city, but elsewhere aristocrats and their

networks of relatives and clients controlled elections. The county seats for Nottinghamshire went uncontested for a hundred years. The members of the House of Commons rarely concerned themselves with the interests of ordinary people. They usually represented the interests of rich country gentlemen and city merchants or the interests of the aristocrats who secured their election.

Many in Britain were very proud of their government of king, lords, and commons, which they said balanced the three great interests in the realm and thus represented all the king's subjects in a fair way. They celebrated this "mixed government" as the source of British stability and success. In truth the British government was an oligarchy—a government controlled by a small number of powerful people and conducted for their benefit. The growing wealth and influence Britain enjoyed had little to do with mixed government, which was a polite fiction.

The Rulers and the Ruled

Eighteenth-century Britain had no written constitution defining and limiting the powers of its most important officials. Written constitutions are a distinctive contribution of the American Revolution to public life. In the absence of a written constitution, Britain was governed by custom and tradition and by the policy preferences of whatever group of aristocrats could secure a working majority in Parliament for policies that the king found acceptable. Many of the functions of government were carried out by a complex and ever-shifting bureaucracy made up of ministers and other officials who were, in theory, appointed by and responsible only to the king.

The most important was the prime minister, the most powerful office in the British government but one that was not described or defined in law until the twentieth century. The office emerged during the eighteenth century and grew in importance, at first because King George I, to whom the Crown had passed, was a German prince who spoke little English. Unable to preside effectively over meetings of his leading ministers and uninterested in the details of government, he accepted one of them, Sir Robert Walpole, as the leader of his government. Walpole held the post for twenty years, maintaining his influence mainly through his use of the royal power of appointment, which he used to build up a party loyal to him. Enjoying the power of an office that did not formally exist, Walpole refused to call himself the prime minister. One of his successors, George Grenville, called it "an odious title."

Walpole and Grenville, along with the others who wielded the powers of prime minister, presided over governments that routinely deprived British subjects of religious freedom, denied them rights of free speech and assembly, taxed them without their consent, searched their homes, shops, and warehouses without just cause or proper warrants, denied many of them the right to bear arms, and in time of war employed roaming armed gangs to force men into naval service.

Their governments were little concerned with the welfare of the king's subjects. Except for men permanently disabled in war, the king's government was indifferent to veterans and to the widows and orphans its wars produced. It took no action to discourage aristocrats and other wealthy landowners from depriving their tenants of land their families had worked for centuries, and indeed facilitated it through acts of Parliament. The total number of landholders in Britain declined dramatically during the eighteenth century. The landless poor streamed into London, filling slums with an impoverished underclass, or migrated to the colonies as indentured servants.

Life was hard for those who remained. Serious efforts to ensure public health were nonexistent. Thomas Percival, a Manchester physician, estimated that half the children born in London before the 1770s died before they reached two. The health of the people was slightly better in the countryside and in provincial towns, but underemployment was chronic and poverty was commonplace. In difficult years as much as a third of the British population was destitute. Private charities, growing in number and resources since the seventeenth century, were insufficient to solve the growing problem of poverty.

Life was held cheap. The use of torture to extract confessions had declined by the eighteenth century, but brutal punishments had not. At the beginning of the eighteenth century, British law recognized sixty capital crimes—crimes for which a convicted person could be executed. By the end of the century there were over two hundred. The Murder Act, passed in 1752, provided that the bodies of executed murderers should be dissected by doctors or hung in chains and left to rot in public view. For lesser crimes, fierce corporal punishment, including public whipping and branding, remained the rule.

Penal transportation to Britain's American colonies was employed as a sentence to rid Britain of people convicted of petty theft and other non-capital crimes. More than half of the all

Robert Dinwiddie was typical of the career bureaucrats who served as royal governors in British America. He rose from customs collector in Bermuda to the more lucrative post of surveyor general of customs in the West Indies before becoming lieutenant governor of Virginia, where he was acting governor in the place of Lord Albemarle and Lord Loudoun, absentee aristocrats who never carried out the duties of their office (© National Portrait Gallery, London).

English migrants to America between 1718 and 1775 arrived as convicts and were sold by the merchants who transported them into indentured servitude, usually for terms of fourteen years. Most were sold to planters in Virginia and Maryland. The planters grumbled but they bought the convicts up. Penal transportation was interrupted by the American Revolution but later renewed by sending convicts to Australia, turning a continent on the opposite side of the planet into a prison from which no one could return.

British and British American merchants also sold West Africans into perpetual servitude in America. The brutal practice of enslaving Africans grew dramatically from the last quarter of the seventeenth century with little opposition in Britain or the colonies. Their appearance, what contemporaries called "heathen" religious practices, inability to speak English, and African customs made them, in the eyes of all but a few people in Britain, suited for nothing but perpetual servitude. For the British and colonial slave traders who took over the British market from the Portuguese, Spanish, and Dutch, the slave trade itself became a source of wealth. Opposition to enslavement on humanitarian and religious grounds began to take shape in the middle of the eighteenth century, but its spokesmen offered no practical alternative to enslavement as a means to procure the labor the colonies needed. Distasteful as enslavement seemed to increasing numbers in Britain, to most it seemed different only in degree from the more familiar experience of the poor, indentured servants, and transported convicts.

Governing the Colonies

To the people of British America, the government that presided over the empire was both distant and almost incomprehensible. Except for merchant sailors, few Americans traveled to Britain. Colonial newspapers, which relatively few colonists read, were often filled with reports of European politics and gossip about royal marriages, but most of it was months old by the time it was published and had little practical importance for British Americans. The few mid-eighteenth-century colonists who concerned themselves with the government in Britain seem to have subscribed to the view that the British government had achieved a happy balance between the interests of the king, the aristocracy, and the commons.

The patchwork of colonies that made up the British Empire were governed by a patchwork of institutions and officers. In Britain, an eight-member body called the Commissioners for Trade and Plantations, often called the Board of Trade, was responsible for advising the Crown and Parliament on colonial affairs. The Board of Trade had no executive powers or important powers of appointment, but it conducted hearings and interviewed colonial officials, merchants, and colonial agents, and the ministry (from which its members were typically drawn) often followed its guidance.

No single government in America governed the colonies on behalf of the king and Parliament. The idea of creating a single government for the colonies was suggested from time to time, but the British never acted on the idea. Each of the British colonies in North America had its own govern-

ment, with a governor, an upper house of the legislature or an appointed governor's council, and an assembly.

The governor was usually a British native appointed by the king and sent to America as the king's representative in the colony. The upper house or council was typically a small group chosen by the governor. It usually included some of the wealthiest and most influential men in the colony. The council advised the governor and, in most colonies, voted to approve or reject laws adopted by the colonial assembly. In some colonies the council also served as a supreme court.

The assembly passed laws for the colony. The assemblies went by a variety of names. In Virginia the colonial assembly was called the House of Burgesses. In Massachusetts it was called the General Court. Elsewhere it was called the House of Delegates. Members of the assembly were elected, although in most of the colonies voting was a privilege of free adult men over twenty-one who owned property. Women, servants, enslaved people, and many people who worked for wages could not vote, and in several colonies the allotment of seats in the assembly did not keep pace with the expansion of the population to the west, leaving the more recently settled areas underrepresented. The opportunity to vote was nonetheless more widely enjoyed in the colonies than in Britain.

William Douglass, a Boston physician who published a history of the British colonies in 1740, compared the organization of their government to the mixed government of Britain. With "the governor, representing the King," he explained, "the colonies are monarchical; by the Council, they are aristocratical; by a house of representatives or delegates from the people, they are democratical. . . . The concurrence of these three forms of government seems to be the highest perfection that human civil government can attain to in times of peace."

The analogy was commonly advanced, but colonial government actually bore little resemblance to the British government. Governors appeared to wield considerable power. They typically appointed the upper houses and could call meetings of the assemblies, veto their legislation, and dissolve them at will. They appointed judges, commanded the militia, and often commanded any of the king's soldiers stationed in their colonies. But the governors were not as powerful as they seemed. Most were British natives who made their livings as colonial officials. Many were appointed without ever having been to the colonies they were to govern. They arrived with no friends on the councils or in the assemblies, which made it difficult for them to get things done. They needed the assemblies to pass laws and the assemblies often controlled their salaries. In practice, the assemblies governed the colonies.

Through the first half of the eighteenth century, the Crown and Parliament devoted little attention to the affairs of their North American colonies. The British government imposed few taxes or regulations, and invested little effort in enforcing the regulations it did impose. The result of this long period of salutary neglect was that the colonists grew used to managing their own affairs. The assemblies established their influence at the expense of the governors. Merchants evaded the customs laws by smuggling or bribing customs officials. By the middle of the century the colonies had become an important source of wealth for Britain. Tobacco, rum, molasses, sugar, and indigo reached British consumers and provided British merchants with goods to trade on the Continent. Timber, tar, and pitch from America's forests reached the Royal Navy, along with hemp for ropes and staves for barrels. In return Britain provided the colonists with credit and sent them woolen fabrics, creamware dishes, buttons, silk, printed cotton, iron goods, clocks, furniture, guns, musket balls, and gunpowder. Money was made and no one looked very hard at how it was done.

Under the circumstances, local government had more influence in the lives of ordinary colonists than the governors or assemblies. In the southern and middle colonies, the county courts, which were dominated by wealthy planters, were the most important institutions of local government. Members of these county courts were usually the officers of the local militia and served on the vestries of churches. In New England, town governments, local courts, and churches had similar influence, but town meetings, in which all the freemen of the town could participate and express themselves, were even more important.

Local government was equally important to the lives of ordinary men and women in Britain. Despite the growing importance of London and the larger towns, the majority of British subjects lived in village communities of a few hundred people, tied to other villages. The parish and the market towns were centers of rural life in Britain, just as church and courthouse were the centers of rural life in America. It was at the local level that the dominant institutions of public life defined and protected the limited rights of the king's subjects in Britain and America alike.

The Rule of Law

Life in Britain and its American colonies was not free, as we understand freedom, but the people of both benefited from the rule of law—the idea that society should be governed by established, just, and widely understood legal principles enforced consistently and without regard to social status, and that those principles apply to rulers as well as the people they rule.

The king's British and American subjects claimed the rule of law was an ancient English tradition confirmed in the Magna Carta, or Great Charter, a thirteenth century agreement between King John and a group of rebellious English barons that limited the powers of the king and guaranteed certain rights to his subjects, including the right to trial by jury and protection against arbitrary or lengthy imprisonment without trial. Magna Carta also limited the power of the Crown to impose taxes, providing that new taxes could not be imposed without the "general consent of the realm."

Magna Carta was over five hundred years old by the middle of the eighteenth century, and its importance as a foundation of British rights was mostly symbolic. More important was the English Bill of Rights of 1689, in which Parliament defined the terms upon which it offered the vacant throne of England jointly to William of Orange and his wife, Mary. The Bill of Rights forbid kings from suspending laws or preventing their execution, and forbid raising an army in time of peace, or imposing taxes without the consent of Parliament. These provisions severely limited the powers of the Crown and provided for the powers of government to be shared by the king and Parliament.

Despite the inequalities inherent in the hierarchical society of Britain and British America, their people benefited from a legal system based on the rule of law, the principle that everyone is accountable to the same laws, enforced by courts—like the Court of Chancery depicted here in about 1725—responsible for administering laws in a fair way (© National Portrait Gallery, London).

To protect the independence of Parliament, the Bill of Rights specified that the "election of members of Parliament ought to be free," though it did not define what a free election would be like, and guaranteed "freedom of speech" in Parliament for members, ensuring that no member could be punished for anything he said there. The English Bill of Rights also guaranteed trial by jury and forbid excessive bail, excessive fines, and "cruel and unusual punishments." This language was repeated in the Eighth Amendment to the Federal Constitution.

The English Bill of Rights was an important foundation for the liberties British Americans claimed as their birthright, but it is as conspicuous for the rights it did not assert as for those it claimed. It did not provide for freedom of speech or expression, including freedom of the press, for the king's subjects, except for a very limited right to petition the king without fear of punishment or penalty. It did not provide for religious freedom. Indeed it required that the no Roman Catholic should sit on the throne and guaranteed a limited right to bear arms for Protestants only. While it asserted the right of trial by jury it did not prohibit torture or warrantless searches, nor did it protect the accused from being forced to incriminate themselves or endure repeated trials for the same alleged offense. It did not guarantee due process, which is the application of laws in a consistent, orderly, and fair way. The English Bill of Rights provided for a very limited right to bear arms, specifying that "subjects which are Protestants may have arms for their defense suitable to their conditions and as allowed by law." The limitations "suitable to their conditions and as allowed by law" gave the British government legal grounds to disarm the king's subjects at will.

Despite these limitations, the English Bill of Rights defined the rights of people in Britain and in British America more clearly than any other document. When Britons and British-American colonists spoke of the "rights of Englishmen," these were the rights they meant. They did not think of these as universal or natural rights, benefitting everyone. They were distinctively British. Possession of these rights was one of many ways eighteenth-century Britons distinguished their country from others, especially France, where the powers of the king were much greater than those of the Brit-

ish monarch and which had no representative legislative body comparable to the British Parliament.

The Conditions of Freedom

The rule of law and a government that recognizes and protects the basic rights of its people are essential to freedom, but freedom requires more than rules and rights to flourish. It requires personal independence—the opportunity to choose how to live your life. Freedom is only meaningful when people have choices, including choices that can improve their circumstances. People who are very poor, who do not have the basic necessities of life and have little or no chance of getting them, are not free. They have no choices that might lead to a better life.

The people of colonial British America enjoyed a higher standard of living than almost any people in the world, and had more personal independence than most people in Britain. While there were unemployed and laboring poor in some American cities, their numbers were small, rarely more than two or three percent of the population. In British America, labor shortages were a frequent problem. In the towns, work was generally available to able-bodied men and women, and at higher wages than in Britain. While acquiring land and setting up a farm required savings, it was within reach for a larger percentage of the population in British America than anywhere in Europe.

Literacy was more widespread in Britain's American colonies than almost anywhere else. Other acquired skills, like the ability to do basic mathematics, seem to have been more common in British America than elsewhere. Eighteenth-century schools focused on those basic skills. Students also learned some Biblical and ancient history, but not much about the history of their own time. John Adams taught such a school when he was a young man. He wrote in his diary that he could look out over his students and imagine he was looking over a whole society in miniature. Among them, he wrote, were "several renowned generals but three feet high," as well as "kings, politicians, divines . . . fops, buffoons, fiddlers, sycophants, fools, coxcombs, chimney sweepers, and every other character drawn in history or seen in the world." He enjoyed thinking how each student "will turn out in future life."

Like nearly everything else in colonial British America, access to education was not enjoyed equally. There were more schools in New England than the south, and the quality of instruction was generally better in New England, where schools were maintained at public expense. There, John Adams wrote with pride, an adult "who cannot read or write . . . is as rare as a comet or an earthquake." Though Adams exaggerated, New Englanders were probably the most literate people in the world in the middle of the eighteenth century. But even in New England, access to education was limited. Everywhere in British America, the education of girls ended before that of boys. Enslaved children did not attend school. It was a crime in some colonies to teach an enslaved person to read or write. The children of laborers and indentured servants received little or no formal education. The children of the poor often did not attend school because their parents could not pay the schoolmaster. They learned only what their parents could teach them. If parents could not read or write their children might never learn to read or write.

Education gives people choices about how to spend their lives by introducing them to ideas they could not have imagined on their own. Education provides people with new skills to earn their living and enrich their lives. Education gives freedom greater value by exposing people to new possibilities. The freedom to live where you like is more valuable if you have learned what other places are like. The freedom to choose the kind of work you do is more valuable if you have learned enough to do something other than the work your parents do. The freedom to worship as you choose is more valuable if you have learned enough about other faiths to make an informed choice. Education is essential to freedom. Without it, opportunities often go unrecognized.

Degrees of Freedom

Although the people of British America enjoyed more freedom than most people in the mid-eighteenth century, it was not enjoyed equally. Freedom was fragmented and limited along social lines. At the bottom of colonial society, enslaved people enjoyed no freedom at all. They had few legal protections. They were bought and sold. They were forced to work for the benefit of their owners all their lives. Their children were enslaved from birth and forced to work as soon as they were old enough to do chores of any kind. Their owners provided them with rough clothes, plain food, and perhaps a crowded cabin or hut to sleep in. Very few enslaved people learned to read or write. Even during their few hours off work, they were rarely permitted to leave their master's property or the surrounding area without a pass. They could be subjected to fierce punishments for the slightest infractions or simply driven harder. Their lives were ruled by violence and threats of violence. House servants and those who lived in towns often had a better life than those who worked in the fields, but no enslaved person had the freedom enjoyed by others.

A small number of white colonists believed slavery was unjust, but most did not. Slavery was brutal and degrading, but so was ordinary life at the lower levels of colonial society. Restrictions on freedom were common among white colonists. Indentured servants enjoyed much more freedom than enslaved people, but little compared to others. The typical indentured servant was a laborer who wanted to come to the colonies to make a better life, but who lacked the money to pay for his passage to America. In return for his passage, an indentured servant agreed to serve a master in the colonies for several years. If he knew a craft he could often bargain for a short period of service. But if he was unskilled, as most were, he was usually set to work in the fields for five to seven years. Transported convicts, who made up a large proportion of indentured servants in the eighteenth century, usually served twice as long. A master could flog his servants and ask magistrates to extend their service if they failed to work hard enough. Indentured servants often died before the end of their service. They were never free.

Apprentices were bound by law to serve their masters for several years, much like indentured servants. Apprenticeship was the usual way to learn a craft, but a young person was required to obey a master's commands just like an indentured servant and could be subjected to the same punishments. Apprentices often lived in the craft shop where

Parliament ordered convicted criminals transported to the American colonies, where they were sold as indentured servants for long terms, in order to rid Britain of what was described as a "criminal class." This portrait of a convict identified only as Addams may have been published to illustrate facial features associated with criminality by the eighteenth-century pseudoscience of physiognomy, whose proponents claimed to be able to predict a person's character from their appearance (©The Trustees of the British Museum).

> JUST arrived in York river, the Brilliant, Captain Miller, from London, with a choice healthy indented SERVANTS, the sale of which will begin at Richmond town on Wednesday the 25th of May; among which are the following tradesmen, viz. blacksmiths, braziers, edgetool makers, bricklayers and plasterers, shoemakers, stone masons, carpenters, joiners and cabinetmakers, cloth weavers, stocking weavers, barbers and peruke-makers, gardeners, farmers, labourers and husbandmen, book-keepers and schoolmasters, tailors, silkdyers, bakers, painters, leatherdressers, sawyers, butchers, a steward, groom, surgeon, &c. I will sell them very cheap, for ready money, or tobacco; and for those on credit, bond and security will be required.
>
> THOMAS SMITH.

British men and women, most of them unable to find work at home, indentured themselves to merchant captains who transported them to the colonies and sold their contracts for terms of service of four or more years—the length of their indentures depending on their skills (The Colonial Williamsburg Foundation).

they worked and were required to do all kinds of menial work in exchange for learning their trade.

Unskilled and lightly skilled workers, whether in towns or in the countryside, were usually free to come and go as they liked, but they often worked alongside indentured servants and were more likely to live in poverty than other colonists. Many worked for farmers and plantation owners in exchange for basic food, plain clothing, and simple shelter. They might be paid some agreed upon amount of money after completing a term of service or finishing some assigned task, but their everyday lives differed little from indentured servants. Sailors and fishermen—very common occupations at a time when most people lived close to the sea—were bound to obey their captains and accepted harsh discipline and rough conditions as a natural part of life.

Women of all ages and social ranks were the largest group of unfree people in British America. Women had few legal rights—none if they were enslaved. Women could not vote, serve on juries, or hold public office. Young women had less access to education than young men. Illiteracy was more common among women and most work was closed to them. An unmarried woman might own property, make contracts, and bring suits in court, but lost these rights when she married. All her property then came under the control of her husband.

Indians had few legal rights. Those who lived near or among the colonists were often treated with hostility. They might own property, but they were not permitted to vote and the courts generally refused to hear their complaints or their testimony. Most Indians lived beyond the frontier, outside the reach of British law.

Men who owned their own farms or craft shops enjoyed more freedom than most other people in British America. They could go wherever they liked. The government required them to pay very little in taxes. They were permitted to vote for a few public offices, though they were not considered eligible to hold most offices themselves. In New England they could express their views in town meetings.

The freest people in British America were the gentry. The gentry included planters and farmers who owned hundreds of acres of land, merchants who owned ships, warehouses and stores, as well as lawyers, physicians, and a growing number of successful entrepreneurs who had created flourishing businesses. The gentry included the wealthiest people in British America. They had the benefit of a better education than most other British Americans. A few of the wealthiest were educated in Britain. Others attended one of the several colleges that had been established in the colonies or were educated by private tutors. Some were largely self-taught. Many accepted public service as a responsibility that went with their wealth and social status. They served as militia officers, on church vestries, and in the assemblies. Many of them were proud and protective of the freedoms they enjoyed. When those freedoms were threatened, they protested, resisted, and ultimately rebelled.

33

Benjamin Franklin dedicated himself to harnessing advances in science to improve everyday life. By 1757, when he traveled to London as agent of the Pennsylvania assembly, his experiments with electricity had established his reputation as America's first great scientist. In this 1767 portrait by English painter David Martin, a bust of Isaac Newton connects Franklin to the founding thinker of the Enlightenment (Pennsylvania Academy of the Fine Arts).

Chapter 3 A World of Ideas

Britain's American colonies grew and prospered during a time of enormous intellectual and practical creativity in Europe known ever since as the Enlightenment. Beginning in the late seventeenth century, European philosophers and scientists dedicated themselves to understanding the natural world and man's place in it. They were building on the ideas and discoveries of philosophers and scientists over previous centuries, but they approached their work with new energy and the conviction that the insights into the natural world offered by philosophy and science could be applied to improve the quality of life for everyone.

The Enlightenment encouraged a new faith in progress—that the conditions of life, the institutions of government, and the organization of society could all be reformed and improved by the deliberate application of reason. The movement bound philosophers and scientists together in a common enterprise aimed at understanding the natural world and harnessing the insights of philosophy and science to improve health and safety, harness power and make work less laborious, relieve suffering and injustice, and reform institutions to make them more rational, humane, and efficient. The philosophers of the Enlightenment disagreed about many things, but they were unified in their conviction that mankind should not be governed by inherited practices and traditions that no longer served the interests of ordinary people.

The Enlightenment was a movement without borders that attracted creative minds all over Europe and even European colonies in the Americas. Influenced by the Enlightenment, Americans embraced new ways of thinking about their rights, as well as the new faith in reason, rational improvement, and progress, and the new spirit of inquiry and experimentation. They eventually applied them to create a new nation unlike any that had ever existed.

Natural Rights

Hundreds of philosophers, scientists, and writers from all over Europe—and eventually America—contributed to the Enlightenment. Many were inspired by two great British thinkers of the late seventeenth century. The first was the scientist Isaac Newton. In his most important book, *Mathematical Principles of Natural Philosophy*, Newton explained that the universe is governed by unchanging laws of nature like the law of gravity. By discovering and describing these laws of nature, he believed, we can understand how the world around us works. Newton's work inspired generations of scientists to study the natural world to understand the principles, or laws, governing the universe. Great advances were made in physics, mathematics, chemistry, biology, astronomy, and other branches of science during the eighteenth century. These advances were applied to engineering, medicine, and other practical activities that improved the quality of life for everyone.

The other British thinker whose work inspired the Enlightenment was the philosopher John Locke. In his book *An Essay Concerning Human Understanding*, Locke explained that everything people know they learn through the use of their senses. Locke taught that people are naturally equal at birth, and that what they become is simply a result of what they learn. Locke's work inspired generations of thought on education and led philosophers and writers to consider the rights of individuals and the proper basis of government. If everyone was born knowing nothing, as Locke said, then people were born equal. No one was born smarter or braver or better in any way than anyone else. If people were born equal, there was no basis to discriminate among people. They should all have the same rights.

Philosophers called these *natural rights*, because they are the result of our natural condition. The theory of natural rights—of rights inherent in the human condition rather than the possession of a particular people, won through their historical experience—had been growing since the seventeenth century. It was shaped by a Dutch jurist, Hugo Grotius, and his German follower, Samuel Pufendorf, and given more complete formulation by a Swiss theorist, Jean-Jacques Burlamaqui, who summarized thinking on natural rights in a book called *The Principles of Natural Law,* published in 1747.

The philosophical literature on natural rights was well known to thoughtful Americans like George Mason, John Adams, and Thomas Jefferson. The idea that all people possess certain fundamental rights seems obvious to us, because we live in a world in which the idea is widely accepted, but it was, as late as 1770, a theoretical construct. No government acknowledged the existence of natural rights before the American Revolution. The acceptance of this idea, and its central role in American thinking about government, is a fundamental reason America is free.

The Science of Government

The development of natural rights theory was only one of many intellectual accomplishments of the Enlightenment. Philosophers also worked to discover the natural laws that govern human behavior in the way the Newtonian laws governed the physical world and to apply those laws to shape social organization and government. Anthropology, sociology, psychology, and economics—fields of inquiry so new that they had not yet been named—are all rooted in this drive to discern patterns in human behavior. Scottish philosophers—Frances Hutcheson, David Hume, Adam Smith, Lord Kames, Thomas Reid, and Adam Ferguson—led the way in these fields, pursuing inquiries

The light of science and reason illuminates young and old in *A Philosopher Lecturing on the Orrery* by English painter Joseph Wright of Derby, depicting a group studying a mechanical model of the solar system. The discovery of natural laws governing the universe led eighteenth-century thinkers to search for natural laws governing society, including universal principles that should form the basis of government (Derby Museums).

David Rittenhouse, portrayed here with a telescope and an astronomical chart, was a Philadelphia clockmaker and self-taught astronomer who embodied the achievements of the Enlightenment in America. In an oration delivered to the American Philosophical Society in February 1775, he expressed hope that beings on other planets were "wise enough to govern themselves," and that "their statesmen are patriots," and their planets were free of slavery (National Portrait Gallery, Smithsonian Institution).

to discover what Hume called "the constant and universal principles of human nature" that would enable men to reduce government to a science.

Challenging centuries of tradition, philosophers of the Enlightenment called on people to consider the purposes, just foundation, and most effective organization of government. European writers who considered these subjects generally agreed that the main purpose of government was to promote the public good, and most thought a just political order would be reasonable, humane, peaceful, and free.

Many thought the only just foundation of government was the consent of the governed.

They theorized that governments originated in an implied contract between the rulers and the ruled, by which the people gave up some of the individual freedom they enjoyed in a "state of nature," in return for enjoying the good order and protection of a society governed for their benefit. This contract theory of government, which was most closely associated with John Locke, defied the traditional view that the rule of kings, the superior status of hereditary aristocrats, and the authority of established churches had been ordained by God, and that ordinary people owed them their obedience.

While Enlightenment ideas about the most effective organization of government differed considerably, most political writers agreed that the best governments balanced the powers and interests of the king, aristocrats and church leaders, and ordinary people. Many Enlightenment thinkers praised the informal British constitution, dividing power between king, lords, and commons, as the ideal of "balanced government." This idea was most closely associated with the French theorist Charles, Baron Montesquieu, whose chief work, *The Spirit of the Laws,* was well known in America.

Montesquieu argued that governments and the laws they enforce should be adapted to the people they govern, and that the distribution of power in government should reflect the natural distribution of influence and wealth in society. No radical, Montesquieu accepted that kings and aristocrats, due chiefly to their wealth, enjoyed more influence than others. Maintaining a just political order, he believed, required a stable government, which could only be maintained if kings, aristocrats, and commoners each held their proper proportion of political power.

While praising Britain's allegedly "balanced constitution," Enlightenment thinkers argued that in many other countries, unchecked monarchical power upset the proper balance of government and resulted in tyranny. In most European countries, established churches supported the claims of monarchs to rule by divine right and demanded obedience to kings and aristocrats. Many philosophers, particularly in France, regarded established churches, with their official dogmas and rigid, authoritarian hierarchies, as major obstacles to the creation of free societies.

The anticlerical ideas of the Enlightenment had little relevance in America, where religious pluralism was increasingly common and where many colonists belonged to dissenting religious traditions—Puritan, Quaker, Presbyterian, and Baptist—that emphasized the individual's relationship with God rather than obedience to a church hierarchy. In America, aspirations for an enlightened, just, and free society tended to merge with the aspiration of seventeenth-century religious refugees to create Godly societies in the New World.

John Adams, Thomas Jefferson, Alexander Hamilton, and James Madison, along with other colonists educated in American colleges in the middle decades of the eighteenth century, were familiar

with the political writings of Locke and Montesquieu, as well as the works of Hume, Hutcheson, and other Scottish philosophers. In Europe their ideas provided topics for academic conversations and coffeehouse debates. In America they became guidebooks to revolution and statecraft.

The Humanitarian Impulse

Confidence that reason and the insights of science could be applied to improve the lives of ordinary people inspired new efforts to relieve suffering, to provide, in a consistent and rational way, for the needs of others, and ultimately to solve problems that had plagued mankind for centuries.

This humanitarian impulse went beyond the kinds of charity encouraged for centuries by the church. Traditional charity sought to alleviate suffering and want by encouraging people to share whatever they could spare with those less fortunate. Its aims were modest, accepting that poverty, illness, and other kinds of distress were unavoidable aspects of life and seeking to relieve the worst of the inevitable suffering. The Enlightenment encouraged people to strive for a world in which the worst of human suffering would be eliminated. People had long talked and written about societies free of poverty and distress, but they had always been utopian fantasies. By the middle of the eighteenth century, people were imagining societies without want as a reality they could shape themselves through the diligent application of reason.

Those who embraced this new humanitarian spirit were confident that many kinds of suffering and want could be eliminated. Their efforts took many forms. Scientific farmers experimented with new crops, new fertilizers, and new ways to till, plant, and harvest, aiming to increase harvests and providing more, better, and cheaper food. They promoted increased reliance on root crops, extolling the virtues of carrots and above all, potatoes—more productive than wheat, wrote economist Adam Smith, easier to grow, and an "agreeable and wholesome variety of food" eaten by "the strongest men and the most beautiful women." A Scottish physician predicted that if the laboring population grew and ate potatoes, "Men would multiply, and poverty . . . would be unknown."

Religious toleration and a spirit of practical improvement established Philadelphia's reputation, in Europe and America, as a city shaped by the humanitarian ideals of the Enlightenment. Philadelphia was not quite as peaceful, orderly, and prosperous as some of its admirers believed, but its wide, straight streets, abundant clean water, diverse population, and rich cultural, civic, and commercial life made it one of the marvels of the age (The John Carter Brown Library).

The ambition to end suffering spurred efforts across a wide range of fields. Physicians, no longer satisfied with treating disease, searched for cures as well as methods to prevent disease through inoculation, improved sanitation, and better diets. Their efforts often failed and the medicines they prescribed sometimes did more harm than good, but smallpox inoculation, systematic effort to provide cities with clean water, and dozens of similar efforts improved the quality of life for countless people. Inventive men applied their creative energy to practical devices—efficient iron stoves for heating, mathematically constructed plows, lightning rods, and fire engines. Ambitious reformers established hospitals, orphanages, asylums for the treatment of the mentally ill, and charity schools for the education of the children of the poor. The results of these efforts were often grim. Underlying problems of disease, poverty, and mental illness did not yield easily to their efforts, but successes fueled new efforts more than failures discouraged them.

This rational humanitarian spirit washed over Britain's North American colonies. George Washington, anxious to make his Virginia plantation a model farm, collected books on innovative agricul-

tural techniques and experimented with new crops and fertilizers. Having suffered through smallpox at nineteen, he advocated inoculation and required soldiers to be inoculated during the Revolutionary War. He bred mules, which can do more work, live longer, and eat less than draft horses, and worked to popularize their use. Thomas Jefferson, whose life was defined by the Enlightenment spirit of rational inquiry and scientific advancement, designed a moldboard plow to cut through soil with minimal effort. In Philadelphia, the center of the American Enlightenment, paved and illuminated streets, water pumps every fifty paces, a hospital, a fire company, and private associations to support education and provide for the less fortunate all testified to a rational, humanitarian spirit.

This newfound confidence in the potential of reason to overcome the miseries that had plagued mankind for thousands of years existed side-by-side with grim assessments of the appalling conditions under which many people lived. "More than half the habitable world," the French philosopher Voltaire wrote in 1771, "is still populated by two-footed animals who live in a horrible condition approximating the state of nature, with hardly

39

enough to live on and clothe themselves, barely enjoying the gift of speech, barely aware that they are miserable, living and dying practically without knowing it." The kind of hopeless poverty Voltaire described was uncommon in Britain's North American colonies, where labor shortages made chronic unemployment rare, but the relative prosperity of the colonists seems to have encouraged reform more than self-satisfied complacency.

The Beginning of Abolitionism

Enslaved people were the one group in Britain's North American colonies whose wretched condition came closest to meeting Voltaire's bleak description. The humanitarian impulse led many people to indignant opposition to slavery. Although slavery had existed for thousands of years, it had developed relatively recently in British North America. The legal status of enslaved people was defined in colonial law in the second quarter of the seventeenth century, but enslaved people made up a small part of the population of British North America before the final years of the seventeenth century, when the importation of enslaved Africans to the North American mainland took off.

Individual colonists expressed distaste for slavery as early as the seventeenth century, recognizing it as inhumane. The earliest vocal opposition to slavery gradually took shape in the middle of the eighteenth century. Quakers were the first to express their opposition to slavery, reflecting their abhorrence of violence—enslavement was usually maintained through violence—and their conviction that all people, regardless of race or gender, possess an "Inner

Light" of goodness. Although some Quakers owned slaves, by the eve of the Revolution that number was very small, and Quakers led all others in principled opposition. Scottish philosopher James Millar wrote in 1771 that "the Quakers of Pennsylvania, are the first body of men . . . who seem to have thought that the abolition of this practice is a duty they owe to religion and humanity."

No one embodied the principles of Quaker benevolence and principled opposition to slavery more fully than Anthony Benezet, who arrived in Philadelphia from London in 1731 as a seventeen-year-old Huguenot refugee who had converted to Quakerism. In Philadelphia he worked to convince his fellow Quakers that slave-owning was contrary to Christianity. He taught school to the children of white Philadelphians by day and taught the children of poor black Philadelphians in his

OBSERVATIONS

On the Inflaving, importing and purchafing of

Negroes;

With fome Advice thereon, extracted from the Epiftle of the Yearly-Meeting of the People called QUAKERS, held at *London* in the Year 1748.

Anthony Benezet

When ye fpread forth your Hands, I will hide mine Eyes from you, yea when ye make many Prayers I will not hear; your Hands are full of Blood. Wafh ye, make you clean, put away the Evil of your Doings from before mine Eyes Ifai. 1, 15.

Is not this the Faft that I have chofen, to loofe the Bands of Wickednefs, to undo the heavy Burden, to let the Oppreffed go free, and that ye break every Yoke, Chap. 58, 7.

Second Edition.

GERMANTOWN:
Printed by CHRISTOPHER SOWER. 1760.

Quaker humanitarianism and a spirit of toleration made eighteenth-century Philadelphia a center of early anti-slavery thought and action. Enslavement, Anthony Benezet insisted in this 1760 pamphlet, was based on nothing but "selfish Avarice" and was contrary to the teachings of Christianity and "to the Rights and Liberties of Mankind" (Library of Congress).

home by night. He opened the first public school for girls in 1754 and devised a special course of study for a deaf girl who attended the school.

Combining the certainties of his religious faith with the rational principle of natural rights, Benezet became the most prolific anti-slavery pamphleteer of the third quarter of the eighteenth century and the most influential abolitionist in the Atlantic world. His work inspired the first generation of British antislavery advocates and persuaded many thoughtful Americans. He not only insisted that slavery was unjust and inhumane, he argued for racial equality. "I have found amongst the negroes," he wrote, "as great a variety of talents as amongst a like number of whites and I am bold to assert, that the notion entertained by some, that the blacks are inferior in their capacities, is a vulgar prejudice, founded on the pride of ignorance of their lordly masters, who have kept their slaves at such a distance, as to be unable to form a right judgment of them."

Deeply attached to the principles of Quaker non-violence and sharing few of the worldly concerns that drove American resistance to imperial authority, Benezet's life work transcended the political controversy that led to the Revolutionary War. But that work marked the beginnings of American abolitionism and inspired the Revolutionary challenge that led to the Pennsylvania Act for the Gradual Abolition of Slavery in 1780. His legacy reaches from the Revolutionary generation straight to our time. A gentle man who never served in public office or commanded men in battle, he was nonetheless among the Revolutionaries, properly understood, who made America free.

Benjamin Franklin

Among the people Anthony Benezet convinced of the evils of slavery was Benjamin Franklin, the American who most fully embodied the spirit of rational improvement inspired by the Enlightenment. Born in Boston in 1706, Franklin learned the printing trade from his brother and moved to Philadelphia as a young man. He traveled to London in 1724 and spent over a year working for printers before returning to Philadelphia. At

By 1816, when American-born painter Benjamin West painted *Benjamin Franklin Drawing Electricity from the Sky*, Franklin's heroic stature as a scientist had merged with his accomplishments as a Revolutionary statesman to make him one of the most widely admired people of his time. West portrayed Franklin harnessing the transforming power of nature (Philadelphia Museum of Art).

once scholarly and practical by nature, Franklin consumed the work of contemporary scientists and philosophers. At twenty-one he organized a club of bookish tradesmen and artisans called the Junto, who met to discuss books and ideas. In 1731, with Franklin's leadership, they founded the Library Company of Philadelphia, the nation's first subscription library. For small annual dues, members had access to what quickly became one of the finest libraries in the Americas.

Franklin built the *Pennsylvania Gazette* into the most successful newspaper in the colonies and threw himself into projects to improve life in Philadelphia and shape the intellectual character of his adopted colony. He was instrumental in founding the Academy and College of Philadelphia, which

41

Evangelical denominations, including the Baptists—pictured here conducting a baptism in the Schuylkill River near Philadelphia—grew dramatically in the last years before the American Revolution. They stressed the relationship between the individual and God, and opposed religious establishments, in which taxes were collected to support an official church (Historical Society of Pennslyvania).

opened in 1751 and is now the University of Pennsylvania. He helped organize the American Philosophical Society and served as its president, overseeing the work of a standing Committee on American Improvements. He started the publication of the Society's proceedings, giving early scientists a way to share their ideas with one another.

Although Franklin delighted in the world of ideas, he turned continuously to their practical application, organizing the first fire company in the city and the first American hospital. He promoted smallpox inoculation, argued for the economic usefulness of paper money, and proposed a system of night watchmen. He developed an improved cast iron stove for heating and experimented with electricity, demonstrating conclusively that lightning is an electrical discharge. He applied that insight to invent the lightning rod, designed to prevent lightning strikes from causing fires by running the electricity to ground.

He retired from business in 1748 and thereafter devoted himself completely to public service. In 1750 he wrote that when he died "I would rather have it said, *He lived usefully,* than, *He died rich.*" He was elected to the legislature and threw himself into the business of government. He secured appointment as postmaster general for Britain's North American colonies, and completely reorganized postal delivery across the continent. All of these accomplishments, large and small, added, as Franklin saw them, to the sum of human happiness. This was the ultimate aim of the eighteenth-century Enlightenment.

Devoted though he was to the future of Philadelphia and the happiness of its citizens, Franklin was even more devoted to the future of the British Empire. In 1757 he traveled to London as agent of the Pennsylvania assembly, which wanted to tax the vast landholdings of the Penn family. His reputation as a scientist opened doors throughout Britain, and Franklin enjoyed the company of the island nation's leading thinkers, writers, and public men. He remained in Britain for five years, and continually expressed his devotion to Britain. The Scottish philosopher David Hume paid tribute to Franklin when he prepared to leave for home in 1762. "I am very sorry," he wrote, "that you intend soon to leave our Hemisphere. America has sent us many good things, gold, silver, sugar, tobacco, etc.; but you are

the first philosopher, and indeed the first great man of letters, for whom we are beholden to her."

When his new friends suggested that the colonies might one day unite and break free of British control, Franklin scoffed at the idea. Americans, he said, would never unite "against their own nation, which protects and encourages them, with which they have so many ties of blood, interest, and affection." The whole idea, he wrote, "is not merely improbable, it is impossible."

American Revival

The Enlightenment reached British America and shaped the way educated Americans thought about human nature, rights, and the world around them at the same time many Americans experienced a profound upheaval in their spiritual lives. The confluence of these two movements—the one intellectual and practical, the other spiritual—had a profound influence on the way Americans thought about themselves and the importance of religious liberty.

By the middle of the eighteenth century, Britain's mainland colonies were home to an extraordinarily diverse array of Protestant denominations. They were organized in something like 1,500 congregations. New England Congregationalists—the descendants of the Puritan migrants of the seventeenth century—accounted for 450 churches. The Church of England accounted for another 300 congregations, most of them in the southern colonies and scattered through Pennsylvania, New Jersey, and New York. The Quakers had about 250 meetings (they did not call their gatherings churches), mostly in Pennsylvania but scattered from Rhode Island to South Carolina. Presbyterians accounted for another 150 churches, mostly in the middle colonies but after mid-century they spread rapidly in the interior parts of the south as Scots-Irish migrants made their way there. Baptist, Lutheran, and Dutch Reformed congregations accounted for about 100 churches each. The Lutheran congregations were concentrated in Pennsylvania, along with some 50 German Reformed congregations.

The religious fervor that brought many religious refugees to the colonies in the seventeenth century had cooled by the early eighteenth century, but the churches remained central to the lives of most colonists. The majority attended church regularly, but the old emphasis on a personal conversion experience that had been so important to the early New England Puritans and to many other Protestants had faded. Religious enthusiasm was rekindled from time to time by revivals, often associated with the arrival of a new minister who called on his congregation to renew its commitment to the faith.

A series of revivals in the mid-1730s, beginning in individual congregations but quickly merging and spreading, set off a general revival since known as the Great Awakening. The revival began in the Connecticut River Valley of New England and in New Jersey, then spread as individual ministers corresponded, coordinated revival meetings, and shared their churches with one another in a concerted effort to rouse the faithful. They employed a deeply personal, spontaneous brand of preaching to appeal to the emotions, calling the faithful to acknowledge their sinful nature and accept God's saving grace.

The revival was led by young clergymen, including Jonathan Edwards and Gilbert and William Tennant, and spread across New England and the middle colonies. A popular young evangelical in Britain, George Whitefield, learned about the revival in America and at the invitation of American ministers came to the colonies to conduct a revival tour that lasted more than a year. Whitefield preached his way from Maine to Georgia, drawing audiences so large no church could hold them. He often preached outdoors, sometimes to thousands of people at a time. His tour reflected how fully British America was tied to a trans-Atlantic world of ideas, as did his intimate friendship with the Philadelphia abolitionist Anthony Benezet, whom he had known in England when they were young.

Revival preaching was soon taken up by enthusiastic lay men and women who lacked formal theological training but who were inspired by their own conversion experience to lead others to salvation in the same way. These lay preachers traveled from town to town, gathering audience as they went and drawing people out of their usual congregations to participate in enthusiastic revival meetings. Some of them denounced the resident ministers in the

towns they visited and argued that the old system of territorial parishes should be discarded in favor of a churches gathered from the faithful.

The revival divided many congregations between the traditional clergy, who prepared their sermons with scholarly care and appealed to the mind as well as the spirit, and revivalists, who denounced what one of them called the "old, rotten, and stinking routine religion" in favor of a religious experience that was highly emotional and enthusiastic, and in which worshipers cried out, wept openly, and even threw themselves on the ground. Ezra Stiles, a Connecticut minister of the old school, concluded that "multitudes were seriously, soberly and solemnly out of their wits."

The radical evangelicals insisted that each person must assert his personal independence in matters of faith and embrace his own relationship with God, without relying on the teachings of educated ministers or participation in the traditional churches as a path to salvation. They ordained their own ministers, without regard to formal training, and preached in fields and private homes to informal congregations gathering white and black, rich and poor, and men and women, without distinction, as souls in need of salvation.

The revivals cooled in New England and the middle colonies after the mid-1740s, as revival ministers gathered their own congregations, built churches, and abandoned the itinerant preaching that had inspired and divided so many communities. The revivals shifted to the southern colonies in the 1750s, with itinerant Presbyterians drawing large crowds, to the disgust of the traditional Anglican clergy and their gentry supporters. The revival reached some of its most receptive audiences in the backcountry of Virginia and North Carolina, regions poorly served by the Anglican Church, where travelling Presbyterian and Baptist preachers found willing converts among ordinary people who had lost touch with traditional religious services. Like the northern revivalists, they preached about the equality of all souls before God and called on each listener to make an independent, personal commitment to accept God's redeeming grace.

The gentry and better educated colonists tended to look on the evangelicals with skepticism. Under the influence of Enlightenment thought, they approached faith in increasingly rational

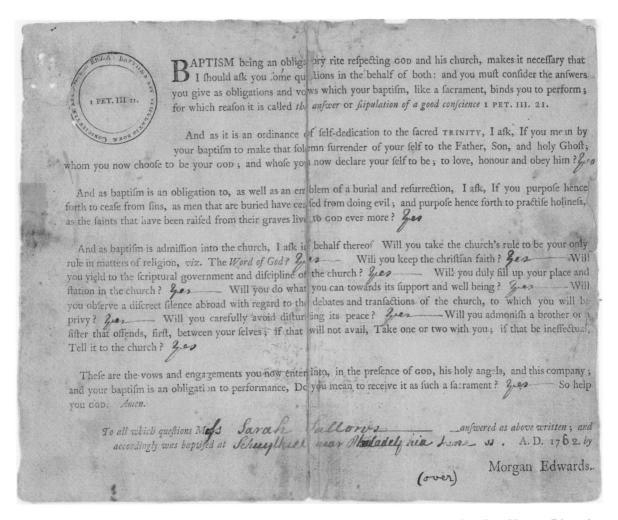

BAPTISM being an obligatory rite respecting GOD and his church, makes it necessary that I should ask you some questions in the behalf of both: and you must consider the answers you give as obligations and vows which your baptism, like a sacrament, binds you to perform; for which reason it is called the answer or stipulation of a good conscience I PET. III. 21.

And as it is an ordinance of self-dedication to the sacred TRINITY, I ask, If you mean by your baptism to make that solemn surrender of your self to the Father, Son, and holy Ghost; whom you now choose to be your GOD; and whose you now declare your self to be; to love, honour and obey him? *Yes*

And as baptism is an obligation to, as well as an emblem of a burial and resurrection, I ask, If you purpose hence forth to cease from sins, as men that are buried have ceased from doing evil; and purpose hence forth to practise holiness, as the saints that have been raised from their graves live to GOD ever more? *Yes*

And as baptism is admission into the church, I ask in behalf thereof Will you take the church's rule to be your only rule in matters of religion, viz. The *Word of God*? *Yes* — Will you keep the christian faith? *Yes* — Will you yield to the scriptural government and discipline of the church? *Yes* — Will you duly fill up your place and station in the church? *Yes* — Will you do what you can towards its support and well being? *Yes* — Will you observe a discreet silence abroad with regard to the debates and transactions of the church, to which you will be privy? *Yes* — Will you carefully avoid disturbing its peace? *Yes* — Will you admonish a brother or a sister that offends, first, between your selves; if that will not avail, Take one or two with you; if that be ineffectual, Tell it to the church? *Yes*

These are the vows and engagements you now enter into, in the presence of GOD, his holy angels, and this company; and your baptism is an obligation to performance, Do you mean to receive it as such a sacrament? *Yes* — So help you GOD. *Amen.*

To all which questions Mrs *Sarah Sallows* _____ answered as above written; and accordingly was baptised at *Schuylkill near Philadelphia June 22* . A.D. 1762 by

Morgan Edwards.

(over)

Sarah Sallows was the twenty-one-year-old daughter of a Philadelphia merchant when Rev. Morgan Edwards baptized her in the Schuylkill River in 1762. She married Robert Shewall, a young merchant who served as a lieutenant colonel in the Pennsylvania Associators during the Revolutionary War. While most evangelicals supported the Revolution, there were exceptions, including Reverend Edwards, who became a loyalist (American Baptist Historical Society).

ways. Advances in natural science had revealed the orderly working of God's creation, they held, and they concluded that God did not interfere in the natural world. Hurricanes, earthquakes, and floods were not evidence of God's displeasure, but were shaped by the laws of nature ordained by God. God's order could be understood through the application of reason, they insisted, and reflected a deity who was benign and forgiving.

This approach to matters of faith was shared, with important variations, by many of the men who led the American Revolution. Some of them regarded God like a great clockmaker, who had created the universe, established its rules, and set them all in motion, and who did not interfere in earthly affairs. Others, including George Washington, shared in this rational view, but believed that God intervened, when He chose, in the affairs of

mankind. During and after the Revolutionary War, Washington referred frequently to God's Providence—His active intervention—on behalf of the American cause.

The revivals weakened the hold of traditional churches on many communities and led many colonists to assert greater personal independence in matters of religion. Church affiliation and religious sentiments became, as a consequence of the revival, much more a matter of personal choice than they had ever been. The Enlightenment, by encouraging men and women to put their trust in reason, also weakened the hold of traditional churches and stirred distrust of established religion. Together these very different movements led to one of the most important achievements of the American Revolution—the establishment of religious liberty as a basic right of free people.

45

When George Washington commissioned Charles Willson Peale to paint his portrait in 1772, he wore his Virginia regimental uniform, recalling his role in the French and Indian War, which Washington then regarded as the most important public service of his life. The mountains in the background are an allusion to the frontier region where Washington's made his reputation as a soldier (Courtesy of Museums at Washington and Lee University, Lexington, Virginia).

Chapter 4 The Frontiers of Empire

Until the middle of the eighteenth century, most of the colonists in Britain's North American colonies lived within one hundred miles of the ocean. The frontier of the British Empire in North America stood on the east side of the Appalachian barrier that stretched from New England to Georgia, in most places less than two hundred miles from the sea.

This began to change in the 1740s as new migrants from Europe, anxious to acquire land, pressed on the frontier. A minority were from England. Most came from Scotland, Ireland, and the various princely states of Germany. Many were economic refugees, escaping poverty or dispossession. They moved quickly into the hinterlands—up the Hudson, into central Pennsylvania, and along the Blue Ridge of Virginia and southward along old Indian paths into the hills of North and South Carolina, settling land above the falls of the rivers flowing east through the tidewater. In some cases they formed communities of immigrant Scots, Scots-Irish, or Germans in the backcountry. Many were fiercely independent people who resented efforts of colonial bureaucrats and eastern gentry to govern them.

Difficult as some of them were to manage, they were part of a population boom that made Britain's North American colonies an increasingly important part of the imperial economy. With a population of some 1.5 million people in 1750, the colonies were no longer an economic backwater. They had become an important market for goods manufactured in England as well as products reimported from continental Europe, India, and beyond, shipped in growing quantities by British merchants who sold American goods in British and European markets and who provided American merchants and planters with credit to buy their goods.

Many of Britain's North American colonists benefited from their place in the web of imperial commerce. New England merchants sold timber, rope, and other supplies to the Royal Navy. New Englanders built an ever increasing number of the merchant ships to serve the imperial market. North Carolinians produced and sold tar and turpentine, essential for building and maintaining ships. North and South Carolinians grew vast amounts of rice, much of which was shipped to Britain's Caribbean colonies to feed the enslaved people who toiled to produce sugar, the most valuable staple produced in the British Empire. The enslaved people of the sugar colonies also ate dried fish, much of it caught and sold by New Englanders. North American merchants bought slaves from African traders on the west coast of Africa and sold their human cargoes in the Caribbean and, in smaller numbers, on the North American mainland. They brought sugar and molasses back to New England, where distillers turned molasses into rum, which was sold all over the Atlantic world. All over the colonies, merchants profited by selling manufactured goods—cloth, finished metal goods from buttons to doorknobs, clocks, books, gunpowder, paint, paper, and glass—shipped from Britain.

The colonists who owned property and participated in the increasingly global market for goods benefitted from their association with the British Empire. Distant as they were from Britain, they were quick to express their loyalty to the Crown and their pride in Britain's victories in a succession of wars, chiefly with France or Spain. They were grateful for the protection of the American coast by the Royal Navy and the broader protection afforded by Britain's standing in a world of predatory imperial powers.

American Empires

By far the largest and most populous of the European empires in the Western Hemisphere belonged to Spain, which claimed most of South and Central America, Mexico, Cuba and several other island in the Caribbean, and most of mainland North America. The Spanish maintained military and trading outposts on the coasts of Florida as well as the southern part of what is now Mississippi and Alabama and the southwest part of Georgia.

The Spanish empire reached across the future states of Texas, New Mexico, and Arizona to southern California, but they had barely explored much of this vast domain, and Spanish settlement was thin everywhere north of Mexico. The Spanish claimed sovereignty over large regions peopled by Indians they exploited when they could, and with whom they traded and fought, but over whom they were never able to establish control. From their northern colonial capital of Santa Fe, in what is now New Mexico, they sought to dominate the Pueblo Indians surrounding them, with no consistent success. They had more trouble with the semi-nomadic Navaho and Apache peoples, and even more with the warlike, nomadic Comanche, who harassed and raided Spanish settlements and preyed on other Indians. The Spanish had barely explored the Pacific coast of North America that would become northern California, Oregon, and Washington, but their claim to it was not yet challenged by other powers.

Except for its military presence in Florida, which pressed close on Georgia, the Spanish Empire in North America was largely unknown to colonial British Americans. Not so the French Empire. France claimed much of North America, including most of what is now eastern Canada and a region extending from the Great Lakes down the Mississippi River to New Orleans. This area was vast but the French hold on most of it was not very strong. The French were mainly interested in trade rather than settlement. French colonists lived along the St. Lawrence River as far as Montreal and were scattered in outposts on the Great Lakes. The settlers in this region, which the French called New France, engaged in a very active fur trade with the Indians.

Although the British controlled the smallest part of North America, there were many more colonists in Britain's North American colonies than in New France. In 1750 the population of the French colonies was about 75,000, less than five percent of the population of Britain's North American colonies. The British navy was generally superior to the French navy and could defend Britain's colonies and threaten those of France. Britain and France fought over territory in North America repeatedly in the first half of the eighteenth century without a decisive result.

The French had one important advantage over the British. Because the purpose of their colonies was mainly to trade, the French seemed to pose little threat to the Indians with whom they traded. The British colonies, by contrast, attracted migrants who carved farms out of the woodlands where Indians hunted. British colonists, pressing their frontier westward, frequently came into conflict with the Indians. The tribes of the Great Lakes, western New York and the St. Lawrence River Valley often sided with the French against land-hungry British migrants. These Indians were fierce and skillful warriors, and their ties to the French balanced the numerical superiority of the British when the British and French went to war.

The Indians constituted a fourth power in North America, not to be underestimated. The most important, from an imperial perspective, were the Iroquois, a confederacy of six Indian peoples who occupied much of what became upstate New York and the eastern Great Lakes region, and south through western Pennsylvania as far as Virginia and Kentucky and southwest into the upper Ohio Valley. They called themselves the Haudenosaunee. The French called them the Iroquois League and the British knew them as the Five Nations. They were, individually, the Mohawk, Oneida, Onandaga, Cayuga, and Seneca peoples. The Tuscarora

Overleaf: Surveyor Lewis Evans, encouraged by Benjamin Franklin, explored the Ohio country and published his findings in this 1758 map, providing a detailed depiction of the region claimed by Britain and France. This version was published in London, and notes that the Ohio country exceeds "in good land all the European Dominions of Great Britain France and Spain" (The Society of the Cincinnati).

Henry Popple's enormous 1733 *Map of the British Empire in America*—to which this smaller map was the index—was the most detailed map of the European empires in North America yet published. It depicted British America bounded to the west by the Appalachian Mountains, beyond which French claims extended from Canada to the Gulf of Mexico (Library of Congress).

people, displaced by the settlement of the Carolinas, migrated north in first third of the eighteenth century and joined the confederacy, which the British sometimes thereafter referred to as the Six Nations.

Each of these peoples had its own language and culture, closely related but distinct. Their confederacy long predated the arrival of Europeans in North America, and served to maintain peace between them, as a kind of cultural union, and as an instrument of mutual support in conflicts with neighboring peoples—with the Hurons and Wyandots to the west and southwest and with other peoples, including the British. Their leaders were as skilled at diplomacy and negotiation as any European, and their warriors were unmatched in the forests and on the waterways of their homeland, which spanned the divide between New France on the north and New England and New York to the east and south.

The Ohio Country

By 1750 the prospect of occupying land to the west of the Appalachians was beginning to stir the imagination of colonists, particularly those in Virginia and North Carolina. Both those colonies had extensive land claims west of the mountains. North Carolina's claim extended to the Mississippi River and included what became Tennessee. Virginia's claim, based on the charter granted to the Virginia Company of London in 1609, ran from "from sea to sea." The original grant to the Virginia Company had been diminished by the grant of Maryland to Lord Baltimore and the grant of Pennsylvania to William Penn, but those colonies had established western limits. The western limit of the Pennsylvania grant was a meandering line five degrees west of the Delaware River. Virginia claimed everything to the west, including what is now the southwest part of Pennsylvania (including the site of Pittsburgh) and everything beyond—including all of what became the states of Ohio, Indiana, Michigan, Illinois, and Wisconsin—as

well as the land south of the Ohio that became West Virginia and Kentucky.

By the 1740s the British and the French were aware of the potential value of the Ohio Country, a swath of forests stretching from what is now northwestern Pennsylvania south and west along the Ohio River and northward from the river across the modern states of Ohio and Indiana to the Great Lakes. It was a region of obvious fertility, much of it level and drained by small rivers, most of them flowing south into the Ohio. It was also the key to controlling the trans-Appalachian West, a larger region embracing later Kentucky and Tennessee, which are also watered by rivers flowing into the Ohio.

Britain and France each claimed the Ohio Valley, but neither had a military hold on the region. Each moved, at very nearly the same time, to assert its claim, setting up a conflict that led directly to an imperial war. In 1749, Virginia colonists formed the Ohio Company and made plans to divide the land up and sell it to settlers. When the French learned of these plans, they sent a military force to occupy the Ohio frontier. In 1753 the French began to build a chain of forts between Lake Erie and the place where the Monongahela and Allegheny rivers join to form the Ohio, where the city of Pittsburgh stands today. Whichever power controlled that point would control the future of the Ohio Valley and the future of the trans-Appalachian West. The contest for the control of the Ohio frontier thus became a contest for future dominance of eastern North America. When he learned about the French forts, the governor of Virginia sent a twenty-one-year-old militia officer, Major George Washington, to the frontier to deliver a message to the French to leave the area.

Young Man Washington

Washington was then almost wholly unknown. He was the third son of a Virginia planter, Augustine Washington, who had died when George was eleven. Augustine had left the

Virginia Governor Robert Dinwiddie dispatched George Washington, then a young major in the militia, to deliver a message to the commander of a French fort south of Lake Erie, in a region claimed by Virginia. Washington's journal of the expedition, published in Williamsburg and republished in London, made his name familiar to government officials in Britain (Darlington Memorial Library, University of Pittsburgh).

THE
JOURNAL
OF
MAJOR *George Washington*,

SENT BY THE

Hon. ROBERT DINWIDDIE, Esq;
His Majesty's Lieutenant-Governor, and
Commander in Chief of *Virginia*;

TO THE

COMMANDANT of the *French* Forces

ON
OHIO.

To which are added, the

GOVERNOR's LETTER:

AND A

TRANSLATION of the *French* Officer's Answer.

WITH

A New MAP of the Country as far as the
MISSISSIPPI.

WILLIAMSBURGH Printed;
LONDON, Reprinted for *T. Jefferys*, the Corner
of St. *Martin's* Lane.

MDCCLIV.
[Price One Shilling.]

best and largest parts of his estate to his two older sons. George was to inherit a modest farm. But he was ambitious. His oldest brother, Lawrence, married into the family of Lord Fairfax, who owned a vast part of northern Virginia. Thanks to the patronage of the Fairfax family, George was made a county surveyor at seventeen and began working on the Virginia frontier, collecting fees for surveying land claims. He was naturally strong and athletic, and the work toughened him in a way that set him apart from the sons of other tidewater gentlemen. He learned to work with rough backcountry people and in time to give commands and see them obeyed. He also developed a conviction that the future of America lay in the west, and he never relinquished it.

Lawrence Washington died from tuberculosis in 1752, leaving George an interest in Mount Vernon, his Potomac River plantation. Lawrence had been a major in the Virginia militia, and George successfully maneuvered to succeed him. The next year the governor, Robert Dinwiddie, sent him to the eastern edge of the Ohio Country to warn the French off. Dinwiddie did not expect the French to obey, but he expected Washington to get a good look at the French force and report on what he learned.

Washington set out in October 1753, making his way through wooded mountains and valleys to a small fort the French had built several miles south of Lake Erie, in what is now northwestern Pennsylvania. The French commander politely told Washington that they were in French territory and that they would not leave. As winter descended, Washington returned with this message and delivered his report to Dinwiddie in Williamsburg in January 1754. The governor was impressed with Washington's written account of his journey and ordered it published. In the narrow, provincial world of colonial Virginia, Washington became a minor celebrity.

Washington urged the governor to build a fort at the forks of the Ohio, where the Monongahela and Allegheny rivers join to become the Ohio River. Dinwiddie immediately sent a party of about forty Virginia frontiersmen to build a small wooden fort at the forks, which they named Fort Prince George. A French force surrounded the fort in April 1754 and forced the Virginians to surrender. The French then knocked down the British fort and built a larger one they named Fort Duquesne, in honor of the governor of New France.

Dinwiddie, meanwhile, promoted Washington to lieutenant colonel and dispatched him, with 160 men, to take command at the forks of the Ohio. Dinwiddie ordered Washington that if anyone attempted to interfere with the building of the fort, Washington was "to restrain all such Offenders, and in Case of resistance to make Prisoners of or kill and destroy them." It was an invitation to start a war, without instructions from London or the knowledge of the king's government. Dinwiddie had issued it to a tough, ambitious young man who was unlikely to back away from a fight.

Washington learned on the march that the French had taken control of the forks. This did not dissuade him. On May 28, 1754, Washington's men encountered a group of French soldiers from Fort Duquesne who had been sent to warn him to depart French territory. Washington ordered a party of forty men, together with a dozen or so Indians, to surround the French. A skirmish began, and within fifteen minutes ten or twelve of the Frenchmen were dead, including their commander. It was the impetuous act of an impetuous young man anxious to earn a reputation as a bold commander. These shots in the wilderness began what Americans call the French and Indian War, a war that spread to Europe and consumed Britain and France in a great war for empire that circled the globe.

Washington expected to be attacked by a larger French force from Fort Duquesne, so he moved his little force to a place called the Great Meadows, where he had his men construct a simple fort he named Fort Necessity. He wrote a hasty letter to his brother Jack that he expected his command "to exert our Noble Courage with Spirit." Describing the skirmish, he wrote, "I can with truth assure you, I heard Bulletts whistle and believe me there was something charming in the sound." This boast was repeated and months later reached King George II in London, the last British monarch to lead troops into battle. He is reputed to have said, "He would not say so, if he had been used to hear many."

A French force of six hundred men along with one hundred of their Indian allies surrounded the little fort on July 3. Washington boldly ordered his men outside the fort and attacked the enemy

In this 1903 painting of Braddock's defeat by Edwin Deming, George Washington catches the bridle of Braddock's horse as the British general is mortally wounded by French soldiers and their Indian allies firing from cover (Wisconsin Historical Society).

but was driven back into the fort. The two sides exchanged fire for several hours, until the Virginians ran low on ammunition and it began to rain. Washington was forced to surrender. The French permitted him and his men to return to Virginia.

Braddock's March

When news of the fighting at Fort Necessity reached Britain, the king's government decided to send troops to capture four French forts on the frontiers between British and French territory: Fort Beauséjour, on the neck of land connecting French Acadia and British Nova Scotia, Fort Saint-Frédéric, on Lake Champlain, between New France and New York, Fort Niagara, on the Niagara River, and Fort

Duquesne. It was a good plan if properly executed.

The British sent a small army under General Edward Braddock to take Fort Duquesne and drive the French off the Ohio frontier. Braddock landed in Alexandria, Virginia, in early 1755. His soldiers were trained to fight on the open plains of Europe, not in the forests of America, where their bright red uniforms made them easy targets for French and Indian riflemen. Benjamin Franklin, met with Braddock and warned him about the dangers of an Indian attack in the wilderness. "These savages," Braddock replied, "may, indeed, be a formidable enemy to your raw American militia, but upon the King's regular and disciplined troops, sir, it is impossible they should make any impression."

American militia joined Braddock's march. So did George Washington, who accompanied the

James Wolfe's death in his moment of victory at Quebec—memorialized in this 1770 painting by Benjamin West—made him a hero throughout the British Empire (National Gallery of Canada, Ottawa).

army as an aide to Braddock. The army struggled through forests and over mountains and rivers for almost two months. Parties worked in advance of the army, clearing a road through wilderness, a task that involved blasting boulders with gunpowder charges as well as cutting down and removing old growth trees to fashion a path twelve feet wide for men and artillery to pass. By the time the army drew close to Fort Duquesne, its soldiers were exhausted.

On July 9, 1755, a force of some 250 French Canadian militia and French Regulars, together with some 650 Indians, attacked Braddock's army on a wooded ridge above the Monongahela River just a few miles from Fort Duquesne. Attacking downhill, the French and Indians fired from the cover of old-growth trees, big enough to provide cover for two or three warriors at a time. Braddock attempted to maintain conventional military discipline and organize his men to fire volleys from compact formations and advance in line of battle, but under withering fire from unseen enemies up the ridge, unit discipline failed. British and provincial troops fell in appalling numbers, many units losing half or more of their men killed and wounded. The Indians fired carefully, taking aim as they did when hunting. "The English people are fools," a Delaware warrior later said, "they hold their guns half man high" while "we take sight and have them at a shot." Washington appealed to Braddock to allow him to take command of the Virginia troops "and engage the enemy in their own way," spread out among the trees and firing from cover, but Braddock refused.

The chaotic battle went on for some three hours. Finally, Braddock fell from his horse, shot through the lungs. As other officers fell, the British Regulars faltered, fell back, and finally fled the battlefield. They "were struck with such a panic" Washington wrote, "that they behaved with more cowardice than it is possible to conceive. . . . they broke and ran as sheep pursued by dogs." Washington and British Lieutenant Colonel Thomas Gage bravely organized the rear guard and held the enemy off while the remnant of Braddock's army retreated.

More than half of the army was killed or wounded. Private Duncan Cameron, a wounded British soldier, hid in a hollow tree from which he witnessed "horrors" more shocking than he had experienced on any European battlefield, as the Indians took the scalps of the dead and wounded alike. General Braddock died in great pain three days after the battle. He was buried in the middle of the road ahead of the column to prevent the Indians from digging up his body and desecrating it. Wagons and marching men packed the earth and disguised his unmarked grave. Remains believed to be Braddock's were found by a road crew in 1804 and reburied nearby.

Braddock's Defeat, also called the Battle of the Monongahela, was long remembered by Americans. Several men who would become generals in the Revolutionary War were at the battle, including Washington, Horatio Gates, Charles Lee, Daniel Morgan, Adam Stephen, and William Crawford. Other future American leaders were there, including frontiersman Daniel Boone. So were many American militiamen whose sons later went to war against the British. In 1755, twenty-five-year-old James Overton was a Virginia militiaman in Braddock's campaign. In 1776, his twenty-three-year-old son

Thomas became an officer in George Washington's army. The men who fought with Braddock saw that the British army, for all of its impressive strength, could be beaten. They witnessed one of the most crushing defeats ever sustained by the British in America and never forgot the lesson.

The rest of the British strategy played out with mixed results. A force of 270 British Regulars and some 2,000 New England troops took Fort Beauséjour, which was poorly defended. A mixed force of New York and New England troops, joined by Mohawk warriors, acquitted itself well against the French on Lake George, but were unable to take Fort Saint-Frédéric. Some 2,500 colonial troops were assembled to take Fort Niagara, but Governor William Shirley of Massachusetts, personally commanding the army, retreated without making an attempt on the fort.

The Great War for Empire

The disastrous outcome of Braddock's campaign overshadowed the others. The defeat left the colonial frontier from New York to Virginia open to Indian attack. Thousands of frontier settlers abandoned their homes and farms and fled east.

The British government had hoped to confine the war to North America with a series of easy victories. It was ill prepared for a general European war, much less a global war for empire, but in 1756 it was drawn into both. British attacks on French shipping led the French to prepare to invade Hanover, the hereditary possession of King George II. Britain quickly concluded an alliance with Prussia to protect Hanover and declared war on France, which was allied with Austria. Most of the other powers in Europe, including Spain, Sweden, and Russia, were either drawn into the war or sought to exploit it to gain some advantage over their rivals. What began with a skirmish on the Ohio frontier became a world war, in which the British and French fought for dominance in India, the Caribbean, and North America. It became a great war for empire, with fighting over much of the known world.

At first the war went badly for Britain. The French were better prepared, since they maintained a standing army of some 200,000 men—Britain had about 30,000—and a navy that was nearly as large, and in some respects technically superior, to the Royal Navy. The new British commander in America, Lord Loudoun, failed in an attempt to take the French fortress of Louisbourg, on Cape Breton Island, which controlled the mouth of the St. Lawrence River. In 1757 the French took advantage of the weakness of the British forces left guarding the American frontier to capture Fort William Henry, a key to the defense of New York and the interior of New England. Britain was threatened with invasion at home and feared the loss of its valuable colonies in the Caribbean.

In 1758 the war turned in Britain's favor. A British naval blockade of France prevented supplies from reaching New France. A British force led by General Jeffrey Amherst captured Louisbourg. The British then took control of French settlements in New Brunswick, Prince Edward Island, and New-foundland. The British were also successful on the Ohio frontier. In the summer of 1758, the British sent General John Forbes with an army of 6,000 men to take Fort Duquesne. George Washington, by then an experienced colonel of the Virginia militia, joined the expedition. The British army marched across Pennsylvania, constructing a road and a series of forts as it moved. Unable to with-stand a siege because they were short of supplies, the French blew up Fort Duquesne and retreated. George Washington and a British force entered the ruins of the fort on November 24, 1758.

British economic and naval power proved to be the difference in the war. During the war the British were able to build warships much faster than the French. By 1759 the Royal Navy had 113 ships of the line—the large warships that decided the outcome of war at sea—and the French had about half that number. The Royal Navy prevented supplies and reinforcements from reaching New France, and in 1759, British General James Wolfe led an army up the St. Lawrence River and captured Quebec, the capital. General Wolfe and the French commander, General Montcalm, were killed in the battle for the city. The French tried to retake Quebec in 1760, but failed. Meanwhile the Royal Navy captured most of the French islands in the Caribbean. Thereafter the Spanish, fearing that the British would become the major power in the world, entered the war on the side of France. Spain was too late and lost Havana and Manila to the Royal Navy.

At a conference in 1763, Britain, Spain, and France agreed to make peace. By the Treaty of Paris, Great Britain secured control of North America east of the Mississippi River, except the city of New Orleans, including all the French possessions in modern Canada. Britain also acquired the French holdings in India. Spain surrendered Florida—then divided into two colonies, called East Florida and West Florida, extending from the Atlantic to the Mississippi River—to the British. In exchange the British returned Havana and Manila and acknowledged Spain's claim to New Orleans and the vast territory west of the Mississippi River. Britain retained Grenada but returned Martinique and Guadeloupe to France.

The British had won a great victory. British colonists from New England to Georgia no longer had to worry about the French threatening the frontier or sending Indian allies to attack their settlements. Colonists in Georgia and the Carolina backcountry no longer had to worry about the Spanish on their frontier or that the Indians to their south and west would secure arms and ammunition from the Spanish. The colonists began making plans to settle the land west of the Appalachian Mountains. Free from foreign threats on the frontier, the colonists looked forward to peace and prosperity. They happily proclaimed their loyalty to their new king, George III.

The Royal Navy established control of the Atlantic by inflicting a crushing defeat on the French navy at Quiberon Bay on the coast of Brittany on November 20, 1759. The French lost seven of the twenty-one ships of the line engaged, leaving the Royal Navy free to devote its strength to the war in American waters (© National Maritime Museum, Greenwich, London).

Our country is in danger, but not to be despaired of. Our enemies are numerous and powerful, yet we have many friends; determine to be free, and Heaven and Earth will aid the Resolution. On you depends the fortunes of America. You are to decide the important question, on which rest the happiness and liberty of millions yet unborn. Act worthy of yourselves.

DR. JOSEPH WARREN
MARCH 6, 1775

THE
SHAPING
OF THE
REVOLUTION

Chapter 5 Protest

Many colonists believed that the return of peace would bring opportunity and prosperity. They no longer had to fear the French to the north or the Spanish to the south, nor did they have to worry about France or Spain arming the Indians and encouraging them to attack settlements on the frontier. The British Empire had triumphed over its enemies. The Royal Navy dominated the sea lanes of the Atlantic world. The empire had extended its hold on India and was expanding trade with Southeast Asia and China. Britain was rich and growing richer, and the colonists expected to share in Britain's success.

The reality proved very different. The sprawling, global conflict had been the most expensive war in European history. Before the war, the British government had operated on an annual budget of about 8 million pounds. At the end of the war, Britain was 137 million pounds in debt. The interest alone was 5 million pounds a year. To pay down the debt, Parliament imposed new taxes on the British people, but a post-war downturn in the economy made it hard to raise revenue. A new tax on cider, one of Britain's favorite drinks, led to protests and rioting.

British officials decided to impose taxes on their American colonists. The British had never collected much tax revenue in America, but they reasoned that the colonists benefitted from the victory as much as any of the king's subjects and ought to pay their share of the costs. Those costs would include troops stationed in America and an aggressive system for collecting taxes, enforcing tax laws, and controlling the territory taken from France and Spain.

This new imperial system of taxation and regulation frustrated and angered many Americans, who were used to managing their own affairs. They, or their parents or grandparents, had come to America to secure a degree of personal independence denied to them in Europe. For generations the colonists had governed themselves with little interference from the British government. They believed that the new laws and policies introduced by the British government violated their rights. They evaded the new laws, protested their enforcement, and demanded their repeal. British officials gave way on some measures, only to follow up with new taxes, new regulations, and military force to compel the colonists to accept their authority.

The Proclamation Line of 1763

The Treaty of Paris more than tripled the size of the British Empire in North America. Britain acquired East and West Florida from Spain. France gave up Newfoundland, Canada, and any claims it had to land between the Appalachian Mountains and the Mississippi River. From the perspective of many American colonists, the war had been fought to secure the land beyond the mountains for settlement, and they looked forward to occupying it as soon as possible.

They were outraged when the British government made a sweeping decision to forbid settlement beyond the mountains. Lord Jeffrey Amherst, the British commander in chief in North America, estimated that the British army would have to station ten thousand men in North America to maintain order among the French colonists and the Indians and to deal with illegal settlers, bandits, and smugglers. This was more than twice as many soldiers as

A young and vigorous king when he assumed the throne in 1762, George III seemed to embody the promising future of Britain and her colonies. The casual pose he struck in his coronation portrait suggests informality and a determination to be an accessible monarch. Symbols of royalty—the mace, scepter, orb, and throne—are absent. His crown is barely visible. The artist, Allan Ramsay, received orders for 176 copies of the portrait, which became one of the most familiar paintings in the English-speaking world during the last part of the eighteenth century (Royal Collection Trust / © Her Majesty Queen Elizabeth II 2022).

LAKE SUPERIOR

L. HURON

L. MICHIGAN

Michillimakinac

N⁰. 60. 2 Bat.

Detroit

L. ERIE

L O U I S I A N A

Fᵗ. Chartres
34.

OHIO R.

VIRGIN

N. CAROLIN

S. CAROLIN

Fᵗ. Prince George
N⁰.2

Fᵗ. Charlotte
N⁰.3

Fᵗ. Augusta
N⁰.4

PART of
EW MEXICO

Tombeche

GEORGIA

Natches

Apalachie N⁰.

Fᵗ. Frede
N⁰.5

W. FLORIDA

Ibbeville 2
21.
Mobile

Pensacola

31.

E. FLORI

Sᵗ. Augustine
9.

L A N D S   R E S E R V E D   F O R   T H E

M I S S I S S I P I   R.

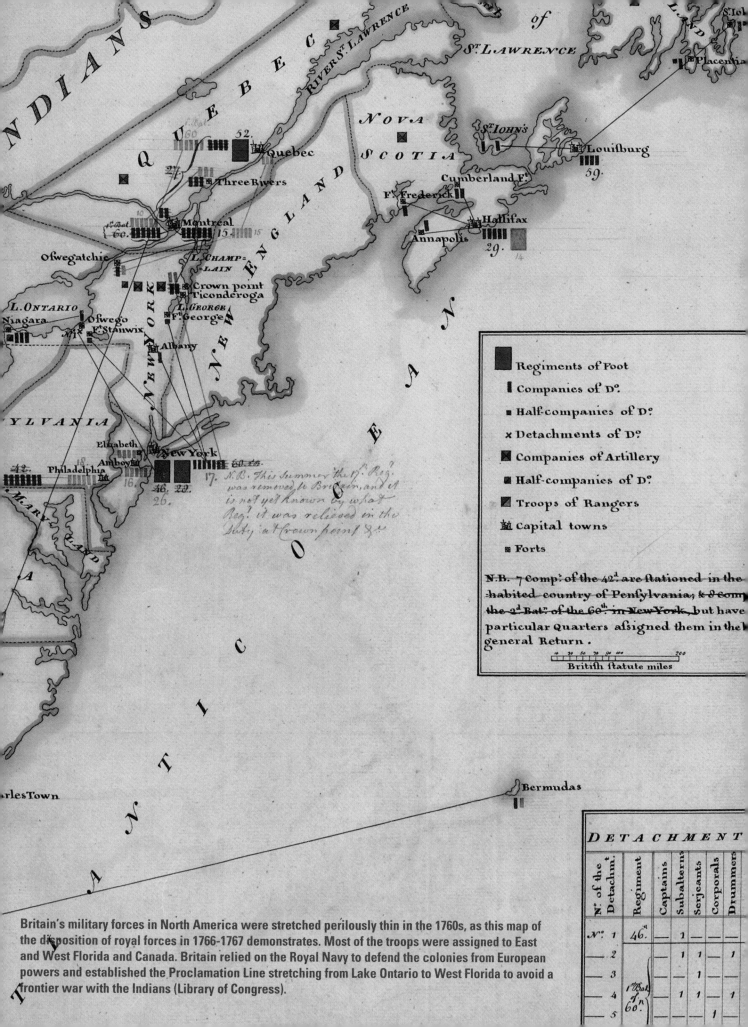

I N D I A N S

Rivers St. LAWRENCE

of St. LAWRENCE

St. Iohn

Placentia

Q U E B E C

NOVA

SCOTIA

1st Bat. 60 · 52 · · Quebec

27

Three Rivers

St. IOHN'S

Louisburg
59 ·

Cumberland Ft.

Ft. Frederick

1st Bat. 60 · 10 · Montreal · 15 · 15

Ofwegatchie

L. CHAMP-
LAIN

Annapolis

Hallifax
29 · 14

N E W   E N G L A N D

Crown point
Ticonderoga
L. GEORGE
Ft. George

L. ONTARIO

Niagara · Ofwego · Ft. Stanwix

O C E A N

Albany

N E W   Y O R K

· · · · · · · · ·
Regiments of Foot

| **Companies of D?**

■ **Half-companies of D?**

× **Detachments of D?**

⊠ **Companies of Artillery**

■ **Half-companies of D?**

◨ **Troops of Rangers**

Capital towns

⊠ **Forts**

Y L V A N I A

Elizabeth
Amboy · New York · 60 · 15 ·
42 · Philadelphia · 18 · 16 · 17 ·
46 · 28 ·
26 ·

N.B. This Summer the 17th Reg.t
was removed to Britain, and it
is not yet known by what
Reg.t it was relieved in the
Duty at Crown point &c.

M A R Y L A N D

N.B. 7 Comp.s of the 42.d are stationed in the
inhabited country of Penfylvania, & 8 comp.s
the 2.d Bat.n of the 60.th in New York, but have
particular Quarters afsigned them in the
general Return.

10 30 50 70 90 100   200
Britifh ftatute miles

A T L A N T I C

arles Town

Bermudas

Britain's military forces in North America were stretched perilously thin in the 1760s, as this map of the disposition of royal forces in 1766-1767 demonstrates. Most of the troops were assigned to East and West Florida and Canada. Britain relied on the Royal Navy to defend the colonies from European powers and established the Proclamation Line stretching from Lake Ontario to West Florida to avoid a frontier war with the Indians (Library of Congress).

D E T A C H M E N T

N? of the Detachm.t	Regiment	Captains	Subalterns	Serjeants	Corporals	Drummers
N? 1	46.x		1			
— 2			1	1		
— 3				1		
— 4	1st Bat. of 60.th		1	1		
— 5						1

the British had ever stationed in North America in peacetime. The cost of maintaining this army would be enormous, and Amherst knew that the cost would increase dramatically if pressure from settlers provoked a war with the Indians who lived west of the mountains and around the Great Lakes.

Amherst managed to provoke the Indians on his own by denying them arms and ammunition and by ending the practice of presenting Indian chiefs with gifts of guns, blankets, and clothing. In May 1763, Indians led by an Ottawa chief named Pontiac attacked Fort Detroit, an important post in the Great Lakes region. The conflict quickly escalated into a general Indian war on the frontier from Niagara through western New York and Pennsylvania, west to the region between the Ohio River and the Great Lakes, and south to the Virginia frontier. What became known as Pontiac's War cost the British about four hundred soldiers killed in action. Another fifty or so were captured and tortured to death. As many as two thousand colonists were killed or taken prisoner by Indians, and twice as many were forced to abandon their homes, mostly on the Pennsylvania frontier. The number of Indian casualties is not known. The conflict burned itself out by the fall of 1764, leaving a legacy of mutual distrust and hatred that persisted for more than thirty years.

In the fall of 1763, while this conflict was at its height, George III issued a proclamation forbidding settlement beyond the Appalachians. The proclamation had been in the works before Pontiac's War began, but frustrated colonists quickly concluded that it was intended to pacify the Indians at the expense of American colonists who wanted to claim western land and occupy it. George Washington called the proclamation "a temporary expedient to quiet the minds of the Indians." His response was among the most moderate. Many colonists regarded the proclamation as a deep betrayal of their interests by the king and his ministers. It was the first serious blow to the reputation of the young George III among his American subjects.

Regulating the Empire

The proclamation forbidding settlement west of the Appalachians was just one in a series of steps the British government took to bring order to the confused and disorganized British Empire in America. The British had always imposed regulations on colonial trade, but for many years these regulations had been lightly enforced and easily evaded.

The British ministry had signaled its intention to enforce regulations on colonial trade more vigorously during the latter part of the French and Indian War, employing writs of assistance to stop smuggling. Writs of assistance were general search warrants. They allowed customs officials to search anywhere for smuggled goods without securing warrants for any specific premises and without evidence suggesting that a crime had been committed—what is now commonly referred to as probable cause. Writs of assistance had been used in Britain and in British America for generations but resentment grew as their use increased.

The writs were issued to individuals and could be used for many years, but they were subject to a limitation: they expired six months after the death of the monarch in whose name they had been issued. King George II died on October 25, 1760, and news reached America the end of December. All writs of assistance would expire on April 25, 1761. When the customs collector in Boston, Charles Paxton, applied for a new writ of assistance, Boston merchants brought suit before the Massachusetts Superior Court, contending that writs of assistance were contrary to the unwritten British constitution and violated the rights of the king's subjects.

The case against the writs was presented by James Otis, Jr., a brilliant young lawyer who refused to accept payment for his services. John Adams, who was in the courtroom, recalled how skillfully Otis argued the case:

Otis was a flame of fire! With a promptitude of Classical Allusions, a depth of research, a rapid summary of historical events & dates, a profusion of Legal Authorities, a prophetic glance of his eyes into futurity, and a rapid torrent of impetuous Eloquence he hurried away all before him. . . . Every Man of an immense crouded Audience appeared to me to go away, as I did, ready to take Arms against Writs of Assistants. Then and there was the first scene of the first Act of opposition to the Arbitrary claims

Samuel Adams led the Massachusetts opposition to British imperial policies in the 1760s. In this portrait by John Singleton Copley, commissioned by John Hancock, he holds the instruction of the Boston town meeting directing their representative to oppose the Sugar Act and points to the Massachusetts Charter (Photograph © 2023 Museum of Fine Arts, Boston).

*of Great Britain. Then and there the Child Inde-
pendence was born. In fifteen years i.e. in 1776. he
grew up to Manhood, & declared himself free.*

Otis won the crowd, but the court decided
in Paxton's favor. Warrantless searches continued,
fueling frustration with the administration of justice and distrust of the British government.

The increased use of writs of assistance was
only one part of an aggressive program of regulation. At the end of the war, the British appointed
new customs collectors with broader powers,
granted the Royal Navy the power to stop and
inspect merchant ships, and increased the authority
of courts to enforce customs laws. Even law-abid-
ing merchants found themselves required to complete new paperwork and obey new regulations
simply to sail from one North American port to
another. Merchants resented these regulations, but
the penalties for ignoring them were high.

The purpose of the old customs laws—the
ones American merchants had frequently evaded—
was to regulate trade. The most important of these
laws was the Molasses Act of 1733. Molasses is a
byproduct of sugar manufacturing. Most of it was
used to make rum, which New Englanders made in
enormous quantities. The Molasses Act imposed a
tax of six pence per pound on sugar and molasses
brought into British America from foreign sources.
The British government wanted the North American colonists to buy these products in Jamaica,
Barbados, or one of Britain's other sugar-producing
colonies, and not from French, Spanish, or Dutch
colonies where they were usually cheaper.

Under the Molasses Act, the cost of foreign
sugar and molasses, with the tax included, was
greater than the cost of British products. The
British assumed New England merchants would
respond to the law by buying British sugar and
molasses. In fact, merchants simply bought these
products at the lowest price they could find. If they
bought them in a foreign colony, they avoided paying the tax by smuggling. They landed the goods
at night or avoided the port towns and landed
their sugar and molasses at some hidden spot on
the coast or along a river. New England merchants
learned to be expert smugglers. The tax collectors
never had enough men to catch them, and the merchants sometimes secretly paid them not to try.

Parliament changed the rules of this game by
passing the Revenue Act of 1764, commonly called
the Sugar Act. As its formal name suggests, the
purpose of the Revenue Act was to raise revenue for
the British government. It did so by imposing new
taxes on foreign cloth, indigo, coffee, and wine, but
the most important part of the law *lowered* the tax
on foreign sugar and molasses to three pence per
pound. For the first time, merchants could buy foreign sugar and molasses, pay the tax, and still pay
less in total than they would have paid for molasses
from the British islands.

The greatest profits were still made from
smuggling foreign sugar and molasses, but the
increased efforts of customs collectors and Royal
Navy ships working to catch smugglers made
smuggling a big risk. Some merchants paid the tax
and made less profit when they sold their molasses
to rum distillers. Other merchants took the risk to
keep smuggling. Either way, they were angry about
British interference in their business.

Taxation Without Representation

Many colonists did not see a reason to complain about a law that *lowered* taxes on sugar and
molasses, but a group of colonial leaders argued
that Parliament had no right to impose taxes of
any sort on the American colonies. Samuel Adams,
a popular leader of the Boston town meeting and
member of the lower house of the Massachusetts
legislature, became a spokesman for this group. "If
our trade may be taxed," Adams wrote,

*why not our lands? Why not the produce of our
lands and everything we possess or make use of? This
we apprehend annihilates our charter right to govern
and tax ourselves. It strikes at our British privileges,
which as we have never forfeited them, we hold in
common with our fellow subjects who are natives of
Britain. If taxes are laid upon us in any shape without our having a legal representation where they are
laid, are we not reduced from the character of free
subjects to the miserable state of tributary slaves?*

James Otis made the argument more directly
in a pamphlet titled *Rights of the British Colonies*

Patrick Henry was an obscure lawyer when he rose to denounce the Stamp Act in the Virginia House of Burgesses. Imagining the scene in the middle of the nineteenth century, artist P.F. Rothermel got the interior of the Capitol in Williamsburg all wrong, but he captured Henry's daring and the shock of members who heard his challenge to the king's authority (Patrick Henry Memorial Foundation).

Asserted and Proved. "The very act of taxing," he wrote, "exercised over those who are not represented, appears to me to be depriving them of one of their most essential rights, as freemen; and if continued, seems to be in effect an entire disfranchisement of every civil right."

This argument was reduced to a simple slogan: "Taxation without representation is tyranny." No one who lived in Britain's North American colonies had a seat in Parliament or the right to vote for a member of Parliament. Parliament was elected by the people of Britain and therefore had the right to tax the people of Britain. The colonists did not get to elect members of Parliament so they were not represented in Parliament. The right to tax the colonists, they argued, belonged to their own colonial assemblies, which were elected by the colonists themselves.

Parliament ignored this argument and charged ahead with its new effort to raise money in America and impose order on the unruly colonists. In 1765 Parliament passed the Stamp Act, which imposed taxes on documents, including licenses, court papers, and documents involved in buying and selling land. The stamp tax was also applied to newspapers, diplomas, pamphlets, and even playing cards. The taxes imposed by the Sugar Act were to be paid by merchants importing sugar and molasses, but the taxes imposed by the Stamp Act were to be paid by nearly everyone. The British had been paying stamp taxes for almost one hundred years. British officials thought the Americans would pay stamp taxes without much complaint.

American colonists protested immediately. Some thought the taxes were too high. Many more agreed with Samuel Adams, and worried that if they paid the stamp taxes, British officials would add more and more taxes, gradually forcing everyone in the American colonies into poverty. What could stop them?

Samuel Adams' cousin, John Adams, called the Stamp Act an "enormous Engine, fabricated by the British Parliament, for battering down all the Rights and Liberties of America." Opposition to the Stamp Act spread through the colonies and unified them in a common cause. In Virginia, a young lawyer with a gift for public speaking named Patrick Henry led the resistance. In a speech to the Virginia House of Burgesses, he warned King George of the fate that had befallen monarchs who trampled on the rights of their subjects. "Caesar had his Brutus," he said, and "Charles I his Cromwell." Henry was interrupted by cries of "Treason!" but he continued, "and George III may profit from their example." Henry introduced a series of resolutions, known as the Virginia Resolves, protesting the Stamp Act. The "Taxation of the People by themselves, or by Persons chosen by themselves to represent them," the resolves asserted, "is the only Security against a burdensome Taxation."

Many protests were peaceful, but others involved violence or threats of violence. In Boston a crowd tore down the office of the man appointed to sell the hated stamps, then marched to his house with a dummy representing the tax collector. They beheaded and burned the dummy and destroyed his house. Secret groups calling themselves "Sons of Liberty" staged violent demonstrations. In New Hampshire, an angry crowd led by Sons of Liberty demanded that George Meserve resign as the stamp tax collector and then made him burn his commission in front of everyone. Meserve later wrote: "I did not know whether I should have escaped from this mob with my life, as some were for cutting off my head, others for cutting off my ears and sending them home with my commission."

In October 1765, representatives from nine colonies met in New York. This Stamp Act Congress adopted what they called a "Declaration of Rights and Grievances" protesting the Stamp Act and insisting that Parliament did not have the authority to tax the colonies—that only the legislatures in each of the colonies could impose taxes on their people.

Colonial resistance to the Stamp Act went beyond formal protests, demonstrations, and mob actions. Merchants in many of the port towns agreed not to buy British products until the Stamp Act was repealed. This was called a non-importation agreement. British merchants complained to Parliament that non-importation hurt business and asked Parliament to repeal the Stamp Act.

Faced with protests in America and pressure at home, Parliament voted in early 1766 to repeal the Stamp Act. The British prime minister, George Grenville, was not pleased. In a speech in Parliament, he said:

Protection and obedience are reciprocal. Great Britain protects America; America is bound to yield obedience. If, not, tell me when the Americans were emancipated? When they want the protection of this kingdom, they are always ready to ask for it. That protection has always been afforded them in the most full and ample manner. The nation has run itself into an immense debt to give them their protection; and now they are called upon to contribute a small share towards the public expense, and expense arising from themselves, they renounce your authority, insult your officers, and break out, I might also say, into open rebellion.

The Empire Divided

At the same time it repealed the Stamp Act, Parliament passed the Declaratory Act, insisting that it had the right to make laws for the colonies "in all cases whatsoever." If Parliament had been wiser, it would have abandoned its efforts to tax the colonies with this symbolic statement. The colonists might then have relaxed and never followed the path from protest and resistance to rebellion and revolution. But British officials did not see this.

Parliament, they reasoned, was the supreme legislature of the whole British Empire and had the right to impose taxes on British subjects wherever they might live. It was nonsense to expect that members of Parliament should be elected in every colony in the empire and travel thousands of miles to London for meetings. And it wasn't necessary. Each member of Parliament, they reasoned, represented everyone in the empire, not just the people who voted for him.

We cannot know whether the British ministers who made this argument believed that members of Parliament who had never seen America,

Mourners carry the Stamp Act to its tomb in this British satirical print, led by William Scott, the author of a critique of American ingratitude, followed by two lawyers bearing flags. Prime Minster George Grenville follows with the little coffin, and after him comes Lord Bute, Grenville's predecessor as prime minister. In the background, trade with America is reviving (The John Carter Brown Library).

including some who could not find the colonies on a map, were qualified to pass fair laws for millions of people thousands of miles away. We know only that they insisted in the Declaratory Act that they had the power to do it. Their reasoning supported an arrogant, overbearing determination to impose their will on the colonists. They regarded the colonists as a subordinate and even inferior people who owed allegiance to the British government but who had few rights that Parliament was obliged to respect. They charged ahead and pushed the colonists from resistance toward rebellion.

In 1767 Parliament adopted a series of new laws known collectively as the Townshend Acts, named for Charles Townshend, the British minister who proposed them. The acts included laws to tighten colonial regulation, taking power out of the hands of local officials and putting it in the hands of judges and bureaucrats appointed by the British government. Among these acts was one giving customs collectors the power to use writs of assistance to search anywhere for smuggled goods, including private storehouses and homes.

The Townshend Acts also included a new revenue law imposing taxes on imported paint, paper, lead, tea, and glass. Unlike the stamp tax, which was to have been paid by ordinary people in the course of everyday business, the Townshend duties were to be paid by the merchants bringing the goods into the colonies. Townshend and his supporters in Parliament referred to the duties as an *external tax*—a fee to take goods into the colonies—as if the tax would be collected outside the colonies, which was simply not the case. Townshend believed that these taxes would be invisible to the ordinary colonist. He reasoned that even if merchants raised their prices to account for the tax, the buyers would not recognize that fact.

He was wrong. The tax burden imposed by the Townshend duties was very small, but the principle at stake, in light of Parliament's claim to the power to legislate for the colonies "in all cases whatsoever," was enormous. A new cycle of protests, riots, and petitions began when the Townshend Acts were announced. In the Virginia House of Burgesses, George Washington introduced a resolution, written by his neighbor George Mason, protesting that the "late unconstitutional Act, imposing Duties on Tea, Paper, Glass, &c. for the sole Purpose of raising a Revenue in *America*, is injurious to Property, and destructive to Liberty." Thousands signed non-importation agreements pledging not to buy British goods until the taxes were repealed.

The colonists reasoned that if they allowed Parliament to tax them without their consent, then Parliament could deprive them of all of their property and all of their political rights as well. This seemed so clear to the Americans that many of them concluded that British officials were carrying out a secret plan—a conspiracy—to deprive American colonists of their rights. This made them suspicious of every act of Parliament. The colonists worried that if they accepted even a small tax, Parliament would follow it with larger and larger taxes and drive them into poverty.

Parliament had brought on a crisis that would end in revolution. The issue at stake was not the cost of the taxes Americans refused to pay. The issue was the role of the colonists in their own government. Parliament had announced, in the Declaratory Act, that the colonists had no right to a voice in making the laws imposed on them. This power rested solely with Parliament. By passing the Townshend Acts, Parliament had announced that it intended to use that power to govern the empire.

"Be united with one spirit, in one cause"

The most thoughtful American response came from a Pennsylvania lawyer named John Dickinson, in a series of essays titled *Letters from a Farmer in Pennsylvania*, published first in Philadelphia newspapers and then reprinted in pamphlets all over the colonies. Dickinson agreed that Parliament had the authority to regulate trade in the empire "for the common good of all." But this authority did not extend to taxing the colonists, because the power to tax, unchecked by representation in Parliament, was the power to destroy. The power to make such laws, Dickinson argued, must rest on the consent of the people, expressed through representatives of their choosing.

Dickinson warned against ignoring the threat posed by the Townshend duties. "Some persons may think this act of no consequence," he wrote, "because the duties are so small." Dickinson called

THE PATRIOTIC AMERICAN FARMER.
J-n D-k-ns——n Esq.r BARRISTER at LAW.
*Who with Attic Eloquence and Roman Spirit hath Aserted,
The Liberties of the BRITISH Colonies in America.*

"I am a Farmer," John Dickinson began his celebrated attack on the Townshend duties. "I have a little money at interest." Dickinson owned a farm, but he was a busy attorney who posed as a disinterested, retiring country gentleman to win the confidence of his readers. This print revealed his true identity as a lawyer steeped in British law (National Portrait Gallery, Smithsonian Institution).

this "a fatal error," explaining that "the authors of this law would never have obtained an act to raise so trifling a sum as it must do, had they not intended by it to establish a precedent for future use. To console ourselves with the smallness of the duties, is to walk deliberately into the snare that is set for us."

It was the principle that mattered, Dickinson explained, not the size of the tax. Without naming Townshend or the other British ministers, Dickinson predicted that future generations would "execrate, with the bitterest curses, the infamous memory of those men, whose pestilential ambition unnecessarily, wantonly, cruelly, first opened the forces of civil discord" between Great Britain and her colonies.

Dickinson urged Americans to "be united with one spirit, in one cause," in asserting their rights. But he discouraged violent protests, which

he called "hot, rash, disorderly proceedings." Armed resistance should be the last resort, after every peaceful means of settling the dispute had been tried, and only when it was clear that the British were intent on destroying American liberties. A war to separate the colonies from Britain, he warned, would be a catastrophe. He hoped that it would never happen, warning that "the calamities attending on war outweigh those preceding it."

The British soon made their intentions clear. In June 1768 customs agents in Boston seized a merchant ship called *Liberty* that belonged to John Hancock, one of city's wealthiest merchants. They charged that the ship was used for smuggling. Hancock was a popular man who supported the resistance to British taxation. Angry Bostonians rioted, forcing the customs collector to flee to a fort in the harbor. The British government decided to meet resistance with military force.

The occupation of Boston convinced Dr. Joseph Warren, portrayed here by John Singleton Copley, that the British ministry intended to impose its will by force. "We are to be governed by the absolute commands of others," he said, "our property is to be taken away without our consent; if we complain, our complaints are treated with contempt; if we assert our rights, that assertion is deemed insolence; if we humbly offer to submit the matter to the imperial decision of reason, the sword is judged the most proper argument to silence our murmurs!" (Photograph © 2023 Museum of Fine Arts, Boston).

Chapter 6 Resistance

On September 30, 1768, a British fleet sailed into Boston harbor and anchored, with the guns of the fleet aimed at the town. Two regiments landed and marched through Boston with their muskets loaded, ready to fire if the colonists resisted. Two more regiments began arriving in November. British officials thought this show of force would quiet the opposition in Boston. It did not. The military occupation of Boston made the city a center of American resistance to British tyranny.

The people of Boston hated having the soldiers in their town. They felt certain the army was there to take away their rights and force them to obey unjust laws. The British troops did not establish a camp in the town. Instead, soldiers were housed in stables, barns, inns, and vacant buildings all over Boston. The people who owned the buildings were not given a choice. A law called the Quartering Act made it legal for the army commanders to occupy property without the owner's permission. The townspeople resented the soldiers. They called the soldiers names like "lobster back" because of their red coats. Angry words led to street fights. Sometimes soldiers started the fights. More often, angry townspeople assaulted soldiers. It was only a matter of time before a tragedy occurred.

Christopher Seider

On February 22, 1770, a market day in Boston, a ten-year-old boy named Christopher Seider

Massachusetts patriots considered armed resistance to the landing of British troops, but decided that the risk was too great. "They will shrink on the day of trial," predicted Thomas Gage, the king's commander in chief in America. "They are a people, who have ever been very bold in council, but never remarkable for their feats in action." The troops landed ready for battle, but were met with silence. This engraving by Paul Revere memorialized the somber event (Courtesy, American Antiquarian Society).

PHILLIS WHEATLEY, NEGRO SERVANT to Mr. JOH

was enjoying a day off from school. Christopher and other schoolboys gathered outside the shop of a merchant named Theophilus Lillie, who was selling British goods without regard to the non-importation agreement. Someone had put a sign up outside the shop that read "IMPORTER." The boys yelled at Lillie's customers, discouraged people from going in the shop, and pelted the building with dirt clods.

Ebenezer Richardson, a customs official who lived down the street, yelled at the boys to go away. He tried to take down the sign, so boys started throwing things at him. Richardson went back to his house. The boys followed him and began yelling, calling him an "informer." It was commonly known that Richardson had been paid for tipping off other customs officers about where smuggled goods were hidden. He was an unpopular man. The crowd of boys outside his house grew to sixty or seventy. They began throwing dirt clods and trash at the house. Some adults joined the crowd, too.

An egg or some piece of trash may have hit Mrs. Richardson or scared her. Whatever happened, Ebenezer Richardson had had enough. He got his musket and loaded it with gunpowder, leaving out the bullet. He went to the door and yelled at the boys that "as sure as there was a God in heaven, he'd blow a Lane thro 'em." Then he fired. The boys scattered. But they returned right away, and began throwing rocks and bricks at Richardson's house, breaking the windows.

Growing angrier, Richardson loaded his musket with swan shot, a kind of ammunition about the size of a pea, used to shoot large birds. He stuck the musket out of an upper window and fired. Richardson hit nineteen-year-old Samuel Gore in the leg. He hit Christopher with at least eleven pellets. One or more passed through his lungs. Bystanders carried the boy into a house where Dr. Joseph Warren tried to save him. Christopher suffered for several hours in great pain. The newspapers said he faced it all with a "manly spirit" and thanked Dr. Warren and the minister who came to pray with him. Christopher died that evening. The people of Boston were furious. Richardson was charged with murder.

Christopher's funeral, held on February 26, was one of the largest in the history of Boston. It was carefully organized by Samuel Adams and others to stir up public passions against the British government and the British troops occupying the town. All "the friends of Liberty," the *Boston Evening-Post* reported, "may have an opportunity of paying their last respects to the remains of this little hero and first martyr to the noble cause."

Christopher's funeral procession wound through the streets of Boston for many blocks. John Adams, a lawyer, wrote that he saw "a vast number of boys walked before the coffin," which was carried on a cart, and hundreds of men, women and girls following behind. A newspaper estimated that four to five hundred boys led the way. The procession, Adams wrote, stretched "farther than can be well imagined." Boston had never seen an event like it. "This shows," Adams wrote, "there are many more Lives to spend if wanted in the Service of their Country."

Sixteen-year-old Phillis Wheatley witnessed the funeral procession, too, and wrote a poem about it. Phillis was born in West Africa and had been captured by slave traders. She was sold in Boston in 1761, when she was about seven. Horrifying as her experience must have been, she was more fortunate than most enslaved people. A tailor named John Wheatley purchased her for a house servant. The Wheatleys helped her learn to read and write, and she became a gifted poet. Her first published poem was printed in 1767, when she was about thirteen. Three years later she wrote a poem about Christopher's funeral, beginning:

In heaven's eternal court it was decreed
How the first martyr for the cause should bleed
To clear the country of the hated brood . . .

The "hated brood" Phillis had in mind was the British army. The soldiers occupying Boston had no part in Christopher's death, but they were in Boston to help enforce the hated tax laws and support men like Christopher's killer, Ebenezer Richardson.

A keen observer, Phillis Wheatley saw that demands for liberty would undermine slavery. "How well the cry for Liberty," she wrote, "and the reverse Disposition for the exercise of oppressive Power over others agree— I humbly think it does not require the Penetration of a Philosopher to determine" (Collection of the Massachusetts Historical Society).

The Boston Massacre

Although a minor customs official had killed Christopher, Bostonians blamed the army of occupation for his death. The army had disrupted the peace of their city and replaced it with the constant threat of force. Relations between soldiers and townspeople, never good, grew steadily worse.

On March 2, a street fight broke out between soldiers and civilians. The next day groups of British soldiers and Boston rope makers fought with clubs and bats. Then on the evening of March 5, a British private, Hugh White, who was standing guard outside the customs house, exchanged insults with a young wigmaker's apprentice named Edward Garrick. White hit Garrick on the side of the head with his musket and knocked him down. A crowd gathered and began throwing things at White and taunting him to fire his musket.

White called for help. Captain Thomas Preston appeared with six armed soldiers. The crowd continued to grow—eyewitnesses report at least forty or fifty people, and some as many as two hundred or more. Henry Knox, a nineteen-year-old bookseller who was in the crowd, warned Preston: "For God's sake, take care of your men. If they fire, you must die." Preston shouted at the crowd to go home. Instead of obeying Preston, people began throwing sticks, snowballs, and chunks of ice at the soldiers.

One hit Private Hugh Montgomery and knocked him down. Montgomery got to his feet, picked up his gun and fired it into the crowd. Within a few moments other soldiers began firing without orders. They shot eleven people, including a ropemaker named Samuel Gray, a sailor named James Caldwell, and a dockworker named Crispus Attucks, who was of mixed African, American Indian, and European descent. The three men died on the spot. The soldiers also shot seventeen-year-old Samuel Maverick and an Irish immigrant named Patrick Carr. Maverick and Carr suffered for a few days before they died.

The angry crowd moved back into the nearby streets and many more armed soldiers arrived to support Preston and his men. The soldiers stopped shooting. Governor Thomas Hutchinson came to the scene and spoke to the crowd from the balcony of the nearby State House. He promised an investigation and asked the people to go home. The sullen crowd broke up. The people of Boston were furious about what they called the "massacre." Preston and several of the soldiers were arrested. Public funerals were held for the five victims. To prevent further bloodshed, the British commander withdrew all his troops from the city and moved them to Fort William on Castle Island in Boston Harbor. The military occupation of Boston ended—at least for a few years.

News of the Boston Massacre spread quickly and angered colonists from New Hampshire to Georgia. Samuel Adams and other patriot leaders made sure that published accounts of the event made it appear that the soldiers were entirely to blame. A pamphlet published by the Boston town meeting titled *A Short Narrative of the Horrid Massacre* described the shooting as an unprovoked attack on peaceful Bostonians. In response, supporters of the army published a pamphlet titled *A Fair Account of the Late Unhappy Disturbance in Boston*. It described the shootings as the result of an ambush planned by street gangs.

Boston lawyers who were sympathetic to the British soldiers refused to defend Captain Preston and his men in court. They worried that angry Bostonians would retaliate against them. Finally John Adams, a cousin of Samuel Adams, agreed to serve as their lawyer. He believed everyone deserves a fair trial, including the services of a lawyer to argue on their behalf. Preston was found not guilty because the jury agreed he did not order his men to fire and that he tried to stop them.

Hugh Montgomery, the soldier who fired first, and another soldier who fired into the crowd were found guilty. The jury agreed that the two soldiers had been afraid they might be killed and so were not guilty of murder. They were convicted of the lesser charge of manslaughter. They were released after having their thumbs branded. This was a sign that they had been found guilty of manslaughter and that if they were found guilty of it a second time they would be executed.

The news that British soldiers had fired on colonists armed only with snowballs and sticks shook the loyalty of many colonists to King George III and his government. They became more convinced than ever that the British government did not care about them and was working to take away their

Paul Revere's engraving of _The Bloody Massacre perpetrated in King Street, Boston_ was copied from a design by Henry Pelham, who issued his own version of the print with the title _The Fruits of Arbitrary Power_. Like many eighteenth-century prints, the image was densely symbolic and not intended to be a literal depiction of the event. Pelham and Revere presented the killings as the inevitable result of the military occupation of their city (Collection of the Massachusetts Historical Society).

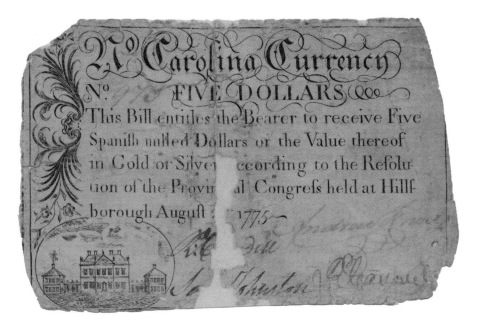

When it was completed in 1770, Tryon's Palace was the most elaborate and expensive public building between Williamsburg, Virginia, and Charleston, South Carolina. This view of the palace—the earliest depiction of the finished building—was engraved on a five dollar bill issued by the North Carolina Provincial Congress in 1775 (North Carolina Collection, Wilson Special Collections Library, UNC-Chapel Hill).

freedom. John Adams later wrote that the "foundation of American independence was laid" on the evening of March 5, 1770, in the streets of Boston.

Christopher Seider's killer, Ebenezer Richardson, was tried for murder in April. The facts in the case were not in dispute. The judge, a royal appointee named Peter Oliver, instructed the jury that Richardson had good reason to fear that the mob was going to kill him and that the shooting was a justifiable homicide. Richardson, Oliver said, was not guilty of a crime. If anyone was guilty, Oliver said, it was "the Promoters of the Effigies and the Exhibitions which draw the people together and caused unlawful and tumultuous assemblies." Oliver thus implied that men like Samuel Adams were responsible for Christopher's death. The jury found Richardson guilty of murder, but Oliver refused to pass sentence on him. Richardson was returned to jail, where he waited for more than year before receiving a full pardon issued by the authority of His Majesty King George III.

Frontier Discontent

Violent resistance to imperial regulations and British authority was not limited to Boston or to the cities and towns of the Atlantic coast where most of the taxes on imported goods were collected. In other parts of British America, colonists resisted the imperial regulations that most touched their lives.

People in the western parts of the colonies, from the New England frontier through New York, Pennsylvania, Maryland, Virginia, the Carolinas, and Georgia were not much concerned about taxes on imported luxuries. Taxes on paint, paper, lead, tea, and glass had little effect on people who didn't paint their homes, use much paper, drink tea, or buy glass for their windows. They used a little lead for bullets, but most of the time they got it without paying taxes. They had other grievances, either against imperial policies or the failure of the empire to respect their rights and respond to their needs.

Often their grievances involved securing ownership of land. People moved toward the colonial frontier in unprecedented numbers in the decade after the French and Indian War. They were intent on acquiring farms where they could support themselves and their families and enjoy personal independence. This ambition was frequently frustrated by imperial regulations, the interference of royal officials, and nearly everywhere by the failure of colonial governments to ensure that ordinary people could acquire secure title to land. Protests, in many cases violent, flared along the colonial frontier from

Vermont, where wealthy absentee New York landowners disputed the claims of ordinary people from New England to the land where they had settled, southward to the Carolinas and Georgia.

The most serious of these protests occurred in North Carolina. For most of the eighteenth century, North Carolina's population was spread along the coast from the lower Cape Fear River, near the South Carolina border, northward along the tidewater rivers and sounds to the Virginia line. Settlers began occupying land in the North Carolina piedmont in the middle of the eighteenth century. After the French and Indian War their numbers increased dramatically. Many of the newcomers came from Virginia, Maryland, or Pennsylvania, and included people of Scots, Scots-Irish, and German as well as English background.

They had little in common with the planters of the North Carolina coast. Many belonged to a Protestant church other than the Church of England, which was the dominant church in eastern North Carolina. They were more likely to be Presbyterians, Baptists, or belong to a German Protestant group. Some newcomers brought slaves with them, but most owned few slaves or none at all. Many were self-sufficient farmers who raised what they needed and produced little to sell.

Most importantly, many of the newcomers lived on land they did not own, at least in the eyes of the colonial government. Until 1763 the northern half of the colony, a region about sixty-five miles wide from the coast to the mountains, was legally the property of John Carteret, 2nd Earl Granville. An English aristocrat who had inherited his claim to the land, Granville never came to America, but his agents operated a land office in North Carolina where settlers could purchase land. When he died in 1763 the land office was closed, just as settlers were arriving in large numbers. Robert Carteret, 3rd Earl Granville, inherited his father's vast land claim. He never saw it and did nothing to make legal settlement possible. Some newcomers bought land from earlier settlers, but most simply staked a claim to undeveloped land by

clearing trees, building a house, and establishing a farm.

To the royal governor, William Tryon, these people were a problem. They paid little or no taxes and seemed to live outside the law. Corruption in local government made the situation worse. County sheriffs collected some taxes from them, often by threats, and then kept the money for themselves. Other local officials charged high fees to register deeds and provide other services. Settlers short of money resisted paying taxes and fees to a government that did little or nothing for their benefit.

The settlers had no peaceful way to resolve these problems because they had little voice in the North Carolina Assembly. Representatives of the tidewater counties controlled the assembly and were slow to give the new settlers a fair voice in government. In 1767 coastal Currituck County, with just 889 taxable residents, elected five members to the assembly, while western Orange County, with some 4,300 taxable residents, was limited to two members. Coastal Pasquotank County, with 792 taxable residents, elected five members, while western Rowan County, with 2,632 taxable residents, elected only two members.

Frontier discontent increased after 1766, when the assembly voted to impose new taxes to fund the construction of an elaborate residence for the governor in the coastal town of New Bern. What became known as Tryon's Palace included meeting rooms for the governor's council and the assembly. The building was a source of pride for the governor and his supporters. Frontier settlers regarded the palace as a symbol of tyranny and objected to paying taxes to build it.

The Regulators

The situation became so bad that, in April 1768, settlers in Orange County met and resolved to take control of local government. Calling themselves Regulators, they demanded the county sheriff and other officials produce copies of tax laws,

(Overleaf) North Carolina's royal governor William Tryon wrote in 1766 that "this province is settling faster than any on the continent." The majority were Scots-Irish and Germans who moved south from Pennsylvania and Virginia seeking land in the North Carolina backcountry. Proudly independent, they resented the tidewater planters who dominated the colony's government. This map was published in 1770 (Library of Congress).

To His
most Excellent Majesty
GEORGE the III.
King of Great Britain, &c. &c. &c.

This Map is most humbly dedicated by

most humble obedient & dutiful Subject

HIS MAJESTY'S

John Collet.

tax collection records, and evidence of how tax money had been used. The Regulators agreed to meet four times a year until their grievances were resolved.

When the county sheriff seized a man's horse for nonpayment of taxes, Regulators tied the sheriff up, took back the horse, and shot holes in the house of a local officeholder and landowner named Edmund Fanning. A close associate of the governor, Fanning was then a Crown attorney, militia colonel, judge, member of the assembly, and county register of deeds. The Regulators accused him of extorting large fees to record land transfers and using his several offices to acquire large tracts of land and enrich himself.

Governor Tryon described the situation in the western counties as "an absolute Insurrection" and the men who led the Regulators as traitors to the king. In fact the Regulators were mostly simple farmers who lacked the money to pay the taxes and fees demanded by government officials. Since many could not obtain deeds to their farms, they lived in fear that the government would take their homes and property. Their petitions to the governor and the assembly accomplished nothing. A petition from Anson County asserted that "we . . . have too long yielded ourselves slaves to remorseless oppression."

In September 1770 a large party of Regulators took over the courthouse in Hillsborough, beat their opponents, and destroyed Fanning's house. When the assembly met in December, it adopted a stern law to punish rioters, in many cases with death, and announced that any group of men who took up arms to prevent the lawful operation of the government would be dealt with as traitors. Under this law sixty Regulators were indicted by a special court convened in New Bern. The accused were ordered to turn themselves in to face trial or become outlaws, subject to being shot on sight by anyone.

By then Governor Tryon had decided to put down the Regulators by force. He raised some 1,300 militia, most in the eastern counties of North Carolina, and marched west to the Hillsborough, in the heart of Regulator country. Among Tryon's aides was John Malcolm, a Boston sea captain recently appointed one of His Majesty's customs officials in North Carolina. On May 14, 1771, the governor's army reached Alamance Creek, west of Hillsborough. Some two thousand

armed Regulators gathered at a nearby plantation and prepared to resist Tryon's army. The governor sent word that he would pardon them if they would surrender their leaders for trial, lay down their arms, and swear their allegiance to King George III. The Regulators responded by asking the governor to remove tax collectors and other officials they said were dishonest.

The governor ordered his little army forward on May 16. As the two sides drew close, Tryon sent John Malcolm forward with a final offer, demanding the Regulators lay down their arms and surrender their leaders for trial. The Regulators, according to a witness, "rejected the Terms offer'd with disdain, said they wanted no time to consider of them and with rebellious clamor called out for battle."

Although outnumbered, Tryon had several cannons, which he used to fire grapeshot, a kind of ammunition made up of dozens of iron balls. "The enemy," Tryon reported to the ministry in London, "took to tree fighting and much annoyed the men who stood at the guns." The two sides exchanged fire for two hours before firing by the Regulators slowed, probably because they were growing short of ammunition. Tryon directed the artillery to cease firing and ordered his men to advance. The Regulators fled the field, leaving behind some three hundred dead and many others wounded. The governor's army lost about sixty men.

Tryon's army took hundreds of prisoners. The governor ordered one of the captured men hanged the day after the battle. Twelve more were tried for treason and six of them were executed. Tryon issued a proclamation offering pardons to other Regulators who would come to his camp, surrender their arms, take an oath to obey the government, pay their taxes, and submit to the law. In the North Carolina legislature, Samuel Johnston, a tidewater planter, introduced a bill requiring the Regulators to turn themselves in or be declared outlaws, liable to be shot on sight. By the end of the year, over six thousand Regulators surrendered their arms and took the required oath.

Others left their farms and moved west, beyond the Proclamation Line and beyond the reach of the king's government. Joining frontier families from Virginia, they settled in the valley of the Watauga River in what is now eastern Tennes-

Josiah Martin called William Tryon's victory over the Regulators "a sacrifice—like a slaughter of defenceless, deluded sheep," and took over as royal governor in August 1771 with "hope to find a field for the exercise of mercy & the display of the Olive Branch" (Image courtesy of Bonhams).

see, where they agreed to "Articles of Association" creating their own local government. Lord Dunmore, the governor of Virginia, learned about the Watauga Association and reported to the British ministry that the Wataugans had set up a "separate state" that "set a dangerous example to the people of America."

William Tryon was rewarded for his conduct with appointment as royal governor of New York. He was replaced by Josiah Martin, an ambitious young British official who soon found that conditions in North Carolina were far worse than reported. Customs officials were corrupt and county officials were just as bad as the Regulators had claimed. Martin removed John Malcolm, whom Martin described as a "hair brained" bully, guilty of "extortions and depredations and violence" against His Majesty's subjects.

Martin toured the backcountry in the summer of 1772 and wrote to the British ministry about the people he met: "I now see most clearly that they have been provoked by insolence and cruel advantages taken of the peoples ignorance by mercenary tricking Attornies, Clerks and other lit-

tle Officers who have practiced on them every sort of rapine and extortion." Martin did his best to deal with the problems of backcountry settlers, but his efforts to reopen the land office and end the confusion and uncertainty about land ownership were unsuccessful.

The struggle between the Regulators and the North Carolina government was just one example of rising discontent about the ineffectiveness and injustice of government in the empire. That government—from county clerks who overcharged for basic services, to customs officials who extorted payoffs from merchants, to a governor who used military force to compel obedience, to the ministry in London, which cared more about the property claims of an English aristocrat than the needs of thousands of colonists—put the interests of the few over those of the many. It enriched aristocrats and office holders but paid little attention to the needs of small farmers, shopkeepers, tradesmen, and laborers. Americans would soon unite to free themselves from the empire and create revolutionary new governments responsive to the interests of ordinary people.

Frederick North, better known as Lord North, was prime minister of Britain from 1770 to 1782. His skill in debate was aided by a powerful memory and a keen sense of humor. King George III praised his "genuine good-natured wit" which even "forced a smile from those against whom it was exercised" (© National Portrait Gallery, London).

Chapter 7 Americans Unite

On March 5, 1770, the new British prime minister, Lord North, asked Parliament to repeal the Townshend duties on paint, paper, lead, and glass. In his remarks, he expressed surprise that "so preposterous a law could originally obtain existence from a British legislature." North explained that law had angered Americans, harmed British commerce, and encouraged the Americans to form "dangerous combinations." He recommended keeping the tax on tea to make it clear that Parliament had the right to tax the colonies. Giving up the tea tax, he said, would invite the Americans "to insult our authority, to dispute our rights, and to aim at independent government."

No one in Parliament that day could have known that just a few hours later, on the other side of the Atlantic Ocean, British soldiers who had been sent to America to intimidate His Majesty's subjects into obedience would shoot and kill several of those subjects in a confrontation remembered as the Boston Massacre. News of the massacre would take several weeks to reach Britain. Shortly thereafter Parliament passed Lord North's bill to repeal the Townshend duties.

The withdrawal of British troops from Boston and the repeal of the Townshend duties removed two of the most important sources of friction between the colonies and the king's government and was followed by several months of calm. The colonial non-importation movement, which had aimed to force Parliament to abandon its efforts to tax the colonies, came to an end. The embargo had cost American merchants and storekeepers a great deal of money in lost sales. They were glad to restock their shelves with British goods. Most colonists were happy to be able to buy imported goods again.

Samuel Adams and other leaders of the American resistance wanted to keep the embargo going, but the remaining tax on tea was not enough to excite much popular opposition. Patriotic Americans simply refused to buy British tea. They drank less expensive tea smuggled into America from Dutch colonies instead. John Adams wrote in his diary in February 1771 about a meeting at John Hancock's house with Joseph Warren and other patriots. "Drank Green Tea," Adams wrote, "from Holland I hope."

The Conspiracy Against Liberty

The period of calm after the repeal of the Townshend duties and the withdrawal of the army from Boston was deceptive. Gangs no longer intimidated shopkeepers accused of selling imported goods and British soldiers no longer traded insults and blows with the people of Boston, but the issues that had divided the British government and the colonies since 1763 had not been resolved.

The British government still maintained that it had the right to make laws for the colonies, and it denied that the colonies had a right to elect members of Parliament to share in making those laws. The colonists denied that Parliament had the right to tax them and insisted that they were only bound to obey laws made by their own assemblies. Unless the British government gave up and returned to the old policy of salutary neglect, allowing the colonies to govern their own affairs without interference from London, another confrontation was bound to happen.

The British government had good reasons to abandon its efforts to tax the colonies and regulate their affairs. The government had spent more in paying tax collectors, customs inspectors, and treasury officials than it had raised in taxes. Sending troops to Boston to keep order and warships to the American coast to catch smugglers added more cost. Non-importation had hurt British manufacturers and merchants and cost the Crown tax revenue it would otherwise have collected at home. The seven-year effort to tax the colonies had lost money, and the British government had no good reason to think that would change soon.

Why, then, did the British government persist? Four explanations seem plausible. The first is folly—that British officials did not understand that the expenses involved in taxing the colonies exceeded the taxes collected and so pressed on with a policy that lost money because they were too ignorant to understand what was happening. The second is stubborn pride—that British officials recognized that the tax program was losing money but persisted because they would not accept being beaten by colonial agitators. The third is distraction—that the future of America, so important in hindsight, did not seem so important to British officials at the time, and they pressed on with an unsuccessful tax program because their attention was focused elsewhere. The fourth explanation is that they persisted in order to create the administrative organization they would need to impose and collect much higher taxes in the future.

Each of these explanations has merit. Ignorance of American affairs shocked Americans who talked to members of Parliament. American Henry Cruger visited London in 1766 and wrote that he spent "every Day with some one Member of Parliament . . . It is surprising how ignorant some of them are of *Trade* and *America.*" In 1769 a British lawyer asked an American whether Philadelphia was in the East or West Indies and said he had "a notion it was upon the coast of Sumatra. Such is their knowledge of America." Men who could not find Philadelphia on a map probably did not calculate the costs and benefits of taxing the American colonies very carefully.

That stubborn pride played a role in Britain's persistence cannot be doubted. Lord North admitted it when he told Parliament that repealing the tax on tea would invite American insults. British officials had spent seven years denouncing their American critics as traitors and their supporters as a vulgar mob. Conceding victory to them would have been too humiliating to accept.

Distractions, too, prevented British officials from reconsidering their American policies. "The great Defect here," Benjamin Franklin wrote from London in 1773, "is, in all sorts of People, a want of attention to what passes in such remote Countries as America . . . and a Disposition to postpone the Consideration even of the Things they know they must at last consider, so that they may have Time for what more immediately concerns them."

The leaders of the American resistance were prepared to believe that many British officials were ignorant, proud, and worried about other things, but they were convinced that the men shaping British policy were planning to impose higher taxes and assume greater control of American affairs, and that if left unchecked they would impoverish Americans and strip them of the traditional rights of Englishmen. They believed that the king's ministers and their supporters in Parliament were engaged in a deliberate conspiracy to deprive Americans of their liberty. This was the only explanation that made sense of British actions. The trouble and expense to which Britain had gone since 1763, it seemed to Samuel Adams, John Hancock, George Washington, Patrick Henry, and many others, was just the beginning of a British campaign that would only end when American colonial governments were powerless to defend American rights. Their worst fears were soon confirmed.

HMS *Gaspée*

British officials may have given up the idea of taxing paint, paper, lead, and glass, but they were determined to enforce the customs laws and collect duties on molasses, sugar, and rum brought into British America from foreign colonies in the Caribbean. They were also determined to stop the illegal trade in foreign tea and other goods, forcing Americans to buy British products.

This would have been a difficult task under the best circumstances. Hundreds of vessels sailed in and out of American ports every year. Any one of them might carry illegal cargo. The Royal Navy had only twenty-four ships to patrol the entire American coast from Florida to Newfoundland. The navy put them under the command of Admiral John Montagu, a tough veteran sailor, and told him to get on with the job. Montagu despised the colonists, and many of them felt the same way about him. John Adams called him a "beast of prey" whose "brutal, hoggish manners are a disgrace to the Royal Navy."

One of Montagu's ships was HMS *Gaspée,* an

Rhode Island merchants commissioned this group portrait to recall an evening of fun in a tavern in Surinam, a Dutch colony on the coast of South America and an important source of smuggled goods. Nicholas Cooke is smoking a pipe and talking with Esek Hopkins, future commander of the Continental Navy. Joseph Wanton, later governor of Rhode Island, is asleep in his chair, and Stephen Hopkins, later a member of the Continental Congress, is pouring a bowl of punch on Wanton's head (St. Louis Art Museum).

armed schooner commanded by a young lieutenant named William Dudingston. A naval officer who captured a ship smuggling goods was entitled to a share of the value of the ship and its cargo when they were sold at auction. An industrious officer could make a lot of money for himself catching American smugglers. Cruising off the coast of Maine and around Cape Cod in late 1771, Dudingston established a reputation as an energetic commander. In January 1772, Montagu ordered him to Rhode Island.

Rhode Island was a smuggler's paradise. The colony surrounded Narragansett Bay—a maze of waterways, scattered islands, and secluded coves that offered smugglers abundant opportunities to land goods out of sight of customs officers. The Rhode Island government was run by merchants, many of whom engaged in smuggling as a normal part of their business, and they had no intention

of cooperating with the Royal Navy or the British government to stop it.

They were sure their charter guaranteed that the colony could make its own laws. They acknowledged the king as the common head of the British Empire and expected the protection of the Royal Navy in time of war, but otherwise they regarded their colony's relationship with Britain as a kind of business arrangement in which, as long as everyone was making money, no one had a reason to complain. Stephen Hopkins, a merchant who served for many years as chief justice of the colony, said in 1757 that "the King and Parliament had no more Right to make Laws for us than the Mohawks."

Joseph Wanton, another merchant, was elected governor in 1769 and immediately wrote to Lord Hillsborough, the secretary of state for the colonies, informing him that the supreme authority

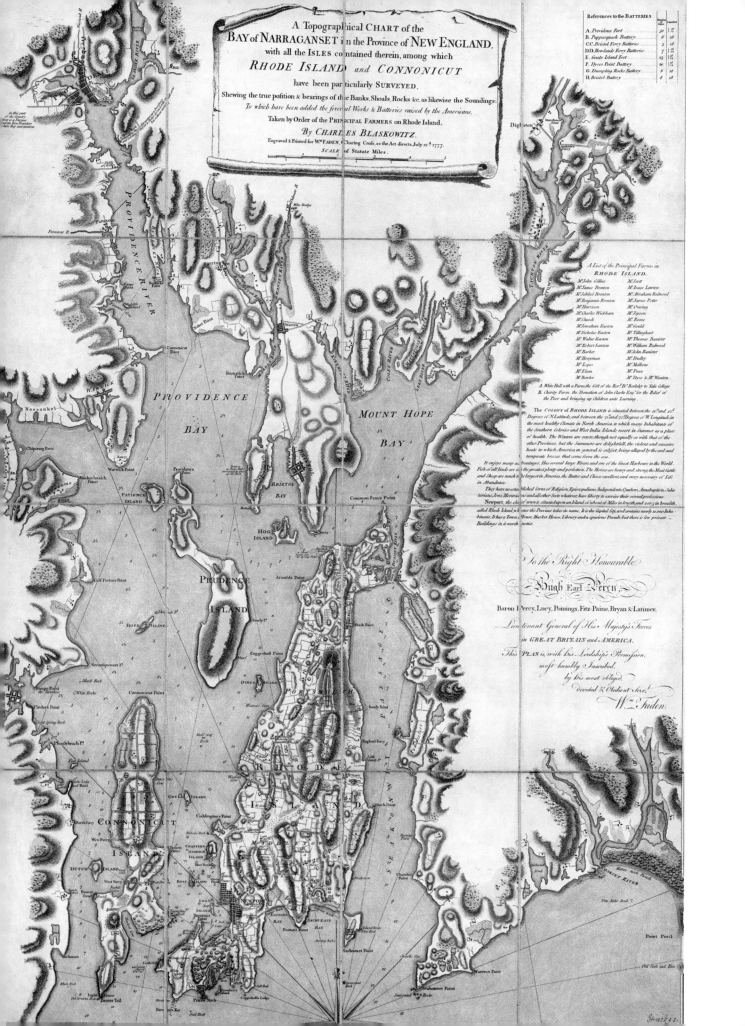

A Topographical CHART of the
BAY of NARRAGANSET in the Province of NEW ENGLAND.
with all the ISLES contained therein, among which
RHODE ISLAND and CONNONICUT
have been particularly SURVEYED.
Shewing the true position & bearings of the Banks, Shoals, Rocks &c. as likewise the Soundings:
To which have been added the several Works & Batteries raised by the Americans.
Taken by Order of the PRINCIPAL FARMERS on Rhode Island.
By CHARLES BLASKOWITZ.
Engraved & Printed for Wm. FADEN, Charing Cross, as the Act directs, July 22d 1777.
SCALE of Statute Miles.

References to the BATTERIES

	Number of Guns	Numbers
A. Providence Fort	50	14
B. Papposquash Battery	6	10
C.C. Bristol Ferry Batteries	3	10
D.D. Howlands Ferry Batteries	7	14
E. Goats Island Fort	15	14
F. Dyers Point Battery	10	14
G. Dumpling Rocks Battery	8	18
H. Bristol Battery	8	18

A List of the Principal Farms in
RHODE ISLAND.

Mr John Collins
Mr James Brenton
Mr Isbbel Brenton
Mr Benjamin Brenton
Mr Harrison
Mr Charles Wickham
Mr Church
Mr Jonathan Easton
Mr Nicholas Easton
Mr Walter Easton
Mr Robert Lawton
Mr Barker
Mr Honyman
Mr Lopez
Mr Elam
Mr Bowler

Mr Scott
Mr Isaac Lawton
Mr Abraham Redwood
Mr James Potter
Mr Overing
Mr Jepson
Mr Rome
Mr Gould
Mr Tillinghast
Mr Thomas Banister
Mr William Redwood
Mr John Banister
Mr Dudley
Mr Mallone
Mr Pease
Mr Dyre & Mr Wanton.

A. White Hall, with a Farm, the Gift of the Revd Dr. Berkley to Yale College
B. Charity Farm, the Donation of John Clarke Esqr for the Relief of
the Poor and bringing up Children unto Learning.

The COLONY of RHODE ISLAND is situated between the 41st and 42d
Degrees of N.Latitude, and between the 71st and 72d Degree of W. Longitude; in
the most healthy Climate in North America, to which many Inhabitants of
the Southern Colonies and West India Islands resort in Summer as a place
of health. The Winters are severe, though not equally so with that of the
other Provinces, but the Summers are delightfull, the violent and excessive
heats to which America in general is subject, being allayed by the cool and
temperate breeze that come from the sea.

It enjoys many advantages. Has several large Rivers and one of the finest Harbours in the World.
Fish of all kinds are in the greatest plenty and perfection. The Horses are boney and strong, the Meat Cattle
and Sheep are much the largest in America, the Butter and Cheese excellent, and every necessary of Life
in Abundance.

They have no established Terms of Religion, Episcopalians, Independents, Quakers, Anabaptists, Saba-
tarians, Jews, Moravians and all other Sects whatever, have liberty to exercise their several professions.

Newport, the chief Town is situated upon an Island of about 16 Miles in length, and 3 or 5 in breadth,
called Rhode Island, whence the Province takes its name. It is the Capital City, and contains nearly 12,000 Inhabitants. It has a Town House, Market House, Library and a spacious Parade, But there is few private
Buildings in it worth notice.

To the Right Honourable
Hugh Earl Percy,
Baron Percy, Lucy, Poinings, Fitz-Paine, Bryan & Latimer,
Lieutenant General of His Majesty's Forces
in GREAT BRITAIN and AMERICA.
This PLAN is, with his Lordship's Permission,
most humbly Inscribed,
by his most obliged,
devoted & Obedient Servt.
Wm. Faden.

PROVIDENCE RIVER

WARWICK

PROVIDENCE BAY

MOUNT HOPE BAY

PATIENCE ISLAND

PRUDENCE ISLAND

HOPE ISLAND

HOG ISLAND

PORTSMOUTH

CONNONICUT ISLAND

RHODE ISLAND

MIDDLETOWN

NEWPORT

Dighton

Point Peril

in the colony rested with the assembly. He added that "the power exercised by the Parliament of Great Britain (in which we are not represented), of raising monies upon us without our consent (which it is possible under a bad administration, may be extended to our last penny), is a real grievance." The British government, the governor informed the king's chief minister for the colonies, could not expect Rhode Island's help in collecting taxes of any sort. Rhode Island officials routinely helped merchants accused of violating the customs laws, and Rhode Island courts regularly let violators and their ships go free.

To Admiral Montagu, in his Boston office, the merchants who ran Rhode Island seemed like a well-organized criminal gang. He urged Dudingston to teach them a lesson. Dudingston quickly captured a sloop smuggling sugar from the French Caribbean and brought her into Newport, where Governor Wanton interrogated him about his authority. In February 1772 Dudingston stopped the sloop *Fortune* and found twelve giant barrels of rum on which, he claimed, no duty had been paid. He seized the rum and the ship and sent them to Boston, beyond the reach of the Rhode Island government. One of the owners of the cargo was a young Rhode Islander named Nathanael Greene. He was so angry at Dudingston, he wrote to a friend, that "I have devoted almost the whole of my time in devising measures for punishing the offender."

Greene was not the only Rhode Islander determined to punish the young naval officer who was making so much trouble. On June 9, 1772, Dudingston set off in pursuit of a merchant ship, the *Hannah*, sailing up the bay toward Providence. The *Hannah's* captain knew the waters well and led a chase that ended with the *Gaspée* stuck on a sandbank while the *Hannah* escaped to Providence. There was nothing for the embarrassed British commander to do but wait for the rising tide to float the *Gaspée* free. He posted a sentry on the deck and the rest of the crew went to sleep.

Late that night a party of about sixty armed men rowed down from Providence. As they approached the ship, Dudingston, called to the deck by the sentry and wearing nothing but his breeches, hailed the boats. Recognizing Dudingston, an eighteen-year-old named Joe Bucklin turned to his friend Ephraim Bowen, who had brought his father's musket, and said "Ephe, reach me your gun, and I can kill that fellow." Bowen said later "I reached it to him accordingly." Bucklin fired, Dudingston fell, and Bucklin exclaimed "I have killed the rascal!"

In fact, Bucklin had shot Dudingston in the groin. The raiders boarded the *Gaspée* and after a brief scuffle, took control of the ship. They promptly herded Dudingston and his men into one of their boats and rowed them to the beach close by, from which the helpless crew watched while the raiders set fire to the *Gaspée* and burned her to the waterline.

"A powerful cause of union"

Mobs had attacked customs officials many times, in Britain and America, and they had even burned boats used by customs collectors. The *Gaspée* was not a customs vessel. She was a ship of His Majesty's Royal Navy. And the men who boarded her, took her commander and crew prisoner, and burned her were not a mob—at least not an ordinary one. The men who boarded the *Gaspée* that night included some of Rhode Island's most important merchants and sea captains, including John Brown, Joseph Brown, Abraham Whipple, Joseph Tillinghast, John B. Hopkins, and Simeon Potter. The rest were sailors, dock workers, and other men who depended on trade, including the trade in smuggled goods, for their livelihood.

They went about their work with calm efficiency, confident in the justice of their actions. Dudingston had defied the authority of the governor of Rhode Island and evaded the Rhode Island courts. The only law the Brown brothers, Whipple, and the others recognized was the law of Rhode Island. In their eyes, Dudingston and his crew were the criminals—pirates sailing Rhode Island waters and stealing the property of Rhode Island merchants under cover of British tax laws that did

British mapmaker Charles Blaskowitz completed the surveys for this map of Narragansett Bay in 1774, shortly after the destruction of the *Gaspée*, and marked "Gaspe Point," on the west shore of the Providence River south of Patuxent (Norman B. Leventhal Map & Education Center at the Boston Public Library).

not legally apply in Rhode Island, at least as far as Rhode Islanders were concerned.

Admiral Montagu was outraged and demanded the men responsible for the destruction of the *Gaspée* be found and punished. Under British law, attacking a ship of the Royal Navy, shooting her commander, and setting the ship on fire was treason, for which the punishment was death. The British government created a commission to investigate the crime. Governor Wanton pretended to cooperate, but Dudingston and his crew were not able to identify their attackers—the whole thing had happened quickly, and in the dark—and no one could be found who could (or would) identify any of the Rhode Islanders involved. And so in the end the British, powerless to impose their will on Rhode Island, did nothing but threaten.

Their threats were ominous. The British government announced that when the men who destroyed the *Gaspée* were found, they would be brought to Britain to stand trial. The British army, if needed, would be sent to impose order so this could be done. The *Providence Gazette* declared this plan "repugnant to every dictate of reason, liberty, and justice." The principle that someone accused of a crime had a right to a trial where the alleged crime occurred before a jury of his peers—that is, of the people of his own community—was a sacred part of the British legal tradition. The announcement that men accused of destroying the *Gaspée* would be taken to Britain in chains was evidence to many colonists that the British government intended to strip all colonists of their rights.

News of the threats spread across the colonies. A writer in the *Providence Gazette* described the British officials responsible for them as "a pack of worse than Egyptian tyrants, whose avarice nothing less than your whole substance and income, will satisfy; and who, if they can't extort that, will glory in making a sacrifice of you and your posterity, to gratify their master the devil, who is a tyrant, and the father of tyrants and liars."

Among those who read the news was a Virginia planter named Richard Henry Lee, a member of one of Virginia's most prominent families. His father had been governor of Virginia, and he had been a member of the Virginia House of Burgesses since 1758. Lee knew all of Virginia's political leaders, but he did not know the leaders of the

resistance in other colonies.

In February 1773 Lee wrote a letter introducing himself to Samuel Adams and suggesting that they begin writing letters to one another to share information and ideas. "To be firmly attached to the cause of liberty on virtuous principles," Lee wrote, "is a powerful cause of union." Lee explained that the British reaction to the destruction of the *Gaspée* was proof of the British government's plans to deprive the colonists of their rights. The plan of "removing Americans beyond the water, to be tried for supposed offences committed here . . . is so unreasonable, and so unconstitutional a stretch of power, that I hope it will never be permitted to take place, while a spark of virtue, or one manly sentiment remains in America." Lee asked Adams for an accurate account of the *Gaspée* affair, explaining that he did not trust reports from "the uncertain medium of newspapers." Adams replied with details Lee did not have.

A few weeks later Lee went to Williamsburg for a session of the House of Burgesses and met with a small group of like-minded members—Patrick Henry, Thomas Jefferson, Lee's brother Francis Lightfoot Lee, and Jefferson's brother-in-law, Dabney Carr—in a private room at the Raleigh Tavern. Jefferson, just twenty-nine years old, had already impressed Lee and Henry as a promising young leader.

They agreed, Jefferson later wrote, that "the most urgent of all measures was that of coming to an understanding with all the other colonies to consider the British claims as a common cause to all." Together they drafted a resolution proposing that each colony appoint a "committee of correspondence" to communicate with the others and agree on a unified response to British actions. Carr presented the resolution in the House of Burgesses, while Patrick Henry and Richard Henry Lee—well known as the best public speakers in Virginia—spoke in support of the resolution, which was adopted by a unanimous vote.

The Virginians sent their resolution to the other colonies. Committees of correspondence were soon formed from New Hampshire to Georgia. This was an important step in establishing a union between the colonies and the future union of independent American states. In this way the destruction of *Gaspée,* which might under other

The East India Company proudly commissioned this painting, *The East Offering its Riches to Britannia,* for its London headquarters to symbolize its domination of trade with India and China. "The East India Company," the *Pennsylvania Gazette* warned, "will leave no Stone unturned to become your Masters. . . . Whole Provinces labouring under the Distresses of Oppression, Slavery, Famine, and the Sword, are familiar to them. Thus they have enriched themselves. Thus they are become the most powerful Trading Company in the Universe" (British Library / GRANGER).

circumstances have remained a local matter, shaped the future of all thirteen colonies and ultimately of the United States.

The East India Company

Events in America were not foremost in the minds of the men in charge of running Britain's far-flung empire. Lord North's government faced financial problems at home and challenges from France and Spain, which had rebuilt their navies and were looking for chances to revenge their defeat in the last war. The declining value of sugar was another serious concern. Sugar, molasses, and rum imported from Britain's island colonies in the Caribbean were worth about four million pounds a year, more than four times the value of the tobacco grown in Maryland and Virginia. The taxes collected on these products were essential to the government.

Most troubling was the precarious condition of the British East India Company. The company was the most important business enterprise in the

We the Ladys
of Edenton do
hereby Solemnly
Engage not to Conform
to that Pernicious Custom
of Drinking Tea, or that we the
aforesaid Ladys will not promote y.e wear
of any Manufacture from England
until such time that all Acts
which tend to Enslave this our
Native Country shall be Repealed

British Empire. The company had enormous assets, including a private fleet of armed merchant ships and a vast network of forts and warehouses. It controlled the importation of cloth and saltpeter (the main ingredient in gunpowder) from India, where it maintained a private army larger than the peacetime army in Britain. In the 1760s the company had used this army to acquire control of Bengal, a region larger than France, from which it collected land taxes. The company also imported spices from Southeast Asia and controlled the importation of tea from China.

Tea consumption in Britain and the colonies had been increasing for decades, but in 1772 and 1773 the company's sales in Britain collapsed due to high prices, heavy taxes, and competition from smuggled Dutch tea, leaving the company with a huge inventory of unsold tea. The company had invested heavily in India, but a terrible famine cut the land tax revenue there at the same time tea sales were declining in Britain. The costs of running the company, including the costs of operating and maintaining its ships and forts and paying its private army, suddenly exceeded the company's income. The East India Company faced bankruptcy.

The East India Company was too big for the government to allow it to fail. Many English aristocrats and prominent merchants had invested in the company and looked to the government for help. To help the company sell its inventory of tea, Parliament adopted the Tea Act. The act, which was passed on May 10, 1773, eliminated the tax of twelve cents collected on every pound of tea brought into Britain as long as the tea was shipped to America, where a tax of three cents per pound was to be collected. This would make East India Company tea cheaper in America than the smuggled Dutch tea the Americans were drinking.

British officials hoped the quick sale of cheap East India Company tea in America would save the company. In the fall of 1773, seven East India Company ships left Britain, carrying more than 1,700 wooden chests filled with more than 600,000 pounds of tea. Four were bound for Boston. The others sailed for Philadelphia, New York and Charleston.

Tea Parties

Patriot leaders were determined not to allow the tea to be sold in the colonies. When the *Polly*, bound for Philadelphia with 697 chests of tea, arrived at the mouth of the Delaware River, a mass meeting was held in the city and agreed that Captain Ayres of the *Polly* should not be allowed to unload the tea. A "Committee for Tarring and Feathering" posted a notice warning the captain to turn his ship around and return to Britain:

You are sent out on a diabolical Service; and if you are so foolish and obstinate as to complete your Voyage, by bringing your Ship to Anchor in this Port, you may run such a Gauntlet as will induce you, in your last Moments, most heartily to curse those who have made you the Dupe of their Avarice and Ambition. What think you, Captain, of a Halter around your Neck—ten Gallons of liquid Tar decanted on your Pate—with the Feathers of a dozen wild Geese laid over that to enliven your Appearance? Only think seriously of this—and fly to the Place from whence you came—fly without Hesitation—without the Formality of a Protest—and above all, Captain Ayres, let us advise you to fly without the wild Geese Feathers.

Captain Ayres wisely stocked the *Polly* with food and water and sailed it back to Britain without unloading his cargo of tea. In Charleston, the merchants to whom the tea had been shipped refused to pay the duty. Customs officials then

On October 25, 1774, fifty-one women in Edenton, North Carolina, signed resolves to stop buying English imports, including tea. After an account of the Edenton Tea Party was published in Britain, London engraver Philip Dawe created this print satirizing the "Patriotic Ladies" and the folly of alienating the American colonists (©The Trustees of the British Museum).

seized the tea from the ships and stored it in a warehouse, where it remained unsold for years. In New York, Governor Tryon, who was worried about the reputation he had earned in North Carolina, agreed to turn the tea ship around. He told the British government that the tea could only have been landed in New York "under the protection of the point of a bayonet, and muzzle of the cannon."

Three tea ships—the *Dartmouth,* the *Eleanor,* and the *Beaver*—arrived in Boston harbor. A fourth tea ship, the *William,* ran aground on Cape Cod. Governor Thomas Hutchinson refused to allow the three ships to leave Boston without unloading their cargo. British Admiral Montagu ordered the Royal Navy warships in the harbor to prevent the ships from sailing. Boston patriots were equally determined to prevent the tea from being unloaded.

On the evening of December 16, 1773, Boston patriots took action. About sixty or seventy men and boys, many of them dressed like Indians and carrying hatchets and axes, boarded the ships, broke open the tea chests, and threw the tea—over 90,000 pounds of it—into the water. No guards had been posted on the ships, and the few sailors on board them offered no resistance. The first mate of the *Beaver* handed the ship's keys to the raiders and supplied them with candles to light the ship's hold. The raiding parties were careful not to damage the ships or anything on board except the tea.

It took the raiders nearly three hours to bring all the tea on deck, break open the chests, and dump the tea overboard. Hundreds of people lined the wharf to watch. Admiral Montagu watched the proceedings but did nothing to stop the raiders. "I could easily have prevented the Execution of this Plan," he wrote the next day, "but must have endangered the Lives of many innocent People by firing upon the Town." When the raiders' work was done, they swept the loose tea off the decks and marched away. When they passed the house where Montagu had been enjoying dinner, the admiral opened a window and called out, "Well, boys, you've had a fine pleasant evening for your Indian caper, haven't you? But mind, you have got to pay the fiddler yet." From the street, one of the "boys" called back: "Never mind, Squire, just come down here, if you please, and we'll settle the bill in two minutes."

The names of the men and boys who participated in what was later called the Boston Tea Party were kept secret for many years. Samuel Gore, the teenager who was shot in the leg on the day Christopher Seider was killed, was one of them. So was Joseph Warren, the doctor who had removed the ball from Samuel's leg, and Paul Revere, a silversmith who was a popular leader of Boston's craftsmen. So, too, was George Hewes, a shoemaker. These and thousands of other ordinary, daring Americans shaped the popular rebellion that made America free.

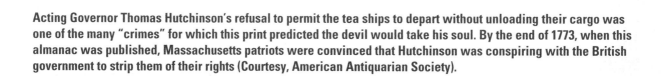

Acting Governor Thomas Hutchinson's refusal to permit the tea ships to depart without unloading their cargo was one of the many "crimes" for which this print predicted the devil would take his soul. By the end of 1773, when this almanac was published, Massachusetts patriots were convinced that Hutchinson was conspiring with the British government to strip them of their rights (Courtesy, American Antiquarian Society).

The Massachusetts CALENDAR;

OR AN

ALMANACK

FOR THE

Year of our Lord Christ 1774;

Being the second after Bissextile or Leap Year

By EZRA GLEASON

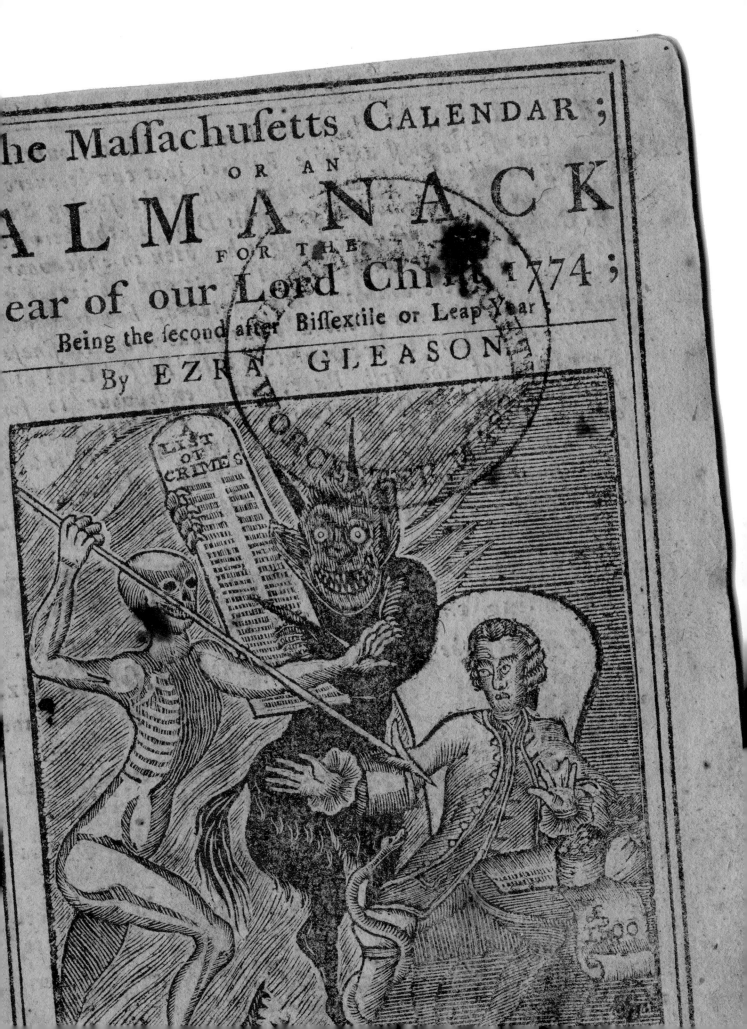

A LIST OF CRIMES

"I wish this cursed place was burned," Thomas Gage wrote from Boston in June 1775, a little more than a year after he replaced Thomas Hutchinson as governor of Massachusetts (Yale Center for British Art).

Chapter 8 Intolerable Acts

Ten years of continuous controversy took a heavy toll on relations between the British government and His Majesty's American subjects. By the beginning of 1774, the surprise and dismay the colonists had expressed a decade earlier had hardened into distrust and anger. Americans in every colony were disgusted with imperial government that invaded their rights but did little to improve their lives. British officials and their supporters, weary from years of arguing with colonists about the supremacy of the British government, spoke openly about sending troops to American to compel obedience.

Moderate voices on both sides of the Atlantic called for discussion and compromise, but the influence of moderates, in Britain and America, was fading. In Britain, the influence of men who favored stern measures and the use of military force was growing. They were supported by writers who laid bare their contempt for the colonists and openly called for expanding imperial authority and limiting the voice of colonists in their own government.

The secret conspiracy against liberty the colonists had long suspected and feared emerged from the shadows as an open assault on the rights of the king's American subjects. With each new act of Parliament, each British speech demanding the colonists be punished, and each British publication expressing contempt for Americans, colonial leaders who counseled moderation and restraint lost credibility. Support for men who believed in the possibility of the colonies maintaining control over their own affairs—of independence within the empire—eroded and finally collapsed.

Ordinary Americans lost faith in cautious leaders and increasingly took matters into their own hands. As moderation failed, colonists were drawn to one side or the other—toward a commitment to American rights or to loyalty to the king and his government. As divisions among the colonist widened, political violence, barely restrained in the past, grew more common and more vicious.

Tar and Feathers

On the night of January 25, 1774, an angry mob dragged John Malcolm from his house in Boston, stripped off his clothes, and coated him with tar and feathers. Malcolm had been deprived of his customs post in North Carolina in 1773 and returned to Massachusetts, where he was assigned to the customs house in Falmouth, on the coast of Maine. There he seized a merchant brig loaded with lumber because of a narrow, technical irregularity in its paperwork. The vessel was promptly condemned by a British admiralty court, and Malcolm received one hundred pounds as his share of the value of the ship and its cargo. A few days later a party of thirty sailors pulled Malcolm out of a house, took his sword, cane, hat, and wig, and then coated him, over his clothes, in tar and feathers. After marching Malcolm through the streets for an hour, they released him.

Malcolm had then returned to Boston, complaining about the humiliating attack. On January 25—a brutally cold day, even for Boston—Malcolm encountered a young boy in the street, pushing a sled. The boy may have said something that infuriated Malcolm. A newspaper reported that the boy had run over Malcolm's foot with his sled.

What happened next is not entirely clear. John Adams wrote that Malcolm "attacked a lad in the street, and cut his head with a cutlass, in return for some words from the boy, which I suppose were irritating. The boy ran bleeding through the street to his relations, of whom he had many. As he passed the street, the people inquired into the cause of his wounds; and a sudden heat arose against Malcolm." Malcolm's superior in Falmouth heard it that way, too, and wrote that what happened to Malcolm "was occasioned by his beating a Boy in the Street in such a manner as to raise a Mob."

The newspaper account of the incident was slightly different. It reported that a Boston shoemaker, George Hewes, came upon Malcolm

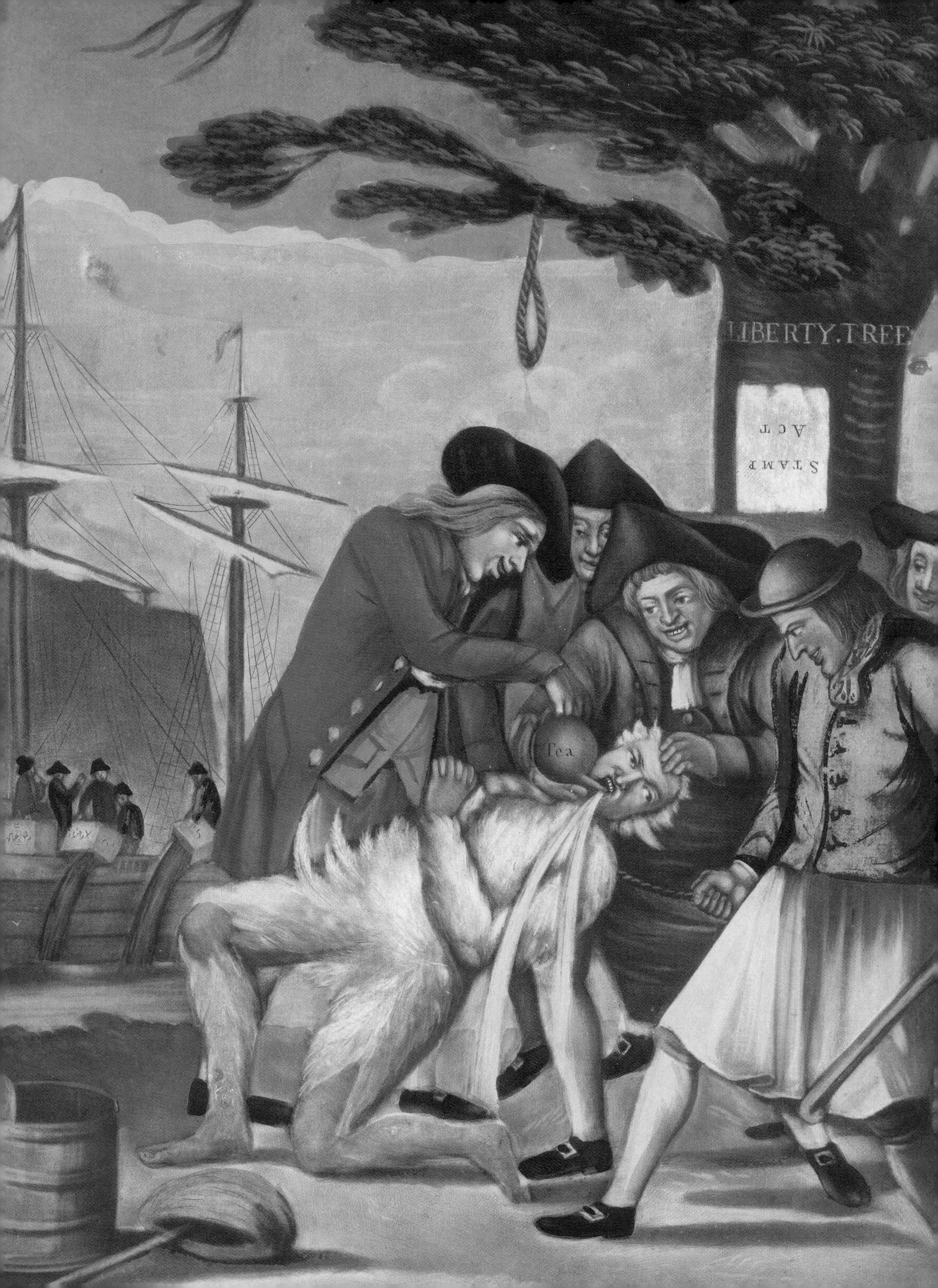
LIBERTY.TREE
STAMP ACT
Tea

"cursing, damning, threatening and shaking a very large cane" at the boy. Hewes intervened, and Malcolm turned on Hewes, calling him an "impertinent rascal." The confrontation quickly escalated, and Malcolm struck Hewes with his cane, gashing Hewes' forehead. Hewes fell to the ground, bloody and unconscious. A Captain Godfrey saw the attack and reported that "after some altercation" Malcolm retreated to his house. Bystanders took Hewes to Dr. Joseph Warren, who dressed the wound and joked grimly with Hewes about his thick skull. "Nothing else could have saved you." The deep scar left by the cane was clearly visible when Hewes died more than sixty-six years later.

The newspaper account says nothing more about the child. Perhaps Malcolm struck him, too, as Adams reported. Or perhaps when Hewes arrived, the boy ran. Whatever happened, the story ran through the city. That night a mob attacked Malcolm's house. Men broke in through a second story window and dragged Malcolm into the street, where they beat him and threw him into a sleigh. When they reached King Street, near the site of the Boston Massacre, unnamed "gentlemen" tried to convince Malcolm's captors to let him go, assuring the crowd that the courts would punish him. The mob, which by then numbered in the hundreds, was unmoved. What had the courts done to punish Preston or his men? What had they done to punish Ebenezer Richardson? Malcolm, they said, "had joined in the murders at North-Carolina" and behaved in a "daringly abusive manner" without being punished. The law had had its chance.

They put Malcolm in a cart, stripped him, and coated him with pine tar and feathers. Then they drove him through the bitter cold night to the Liberty Tree—an elm on the Boston Common—where they demanded he renounce his office and, according to a report friendly to Malcolm, ordered him to curse the king and the governor. Malcolm stubbornly refused, so they drove him through the city to the gallows near Boston Neck and threatened to hang him. Along the way, according to a later report, the mob forced Malcolm to drink hot tea until he vomited, taunting him to drink to the royal family. When he still defied the mob, they beat and whipped him and threatened to cut off his

ears. Broken, Malcolm finally gave up and agreed to do whatever the mob wanted. His tormenters drove him through the streets and dumped him in front of his house.

Franklin in London

News of the Boston Tea Party reached London about the time the mob was dragging John Malcolm through the streets of Boston. A few days later, Benjamin Franklin, the London agent of the Massachusetts assembly and the most famous American subject of the king, was called before the Privy Council—the king's senior advisors—and subjected to a different kind of political attack.

The official reason for the hearing was to ask Franklin questions about a petition from the Massachusetts Assembly requesting the removal of Governor Thomas Hutchinson and Lieutenant Governor Andrew Oliver. More than a year before, the two men had written to British officials about ways to impose order on America. Hutchinson had said that it was impossible that colonists should enjoy the same rights as subjects in Britain. Governing the colonies properly required, in Hutchinson's words, an "abridgment of what are called English liberties." Oliver suggested stripping the assembly of the right to choose the governor's council, which should be appointed by the king instead.

Someone in the British government passed copies of the letters to Franklin, who sent them to the assembly. In May 1773 they were published in the *Massachusetts Gazette*. The public was outraged. To Samuel Adams and other patriot leaders, the letters were evidence that British officials and their American allies intended to take away the rights of British colonists. Angry members of the assembly petitioned the king to remove Hutchinson and Oliver.

The privy counselors had no intention of recommending that the king remove either man, but they wanted Franklin to face them while they denounced him and his disloyal associates in America. Thirty-five members of the Privy Council attended the hearing. The hall was packed with spectators, including members of the House of

After his ordeal at the hands of a Boston mob, John Malcolm traveled to London, where he presented Parliament with a patch of his skin still coated with tar and feathers. This print was published in London soon after. The destruction of the tea in the background is the earliest depiction of what later became known as the Boston Tea Party (The John Carter Brown Library).

Benjamin Franklin stood proudly while members of the Privy Council laughed and applauded as Alexander Wedderburn tried to humiliate him. The "indecency" of the council's behavior was shocking, wrote Lord Shelburne, one of the few men present who opposed the ministry's heavy-handed conduct in America (© Courtesy of the Huntington Art Museum, San Marino, California).

Commons and at least one general, Thomas Gage. Alexander Wedderburn, the king's solicitor general, represented the ministry. In a speech lasting an hour, Wedderburn attacked Franklin's personal character, mocked his international reputation as a scientist, and accused Franklin of trying to subvert His Majesty's authority in America. Franklin, he said, was a thief who had constantly misled the king's subjects and was a "prime conductor" of the opposition to British authority in America.

Addressing the lords, Wedderburn accused Franklin and his American friends of "perpetually offering every kind of insult to the English nation. Setting the King's authority at defiance; treating the parliament as usurpers of an authority not belonging to them, and flatly denying the Supreme Jurisdiction of the British empire." These traitors, he added, "in form of a Committee of Correspon-

dence, have been inflaming the whole province against his Majesty's government."

Franklin and Americans like him, Wedderburn charged, had encouraged the colonists "to destroy the ships of England, to attack her officers, to plunder their goods, to pull down their houses, or even to burn the King's ships of war." Governor Hutchinson was not to blame for the strained relations between the British government and the colonies. The blame, Wedderburn argued, belonged to Franklin and the disloyal agitators who constantly misled His Majesty's subjects and had just recently "destroyed the cargo of three British ships."

The members chuckled with pleasure as Wedderburn abused Franklin. Many laughed out loud. Lord North listened silently. So did Franklin, who remained standing while Wedderburn spoke, his expression calm and unmoving. When Wedderburn announced that he was ready to question the witness, Franklin replied through his lawyer that he did not wish to be examined, and quietly left the room. Franklin worried for several days that he would be arrested and charged with some crime, but the government was not yet prepared to go that far.

Wedderburn's attack on Franklin reflected the government's anger about the destruction of the tea and its frustration at the refusal of Americans to accept the government's supremacy. It also reflected something more important. British officials like Wedderburn and Lord North believed that the problems in the colonies were the work of a small group of troublemakers, including Franklin, Samuel Adams, John Hancock, Patrick Henry, and John Dickinson, who misled ordinary people into resisting the king's government. Distant, unruly colonists could not be governed like the king's subjects in Britain. The government had been too lenient with them. All of that was about to change, starting with Massachusetts.

"War with all America"

On March 7, 1774, Lord North presented a bill in Parliament to close the port of Boston and to keep it closed until Bostonians paid the East India Company for the lost tea and law and order had been restored in the city. The issue, he said, was larger than the tea or even the right of Parliament to tax the colonies. In Boston, he explained, Britain and Massachusetts were "considered as two independent states." The issue to be resolved by the Boston Port Act was whether the British government actually had any authority in America.

Moderates in Parliament warned that the bill would "create that association of the Americans which you have so much wished to annihilate" and predicted a rebellion if the bill became law. Edmund Burke, a member of the House of Commons who was convinced that the opposition in America was a popular movement and not simply the work of a few rabble rousers like Samuel Adams, said the bill amounted to a declaration "that you wish to go to war with all America." North answered that if the act provoked a rebellion, it would be America's fault. Americans could not be reasoned with, another member said, because

they preferred "to decide the matter by tarring and feathering." Anger won. The Boston Port Act became law. Nothing but food and firewood could be shipped to Boston, and every ship carrying them was to be unloaded at Salem and the goods brought into Boston by land. Nothing could be shipped out.

Parliament piled on other laws to bring Massachusetts to heel. The Administration of Justice Act made it possible for royal officials charged with offenses in Massachusetts to be tried in Britain. John Adams called this the "Murder Act," because he believed it would make it possible for royal officials to get away with any crime. The Massachusetts Government Act deprived the people of the right to elect the upper house of the legislature. The king would appoint the members instead. The Quartering Act, which applied to all of the colonies, allowed British commanders to house their troops in unoccupied buildings if the colonial authorities did not provide barracks. Many colonists feared this would soon lead to the army taking over private homes.

Members of Parliament competed with one another in expressing their contempt for Americans. If Americans resisted the laws, one member said, "I would burn and set fire to all their woods, and leave their country open to prevent that protection they now have." As for Boston, he said that "nest of locusts" should be destroyed as the Romans destroyed ancient Carthage. Beyond Parliament, the king's supporters denounced America and Americans. Samuel Johnson, famous for writing the first major dictionary of the English language, wrote that Americans were "a race of convicts, and ought to be thankful for any thing we allow them short of hanging." In a widely circulated pamphlet, Johnson wrote that Americans were not entitled to a voice in government, having "voluntarily resigned the power of voting" when they or their ancestors left Britain. If they resisted the new laws, Johnson suggested that the British arm the Indians and encourage them to attack the colonists. These statements circulated widely in the colonies, and confirmed the colonists' worst fears about the government in London.

The Boston Port Act called for the British army to occupy Boston until order was restored and the colonists paid for the tea dumped into the harbor. The first regiment arrived in May.

The troops were commanded by Lt. Gen. Thomas Gage, who was both commander in chief of His Majesty's army in America and the new royal governor of Massachusetts.

Gage had served in America for many years, married the daughter of a wealthy New Jersey family, and owned property in America. He knew the colonies better than most British officials and had very definite ideas about how to keep the colonists in line. They had to be treated with firmness. Town meetings and other popular institutions stirred resistance to authority and should be discouraged. "Democracy is too prevalent in America," he had written in 1772, and the British government should devote "the greatest attention to prevent its increase." The government, he insisted, should never retreat from its policies because of local opposition. Yielding bit by bit to colonial protests only encouraged the colonists to resist the law.

Gage intended to enforce the law without yielding. He closed the port of Boston on June 1. On his orders, a sixteen-gun sloop-of-war patrolled the entrance to the harbor and the wharves were guarded by a sixty-four-gun ship-of-the-line, with thirty-two guns aimed at the city. Two weeks later more troops arrived and pitched their tents on the Boston Common, displacing the herd of cows that normally grazed there. Dock workers and sailors went unemployed, and very soon artisans and manual laborers were out of work as the materials they used and the money to pay them vanished. With no work to do and no money in their pockets, they grew angrier every day.

The Common Cause

Thomas Gage tried to stop town meetings but the townspeople defied him and met anyway. The Boston town meeting framed the problem in a letter sent to the other colonies. The British government's attack on the rights of Americans, they said, "though made immediately upon us, is doubtless designed for every other colony" as well. "The single question then is," the letter continued, "whether you consider Boston as now suffering the common cause?"

The same answer came back from all over the colonies. In Farmington, Connecticut, the people erected a liberty pole, burned the port bill, and denounced the ministry as "pimps and parasites" in league with the devil. The people of Durham, New Hampshire, sent a few cattle and money they had collected to help Bostonians through the ordeal. Other towns and parishes throughout New England sent food. The people of Savannah sent sixty-three barrels of rice to Boston along with money. In New York, a popular meeting condemned the port bill and protestors dragged effigies of Lord North, Alexander Wedderburn, and the devil through the street and then set them on fire.

New Yorkers also called for representatives of each colony to meet to consider a common response to the crisis. Colonists elsewhere echoed this call, although their leaders had different ideas about what a general congress should do. Some were in favor of a new non-importation agreement, while others were for stopping all trade with Britain and Britain's Caribbean colonies. Most farmers disliked that idea. Merchants in New York, Philadelphia, and Charleston opposed anything that would obstruct trade and looked to a general congress to support them. Some thought a general congress should prepare a petition to the king. Each colony had internal disputes, local concerns, and reasons to distrust the other colonies.

The Virginia House of Burgesses was meeting in Williamsburg when news of the Boston Port Bill arrived in mid-May along with a disturbing rumor that the British government intended to arrest Samuel Adams, John Hancock, and other Massachusetts leaders and take them to Britain in chains to stand trial for crimes against the state. In response, Richard Henry Lee, Patrick Henry, Thomas Jefferson, and several others members met privately and agreed to support the patriots in Massachusetts. The next day, at their urging, the House of Burgesses declared June 1 "a day of Fasting, Humiliation, and Prayer" for its members "devoutly to implore the divine interposition,

In Maryland, popular resistance to imperial policies was stoked by Anne Catharine Green, publisher of the *Maryland Gazette*. When the brig *Peggy Stewart* arrived in Annapolis with a cargo of tea in October 1774, an angry crowd forced the owners to burn the vessel and the tea with it, then publish an apology for their "daring insult" in her newspaper. Charles Willson Peale portrayed her as a genteel widow, with a copy of her newspaper almost hidden beneath the table (National Portrait Gallery, Smithsonian Institution)

106 In this detail of a London print titled *The Alternative of Williamsburg* and attributed to Philip Dawe, a crowd of Virginians, including women, children, and an African American, looks on as wealthy merchants sign a non-importation agreement under threat of being tarred and feathered if they refuse (The Museum of Fine Arts, Houston).

for averting the heavy Calamity which threatens destruction to our Civil Rights, and the Evils of civil War." Governor Dunmore, who held that the authority to issue proclamations rested with the governor alone, and who regarded an expression of solidarity with the riotous colonists of Massachusetts as disrespectful to the king's government, promptly dissolved the House of Burgesses.

Dissolving the House of Burgesses was within Dunmore's power, but it was a serious miscalculation. Instead of going home, as Dunmore expected, the burgesses simply moved down the street to the Raleigh Tavern, where they met without the sanction of the governor. As a meeting of private individuals they could not pass laws, but doing so was not their goal. They agreed to consult with their constituents and reconvene at the tavern on August 1. This mild act of rebellion set in motion a series of events that led to the collapse of royal authority in Virginia.

In June and July, Virginians gathered in county conventions to discuss the crisis. Though many of them deplored the destruction of the tea, they regarded the closing of the port of Boston, the changes imposed on the Massachusetts government, and the military occupation of Boston as an intolerable invasion of American rights and a threat to everyone in the colonies. Many of these popular conventions adopted resolutions condemning the actions of the British government.

The boldest were the Fairfax Resolves, written by George Mason and adopted by a public meeting in Alexandria presided over by George Washington. Mason argued that the colonists possessed the same rights as their ancestors who had first settled Virginia—the rights of Englishmen—among whom the most sacred right was the right to participate in the making of the laws under which they lived. They acknowledged that it was impractical for the colonies to be represented in the British Parliament, which was why the power to make laws for the colonies belonged to the colonial legislatures. For Parliament to make those laws was "totally incompatible with the Privileges of a free People, and the natural Rights of Mankind."

The Virginia Convention met at the Raleigh Tavern on August 1. It chose delegates to a general congress to meet in Philadelphia, adopted a non-importation agreement for Virginia effective

immediately and a non-exportation agreement to go into effect in a year if the grievances of the colonies had not been resolved. The convention agreed to meet again in the spring of 1775. The agreement to meet again without a call from the royal governor was revolutionary. When the convention met in 1775 it assumed the functions of the House of Burgesses, bypassing the royal governor and effectively separating the government of Virginia from the British Empire.

Maryland and North and South Carolina held their own conventions and dispatched delegates to Philadelphia, as did the colonies to the north. Georgians, their tiny colony pressed between the British military outpost in East Florida and hostile Creek Indians to the west and dependent on the one for defense against the other, decided not to send a delegation to the Continental Congress.

The Continental Congress

The delegates from the other twelve colonies arrived in Philadelphia in little groups during the last days of August and the first days of September. Until all the delegates arrived, those who arrived early occupied their time seeing the sights of Philadelphia, socializing with Philadelphians who welcomed the delegates into their homes, and talking among themselves. It would be difficult to overestimate the interest the delegates took in meeting one another. A few of them had corresponded. Richard Henry Lee and Samuel Adams had been trading letters for more than two years and must have greeted one another like old friends, though they had never seen each other.

Others were complete strangers, known to one another by reputation and rumor. Several delegates commented, with undisguised excitement, that they had met John Dickinson, "the celebrated Pennsylvania farmer," whose eloquent pamphlet against the Townshend Acts they had all read. Some were surprised to see him arrive in an elegant coach pulled by four horses—the opposite of the simple, bookish farmer whose pose he had assumed in his *Farmer's Letters*. John Adams noted that Caesar Rodney of Delaware was "the oddest looking Man in the World," tall and thin, "his face is not bigger than a large Apple." But Adams

107

found Rodney full of "Sense and Fire, Spirit, Wit and Humour." Much of the work of the First Continental Congress was done in these encounters, as the leaders of twelve very different colonies met and took the measure of one another.

George Washington and Patrick Henry traveled north together and were among the last to arrive. Each caused a considerable stir among the delegates. Washington's presence was commanding. He was tall and athletic, and stood out in a room full of stout, middle-aged men. He seemed younger than forty-two, yet his seriousness attracted the attention of much older men. Washington talked privately with members to persuade them that the colonies needed to prepare to defend themselves together. "Shall we supinely sit," he wrote, "and see one Provence after another fall a Sacrafice to Despotism?" Men who had never met Washington were impressed by his good judgment and determination as well as by his military experience.

Many delegates were drawn to Patrick Henry, whose reputation as a public speaker had preceded him. In a private moment, John Adams told Henry he did not expect the British government to soften its position. He expected "double vengeance," and concluded, "We must fight." Henry nodded. "By God," he said, "I am of your opinion."

When Congress convened in Carpenters' Hall on September 5, Henry made a speech that confirmed his reputation as an orator. He called on the delegates to set aside their provincial concerns and embrace a common purpose and a common destiny. "The distinction between Virginians, Pennsylvanians, New Yorkers and New Englanders," he said, "are no more. I am not a Virginian, but an American." The crisis had dissolved the old order, he said. "Government is at an End. All Distinctions are thrown down. All America is thrown into one Mass."

Saying it out loud did not make it true. There remained enormous differences between Virginians and Pennsylvanians and even more differences between New Englanders and Carolinians. But saying it raised the possibility that one day it might be true—that the colonies of British North America might somehow form a single nation. Neither Henry nor anyone else understood how this might happen, but they had come together to deal with common concerns, and every day they worked together the closer together they would be drawn until somehow they would be more American than anything else. Their shared labors, shared ideals, and the shared experiences of thousands of soldiers and citizens over a war that would last for eight years would create an American national identity.

The issue that led Henry to suggest that all America had been thrown into "one Mass" was how votes in Congress should be apportioned. As a delegate from the most populous colony, Henry naturally favored a system based on population. Delegates from the least populous colonies preferred that each colony have one vote. Delegates from South Carolina—immensely wealthy but lightly populated compared with others—preferred a system that gave greatest weight to property.

This would remain an issue throughout the American Revolution and remains an issue today. The Federal Constitution ratified in 1788 was a compromise—giving weight to population in the House of Representatives and giving each state two votes in the Senate. The Continental Congress was incapable of reaching such a compromise. It had been called as a meeting of delegates from colonies determined to maintain their autonomy in the face of an unprecedented challenge from the British government that threatened to strip them of local control. If Congress was to do business at all, each colony had to have an equal voice. Rhode Island and New Hampshire would never consent to Virginia having more votes in Congress. Virginia accepted that as the price of unity—the first of many compromises upon which our union of diverse states and diverse people is based.

Some delegates, led by Samuel Adams, were ready to declare independence immediately. Most, however, were not. They remained loyal to the king and wanted to persuade the British government to compromise. Congress sent a petition to the king expressing their loyalty while asserting the colonists' rights to "life, liberty and property." The petition asked the king to intervene with Parliament on their behalf. Delegates who favored independence had no faith that the king would do so, but they agreed to the petition as the price of maintaining a different kind of unity—the union of men who still hoped for reconciliation with those who had had given up hope and expected war. John Adams, Samuel Adams, Patrick Henry, Richard Henry Lee, and their circle of determined patriots had identi-

Paul Revere was an artisan—a man who worked with his hands—but nonetheless regarded himself as a gentleman, a status plainly asserted in this elegant portrait by fellow Bostonian John Singleton Copley. Moving as easily among Boston's craftsmen and store-keepers and its radical lawyers and merchants, he was a central figure in the resistance (Photograph © 2023 Museum of Fine Arts, Boston).

fied the delegates they did not trust, whose loyalty to the king exceeded their attachment to liberty, and they agreed to make the effort those delegates demanded. The first tentative American union was built and maintained by such compromises.

After thorough discussion, the delegates endorsed the Suffolk Resolves, recently adopted in Boston. Congress agreed that the colonists should refuse to buy any British goods until the Intolerable Acts were repealed. The more cautious delegates were not enthusiastic about this boycott. The idea was unpopular with merchants, whose livelihood would be disrupted by it. The cautious delegates accepted this Continental Association as a compromise that would preserve their influence in Congress. It was to go into effect on December 1, 1774, giving merchants a chance to complete pending transactions and the petition to reach the king.

The delegates had convened to deliberate on common measures to resolve grievances with the British government, but they accomplished much more. They established a system for working together. Conscious, as John Rutledge of South Carolina pointed out, that they had "no coercive or legislative Authority" and that their constituents were "bound only in Honour, to observe our Determinations," they worked to ensure that their resolutions would command the widest possible respect in the colonies. In this way, the inherent weakness of the Continental Congress became, at the start, a most valuable asset. Without power, it had to forge consensus. Congress adjourned on October 26, agreeing to meet again in 1775 if Parliament had not repealed the Intolerable Acts.

Silas Deane of Connecticut wrote home that "I never met, nor scarcely had an Idea of Meeting with Men of such firmness, sensibility, Spirit, and Thorough Knowledge of the Interests of America as the Gentlemen from the Southern provinces appear to be." Patrick Henry was "the compleatest Speaker I ever heard," rivaled only, it was said, by Richard Henry Lee—"they are stiled the Demosthenes, and Cicero of America."

Deane was most impressed with the Virginian who said the least. "Col. Washington," Deane wrote, has "a very young Look, & an Easy Soldierlike Air." His youthfulness puzzled Deane, who knew that Washington had fought in the first years of the French and Indian War and "was with

Braddock, and was the means of saving the remains of that unfortunate Army." Washington spoke modestly, Deane observed, but with a "determined Stile."

Deane reported a story about Washington that was whispered among the delegates: "It is said That in the House of Burgesses in Virginia, on hearing of the Boston port Bill, he offered to raise and Arm, and lead One Thousand Men himself at his Own Expence for the defence of the Country were there need of it. His Fortune is said to be equall to such an Undertaking." Washington had made no such speech, but what is important about the rumor is that men who met him in Philadelphia readily believed it.

The Country in Arms

The Boston Port Bill had a consequence its authors in London did not anticipate. The law was intended to punish Bostonians for the destruction of the East India Company's tea, but closing the port also crippled the economy of much of rural eastern Massachusetts, for which Boston was the commercial center. The economic slowdown focused the anger of people in small towns and villages—people who had never been as deeply involved in resisting the tax laws and customs regulations as Bostonians—on the British government. As a result the Massachusetts countryside was soon filled with angry patriots ready to resist British tyranny. That tyranny was represented by General Thomas Gage and the army of occupation in Boston.

General Gage wrote to London in August of the growing resistance outside Boston, where colonists were casting musket balls and collecting gunpowder. Gage was a practical military man, and understood that controlling the colony depended on denying rebellious colonists arms and ammunition. Most militiamen had their own guns, but they relied on common stores of gunpowder and musket balls, which were in short supply. Little gunpowder was made in the colonies, chiefly because saltpeter, the main ingredient, was hard to produce. Much of the gunpowder used in the colonies was manufactured in Britain using saltpeter from India.

Each town had its own gunpowder, but the

largest supply in New England belonged to Massachusetts. It was stored in the Provincial Powder House, a stone tower on an isolated hilltop six miles from Boston—far enough from the city that if the powder exploded, nothing else would be lost. The isolation of the tower served the British well. On September 1, 1774, British troops seized the powder house and carried 250 half barrels of gunpowder back to Boston before more than a few colonists knew what had happened.

News that the British army had taken the powder spread quickly through eastern Massachusetts and into New Hampshire, Connecticut, and Rhode Island. With it went a rumor that militia had fought them and at least six Americans were dead. An even more extraordinary rumor, that the Royal Navy had bombarded Boston, was mixed with it. Militiamen from all over southern and eastern New England, in ones and twos and whole companies, set off for Boston in the belief that the colonies were at war. How many thousands set out is not clear. More accurate reports—there had been no fighting after all, the British army was not on the march, the fleet had not fired on the city—caught up with most men on the road, and they turned back. Some four thousand reached Cambridge, just outside Boston, before they learned what had happened.

Dr. Joseph Warren wrote that he was delighted by the energy and "resolution" of the country people. Thomas Gage was surprised by the fury he had caused and realized that his army of three thousand men could not maintain control if the colonists started an armed rebellion. He wrote to the ministry in London asking for more troops. "If you think ten Thousand Men sufficient," he wrote, "send Twenty." As for money, he continued, "if one Million is thought enough, send two." No one in the government took him seriously. The standing army in Britain consisted of just twelve thousand men. The government sent Gage four hundred marines.

Gage pushed ahead with his plan. In December he sent troops to take the gunpowder and arms stored at Fort William and Mary in the harbor of Portsmouth, New Hampshire, sixty miles from Boston. Paul Revere rode north to warn the townspeople that the soldiers were coming. Four hundred New Hampshire militiamen occupied the fort and carried away one hundred barrels of gunpowder before the British arrived.

In February 1775 the British tried to seize cannons kept at Salem, a town north of Boston. Warned that the troops were coming, local patriots hid the cannons. The soldiers were slowed by angry townspeople, including a young woman named Sarah Tarrant who shouted from her window: "Go home, and tell your master he sent you on a fool's errand and has broken the peace of our Sabbath. What do you think? We were born in the woods to be frightened by owls?" When a soldier pointed his musket at her, she shouted, "Fire, if you have the courage, but I doubt it." The British troops left empty handed.

Shortly thereafter Gage sent two officers disguised as farmers to map the roads and farm lanes in the countryside outside Boston where the army would have to operate in the event of war. The country people watched them with suspicion from the moment they left the city. Their rough brown clothes were not enough of a disguise to fool anyone. When they stopped at an inn in Watertown for dinner, the African-American serving woman looked at them with thinly veiled amusement. "We observed to her that it was a very fine country," one of them later remembered saying. "So it is," she replied, "and we have brave fellows to defend it." Everyone in the countryside, it seemed, was watching and waiting.

At the end of March, British guards on Boston Neck searched a wagon leaving Boston and found 13,425 musket cartridges—musket balls and individual charges of powder wrapped in paper, ready to load and fire—along with some 5,000 loose musket balls. The guards seized the ammunition, ignoring the protests of the owner, who claimed it was private property. The people were preparing for war, and there was little Thomas Gage could do to stop them.

The king's ministers in London had assured Gage that the colonists would not fight. Lord George Germain, an ally of Lord North, said that the people of Massachusetts were nothing but "a tumultuous and riotous rabble," led astray by a few treacherous men. Get rid of them, the king's ministers told Gage, and the resistance would collapse. Gage had learned how wrong they were. Ordinary colonists, many thousands of them armed, were as determined to defend their rights as their leaders.

Patrick Henry, wrote Thomas Jefferson, "captivated all with his bold and splendid eloquence." The greatest orator of his generation, Henry often spoke on behalf of the small farmers and religious dissenters of the Virginia backcountry (Mead Art Museum at Amherst College).

Washington called on the men of the county to join the militia. Other counties repeated the call. In March, when the Virginia Convention met at St. John's Church in Richmond, military preparations were the main topic of discussion. Patrick Henry offered a resolution that "this colony be immediately put into a posture of defense." Richard Henry Lee and Thomas Jefferson spoke in support of Henry's resolution, but several speakers argued that Virginia should not do anything to provoke the British. Some warned that if Virginia angered the British it might suffer the same fate as Massachusetts.

Henry disagreed. He knew that the British army would overwhelm the Massachusetts patriots unless other colonies helped them. Virginia was the largest colony and had the largest population. Other colonies, Henry believed, would follow Virginia's lead. When he rose to speak again, his aim was to persuade the convention to prepare for war.

Henry began in a low tone, but his voice became louder and more determined with each sentence. A Baptist minister who was there recalled: "His voice rose louder and louder, until the walls of the building and all within them seemed to shake and rock." Americans had a choice, Henry said, between submitting to British tyranny and fighting for their liberty:

If we wish to be free—if we mean to preserve inviolate those inestimable privileges for which we have

"It is to no purpose to attempt to destroy the opposition . . . by taking off our Hancocks, Adams, and Dickinsons," an American warned a member of Parliament in December. "Ten thousand patriots of the same stamp stand ready to take their place."

Liberty or Death

General Gage comforted himself with the thought that an armed conflict, if it came, would be limited to New England. No help would come to New England rebels from the South. The southern planters, Gage wrote, "can do nothing. Their numerous slaves in the bowels of their country, and the Indians at their back, will always keep them quiet."

Events soon proved Gage wrong. In January 1775, a meeting in Fairfax County led by George

*been so long contending—if we mean not basely
to abandon the noble struggle in which we have
been so long engaged, and which we have pledged
ourselves never to abandon until the glorious object
of our contest shall be obtained—we must fight! I
repeat it, sir, we must fight! An appeal to arms and
to the God of hosts is all that is left us!*

*They tell us, sir, that we are weak; unable to cope
with so formidable an adversary. But when shall
we be stronger? Will it be the next week, or the next
year? Will it be when we are totally disarmed, and
when a British guard shall be stationed in every
house? Shall we gather strength by irresolution and
inaction? Shall we acquire the means of effectual
resistance by lying supinely on our backs and hug-
ging the delusive phantom of hope, until our enemies
shall have bound us hand and foot?*

*Sir, we are not weak if we make a proper use of
those means which the God of nature hath placed
in our power. The millions of people, armed in the
holy cause of liberty, and in such a country as that
which we possess, are invincible by any force which
our enemy can send against us. Besides, sir, we shall
not fight our battles alone. There is a just God who
presides over the destinies of nations, and who will
raise up friends to fight our battles for us. The battle,
sir, is not to the strong alone; it is to the vigilant, the
active, the brave. Besides, sir, we have no election.
If we were base enough to desire it, it is now too late
to retire from the contest. There is no retreat but in
submission and slavery! Our chains are forged! Their
clanking may be heard on the plains of Boston! The
war is inevitable—and let it come! I repeat it, sir, let
it come. . . .*

*Gentlemen may cry, Peace, Peace—but there is no
peace. The war is actually begun!*

*The next gale that sweeps from the north will bring
to our ears the clash of resounding arms! Our brethren are already in the field! Why stand we here idle?*

*What is it that gentlemen wish? What would they
have? Is life so dear, or peace so sweet, as to be purchased at the price of chains and slavery? Forbid it,
Almighty God! I know not what course others may
take; but as for me, give me liberty or give me death!*

The members of the convention were speech-
less. A young man named Edward Carrington,
who was standing in the crowd outside the church,
was so moved that he turned to a friend and asked
to be buried at that spot, beside the open window
where he had listened to Patrick Henry speak. He
was buried there thirty-five years later. The convention approved Henry's resolution. Virginians
prepared for war.

Henry's charge that the British were trying to
reduce the colonies to slavery—an idea that echoed
through the long controversy between the colonies
and Britain—had special meaning for the many
thousands of Americans who were already enslaved.
For African Americans, slavery meant much more
than just being deprived of political rights. It
meant being deprived of all rights. For them, slavery was not a danger to be avoided. It was a real
condition to be escaped.

There were white colonists who understood
that the natural rights they claimed belonged to
people of all races. A few weeks after the Boston
Tea Party, townspeople of Medfield, Massachusetts,
adopted a resolution that it was "greatly absurd for
us to plead for liberty" while enslaved people "have
not the least Shadow of Liberty" remaining. Boston
leader James Otis wrote: "The colonists are by the
law of nature free born, as indeed all men are, white
or black." In a statement published in the most
widely read newspaper in the southern colonies,
Richard Henry Lee's brother Arthur wrote: "freedom is unquestionably the birth-right of all mankind, of Africans as well as Europeans."

Some African Americans saw the dispute
between Britain and the colonies over rights as an
opportunity to claim their own rights. In 1773,
four African-American men published a pamphlet
in which they spoke for the enslaved people of
Massachusetts. "We expect great things," they
wrote, "from men who have made such a noble
stand against the designs of their fellow-men to
enslave them."

113

Tyranny, like hell, is not easily conquered;
yet we have this consolation with us,
that the harder the conflict, the more
glorious the triumph.

THOMAS PAINE
DECEMBER 19, 1776

THE
GLORIOUS
CAUSE

In *The Battle of Bunker's Hill,* American artist John Trumbull depicted the battle as a drama in which brave men—British as well as American—sacrificed themselves in the service of their countries (Yale University Art Gallery).

Chapter 9 Colonists at War

Late on the evening of April 18, 1775, nine hundred British Regulars set out through the dark streets of Boston. They were headed for Concord, a village sixteen miles west, where spies reported the colonists had accumulated a store of arms and ammunition, including two brass field cannons smuggled out of Boston. General Gage thought the soldiers might run into trouble, so each man carried thirty-six rounds of powder and ball. The men moved quietly to avoid waking the townspeople. A dog barked as they passed. A soldier quickly killed the dog with his bayonet.

The British hoped to surprise the colonists, but that was impossible. Patriot spies had already reported the army's plan to Joseph Warren, who dispatched Paul Revere on a ride between Boston and Concord to warn the country people that the Regulars were on the march. Thanks to Revere and the other riders, the countryside was soon filled with militiamen marching or riding through the night to join their companies. British soldiers could see them moving in the darkness. Major John Pitcairn, commanding the troops at the head of the column, ordered his men to stop and load their muskets. He did not intend to face an ambush unprepared.

Pitcairn's men reached Lexington, about nine miles from Boston, as dawn broke on April 19. The Lexington militia—a company of about eighty men, commanded by a farmer named John Parker—was formed in a line on the Lexington Green. Parker saw that he was badly outnumbered, but he was determined to make a show of resistance to let the soldiers know that the colonists would protect their homes and property. One nervous militiaman said, "There are so few of us it is folly to stand here." Paul Revere, who was on the scene, reported that Parker told his men "Let the troops pass by, and don't molest them, without they begin first."

Pitcairn ordered his leading companies off the road and into a line of battle facing the Lexington men. A British officer, probably Pitcairn, shouted to Parker and his men to lay down their weapons. Parker knew that resisting such a large British force would be useless. After a tense moment he ordered his men to disperse, but without laying down their arms. Most of the militiamen began to scatter, retreating from the Regulars or moving off to the sides in small groups. A few Americans stubbornly held their ground and glared at the British soldiers.

A moment later someone fired a shot. Most witnesses agreed that it did not come from either line. British soldiers said they saw a flash from behind a wall. Someone else said they saw a shot fired from a window of the nearby tavern. Some in the militia thought the first shot was fired by a British officer on horseback. Whoever fired first, the Regulars responded, without orders, by firing on Parker's retreating men.

A few of the militia fought back. Jonas Parker stood his ground, his musket balls in his hat at his feet, and fired on the Regulars. He was shot down. As he struggled, wounded, to reload his musket, an advancing British soldier ran him through with a bayonet. Jonathan Harrington retreated, but was shot down in his own front yard. He crawled to his door and died there, with his wife and son watching. As the smoke cleared, eight Americans lay dead and another nine wounded.

The British officers got their men back into line and marched on. By the time they reached Concord, seven miles away, about three hundred militiamen were waiting. As the Regulars approached, the militia retreated westward. across the Old North Bridge over the narrow Concord River. They watched as the British troops occupied the town and went from house to house, looking for arms. The patriots had removed nearly all the weapons from the town. The British soldiers found a few iron cannon barrels and some musket balls, but little else.

The militia, their number grown to about five hundred, confronted the Regulars at the Old

Connecticut soldiers Ralph Earl and Amos Doolittle visited Lexington and Concord a few weeks after the battles. They talked to eye-witnesses, then Earl sketched the scenes and Doolittle, an aspiring silversmith, engraved views of the fighting. *The Battle of Lexington* (detail above), depicts Parker's men dispersing when the Regulars opened fire (The Connecticut Historical Society). *A View of the South Part of Lexington* (below), depicts the running fight between Concord and Lexington, in which militia fired on the Regulars from the cover of trees, buildings, and stone walls, inflicting heavy casualties (Chicago History Museum).

North Bridge. The militiamen marched toward the bridge and fired on the British soldiers in line on the opposite side. The Regulars retreated in confusion as the militia killed three and wounded nine, including four officers. The British commander ordered his men back on the road and headed toward Boston.

The march turned into a bloody running battle. Militia used side roads and country paths to get ahead of the Regulars and fired on them as they passed. Companies of exhausted British soldiers stopped to fire back, but the Americans vanished into woods and over hills only to reappear farther down the road. Stone walls, a British officer wrote, "were all lined with people who kept up an incessant fire upon us." Large parties of militia shot down redcoats at Meriam's Corner and at a bend in the road on Elm Brook Hill. John Parker and men from the Lexington militia—survivors of the morning fight on Lexington Green—ambushed the Regulars from a hillside overlooking the road.

Colonists shot at the soldiers from the windows of roadside houses. Soldiers sent ahead to search houses for armed colonists were killed inside. Others killed anyone they found, armed or not, then looted their possessions and set their houses on fire. "We were totally surrounded with such an incessant fire as it's impossible to conceive," a British officer wrote. As the number of dead and wounded mounted, the marching column disintegrated into a frightened rabble. Many of the British soldiers, their ammunition gone, considered surrendering.

General Gage had worried that something bad would happen, and about the time Pitcairn's men reached Concord he had ordered a whole brigade of British troops, about 2,000 men, to march west in support. The fresh troops met the exhausted, frightened survivors just east of Lexington and the column turned and marched toward Boston. The militia harassed them the whole way, but the Regulars managed to get back to city. The colonists had killed or wounded 272 of the king's soldiers. The dead were scattered along the road. Colonists took their weapons, stripped the bodies, and buried many of them in shallow graves where they fell. The Regulars had killed over 100 colonists, but had accomplished nothing of any military importance.

They had been sent to Boston to impose order and had started a war instead.

As night came militia companies took up positions around Boston. In the days that followed, militia companies from all parts of the New England joined the patriots surrounding Boston. Unexpectedly faced with organizing an army, Massachusetts leaders asked Artemas Ward, a veteran officer of the French and Indian War, to take charge. Ward had no experience commanding an army, but he did his best to organize the militia surrounding Boston. It was a difficult task. Few of the Americans had much training and their officers lacked the experience needed to train them.

"The frenzy that has been so long growing"

Colonists elsewhere, their patience with the British government exhausted, turned on their royal governors. On April 24, a party of North Carolina patriots entered the grounds of the governor's palace at New Bern and carried off six cannons. Governor Josiah Martin expressed contempt for what he called "false patriotism or democratic zeal" among the people. On May 18, Martin wrote to Lord Dartmouth, British secretary of state for the colonies, that "the frenzy that has been so long growing among the People of these Colonies seems daily I think to spread wider and wider and is continually breaking forth in new and dangerous outrages." A few days later he abandoned the governor's palace and took refuge in Fort Johnston on the lower Cape Fear River. The assembly, which convened as the North Carolina Provincial Congress, assumed governing authority.

Martin assured the ministry in London that the people of the western counties who had been involved in the Regulator Movement remembered "the solemn Oath of Allegiance" they had taken when the rebellion was crushed and would remain loyal to the Crown. Martin had carefully courted some of the highland Scots in the interior—many of them very recent immigrants—but his claims to have won over all of the former Regulators were wishful thinking.

In late May the people of Mecklenburg County, in the North Carolina piedmont, adopted resolutions declaring all laws passed by Parliament

Paid *Six-Pence a Day*—the title of this satirical print—British soldiers in America earned less than common laborers or chimney sweeps, while facing armed American rebels and the grim threat of famine (The Society of the Cincinnati).

and all commissions granted by the Crown to be null and void, provided for the appointment of militia officers and other local officials, the legal collection of just debts and taxes, and other functions of government until the Provincial Congress should direct otherwise. The final resolution reflected the sentiments of the county. It instructed Colonel Thomas Polk and Dr. Joseph Kennedy to secure three hundred pounds of powder, six hundred pounds of lead—enough for ten thousand musket cartridges—and one thousand gun flints. Mecklenburg County prepared for war.

In Virginia, popular anger at the removal of the colony's gunpowder from the magazine in Williamsburg led to a confrontation between patriots and the royal governor. Royal marines removed the powder on April 20 and took it to a Royal Navy ship in the James River. When an angry crowd protested, Governor Dunmore announced that if

attacked he would "declare Freedom to the Slaves, and reduce the City of Williamsburg to Ashes." When news of the fighting outside Boston reached them on May 2, the Hanover County militia, commanded by Patrick Henry, marched on Williamsburg to demand the return of the powder. Dunmore fled to the protection of a Royal Navy vessel, leaving the government of the colony in the hands of patriots. From New England to Georgia, patriots secured arms and ammunition in anticipation of war.

News of the fighting in Massachusetts prompted patriots on the northern frontier to take dramatic action of their own. The people living in the mountains and valleys between the Connecticut River and Lake Champlain had their own grievances. Like settlers along much of the colonial frontier, they were entangled in disputes over land titles. Many held titles issued under grants issued by New Hampshire that were contested by New York landowners, who claimed the region for New York. Popular leaders among the settlers, including Ethan Allen, were regarded as outlaws by New York officials. On May 9, 1775, a group of fewer than one hundred backwoodsmen under Allen's command, calling themselves the Green Mountain Boys, seized control of Fort Ticonderoga, a British fortress on Lake Champlain guarding the main route from Canada into New England and New York. The fort was armed with dozens of cannons, but the small group of British soldiers inside was not expecting an attack. Allen led his men over the wall and forced the surprised British to surrender without firing a shot. A Connecticut officer named Benedict Arnold took part in the attack and received some of the credit for the victory.

The Second Continental Congress convened in Philadelphia on May 10. The city's residents were already making preparations for war. "Uniforms and Regimentals are as thick as Bees," John Adams wrote. "The Martial Spirit throughout this province is astonishing." Among the delegates was Benjamin Franklin, who had returned from London just five days before Congress met. Franklin was the most famous man in Congress, but John Adams took the lead, announcing that the Massachusetts Provincial Congress had decided to frame a constitution for itself, and urging Congress to recommend that every colony call a convention to "set up governments of their own, under their own authority, for the people were the source all authority and all power."

Congress was not ready to take such a radical step that implied that the king was no longer sovereign in the colonies. The speech was nonetheless one of the most important of the Revolution. The idea of calling conventions representing the people to frame written constitutions had been suggested by political thinkers, but it had never been tried. No such convention had ever been called, and indeed no written constitution governed any nation in the world.

Over the next twelve years, Americans would call many conventions to frame constitutions of government, culminating with the Federal Convention in the summer of 1787. The written constitution framed by a convention of delegates called together for that purpose has proved to be one of the most important contributions of the American Revolution to the science of government and has been imitated hundreds of times since. The American Revolution was the beginning of modern constitution making, a movement that has reshaped governments in every part of the world.

On June 12, 1775, General Gage issued a proclamation offering a pardon to rebels who would lay down their arms, "excepting only from the benefit of such pardon, Samuel Adams and John Hancock," whose offenses he deemed too great to forgive. The proclamation condemned "the infatuated multitudes, who have long suffered themselves to be conducted by certain well-known incendiaries and traitors, in a fatal progression of crimes, against the constitutional authority of that state," and who "have at length proceeded to avowed rebellion." Gage warned that any colonist who had "appeared in arms against the king's government" and failed to lay down his arms, concealed or protected those in arms, or provided them with "money, provision, cattle, arms, ammunition, carriages, or any other necessity," or held secret correspondence with them would henceforth be regarded as "rebels and traitors, and as such to be treated."

Bunker Hill

Several weeks passed after Lexington and Concord with no further fighting around Boston. After consulting with his officers, General Ward directed the army to take control of Charlestown Neck, a peninsula overlooking Boston Harbor from the north. There were two large hills on the peninsula. The largest was Bunker Hill, rising to 110 feet. A little to the south and closer to Boston Harbor was Breed's Hill, which was 75 feet high. From the top of Bunker Hill, American troops could watch British movements and avoid being surprised.

General Ward ordered General Israel Putnam and Colonel William Prescott to fortify Bunker Hill on the night of June 16–17. By working at night they could avoid being seen from British ships in the harbor. When they reached the Charlestown Neck, Putnam and Prescott decided that Breed's Hill would make a stronger position. They directed their men to build a square earth redoubt, a kind of small fort, at the top of Breed's Hill. The redoubt was about 130 feet on each side and had earth walls about six feet high. The battle that followed would be called the Battle of Bunker Hill, but most of the fighting took place on Breed's Hill.

When the sun rose on June 17 and General Gage saw what the colonists were doing, he organized an attack to drive them away. He sent 1,500 British soldiers over to Charlestown Neck by rowboat. Gage placed these soldiers under the command of William Howe, an experienced British general who had just arrived in Boston. Gage sent an additional 700 men over as a reserve force for Howe to use if needed.

European generals usually attacked fortified enemies by advancing quickly in narrow columns, which made it hard for defenders to shoot down all but the men at the front of the column. If the column moved fast it could reach the fortified line of the enemy and then fan out, overwhelming the defenders with bayonets. This tactic had worked for the British many times.

General Howe chose not to use this method. He had little respect for the New England militiamen

and expected them to run at the sight of advancing British troops. Howe organized his men in long lines, parallel to the American fortifications, and ordered the British soldiers to advance across open fields. They were to hold their fire until they reached the American lines and then fire their weapons and attack the Americans with their bayonets.

The first British attack fell on the American line between Breed's Hill and the water, where Col. John Stark of New Hampshire was in command. Stark ordered his men to hold their fire until the British were just 150 feet away. Officers ordered their men not to fire "until you see the whites of their eyes." At that range they could not miss. When the Americans fired, whole rows of British soldiers fell dead and wounded. Within a few minutes the British soldiers were forced to retreat.

Howe realized that the colonists were not going to run after all. He quickly organized a second attack and arranged his men in columns. The columns moved quickly up the south side of Breed's Hill toward the redoubt. The colonists held their fire until the British were within 150 feet of their position. Then they began what a British officer called "an incessant stream of fire." In a few minutes the second British attack was forced to retreat, leaving piles of dead and wounded men behind.

Howe had enough fresh soldiers left for one more attack. He organized his men in columns and ordered them to march quickly and not stop before reaching the redoubt. As soon as the British came within close range, American fire tore into the their columns. The British marines were stopped by American fire, but elsewhere the Americans ran out of ammunition and were powerless to stop the British soldiers, who came over the walls of the redoubt. American officers ordered their men to retreat, but not every-

This civilian canteen, carried by a New England soldier at Bunker Hill, is a reminder that the battle was fought in the unforgiving heat of midsummer (The Society of the Cincinnati).

Part of Winter Hill

MISTICK RIVER

A PLAN
of the
BATTLE,
on
BUNKERS HILL
Fought on the 17.th of June 17
BY
an Officer on the Spot

¼ of a Mile.

BUNKERS HILL

Charlestown Point

Hither the Ships ought to have come

Will's Creek

School Hill

CHARLESTOWN

Howe

the Glasgow

the Lively

a Transport

the Somerset

Phipp's Farm

CHARLES RIVER

Floating Batteries

the North End

North Battery

Bartons Point

Burgoyne & Clinton

the Ferry to Charlestown

Mill Dam

Clarke's Wharf

ARLES

BEACON HILL

Redoubt

THE TOWN

the Dock

BOSTON

Redoubt and 8 12 Pounders

Long Wharf

VER

THE COMMON

OF

HARBOUR

Batteries

Fox's Hill

the Fort with some Field Pieces

South Battery

Redoubt and four 12 Pounders

BOSTON

Battery

Windmill Point

General Gage ordered his troops to make a frontal assault on the rebel position on the Charlestown Neck. He might have landed his soldiers at the narrow part of the neck and captured the entire American force. This map was published in London along with a report on the battle (The Society of the Cincinnati).

one was able to get out. A fierce hand-to-handle struggle took place inside the redoubt. The British used their bayonets. The Americans, who had few bayonets, used their muskets as clubs. Dozens on both sides were killed and wounded in these final minutes of the battle.

The Americans retreated to Bunker Hill and then, after a short halt, marched off the Charlestown Neck, leaving the British in control of the battlefield. From a military point of view, the British had won, but the cost was shocking to them. They had lost 226 men killed and 828

123

and many other ways, the memory of the American Revolution drew Americans together and shaped our national identity.

Despite losing the battle, American leaders were pleased. Understanding that the British could not replace so many lost soldiers easily, Brig. Gen. Nathanael Greene of Rhode Island said, "I wish we could sell them another hill at the same price." The battle had proved that Americans could stand up to the British in battle. Some Americans imagined winning the war quickly.

Washington Takes Command

The success of the New England militia around Boston led many Americans to believe that the war could be won with part-time volunteer soldiers. Others saw that defeating the British army would require that the Americans create an army of their own, made up of men who would serve for as long as necessary to win the war. The Second Continental Congress, meeting in Philadelphia, decided to establish such an army. Because it would fight for the liberty of all Americans and would include men from every colony, Congress named it the Continental Army.

Congress appointed George Washington to lead the new Continental Army. Washington had done much more listening than talking in Congress, but each day he wore his uniform—the blue uniform of a colonel of the Virginia militia. This was Washington's way of reminding the other members that America, and not just New England, was at war, and that he was ready to serve in an American army to fight for the liberty of America.

Congress chose Washington because of his experience as an officer in the French and Indian

wounded. The Americans lost far fewer men. Their records are not as accurate as those of the British, but it seems the Americans lost 140 men killed and 271 wounded. Among the American dead, killed during the hand-to-hand fighting inside the redoubt, was Joseph Warren, a friend to Samuel Adams and John Hancock and one of the most respected leaders of the patriot cause.

Warren was the first martyred hero of the Revolutionary War. In time Americans who honored the sacrifices made for freedom gave Warren's name, and that of other heroes of the war, to towns and counties in every part of the country. In this

Henry Knox, a twenty-five-year-old Boston bookseller, volunteered his services as an artillery officer in the summer of 1775. Knox had learned most of what he knew about artillery by reading books. Knox served as the commander of Washington's artillery through the entire Revolutionary War (Metropolitan Museum of Art).

War and because congressmen recognized that he was a thoughtful, careful man. Members of Congress also believed that appointing a Virginian would help win the support of the southern colonies for a war being fought in New England. It helped that Washington looked and acted like a general. He was much taller than most men of his time and he was athletic. Thomas Jefferson, who knew Washington well, later said he was "the best horseman of his age." Washington was used to giving orders and was the kind of man people respected and obeyed. He was a natural leader.

Congress voted to make Washington commander in chief of the Continental Army on June 15, 1775. Congress offered to pay him five hundred dollars a month, but Washington refused to accept any pay. He said he would keep track of his expenses and would ask Congress to pay him back at the end of war, but that he would not accept a salary for serving his country.

Two days later Washington wrote to his wife, Martha, to tell her that he had been appointed to command the army. "It has been determined in Congress," he explained,

> that the whole Army raised for the defence of the American Cause shall be put under my care, and that it is necessary for me to proceed immediately to Boston to take upon me the command of it. You may believe me my dear Patcy, when I assure you, in the most solemn manner, that, so far from seeking this appointment I have used every endeavor in my power to avoid it, not only from my unwillingness to part with you and the Family, but from a consciousness of its being a trust too great for my Capacity and that I should enjoy more real happiness and felicity in one month with you, at home, than I have the most distant prospect of reaping abroad, if my stay were to be Seven times Seven years. But, as it has been a kind of destiny that has thrown me upon this Service, I shall hope that my undertaking of it, is designed to answer some good purpose.

The claim that he had tried to avoid the appointment reflected Washington's modesty, but it was not entirely true. By wearing his uniform each day, he had made it clear he was prepared

to serve. But just what was he being asked to do? What was the goal of the new Continental Army?

His letter to Martha provides a hint. "I shall rely," he wrote, "on that Providence which has heretofore preserved and been bountiful to me, not doubting but that I shall return safe to you in the fall." Perhaps this was little more than wishful thinking, but it seems clear that Washington believed he had been appointed for a very specific purpose: to force the British army out of Boston. Once that was accomplished, he expected to go home to Mount Vernon. At least he hoped so.

The war had begun, it seemed, with a very limited aim. It was not yet a war to separate the colonies *from* the British Empire and to establish their independence as a separate nation. The war had begun as a military conflict to establish the independence of the colonies *within* the British Empire—to force the British government to accept that the colonies had a special relationship to Britain in which they acknowledged a common king, a shared tradition of British law, and a commitment to defend the empire, but that otherwise the colonies would govern themselves.

In the summer of 1775 many Americans still hoped for reconciliation between the colonies and the British government on terms favorable to the colonies. As events unfolded it became clear that the British government would never accept such terms. If the colonies were going to govern themselves, they would have to establish their independence *from* the British Empire, freeing themselves from British rule in a war for independence. In the summer of 1775 few colonists were prepared for such a war.

Creating the Continental Army

Washington arrived in Cambridge, just outside Boston, on July 2, and took command of the army. He was disappointed by what he found. "Confusion and Discord reigned in every Department," Washington wrote to a friend. The army included over fourteen thousand men gathered from all over New England. That was a large force, but the men were badly equipped and badly organized. Few of the men had uniforms. Most wore the sort of clothes they wore at home. They were

armed with all sorts of muskets, many of which were old and in poor repair.

What was worse, the men did not behave like soldiers. Without uniforms, it was hard to tell the difference between a colonel, who commanded a regiment, and an ordinary private soldier. Few men listened to orders unless they knew the man giving them. Officers, who in many cases were elected by their men, were often uncomfortable giving orders. Few of them knew enough about running an army to give good orders anyway. The New England officers, Washington wrote to his cousin in Virginia, "generally speaking are the most indifferent kind of People I ever saw." He added that "the Men would fight very well (if properly Officered) although they are an exceeding dirty and nasty people."

It would take time, but Washington began to form these men into a true army. Since few officers or men had uniforms, he instructed officers to wear ribbons of different colors to indicate their rank. Generals were to wear ribbons across their chests. Colonels and majors were to put a red ribbon on their hats, captains yellow, and lieutenants green. Sergeants were ordered to wear a red cloth knotted around their right shoulder, corporals a green one. This system helped officers and men organize themselves more effectively and made the chain of command visible to everyone.

Washington and his senior officers reorganized the army camp and the system for providing the army with food, uniforms, blankets, ammunition, and other supplies. They stopped men from wandering away from camp whenever they wanted and began teaching them how to march and fight like soldiers. It was not easy. New England farmers were proudly independent and were not used to taking orders.

A few weeks later the first men from outside New England arrived. They were expert riflemen who came from the backwoods of Pennsylvania, Maryland, and Virginia. Unlike the plain New England farmers who made up most of the army, these men were experienced hunters and Indian fighters who lived on the frontier. They were expert marksmen. Their guns were far better than those carried by the ordinary American or British soldier,

and they knew how to use them. Most American and British soldiers carried muskets, the basic infantry weapon of the time. Musket barrels were simply straight metal tubes, smooth on the inside. Muskets were not very accurate beyond one hundred feet and a musket ball, which weighed about an ounce, fell harmlessly to the ground at about four hundred feet.

Rifles were different. Their barrels had spiral grooves inside, which made the rifle ball spin as it came out. This spinning action made the balls fly straight and made rifles very accurate. Gun makers in Pennsylvania and Virginia had perfected rifles for use on the frontier. Rifles were expensive and took much longer to load than muskets, but in the hands of an expert, a rifle could do things no musket could ever do. The expert riflemen who joined Washington's army could hit targets six or seven inches in diameter from 750 feet. Few of the New England farmers in the army had ever seen a rifle and they were amazed that the riflemen could hit small targets from so far away.

The riflemen were used to doing whatever they liked and did not care for taking orders, so they caused some problems for Washington, but they helped make the Continental Army an American army and not just a New England one. The Continental Army slowly became a real army, but Washington worried about whether his army would be able to stand up to the British in a major battle. He had trouble getting men to keep careful watch on the enemy to avoid a surprise attack. "It is among the most difficult tasks I ever undertook in my life" he complained privately, "to induce these people to believe that there is, or can be, danger till the Bayonet is pushed at their Breasts."

Supplying the army was another constant challenge. The army never had enough gunpowder or ammunition. In early August, Washington wrote to the governors of Connecticut and Rhode Island asking them to find gunpowder, lead, and gun flints for the army. A few weeks later he told Richard Henry Lee that he had only 184 barrels of gunpowder—enough to issue twenty-five rounds of ammunition to each soldier and barely any to the artillery.

Continental soldiers arrived in the army camp outside Boston in a variety of makeshift uniforms, from the simple hunting attire of backcountry riflemen to the brown and buff uniforms of the Pennsylvania regiments depicted in this contemporary print. Many soldiers arrived in civilian clothes (The John Carter Brown Library).

As summer gave way to fall, Washington's army built earthworks surrounding Boston. The British did not march out to challenge the Americans, fearing another Bunker Hill. But Washington could not force them to leave Boston. The only land approach to the city was through Boston Neck, a narrow strip of land the British army could easily defend. British ships controlled the harbor, making it impossible for Washington to attack by water. The war was not going to end that fall as Washington and many others had hoped.

The challenges Washington faced just to keep his army in the field were overwhelming. "Could I have foreseen what I have, and am likely to experience," he wrote to a friend that November, "no consideration upon earth should have induced me to accept this command." In January he admitted that "I have often thought how much happier I should have been, if, instead of accepting of a command under such circumstances, I had taken my musket on my shoulder and entered the ranks, or, if I could have justified the measure to posterity and my own conscience, had retired to the back country, and lived in a wigwam." But he gave no thought to resigning.

The Invasion of Canada

Other than the army trapped in Boston, the British had few troops anywhere in the thirteen colonies. The British held Canada, taken from the French in the last war and guarded by garrisons of a few hundred British Regulars and local militia. Congress decided to send two small forces, rather grandly called armies, to drive the British out of Canada. Few British colonists had settled in Canada since the end of the French and Indian War. The colonists there were mostly of French background. Congress reasoned that these conquered French colonists had no love for the British and would gladly join the thirteen colonies in their rebellion against British authority if American troops drove the British garrisons out. Without Canada to use as a base, American leaders thought, the British would have a hard time regaining control of the colonies.

Congress chose two promising leaders to command the invasion—Benedict Arnold, who

had helped capture Fort Ticonderoga, and a New Yorker named Richard Montgomery. Arnold was to take a force of about one thousand men and go by small boats and then on foot through the wilderness of what would become Maine until he reached the St. Lawrence River in Canada. He would then attack and hold Quebec, the capital of Canada. Montgomery was to lead another small army from Fort Ticonderoga up Lake Champlain and then overland to take Montreal.

Montgomery was a brave and handsome soldier who many expected to become a hero in the war. He had an easier time with his assignment. He captured Montreal on November 13, 1775. Arnold's route through the wilderness was longer and harder. His supplies ran low and his men were soon exhausted by their forty-five-day journey through the forest. By the time Arnold reached the St. Lawrence River he had only 675 men. The rest had turned back or been left sick or dead along the way.

Some 1,800 British troops held Quebec, sheltered behind fortified walls. Arnold could not take the city with his little force, so he waited for Montgomery, who arrived from Montreal in December. On December 31 their combined forces attacked the city. Arnold and his men made it over the wall but were stopped inside. Arnold was shot in the leg. Montgomery and his men, attacking the city on the other side, fared worse. Over fifty Americans were killed and about four hundred were captured. Within two hours the battle was over. Among the dead was Richard Montgomery, who would be remembered, along with Joseph Warren, as one of the war's first heroes.

Few French Canadian colonists, the Americans found, were interested in joining their rebellion. They looked on the war as a quarrel among the British and wanted no part of it. The Americans who survived the unsuccessful attack on Quebec remained in Canada until the spring of 1776 and then made their way south to Fort Ticonderoga in defeat.

"The Noble Train of Artillery"

The Continental Army, meanwhile, made no progress in driving the British army out of Boston. The British were equipped with sufficient artillery

The death of Richard Montgomery at the Battle of Quebec deprived the Continental Army of one of its most promising young leaders (Yale University Art Gallery).

Congress voted to present Washington with a gold medal commemorating victory in the siege of Boston. Bronze versions like this one were struck from the original dies. The medal depicts Knox's cannons on Dorchester Heights, commanding the British warships in the harbor (Boston Public Library).

BOSTONIUM RECUPER

to keep Washington's army at a safe distance, and while Washington had his own artillery, it consisted mainly of light cannons. Washington needed heavy guns capable of reaching British warships in Boston harbor. With heavy artillery—chiefly eighteen and twenty-four pounder guns—the Continental Army could make it impossible for the Royal Navy to remain in the harbor. The British army would then have no choice but to evacuate Boston. Unfortunately, the army had no heavy artillery.

In the fall of 1775, twenty-five-year-old Henry Knox suggested a solution. Knox was an imposing young man, over six feet tall and weighing some 250 pounds. He grew up in Boston and as a member of a street gang had acquired a reputation for toughness. He joined a volunteer artillery company when he was eighteen and shortly after that witnessed the Boston Massacre. He testified at the trial of the British soldiers that he had tried to convince them to go back inside and not confront the gathering mob. In 1772 he helped organize a special militia group called the Boston Grenadier Corps. About the time he turned twenty-three, a shotgun he was handling went off accidentally and blew two fingers off his left hand.

Knox owned a small bookstore in Boston, and before the war he had studied books on artillery. He told Washington that they could get the heavy cannons the army needed from Fort Ticonderoga, which Ethan Allen and his Green Mountain Boys had captured in May. The problem was that these cannons were three hundred miles away. Knox volunteered to go get them.

The idea of hauling sixty tons of heavy artillery and ammunition overland seemed, in some respects, preposterous, but if it could be done at all it had to be done in winter, when the roads were frozen hard enough to bear the weight of the heavy guns, which could be hauled most of the way on sleds. If they waited until spring the task would be impossible. The guns would then have to be hauled in wagons, and the wheels would sink deep in the mud under the enormous weight. Washington ordered Knox to move quickly.

Knox and a small party of soldiers reached Ticonderoga on December 5, dismantled most of the fort's useful guns, loaded them on sleds constructed for the purpose, and started back. Horses,

which Knox hired from local farmers, pulled the sleds most of the way. It took Knox over forty days to move what he called his "Noble Train of Artillery" across the frozen Hudson River and dozens of other streams and through the backcountry hills of New York and western Massachusetts.

John P. Becker, a twelve-year-old boy from Saratoga, New York, was one of the drivers. His father, a farmer, had worked as a hired teamster during the French and Indian War. Father and son drove teams pulling Knox's guns and equipment through New York east to Springfield, Massachusetts. John remembered later that his father drove four horses to haul a heavy iron nine pounder gun, and that larger eighteen and twenty-four pound guns required at least eight horses. He watched as a heavy eighteen pounder broke through the ice on the frozen Hudson and sank to the bottom. They managed to pull it out and keep going. He remembered, too, that the people of Westfield, Massachusetts, who had never seen cannons before, treated the teamsters to whiskey and cider as they passed through town. America is free because of the determination and ingenuity of Henry Knox and his men—including young men like John Becker.

Knox reached Washington's headquarters on February 27 with forty-five cannons and fourteen mortars—a short, heavy gun used to fire high arcing shots into enemy positions. It was an amazing accomplishment. On the evening of March 4, Washington's army rolled the artillery into position on Dorchester Heights, overlooking Boston Harbor. From there, cannon fire could reach the Royal Navy ships in the harbor. The British admiral told General Howe, who had taken over command from General Gage, that his ships could not stay in the harbor. Howe agreed and loaded the British army on the ships and sailed away, leaving Boston in the hands of Washington's army.

Americans rejoiced when they learned the good news. Congress voted to award George Washington a gold medal for achieving this great victory. Some colonists thought the war was ending. George Washington was more cautious. As he watched the British sail away, he knew they would return soon enough, in greater numbers, to try to crush the American rebellion. While others celebrated, Washington's thoughts turned to how to defend America against the coming attack.

In the debate over independence, Thomas Jefferson said that "John Adams was our Colossus on the floor. He was not graceful, nor elegant, nor remarkably fluent; but he came out occasionally with a power of thought and expression that moved us from our seats." At Jefferson's request, Adams sat for this portrait by Mather Brown in 1788 (Boston Athenaeum).

Chapter 10 Separation

Some colonists still hoped for reconciliation. They regarded the armed conflict as an unnatural war brought on by British officials driven by greed and a desire for power. The king, they hoped, would ultimately recognize that he was being poorly served by his ministers and would end the civil war within his kingdom by withdrawing the army from America and allowing the colonists to govern themselves. They hoped, in short, for independence while remaining within the British Empire.

Members of Congress who preferred reconciliation, or who doubted the colonists could win an armed struggle, convinced the others to send a final petition to George III. What became known as the Olive Branch Petition was drafted by John Dickinson and approved on July 5, 1775. It asked the king to end the fighting by withdrawing his army and instructing Parliament to repeal "such statutes as more immediately distress any of your Majesty's colonies." The petition was presented to the king in August. He ignored it. Whatever small chance there had ever been for a peaceful reconciliation on terms acceptable to most of the colonists evaporated at that moment.

The British treated the armed conflict in America as a war for independence from the start. When news of Bunker Hill reached London, Lord North advised the king that the war in America should be treated "as a foreign war." British officials directed their agents on the American frontier to persuade the Indians "to take up the hatchet against his Majesty's rebellious subjects" and began negotiations with small German states to hire their soldiers, who had a reputation for ruthless efficiency, to put down the rebellion in America. On August 23, 1775, the king issued a proclamation declaring the colonies in rebellion and patriot leaders as traitors. Then in October the king made a speech to Parliament in which he announced that "the rebellious war . . . is manifestly carried on for the purpose of establishing an independent empire."

Parliament followed with a sweeping new law, the American Prohibitory Act, which declared all American ports closed and that all ships and cargoes owned by Americans were the property of the Crown as if they belonged to "open enemies." Opponents of the bill in Parliament called it a declaration of war on the colonies, which it was. The act applied to the ships and cargoes of every American merchant, even those who opposed the patriots and complied fully with customs laws. The king signed the act on December 22, 1775, and copies of the new law reached America in late January. It drove merchants, shopkeepers, and nearly everyone else dependent on maritime trade into the patriot camp.

"Independency is an Hobgoblin"

British measures in the second half of 1775 essentially severed the bonds between Britain and the rebellious colonies. Britain had decided to treat Americans as independent before they were willing to declare themselves independent. John Adams, who quickly became the most active proponent of independence in the Continental Congress, recognized this fact, describing the American Prohibitory Act, "or piratical act, or plundering act," as an "Act of Independency." The law had ejected the colonies from royal protection, he wrote, "and makes us independent in Spight of all our supplications and Entreaties." Adams was puzzled that so many Americans were reluctant to accept the king's gift.

In the weeks and months after the American Prohibitory Act became known in the colonies, Congress divided between those who followed John and Samuel Adams, Richard Henry Lee, and Patrick Henry in favoring separation from Britain and the establishment of an independent government, and those who followed John Dickinson and other moderates who held on to the hope of reconciliation. The possibility of reconciliation, to the extent that it was ever more than an illusion, was fading quickly. Yet the prospect of separating from Britain remained fearful to people in and out of Congress. "Independency is an Hobgoblin" of such frightening appearance, John Adams wrote in late March 1776, "that it would throw a delicate Person into Fits to look it in the face."

Frightened or not, Congress had little choice but to make decisions and take actions as if the United States was already an independent nation. When it created the Continental Army, Congress had voted to issue two million dollars in paper money to help pay for the war. By early fall it was clear that the British army could not be forced out of Boston before the end of the year, and Congress

The Continental Congress issued paper money to help finance the war—so much that its value quickly declined. In 1778 Continental money was worth no more than one-fifth of its face value compared to Spanish silver dollars, which merchants preferred in payment. By 1780 the Continental dollar was worth no more than one-fortieth of a Spanish silver dollar (The Society of the Cincinnati).

None of these things were manufactured in America in sufficient quantity to conduct a war. Congress worked to organize domestic manufacturing, created a navy to raid British supply ships, and sent agents to Europe to acquire supplies there. Congress amended its own resolutions to allow merchants importing military supplies to export anything to pay for them. To secure sufficient manpower to conduct a longer war, Congress urged each of the colonies to enroll all free men between the ages of sixteen and fifty for militia service, and then, at the request of General Washington, agreed to raise an army of more than twenty thousand men to serve through the end of 1776.

By the end of 1775, Congress had raised an army, created a navy, issued money, regulated commerce, encouraged manufacturing, and dispatched representatives to secure the support of foreign governments. Although it lacked the authority to levy taxes, Congress had become, in most other respects, the government of an independent nation.

began preparing for a much longer war than most members had imagined after Lexington and Concord. This meant providing the army with a steady supply of guns and ammunition, food, uniforms, tents, and gunpowder.

Congress also recommended that each of the colonies set up governments of their own. These would be, in all but name, fully independent governments, locally elected, without a single royal appointment. The necessity of creating independent governments came to the fore in late October, when New Hampshire leaders asked Congress for advice about establishing a formal government. Unlike Massachusetts, Connecticut, and Rhode Island, New Hampshire had no colonial charter defining the powers of its colonial government. New Hampshire was a royal colony, with a governor appointed by the king. The last royal governor, John Wentworth, had fled the colony in June. The colonial assembly had worked to maintain order, but it lacked a frame of government. A congressional committee recommended that New Hampshire leaders "call a full and free representation of the people" to "establish such a form of government, as, their judgment, will best produce the happiness of the people."

Despite these developments, many Americans refused to assert independence. The Pennsylvania assembly ordered its delegates to Congress to oppose any proposal "that may cause or lead to a Separation from our Mother Country, or a Change of the Form of this Government." The New Jersey and Delaware assemblies did the same. The Maryland Convention, which was running the province in the absence of a royal government, declared that the people of Maryland "being thoroughly convinced that to be free subjects of the king of Great Britain . . . is to be the freest members of any civil society in the known world, never did, nor do entertain any views or desires of independency."

Loyalists

During the decade of controversy over the authority of the king's government in America, colonists expressed a wide range of views between subjection and deference to the king's ministers to rebellion and defiance of royal authority. Most found some middle ground and hoped the problems would go away. War made the middle ground untenable for many colonists, especially those who lived in the cities and larger towns where others were politically active on one side or the other. The

pressure of events—the military occupation of Boston, the killing of colonists and the king's soldiers, threats of arrests and executions, mob violence, and the economic chaos of embargoes, boycotts, and the constant threat of property loss—led people to identify with one side or the other.

War dissolved the uncertainties and varieties of opinion and divided Americans between two warring camps. Americans became either whigs or tories—British labels for adherents to the traditional party of parliamentary supremacy and the traditional party of royal authority. The Revolutionaries called themselves whigs, patriots, and more often as the war continued, Americans. They called their opponents tories, loyalists or simply the "king's men."

Loyalists had as many reasons for their loyalism as patriots had for supporting the Revolution. Some were sincere monarchists who believed that the king ruled because it was God's will. Others were proud to live in the British Empire and participate in its success. Still others were loyal to the king because they could not imagine the rebellion would succeed. Some of these shared patriot concerns about the British government's actions, but they believed military resistance would fail and the best course was peaceful protest and negotiation. Self-interest played a part in most decisions. Many loyalists simply wanted to be on the winning side. Some of them hoped for rewards for their loyalty.

Others were influenced by family, local gentry, church, or community, or chose the king's side because their local rivals or competitors were on the patriot side. Some of the former North Carolina Regulators, for example, became loyalists because they hated the eastern North Carolinians who had joined Tryon's army and marched against them. They may have distrusted the king's ministers, but they could not forgive the North Carolinians who had fought them, and refused to join them in resisting British oppression they had felt as keenly as anyone. This was often a very personal choice. Thousands of former Regulators were uncompromising patriots.

Some people became loyalists because they had been victimized by patriots. Among the victims was twenty-five-year-old Thomas Brown, who had recently arrived in Georgia from England. With family money and the labor of seventy-four

indentured servants he brought from England, Brown had carved a new settlement out of the forest in the backcountry near Augusta. He had a fine new house, barns, stables, and dozens of tenants. The troubles in New England seemed far away, with what he said was "no connection or concern" to him. When local patriots asked him to join their association, he declined.

Brown's success undoubtedly aroused the jealousy of his hardscrabble neighbors, and he may have treated them, in turn, with disdain. One day in August 1775 a group of 130 armed men marched to his house to force him to sign their association. Brown met them on the porch and explained that he "could never enter into an Engagement to take up arms against the Country which gave him being." Brown waved a pistol and sword at the crowd. Six men rushed and overpowered him and someone knocked him unconscious with the butt of a rifle. Armed men threw Brown, still unconscious, into a wagon and drove him to Augusta, where his tormenters beat him and tied him to a tree, poured tar over his feet and lit the tar on fire, burning off two of his toes. They left him to die, but a doctor bandaged Brown and set his broken bones. Somehow he survived.

Brown might have stayed out of the war, but his ordeal made him an active enemy of the patriot cause. As soon as he was able, Brown organized hundreds of his backcountry neighbors into a loyalist militia that fought with fierce—some said savage—determination against the patriots. "Burnfoot" Brown, as his enemies called him, encouraged the Creek Indians to attack frontier settlements and commanded troops loyal to the king for the rest of the war.

Brown's ordeal was unusually brutal, but the hatred that drove it was not. Throughout the colonies, the conflict between patriots and loyalists fed on personal animosities, family feuds, ethnic and religious distrust, and the antagonism between landlords and tenants and between wealthy landowners and their less successful neighbors. The disorder and lawlessness of war dissolved the restraints that kept personal hatred in check, especially in regions—including parts of northern New Jersey, Westchester County in New York, and the backcountry of the Carolinas and Georgia—where active warfare was most prolonged.

In quieter places, worried people managed to hide their political views from potentially hostile neighbors and tried to avoid provoking either side. They prayed that the violence and destruction of the war would pass them by. If they were lucky it did, but over a war lasting eight years it was difficult to avoid signing an oath, answering a call to a militia muster, cooperating with passing troops, or selling supplies to one army or the other. Any of these actions marked a man and his family as either loyalist or patriot.

Civil War

Armed conflict spread throughout the colonies in the fall of 1775. Few British soldiers were stationed in the colonies outside Boston. The fighting elsewhere was mostly between patriots and loyalists. The first fight took place in southeast Virginia, where the royal governor, Lord Dunmore, made use of royal navy sailors and two companies of British Regulars to ransack the region looking for arms. Skirmishes with patriot militia prompted Dunmore to raise a loyalist force of several hundred men, including some three hundred former slaves. Dunmore offered to emancipate them if they served under his command. Dunmore established his headquarters in Norfolk and fortified the crossing of the Elizabeth River at Great Bridge, the only practical approach for rebel militia. He announced that he would soon reduce Virginians "to a proper sense of their duty."

Virginia troops occupied the opposite side of the river on December 2 and reinforcements from Virginia and North Carolina arrived in a steady stream. On December 9, Dunmore ordered troops, including British Regulars, to cross the bridge and make a preemptive attack on the rebels. Protected by earthworks, the patriots repulsed the attack, inflicting heavy losses on Dunmore's men, who retreated to Norfolk and boarded navy ships. When the patriots refused to allow Dunmore's fleet

James DeLancey, from a wealthy New York family, commanded a loyalist regiment known as "DeLancey's cowboys" that seized supplies, chiefly cattle, to feed the king's troops. This is one of the only known portraits of a loyalist in uniform painted in America during the war (The Society of the Cincinnati). **137**

Above: Lt. Henry Gray, who manned a gun at Fort Sullivan, painted this watercolor of the battle shortly after the victory. It is one of the few eyewitness depictions of battle in the Revolutionary War (Image courtesy of The Gibbes Museum of Art/Carolina Art Association).

Below: News of the repulse of the British squadron at Charleston shocked the British, who expected the powerful Royal Navy to crush American resistance. This *Plan of the Attack of Fort Sulivan* was published in London less than two months after the defeat (The Society of the Cincinnati).

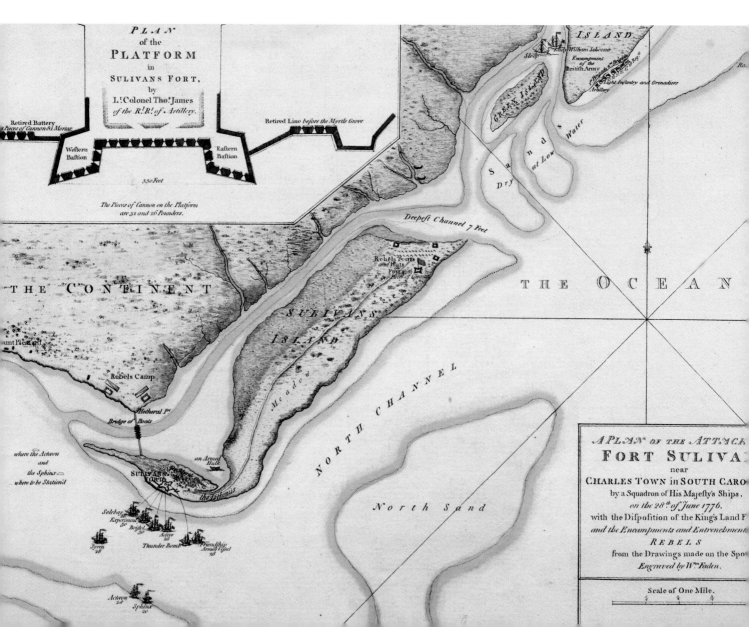

to take on water and supplies before departing, the British set fire to Norfolk, reducing the town to ashes.

The royal governor of South Carolina also fled to the protection of a Royal Navy vessel, leaving the patriot committee of safety in control of Charleston, but the loyalties of South Carolinians were divided. Many plantation owners in the tidewater were ardent patriots, but some settlers in the backcountry were less inclined toward armed rebellion. Few people in the backcountry drank tea or consumed the sorts of things the British wanted to tax. Their main concern was protection from Indians who threatened their settlements. Many of them distrusted the wealthy planters of the tidewater and gravitated toward loyalism.

Backcountry leaders in South Carolina gathered their neighbors to form loyalist militias to maintain order and resist domination by the low country planters who had taken over the colonial government. When some 500 patriotic militia seized gunpowder held in the frontier crossroads community of Ninety Six, a force of about 1,900 loyalist militia laid siege to them on November 19, while another patriot force marched through the backcountry capturing loyalist leaders and breaking up a loyalist camp. After three days of fighting the loyalists gave up the Siege of Ninety Six and retreated.

No one knew how many loyalists there might be, but the royal governors of the southern colonies who fled to Britain claimed that many thousands of colonists in the South would fight for the king and could be organized to defeat the rebellion. British political and military leaders held on to this idea until the last year of the war, convinced that loyalists were a reservoir of manpower and political support they needed to restore royal authority.

The British sent agents to the North Carolina backcountry to organize Scottish settlers who were loyal to the king into a small army that would march to the coast to meet a British naval squadron. Together, the loyalists and the British navy would defeat the patriots and restore the king's government in North and South Carolina. About 1,600 armed loyalists gathered in the Scottish settlements in North Carolina in January and the next month marched toward the coast.

At dawn on February 27, 1776, they encountered patriots sent to block their march at Moores Creek, near Wilmington. The patriots had removed the floor of the bridge across the creek to make it difficult for the loyalists to cross. The fearless Scotsmen who tried to cross on the remaining wooden structure of bridge were easy targets for the patriots, who were waiting on the other side of the creek. Dozens of loyalists were killed and the patriots captured most of the rest as they retreated. The British squadron sailed late and reached North Carolina three months after the loyalists were defeated.

The antagonism between patriots and loyalists that led to the fighting at Great Bridge, Ninety Six, and Moores Creek manifested itself in organized skirmishes and isolated acts of violence all across the colonies in the late 1775 and early 1776. This pattern continued in many regions until the war came to an end in 1783. The Revolutionary War was a civil war between patriots and loyalists as well as a war for independence fought against the British.

The British squadron that was to have coordinated with loyalists in North Carolina sailed late and reached the coast near Wilmington three months after the loyalists were defeated. The squadron sailed on to attack Charleston, South Carolina. On June 28, the British opened fire on Fort Sullivan, a half-completed log and sand fort guarding Charleston Harbor. British ships fired on the fort for ten hours. The fort's crude walls, made of palmetto logs, did not splinter when hit. British cannon balls buried themselves harmlessly in the sand. Patriots led by Col. William Moultrie returned fire with twenty-five guns, punishing the British squadron. Sir Peter Parker, the British commander, finally decided to sail away without capturing Charleston. The Battle of Fort Sullivan—the first great victory of American forces in battle since the war's first day—proved that determined patriots could even defeat the Royal Navy, the largest and most powerful navy in the world.

Common Sense

Despite early patriot victories, skeptics argued that fighting a war for independence was foolish. The British military was simply too powerful for the colonists to defeat. Even if they could raise an army large enough to contend with the British army, they could not supply it. And without a navy to confront the Royal Navy, victory was impossible. Some kind of compromise, with the British allowing the colonies to tax themselves, seemed to the skeptics like the only practical solution. Optimistic men argued that the colonists could win their independence. Britain, though powerful, was a long way off. The British would find it difficult to fight a war across an ocean. They would also find it difficult to put down a rebellion in thirteen colonies spread across more than a thousand miles of the Atlantic coast. Americans might lack arms, gunpowder, and other military supplies, but they could build armories and powder mills. The people, they said, were motivated by "the sacred cause of liberty," and would keep fighting until the British gave up and acknowledged American independence.

Between the skeptics and the optimists were many people who were undecided. They hoped most for peace and security. They wanted the British to abandon their efforts to control the colonies and agree that the colonists had a right to govern themselves. They were not confident the colonies could win their independence in war, and they were not sure independence was such a good idea. The world was filled with predatory powers. Without the protection of the Royal Navy, former colonies might fall victim to Spain, France, or some other European colonial power. Should the colonies declare their independence or remain within the empire?

The most powerful answer to this question came from a most unlikely person. Thomas Paine was an Englishman who arrived in America, almost penniless, in 1774. He was thirty-seven and had failed as a teacher, storekeeper, tax collector, and as a stay maker, making ropes for ships' rigging. Along the way he had learned to write well. He arrived in Philadelphia with a letter of introduction from Benjamin Franklin and found work editing a magazine.

Paine was appalled by the poverty of ordinary people in Britain and the miseries inflected on them by a political order that favored the monarch and his aristocratic supporters. He was disgusted by the cruelty and injustice of laws that allowed wealthy landowners to drive small farmers from the land and force them to work as agricultural laborers or join the thousands of hungry, ragged people crowding London. He was angered by the degrading poor laws, the savage operation of the criminal law, and the grotesque inequity of the British political system. Yet he was an optimist. Deeply influenced by the humanitarian idealism of the Enlightenment, he was convinced that the world might be made anew and that America could lead a revolution that would promote the spread of liberty, equality, and respect for natural and civil rights around the world.

Paine listened to Americans debate the wisdom of declaring independence or maintaining their allegiance to King George III. Then he wrote a simple pamphlet making the argument that independence was the only choice left to America. George III, Paine explained, did not care about the interests of the colonists. He was a tyrant, like most kings, and did not deserve the loyalty of the colonists. Unless Americans aimed at independence, no foreign government would help them. Whether they wanted it or not, the colonies were at war with Britain, and the only logical goal was independence. Independent America could trade with the whole world, avoid the endless wars of Europe, and provide a better life for its people.

Paine called his pamphlet *Common Sense.* It was daring and provocative. Paine mocked the idea of monarchy. In England, Paine wrote, "a King hath little more to do than to make war and give away places; Of more worth is one honest man to society, and in the sight of God, than all the crowned ruffians that ever lived."

Paine thought the idea of Britain ruling over America was unnatural. "There is something absurd," he wrote, "in supposing a Continent to be perpetually governed by an island. In no instance hath nature made the satellite larger than its primary planet; and as England and America, with respect to each other, reverse the common order of nature, it is evident that they belong to different systems. England to Europe: America to itself."

COMMON SENSE;

ADDRESSED TO THE

INHABITANTS

OF

AMERICA,

On the following interesting

SUBJECTS.

I. Of the Origin and Design of Government in general, with concise Remarks on the English Constitution.

II. Of Monarchy and Hereditary Succession.

III. Thoughts on the present State of American Affairs.

IV. Of the present Ability of America, with some miscellaneous Reflections.

A NEW EDITION, with several Additions in the Body of the Work. To which is added an APPENDIX ; together with an Address to the People called QUAKERS.

N. B. The New Addition here given increases the Work upwards of one Third.

Man knows no Master save creating HEAVEN,
Or those whom Choice and common Good ordain.
THOMSON.

PHILADELPHIA PRINTED.

And SOLD by W. and T. BRADFORD.

Common Sense was the most widely circulated pamphlet of the American Revolution. As many as fifty thousand copies may have been printed during the war—the precise number cannot be known, because few printers' records survive (The Society of the Cincinnati).

Considering the history and social diversity of the colonies, Paine pointed out that

Europe, and not England, is the parent country of America. This new World hath been the asylum for the persecuted lovers of civil and religious liberty from every part of Europe. Hither have they fled, not from the tender embraces of the mother, but from the cruelty of the monster; and it is so far true of England, that the same tyranny which drove the first emigrants from home, pursues their descendants still.

Paine called on Americans to recognize that the future of the world depended on their struggle. "The Sun never shined on a cause of greater worth," he wrote. "'Tis not the affair of a City, a County, a Province, or a Kingdom; but of a Continent—of at least one eighth part of the habitable Globe. 'Tis not the concern of a day, a year, or an age; postcrity arc virtually involved in the contest, and will be more or less affected even to the end of time, by the proceedings now."

To those who argued in favor of reconciliation, Paine asked: "Tell me whether you can hereafter love, honour, and faithfully serve the power that hath carried fire and sword into your land? If you cannot do all these, then are you only deceiving yourselves." Regardless of the answer, he explained, no compromise was possible. "Britain hath not manifested the least inclination towards a compromise, we may be assured that no terms can be obtained worthy the acceptance of the Continent, or any ways equal to the expence of blood and treasure we have been already put to." The conclusion, Paine wrote, was inescapable: "Every thing that is right or reasonable pleads for separation. The blood of the slain, the weeping voice of nature cries, 'TIS TIME TO PART.'"

Paine wrote *Common Sense* for ordinary people. He quoted the Bible, which nearly every literate American read. He wrote in simple sentences everyone could understand, and he inspired ordinary people with his ideas. The effect of the pamphlet was amazing. Thousands of copies were sold within weeks. It was passed from hand to hand, and read aloud in the army. Colonists who had been reluctant to support independence were persuaded by *Common Sense*.

Independent States

As spring came, the members of Congress remained divided and uncertain. The delegates of the four New England colonies and Virginia were all in favor of declaring American independence, but many of the other delegates and the people they represented were divided, uncertain, or openly opposed to separating from the empire. John Adams, who was determined to declare independence, understood the conflicting emotions the idea of separation produced. "Hope fear, joy, sorrow, love, hatred, malice, envy, revenge, jealousy, ambition, avarice, resentment, gratitude, and every other passion, feeling, sentiment, principle, and imagination were never in more lively exercise than they are from Florida to Canada, inclusively."

A step that seems inevitable to us, in hindsight, did not seem so to many Americans in 1776. They could not see, as we can, the consequences of American independence: their ultimate victory, the establishment of a continental republic and its steady rise in economic and political influence, the development of an American national identity, and the expansion of natural and civil rights to ordinary Americans, ultimately including the enslaved, women, and the broad range of people who had been disadvantaged, discriminated against, and exploited for centuries. They did not know, as we do, that the independent United States would become a refuge for oppressed and impoverished people from every part of the world and a model for the world of what free people can accomplish. They could not imagine that in the twentieth century, the United States would become the most powerful nation in the world, and would use that power to defend the Earth against tyrants intent on world domination.

They could see great risks and the potential for calamity. The New York and Pennsylvania delegates were under strict orders from their assemblies, which distrusted the radicalism of New England, to oppose independence. The Maryland delegation was under similar orders. Adams could make no sense of Maryland. "So eccentric a Colony," he wrote, "sometimes so hot, sometimes so cold," that he could not predict what it would do.

It soon became clear that the people of Pennsylvania, or at least Philadelphia, were more determined than their assembly for separation from Britain. A popular meeting in the State House yard called for independence and condemned the assembly. On June 5 the assembly relented and appointed a committee to prepare new instructions for the Pennsylvania delegates to Congress, permitting them to vote with the other delegates.

That was enough for the advocates of independence in Congress. On June 7, 1776, Richard Henry Lee introduced a resolution:

That these United Colonies are, and of right ought to be, Free and Independent States, that they are absolved from all allegiance to the British Crown, and that all political connection between then and the State of Great Britain is, and ought to be, totally dissolved.

Despite their new instructions, the Pennsylvania delegates were still divided. Maryland remained uncertain and New York was forbidden to vote for independence. Delaware's vote depended on who was in attendance. No one knew how New Jersey's delegates would vote. Under the circumstances further consideration of the matter was postponed until July 1. In the meantime Congress appointed a committee of five to prepare what was called "a declaration of independence." The members of the committee were John Adams, Benjamin Franklin, Thomas Jefferson, Robert Livingston of New York, and Roger Sherman of Connecticut.

Franklin and Adams were the most prominent members of the committee, but neither of them showed any interest in drafting the declaration. Adams convinced Jefferson to do the work, explaining that "a Virginian ought to appear at the head of this business." Adams said that he could not do it because "I am obnoxious, suspected, and unpopular." Finally, Adams insisted, "You can write ten times better than I can." Adams was not as unpopular as he claimed, and he was a skilled writer. In

truth, Adams had to spend June politicking for votes for independence and left the work of writing the declaration to the shy, bookish Virginian.

While Jefferson wrote, Adams devoted his time to winning over reluctant delegates. When July 1 came, Adams spoke once more in favor of independence and John Dickinson spoke eloquently on the other side. New Jersey and Maryland joined the majority for independence. Delaware remained divided, but one of the delegates in favor of independence sent a messenger to persuade the absent Caesar Rodney to ride to Philadelphia to break the tie. Rodney's wife was ill and he was suffering from cancer, but he rode through the rain to reach Philadelphia the next day. New York's delegates were still forbidden to vote for independence, but they agreed to abstain. The South Carolina delegation wavered, but Richard Henry Lee persuaded its leaders to vote in favor of independence if Delaware and Pennsylvania did so. In the seven-member Pennsylvania delegation, four delegates were still opposed to the Lee resolution, but John Dickinson and Robert Morris agreed to withhold their votes and allow the delegation to support independence by a vote of three to two.

Lee's resolution in favor of independence ultimately passed, with twelve states in favor and New York abstaining. In a long life devoted to public service, this was John Adams' finest moment. A New Jersey delegate to Congress, Richard Stockton, said that "the man to whom the country is most indebted for the great measure of independency is Mr. John Adams of Boston. I call him the Atlas of American independence. He it was who sustained the debate, and by the force of his reasoning demonstrated not only the justice but the expediency of the measure." On July 3, Adams wrote to his wife, Abigail: "Yesterday the greatest Question was debated which ever was debated in America, and a greater perhaps, never was nor will be decided among Men."

Chapter 11 The Declaration of Independence

John Adams expected Americans would forever celebrate the second of July—the day Congress voted to separate from Britain—as a national holiday, with fireworks, feasts, speeches, and parades. The adoption of a formal document declaring independence on July 4 seemed to him, and to many others, as an afterthought. That document might have been an afterthought, little remembered or discussed, if it had not been written by a man who had read widely and thought deeply about the relationship between people and their government and who possessed an extraordinary gift for expressing his ideas.

With characteristic modesty, Thomas Jefferson later explained that the Declaration of Independence was not an original work and that it simply reflected the common views of Americans and the principles of widely read philosophers, among whom Jefferson named Aristotle, Cicero, Algernon Sydney, and John Locke. The aim of the Declaration, Jefferson wrote many years later, was "not to find out new principles, or new arguments never before thought of, not merely to say things which had never been said before; but to place before mankind the common sense of the subject, in terms so plain and firm as to command their assent."

Jefferson seized the occasion in a way neither Franklin nor Adams would have done. He recognized that the formal announcement that the colonies had separated from Britain was an opportunity to do something more and in the long term much more important: to declare that the united colonies had formed a new nation, to describe the principles upon which they had done so, and to define the aims of the nation so created. In doing so, he created one of the world's most important expressions of the aims of civil society and the purposes of government.

Jefferson's modest insistence that the ideas expressed in the Declaration were derived from the work of ancient and modern philosophers and the "common sense of the subject" cannot disguise the deeply original way he applied those ideas. The Declaration translated the philosophical speculations of the eighteenth century into a practical prescription for the conduct of free society.

While the largest part of the Declaration was devoted to a list of the "Injuries and Usurpations" George III had visited on the colonies in the recent past, the most important parts were entirely forward looking—a declaration that Americans constituted "one people," that this new nation would assume a "separate and equal station" among "the Powers of the Earth," and that the nation would be dedicated to ideals of universal equality and natural rights. The consequences of these commitments for government and for the lives of ordinary Americans all had to be worked out. Thomas Jefferson and the men who subscribed their names to the Declaration understood this. They mutually pledged their lives, their fortunes, and their honor to advancing those aims. The fulfillment of those aims remains our national purpose today.

Debating the Declaration

Thomas Jefferson wrote the Declaration in the quiet of a rented room over the last three weeks of June 1776. Jefferson shared his draft with John Adams and then with Franklin, and then with all four members of the committee. They suggested minor changes, but the Declaration presented to

Thomas Jefferson was just thirty-three when he wrote the Declaration of Independence. He had come to Congress, John Adams remembered, with "a reputation for literature, science, and a happy talent at composition. Writings of his were handed about remarkable for the peculiar felicity of expression. Though a silent member in Congress, he was so prompt, frank, explicit and decisive . . . that he soon seized upon my heart." Jefferson sat for this portrait by Mather Brown in 1786 (National Portrait Gallery, Smithsonian Institution).

Congress on June 28 was Jefferson's work. Josiah Bartlett, a New Hampshire delegate, thought the draft declaration "a pretty good one. I hope it will not be spoiled by canvassing in Congress."

Congress took up consideration of the Declaration on July 2 and debated the wisdom of the draft clause by clause, changing and deleting for two days. Franklin and Jefferson said little. Franklin had no skill in debate, and Jefferson thought defending his own words was inappropriate. The task of arguing for Jefferson's draft fell to Adams.

The delegates scrutinized every phrase. The draft denounced the king for sending "Scotch and other foreign mercenaries" to impose Britain's will on America. "Scotch" was cut because the Scots were not really "foreign" and in deference to the many thousands of Scots migrants in America. The delegates also cut a passage that reflected the deep disappointment many Americans felt about the path that British had taken: "We might have been a great and free people together; but a community of grandeur and freedom it seems is below their dignity."

The most dramatic passage deleted from the draft denounced the king for permitting the African slave trade to continue. The king, Jefferson wrote, had "waged cruel war against human nature itself, violating its most sacred rights of life and liberty in the persons of a distant people who never offended him, captivating and carrying them into slavery in another hemisphere, or to incur miserable death in their transportation hither." The passage filled a fourth of the long section of Jefferson's draft dealing with the king's misdeeds.

While the Crown had vetoed colonial acts abolishing the African slave trade, Jefferson's fellow delegates refused to blame the king for the trade's injustice. Those who regarded slavery with disgust thought heaping shame on the king hypocritical. Those inclined to defend slavery regarded Jefferson's condemnation as a personal assault. The passage pleased almost no one and was removed.

On July 4, all of the delegates present except for John Dickinson—still hoping for reconciliation—voted to approve the revised Declaration. The text was handed off to printer John Dunlap, who printed the Declaration late that night. It was read aloud in the State House yard on July 8, and the bells of Philadelphia's churches rang late into the night. The next day the Declaration was read,

by George Washington's command, to the troops gathered around New York City. The war they had been fighting for more than a year now had a clear purpose. What had started as armed resistance to the British army had become a war for independence.

On July 10 the Declaration was read to a crowd gathered on the New York common. Shortly thereafter New Yorkers pulled down the gilded equestrian statue of George III that stood there. The gold leaf was scraped off and the four thousand pounds of lead beneath was broken up, loaded on wagons, and carted off to Connecticut to be cast into musket balls to shoot at the king's soldiers. "It is hoped," a Massachusetts lieutenant named Isaac Bangs wrote, "that the Emanations of the Leaden George will make as deep an impression in the Bodies of read Coated and Torie Subjects . . . as the superabundant Emanations of the Folly and pretended Goodness of the real George have made upon their Minds, which have effectually poisoned and destroyed their souls."

One People

The Americans who listened to the Declaration of Independence read aloud that summer—a ritual repeated in communities from Exeter, New Hampshire, to Savannah, Georgia—heard ideas about the nature of government and the natural rights of mankind that had never been expressed in an official statement of national purpose. The ideas in the Declaration may have been drawn, as Jefferson wrote, from the philosophy of Greek and Roman antiquity and the contemporary political philosophy of the Enlightenment, but the United States was the first modern nation to put those ideas into practice.

The first part of the Declaration explained that the purpose of the document was to express to the world why the colonies severed their connection with Britain:

When in the Course of human Events, it becomes necessary for one People to dissolve the Political Bands which have connected them with another, and to assume among the Powers of the Earth, the separate and equal Station to which the Laws of Nature and Nature's God entitle them, a Decent Respect to the Opinions of Mankind requires that they should declare the causes which impel them to that Separation.

Jefferson packed several assumptions into this long sentence. The first was that the colonists were "one People," which was not yet true. The colonists still identified very closely with their colonies, and the idea that they constituted a nation in the sense that Englishmen or Frenchmen belonged to a single nation had barely occurred to anyone. The colonists were loosely tied by a common language, though many recent arrivals—particularly the Germans who had been pouring into the middle colonies for a generation—spoke little English. The colonists were nearly all Christians and overwhelmingly Protestant, but they belonged to many Protestant denominations and sects, some of which were mutually antagonistic. The colonists were scattered from the subtropical lowlands of coastal Georgia to the mountain valleys of New England, a vast expanse of territory that was in no sense a single land.

The thing that most closely bound them together—common allegiance to the British Crown—they were in the act of discarding. But perceptive leaders understood that the shared experience of resistance and war was binding the colonists together in a new way. Americans may not have been one people in 1776, but shared principles and the shared experience of a war that would last for eight years and touch every part of the new nation would make them one people, with common ideals, shared history, heroes, and symbols. In time the Declaration of Independence itself would become a part of that shared national identity and its draftsman, Thomas Jefferson, would be recognized as one of the central figures in our national history.

The Powers of the Earth

Jefferson's second assumption was that other peoples constituted "the Powers of the Earth," distinguished by their "separate and equal station" in the world. This was true but did not describe the global situation in a comprehensive way, as Jefferson and his peers understood. The world that they knew was dominated by a small group of great powers, among which Britain, France, Spain, Austria, and Russia predominated, to which might be added minor powers including Holland, Prussia, and Sweden.

The great powers were, in varying ways, imperial powers that exercised dominion over large areas of the globe and over peoples who enjoyed few rights. Most of their peoples were subjects who were either exploited or ignored by the powers that dominated them. The united colonies had no intention of being dominated. The Declaration expressed the bold intention to assume a separate and equal place among "the Powers of the Earth."

The extraordinary nature of this intention is easily lost on us, because our world is divided into hundreds of independent, sovereign states, each in principle separate from and equal to all the others. The modern United Nations, an assembly of the world's sovereign states, has 193 members. Most of them are, in reality, too small or too weak, economically or militarily, to be wholly independent of the modern great powers, but nearly all of them maintain sovereign authority over their territory—they have governing bodies that make laws, institutions to enforce those laws, exert at least some control over their boundaries, and engage in relations with other sovereign states.

The eighteenth-century world was not divided in this way into separate and equal sovereign states. Much of the world was still occupied by indigenous peoples for whom the concept of sovereign statehood had no meaning, or as in much of North America, indigenous peoples who had a sense of identity, belonging, place, and subordination to custom and tradition that was comparable, but far from identical, to the European idea of sovereign statehood.

Much of Europe, including most of what we know as Germany, still consisted of semi-feudal fiefdoms, some of them separate from others, but many of them subordinate to or dependent on some imperial power in a way that compromised their equality with the fully independent states. The same was true of much of Asia and Africa, which were home to monarchical states of varying

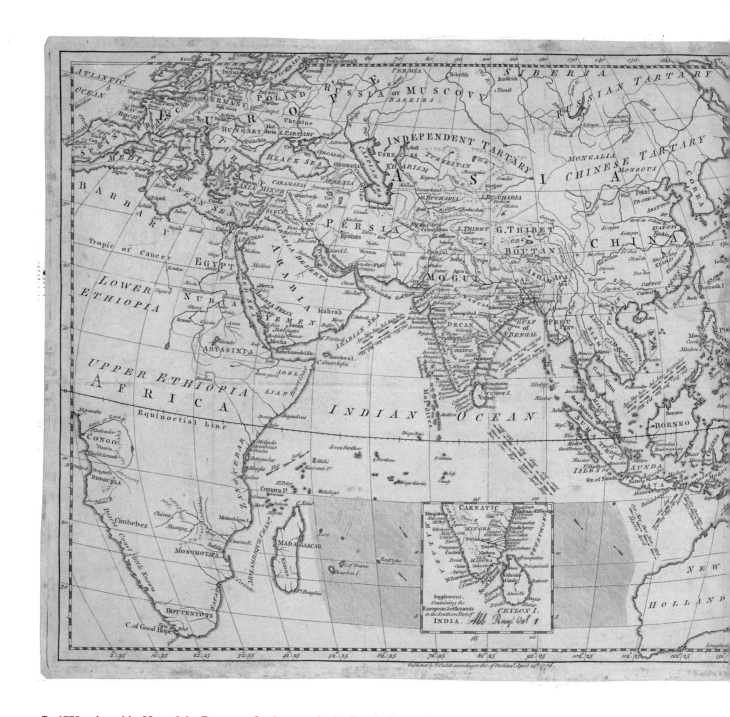

By 1776, when this *Map of the European Settlements in the East Indies and on the Eastern Coast of Africa* was published, European navigators had explored the coasts of most of the inhabited world and the major colonial powers were extending their dominion over the world's people. Americans were the first to declare their independence from colonial subjection and win a war of national liberation (Norman B. Leventhal Map & Education Center at the Boston Public Library).

independence, ranging from the vast but diffuse authority of the "Celestial Empire" of the Chinese emperors to the dependent kingdoms and vassal states spread across the Eastern Hemisphere. The leaders of the American Revolution had no intention of creating a client state dependent on any of the great powers.

The idea of creating a new, independent, sovereign state was unprecedented. Most of the established states, and all of the "Powers of the Earth," were several centuries old, and each claimed to be rooted in customs and traditions reaching back to antiquity. Creating new, independent, sovereign states was a subject of theoretical speculation for the political and legal thinkers of the Enlighten-

ment. The most important was the Swiss jurist Emer de Vattel, whose 1758 treatise, *The Law of Nations*, was the standard work on international law for more than fifty years. "Every nation which governs itself," Vattel wrote,

without dependency on any foreign country, is a sovereign state. Its rights are by nature the same as those of every other state. These are the moral persons who live together in a natural society subject to the law of nations. For any nation to make its entrance into this great society, it is enough that it should be truly sovereign and independent, that is to say, that it governs itself under its own authority and its own laws.

Jefferson and most of the other leaders in the Continental Congress were intimately familiar with Vattel's work. Those who were not could refer to the copy presented to Congress by Benjamin Franklin, who wrote to Vattel's English editor in December 1775 that the book "has been continually in the hands of the members of our congress." The United States was the first new state established in the world on the basis of sovereign independence as Vattel defined it. What Vattel imagined, Americans created. America is free because they did so.

Asserting the independent place of the United States among "the Powers of the Earth" was an essential step in securing financial and military assistance from Britain's European rivals, most of all France. The French were anxious to revenge their defeat in the French and Indian War, recover some of their lost colonies, and establish the French navy as the equal, if not the superior, of the British Royal Navy. Although the French Crown had no sympathy for American ideas about natural rights, universal equality, or representative institutions, influential French officials—most important of all the comte de Vergennes, the king's foreign minister—saw providing the American rebels with arms and military supplies as a way to embarrass the British and perhaps even separate Britain's North American colonies from the British Empire without going to war.

The French began shipping gunpowder and ammunition to the Continental Army, mostly delivered to Caribbean ports where it was loaded on American vessels, early in the war. Congress dispatched agents to Europe to ensure the continued flow of these supplies and to press France for arms and other supplies. In the fall of 1776, Congress dispatched Benjamin Franklin to France to seek more extensive aid and a military alliance that would bring France—the preeminent military power on the European continent—into the war against Britain. Franklin's experience as a colonial agent in London had prepared him for this role, and his international reputation as a scientist and philosopher ensured him attention at Versailles, the palace of King Louis XVI and a symbol of the dazzling power of one of the world's most powerful monarchs.

Popular Sovereignty

For thousands of years, monarchs had ruled the peoples of the world. Although those monarchs, from the pharaohs of Egypt to the emperors of China, varied considerably, nearly all of them claimed their right to rule was ordained by divine power. In Britain, reverence for the divine nature of royal authority had eroded in the seventeenth century, when Parliament tried and executed one king and drove a second into exile, then limited the authority of his hand-picked successor with a bill of rights that assured that the king would share governing authority with Parliament. King George III nonetheless claimed to rule over his empire "by the Grace of God," and anyone who challenged that authority risked arrest, trial, and execution for treason.

The delegates who signed the Declaration of Independence took that risk. The longest part of their Declaration listed the "repeated Injuries and Usurpations" committed by the king, charging that he had blocked legislation, interfered with their assemblies, discouraged immigration, deprived colonists of due process, and sent a standing army to the colonies to impose his will. He had, they said, "plundered our Seas, ravaged our Coasts, burnt our Towns, and destroyed the Lives of our People," and was in the process of sending foreign mercenaries to complete "the Works of Death, Desolation and Tyranny, already begun with circumstances of Cruelty and Perfidy scarcely paralleled in the most barbarous Ages, and totally unworthy the Head of a civilized Nation." He was a tyrant, Congress concluded "unfit to be the ruler of a free people," and had forfeited the allegiance of the colonies, which would henceforth be "Free and Independent States."

In our age of unfettered expression, when severe criticism of government officials is published every day, the boldness of these charges may be hard to grasp. Nothing quite like it had ever been published. But the charges leveled at the king were modest compared to the extraordinary claim the Declaration makes about the source of government power.

The Declaration of Independence claims that the authority to govern is derived "from the Consent of the Governed." Like many of the ideas in the Declaration, this one had been proposed and discussed by political thinkers for generations before the American Revolution. The idea was common among radical thinkers in Britain during the English Civil War of the 1640s that resulted in the overthrow and execution of King Charles I. John Locke explained in his *Second Treatise of Government*, published in 1690, that the "liberty of man, in society, is to be under no other legislative power, but that established, by consent, in the commonwealth; nor under the dominion of any will, or restraint of any law, but what that legislative shall enact, according to the trust put in it."

Locke and others appealed to the idea that sovereignty originates with the people to justify the English Glorious Revolution of 1688, in which King James II was driven from the throne and the sovereign power of the monarchy transferred to William of Orange and his wife, Mary. They claimed popular sovereignty as the ultimate foundation of royal sovereignty, not as a power to replace monarchy with a new form of government.

Today we take it for granted that the authority of government is based on the consent of the people, and that acting together, a people can change their form of government, but in 1776 this was a radical idea. The Declaration makes this claim in its most familiar passage:

> *We hold these truths to be self-evident, that all Men are created equal, that they are endowed by their Creator with certain unalienable Rights, that among these are Life, Liberty and the Pursuit of Happiness. That to secure these Rights, Governments are instituted among Men, deriving their just Powers from the Consent of the Governed, that whenever any Form of Government becomes destructive of these Ends, it is the Right of the People to alter or to abolish it, and institute new Government, laying its Foundation on such Principles and organizing its Powers in such Form, as to them shall seem most likely to effect their Safety and Happiness.*

Original Meanings

Familiar as it is, this passage, like others in the Declaration of Independence, demands study and reflection to understand the full meaning attached to it by Thomas Jefferson and the members of the Continental Congress who voted to adopt the Declaration. The Declaration is a short document, with no references to other documents or works of political philosophy that might help us understand what Jefferson and his fellow delegates meant by self-evidence, equality, unalienable rights, liberty, "Pursuit of Happiness," and the other words and phrases they used.

That task would be somewhat easier if we understood more about what Jefferson read and thought in the years before he wrote the Declaration. Unfortunately his family home burned down in 1770, taking with it, Jefferson wrote to a friend, "every paper I had in the world, and almost every book." That leaves us with limited sources, including what Jefferson wrote and said between 1770 and 1776, what his teachers and close associates wrote and said, and what Jefferson himself later wrote about the Declaration. Jefferson lived for exactly fifty years after the Declaration was adopted. Remarkably, Jefferson and John Adams both died on July 4, 1826—the fiftieth anniversary of the adoption of the Declaration. During those fifty years, both of them wrote about the writing and adoption of the Declaration, though neither discussed its meaning in much detail.

We can also infer what Jefferson and the other delegates meant from public documents of the time that use similar language, like the Virginia Declaration of Rights drafted by George Mason and adopted by the Virginia Convention while Jefferson was working on his draft of the Declaration of Independence. Finally, we can infer what Jefferson and the other delegates meant by studying the works of political philosophy we know or believe that they studied, familiarizing ourselves with the intellectual world in which Jefferson and his colleagues lived. By doing so, we can identify the sources for their ideas in books that discuss those ideas in detail and not just in a few brief, inspiring phrases.

This kind of study can bring us closer to understanding the original meaning of the Declaration of Independence, but because our sources are limited and incomplete we will never understand the document in exactly the way Jefferson and his contemporaries understood it. We are likely to find, as is often the case with important public documents, that there was no one original meaning. As much as they had in common, Thomas Jefferson, John Adams, Benjamin Franklin, and the other delegates to the Continental Congress had different ideas about political philosophy, and each understood the Declaration in his own way. So did the thousands of Americans who read the Declaration in the summer of 1776 or heard it read aloud, and so have the millions of Americans who have read it since.

While studying the meaning of the Declaration in this way cannot lead us to definitive answers, the exercise brings us much closer to understanding what the leaders of the Revolutionary generation thought about political and personal independence, the nature of republics, and the meaning of liberty, equality, and rights. Studying what Jefferson and his contemporaries thought about these subjects helps us understand the principles that make America free and that can help us maintain that freedom. While we may come up with differing interpretations of the original meaning of the Declaration of Independence, the effort leads to deeper understanding of the accomplishments of the Revolutionary generation and of the work that remains to be done to create a more just society.

"Life, Liberty and the Pursuit of Happiness"

The Declaration based the right of the people to abolish or alter their government on what it claimed was the self-evident truth that "all Men are created equal" and possess "unalienable rights." European philosophers and political radicals had been speculating about universal equality and universal natural rights for decades, but the American Revolutionaries were the first people in modern times to base a system of government on the principle of universal equality and to define the purpose of government as promoting and defending the rights of a sovereign people to "Life, Liberty and the Pursuit of Happiness."

Whatever else they were in 1776, those truths were not self-evident, at least in the sense that they were truths any rational person then living would acknowledge. They were declared in darkness, in a world where equality was almost unknown and the rights we cherish were barely recognized. It was a world where daily experience suggested that the mass of mankind was made to suffer without recourse, without rights, the lives of ordinary people held cheap by men who claimed that the right to rule and to high status and wealth was a birthright of the few, whom the many were created to serve. The darkness of that world was too great to be dispelled in one movement, or even a few decades. Reforming it has been the work of many generations, and its heroes—men and women of all races—are the common creators of free society.

The Declaration refers to unalienable rights—rights that cannot be sold, given away, or taken away. We would be more likely to call these *natural rights* or *human rights.* They include the basic rights inherent in the human condition. They are not granted by government and do not depend on government for their existence. They are based on what the Declaration calls the "Laws of Nature and Nature's God."

The Declaration lists life, liberty, and the pursuit of happiness among these natural rights. The right to *life* is the most fundamental, implying, at the very least, that every person has a right to defend himself or herself against aggression and to provide for their own basic needs.

Liberty is the absence of restraint or interference, including interference in what people choose for themselves as long as those choices do not endanger the lives or compromise the rights of others to make choices for themselves. Thus the rights of conscience—to make personal judgments, especially about matters of faith, morality, and ethics—are natural rights. So are the choices people make about religion and their expression in practice, as long as those practices do not endanger the lives or comparable rights of others. Likewise the right to express our judgments is also a natural right.

Jefferson may have based his ideas about the unalienable right to liberty of conscience and judgment on the work of Scottish philosopher Frances Hutcheson, who wrote in his *System of Moral Philosophy,* published in 1755, that "no man can really change his sentiments, judgments, and inward affections, at the pleasure of another; nor can it tend to any good to make him profess what is contrary to his heart. The right of private judgment is therefore unalienable."

The third natural right named in the Declaration is *the pursuit of happiness.* This phrase seems odd to many modern readers because happiness now refers mainly to personal satisfaction or pleasure, often of a short-lived kind. In the eighteenth century, happiness included satisfaction and pleasure but it also included something richer and more complicated. It also referred to the sense of personal fulfillment achieved by virtuous deeds—sacrificing private gain and setting aside selfish motives for the good of other people.

The right to pursue happiness was thus a right to seek fulfillment by doing good for others, or what people in the eighteenth century called benevolence. By doing so an individual could secure for himself or herself dignity, respect, appreciation, honor, fellowship, community, and love. We do not need these things to be free—that is, to live and exercise our liberty—but we need them to be truly happy.

In writing this passage of the Declaration, Jefferson could have followed John Locke's assertion that our rights to life, liberty, and *property* are the most fundamental. Some historians contend that Jefferson substituted pursuit of happiness for property, or even that possessing property is an essential aspect of happiness, and so is embraced by pursuit of happiness. It seems just as plausible to conclude that Jefferson left the right to property out, remembering that the Declaration says that life, liberty, and the pursuit of happiness are "among" our unalienable rights, implying that there are others. Our right to possess property is certainly among those other natural rights.

The catalogue of the king's "abuses and usurpations" that makes up the largest part of Declaration documents the British government's violations of the political or civil rights of the colonists. The list is presented to justify the claim that the king had become a tyrant and thus abandoned his responsibility to defend the natural rights of his subjects.

Unlike natural rights, which exist independent of government, political or civil rights are based on the consent of the sovereign people to be bound by laws designed to protect their lives, promote their interests, and resolve their disputes. Natural rights are universal, but civil rights may differ from one political system to another. Britain's North American colonies had long enjoyed rights to participate in making the laws, to the swift and fair administration of justice, and to freedom from excessive taxation, military occupation, and expensive, invasive government regulation. Although the Declaration of Independence did not describe the governments the independent states would form or the laws they would enact, the list of the king's abuses reflects the civil rights the Revolutionary generation valued most highly.

The signers of the Declaration of Independence pledged to support it with their lives, their fortunes, and their "sacred honor." Benjamin Rush, one of the signers, recalled the "pensive and awful silence which pervaded the house when we were called up, one after another, to the table of the President of Congress to subscribe what was believed by many at that time to be our own death warrants." That ceremony, on August 2, 1776, is depicted in this painting by French artist Charles-Edouard Armand-Dumaresq (White House Collection/White House Historical Association).

Created Equal

The Declaration of Independence appealed to the principle of universal equality at a time when the natural rights of many colonists were routinely violated and when the majority, including all women, were excluded from the enjoyment of civil rights.

The natural rights of enslaved Americans were ignored. The law deprived them of control over their lives and did little to protect them from attack. Killing an enslaved person was a serious crime under the laws of most of the colonies, but those laws were only rarely enforced. Indeed enslavement was maintained by violence and the threat of violence. The dehumanizing brutality of slavery sought to deprive the enslaved of independent thought and self-esteem in order to make them obedient, and their constant subordination to the will of their enslavers made personal fulfillment—the pursuit of happiness—impossible.

153

In CONGRESS, July 4, 1776.

THE UNANIMOUS

DECLARATION

OF THE

THIRTEEN UNITED STATES OF AMERICA.

WHEN, in the Courſe of human Events, it becomes neceſſary for one People to diſſolve the Political Bands which have connected them with another, and to aſſume, among the Powers of the Earth, the ſeparate and equal Station to which the Laws of Nature and of Nature's GOD entitle them, a decent Reſpect to the Opinions of Mankind requires that they ſhould declare the Cauſes which impel them to the Separation.

We hold theſe Truths to be ſelf-evident, that all Men are created equal, that they are endowed, by their Creator, with certain unalienable Rights, that among theſe are Life, Liberty, and the Purſuit of Happineſs.—That to ſecure theſe Rights, Governments are inſtituted among Men, deriving their juſt Powers from the Conſent of the Governed, that whenever any Form of Government becomes deſtructive of theſe Ends, it is the Right of the People to alter or to aboliſh it, and to inſtitute new Government, laying its Foundation on ſuch Principles, and organizing its Powers in ſuch Form, as to them ſhall ſeem moſt likely to effect their Safety and Happineſs. Prudence, indeed, will dictate, that Governments long eſtabliſhed, ſhould not be changed for light and tranſient Cauſes; and accordingly all Experience hath ſhewn, that Mankind are more diſpoſed to ſuffer, while Evils are ſufferable, than to right themſelves by aboliſhing the Forms to which they are accuſtomed. But when a long Train of Abuſes and Uſurpations, purſuing invariably the ſame Object, evinces a Deſign to reduce them under abſolute Deſpotiſm, it is their Right, it is their Duty, to throw off ſuch Government, and to provide new Guards for their future Security. Such has been the patient Sufferance of theſe Colonies; and ſuch is now the Neceſſity which conſtrains them to alter their former Syſtems of Government. The Hiſtory of the preſent King of Great-Britain is a Hiſtory of repeated Injuries and Uſurpations, all having in direct Object the Eſtabliſhment of an abſolute Tyranny over theſe States. To prove this, let Facts be ſubmitted to a candid World.

He has refuſed his Aſſent to Laws, the moſt wholeſome and neceſſary for the public Good.

He has forbidden his Governors to paſs Laws of immediate and preſſing Importance, unleſs ſuſpended in their Operation till his Aſſent ſhould be obtained; and when ſo ſuſpended, he has utterly neglected to attend to them.

He has refuſed to paſs other Laws for the Accommodation of large Diſtricts of People, unleſs thoſe People would relinquiſh the Right of Repreſentation in the Legiſlature, a Right ineſtimable to them, and formidable to Tyrants only.

He has called together Legiſlative Bodies at Places unuſual, uncomfortable, and diſtant from the Depoſitory of their public Records, for the ſole Purpoſe of fatiguing them into Compliance with his Meaſures.

He has diſſolved Repreſentative Houſes repeatedly, for oppoſing with manly Firmneſs his Invaſions on the Rights of the People.

He has refuſed for a long Time, after ſuch Diſſolutions, to cauſe others to be elected; whereby the Legiſlative Powers, incapable of Annihilation, have returned to the People at large for their exerciſe; the State remaining, in the mean Time, expoſed to all the Dangers of Invaſion from without, and Convulſions within.

He has endeavoured to prevent the Population of theſe States; for that Purpoſe obſtructing the Laws for Naturalization of Foreigners; refuſing to paſs others to encourage their Migrations hither, and raiſing the Conditions of new Appropriations of Lands.

He has obſtructed the Adminiſtration of Juſtice, by refuſing his Aſſent to Laws for eſtabliſhing Judiciary Powers.

He has made Judges dependent on his Will alone, for the Tenure of their Offices, and the Amount and Payment of their Salaries.

He has erected a Multitude of new Offices, and ſent hither Swarms of Officers to harraſs our People, and eat out their Subſtance.

He has kept among us, in Times of Peace, Standing Armies, without the Conſent of our Legiſlatures.

He has affected to render the Military independent of and ſuperior to the Civil Power.

He has combined with others to ſubject us to a Juriſdiction foreign to our Conſtitution, and unacknowledged by our Laws; giving his Aſſent to their Acts of pretended Legiſlation:

For quartering large Bodies of Armed Troops among us:

For protecting them, by a mock Trial, from Puniſhment for any Murders which they ſhould commit on the Inhabitants of theſe States:

For cutting off our Trade with all Parts of the World:

For impoſing Taxes on us without our Conſent:

For depriving us, in many Caſes, of the Benefits of Trial by Jury:

For tranſporting us beyond Seas to be tried for pretended Offences:

For aboliſhing the free Syſtem of Engliſh Laws in a neighbouring Province, eſtabliſhing therein an arbitrary Government, and enlarging its Boundaries, ſo as to render it at once an Example and fit Inſtrument for introducing the ſame abſolute Rule into theſe Colonies:

For taking away our Charters, aboliſhing our moſt valuable Laws, and altering fundamentally the Forms of our Governments:

For ſuſpending our own Legiſlatures, and declaring themſelves inveſted with Power to legiſlate for us in all Caſes whatſoever.

He has abdicated Government here, by declaring us out of his Protection, and waging War againſt us.

He has plundered our Seas, ravaged our Coaſts, burnt our Towns, and deſtroyed the Lives of our People.

He is, at this Time, tranſporting large Armies of foreign Mercenaries to complete the Works of Death, Deſolation, and Tyranny, already begun with Circumſtances of Cruelty and Perfidy, ſcarcely paralleled in the moſt barbarous Ages, and totally unworthy the Head of a civilized Nation.

He has conſtrained our Fellow-Citizens, taken Captive on the high Seas, to bear Arms againſt their Country, to become the Executioners of their Friends and Brethren, or to fall themſelves by their Hands.

He has excited domeſtic Inſurrections amongſt us, and has endeavoured to bring on the Inhabitants of our Frontiers, the mercileſs Indian Savages, whoſe known Rule of Warfare, is an undiſtinguiſhed Deſtruction, of all Ages, Sexes, and Conditions.

In every Stage of theſe Oppreſſions we have Petitioned for Redreſs in the moſt humble Terms: Our repeated Petitions have been anſwered only by repeated Injury. A Prince, whoſe Character is thus marked by every Act which may define a Tyrant, is unfit to be the Ruler of a free People.

Nor have we been wanting in Attentions to our Britiſh Brethren. We have warned them, from Time to Time, of Attempts by their Legiſlature to extend an unwarrantable Juriſdiction over us. We have reminded them of the Circumſtances of our Emigration and Settlement here. We have appealed to their native Juſtice and Magnanimity, and we have conjured them by the Ties of our common Kindred to diſavow theſe Uſurpations, which would inevitably interrupt our Connexions and Correſpondence. They too have been deaf to the Voice of Juſtice and of Conſanguinity. We muſt, therefore, acquieſce in the Neceſſity, which denounces our Separation, and hold them, as we hold the Reſt of Mankind, Enemies in War, in Peace Friends.

We, therefore, the Repreſentatives of the UNITED STATES OF AMERICA, in GENERAL CONGRESS Aſſembled, appealing to the Supreme Judge of the World for the Rectitude of our Intentions, do, in the Name, and by Authority of the good People of theſe Colonies, ſolemnly Publiſh and Declare, That theſe United Colonies are, and of Right ought to be, FREE AND INDEPENDENT STATES; that they are abſolved from all Allegiance to the Britiſh Crown, and that all political Connexion between them and the State of Great-Britain, is, and ought to be, totally diſſolved; and that as FREE AND INDEPENDENT STATES, they have full Power to levy War, conclude Peace, contract Alliances, eſtabliſh Commerce, and to do all other Acts and Things which INDEPENDENT STATES may of Right do. And for the Support of this Declaration, with a firm Reliance on the Protection of DIVINE PROVIDENCE, we mutually pledge to each other our Lives, our Fortunes, and our ſacred Honour.

John Hancock.

GEORGIA,	Button Gwinnett, Lyman Hall, Geo. Walton.	VIRGINIA,	George Wythe, Richard Henry Lee, Th⁵. Jefferſon, Benj⁴. Harriſon, Th⁵. Nelſon, jr. Francis Lightfoot Lee, Carter Braxton.	DELAWARE,	Cæſar Rodney, Geo. Read.	MASSACHUSETTS-BAY,	Sam¹. Adams, John Adams, Rob¹. Treat Paine, Elbridge Gerry.
NORTH-CAROLINA,	Wm. Hooper, Joſeph Hewes, John Penn.			NEW-YORK,	Wm. Floyd, Phil. Livingſton, Fran⁵. Lewis, Lewis Morris.	RHODE-ISLAND AND PROVIDENCE, &c.	Step. Hopkins, William Ellery.
SOUTH-CAROLINA,	Edward Rutledge, Th⁵. Heyward, junr. Thomas Lynch, jun⁵. Arthur Middleton.	PENNSYLVANIA,	Rob¹. Morris, Benjamin Ruſh, Benja. Franklin, John Morton, Geo. Clymer, Jas. Smith, Geo. Taylor, James Wilſon, Geo. Roſs.	NEW-JERSEY,	Rich⁴. Stockton, Jno. Witherſpoon, Fra⁵. Hopkinſon, John Hart, Abra. Clark.	CONNECTICUT,	Roger Sherman, Sam¹. Huntington, Wm. Williams, Oliver Wolcott.
MARYLAND,	Samuel Chaſe, Wm. Paca, Thos. Stone, Charles Carroll, of Carrollton.			NEW-HAMPSHIRE,	Joſiah Bartlett, Wm. Whipple, Matthew Thornton.		

IN CONGRESS, January 18, 1777.

ORDERED,

THAT an authenticated Copy of the DECLARATION OF INDEPENDENCY, with the Names of the MEMBERS OF CONGRESS, ſubſcribing the ſame, be ſent to each of the UNITED STATES, and that they be deſired to have the ſame put on RECORD.

By Order of CONGRESS,

JOHN HANCOCK, Preſident.

BALTIMORE, in MARYLAND: Printed by Mary Katharine Goddard.

The logic of the Declaration was inescapable, although many people dependent on enslavement as a source of wealth would seek to escape it: if all men were created equal and endowed with unalienable natural rights, slavery would have to be abolished and the natural rights of former slaves protected and promoted.

The only alternative was to prove that Africans and their American descendants were not men and women in the same way that the Europeans and their American descendants were—that they were naturally inferior and that their inferiority meant they did not possess natural rights. Such racist views were widely held in the eighteenth century, even by otherwise sophisticated thinkers. Scottish philosopher David Hume, who had no personal experience with Africans, thought that the races of mankind had different origins, and wrote that he was "apt to suspect the Negroes, and in general all other species of men, to be naturally inferior to the whites."

Others like Pennsylvania abolitionist Anthony Benezet insisted that Africans and their descendants had the same natural capacities as Europeans and their descendants and possessed the same natural rights. Frances Hutcheson, the Scottish philosopher whose ideas influenced Jefferson and other American Revolutionaries, argued against slavery, insisting that there could be no "right to assume power over others, without their consent."

Among those who insisted that Africans and their descendants possessed natural rights were Africans themselves, including Ignatius Sancho. Born on a slave ship sailing for the Caribbean, he was later freed and became a successful London shopkeeper, writer, and opponent of slavery. Sancho and others who argued for the abolition of slavery expected America to become a haven for justice and equality.

Thoughtful people on both sides of the Atlantic recognized that talented men and women of African descent like Ignatius Sancho and Phillis Wheatley proved that people born in Africa and their descendants, enslaved and free, possessed natural abilities in the same way as Europeans and their descendants and possessed the same natural rights. Others recognized that the possession of talents had no bearing on the possession of natural rights.

Principled opposition to slavery, which had previously been expressed by a few, mostly on religious grounds, attracted support as the idea of universal natural rights took hold. The controversy between the colonies and Britain accelerated thinking on both sides of the Atlantic about natural rights and fed the early development of the anti-slavery movement in America and in Britain.

People in Britain who were most uncomfortable with slavery tended to be vocal defenders of American rights and supporters of the American cause. Some of them saw the Revolution as a truly radical movement based on the natural rights of all mankind. This was the view of the English radical Richard Price, a great friend and admirer of Benjamin Franklin. Englishmen like Price who believed that governments should be based on natural rights recognized the American Revolution as a truly and deeply radical moment in world history that would ultimately transform the lives of people everywhere.

Since principled opposition to slavery rested on the idea of natural rights, it is not at all surprising that the first statute abolishing slavery ever written was adopted, not in Britain, but in what might justly be described, at that moment, as the most culturally diverse, philosophically sophisticated, and forward-looking place in the western world: Pennsylvania. With a founding creed based on Quaker ideas of moral equality, tolerance, charity, and non-violence, eighteenth-century Pennsylvania attracted settlers and religious refugees from several parts of western Europe, including people from differing cultural and legal traditions. The idea that universal equality and natural rights were the basis of government was accepted more readily there than anywhere else and led logically to the Pennsylvania Act for the Gradual Abolition of Slavery, adopted in 1780.

Slavery was abolished by law in the states north of Pennsylvania during the Revolutionary

In 1777, shortly after the American victories at Trenton and Princeton, Congress commissioned Mary Katharine Goddard, the publisher of the *Maryland Journal*, to produce a new broadside of the Declaration of Independence listing the names of the signers for the first time. She boldly included her own name at the bottom—"Baltimore, in Maryland: Printed by Mary Katharine Goddard" (Library of Congress).

generation and as a direct consequence of the Revolutionary appeal to universal natural rights. Securing the adoption of those laws required, in some cases, lengthy debate and compromises resulting in gradual abolition schemes that prolonged the bondage of enslaved Americans, but which ultimately extinguished slavery in the middle states and New England.

While other Americans considered the meaning of the Declaration of Independence and debated measures to fulfill its ideals, thousands of African Americans served in the armed forces that won American independence. As many as nine thousand served in the Continental Army and Navy, in the militia, on privateering vessels, and as teamsters or servants to officers. This was about four percent of the men who served, but their terms were typically much longer than that of whites. During the latter stages of the war, when white recruitment slowed, black soldiers, sailors, and support personnel probably accounted for between fifteen and twenty percent of the effective strength of the armed forces. America is free thanks to their service.

"Posterity will triumph"

The Declaration of Independence did not describe the independent states as they were. It reflected ambitions for what they might and should become—free republics in which natural and civil rights would be respected and citizens would devote themselves to the public good. Declaring that all men are created equal was not hypocrisy—it was an aspiration to which the delegates pledged themselves. All that their pledge implied was not clear to them.

The Declaration of Independence was a beginning. The Declaration did not make the American states independent. There remained a war to fight and win. "I am well aware of the toil and blood and treasure, that it will cost us to maintain this Declaration, and support and defend these States," John Adams wrote home.

Declaring Americans one people did not make them so. Americans would become one people when they had a national identity, made up of shared experiences, heroes, victories, suffering,

symbols, and ideals. The long war for independence supplied many of them. Generations of historical experience would supply many more.

Declaring universal equality and rights to life, liberty, and the pursuit of happiness self-evident and those rights unalienable did not immediately change the lives of the women and men for whom those rights were routinely ignored. Inequality remained the norm, and whatever rights people might possess in the imagination of philosophers, few enjoyed those rights in practice.

In the years that followed the Declaration of Independence, Americans made remarkable progress in fulfilling its high ideals. They devised state constitutions reflecting the consent of the governed—or at least those who possessed sufficient property to vote and hold public office. They created republican governments responsive to the will of the people and dedicated to their interests—governments that would become increasingly democratic in the early nineteenth century. They began the process of dismantling established religions, ensuring greater liberty of conscience than enjoyed anywhere in the world. And they began the process of dismantling slavery.

Generations of Americans would have to dedicate themselves to fulfilling the aspirations

On July 9, 1776, a crowd of New Yorkers pulled down the equestrian statue of George III dedicated in 1770. The broken parts of the lead statue were carted to Connecticut, where they were cast into thousands of musket balls for the Continental Army. This imaginative depiction of the scene was painted by William Walcutt in 1857 (Lafayette College Art Collection, Easton, PA).

expressed in the Declaration before most Americans would enjoy their natural and civil rights. Progress has been uneven and often frustrating, slowed by complacence and timidity as well as selfishness, bigotry, and intolerance. But progress we have made, and we will continue to make.

All of this is clear to us in hindsight. At the time the path ahead was dark. "Yet through all the gloom," John Adams wrote home to Abigail, "I can see the rays of ravishing light and glory. I can see that the end is more than worth all the means. And that posterity will triumph . . ."

157

Captured at Fort Washington in November 1776, Major Otho Holland Williams of Maryland was imprisoned that winter in an unheated cell just sixteen feet square. One of his captors asked him what trade he had worked in before the war. A profession, he replied, "which had taught him to rebuke and punish insolence" (Society of the Cincinnati of Maryland).

Chapter 12 An Army of Free Men

Separation from the British Empire turned the war with Britain into a war for independence. To win, the British would have to conquer and occupy the United States, imposing their will by force, or they would have to break the will of the Americans by occupying their cities, ravaging their countryside, controlling the coast, and strangling American commerce. Conquest and occupation were not practical, because the continent was vast and the British army was simply not large enough to occupy it all. Britain fought to break American will to resist. Optimistic British leaders hoped to do so quickly by attacking the rebellious colonies with overwhelming force.

The only course that could lead to a patriot victory was for Americans to fight until Britain wearied of the war and abandoned the struggle. Whatever happened, it would be a fight to the finish, with little chance of a compromise by either side or of a negotiated settlement. John Adams predicted as much, writing to Samuel Chase, a delegate from Maryland, in July 1776: "A Bloody Conflict We are destined to endure. This has been my opinion, from the Beginning."

When Congress declared the independence of the United States, the new nation was almost free of British troops, but George Washington knew that the British would return, with a much larger army and a fleet of powerful warships, to reclaim the colonies. When they came, Washington expected they would attempt to take New York City, which has the finest natural harbor on the American coast. With New York as its base, the Royal Navy would try to blockade the ports and stop ships carrying supplies from reaching the Continental Army. The British army, meanwhile, would try to destroy the Continental Army, take control of the major rivers and roads, occupy the most important cities and towns, and restore royal government. Washington's job was to stop them.

The Challenges of Command

Washington marched the Continental Army from Boston to New York in the spring of 1776 and began to prepare. To defend America against British invasion, he had an army of ordinary people—farmers, tradesmen, dock workers, sailors, and other working men. Most of them were young, and though most were used to hard work, very few had any military experience. That spring thousands more young Americans like them joined regiments raised in each colony for Continental service. The Continental Army became, for the first time, a truly American army and not simply a New England army with a few men from other colonies as it had been through the Siege of Boston.

The men were all volunteers. Some were lured into joining the army with bounties—fifty or a hundred dollars paid at enlistment—or they were unemployed and tempted by the promise of a soldier's pay. Most were committed, for reasons of their own, to the common cause. The majority could read and write, but few had read the philosophical works of writers like John Locke. More than a few had read, or heard about, pamphlets like John Dickinson's *Letters from a Farmer in Pennsylvania,* but their views were not, for the most part, very sophisticated. It was enough that the British government had been bullying the colonists for as long as they could remember—the typical Continental soldier was under twenty, and had been a small child at the end of the French and Indian War—and that the British government was sending an army to force the colonists to obey laws the colonists had no part in making.

The junior officers—the lieutenants and captains—were slightly older, somewhat more experienced, and generally better educated. They were mostly in their twenties. Some had their own farms or had made a start in business. Some were the sons

The officers of the Continental Army were all volunteers. Most were men in their twenties, with no prior military experience. They risked their lives—and many lost their lives—in a war for independence against one of the world's great powers. Miniatures like these are often the only portraits we have of them (The Society of the Cincinnati).

of gentlemen. Many had delayed making their start as farmers, craftsmen, shopkeepers, or merchants in order to fight for the cause. A few of them were college educated and left behind diaries and letters, littered with references to heroes from classical antiquity and high-sounding ideas from books they had read, but young men with heads stuffed with Plutarch and Cicero, anxious to win honor like the Spartans at Thermopylae, were the exception.

Among the officers was a class of men distinct from the bright, enthusiastic young junior officers. They were older and much more experienced men in their thirties or forties. They were farmers and artisans mostly, but among them were men who had served in the French and Indian War or fought the Indians on the frontier, professional hunters at ease with guns and used to sleeping on the ground, merchant seamen accustomed to dealing with rough men and difficult circumstances, and plantation masters used to giving orders and having them obeyed. Despite his gentlemanly manners and refinement, George Washington liked these tough, practical men, and relied on them.

One of them was John Glover, a merchant seaman from Marblehead, Massachusetts, who led a regiment of sailors and fishermen raised in the coastal towns north of Boston and commanded them with the inflexible severity of a ship's captain in a storm. Washington needed officers like Glover, because the army he commanded was unlike any army the world had known. His men were not the subjects of a king. They were the citizens of a republic, and their service could not be imagined as an obligation owed by a subject to a sovereign monarch. It was service freely given by one citizen to all.

Commanding the world's first army of free men presented George Washington with challenges no general had ever faced and no general in history has faced since without his example to guide them. Imposing tough European standards of military discipline on his men conflicted with the personal independence his men had enlisted to secure. Instilling "proper discipline and Subordination" on such men, Washington wrote to John Hancock on February 9, 1776, "is a Work of great difficulty."

That difficulty, Washington found, was compounded by the rough sense of equality shared by many of his soldiers, especially those from New England who had elected their officers, and among the riflemen from Virginia and Pennsylvania whose independent spirit led them to resist any military discipline. Washington needed to shape his men into a cohesive army, toughened by discipline, accustomed to the hardships of military service, and prepared to meet the terrors of battle.

To add to Washington's problems, his army of free men was short of nearly everything—muskets, cannons, uniforms, tents, knapsacks, gunpowder, bullets, and all the other supplies an army needs. Nowhere in the colonies was there an armory capable of producing muskets. American gunsmiths made fine rifles, one at a time, but were completely unable to supply an army with the thousands of muskets needed to fight a war. There were only a few gunpowder mills in America. They made enough gunpowder for local hunters. They did not produce enough gunpowder for an army at war.

Americans had the skills to sew uniforms, tents, knapsacks, and other things made of cloth, but most of the cloth Americans used before the war came from Britain. By the spring of 1776 there wasn't much new cloth left in America to use. Some of the new regiments arrived in New York in fancy uniforms made back home. Before long the uniforms would be torn and dirty and replacing them would be nearly impossible.

The problem of supplying the army weighed heavily on Washington as he set his men to building earthwork forts to defend New York from the attack he knew was coming. New York is an island city, surrounded by a maze of rivers and waterways. It would be difficult—perhaps impossible, Washington knew—to defend those waterways from the Royal Navy.

Washington gathered about nineteen thousand men in and around New York by early July 1776. About nine thousand were part of the Continental Army, which included men from all over the newly independent states. The rest were militia from New York and nearby states. He kept the men busy building fortifications on Manhattan, on the New Jersey side of the Hudson River, and across the East River on Long Island, near the little town of Brooklyn. Washington and his army waited for the British.

They did not have long to wait. On June 25, 1776, three British warships arrived in New

York Harbor carrying General William Howe and a small force of British soldiers. Four days later, forty-five more ships arrived, and a day after that eighty-two more ships. It looked, said one amazed American, like "all London was in afloat."

General Howe's Army

General Howe's aim was to capture New York City, defeat Washington's army, and force the rebels to lay down their arms and accept British authority. To accomplish this he had an army of some thirty-two thousand professional soldiers, the most powerful force Britain had ever sent overseas. His men were fully armed, well supplied, and supported by a fleet of thirty warships, in addition to hundreds of transports and support vessels, all under the command of his brother, Admiral Richard Howe. The army set up camp on Staten Island, southwest of Manhattan, and rested for several weeks while General Howe planned his attack.

The British government had directed the Howe brothers to try to convince the colonists to accept British authority without further fighting. To start a dialogue, Admiral Howe sent an aide under a flag of truce with a letter addressed to "George Washington, Esquire," as if he was just a gentleman farmer and not a general commanding an army. Washington's aides sent the aide and the letter back, saying that there was no such person with the army. The admiral sent the letter again, addressing it to "George Washington, Esquire, etc., etc." Washington's staff refused it again. The admiral's frustrated secretary wrote in his private journal that Washington was nothing more than "a little paltry colonel of militia at the head of banditti or rebels."

Howe then sent a note to "General Washington" asking him if he would receive an officer with a message. Washington agreed, and he met a few days later with a British colonel named James Paterson. Henry Knox, who was present for the meeting, wrote that Paterson was completely intimidated by Washington but managed to explain that General Howe would pardon the rebels if they surrendered their arms and went home. Washington listened politely and said that the Americans had done nothing wrong by defending their liberty and did not ask to be pardoned. Paterson, Knox wrote, sat "awestruck as if before something supernatural" while Washington spoke of liberty and republicanism like a character out of Roman history.

Admiral Howe then tried writing to Benjamin Franklin. The two had met in London on Christmas Day, 1774, when Franklin accepted a surprise invitation to play chess with the admiral's sister. The admiral, a member of Parliament, had come over to meet Franklin, hoping to use the famous colonist to work out some compromise that would settle the differences between Britain and the colonies. Howe assured Franklin that his service to the empire could be of infinite value and hinted that he could expect a handsome reward from the British government for his assistance. "This to me," Franklin wrote, "was what the French call Spitting in the Soup." The conversation ended with courtesy on both sides. Less than two years later they were enemies. Franklin responded to Admiral Howe just as Washington had responded to General Howe. He added that it was impossible for Americans to think of making peace with an enemy who "is even now bringing foreign mercenaries to deluge our settlements with blood."

The "foreign mercenaries" Franklin mentioned were part of General Howe's army, which included eight thousand hired soldiers from one or another of the many small countries that would later become part of Germany. The largest part came from Hesse-Kassel, a small country ruled by Frederick II, an uncle of Britain's King George III. Frederick II and rulers of other German states made a large part of their income selling the use of their soldiers. So many of these soldiers came from Hesse-Kassel that Americans called them all Hessians.

By the end of the Revolutionary War, about thirty thousand of these hired German soldiers had served with the British army in America. About seven thousand of them died during the war. About seventeen thousand returned home. The other six thousand stayed in America. Most of those deserted from the army. Many of the deserters settled in parts of Pennsylvania, Maryland, and Virginia where many German-speaking people already lived. Like the American soldiers they came to fight, the Hessian deserters simply wanted the freedom to build a better life.

British and Hessian troops crossed the Harlem River and landed near the northern end of Manhattan to attack Fort Washington, on the high ridge in the right distance. This watercolor, one of the few eyewitness depictions of a Revolutionary War battle, was painted by a British officer (New York Public Library).

In 1776, however, Americans hated them. In battle the Hessians could be merciless. Few of them spoke English or understood why the Americans were fighting. The right to protest against the government was unknown in most of Europe. To the Hessians, the American rebels were simply traitors to their king who deserved the harshest treatment. British officers sometimes had to restrain Hessians from abusing or killing captured American soldiers.

The Contest for New York City

On August 22, Admiral Howe's fleet ferried thousands of British and Hessian troops from Staten Island to Long Island. Washington moved most of his army to Long Island to meet them. On August 27, the armies met in the Battle of Brooklyn, one of the largest battles of the war. Washington's army fought bravely but was outmaneuvered by the British, who marched undetected around Washington's flank. A determined stand by the Maryland Continental Line saved the army from destruction, although hundreds were killed or captured. Among the captured was Maj. Gen. William Alexander of New Jersey, who commanded the heroic defense.

Washington's army retreated to fortified lines close to the East River near the village of Brooklyn. Unwilling to attack the Americans head on and risk a second Bunker Hill, General Howe prepared for a siege. Washington refused to be pinned down. On the night of August 29–30 he ordered the army to retreat across the East River to Manhattan. John

Glover's regiment of sailors and fishermen ferried the army across the river under the cover of fog and darkness without the loss of a single man. The British were shocked the next morning to find the American defenses empty.

The British crossed to Manhattan a few weeks later and defeated the Continental Army at the Battle of Kip's Bay on September 15. Washington's men fought better at Harlem Heights on September 16 but could not save the city from capture. British troops occupied New York City that same day.

Among the men who lost their lives in the defense of New York City was a young Connecticut captain named Nathan Hale. A graduate of Yale College, Hale was a schoolteacher before the war. In early September he volunteered to cross over to Long Island to spy on the British. Within a short time he was arrested, probably after someone Hale knew recognized him. Papers showing the location and strength of various British positions were found in his possession. General Howe ordered him executed as a spy. Before he was hanged, British officers asked him if he had anything he wanted to say. Hale's final words were a perfect expression of patriotism: "I only regret that I have but one life to lose for my country."

The last position on Manhattan Island held by the Continental Army was Fort Washington, a large earthwork fort on the northern end of the island. Washington's officers believed it could hold out against attack for weeks, and if it were in danger of being captured the soldiers inside could cross the Hudson River to the safety of New Jersey.

British and Hessian soldiers attacked the fort from the north on November 16. Among the first Americans killed was a Pennsylvania artilleryman named John Corbin who was serving with a cannon crew several hundred yards north of the fort. His wife, Margaret, was nearby. She was one of hundreds of women who traveled with the army, cooking, mending uniforms, and nursing the sick in exchange for rations. In battle the wives of artillerymen often carried water, which was essential to sponge out the guns between rounds, smothering the sparks that remained after a cannon was fired. When John Corbin was killed Margaret took his place in the cannon crew. A few minutes later she fell horribly wounded as Hessian troops overran

the battery. Congress later awarded her a soldier's pension, recognizing a female combat veteran for the first time in our history.

Within an hour of launching their final attack, the British and Hessians entered Fort Washington and forced the American garrison to surrender. George Washington watched, appalled, from the New Jersey side of the Hudson. It was the worst defeat he ever suffered, though he suffered at a distance. The British captured over 2,800 American soldiers. Three-fourths of them would die as prisoners, many crowded into a building that had been a sugar warehouse before the war, or shoved below the decks of rotting ships anchored off New York City. The British were indifferent to their suffering.

America is free because of the sacrifices of people like Nathan Hale, John and Margaret Corbin, and the thousands of ordinary Americans who suffered and died in British prisons, hungry, ragged, and worn down by illness and abuse. Hale was idealistic and inspired by the heroes of classical antiquity about whom he had read. We can never know for sure what inspired John and Margaret Corbin. They came from the rough backcountry of Pennsylvania. Margaret was an orphan whose parents were killed by Indians when she was five. British taxes on luxuries like paint, paper, or tea did not matter much to people like John and Margaret, who could never afford luxuries.

They probably valued personal independence. What little they had—a bedstead, a few pots, a gun—belonged to them. If they liked they could go south or west toward the Ohio frontier where the British had drawn a line forbidding settlement—a symbol of their intention to impose much tighter control on their restless, unruly subjects. The Corbins gave everything for the promise of freedom. John lost his life. Margaret—her arm crippled and her face badly disfigured—was never able to care for herself again. She lost the personal independence she was probably fighting to secure for herself, her husband, and for the family she never had.

The Crisis

After the surrender of Fort Washington, the few thousand men left in the army retreated south

No eighteenth-century image of Margaret Corbin survives. Sculptor Tracy H. Sugg imagined her as a tough, determined young woman, serving her cannon only moments before she fell (Courtesy Tracy H. Sugg, Sculptor).

through New Jersey. Howe sent one of his most aggressive generals, Lord Cornwallis, to pursue Washington, but he ordered Cornwallis to stop at New Brunswick, about halfway across the state. Howe seems to have reasoned that there was no value in wasting his men crushing a rebel army that was about to dissolve anyway. The remains of Washington's army, mud soaked and exhausted, crossed the Delaware River into Pennsylvania on December 7, 1776, leaving the British in control of most of New Jersey.

At that moment, the Revolutionary War seemed to be coming to an end. New Jersey loyalists came out in large numbers to swear their allegiance to the British government. A British cavalry patrol commanded by a young officer named Banastre Tarleton captured Maj. Gen. Charles Lee, Washington's senior subordinate. Congress, fearing the British would occupy Philadelphia within a few days, fled to Baltimore. General Howe believed the American rebellion was almost over. With the weather growing worse by the day, he ordered his army to go into winter quarters at New Brunswick. He posted soldiers at Trenton and Princeton, close to the Delaware River, and settled in to wait for the end of the war.

Washington's options grew fewer every day. On December 18, he wrote his brother Samuel Washington that unless something could be done to increase the size of the army and improve its condition, "I think the game will be pretty well up." Morale was low. At the end of the year, the enlistments of all but 1,400 soldiers would expire. He knew that most of the men would choose to go home to help their families through the winter rather than stay and fight.

Thomas Paine, the author of *Common Sense*, issued a new call to action in a pamphlet called *The Crisis*. Washington found it so inspiring that he had it read to his entire army:

These are the times that try men's souls. The summer soldier and the sunshine patriot will, in this crisis, shrink from the service of his country. But he that stands it now deserves the love and thanks of man and woman. Tyranny, like hell, is not easily conquered; yet we have this consolation with us, that the harder the conflict, the more glorious the triumph.

Washington Crosses the Delaware

Almost everyone thought that Washington would have to stop for the winter and try to rebuild his army in the spring. But Washington knew that unless he could do something to rekindle hope in the minds of his soldiers and the American people, there would be no army to rebuild. Instead of seeking a safe place to spend the winter, Washington began looking for an opportunity to strike a blow.

He decided to cross the Delaware River and mount a surprise attack. He asked John Glover, whose regiment had saved the army after the Battle of Brooklyn, if they could get the army across the icy Delaware at night. Glover told Washington "you need not be troubled about that, General, as his boys could manage it." The next day Washington sent secret orders to the senior officers of the army, laying out his plan.

Washington's target was the Hessian garrison in Trenton, New Jersey, just across the Delaware River. The Hessians were proud, professional soldiers who kept careful watch, even on Christmas Day. They had to, because New Jersey militiamen were in the area. Forty or fifty of them appeared out of the woods around nightfall on Christmas and attacked a Hessian outpost, wounding six men. A nervous Hessian major suggested to the Hessian commander, Colonel Johann Rall, that the garrison should be ready to retreat from Trenton if the Americans appeared in larger numbers. "Fiddlesticks," Rall replied, "these clodhoppers will not attack us." A winter storm, with snow, sleet, and howling wind, hit Trenton later that evening. The Hessians relaxed and took cover, convinced that the Americans would never attack in such bad weather.

As the storm hit, Washington's army was marching toward the Delaware River crossing. The river was filled with large chunks of floating ice. Washington's plan was for the army to cross at three places during the night, but at two of them the river was so choked with ice that it was impossible to get across. Only the men with Washington made it across the Delaware. Henry Knox organized the soldiers at the crossing point. Glover and his Massachusetts sailors and fisherman, along with Pennsylvania and New Jersey soldiers who had worked on the river before the war, ferried

Thomas Sully was the first artist to paint Washington's dramatic night crossing of the Delaware River before the Battle of Trenton. Sully visited the site of the crossing to sketch the scene and was careful to depict the square-ended Durham boats used in the crossing. In the background, Henry Knox, with his sword drawn, directs troops toward the waiting boats (Photograph © 2023 Museum of Fine Arts, Boston).

Washington's men over to New Jersey. The storm blotted out the moon and stars and made it so dark it was impossible to see the opposite shore.

Once across, the Americans marched toward Trenton, nine miles away. Knox had managed to get eighteen cannons across the river—a large number for Washington's little army of 2,400 men. Knox had even brought over extra men to work the cannons he expected to capture from the Hessians during the attack. Washington had planned to attack Trenton at first light, but the difficulty of

the crossing and the bad weather delayed him. It was nearly eight o'clock on that dark, gray morning before he was in position to attack.

Washington's army struck from the west and the north, pushing the Hessian outpost guards back toward the little town. Colonel Rall quickly organized the three Hessian regiments in the center of town and got his cannons into position to fire at the advancing Americans. Knox's artillery responded, driving the Hessians away from their cannons, which the Americans captured. Rall led a counterattack that recaptured the cannons but in the process he led his men into a trap. American troops had nearly surrounded the town and fired into Rall's men from three directions.

"Here succeeded a scene of war," Henry Knox wrote a few days later, "of which I had often conceived but never saw before." In the chaos even the residents of Trenton were drawn into the battle. A Hessian later wrote that the people of Trenton shot at them from their houses, and remembered a woman who fired out of her window and killed a Hessian captain. In the confusion, noise, and smoke of battle, Colonel Rall was shot. The disorganized Hessians retreated to the east edge of the town but soon laid their flags on the ground and surrendered. Rall and 22 of his men died in the battle. Washington took 896 prisoners, including at least 86 wounded men. He captured six fine brass cannons and enough supplies to outfit several American brigades. Only two American officers and two privates were wounded in the battle, but several more died from illness brought on by the cold and wet and exhaustion. Washington decided not to risk his tired little army by marching to attack another British outpost and crossed back across the Delaware to safety.

General Howe rushed troops to the river, but Washington had gone. Howe was surprised by this daring raid but dismissed Washington's victory at Trenton as a fluke. The Hessians, after all, were mercenaries. Washington would meet a very different fate, Howe believed, when he faced the king's troops in an open battle.

"The day is ours!"

Washington put Howe's confidence to the test in early January. On December 30, he crossed the Delaware again. This time the British, led by General Cornwallis, marched to meet him. On the night of January 2, the two armies were separated by a small creek near Trenton. Cornwallis thought he had the Americans trapped. "We've got the old fox safe now," he said. "We'll go over and bag him in the morning." He planned to attack at dawn, but during the night Washington and his army slipped away, leaving their campfires burning to fool the British. In the morning Cornwallis was surprised to see that the Americans were gone.

Washington's army marched north through the night, and in the morning surprised British troops at Princeton. In the opening minutes of the battle the British drove the Americans, as they had driven them in every encounter. The British charged with bayonets, and the Americans—most of them without bayonets with which to resist the British in a desperate, hand-to-hand battle—withered and fell back. Brig. Gen. Hugh Mercer, Washington's friend, fell mortally wounded. British soldiers stabbed him repeatedly with bayonets. The center of Washington's army disintegrated in panic.

What happened then proved to be the great moment in George Washington's life. It was the moment for which all his experiences—his years in the saddle, the rugged outdoor life of a youthful backcountry surveyor, the fierce combat of the French and Indian War, and the daily work of managing a great plantation, giving orders and seeing them obeyed—had prepared him.

He rallied his men, and with a calm determination that astonished everyone who watched, Washington drew his men back into a compact line of battle. His casual, unstudied indifference to danger brought to men's minds the courage of an ancient Rome general. In an instant that must have seemed interminable to his men, Washington surveyed the oncoming British line as it closed to within one hundred feet. "I shall never forget what I felt," a young officer wrote, "when I saw him brave all the dangers of the field and his important life hanging as it were by a single hair with a thousand deaths flying around him. Believe me, I thought not of myself."

Washington dressed his line and sent it forward to deliver what a participant termed "a heavy platoon fire on the march." The fire of Washington's compact line shattered the British advance. The redcoats wavered, then broke. For the first time in the war, Americans cheered as the British turned their backs and ran. "It's a fine fox chase, my boys!" Washington shouted as he spurred his horse and took off after them. By the time he drew rein, the surviving remnant of the British force was in full flight toward Trenton. For Washington, this must have been one of the most satisfying moments in the war.

James Peale fought in the Battle of Princeton and later painted this view of the battle from memory. In the foreground, Capt. Joseph Moulder's artillery battery is holding the British at bay while George Washington organizes the counterattack that swept the British from the field (Princeton University).

In hindsight—the ability to consider all that would come after is our great advantage—we can see the importance of what happened. This was a moment that made American victory in the war possible. Defeat at Princeton forced the British army, a vast invasion force sent to crush the American rebellion in one campaign, to retreat to New York. The victory rallied the American people, who saw that the British were not invincible. Paired with the victory at Trenton, the victory at Princeton became a part of our national identity. It secured Washington's reputation as a national hero.

It was one of the pivots around which our national history has turned. Everything afterwards flowed through this victory. Every proud moment to come was made possible by this improbable moment when Washington rallied his broken and disorganized men, led them forward by sheer will, and routed the British. It took a British historian to see the true significance of the achievement. Sir George Otto Trevelyan wrote: "It may be doubted whether so small a number of men ever employed so short a space of time with greater and more lasting effects upon the history of the world."

Because of this proud moment the war would have others. Washington led his army north. They made their winter camp around Morristown, in the New Jersey hills west of New York City. The British decided they could not drive Washington out of New Jersey and withdrew their army to the area around New York City for the winter.

News of the victories at Trenton and Princeton revived the spirits of patriots throughout America. Heading home to Connecticut that January, John Chester wrote to a friend, "You cannot Conceive the Joy and Raptures the people were universally in as we passed the road. 'Tis good to the be the messenger of Glad Tidings." After months of effort, the British had only managed to take New York City. They had beaten Washington's army repeatedly, but Washington had managed to keep his army of free men together. His victories at Trenton and Princeton raised the spirits of the army and convinced many Americans that it was possible to defeat the British and win the war.

*Almost every one has heard of the
soldiers of the Revolution being tracked by
the blood of their feet on the frozen ground.
This is literally true; and the thousandth
part of their sufferings has not,
nor ever will be told.*

SERGEANT JOSEPH PLUMB MARTIN
*Narrative of some of the Adventures,
Dangers and Sufferings of a Revolutionary Soldier*
1830

REPUBLICS
AT WAR

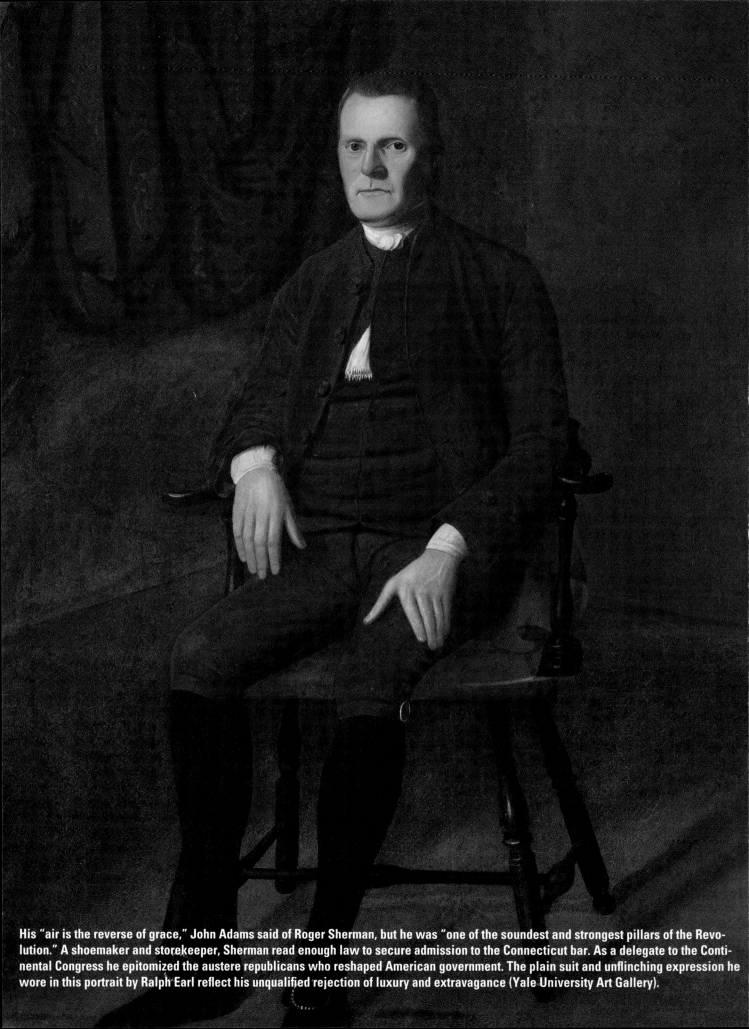

His "air is the reverse of grace," John Adams said of Roger Sherman, but he was "one of the soundest and strongest pillars of the Revolution." A shoemaker and storekeeper, Sherman read enough law to secure admission to the Connecticut bar. As a delegate to the Continental Congress he epitomized the austere republicans who reshaped American government. The plain suit and unflinching expression he wore in this portrait by Ralph Earl reflect his unqualified rejection of luxury and extravagance (Yale University Art Gallery).

Chapter 13 American Republics

The war of the American Revolution was a new kind of war, although this was not immediately apparent, even to many of those involved. The weapons, tactics, and most of the strategies employed differed only slightly from those of the imperial wars that preceded it. As in other imperial conflicts of the eighteenth century waged on the periphery of the European state system, armies were smaller than those deployed on the European continent and commanders were reluctant to risk large-scale battles because reinforcing, resupplying, and otherwise maintaining their armies was expensive and involved moving men and materials vast distances. As in earlier conflicts in North America, naval power was crucial in the Revolutionary War and the combatants waged a brutal struggle on the frontier in which the Indians played an important part.

What made the Revolutionary War different was that it was an ideological conflict waged by Revolutionaries intent on overthrowing British rule and creating republics in its place. It was more than a colonial rebellion orchestrated by the colonial gentry to wrest power from distant imperial overlords and their local subordinates. Such rebellions had happened before and have happened many times since. The Revolution was a struggle for autonomy, both local and personal, aiming to free the colonies from restraints imposed by their British rulers and to free individuals from unnecessary restraints imposed by governments.

The Revolutionary War was a struggle for independence, for the individual colonies and for individual Americans, seeking to establish autonomy for the states and liberty for themselves. Few ordinary Americans—the kinds of people who fought and won the war—knew much, if anything, about political philosophy, but they knew that they wanted to be free to make their own choices without the burdens of heavy taxes or restraints imposed by bureaucrats on another continent or by heavy-handed rulers at home.

The Idea of a Republic

This Revolutionary drive for autonomy was balanced by a Revolutionary desire for a new kind of social order that reflected the interests of ordinary people rather than the interests of a monarch. In place of a sovereign king and privileged aristocrats the Revolutionaries vested sovereignty in the people. Their new governments derived their power from the consent of the governed. Inspired by the republics of classical antiquity—the Greek city-states of Athens and Sparta and above all, the Roman Republic—Revolutionary leaders sought to create American republics that would rival the republics of ancient times.

The differences between the monarchy under which they lived and the republics they imagined were immense. Monarchies were tied together by patronage—by favors bestowed by the king on his relatives and other aristocrats, by favors bestowed by aristocrats on local gentry, and by the subordination of ordinary people to the gentry, aristocrats, and the king. Beyond patronage, monarchies maintained themselves through force and fear. Continental monarchies relied heavily on their armies to intimidate their subjects as well as their enemies. The British regarded large standing armies with grave suspicion. Their pride in British liberty rested in large part on the fact that their peacetime army was small compared to those on the Continent and rarely used to coerce the king's subjects. "It is dangerous to our liberties and destructive to our trade," said William Pitt the Elder, the greatest parliamentary leader of the eighteenth century, "to encourage great numbers of our people to depend for their livelihood upon the profession of arms." American

Republican political ideas were shaped by a flowering of interest in classical history and culture among educated people in America and Europe during the second half of the eighteenth century. Among the classical figures they most admired was Cincinnatus, a general who defended the Roman Republic from invaders and then returned to his family and his farm—a scene depicted in this painting from about 1775 attributed to Angelica Kauffmann—without accepting rewards for his service. Cincinnatus symbolized unselfish patriotism (The Society of the Cincinnati).

anger over the military occupation of Boston was shaped by traditional British opposition to using the army to police and intimidate civilians.

Republics were held together by public virtue—by the devotion of their citizens to the common good and their willingness to sacrifice their selfish desires for the good of all. The central idea of a republic is attachment to the *res publica,* a Latin phrase meaning public things or public matters. Educated Americans of the Revolutionary generation were well acquainted with the works of Livy, a Roman historian, and Plutarch, author of *Lives of the Noble Grecians and Romans,* a collection of biographies of virtuous heroes of antiquity.

Many of the heroes memorialized by Livy and Plutarch had achieved enduring fame by sacrificing their selfish interests to support the public good.

These and other works taught that republics are fragile—at constant risk of being destroyed from without and from within. If men refused to serve in its defense, a republic would fall prey to foreign enemies. Thus the most essential virtue in a republic was the willingness of citizens to take up arms in its defense, either as volunteers or in response to a mandate that fell broadly on men without regard to social status.

Republics also called on their citizens to set aside their private desires for the good of the whole by accepting and obeying laws made by their elected representatives that might be contrary to their selfish interests and by accepting the outcome of elections when the outcome was contrary to their personal wishes. Republican citizenship called on men to serve, to participate in public life, and to subordinate themselves to the rule of law. If men refused to subordinate their selfish desires for the common good, a republic would be torn by internal disputes and collapse in disorder.

While inspired by ancient republics, the Revolutionaries were deeply influenced by the insights of seventeenth and eighteenth-century political philosophy and more recent efforts to devise a scientific understanding of society comparable to the Newtonian understanding of the natural world. By applying these insights, the Revolutionaries hoped to construct modern republics held together by benevolence—a desire to do good by improving the lives of others through humane and charitable deeds—rather than republics held together by service in arms.

The enthusiasm of educated Americans for republican ideals led them to employ symbols drawn from classical antiquity to represent their republics. Among the most common was *Libertas*, the female embodiment of Liberty, who was often portrayed holding a rod, or *vindicta*, used

in a ceremony to free slaves from bondage, or a longer staff holding aloft the *pileus*, or liberty cap, worn by former slaves as a sign of their freedom. Another was a *fasces*, a bundle of sticks—individually weak, but unbreakable when bound together. Fasces were a common Roman symbol of strength in unity. American republicans named the upper houses of their legislatures senates after the Roman Senate, the chief governing body of the Roman Republic. They celebrated George Washington, who unselfishly refused to accept pay for serving as commander in chief of the Continental Army, as a modern Cincinnatus, comparing him to a hero of the Roman Republic who led the army to victory and then returned to his farm, refusing rewards for his service.

Ordinary Americans who knew little about classical republics imagined that a state without kings and lords should be governed like their counties, towns, and churches were governed—by local officials often chosen by freeholders and other ordinary people. They imagined a social order in which Americans would be equal citizens rather than subjects—a radically new kind of society without kings or aristocrats.

Written Constitutions

To create that new social order, defend the rights of the people, and protect their independence in a world of hostile powers, the Revolutionaries had to create new governments to replace the British government they had rejected. Like most of the governments in the world, the British government was based on traditions that extended back hundreds of years. Britain had no written constitution. When Britons spoke of their constitution—which many did with pride—they were referring to agreements between the Crown and its subjects, of which the Magna Carta is the most important, to acts of Parliament, like the English Bill of Rights of 1689,

Overleaf: The evolution of constitutionalism is reflected in this proposed constitution rejected by the people of New Hampshire. The legislature adopted a temporary constitution in January 1776, to remain in force "during the present unhappy and unnatural contest with Great Britain." In 1778 a special constitutional convention met in Concord and submitted this draft constitution to the people in 1779. The people rejected it. Many were probably concerned that the proposed president of the council—the senior executive official—might abuse his authority like the colony's royal governors. Another convention met in Exeter in 1781 and submitted another draft constitution to the people. Revised, resubmitted, and finally approved by popular vote in 1783, the new constitution went into operation in 1784 and remains in force today (Library of Congress).

A DECLARATION

of RIGHTS, and PLAN of Government for the State of New-Hampshire.

WHEREAS by the tyrannical Administration of the Government of the King and Parliament of Great-Britain, this State of New-Hampshire, with the other United-States of AMERICA, have been necessitated to reject the British Government, and declare themselves INDEPENDENT STATES; all which is more largely set forth by the CONTINENTAL CONGRESS, in their Resolution or Declaration of the fourth of July A. D. 1776.

AND WHEREAS, it is recommended by the said CONTINENTAL CONGRESS to each and every of the said United-States to establish a FORM of GOVERNMENT most conducive to the Welfare thereof. We the DELEGATES of the said State of NEW-HAMPSHIRE chosen for the Purpose of forming a permanent PLAN of GOVERNMENT subject to the Revisal of our CONSTITUENTS, have composed the following DECLARATION of RIGHTS, and PLAN of GOVERNMENT; and recommend the same to our CONSTITUENTS for their Approbation.

A DECLARATION of the RIGHTS of the PEOPLE of the STATE of NEW-HAMPSHIRE.

First, WE declare, that we the People of the State of New-Hampshire, are Free and Independant of the Crown of Great-Britain.

Secondly. We the People of this State, are intitled to Life, Liberty, and Property; and all other Immunities and Privileges which we heretofore enjoyed.

Thirdly. The Common and Statute Laws of England, adopted and used here, and the Laws of this State (not inconsistent with said Declaration of INDEPENDENCE) now are, and shall be in force here, for the Welfare and good Government of the State, unless the same shall be repealed or altered by the future Legislature thereof.

Fourthly. The whole and intire Power of Government of this State, is vested in, and must be derived from the People thereof, and from no other Source whatsoever.

Fifthly. The future Legislature of this State, shall make no Laws to infringe the Rights of Conscience, or any other of the natural, unalienable Rights of Men, or contrary to the Laws of GOD, or against the Protestant Religion.

Sixthly. The Extent of Territory of this State, is, and shall be the same which was under the Government of the late Governor John Wentworth, Esq; Governor of New-Hampshire. Reserving nevertheless, our Claim to the New-Hampshire Grants, so called, situate to the West of Connecticut River.

Seventhly. The Right of Trial by Jury in all Cases as heretofore used in this State, shall be preserved inviolate forever.

A PLAN of Government for the State of New-Hampshire.

First, THE State of New-Hampshire shall be governed by a COUNCIL, and House of REPRESENTATIVES, to be chosen as herein after mentioned, and to be stiled the GENERAL-COURT of the State of New-Hampshire.

Second. The COUNCIL shall consist for the present of twelve Members to be elected out of the several Counties in the State, in Proportion to their respective Number of Inhabitants.

Third. The Numbers belonging to each County for the present, according to said Proportion being as followeth, viz.—To the County of Rockingham, five—to the County of Strafford, two---to the County of Hillsborough, two---to the County of Cheshire, two---to the County of Grafton, one.

Fourth. The number for the County of Rockingham, shall not be increased or diminished hereafter, but remain the same; and the Numbers for the other Counties shall be increased or deminished as their aforesaid Proportion to the County of Rockingham may chance to vary.

Fifth. The House of REPRESENTATIVES shall be chosen as follows. Every Town or Parish, choosing Town Officers, amounting to one hundred Families, and upwards, shall send one Representative for each hundred Families they consist of, (or such lesser Number as they please) or class themselves with some other Towns or Parishes that will join in sending a Representative.

Sixth. All other Towns and Parishes under the number of one hundred Families, shall have Liberty to class themselves together to make the number of one hundred Families or upwards, and being so classed, each Class shall send one Representative.

Seventh. The number of COUNCILLORS belonging to each County shall be ascertained and done by the General-Court every Time there is a new Proportion made of the State Tax which shall be once in seven Years at the least, and oftner if need be.

Eighth. All the Male Inhabitants of the State of lawful Age, paying Taxes, and professing the Protestant Religion, shall be deemed legal Voters in choosing COUNCILLORS and REPRESENTATIVES, and having an Estate of Three Hundred Pounds equal to Silver at six Shillings and eight Pence per Ounce, one half at least whereof to be real Estate, and lying within this State, with the Qualifications aforesaid, shall be capable of being elected.

Ninth. The Selectmen of each respective Town and Parish, choosing Town Officers containing one hundred Families or upwards, and also of each respective Class of Towns classed together as aforesaid, shall notify the legal Voters of their respective Towns, Parishes, or Classes, qualified as aforesaid, in the usual Way of notifying Town-Meetings, giving fifteen Days notice at least, to meet at some convenient Place on the last Wednesday of November annually, to choose COUNCILLORS and REPRESENTATIVES.

Tenth. And the Voters being met, and the Moderator chosen, shall proceed to choose their Representative or Repepresentatives, required by this Constitution by a Majority of the Voters present, who shall be notified accordingly, and a Return thereof made into the Secretary's Office, by the first Wednesday of January then next.

Eleventh. And such Representatives shall be paid their Wages by their Constituents, and for their Travel by the State.

Twelvth. And in the Choice of COUNCILLORS each Voter shall deliver his Vote to the Moderator for the number of COUNCILLORS respectively required, with the Word COUNCILLORS writen thereon, & the Voters Name endorsed to prevent Duplicity.

Thirteenth. These Votes shall be sealed up by the Moderator, and transmitted by the Constable to one of the Justices of the Inferior Court of Common Pleas for the County, before the second Wednesday in December next following.

Fourteenth. And the said Justices of the Inferior Court shall meet together on the said second Wednesday of December annually, to count the Votes, and the Persons that have most Votes to the Number of COUNSELLORS required, shall be declared duly elected, and shall be notified by the said Justices accordingly, and a Return thereof shall be made by them into the Secretary's Office by the first Wednesday in January annually.

Fifteenth. And in Case any two Persons shall have a like Number of Votes, the said Justices may determine the Choice in Favour of which they please.

Sixteenth. The COUNCIL and House of REPRESENTATIVES so chosen and returned as aforesaid, shall meet on the first Wednesday in January next after their being chosen, at such Place as the present, or future General-Court may from Time to Time appoint; and being duly sworn, shall hold their respective Places until the first Wednesday in January then next.

Seventeenth. The COUNCIL shall choose their President, vice President, and Secretary; and the House of REPRESENTATIVES shall choose their Speaker and Clerk.

Eighteenth. The COUNCIL and House of *Representatives* respectively, shall determine all disputed Elections of their own Members, regulate their own Proceedings; and on any Vacancy, order a new Election to fill up such Vacancy.

Nineteenth. The said General-Court elected and constituted as aforesaid, shall be invested with the Supreme Power of the State. And all Acts, Resolves, or Votes, except Grants of Money, Lands, or other Things, may originate in either House; but such Grants shall originate in the House of *Representatives* only.

Twentieth. The said COUNCIL and House of *Representatives* respectively, shall have Power to adjourn themselves from Day to Day, but not longer then two Days at any one Time, without Concurrence of the other.

Twenty-first. The PRESIDENT of the COUNCIL shall hold public Correspondence with other States, or Persons; call the Council together when Occasion shall require; and with Advice of three or more of the Council shall from Time to Time call the General-Court together if need be, before the Time they were adjourned to: And also point out the principal Business of their Session.

Twenty-second. The Military and Naval Power of the State shall be regulated, and all proper Officers thereof appointed, as the Legislature by Law shall direct from Time to Time.

Twenty-third. The Judges of the Superior and Inferior Courts, Judges of Probate, Judge of Admiralty, Judge of the Maritime Court, Justices of the Peace, Sheriffs, Coroners, Attorney-General, Treasurer of the State, and Delegates to the CONTINENTAL CONGRESS, shall be appointed by the said General-Court, and commissionated by the President of the Council.

Twenty-fourth. The Appointment of Registers of Deeds, County Treasurer's, Clerks of Courts, Registers of Probate, and all other Civil Officers whatsoever, not before mentioned, shall be regulated by the Laws that now are, or that hereafter may be enacted.

Twenty-fifth. All Civil Officers of the State, shall be suitably compensated by Fees or Salaries for their Services.

Twenty-sixth. No Member of the General-Court shall be Judge of the Superior Court or Inferior Court, Judge or Register of Probate, or Sheriff of any County, or Treasurer of the State, or Attorney-General, or Delegate at the CONTINENTAL CONGRESS.

Twenty-seventh. And no Member of the Council, Judge of the Superior Court, or Sheriff, shall hold a Commission in the Militia, Army, or Navy of this State.

Twenty-eighth. No Member of the House of Representatives shall hold any Salary under the Government.

Twenty-ninth. The President of the Council, with Advice of Council, may grant Reprieves not longer than six Months, but the General-Court only shall have Power to pardon Offences against the State.

Thirtieth. A Quorum of the Council, and a Quorum of the House of Representatives, shall consist of a Majority of each House.

Thirty-first. This DECLARATION of RIGHTS, and PLAN OF GOVERNMENT, shall be the force of Law, and be esteemed the fundamental Law of this State.

Thirty-Second. The General-Court shall have no Power to alter any Part of this Constitution; but in case they should concur in any proposed Alteration, Amendment, or Addition, the same being agreed to by a Majority of the People, shall become valid.

STATE OF NEW-HAMPSHIRE.

IN CONVENTION, June 5th, 1779.

Voted, THAT the foregoing BILL of RIGHTS, and PLAN of GOVERNMENT, be printed, and dispersed throughout this State, for the People thereof, to give their Opinion thereon.

Voted, That Colonel *Thornton,* and Colonel *Bartlett,* be a Committee to get this Plan of Government printed, and transmit two or more Copies of the same to each and every Town, Parish and Place in this State, to which Precepts for this Convention were sent, and publish the same in the *New-Hampshire* News-Papers.

Voted, That the Selectmen of the several Towns, Parishes, and Districts in this State, upon the receipt of the same, are desired to notify and warn the legal Inhabitants paying Taxes in such Town, Parish, or Place, to meet at some suitable Place therein, giving them at least fifteen Days notice, for the Purpose of taking said Plan under Consideration; and make return of the Number of Voters present at such Meeting, and how many voted for receiving said Plan, and how many for rejecting the same, unto this Convention at *Concord* in this State, on the third Tuesday in September next.

By order of the Convention,

JOHN LANGDON, President, P. T.

E. Thompson, Secretary.

EXETER; Printed by *Zechariah Fowle,* 1779.

ces upon this Constitution were
For it about — 1200
against it about — 1700

and to decisions of English courts. This informal constitution had evolved over many generations.

While Revolutionary leaders in America valued aspects of this informal British constitution, particularly the rule of law and the idea that people possess rights like those guaranteed by the Magna Carta that government cannot violate, many came to believe that tradition was not enough to protect the rights of the people. Revolutionary leaders concluded that they had to define the purpose, organization, authority, and responsibilities of government in written instruments which they called constitutions.

The idea that governments should be defined by written constitutions is one of the most important contributions of the American Revolution to the world. Since the American Revolution, many nations—particularly nations establishing their independence from colonial rule and those emerging from authoritarian domination—have followed the American model and created written constitutions.

The basic principles of American constitutional government were worked out between 1775, when royal authority in America collapsed, and 1791, when the first ten amendments to the Federal Constitution we call the Bill of Rights were ratified by the states and became a part of the Federal Constitution. Since then, our constitutional tradition has developed through a constant process of constitutional innovation and reform. Each new state admitted to the union has established its own constitution, and many states have revised or rewritten their constitutions over the last two centuries. These state constitutions are all republican in nature and establish governments similar in form, but each reflects conditions, expectations, and needs distinctive to the state for which it was created. The Federal Constitution, ratified by the states in 1788, has been amended repeatedly, and its provisions have been subjected to continuous review and interpretation by the courts, to which our constitutions assign the role of applying the law.

American constitutionalism was shaped by the British constitutional and legal tradition and the experience of the imperial crisis in the decade before the Revolutionary War, in which the British government repeatedly violated rights Americans claimed were guaranteed to them under the informal British constitution. From this experience—in which the British denied that the colonists possessed rights those colonists insisted they possessed—emerged the simple idea that legal rights should be clearly defined in written instruments that no government could set aside by normal legislation. To protect their rights in the future, Americans devised the idea of a constitution, deriving its power from the sovereignty of the people, and approved—or ratified—by special conventions, made up of delegates chosen by the people for this purpose. Once ratified, such a constitution could only be changed by the consent of substantial majorities. These conditions made constitutions superior to ordinary legislation.

The first constitutions were established in the newly independent states to replace colonial governments that had ceased to function effectively in the first months of the Revolutionary War—particularly in colonies for which governors were appointed by the Crown. By early in 1776 the royal governors had fled, leaving the colonial legislatures to continue functioning, in several cases without formal legal authority. In Virginia, the members of what had been the House of Burgesses met as the Virginia Convention. Elsewhere the assemblies reorganized themselves in similar ways. In North Carolina, governing authority was assumed by the North Carolina Provincial Congress. This pattern was followed elsewhere, where the power to make law and, in the absence of a governor, to provide for its execution, was assumed by provincial congresses and conventions. Most of these bodies assumed responsibility for drafting constitutions.

What followed was a period of constructive statecraft unlike any in history. Under the necessity of establishing republican governments protecting individual rights while facing the unprecedented challenges of war with one of the world's great powers, the independent states devised new constitutions, each drawing on the experience of the others and the ideas of creative statesmen who had devoted a great deal of thought to the principles of government over more than a decade of political controversy with Britain.

Thoughts on Government

The creation of American republics during the American Revolution was shaped by circumstances—by the need to provide stable governments, maintain the rule of law, and meet the demands of war—but it was also shaped by men who were aware that those circumstances presented Americans with unique opportunities to create just and lasting governments based on the insights of philosophy, history, and science. The most influential of these was John Adams, who devoted much of his life to studying the principles and practices of republican government.

In November 1775, Richard Henry Lee asked Adams for his thoughts on the proper organization of government in the event the colonies formally separated from Britain. Adams wrote Lee a brief description of how an independent state government might be organized. In March 1776, John Penn and William Hooper, North Carolina delegates who were returning home to help draft a state constitution, asked Adams for his advice on organizing their new government. Adams, he later explained, thought this was an opportunity "providentially thrown in his Way" to influence the republics to be formed in the South, and "concluded to borrow a little Time from his sleep" to write a more detailed description of the principles and proper organization of republican governments. Other delegates heard about the document and asked for copies, and finally Adams—tired of copying and recopying—asked Richard Henry Lee to have it printed. Adams' advice was published anonymously in April as *Thoughts on Government: Applicable to the Present State of the American Colonies.*

His purpose, Adams wrote, was not to dictate, but rather to "mark out a Path, and putt Men upon thinking." The proper end of government, Adams wrote, is the happiness of the governed, and "all sober inquiries after truth, ancient and modern" had found that true happiness was found only in virtue, or the natural inclination to do good for others. Adams concluded that the best form of government was one that encouraged virtue and discouraged vice, the equally natural tendency of people to behave selfishly.

A monarchy could not do this, he reasoned, because it was based on the "honor of a few." Mon-archies served the interests of kings and aristocrats and assumed that ordinary people could never rise above petty, selfish concerns and that they had to ruled by their social superiors. The greatest writers, Adams wrote, had agreed that "there is no good government but what is republican," because republics rested on the idea that all people are capable of virtue.

Republics, Adams explained, could take many different forms, but successful ones had certain common characteristics. The first was the rule of law. A republic, Adams wrote, is "an empire of laws, not of men." The purpose of law was to secure the people's rights to life, liberty, and property, all of which are essential for human happiness. Laws must, moreover, be clear and fair and govern all equally. They must also be wisely administered.

Some British writers of the eighteenth century claimed that British attachment to the rule of law made their government republican in spirit while its monarchy and hereditary aristocracy provided the stability that had made it possible for Britain to flourish. They boasted that Britain's mixed government of king, lords, and commons ensured conditions that benefited all British subjects. This claim ignored the spread of grinding poverty, particularly in London, and it ignored the fact that the House of Commons was chosen by a small group of qualified voters in elections generally dominated by the aristocracy. The House of Commons did not, in fact, represent the interests of ordinary people.

The second essential characteristic of a republic is that it rests on the sovereignty of the people and should reflect the will of the people. Eighteenth-century monarchies claimed that the common good was the end of government, but with power concentrated in the hands of a king and his aristocratic supporters, monarchical governments generally pursued policies to benefit the few. In a republic, Adams explained, governments should benefit the many and reflect the will of the people expressed through representative institutions.

The most important is the legislative, or law-making, institutions. Adams and the creative state builders of the American Revolution devoted much of their intellectual energy to the proper construction of legislatures. They were concerned about the execution and administration of the law, functions carried out by executives and courts, but the law-making power attracted most of their attention. The legislature was, for them, the central institution of republican government.

Adams favored dividing the legislative powers of government between two bodies—a lower house or popular assembly, elected by the people at large and reflecting their will, and a upper house chosen, Adams suggested, by and from among the members of the lower house. The larger lower house, or assembly, Adams explained, should "feel, reason, and act" like the people. Adams warned against vesting all legislative authority in a popular assembly. A single assembly elected on a popular basis, he wrote, "is liable to all the vices, follies, and frailties of an individual; subject to fits of humor, starts of passion, flights of enthusiasm, partialities, or prejudice, and consequently productive of hasty results and absurd judgments."

Like many political thinkers, Adams worried that an unchecked democracy posed as much danger to rights as an unchecked monarchy or aristocracy. A government based solely on majority rule, he thought, would inevitably trample on the rights of minorities and would have a tendency to change policies with each shift in popular opinion, leading to instability and chaos. Since ancient times, governments largely or wholly democratic had never lasted for long. They had tended toward anarchy, from which dictatorships had emerged to restore order. The function of the smaller upper house Adams proposed was to curb the disorderly tendencies of the popular assembly, insulating the legislature from sudden, emotional shifts in popular opinion. He suggested that the members of the upper house should be elected by and from among the members of the lower house.

Despite his concern about curbing the excesses of popular assemblies, Adams' ideas about the organization of legislative power were extraordinarily democratic. All legislators, he proposed, should be elected annually. Yearly elections would teach representatives "humility, patience and moderation, without which every man in power becomes a ravenous beast of prey." Yearly elections would also impress upon the people a sense of their responsibility as citizens and "a conscious dignity becoming freemen." Their direct and personal role in government, he predicted, would make common people "brave and enterprising." Adams was

excited, he wrote, to

have been sent into life at a time when the greatest lawmakers of antiquity would have wished to live. How few of the human race have ever enjoyed an opportunity of making an election of government . . . for themselves and their children! When, before the present epocha, had three millions of people full power and a fair opportunity to form and establish the wisest and happiest government that human wisdom can contrive?

The Virginia Declaration of Rights

Adams' excitement was shared by other Revolutionary leaders, who recognized that they had a historic opportunity to break the hold of kings and aristocrats on the world and begin an era of expanding freedom in which governments would be dedicated to advancing the interests of the people. This excitement bound many of them together, despite wide differences in character and experience.

Adams sent a copy of *Thoughts on Government* to Patrick Henry, whose populist appeal and oratorical gifts contrasted with Adams' scholarly statecraft, assuring Henry that he considered it "an Honour and an Happiness, that my opinion So often co-incides with yours." Different though they were, Adams recognized that they both aimed at empowering ordinary people:

The Dons, the Bashaws, the Grandees, the Patricians, the Sachems, the Nabobs, call them by what Name you please, Sigh, and groan, and frett, and Sometimes Stamp, and foam, and curse—but all in vain. The Decree is gone forth, and it cannot be recalled, that a more equal Liberty, than has prevail'd in other Parts of the Earth, must be established in America.

Henry responded with enthusiasm. "I am not without hopes it may produce good here where there is among most of our opulent families a strong bias to aristocracy." He encouraged Adams to share his views more widely and "assail the strong Holds of tyranny."

Republican reform had what Henry called "many and powerfull Enemys" in the Virginia Convention, which met for the fifth and final time between May 6 and July 5, 1776 to prepare a republican constitution for the state. The wealthy, go-slow men distrusted Henry and his allies. Carter Braxton, among Henry's most active opponents, published a response to Adams' *Thoughts on Government* in the *Virginia Gazette:*

The systems recommended to the colonies seem to accord with the temper of the times, and are fraught with all the tumult and riot incident to simple democracy . . . The best of these systems exist only in theory, and were never confirmed by the experience, even of those who recommend them. I flatter myself, therefore, that you will not quit a substance actually enjoyed, for a shadow or phantom.

Braxton urged Virginians to craft a government based on the familiar principles of Britain's mixed government, with an assembly elected every three years, an upper house elected by the members of the lower house to serve for life, like British lords, and a governor elected by

the whole legislature, to serve for life. The battle lines were drawn.

The leading role in the Virginia Convention was assumed by an unlikely Revolutionary: George Mason, a bookish Fairfax County planter, older than most of his peers. Temperamental and impatient, Mason suffered through most of his adult life from gout, which compounded his natural irritability. He was known as "Colonel" Mason, but the militia title was a courtesy—a less military character is hard to imagine. Although he was a deep student of political thought, he regarded public office as a burden. Mason could never bring himself to sit in public assemblies and listen to the endless harangues of little men about little problems. Although he served several terms in the Virginia legislature,

George Mason, a scholarly planter and lifelong student of political and legal thought, valued his personal independence and his books far more than popular acclaim. His only life portrait—by John Hesselius, who painted many of Mason's neighbors—is lost. Fortunately Mason's son had this copy of the original painted by Dominic Boudet around 1811 (Courtesy of the Board of Regents, Gunston Hall).

[12]

THE

DECLARATION of RIGHTS.

Made by the Representatives of the good people of Virginia, assembled in full and free Convention; which rights do pertain to them, and their posterity, as the basis and foundation of Government.

FIRST, THAT all men are by nature equally free and independent, and have certain inherent rights, of which, when they enter into a state of society, they cannot, by any compact, deprive or divest their posterity; namely, the enjoyment of life and liberty, with the means of acquiring and possessing property, and pursuing and obtaining happiness and safety.

2d. That all power is vested in, and consequently derived from, the people; that magistrates are their trustees and servants, and at all times amenable to them.

3d. That government is, or ought to be instituted for the common benefit, protection and security, of the people, nation, or community, of all the various modes and forms of government that is best, which is capable of producing the greatest degree of happiness and safety, and is most effectually secured against the danger of maladministration; and that wherever any government shall be found inadequate or contrary to these purposes, a majority of the community hath an indubitable, unalienable, and indefeasible right, to perform, alter, or abolish it, in such manner as shall be judged most conducive to the public weal.

4th. That no man, or set of men, are intitled to exclusive or separate emoluments or privileges from the community, but in consideration of public services; which, not being descendible, neither ought the offices of magistrate, legislature, or judge, to be hereditary.

5th. That the Legislative and Executive powers of the state should be separate and distinct from the judicary; and that the members of the two first may be restrained from oppression, by feeling and participating the burthens of the people, they should at fixed periods, be reduced to a private station, return into that body from which they were originally taken, and the vacancies be supplied by frequent, certain, and regular elections, in which all, or any part of the former members, to be again eligible, or ineligible, as the laws shall direct.

[13]

6th. That elections of members to serve as representatives of the people, in Assembly, ought to be free, and that all men, having sufficient evidence of permanent common interest with, and attachment to, the community, have the right of suffrage, and cannot be taxed or deprived of their property for public uses without their own consent, or that of their representatives so elected, nor bound by any law to which they have not, in like manner, assented for the public good.

7th. That all power of suspending law, or the execution of laws, by any authority without consent of the representatives of the people, is injurious to their rights, and ought not to be exercised,

8th. That in all capital or criminal prosecutions, a man hath a right to demand the cause and nature of his accusation, to be confronted with the accusers and witnesses, to call for evidence in his favor, and to a speedy trial by an impartial jury of his vicinage, without whose unanimous consent he cannot be found guilty, nor can he be compelled to give evidence against himself; that no man be deprived of his liberty, except by the law of the land, or the judgment of his peers.

9th. That excessive bail ought not to be required, nor excessive fines imposed, nor cruel unusual punishments inflicted.

10th. The general warrants, whereby any officer or messenger may be commanded to search suspected places without evidence of a fact committed, or to seize any person or persons not named, or whose offence is not particularly described and supported by evidence, are grievous and oppressive, and ought not to be granted.

11th. That in controversies respecting property, and in suits between man and man, the ancient trial by jury is preferable to any other, and ought to be held sacred.

12th. That the freedom of the press is one of the great bulwarks of liberty, and can never be restrained but by despotic governments.

13th. That a well regulated militia, composed of the body of the people trained to arms, is the proper, natural, and safe defence of a free state; that standing armies, in time of peace, should be avoided, as dangerous to liberty; and that, in all cases, the military should be under strict subordination to, and governed by, the civil power.

14th. That the people have a right to uniform government; and therefore, that no government separate from, or independent of the government of Virginia, ought to be erected or established within the limits thereof.

15th. That no free government, or the blessing of liberty, can be preserved to any people but by a firm adherence to justice, moderation, temperance, frugality, and virtue, and by frequent recurrence to fundamental principles.

The Virginia Constitution of 1776, which included the Declaration of Rights drafted by George Mason, was adopted like any other legislation. By 1784, when this pamphlet edition was published, Thomas Jefferson, James Madison, and other Virginia leaders advocated calling a convention to draft a new constitution that would be submitted to the people for ratification. They were motivated, in part, by the idea that a constitution should rest on a broader foundation of popular approval than ordinary laws (British Library / GRANGER).

Mason never relished it, and he once described an effort to secure his reelection "as an oppressive and unjust Invasion of my personal Liberty."

Assigned to a committee to draft a bill of rights for the new constitution, Mason grumbled about parliamentary procedures and "useless" committee men and wrote the Virginia Declaration of Rights, the most important part of the Virginia Constitution, more or less on his own. "All men are born equally free and independent," the declaration begins, "and have certain inherent natural rights, of which they can not by any compact, deprive or divest their posterity; among which are the enjoyment of life and liberty, with the means of acquiring and possessing property, and pursuing and obtaining happiness and safety." Aristocrats, cautious men, and closet loyalists blanched at the opening words. "A certain set of aristocrats for we have such monsters here," wrote Thomas Ludwell Lee, "finding that their miserable system cannot be reared on such foundations . . . kept us at bay on the first line."

The Virginia Declaration of Rights proved to be one of the most influential state papers of the American Revolution. It asserts that the power of government "is derived from the People," who retain "an indubitable, inalienable, and indefeasible Right" to "reform, alter or abolish" any government at will. It calls for "frequent, certain, and regular elections" of the legislators and the governor, that they "may be restrained from oppression," rejecting Braxton's call for an aristocratic upper house and a governor serving for life.

The Virginia Declaration of Rights outlines the most basic civil rights, including the rights to a speedy trial by jury, and against self-incrimination, excessive bail, general warrants, unlawful seizure of property, and unjustified imprisonment. It asserts that "the freedom of the press" is "one of the great bulwarks of liberty, and can never be restrained but by despotic governments." The declaration also provides for religious toleration, asserting that "all men are equally entitled to the free exercise of religion" and that all should practice "Christian forbearance, love, and charity toward each other," but it did not end Virginia's official support of the Anglican church. It also provided that "a well-regulated militia, composed of the body of the people, trained to arms, is the proper, natural, and safe defense of a free state; that standing armies, in time of peace, should be avoided as dangerous to liberty; and that in all cases the military should be under strict subordination to, and governed by, the civil power." The Virginia Declaration of Rights influenced similar declarations adopted in Pennsylvania, North Carolina, Maryland, Delaware, Massachusetts, and Vermont, and ultimately shaped the Bill of Rights attached to the Federal Constitution.

The main body of Virginia's constitution followed the Declaration of Rights and was an unqualified rejection of Carter Braxton's vision of a mixed government dominated by the rich and well born. Two members of the lower house, or House of Delegates, were to be elected annually from each county. The twenty-four members of the upper house, or Senate, were to be elected by the people every three years. The governor was far from the royal surrogate Braxton proposed. Instead of being elected for life, the constitution provided that the governor would be elected by the legislature each year and could only serve three consecutive terms before being disqualified from serving again for four years.

The new constitution concluded with a practical measure to launch the new state government,

empowering the members of the convention to elect the first governor of the Commonwealth of Virginia. They chose Patrick Henry, the state's leading champion of popular sovereignty.

The Pennsylvania Constitution of 1776

The work of the Virginia Convention was widely admired and imitated in the flurry of constitution-making that followed American independence. Connecticut and Rhode Island, which had long governed themselves under their colonial charters, made minor revisions to those documents, deleting references to the king, and continued on much as they had done for generations. Elsewhere independence touched off a period of constitution writing that continued for more than a decade.

Each of the constitutions adopted in these years reflected local and particular circumstances of its state. In Maryland, where the traditional political leaders among the gentry continued to hold sway, the constitution provided for the annual election of members of the lower house—styled the House of Delegates as in Virginia—but provided five-year terms for members of the Maryland Senate. In New York, where a constitution was adopted in April 1777, members of the assembly were given one-year terms and senators four-year terms. The assemblymen, senators, and governor were all to be elected by popular vote.

South Carolina adopted a provisional government in the spring of 1776 and got around to adopting a constitution in the spring of 1778. Like the governments established in most states, it consisted of a lower house, called the South Carolina House of Representatives, and a smaller upper house, the South Carolina Senate. The members of both houses were to be elected annually, which mirrored the broadly democratic character of most of the revolutionary legislatures. Other provisions of the South Carolina constitution made it relatively undemocratic. Candidates for the South Carolina Senate had to have an estate worth two thousand pounds in the district from which they was elected. Landowners could even represent senate districts in which they did not reside as long as they owned property in the district worth seven thousand pounds. The distribution of seats in the legislature also favored the long-established plantation districts of eastern South Carolina over the rapidly growing interior. These requirements helped ensure that the wealthiest landowners would maintain their influence in the new government.

The constitution adopted in Pennsylvania, by contrast, overturned the influence of the state's traditional rulers. Pennsylvania had been dominated since its founding by wealthy Quakers. Although the Quakers were among the most humane groups in eighteenth-century America—pacifist, tolerant, philanthropic, committed to religious liberty, and generally opposed to enslavement—they jealously resisted the growing influence of others in Pennsylvania affairs. The Quaker-dominated assembly had long resisted increasing the representation of the backcountry counties, which were filling up with Presbyterians, Lutherans, and other non-Quakers. Like the gentry elsewhere, wealthy Quakers were slow and in many cases reluctant to embrace open resistance to British policies, and their pacifism made them opponents of waging war for American rights.

In the spring of 1776 they were swept out of office, replaced by a group of political leaders intent on reforming Pennsylvania government to provide the people of the hinterland with a much larger share of political influence and to break the hold of the old Quaker gentry on the state. Thomas Smith, himself a supporter of reform, was appalled by the character of the delegates and their ignorance about the principles of government. "Not a sixth part," he wrote, "ever read a word on the subject but I believe we might have at least prevented ourselves from being ridiculous in the eyes of the world."

The Pennsylvania convention crafted a constitution wholly unlike the one Adams had recommended in his *Thoughts on Government*. Instead of a legislature with two houses—a larger one, elected frequently by the people, and a smaller one, somewhat insulated from popular pressure by being elected by the members of the larger house from their own number—the Pennsylvania Constitution of 1776 vested all legislative authority in a single legislature, to be elected annually. Unlike other state constitutions which required at least modest property ownership as a prerequisite to voting, the Pennsylvania constitution provided that any man twenty-one years of age who had resided in the state for a year and paid his taxes during that time would be allowed to vote.

This was a major departure from the traditional basis of voting in Britain and the colonies. Today we regard voting as a basic right of which few, if any, citizens should be deprived. Many states deprive convicted felons of the right to vote and all states deny the vote to people under the age of eighteen and most people suffering from severe mental disabilities, but there are movements in some states to expand voting rights to these groups and in some places there is agitation to allow non-citizens to vote.

Voting, which we now regard as a right few are denied, was, in the eighteenth century, a privilege to which relatively few were admitted. Before the American Revolution, the right to vote was a privilege of men who owned property. Since most laws either protected property or deprived people of it through taxation, the right to vote was restricted to those whose personal interests were most clearly involved. It was also restricted to those whose property made them, in principle at least, independent of others and who could therefore cast votes reflecting their interest or the best interest of society. Dependent people—people who owned little or no property and therefore relied on others for wages, indentured servants, apprentices, the enslaved, women, and children—were not afforded the privilege of voting because they could not be expected to act independently.

Our way of thinking about voting—as a right few can justly be denied—is a legacy of the American Revolution, which was conducted to secure personal independence as well as national independence. The Revolution replaced subjection to a sovereign king with the sovereignty of the people and made voting an expression of citizenship. At the same time, the Revolution brought an end to indentured servitude and other forms of bound labor. In the decades after the Revolution, the assumption that people who work for wages are incapable of acting independently eroded, as a more recognizably modern relationship between employers and employees replaced the traditional relationship between master and servant.

To help ensure the independence of voters, the Pennsylvania constitution provided that

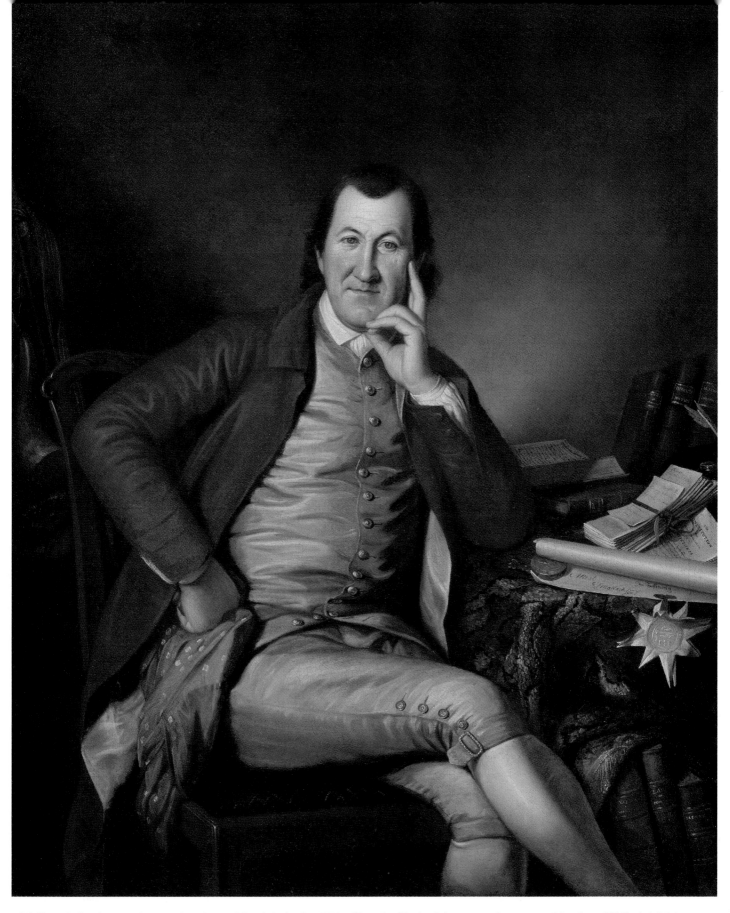

A failure in business who was imprisoned for debt in the 1760s, Timothy Matlack became a brewer and leader of Philadelphia's shopkeepers and artisans. A tireless Revolutionary, he championed the rights of tradesmen and working people. Matlack was one of the draftsmen of the Pennsylvania Constitution of 1776, which sits on the table beside him. Matlack sat for this portrait by Charles Willson Peale in fine clothes, but ignored genteel conventions by wearing his hair naturally, as tradesmen often did. The Revolution offered men like Matlack opportunities to play major roles in public life (Photograph © 2023 Museum of Fine Arts, Boston).

All elections, whether by the people or in general assembly, shall be by ballot, free and voluntary: And any elector, who shall receive any gift or reward for his vote, in meat, drink, monies, or otherwise, shall forfeit his right to elect for that time, and suffer such other penalties as future laws shall direct. And any person who shall directly or indirectly give, promise, or bestow any such rewards to be elected, shall be thereby rendered incapable to serve for the ensuing year.

The Pennsylvania constitution included other provisions to ensure that legislation should be entirely transparent. It opened the doors of the legislature to "all persons who behave decently," except on rare occasions when public business required the legislature to deliberate in private. The constitution also specified that the proceedings of the legislature should be published weekly when it was sitting, including the votes of each member, that all bills should be printed for public consideration before a final vote was taken, and that "for the more perfect satisfaction of the public, the reasons and motives for making such laws shall be fully and clearly expressed in the preambles."

Like other Revolutionary state constitutions, the Pennsylvania Constitution of 1776 reflected concern that executive power was most likely to be abused. Several states, including Virginia, had attempted to solve this problem by providing for the annual election of governors and limiting the number of terms they might serve. Pennsylvania attempted to solve the problem by abolishing the post of governor and vesting executive power in a supreme executive council consisting of councilors elected by each county who could serve no more than three years in seven.

The Pennsylvania Constitution of 1776 had many critics. "No country ever will be long happy," John Adams wrote, "which is thus governed." To his wife, Abigail, he wrote that "we live in an Age of political Experiments. Among many that will fail, some, I hope, will succeed. But Pennsylvania will be divided and weakened, and rendered much less vigorous in the cause by the wretched ideas of government which prevail in the minds of many people in it."

Citizens

The transformation of government that swept over the independent states during the war years resolved uncertainties about government created by the sudden collapse of royal authority, reorganized governments along republican lines—all more responsive to popular will than the colonial governments they replaced—and defined natural and civil rights those governments would protect. This revolution in government had broad support, but it was shaped by a relatively small group of men. Most of them were comfortable and many were wealthy. Some, like John Adams and George Mason, were gifted intellectuals, well read in the law, political philosophy, and history. The revolution in government was their great achievement.

The revolution in government set in motion a much more important revolution that was shaped by ordinary Americans. The creation of republics based on the principle of universal equality changed subjects into citizens. Citizenship—to the surprise and dismay of wealthy, educated men who expected the people to defer to them—empowered ordinary people to assert themselves continuously in public affairs, fueling political movements that have shaped public life, in ever shifting ways, rising and falling in intensity, for nearly two hundred and fifty years.

Among the first were religious dissenters in Virginia. Shortly after the draft of the Virginia Declaration of Rights appeared in newspapers, fifty members of a Baptist church in Occoquan petitioned the Virginia Convention demanding freedom of worship, exclusion from taxation to support the Anglican clergy, and the right to marry without the involvement of the Anglican church—rights they argued were among "the liberties of mankind" to which all were entitled. This was just the first such petition. When the Virginia House of Delegates met for the first time that fall, it received petitions demanding religious liberty and calling for the end of Virginia's religious establishment signed by more than eleven thousand men. The petitioners said that they based their hopes on the "declaration of the Honourable House with regard to equal liberty."

In Massachusetts, where state government functioned under a slightly revised version of the colonial charter until 1780, citizens began demanding a state constitution to ensure that government reflected their needs. In western Massachusetts, where the population had grown rapidly in the years before the war, citizens demanded more local control of government. They resented the fact that the legislature appointed their judges and forced the courts to remain closed until government was reorganized on a more just basis. Petitioners from Pittsfield demanded a government based on such "a Broad base of Civil and religious Liberty as no length of time will corrupt and which will endure as long as the Sun and Moon shall endure."

Everywhere Americans began asserting their rights to individual liberty—personal autonomy, free of government interference or legal restrictions—and to an equal share in public life. The new state constitutions were all very vague about the privileges and responsibilities of citizenship, but ordinary Americans were not. They asserted that citizenship was based on the principle of universal equality and refused to defer to their traditional governors at home just as they refused to defer to King George and his ministers.

The empowerment of ordinary people as citizens reshaped public life. Wealthy landowners and lawyers continued to dominate public office as they had done for decades, but the Revolution changed the relationship between these gentlemen of property, education, and refinement, and the citizens they represented. Before annual elections, a Pennsylvania writer commented, "a poor man has rarely the honor of speaking to a gentleman on any terms, and never with familiarity but for the few weeks before the election. How many poor men, common men, and mechanics have been made happy . . . the right of annual elections will oblige every gentlemen to speak to you once a year" because "you can bestow something upon them."

The same spirit brought men of middling property into public life in increasing numbers. In the North Carolina constitutional convention, wealthy tidewater planter Samuel Johnston looked with dismay at the rough, unsophisticated, uncultured men who were pushing their way into office. "Everyone who has the least pretensions to be a gentleman is borne down," he complained privately, by "a set of men without reading, experience, or principles to govern them."

The new men who sought and secured seats in the independent state legislatures during the war years were often well off financially and owned considerable property, but they were distinguished from the gentry that had long dominated political office by their lack of social distinction. Many of them were successful tradesmen and businessmen. They owned iron furnaces, grist mills, taverns, and ferries. Some were prosperous farmers. Many of them lacked the kind of genteel education and social refinement that distinguished the gentry, and few were connected to the established gentry families by marriage. They never learned Latin or Greek, did not read European magazines, novels, or plays, nor did they know how to fence or dance a minuet. They were practical men of affairs, not gentlemen of leisure. As British subjects they had stood below the gentry in the finely graded hierarchy that divided society from the king and his aristocratic followers down to servants and slaves. In the new republics they were simply successful citizens in a society of equals. At elections they often appealed to ordinary citizens more effectively than the traditional gentry.

Before the American Revolution, life was based on inequalities. Below the king, all were subjects, but their subjection was never equal. At each layer in the social hierarchy the king's subjects possessed privileges associated with their status. The most substantial of those privileges were hereditary. The American Revolution did not make all Americans equal in status, but it eliminated legal privileges associated with status and made equality the standard for relations between individuals and between individuals and government. Beginning with the Revolution, men—and increasingly, women—regarded themselves as the equals of others.

"We are convinced of our right to be free"

The enslaved were no exception. Before the Revolution, judges and lawyers debated whether slaves were subjects or simply human property, but they were subject to law. Free blacks who lived in the colonies were indisputably subjects of the Crown, but in the finely graded hierarchy of colonial society they occupied an uncertain status that was, in many respects, below that of white

187

indentured servants. Subjecthood was an unequal status, but it was universal within the royal domain. All were subjects—even the Indians who lived on and beyond the margins of colonial society—and thus alike in their inequality.

The status of Indians in the new nation was complicated. Most lived outside the reach of conventional legal institutions and could not be subordinated to law in the same way as people who lived within the frontiers of the new states. Many were at war with white settlers on the frontier and many were allied with the British. Those Indians allied with Americans or who lived peacefully within the frontiers of the new states were few enough that the question of whether they were, or could be, equal citizens did not occupy much attention. Most of the whites who did not regard Indians as intractable enemies—who imagined a future in which whites and Indians might live in peace—could only imagine such a future if the Indians abandoned their traditional culture and became settled farmers, embracing white ideas of property ownership. Living on and beyond the margins of white society, few Indians expressed an interest in citizenship.

This was not the case with the enslaved, who lived within the bounds of every state and who longed for emancipation and equality. Emancipation began, wrote Ira Berlin, "in the flames of the American Revolution." It was driven by black Americans, enslaved and free, who embraced the Revolutionary ideal of universal equality and drove it toward its logical conclusion in the abolition of slavery and the achievement of citizenship.

The legal and cultural conventions that supported slavery in British America came apart piece by piece in the eighty years that followed the Declaration of Independence, inspired by its idealism. Enslaved women and men wanted to escape from slavery and they seized every means available to do it. Before the Revolution flight was the most viable means, and in some cases the only one. Some slaves who earned money and were allowed to keep it by indulgent enslavers purchased their freedom or the freedom of others. The Revolution dramatically expanded the ways in which the enslaved could escape slavery, including military service, law suits, and state-mandated emancipation.

The Revolutionary War accelerated the erosion of slavery by providing enslaved Americans opportunities to free themselves. Some simply left their enslavers in the chaos of war and found a haven in the camp of a nearby army, whether British or American. The British extended offers of freedom in exchange for military service to secure manpower and to punish their enemies—the British promised to return the slave property of loyalists, though sifting out men enslaved by the king's friends rarely proved practical. These offers were motivated by military expediency rather than abolitionist sentiment. Lord Dunmore, the first British official to extend such an offer, enslaved men and women himself.

Americans, always short of soldiers, made similar offers, the terms varying according to local and even individual circumstances. White Americans liable for military service in some places could present slaves as substitutes, though wary enrolling officers often wanted to know what inducement the enslaved man had been offered. Emancipation or its prospect at discharge was commonly regarded as sufficient. In an effort to discourage runaways, the Virginia legislature amended the state's militia law in 1777 to require black volunteers to prove that they were free men. Hard pressed recruiters probably ignored the law. Reluctance to enlist the enslaved, runaways, and free blacks declined as manpower shortages grew worse, so that by the last stages of the war black soldiers made up an important part of Washington's army.

Others emancipated themselves in court. In 1781, an enslaved woman who later called herself Elizabeth Freeman brought suit in Great Barrington, Massachusetts, to secure her freedom. A local attorney, Theodore Sedgwick, took her case, arguing that under the provision of the Massachusetts constitution that "all men are born free and equal," slavery had no legal basis in the state. The case reached the state supreme court, which ruled that slavery was contrary to the natural rights of mankind and the legal equality promised in the new constitution. Others brought suit in Massachusetts, or simply left their enslavers, who had no legal mechanism to return them to slavery.

The enslaved embraced state-mandated emancipation as well. Slavery was common in all thirteen states, and deeply entrenched in the economies of Connecticut, New York, New Jersey, and Pennsylvania, as well as the states to the south. Support for slavery crumbled first where it was of marginal economic importance. Vermont, a frontier region between New Hampshire and New York claimed by both, asserted its independence in 1777, adopting a republican constitution that no male "born in this country, or brought from over sea" ought to be held in servitude after the age of twenty-one. For females the age was eighteen. There was enough ambiguity in the law to facilitate the continued enslavement of a few. Regardless of the complicated and somewhat messy application of abolition in Vermont, it attracted free black settlers, including veterans, after the war.

Twenty enslaved men petitioned the New Hampshire legislature for the abolition of slavery in 1779, declaring that "private or public tyranny and slavery are alike detestable to minds conscious of the equal dignity of human nature." The legislature tabled the petition, but New Hampshire's constitution of 1784 declared that "all men are born equally free and independent" and possess natural rights, "among which are the enjoying and defending life and liberty." By then many enslaved men had secured their freedom through military service. Slavery lingered in New Hampshire: the 1790 census counted 158 enslaved people, but the 1800 census found only 8.

State-sponsored abolition was more difficult to achieve in states where slavery was more important to the economy, as it was in Pennsylvania, New Jersey, New York, and Connecticut. All four ultimately adopted statutes providing for gradual emancipation, rejecting calls for immediate abolition in an effort to secure the acceptance of slaveowners. The Pennsylvania Act for the Gradual Abolition of Slavery, adopted in 1780, was the first of these statutes. A reflection of the humanitarian tradition of Pennsylvania Quakers and the religious and philosophical opposition to enslavement of Anthony Benezet, Benjamin Franklin, and others, the statute served as a model for the other states. The purpose of the law was to admit those who would otherwise be enslaved to "the common blessings" to which they were "entitled . . . by nature."

The act freed almost no one immediately. It provided that children born to enslaved women would have the status of indentured servants until they were twenty-eight, when they would be become free men and women. Others would remain slaves for life unless freed by their enslavers.

The act also provided that enslaved people brought into Pennsylvania would be free after six months of continuous residence. If strictly enforced, the law would achieve the extinction of slavery in Pennsylvania by slow degrees. It avoided the question of whether the children born to slave women were citizens or would become citizens when they were released from their indenture at twenty-eight. Many enslaved men and women in Pennsylvania and other states devised ways to free themselves without waiting for the law, often by running away.

Despite the limitations imposed on black military service, the difficulties the enslaved experienced in getting their appeals heard in courts and legislatures, and the limitations of state-sponsored emancipation, the free black population grew dramatically during and after the war. The success of so many free black Americans eroded the most common argument against emancipation and black citizenship—that African Americans were incapable of taking care of themselves and lacked the moral and intellectual capacity to make use of freedom. This position had been so common before the Revolution that whites rarely had any reason to articulate it. Only when challenged by early opponents of slavery did slaveowners and others who benefitted from enslavement dismiss the capacities of the people whose enslavement supported and enriched them. If any truth was self-evident to them, it was that all men were not born equal.

Many of the enslaved continued to suffer enslavement without seeking to escape because of the constant fear of punishment and because the idea of equality was so alien to their lives. They sought ways to improve their daily existence or engaged in forms of resistance—feigning illness or injury, malingering, breaking tools, and petty sabotage—to avoid labor for a day or a week. Like many white Americans, they were averse to risk, willing to accept the evils of the life they knew rather than face the dangers of a different one.

Although most of the enslaved remained in chains, enough claimed their freedom for many Americans to imagine, for the first time, a world without slaves. For most of history, the idea of a world without slavery was simply inconceivable. The prospect terrified most slaveowners at the same time it inspired the men and women they enslaved. It led thousands to free themselves, demolishing

the slaveowner's argument that the men and women they enslaved did not want to be free—that they were content with their status and while they might enjoy lighter burdens and petty privileges, they did not want the kind of personal independence that white Americans demanded.

No Americans embraced the Declaration's claim of universal equality founded in human nature more forcefully or more persistently than black Americans—most of all black abolitionists. In the years after the Revolution they blended the assertion of equality as a natural right with the claims of evangelical Christianity to the universal equality rooted in the teachings of Nature's God. They made the long crusade to abolish slavery about equality.

That abolition was based on the principle of universal equality now seems so obvious that we can scarcely imagine abolition on any other grounds, but other powerful arguments against slavery—economic inefficiency, its tendency to corrupt the moral and ethical sensibilities of slaveowners, or the revoltingly inhumane violence inherent

Jean Baptiste Antoine de Verger, a lieutenant in the French army, painted this watercolor of American soldiers in his diary. Like other French officers, he was fascinated by the African Americans in the American army. His portrait of a soldier of the First Rhode Island Regiment, at left, is an accurate depiction of the unit's distinctive white uniform and is one of the few wartime images of an African American soldier. Verger portrayed the others—a Pennsylvania Continental, a backcountry rifleman in homespun linen and armed with a hatchet, and an artillerist with a priming horn and a linstock, used to fire cannon—with similar attention to detail (Brown University).

in it—might have prevailed if black abolitionists had not pressed continuously for equality and the privileges of citizenship. Slavery was, in fact, abolished elsewhere in the world without reference to equality. The claim that "all men are created equal" became the defining ideal of the United States because African Americans and their allies made it so. American is free because they did.

The grim reality that America's victory in a long war of national liberation rested on the suffering and sacrifice of people committed to the cause is the message of the final version of Charles Willson's Peale's *George Washington at the Battle of Princeton*. The triumphant charge that swept the British from the field and the death of his friend Hugh Mercer appear in the background, as if drawn from Washington's own memory (Princeton University).

Chapter 14 A People's War

From its winter quarters in Morristown, New Jersey, George Washington's army kept watch over the British army in New York City. The character of the war was changing, and with it the way Washington understood the men under his command. The martial enthusiasm that had led thousands of young men to enlist in the Continental Army and state regiments in the first year of the war was gone. Many of the men were gone, too—killed, grievously wounded, or captured.

The captured men had been herded into makeshift prisons in and around New York City. They had been crowded into sugar houses—large buildings where merchants had stored molasses and sugar shipped from the West Indies. The British fed them on rotten salt meat and ship's biscuits infested with insects and ignored their suffering. British soldiers were not inclined to treat traitors to the king like prisoners of war. They resisted the temptation to hang them only because the rebels held British prisoners, and once the hanging began there might be no end to it. When the sugar houses were full the British shoved their prisoners into hulks—rotting, dismasted ships moored in a stagnant backwater in the East River. The prisoners packed into HMS *Jersey* and the other hulks listing off Brooklyn starved in a city where food was abundant, their miserable lives punctuated by the daily ritual, in summer's heat and winter's cold, of burying their dead comrades in shallow graves scooped from the stinking mud of Wallabout Bay.

In the winter quarters at Morristown, the ranks were thin. Many men whose enlistments had expired were gone. Some reenlisted in the late spring, after crops were planted, but others had had enough of war. Those who remained were housed in drafty cabins and poorly fed, not because food was scarce but because the army had not developed a reliable system for getting food to them. Men who had gone to war in the spring and summer of 1776 in bright new uniforms had worn them to rags. Yet they faced their task with grim determination.

George Washington's view of them was changing. During the war's first year and more, Washington had assumed that ordinary men enlisted in the army for pay and had to be subjected to stern discipline to keep them to their duty. Discipline, he was certain, was the essential characteristic of a successful army. But most his men were short-term recruits who would decline to reenlist if they were subjected to corporal punishment, and others might simply desert—their spirit of personal independence and love of liberty overwhelming their unselfish commitment to the cause.

A revolution predicated on the idea that all men are created equal and possess certain inalienable rights, including rights to life and liberty, was hard pressed to justify executing men for desertion or imposing savage punishments for infractions of military discipline, yet the pragmatic Washington needed men who would follow orders without question and who would sacrifice their lives at his command. The war, he was convinced, could not be won otherwise.

The mutually exclusive demands of personal liberty and military discipline were difficult to reconcile. Washington did so by appealing to the idea of honor. In the bleak winter of 1776, when the enlistments of most of his soldiers were about to expire, Washington addressed them in a way that revealed a Revolutionary shift in his thinking. "My brave fellows," he began, "you have done all I asked you to do, and more than could be reasonably expected; but your country is at stake, your wives, your houses, and all that you hold dear. . . . If you will consent to stay one month longer, you will render that service to the cause of liberty, and to your country, which you can probably never do under any other circumstances." When the men stepped forward to volunteer an officer asked Washington if they should be formally enrolled. "No," Washington replied, "men who will

volunteer in such a case as this, need no enrollment to keep them to their duty."

The force Washington believed would "keep them to their duty" was honor—a personal commitment to moral and ethical conduct, even at the expense of selfish interests. Honor was traditionally regarded as an attribute of gentility, on the entirely practical grounds that ordinary people could not afford to set aside their selfish interests for the good of others. They had to struggle simply to survive or to provide for their families and could not be expected to sacrifice their interests for any larger community. By contrast, gentlemen—using that term in the pre-modern sense to refer to men of sufficient means that they could afford to set pecuniary interests aside and of sufficient education or understanding to distinguish the public good from private interests—could be motivated by honor. Officers were traditionally drawn from the aristocracy and the gentry because these groups were assumed to be motivated by honor. Commanding the Continental Army in his failed defense of New York and the retreat through New Jersey convinced Washington that the ordinary soldiers who reenlisted in that crisis were motivated by honor as surely as any officer.

The idea that ordinary men were motivated by honor was tested every day in the sugar houses and the prison hulks where the British offered prisoners the possibility of relief if they would join His Majesty's navy or enlist in His Majesty's army. Many agreed, if only to escape torment—how many will never be known—but many thousands more refused. They had nothing left but life and honor, and they refused to sacrifice their honor to save their lives. The honor of ordinary Americans—despite the suffering that continued as long as the war, despite the failures of their leaders, and despite the injustice and cruelty they endured—made victory possible. Without it, America would not be free.

Amphitrite

On April 20, 1777, a heavily armed French merchant ship, *Amphitrite,* arrived in Portsmouth, New Hampshire. She carried 52 brass field cannons, more than 20,000 cannon balls, 6,132 muskets, more than 250,000 gun flints, 24,000 pounds of lead musket balls, 12,000 pounds of gunpowder, 925 tents, and assorted uniforms, blankets, tools, tin plates, and other military supplies.

The French had gone to great pains to disguise the fact that they were supplying arms, ammunition, and other supplies to the Americans to avoid the British accusing them of doing so and causing an international incident that might lead prematurely to war. In fact, the British government had spies in France and America. King George III and his ministers were well aware that the French were equipping the rebels, but they were no more ready to accuse the French than the French were ready to be accused. Neither side was ready for an expensive war against the other.

Despite the arrival of French arms in America, the British looked forward to ending the rebellion by the end of 1777. The French, on the other hand, looked for a prolonged war in America—a war in which most of the British army would be tied up fighting the rebels and a large part of the Royal Navy would be occupied supporting army operations and patrolling the American coast— leaving the French navy free to pick off Britain's island colonies in the Caribbean, take control of the English Channel, and perhaps even mount an invasion of Britain, something that had not happened since the Norman conquest of England more than seven hundred years earlier. The French ministry was impressed by news of the American victories at Trenton and Princeton, but was looking for more evidence that the Americans were capable of sustaining the war.

The French provided America with thousands of long arms, like this Model 1766 Charleville musket, along with bayonets, cannon barrels, ammunition, gunpowder, uniforms, knapsacks, tents, and other military supplies, without which the Continental Army could not have sustained the war (The Society of the Cincinnati).

None of this was a secret to George Washington, who understood that the French government would only do as much for the American cause as it seemed in its interest to do. He was relieved to get the arms from the *Amphitrite*. Many soldiers whose enlistments had expired had taken their muskets home with them. At his request, Congress had called on the states to raise new regiments and enlist the men for three years, but the states were desperately short of muskets and many new recruits arrived at the army camp at Morristown that spring without arms.

The cannons and muskets that arrived on the *Amphitrite* were military surplus—outdated weapons the French were no longer issuing to their troops for field use. The French government ultimately shipped over one hundred thousand surplus military muskets to America in support of the rebellion. Americans referred to the most common of these as Charleville muskets because many bore the mark of the royal armory at Charleville, though muskets of this design were made at other French armories. The Charleville muskets were easily distinguished from the standard British infantry musket and most other weapons by three bright metal bands fixing the barrel to the stock. British officers recognized them in the hands of the rebels when the armies met in battle.

As spring came, Washington knew that the British would renew their efforts to defeat his army and win the war. Benjamin Franklin had arrived in Paris on his mission to persuade the French to join the war as an ally of the United States. A successful defense might be enough to draw the French into the war.

Danbury

That defense depended on many things, not least keeping the army supplied, which was a constant challenge for George Washington and his officers as well as for the Continental Congress. Much of the food and other supplies Washington's army used were purchased in Connecticut and adjacent areas of New England and stockpiled in Danbury, in the western part of the state, then brought by wagon across the Hudson and southwest to the army encampment at Morristown.

In April, Howe sent a force of some 1,900 men to destroy the supplies stored in Danbury. The Royal Navy landed the raiders on the Connecticut coast from which they marched north toward Danbury, twenty-five miles away. A messenger rode to the home of Henry Ludington, colonel of the militia in nearby Dutchess County, New York, to get him to call out his men. It was dark and raining, and the exhausted messenger did not know the area. According to a local tradition, Ludington sent his sixteen-year-old daughter, Sybil, to sound the alarm. She rode forty miles that night, going from house to house, calling out the militiamen. Sybil made it home the next morning.

The British reached Danbury, and the next day burned several thousand barrels of beef, pork, and flour, along with thousands of shoes, tents, and other supplies, as well as the wagons needed to haul them to Washington's army. American troops entered Danbury just as the British and Hessians left, too late to save the supplies or the town. Joseph Plumb Martin, a Continental soldier, later remembered that "the town had been laid in ashes, a number of the inhabitants murdered and cast into their burning houses, because they had presumed to defend their persons and property . . . . I saw the inhabitants, after the fire was out, endeavoring to find the burnt bones of their relatives amongst the rubbish of their demolished houses."

Scenes like this were repeated wherever the war went, and as the war stretched on for years it reached and scarred communities and families from Maine to the Florida frontier, leaving behind destruction and sadness and bitter anger. In Britain men might imagine that reconciliation was still possible, but that was already a fantasy, and every day the war continued, obstinate and bloody, the more a fantasy it became.

As the British and Hessians marched away, Continental troops and Connecticut militia converged on them, attacking their rear guard three miles south of Danbury and then engaging the enemy in a running battle all the way to the coast, with Americans led by Benedict Arnold firing on the marching column, retreating, and reforming to attack again down the road, much as the Massachusetts militia had done during the British retreat from Lexington and Concord. Most of the British—many had not slept for three days, and some had fallen on the road from exhaustion—managed to escape to their transports. About 150 of them were wounded, killed, or captured. The British never attempted another inland raid of the kind.

Among the American dead was twenty-five-year-old Samuel Elmer, Jr. A lieutenant on furlough when the Danbury Alarm sounded, he rode south and volunteered for service. In the final moments of the battle he was killed rallying his men along a stone wall. He was buried where he fell. His grief-stricken father later moved Samuel's body to a local burying ground, and placed a gravestone there with this inscription, expressing the hope that his son's sacrifice would be remembered:

Lieutenant Samuel Elmer,
son of Col Samuel Elmer of Sharon,
was killed at Fairfield,
fighting for the liberties of his country,
April 28, 1777 in the 25th year of his Age.
Our youthful Hero bold in Arms
His Country's cause his bosom warms

To have her right Fond to Engage
And Guard her from a Tyrant's rage
Flies to ye Field of Blood & Death
And gloriously resigns his Breath

America is free because Samuel Elmer, Jr., and many other young men like him gave their lives to make it free.

"Thus was I, a slave . . . fighting for liberty"

Among the soldiers in action that day was Jeffrey Brace, an enslaved man who had just enlisted in the Connecticut Continental Line. We know his story because in 1810 an idealistic young lawyer helped him write his memoirs—the story of a free African forced into slavery who fought in the Revolutionary War and lived the rest of his life as a free man. He had been born in what is now Mali in about 1742. Taken by slave traders when he was about sixteen, he survived the brutality, starvation, and violence of the Middle Passage and the cruelty of slave brokers in the British island colony of Barbados. After two months spent imprisoned in a filthy warehouse he later called a "house of subjection," he was sold for service on a privateer—a privately owned ship fitted with cannons to attack enemy merchant ships during the French and Indian War.

He proved to be a brave privateer—his shipmates named him Jeffrey, after British general Jeffrey Amherst—but when the war ended his enslaver had no further use for him and he was sold as a slave to a Connecticut man who forced him to work outside in winter with neither coat nor shoes and beat him mercilessly for imagined wrongs. A neighbor was so appalled that he took Jeffrey in and threatened to lodge a criminal complaint against his enslaver if he interfered. After a brief respite, Jeffrey was passed from one enslaver to another, enduring more brutality. Finally in 1768 he landed in the house of an elderly widow, Mary Stiles, where he did domestic chores. She taught him to read and introduced him to the Bible. He committed long sections of it to memory and could recite them for the rest of his life. When she died, Jeffrey—then called Jeffrey Stiles—passed to her son, Benjamin Stiles.

No portrait of Jeffrey Brace is known, and it is not likely that one was ever made. Historical artist Don Troiani painstakingly recreated the uniform and equipment of the African American soldiers of the Sixth Regiment of the Connecticut Continental Line in this modern painting memorializing their service (Courtesy Don Troiani).

By 1775 he had been in New England for more than a decade, but his memoir makes no mention of colonial resistance to British regulation and taxation, the military occupation of Boston, nor any of the other events leading to the war for independence. Yet when the opportunity presented itself, Jeffrey enlisted in the Sixth Regiment of the Connecticut Continental Line. In his words, he "entered the banners of freedom . . . to liberate freemen, my tyrants."

Why did he enlist? He did not say, but we can assume that Benjamin Stiles agreed to free him if he served in the Continental Army. Some New England enslavers agreed to free their slaves in exchange for all or part of their military wages— essentially permitting the enslaved to purchase their freedom. Others agreed to free slaves who entered the army as a contribution to the Revolutionary cause. Still others did so because they realized that slavery was inconsistent with the principles of the Revolution. Rachel Johnson of Wallingford freed Dolly in 1778, insisting that "I believe all mankind should be free." Abijah Holbrook of Torrington explained that "all mankind by nature are entitled to equal liberty and freedom" when he freed Jacob and Ginne Prince.

Jeffrey had been with his regiment no more than a few weeks when they pursued the British and Hessians out of Danbury. "We beat them back," Jeffrey said. "The fight was continued all day, and the victory was sometimes doubtful." At thirty-five he was one of the oldest men in the regiment and one of the few who had experience in battle. After the fighting he was assigned to the regiment's light infantry company, a select group of skilled soldiers distinguished for their courage, height ("I then wanted but a quarter of an inch of being six feet three inches," he wrote) and athletic ability. The light infantry wore distinctive leather helmets and were sometimes referred to, as they are in Jeffrey's memoir, as "leather caps." He remained in the light infantry for the rest of the war. "Thus was I," he concluded, "a slave, for five years fighting for liberty."

Every soldier in the Continental Army had his own story—his own reasons for fighting and his own hopes for the future. America is free because of their sacrifices and their courage. Jeffrey said that his abusers had beaten him in order to make

him docile and obedient, because they believed that "the thought of liberty must never be suffered to contaminate itself in a negro's mind." The thought of liberty had never left his mind. When the Continental Army disbanded in 1783, Jeffrey secured his freedom. He began calling himself Jeffrey Brace, adopting an Americanized version of his African name. For the first time in decades, he wrote, he "enjoyed the pleasures of a freeman; my food was sweet, my labor pleasure." He settled in Vermont, where the new state constitution called for the gradual abolition of slavery, acquired land, and raised a family. His life was never easy. Even on the New England frontier, he could not escape bigotry and exploitation. But for him, as for many others, the American Revolution was a turning point between slavery and freedom. America is free because enslaved men like Jeffrey Brace fought, and many died, to make it so.

Burgoyne

John Burgoyne, an ambitious general who had been at the Siege of Boston and sized up the Americans, devised a plan he believed would end the war. He proposed leading an army down the Lake Champlain-Hudson River corridor connecting Canada and New York. The rivers and lakes in the corridor provided a nearly continuous water route from the St. Lawrence River to the Hudson. By taking control of the Hudson River Valley, Burgoyne expected to cut off the flow of men and supplies from New England that sustained Washington's army. Burgoyne was so sure of success that before leaving Britain he bet a friend a large amount of money that he would return a victorious hero.

The plan seemed good to British leaders looking at maps in London, but carrying it out would prove much more difficult than they imagined. Burgoyne's army would have to pass through hundreds of miles of forest and unsettled country, carrying most of its food and other supplies with it. There was little hope of collecting supplies from farms along the way. Burgoyne would also have to take control of a series of forts. The most important, Fort Ticonderoga, dominated the southern end of Lake Champlain and controlled the portage between Lake Champlain and Lake George. The

Joshua Reynolds, one of the most talented British painters of the eighteenth century, caught all of John Burgoyne's ambition and swagger in this portrait completed in 1766 (Copyright The Frick Collection).

latter stretches thirty-two miles to the south. A narrow finger of Lake Champlain, South Bay, parallels Lake George. From the south end of the lakes, Burgoyne would have to cross a heavily forested region guarded by forts to reach the Hudson, where Fort Edward barred access to the river. Once he reached the Hudson, Burgoyne would have to pass a rough, easily defended area before reaching Albany.

American troops manned these forts in the summer of 1777. Among them was Acquilla Cleaveland, a private in a New Hampshire ranger company, who wrote to his wife, Mercy, on June 10 that they had been patrolling the west shore of Lake Champlain for sixty miles north of Fort Ticonderoga, but had seen only one Indian scouting party, near Split Rock Mountain. They had no reports of British movements to the north. "By what we herd they will not trouble us here this summer." He was more worried about smallpox, which he said loyalists were trying to spread to American troops. Food was expensive, he wrote, and promised recruitment bounties remained unpaid. He concluded:

My Dear wife after my regards to you, I don't know when I shall see you but would have you do as well as you can remember that god is as able to support you now as ever if you trust in him. I shall come home as soon as I can get a chance. And so I remain your loving husband till Death.

A week later, on June 17, Acquila Cleaveland was killed by a party of Mohawks sent south by the British.

That same day, Burgoyne's army moved south from St. John's, Canada. It consisted of over 7,000 men, including about 3,900 British soldiers and 3,100 Hessians. Shortly after setting out, Burgoyne issued a statement to the Americans, encouraging them to repent and support his army, warning those who did not that "the Messengers of Justice and of Wrath await them in the field, and Devastation, Famine, and every . . . Horror." Among the horrors he threatened was "to give stretch to the Indian Forces under my direction, and they amount to thousands, to overtake the harden'd enemies of Great Britain and America."

These were foolish threats to make, and reflected the fact that neither Burgoyne nor the British officials who supported his campaign had any respect for the Americans they were facing. With Washington occupied by Howe in New Jersey, Burgoyne expected to take control of the Hudson Valley without a serious fight. Opposing him, Burgoyne believed, would be an undersized force of dispirited militia. Howe encouraged this kind of thinking, assuring the ministry in London that the "friends of Government" in upstate New York "will be found so numerous and so ready to give every aid and assistance in their power" that Burgoyne would have no problem imposing his will.

This was the old delusion that loyalists would rise to support the Crown as soon as the king's army appeared that had already led to British failures in Virginia, the Carolinas, and New Jersey. Exiled royal governors assured the British ministry that the rebellion was led by a few incendiaries capable of raising mobs in port towns like Boston, but that the "substantial men" in most communities were loyal to the Crown and anxious to show it. Aristocratic British officers assumed the same thing. Their dealings were almost exclusively with prosperous landowners and merchants, men whose success attached them to the established way of doing things. British leaders simply could not conceive that, in America, ordinary people were not inclined to defer to the judgment of the local gentry, and so the British continuously underestimated the anger they stirred.

Burgoyne had his proclamation printed and sent agents to distribute it along the frontier. Threats of descending on rebels with fire and sword only hardened popular resentment. So did encouraging the Indians to make war on Americans. When he reached Lake Champlain, Burgoyne called a meeting of chiefs and leading warriors of the Iroquois, Ottawa, and Abenaki peoples. Addressing them through an interpreter, Burgoyne told them that King George regarded them with great satisfaction and asked them to join in punishing the king's enemies. "Warriors," he said, "you are free—Go forth in might of your valour and your cause; strike at the common enemies of Great-Britain and America—disturbers of public order, peace, and happiness." Scalps might be taken, he added, but only from the dead and not from aged men, women, or children. Some five hundred Indians joined Burgoyne's army as it moved south.

Facing Burgoyne was the army of Major General Philip Schuyler, commander of the Northern Department, a largely autonomous post in which he was responsible for defending the new nation from an attack down the Lake Champlain-Hudson River corridor. Maintaining military control of this region was a desperate challenge. To the west of Albany, in the Mohawk River Valley and northward to the Great Lakes, was the land of Iroquois, a confederacy of powerful, warlike Indian tribes more likely to fight with the British than the Americans because they knew that the British, at least for the moment, valued their trade more than the vast forests they inhabited, which the Americans coveted. To the east, in the mountain valleys between New York and New Hampshire was a region—what would become Vermont—claimed by both states and peopled by New Englanders who seemed as likely to take up arms against New Yorkers as to fight the British. To the south, along the Hudson all the way to Manhattan, New Yorkers were divided between patriots and loyalists.

To maintain control of this critical, complex, and confusing region, Schuyler had only a fragment of the armed strength of the United States. Most of the available manpower was funneled to Washington's army. Schuyler had Continental troops raised in New York and other units, mostly militia, from New York and adjacent parts of Connecticut and western Massachusetts. They were barely sufficient to man the frontier outposts spread across a wide arc from the hazy borderlands of Vermont to the Mohawk River Valley. Adding to his difficulties was the distrust many New Englanders felt for New Yorkers, and their resistance to being placed under the command of New York officers, including Schuyler himself. Arms and gunpowder were in desperately short supply, and providing his men with food, clothing, and other necessities was a continuous problem.

"A wild and unknown country . . ."

It proved an even more critical problem for Burgoyne, who set off up Lake Champlain on June 20, full of bravado and unjustified confidence, into what one of his officers called "a wild and unknown country." The army used the lake to move south, loading men and supplies on hundreds of flat-bottomed boats called bateaux. Each bateau was thirty to thirty-two feet long and six or seven feet wide amidship, with a prow on each end, and could carry about twenty-four men.

One of those men, Lieutenant August Wilhelm Du Roi, a mercenary from the German duchy of Brunswick-Wolfenbüttel, kept a journal during the campaign that provides insights on the war that seem to have escaped many of his superiors. "No finer or more beautiful sight can be imagined," he wrote "than a fleet of about eight hundred boats propelled on smooth water by hundreds of oars." But the deep woods on either side of the lake filled him with foreboding. "The banks of the lake are covered by the thickest woods, and every time a camp had to be pitched, trees had to be cut down and the place cleared."

Burgoyne's army landed near Fort Ticonderoga, the great fort guarding the point in the lake system where Lake Champlain connected with South Bay on the east and Lake George on the west, both providing a water route that reached close to the Hudson. Fort Ticonderoga was an impressive masonry structure constructed according the principles of the leading military engineers of its time. Properly manned, armed, and supplied, it was regarded as impregnable. The British found that the American commander, Arthur St. Clair, had left a nearby hill, Mount Defiance, unguarded. Mounting artillery near the crest, the guns rendered Ticonderoga untenable. St. Clair evacuated the fort, and Mount Independence, on the opposite side of the lake, on July 6.

The rebels had built a bridge connecting Ticonderoga and Mount Independence. It was seven hundred feet long and built in water that was as deep as twenty-five feet and swept by a heavy current. The work, Du Roi calculated, was staggering, and had been carried out in a place remote from forges and sawmills, which had to be constructed. "Such perseverance," he wrote, "is seldom found in history, except in a republic, where a general participation in a common cause would inspire and hold it. It is rarely, if ever, found in monarchies."

Burgoyne's army continued down South Bay to Skenesborough, then set off overland toward the Hudson. That's when problems began, and a campaign that had seemed destined for triumph

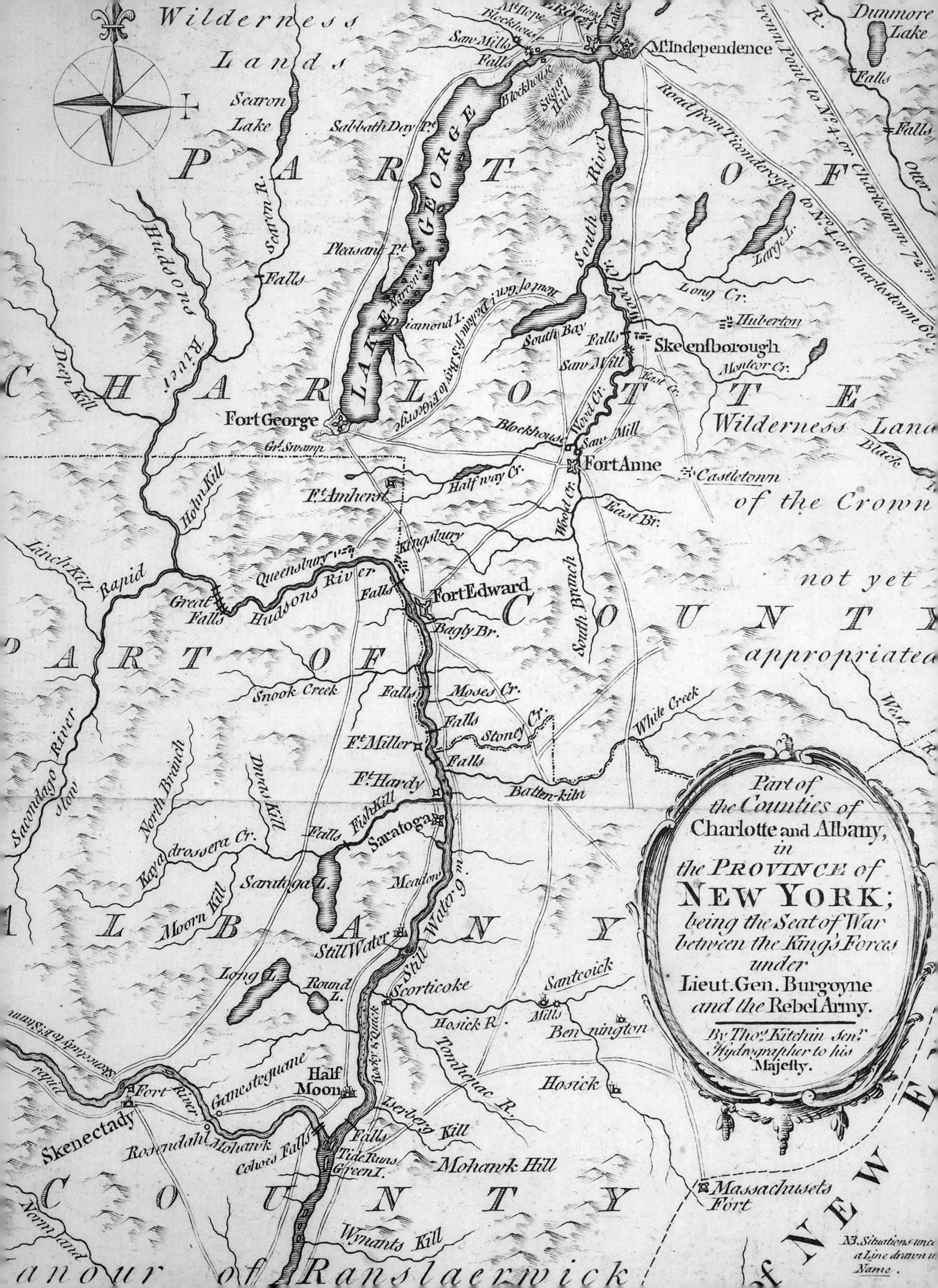

Part of
the Counties of
Charlotte and Albany,
in
the PROVINCE of
NEW YORK;
being the Seat of War
between the King's Forces
under
Lieut. Gen. Burgoyne
and the Rebel Army.
By Thos. Kitchin Senr.
Hydrographer to his
Majesty.
Wilderness Lands
Mt. Independence
Saw Mills
Falls
Blockhouse
Sugar Hill
Dunmore Lake
Searon Lake
Sabbath Day Pt.
LAKE GEORGE
South River
Road from Ticonderoga to No. 4 or Charlestown 72 m.
PART OF
Searon R.
Hudsons River
Pleasant Pt.
Large L.
Falls
Long Cr.
Diamond I.
South Bay
Huberton
Skeensborough
Saw Mill
Deep Kill
Fort George
Gt. Swamp
CHARLOTTE
Wilderness Land
Blockhouse
Wood Cr.
Fort Anne
Castletown
Ft. Amherst
Half way Cr.
of the Crown
East Br.
Holm Kill
Kingsbury
Queensbury
Hudsons River
Rapid
Great Falls
Fort Edward
not yet
COUNTY
South Branch
Bagly Br.
appropriated
PART OF
Snook Creek
Moses Cr.
Stoney Cr.
White Creek
Ft. Miller
Ft. Hardy
Batten-kiln
Sacondaga River
North Branch
Fish Kill
Saratoga
Kayadrossera Cr.
Saratoga L.
Meadows
Moon Kill
ALBANY
Still Water
Long L.
Round L.
Scorticoke
Santcoick
Hosick R.
Mills
Bennington
Tomhenac R.
Hosick
Half Moon
Ganestequane
Fort River
Skenectady
Rosendahl
Mohawk
Cohoes Falls
Falls
Tide Runs
Green I.
Mohawk Hill
Iserberg Kill
Massachusets Fort
COUNTY
NEW
Wynants Kill
Manour of Ranslaerwick
N.B. Situations unce[rtain] a Line drawn u[nder the] Name.

suddenly started to take on an entirely different character. His march took him down what Ebenezer Elmer, a New Jersey lieutenant, described as "the worst and most disagreeable swampy road that ever was." Americans led by Thaddeus Kosciuszko, a Polish engineering officer who had volunteered for service in the Continental Army, made it worse by blocking it with fallen trees and dammed streams, making it nearly impassable. American riflemen harassed the advancing army and faded into the forest. It took the British army, loaded down with heavy artillery, twenty-two days to travel just twenty miles.

"The woods here are immense," Du Roi wrote, "and a European can hardly get an idea of their extent without having seen them. They are marshy, full of underbrush and almost impassable, large trees having fallen down, barring the way." Under these conditions, "each soldier must do his best to seek cover behind a tree and advance without command . . . to which our regular troops are not accustomed. The rebels, who have been hunting in the woods from childhood on, and consequently are good shots, have, and always will have, the advantage over us." The British nonetheless had to attack, Du Roi concluded:

They came over to fight the rebels, and the rebels can always select the best places from which to defend themselves. Whenever the attack proves too serious, they retreat, and to follow them is of little value. It is impossible on account of the thick woods, to get around them . . . or to force them to fight. Never are they so much to be feared as when retreating. Covered by the woods, the number of the enemies with which we have to deal, can never be defined.

Du Roi was a proud professional soldier, and he was certain that the rebels would be defeated if confronted "on a plain, by troops arrayed in battle order according to the rules." But the Americans refused to oblige, Du Roi wrote, "knowing too well the advantages of their own way of fighting."

George Washington—who never forgot the lessons of Braddock's march into the wilderness of western Pennsylvania—believed that "Burgoyne's

Army will meet, sooner or later an effectual Check" and that his success in penetrating so far south "will precipitate his Ruin." Washington believed that by detaching troops to gather supplies, Burgoyne was pursuing a "Line of Conduct . . . most favorable to us," offering the opportunity to defeat him in detail.

To collect supplies, Burgoyne sent a detachment of about one thousand men eastward, toward the region that later became Vermont, to gather supplies in an area of scattered farms on what became the border between New York and Vermont. Militia from Vermont, New Hampshire, and Massachusetts attacked them near Bennington on August 16, 1777. Seeing the British force, their commander, General John Stark, is said to have told his men: "There are your enemies . . . we must have them in half an hour, or my wife sleeps a widow this night." Over two hundred of the British and Hessians were killed or wounded and over seven hundred captured. Only a few made it back to Burgoyne's army.

Burgoyne's expectation that loyalists in large numbers would turn out to support him proved to be a mirage. "I believe that the English have counted too much on the probability that the inhabitants of the province of New York would declare themselves for the king," Du Roi wrote, "submit to his sovereignty and even take part against the other rebellious colonists." Plain as this appeared to a Hessian observer, it was never clear to Burgoyne or to the generals who later devised plans for subduing the colonies, most of which depended on the support of loyalists.

The Indians proved to be an enormous liability for Burgoyne. By "marauding and cruelties," Du Roi wrote, the Indians had forced many farmers to seek shelter behind rebel lines, often taking the livestock with them. "It did not make any difference to the Indians, if they attacked a subject loyal to the king, or one friendly to the rebels; they set fire to all their homes, took away everything . . . It would certainly have been better, if we had not had any Indians with us." Despite Burgoyne's injunctions, the Indians killed women and children, leading men who might have stayed out of the fighting to join the American forces.

Burgoyne's army hacked its way through forests and swamps between Fort Anne and Fort Edward to reach the Hudson River (The Society of the Cincinnati).

Among the dead was Jane McCrea, a young woman engaged to be married to a loyalist officer serving with Burgoyne and whose brothers were serving with the American troops. She was killed and scalped by an Indian serving with the British. Word of her murder inflamed the region, discouraging loyalists who believed their families were safe and driving others to join the American forces.

The small British army that was supposed to march down the Mohawk Valley to meet Burgoyne near Albany did not get far before being forced to turn back. No help came from the British in New York City either. General Howe spent the summer and early fall maneuvering to take Philadelphia and left a force under General Sir Henry Clinton to move up the Hudson to support Burgoyne. Clinton started late. He captured two American forts along the Hudson but never reached Burgoyne, who had to face the American forces on his own.

Saratoga

By the time Burgoyne's army reached the Hudson and began moving south toward Albany, autumn was approaching. Ever a gambler, Burgoyne decided to forge ahead and make his winter quarters in Albany, where, in due course, he expected to be supplied from New York City. The alternative was to retreat to Fort Ticonderoga and renew his campaign in the spring. He remained confident in defeating the American forces gathered to block his advance, but he did not know that as he had inched his way south the forces gathered to oppose him had grown considerably.

Schuyler stationed his troops near Stillwater, beside the Hudson a few miles south of his own Saratoga estate. Burgoyne's troops destroyed Schuyler's house and mills as he approached. Schuyler's army was plagued by desertion and illness, but he explained to Washington that "if we by any Means could be put in a Situation of attacking the Enemy and giving them a Repulse, their Retreat would be so extremely difficult that in all probability, they would lose the greater part of their Army."

Schuyler was not to command that attack. Congress, frightened by the evacuation of Ticonderoga and worried that Schuyler would lose Albany without a fight, relieved him and turned

the Northern Army over to Horatio Gates, who had spent weeks in Philadelphia criticizing Schuyler and angling for the command. "We shall never defend a Post, untill We shoot a General," John Adams wrote to Abigail. Losing his command was humiliating to Schuyler, but he remained to offer whatever assistance he could as the armies prepared for battle on his own home ground. The American army grew to some fifteen thousand men and included soldiers sent by George Washington and men gathered from all over New York and western New England. Washington sent some of his best

In contrast to the fine uniforms worn by General Gates and most of his senior officers in John Trumbull's *Surrender of General Burgoyne at Saratoga*, a Brunswick officer wrote that "not one" American enlisted man "was properly uniformed but each man had on the clothes in which he goes to the field, to church, or to the tavern. But they stood like soldiers, erect, with a military bearing . . . so still that we were greatly amazed" (Yale University Art Gallery).

troops to help Gates, including Daniel Morgan's Virginia riflemen.

The armies fought at a place called Freeman's Farm on September 19. The battle was a tactical victory for the British, but Burgoyne lost men he could not replace and the Americans continued to block his path toward Albany. A tactical victory did Burgoyne little good. He needed to break the American army and open the road south. The fate of the campaign he had drawn up with such confidence on a map in London came down to winning a battle against an American army with twice his numbers, deep in hostile country, on the ground of his enemy's choosing—a hilly region that favored defense. He had to do it without the support of his Indian allies, who had abandoned him, or the loyalists, who had never turned out in sufficient numbers to make any difference at all. He had to do it without help from the direction of New York City.

Time had become his enemy. Burgoyne lost precious days waiting for some news that the British were pressing north from New York City to come to his aid, but heard nothing. General

Riedesel, who commanded Burgoyne's German mercenaries, advised retreat. Burgoyne decided to make a reconnaissance in force on October 7 to test the American lines on Bemis Heights, but it was too little, too late. His men were repulsed. General Simon Fraser, one of Burgoyne chief lieutenants, was killed by an American rifleman, and the British army was forced to retreat to its fortified lines, pursued by Americans led by Benedict Arnold. Samuel Woodruff, a Connecticut private, later said that Arnold "behaved more like a madman than a cool and discreet officer." Arnold was badly wounded. The British managed to hold their ground, but Americans took the Hessian redoubt on the British right flank, forcing Burgoyne to retreat to a defensive position a short distance up the Hudson. Over the next few days the Americans surrounded Burgoyne's army. Outnumbered, burdened by hundreds of wounded men, and running out of supplies, Burgoyne had no choice. He surrendered his army, with its forty-two cannons and over seven thousand muskets, on October 17, 1777.

Lafayette

While Burgoyne was moving slowly south down the Hudson toward defeat, George Washington and most of his army kept watch on the main British army under General Howe, which remained in New York City through the summer. Howe's inactivity puzzled Washington. Then in August, most of Howe's army boarded ships in New York Harbor and sailed off. Washington did not know where they were going. Suspecting that Howe was going to attack Virginia or sail up the Delaware River to attack Philadelphia, Washington moved the army to eastern Pennsylvania.

While Washington was waiting to see where Howe was going, a young French aristocrat arrived at his headquarters. His name was Marie Joseph Paul Yves Roch Gilbert du Motier, marquis de Lafayette. His family called him Gilbert. Others called him Lafayette. Orphaned at twelve, he was the heir to a substantial fortune. Like many young French aristocrats, he entered the army and by eighteen was promoted to captain.

In some respects, eighteenth-century France was a vast armed camp. France maintained the largest standing army in Europe. The military consumed an enormous share of the nation's wealth, and the largest part of the taxes collected in France was devoted to it. Achievement in arms was the chief source of social distinction for the aristocracy, which monopolized the officer corps—young men who sought commissions had to demonstrate their aristocratic lineage. Glory in war was their ideal, and advancement in rank and prestige their constant aim.

Soon after his promotion to captain, Lafayette decided to volunteer for service with the Continental Army. Such a thing would be unthinkable today, but in the eighteenth century army officers volunteered their services to other nations at war in order to gain practical experience. Formal military education was then in its infancy and extended no further than engineering and artillery, the military arts that required the most technical training. Service in foreign wars offered opportunities for glory as well as experience. In the first years of the Revolutionary War, a steady stream of French army officers presented themselves to American diplomats in Paris seeking promises of high rank and generous pay to fight with the rebel army against Britain. Most of them were indifferent to the American cause.

Lafayette was different. He told Silas Deane, then in Paris, that he wanted only to advance the cause of freedom and asked to be allowed to serve at his own expense. Deane promised Lafayette a general's commission and assured the wealthy marquis a warm welcome from Congress. Lafayette's father-in-law appealed to the king to forbid Lafayette to leave, but Lafayette used a bit of his vast wealth to purchase a ship and slipped away. Congress voted to make him a major general, although the members—having learned from Deane that the king expected Lafayette to return home immediately—may have considered the appointment an honorary one.

Lafayette did not. He immediately presented himself to Washington and offered to serve in any capacity Washington wished. At nineteen, he remains the youngest major general in our nation's history. Washington was probably dismayed that Congress had made the young man a major gen-

Sculptor Samuel A. Murray captured Lafayette's energy and aristocratic bearing in this model for a statue honoring the youngest major general in American history (The Society of the Cincinnati).

eral, but he soon embraced Lafayette like a son and offered him command of a division. Lafayette accepted and asked for one, he said, "composed entirely of Virginians," to honor Washington. Like Washington, he served without pay. He also paid his staff, replaced the uniforms of his ragged soldiers, and bought food and supplies for his men. By the end of the war Lafayette had spent nearly $250,000 of his own money. He never complained about it, insisting that the world must have "a people who are entirely free." He became, in time, one of the most celebrated heroes of the American Revolution. When he toured America in 1824–1825 he was greeted everywhere with wild enthusiasm. He outlived every other general of the war. An American flag stands over his grave in Paris.

Other enthusiastic French volunteers, among them Louis Duportail, a military engineer, brought special skills and experience to the Continental Army. Two of the most distinguished foreign volunteers were Thaddeus Kosciuszko, a military engineer, and Casimir Pulaski, a cavalry officer. Both were from Poland. Kosciuszko—who had commanded men who slowed Burgoyne's march southward—was as devoted to freedom as Lafayette and later led a revolution in his native country. Thomas Jefferson called him "as pure a son of liberty as I have ever known."

Brandywine and Germantown

Reluctant to sail up the Delaware River and face the American forts guarding the river a few miles below Philadelphia, Howe sailed south to the Virginia Capes, entered the Chesapeake Bay, and landed his army in northern reaches of the bay, intending to march overland to take Philadelphia from the south or west. Washington moved south and barred Howe's way at Brandywine Creek, close to the border between Pennsylvania and Delaware.

Washington was anxious—perhaps too anxious—to cross the creek and attack the enemy as he approached. On the morning of September 11, 1777, Washington sent William Maxwell's brigade across Brandywine Creek to engage the leading elements of Howe's army under Hessian General Knyphausen. The Americans managed to push Knyphausen back, acquitting themselves well. What

was not evident, mainly because the Continental Army lacked adequate cavalry to scout the enemies positions, was that the main body of Howe's army had moved upstream and crossed the creek miles above the scene of the early fighting, heading to the right flank and rear of Washington's army.

Washington grasped what was happening in time to turn his right flank to meet Howe's advancing army and move other troops to resist them. The battle was joined near the Birmingham Friends Meeting House, a Quaker meeting house in the rear of Washington's original line along the creek. The British resorted to a bayonet charge to dislodge Washington's men, who fought stubbornly before withdrawing from the battlefield. Washington had been outgeneraled, but his men had not been outfought.

Howe marched northwest and after two weeks of maneuver captured Philadelphia without a fight. Congress, anticipating the loss of the city, had already packed up and moved to Lancaster. On October 4 Washington made a surprise attack on Howe's camp at Germantown, just outside Philadelphia. The British repulsed Washington's army after fierce fighting. The Battle of Germantown, though another defeat for Washington's army, proved that the Americans still possessed the will to fight. Howe had captured the largest city in the United States, but he had not broken the spirit of Washington's army.

The American defeat at Germantown was as important, in one way, as the American victories at Trenton and Princeton of a year earlier. It discouraged Howe from attacking the Continental Army once it had established a fortified winter camp at Valley Forge, in the hills west of Philadelphia. Having achieved his immediate aim, Howe settled in for the winter himself. It only gradually occurred to him and to the rest of the British high command that according to the strange logic of this war, capturing Philadelphia—the largest city in British North America and the capital of the rebellion—meant almost nothing. The supplies that had flowed to the American army through the city simply flowed to Washington's men through other channels. Philadelphia was no more essential to the American cause than New York City.

Washington's winter camp at Valley Forge, in a hilly region west of Philadelphia, was easily defended against attack but close enough to the city to keep watch over the British. The army remained there for more than six months. Washington used the time to train his army, taking advantage of the knowledge of a European volunteer named Friedrich von Steuben, a veteran of the celebrated Prussian army of Frederick the Great. Steuben took over the task of teaching American soldiers to march and fight like the most disciplined armies of Europe. It was a challenging job. John Laurens, a young South Carolina officer, wrote to his father that Steuben "appears to be a man profound in the Science of war" who "seems to understand what our Soldiers are capable of." He would "not give us perfect instructions absolutely speaking, but the best which we are in condition to receive." As the months passed Steuben gradually trained the men of the Continental Army to march and fight as well as the British.

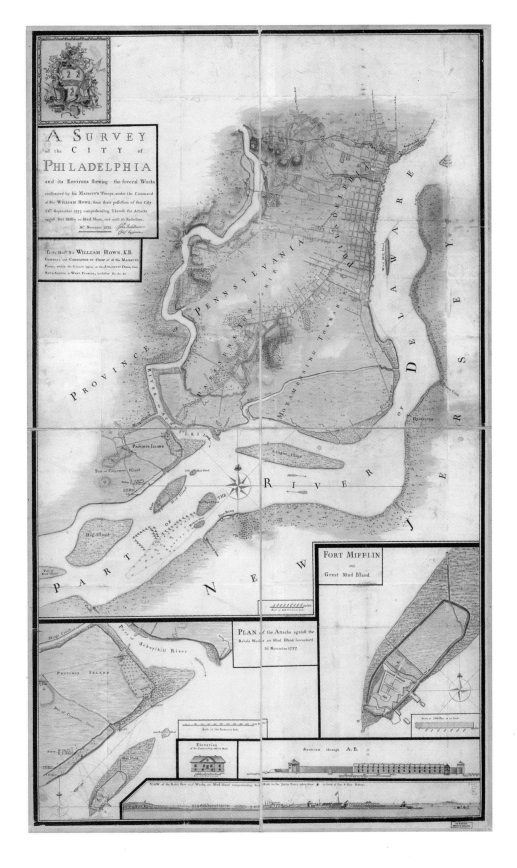

After taking Philadelphia, depicted in this map by John Montrésor, Howe's chief engineer, the British turned on the American forts blocking British vessels from reaching the army with supplies. Howe sent 1,200 Hessians to attack Fort Mercer on Red Bank on October 22. Some 400 American defenders, including a large number of African American soldiers, repulsed the attack, inflicting the heaviest losses sustained by the British army in battle since Bunker Hill (Library of Congress).

Louis XVI succeeded his grandfather Louis XV as king of France in 1774, when he was twenty years old. Antoine-François Callet painted this larger-than-life portrait of the king in 1779. Callet and his assistants painted twelve copies for the king to present as diplomatic gifts and to symbolize his authority in the residences of French ambassadors abroad (Château de Versailles, © RMN-Grand Palais / Art Resource, NY).

Chapter 15 The French Alliance

The outcome of the campaigns of 1777 might have led the British government to conclude that persisting in the war was folly. Burgoyne's humiliating surrender and Howe's failure to destroy Washington's army—despite taking Philadelphia—led the king's ministers to question whether the war could be won. Lord North was plagued by doubts. "I am very melancholy notwithstanding our victory," he wrote when he received the news of Brandywine, adding that the "best use we can make of it is to get out of this dispute as soon as possible." Lord George Germain, the secretary of state for the American department and one of the architects of British strategy, concluded that conquering the colonies was impossible. He suggested a strategy of naval blockade and coastal raids to wear down Americans' will to fight. Lord North offered to resign, admitting that his government had failed and urging the king to appoint a new prime minister. The king refused to accept North's resignation. He was determined to continue the war.

Parliament authorized more than thirteen million pounds in additional military spending. Most of that money was consumed shipping food and basic supplies to the army in America. Each year the war continued, every British Regular and Hessian mercenary consumed one-third of a ton of food and supplies. After losing New York and Philadelphia, Washington retreated into the interior, where he drew his supplies from the hinterland while denying the British the same sources of food and forage. Washington's patrols barred the British from gathering provisions in the countryside. Most of the supplies the British army required—food for men and horses, as well as powder, shot, and equipment of every description—had to be brought from bases in Nova Scotia, Ireland, and England. Providing those supplies consumed nearly all of the thirteen million pounds—about thirteen percent of Britain's national revenue—every year the war continued.

Britain could not sustain that level of spending indefinitely, but it might be able to sustain it longer than the Americans could keep armies in the field. War weariness had begun to take a toll on Americans by the end of 1777. Recruiting had slowed. Routine trade was disrupted. Imported goods had become scarce or disappeared from the market. Prices were rising as a consequence of real scarcity and the reliance of Congress and the states on paper money which declined in value as soon as it was issued.

A strategy based on blockading American ports, intercepting American shipping, preventing supplies from reaching American armies, and raiding American ports, British ministers reasoned, might win the war and restore the colonies to the British Empire, though how long that might take was not clear to them. They persisted in order to preserve the empire, without calculating the ultimate cost of victory, if indeed victory could be won. Preserving the empire, they were convinced, was essential to national greatness.

During the imperial crisis that preceded the war, Americans had contended for independence *within* the British Empire. They had since concluded that the liberty they sought and the natural and civil rights they claimed required independence *from* the British Empire and indeed independence from the whole imperial system that dominated the Atlantic world at the end of the eighteenth century and was rapidly spreading around the globe. That imperial system, which reached its height in the late nineteenth century before disintegrating in the twentieth century, no longer dominates the world, though many nations bear deep scars from it. As a consequence the extraordinary implications of America's rejection of empire are not as clear as they once were. In the eighteenth century, the great powers were either imperial powers or had imperial ambitions, and other states were mostly clients of, or somehow dependent on, one of the

With a regular army of over two hundred thousand men, led by aristocratic officers for whom glory in war was a path to social distinction and recognition, France was the most formidable military power in Europe in the 1770s (Château de Versailles, © RMN-Grand Palais / Art Resource, NY).

imperial powers. Independence from the imperial system was unusual and difficult to maintain.

To achieve independence *from* empire, Revolutionary leaders concluded that they needed the military support of France—Britain's chief imperial rival. Their bid to secure it, and then to benefit from it, and ultimately to detach from it, was fundamental to the achievement of independence.

Empire and Revolution

The European empires of the eighteenth century secured wealth for kings and their favored subjects by monopolizing trade with their colonies. To do so, they exercised dominion—control of people and the land those people occupied—to compel compliance with the regulations they imposed. They maintained dominion over their colonial

subjects by appealing to their interests—usually the interests of the wealthiest among them—and by force or threats of force. They employed these tactics in dealing with indigenous peoples as well as migrants, whether in America or Ireland, Africa or India.

None of the imperial governments ever properly calculated the costs of maintaining dominion because eighteenth-century governments did not possess the data to do so. In the absence of hard facts, governments depended on instinct and guesswork and made decisions based on ideas of national honor that were shaped more by dynastic rivalries and religious prejudices than by rational assessments of national interest. Despite mounting evidence to the contrary, they were convinced that the productive capacity of the world was fixed, and that a steady income could be extracted from each part of it, much as a landed estate in Britain or France could be expected to produce a certain steady annual income in rents. Empires were conceived in much the same way, and indeed the British Empire was sometimes referred to as the national estate.

Only the most advanced thinkers, like Adam Smith, whose *Inquiry into the Nature and Origins of the Wealth of Nations* was published in 1776, recognized that dominion was not the basis of national wealth. Smith devoted the last pages of the book to arguing that the war in America was adverse to Britain's interest. It would be cheaper, Smith wrote, to acknowledge American independence and for Britain to trade with the new nation on equitable terms, dominating the American import market as it had always done and reaping all the profits of colonial trade with none of the expenses of dominion.

The British Empire in North America had always been chaotic and disorganized, consisting of colonies established by corporate charters, proprietary grants, and royal initiatives, but it was a source of wealth for Britain that, before the imperial crisis that preceded the war, cost Britain little to maintain. Benjamin Franklin had made this point in testimony given to the House of Commons in 1766. "Numerous as the people are in the several old provinces," he explained, "they cost you nothing in forts, citadels, garrisons or armies, to keep them in subjection. They were governed by this country at the expence only of a little pen, ink, and paper. They were led by a thread."

Franklin was right with regard to the cost of maintaining the subjection of the colonists—although they were occasionally unruly and avoided imperial regulations when doing so was in their interest—but the price of dominion included the growing costs of the military establishment required to preserve and extend the royal domain in a world increasingly dominated by predatory imperial powers. For Britain, that was the cost of maintaining the world's largest and most powerful navy, capable of establishing control of the sea lanes between Britain and its colonies while also defending the British homeland from invasion.

Although France had lost much of its overseas empire in the French and Indian War, its leaders were equally committed to empire. They were anxious to acquire new overseas possessions and to limit the size of Britain's empire and the wealth

it provided to the British Crown. France invested heavily in its navy in the years after the French and Indian War with the intention of challenging Britain's naval dominance, depriving Britain of colonies, and limiting the income Britain secured from its empire.

Despite the mounting costs of dominion, the European empires were extending their reach in the last half of the eighteenth century. Britain and France competed for dominion in India, and in the years following the Revolutionary War in America, Britain extended its influence over large parts of the Indian subcontinent. The American Revolution took place during a period of expanding imperial horizons and ambitions. A few weeks after the Boston Massacre, Captain James Cook, a British explorer, reached the east coast of Australia, which he claimed for the Crown. Imperial dominion was expanding even as Americans fought to overthrow it.

The American Revolution, with its demands for local independence and autonomy, popular sovereignty, and universal liberty, challenged the European imperial system. Two hundred and fifty years later, it is clear that the American Revolution was the beginning of a revolution in world affairs, in which imperial dominion would disintegrate as more and more of the world's peoples demanded and secured their independence and assumed a separate and equal station among the powers of the Earth. The United States was the first nation in modern times to wage a war for independence from imperial control.

Despite wide popular support for independence, American leaders were convinced they could not achieve that goal without the support of Britain's imperial competitors. To sustain their war for independence, Americans needed muskets, cannons, and above all else, gunpowder, which they could not manufacture in sufficient quantities. France, Spain, and Holland were the only powers capable of supplying them.

The Americans also needed naval support. "Without a decisive naval force we can do nothing definitive," George Washington wrote. "And with it, everything honorable and glorious." The war could not be won as long as Britain's Royal Navy occupied major American ports, disrupted American shipping, and ensured the flow of reinforcements and supplies to British land forces.

An American navy was not the answer. Congress established the Continental Navy in 1775, but its mission was limited. Congressman Samuel Chase of Maryland called it "the maddest idea in the world" to think that the United States could challenge the Royal Navy. The warships of the Continental Navy were suited to intercepting British supply vessels, raiding isolated and lightly defended posts, and occasionally challenging small vessels of the Royal Navy, but wholly incapable of securing control of the American coast. France was the only nation capable—and under the right circumstances, that might be willing—to provide the naval support the United States needed.

Franklin in Paris

King Louis XVI of France and his ministers were imperialists with no sympathy for the aims of the American rebels and no inclination to champion natural rights, republicanism, or ideals of universal natural and civil rights, liberty, equality, or citizenship. They had no interest in American independence except that they believed that the loss of the thirteen rebellious colonies would reduce British power. As desirable as that might be to France, they regarded the American rebellion with skepticism.

Persuading the king's government was the task of Benjamin Franklin, who arrived in France in December 1776. Franklin was well known in France as a man of science. King Louis XV had personally endorsed the publication of Franklin's work on electricity in 1752 and written to Franklin congratulating him on his discoveries. European philosophers and scientists regarded Franklin as one of their own. In 1772 he had been elected to the French Royal Academy of Science, one of only eight foreigners ever so honored. European diplomats thought of Franklin as a fellow diplomat. During his last years in London, before the war, Franklin had been regarded as the unofficial representative of Britain's American colonies in Europe.

Franklin was celebrated from the moment he arrived in France. Frenchmen concerned about corruption and materialism in their own country imagined America as a land of virtue and simplicity. They saw Franklin as a symbol of all they imagined and admired about America. He arrived wearing a fur cap for warmth, a pair of spectacles, and modest clothes, and found that this plain, practical dress commanded attention and respect. In a country where men of means dressed in fine clothes and wore wigs or had their own hair dressed with powder and tied with ribbon, Franklin appeared in a simple suit, with what was left of his hair in its natural state, even when he was presented to the king. An aristocratic admirer provided Franklin with an elegant house in a Paris suburb where Franklin entertained a constant stream of visitors. Crowds followed him when he went out, and artists competed to paint his portrait, carve his likeness in stone, or cast it in bronze. Prints of Franklin were suddenly everywhere in Paris, and his face appeared on handkerchiefs, snuffboxes, clocks, dishes, and souvenirs of every kind.

Franklin exploited his celebrity to keep the American cause before the king's government. The king was willing to provide the American rebels with gunpowder and surplus muskets and cannons as long as it was done quietly, but he had no interest in supporting an effort to overthrow a fellow monarch, even a British one. The queen, Marie Antoinette, was outspoken in her contempt for the American rebels. The French foreign minister, the comte de Vergennes, on the other hand, supported an alliance with the United States under circumstances that clearly favored France, which meant circumstances in which French intervention would embarrass Britain, create a balance of power in Europe, and diminish the wealth Britain derived from its empire. Franklin bided his time until the circumstances were right.

"A little revenge"

That moment came on December 4, 1777, when a detailed report of Burgoyne's surrender and of the Battle of Germantown reached Paris. For weeks, British sources had been reporting that the Americans had run from Burgoyne or that their army had surrendered to him. The report from America contradicted those claims. Americans had not fled from Burgoyne—they had trapped him and forced him to surrender. As for Howe, he had taken Philadelphia but not the American forts controlling the lower Delaware River, up which his

The king's foreign minister, the comte de Vergennes, was more concerned with establishing a balance of power in Europe than in reclaiming national honor in a war of revenge against Britain. Restrained in his goals and more farsighted than many of his contemporaries, Vergennes nonetheless imagined the United States as a client of France and failed to control the crippling expenses of a global naval war with Britain (Château de Versailles, © RMN-Grand Palais / Art Resource, NY).

Celebrating American independence, this French print from 1778 depicts America—represented as an Indian woman—kneeling before Libertas, the goddess of liberty, identified by her rod with a pileus, or liberty cap. On the left are Mercury, god of commerce, and Ceres, goddess of agriculture. Minerva, goddess of wisdom and war, is at center with her spear poised. At right, Courage, his helmet decorated with the Gallic rooster—a symbol of France—attacks a crowned figure holding a chain, representing Britain. Behind Courage, the allegorical figure Prudentia—a female representing prudence and the application of principle—stands beside the robed figure of Benjamin Franklin, who uses a ceremonial rod called a vindicta to free America (The Society of the Cincinnati).

supplies would have to be brought. Like Burgoyne, he was cut off and might be forced to surrender as well. At that moment the loss of Philadelphia did not appear to endanger the American cause any more than the loss of Ticonderoga. Franklin summarized the situation in his typically witty way: Philadelphia had captured Howe. John Adams wrote that the Battle of Germantown had "more Influence upon the European Mind than that of Saratoga—altho the Attempt was unsuccessfull, the military Gentlemen in Europe considerd it, as the most decisive Proof that America would finally succeed." Vergennes commented that Howe's surrender "seems very possible."

On December 6, Conrad-Alexandre Gérard, first secretary to the Council of State and Vergenne's deputy, called Franklin to a meeting at Versailles. He said that recent developments demonstrated the ability of the American states to maintain their independence, and invited Franklin to renew his "former proposition of an alliance," which would be looked on with favor. For months, Franklin had been working to convince Vergennes that Americans were worthy allies who would fight until they won their independence. Vergennes was suddenly worried that he had waited too long, and that Americans were about to win their independence before France could join the war and share in the victory. Within weeks, Vergennes agreed that France would recognize the independence of the United States and join the war as an ally of the United States.

On February 6, 1778, the three American diplomats in Paris—Franklin, Silas Deane, and Arthur Lee—signed a Treaty of Amity and Commerce, in which France recognized the United States as a sovereign nation and the two nations agreed to establish close commercial ties. France opened several ports in France and the West Indies to American merchants. They also signed a Treaty of Alliance, which provided that the United States and France would make war and peace together in the event war broke out between Britain and France. In the event of such a war—which was a certainty, given French recognition of American independence—the parties agreed that British acknowledgment of American independence would be a condition of peace. Gérard signed the treaties on behalf of the king. Franklin wore a rust red velvet coat to the ceremony, somewhat old and worn. When Deane asked him why he wore it, Franklin replied "a little revenge," adding "I wore this coat on the day Widderburn abused me at Whitehall." Congress ratified the two treaties in May. Relations between Britain and France deteriorated quickly, and the two nations were at war by the end of June.

Whether the United States could have prevailed in the Revolutionary War without the intervention of France has been a subject of debate for more than two hundred years. Many American leaders, including Franklin, Patrick Henry, Samuel Adams, and most important of all, George Washington, did not think so. They recognized that playing the imperial ambitions of France against those of Britain involved risks, including the risk that the United States might become a minor state dominated by France and dependent on it. They weighed those risks and took them.

The Carlisle Commission

The British government was not prepared for a war with France and used informal channels to sound Franklin out about the possibility of a negotiated peace. George III met with James Hutton, one of Franklin's many British friends, who visited Franklin in Paris early in January 1778. Hutton wrote to Franklin at the end of the month, assuring him that any resolution of the conflict "short of absolute Independency" would be considered in London and asking for a "hint of anything practicable." Knowing that his reply would reach Lord North, and probably the king, Franklin unleashed his disdain:

You have lost by this mad War, and the Barbarity with which it has been carried on, not only the Government and Commerce of America, and the publick Revenues and private Wealth arising from that Commerce; but what is more, you have lost the Esteem, Respect, Friendship and Affection of all that great and growing People, who consider you at present, and whose Posterity will consider you as the worst and wickedest Nation upon Earth.

Franklin added that "a Peace you may undoubtedly obtain, by dropping all your Pretensions to govern us," and by offering Americans compensation for Britain's "bullying and barbarity." Franklin suggested Britain turn over Canada, Nova Scotia, and East and West Florida as compensation for the "needless and cruel" conduct of the British army and navy since the war began.

Lord North was prepared to accept almost any peace that would preserve the king's formal role as sovereign, even if that meant conceding that the colonies had the right to govern themselves. Peace commissioners, including General Howe and his brother, Admiral Lord Howe, two former colonial governors, and the young earl of Carlisle were appointed and instructed to meet with any individual or government in the colonies willing to discuss peace. The commissioners were even authorized to "admit of any claim or title to independency" during their talks as long as the Americans would consider reconciliation. As a sign of good faith, Parliament repealed the tax on tea and the Massachusetts Government Act. The Americans might even continue under their Articles of Confederation as long as they would acknowledge George III as their king.

What the British government was willing to discuss in the spring of 1778 was nothing less than independence within the empire, which is what all but the most radical American leaders had demanded before the war. The Carlisle Commission was authorized to offer America much the same status that would be afforded to Canada by the British North America Act, passed by Parlia-

Not yet thirty when appointed to lead the peace commission, Frederick Howard, earl of Carlisle, faced an impossible task. After the commission cast aspersions on the motives of France, Carlisle wisely declined Lafayette's challenge to a duel (Museum of the Shenandoah Valley).

ment in 1867, which made Canada a self-governing dominion within the British Empire.

That the First Continental Congress would have accepted that offer in 1774 cannot be doubted, but much had happened since to make reconciliation impossible. Henry Laurens, the president of Congress, suggested that the proposals, if not the commissioners, should be returned "decently tarred and feathered." Washington responded with cold bitterness of a general who had watched many men suffer and die. Reconciliation was impossible. "The injuries we have received from the British Nation," he wrote, "were so unprovoked; have been so great and so many, that they can never be forgotten." Patrick Henry wrote to Richard Henry Lee that the appointment of the commission was a sign that Britain was "baffled, defeated" and "disgraced." He urged Congress to reject British overtures, insisting that America could "find no safety" until Britain was "thoroughly purged by a revolution, which shall wipe from existence the present king with his connexions."

Congress rejected the commission's proposals, suggesting that peace talks might begin once Britain acknowledged American independence and withdrew its army and navy. The commissioners quietly let it be known that American leaders who helped restore the king's authority would be rewarded and when that failed they issued a proclamation aimed at the American people. Even Lord Carlisle saw that hope of success was ridiculous. "The common people hate us in their hearts," he wrote to his wife, "notwithstanding all that is said of their secret attachment to the mother country."

The commissioners left America in November 1778, having accomplished nothing except enraging the French officers in Washington's army by calling the alliance with France an "unnatural connection" tying Americans to "a power that has ever shewn itself an enemy to all civil and religious liberty" and intent on making America "the instruments of her ambition." Lafayette challenged Carlisle to a duel, which he proposed they fight in the sight of the British and American armies. "I have nothing very interesting to do here," he wrote to a fellow Frenchman, and "killing Lord Carlisle . . . will have a good effect in America." Carlisle declined the challenge.

Monmouth

Parliament was disappointed by the failure of the Carlisle Commission, but George III was not surprised. "Farther concession" to the Americans, he wrote to Lord North, "is a joke." Having extended an offer of reconciliation and been rebuffed, the king was determined to pursue the war to a successful conclusion. While seeking a negotiated peace with America, the British prepared for war with France.

The greatest threat was to Britain's colonies in the West Indies, all of which were exposed to attack from the sea. Defending them was more important to Britain's financial interests than prosecuting the war on the American mainland. Delay might prove fatal. The British ministry accepted

General Howe's resignation—he had lost the confidence of his officers and the government—and turned the army over to General Sir Henry Clinton, Howe's senior subordinate. The ministry ordered Clinton to abandon Philadelphia—the French navy might blockade the Delaware River and make the army difficult to supply—and return to New York City, where he was to detach several thousand men and send them to the West Indies. Clinton was to hold New York City and use it as a base from which to intercept American shipping and raid American ports. The king's ministers in London also ordered Clinton to detach troops to operate in Georgia and South Carolina. They were convinced that loyalists in the South would support the reestablishment of royal authority.

Clinton decided to return to New York by land, in a rapid retreat across New Jersey through the unsparing heat of the Middle Atlantic summer. Washington's senior subordinate, Charles Lee—he had been captured in 1776 and just recently exchanged—urged Washington to let Clinton go. But Washington seized the opportunity to strike a quick blow at Clinton's flank or rear on the march. Washington broke camp at Valley Forge and after several days of hard marching caught up with Clinton between Englishtown and Monmouth Court House, New Jersey, on June 28, 1778.

Charles Lee led the attack, but ordered his men to retreat as soon as the British counterattacked. Washington, coming forward with the rest of the army, was surprised and angry to see Lee's men coming back down the road. Corporal Joseph Plumb Martin, who witnessed the scene, later wrote that Washington seemed "in a great passion." Washington rallied Lee's men and ordered reinforcements to form a line of battle to stop the British, then rode forward a short distance to observe the enemy advance, Martin wrote, "while the shot from the British Artillery were rending up the earth all around him."

For hours the two armies struggled in the heat as the British mounted successive attacks on the American position, which the Americans repulsed with disciplined volleys and expertly managed artillery fire. Alexander Hamilton, then Washington's military secretary, said that he "had never known, or conceived, the value of discipline till that day." Thanks to months of training at Valley Forge,

Best known for *Washington Crossing the Delaware*, Emanuel Leutze painted this heroic version of Washington rallying his retreating troops at the Battle of Monmouth. Maj. Gen. Charles Lee, who ordered the retreat, slumps in his saddle at left, while the men at left reform their lines to face the advancing British (Monmouth County Historical Association).

American troops marched, deployed in line of battle, exchanged fire, adjusted their lines, and maintained order as capably as their British opponents.

During the battle, Joseph Plumb Martin remembered seeing

a woman whose husband belonged to the Artillery . . . attended with her husband at the piece the whole time; while in the act of reaching for a cartridge and having one of her feet as far before the other as she could step, a cannon shot from the enemy passed directly between her legs without doing any other damage than carrying away the lower part of her petticoat.

While Martin did not record her name, she may have been Mary Ludwig Hays, whose husband William Hays served in Proctor's Artillery. Like Margaret Corbin, who was wounded at Fort Washington, and other wives of artillerymen, Mary Hays brought water and ammunition up from the rear to serve the guns. Called Molly, she may be the basis for the story of "Molly Pitcher," said to have carried water to thirsty soldiers during the battle. Whether Hays or another woman inspired the legend of Molly Pitcher is less important than the fact that there were more heroic woman in the Revolutionary War than we will ever be able to document. There were hundreds of Molly Pitchers. The legend took shape in the middle of the nineteenth century, when the last veterans of the Revolutionary War—men and women—were passing from the scene. Stories of their heroism, real and imagined or some combination of the two, filled the emptiness they left behind.

The Battle of Monmouth ended in a tactical standoff, with the exhausted combatants facing one another. During the night the British army left the battlefield and continued its march toward New York City. Washington could claim to have won the field, but the ground had no strategic value and would have been his the next day without a fight. From a political standpoint, however, the battle was a smashing American victory. American generals mismanaged their troops at various points in the battle, but enlisted men conducted themselves with courage and skill, demonstrating that the Continental Army could fight British Regulars in the open field without the element of surprise they had enjoyed at Trenton, Princeton, and Germantown. The battle confirmed Washington's position as the preeminent American military leader.

It also seems to have intimidated Clinton, a cautious and unimaginative general less interested in achieving victory than in avoiding defeat. After Monmouth, Clinton never risked his army in a general engagement with Washington, though such a battle was the only way that the British army could win the war short of waiting the Americans out, holding on to New York City until the Americans were no longer able to keep the Continental Army in the field. With a growing minority of British leaders inclined to make peace, the prospect of success in such a prolonged war of attrition was not good. Clinton does not seem to have thought the problem out that far. Like Howe, he was confused by the unorthodox circumstances of the conflict, which seemed to defy the axioms of war.

"The french . . . left us in a most Rascally manner"

Clinton might have avoided the risk of battle by withdrawing to New York by sea, but he was concerned that a convoy might be captured by the French fleet under the command of Admiral Charles, comte d'Estaing, which was reportedly on its way to America. The French arrived off New York Bay a few days after Clinton reached the city. Admiral d'Estaing commanded twelve ships of the line and four frigates, armed with a total of 834 cannons. His fleet outgunned Admiral Howe's nine ships of the line, which lay at anchor inside the bay, by 300 guns. The Frenchman was anxious to attack but could not get his fleet across the bar at the mouth of the bay. His ships drew too much water.

After conferring with Washington, d'Estaing sailed for Newport to cooperate with American troops to take the city from the British, who had occupied it since 1776. Washington detached troops under Lafayette and Nathanael Greene, including John Glover's brigade, to support John Sullivan, whose troops had been stationed in Rhode Island since the spring. A call for militia swelled American force to ten thousand men. Admiral d'Estaing had four thousand infantry in addition to his fleet. The British had only three thousand men in Newport.

With success apparently imminent, Sullivan crossed onto Aquidneck Island—Newport is located at the southern end of the island—to lay siege to the town. Admiral d'Estaing was offended that Sullivan's command crossed to the island before his own men—they had agreed to do so on the same day. Meanwhile Admiral Howe, having been reinforced, sailed to reinforce the Newport garrison and face d'Estaing, who reembarked his troops and prepared for a naval battle. Before it took place, a storm scattered and damaged the ships of both fleets. Howe withdrew to New York to refit and d'Estaing, despite pleas from Sullivan, Greene, and Lafayette, sailed off to Boston. The admiral had found Sullivan insufferable and refused to return.

A campaign that had begun with such promise turned into a disaster. Col. Israel Angell of the Second Rhode Island Regiment (who had lost an eye at Monmouth) wrote in his diary that "the french . . . left us in a most Rascally manner." General Sullivan—a blunt New Hampshire lawyer—issued general orders "lamenting the sudden unexpected departure of the French fleet," but added "hopes the Event will prove America able to procure that by our own Arms which his Allies refuse to assist in Obtaining." The insult infuriated Lafayette. The militiamen, mostly enlisted for a few weeks, departed in droves, reducing the army to

Honor, in life and death, was a consuming ideal of the French nobility. In this allegorical portrait, the spirit of Thomas François Lenormand de Victot, a navy lieutenant who served under Admiral d'Estaing at Newport and Savannah, protects his sailors from Death. Lenormand fell ill and died in Martinique in 1782 (The Society of the Cincinnati).

between four and five thousand men, facing a British army of over six thousand.

Outnumbered and without naval support, Sullivan had little choice but to withdraw from the island. On the morning of August 29 the Americans took up on a line across the island north of Newport and met their British pursuers in a spirited defense, repulsing attacks on the two roads leading back to the mainland. As at Monmouth, American troops—regardless of the miscommunications and mistakes of their generals—performed with skill and courage. The Americans recrossed to the mainland without difficulty. Washington asked Sullivan to be conciliatory, reminding him that the French were "a people old in war, very strict in military etiquette, and apt to take fire where other are scarcely warmed." But the damage was done. Admiral d'Estaing assured his acquaintances in Boston that he bore Americans no ill will, then sailed for the Caribbean.

The allies had made a troubled start. A few weeks later, however, spirits lifted when a large cargo of uniforms arrived from France—enough to outfit most of Washington's army. Some of the coats were blue—they went to North Carolina, Maryland, New Jersey, and New York units. Those from Virginia, Delaware, Pennsylvania, and Massachusetts, and New Hampshire got brown coats. For the first time, most of the army had uniforms to wear.

Savannah

The British ministry, convinced that loyalist sentiment was strong in Georgia and South Carolina, directed General Clinton to send a force to occupy Georgia and, in due course, restore the king's authority in South Carolina. Clinton dispatched three thousand men under Lt. Col. Archibald Campbell in December 1778. Maj. Gen. Robert Howe had seven hundred Continentals and a few militia with which to oppose them. Campbell landed near Savannah, brushed Howe's force aside, and took the city, capturing over 450 men and more than seventy artillery pieces. Campbell moved inland and took Augusta at the end of

January 1779. Two weeks later, on February 14, American militia from the Carolinas and Georgia attacked and routed a party of loyalists on their way to join Campbell. The Battle of Kettle Creek was of no lasting strategic importance, but it was a forecast of the bitter fighting between patriots and loyalists that would characterize the war in the southern backcountry. A few weeks later British Regulars defeated Georgia and North Carolina troops at the Battle of Brier Creek.

The British made forays into South Carolina during the spring and summer of 1779—not in sufficient strength to take Charleston, but serious enough to alarm the governor, John Rutledge, who sent an appeal to Admiral d'Estaing for aid. The admiral, with a fleet of twenty ships of the line, thirteen other warships, and infantry transports arrived off the Georgia coast on September 8. The French joined forces with the little American army under Maj. Gen. Benjamin Lincoln, who had been sent south to replace Howe. Together they laid siege to Savannah, which the British under Gen. Augustine Prevost had enclosed within fortified lines. Estimates vary, but Prevost probably had no more than three thousand men.

French heavy artillery opened fire on October 4 and bombarded the British lines for four days. French engineers advised d'Estaing that it would probably take ten days to force a British surrender. Worried that a British fleet might arrive at any time, the admiral was not willing to wait that long, and decided to storm the British works. General Lincoln agreed. The attackers had about 4,500 men—3,500 French and the rest South Carolina and Georgia Continentals, Charleston militia, and American cavalry under Brig. Gen. Casimir Pulaski, a Polish volunteer. The attack was set for four o'clock on the morning of October 9. Unfortunately the element of surprise was lost. An American deserter told the British that the main attack would fall on the Spring Hill Redoubt, on the west side of their lines, which the British promptly reinforced.

The attack on the redoubt was led by light infantry under Col. John Laurens and the Second South Carolina Continentals, under Lt. Col. Francis Marion. Marion's men were the first to

reach the parapet and plant their colors there, but they were driven back into the ditch surrounding the redoubt. The parapet was too high to scale. Men who tried were cut down by fire from above and by crossfire from the works on either side of the redoubt. As attackers piled into the ditch, the British left the protection of the redoubt and engaged them with pistols, bayonets, pikes, swords, and fists. The fight for the redoubt lasted nearly an hour. When the attackers retreated, they left behind at least 170 dead and wounded men. The total allied casualties—over 800—constituted one fifth of the men engaged. As many as half of the men who attacked Spring Hill Redoubt were killed, wounded, or captured.

The Battle of Savannah was the most costly battle since Bunker Hill. Among the mortally wounded was General Pulaski, who had led his cavalry in a charge west of the redoubt, and Sgt. William Jasper, a courageous soldier who had exposed himself to enemy fire to replace the fallen colors at Fort Sullivan in 1776. General Lincoln wanted to resume the siege, but d'Estaing—wounded twice in the battle—refused. He embarked his men and sailed away. Lincoln retreated to South Carolina.

When he learned of the outcome of the siege, the severe casualties inflicted on the French and American troops, and d'Estaing's abandonment of his American allies, British General Clinton did not disguise his pleasure, writing "I think that this is the greatest event that has happened the whole war." Equally delighted, George III ordered cannons fired at the Tower of London and St. James Park—the first time cannon had been fired in London to celebrate victory since the end of the French and Indian War.

"I have not yet begun to fight!"

The French alliance turned the American Revolutionary War into a global war for empire. Unsuccessful at Newport and Savannah, the French navy took the island colonies of Dominica, St. Vincent, and Grenada from the British and threatened the even more valuable British colonies of Barbados

Admiral d'Estaing's chief engineer drew this richly detailed map shortly after the Siege of Savannah. The French began siege works from which they bombarded the British lines without effect. D'Estaing then abandoned siege tactics and organized a disastrous frontal assault on the Spring Hill Redoubt (The John Carter Brown Library).

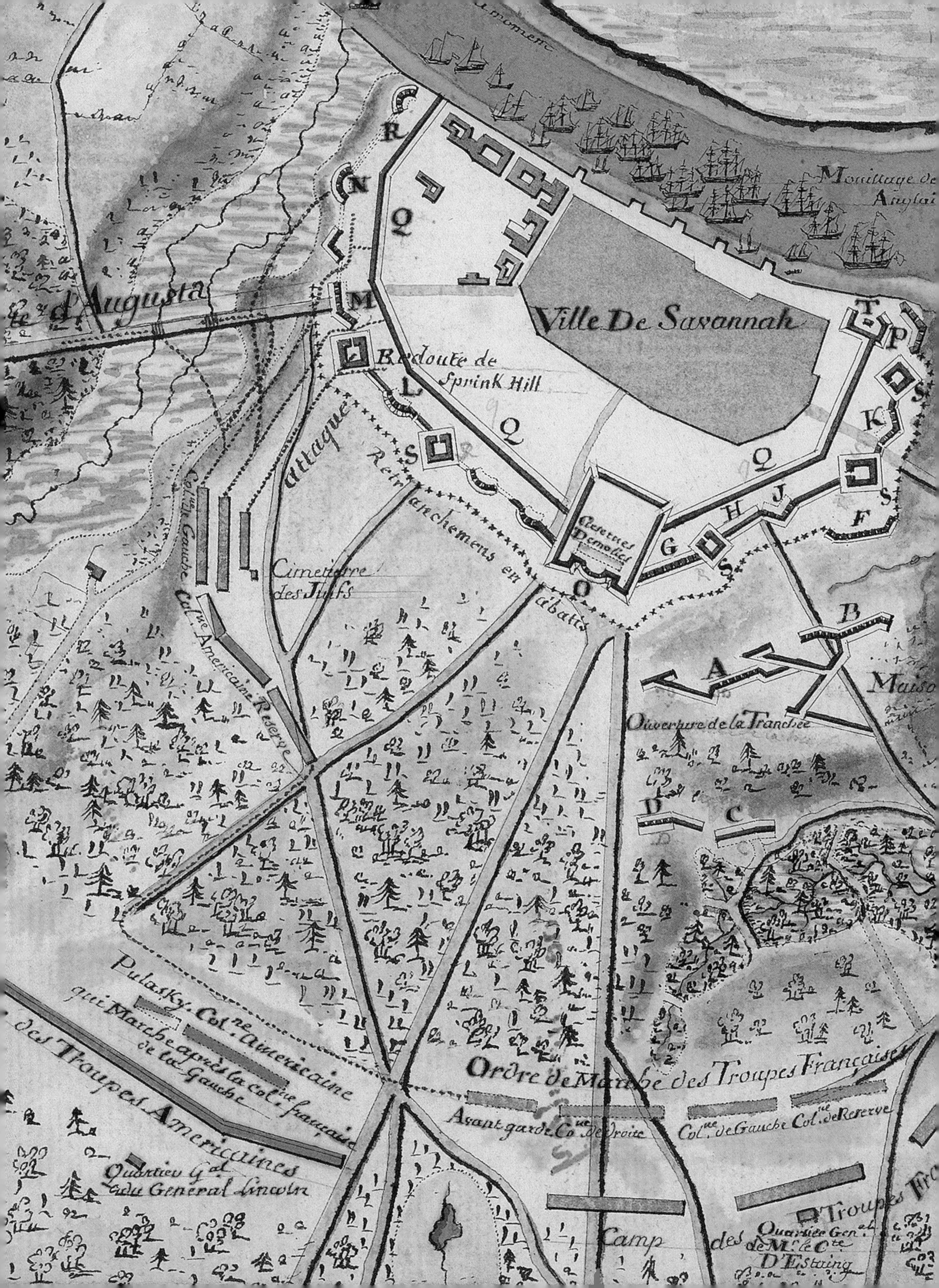

d'Augusta
Ville De Savannah
Mouillage de
Anglai
Redoute de
Sprink Hill
attaque
Retranchemens en abatis
Casernes Demolies
Cimetierre
des Juifs
Col.ne de Gauche
Col.ne Americaine Reserve
Ouverture de la Tranchee
Maiso
Pulasky Col.ne Americaine
qui Marche après la Col.ne française
de la Gauche
des Troupes Americaines
Quartier G.al
du General Lincoln
Ordre de Marche des Troupes Françaises
Avant garde Col.ne De Droite
Col.ne de Gauche Col.ne de Reserve
Camp des Troupes Fr
Quartier Gen.al
de M.r C.te
D'Estaing
R
N
Q
M
L
S
O
G
H
J
F
K
P
T
A
B
C
D

and Jamaica. Depriving Britain of its empire in the West Indies was far more important to the French government than securing American independence, to the mounting frustration of American officials.

On the other hand, protecting its far-flung possessions was far more important to the British government than suppressing the American rebellion. French and British fleets clashed from the English Channel to the Caribbean to the Bay of Bengal in an imperial war that drew British strength and attention away from North America. When Spain joined the war in 1779—as an ally of France but not of the United States—Britain diverted resources to the defense of Gibraltar, the fortress at the entrance to the Mediterranean Sea it had held since 1713. Heedless of expense, the British successfully defended Gibraltar in a siege that went on for more than three and a half years, consuming resources that might have been devoted to North America. Together France and Spain threatened to invade England, forcing the British to keep the powerful warships of the Channel Fleet in home waters. Determined to protect the rest of its empire, the British failed to recover its lost colonies in North America. Honor, as much as any rational calculation of cost, shaped their conduct.

The extent to which honor shaped the thinking of the combatants is illustrated by one of the most dramatic incidents of the war. The French alliance opened French ports to American privateers and warships of the Continental Navy, making it possible for Americans to carry their war for independence to British waters. In early 1779, the French government presented John Paul Jones, a Continental Navy captain, with an old French merchant ship that had been converted to a forty-two-gun man of war.

The witty proverbs Benjamin Franklin had published decades before in *Poor Richard's Almanac* were making the rounds in France ("Early to bed, and early to rise, makes a man healthy, wealthy and wise" and "There are no gains, without pains" are two of the many still repeated today). Jones named the ship *Bonhomme Richard* in Franklin's honor. Jones may have also meant it as a friendly jab at the elderly Franklin. The old ship was well past its prime—rotten, leaky, and armed with cast-off French guns of poor quality.

Determined to cover himself in glory, Jones sailed *Bonhomme Richard* around the British Isles in the summer of 1779, capturing sixteen ships. On September 23, while sailing near the English coast, Jones sighted a convoy of cargo ships homeward bound from the Baltic Sea. Sinking and capturing them would have been a major accomplishment, but they were guarded by a new fifty-gun warship, HMS *Serapis,* commanded by Capt. Richard Pearson, which broke off from the convoy to engage the enemy.

The battle was joined as night fell. The two ships opened fire almost simultaneously. Two of the old cannons on the *Richard* blew up, and careful fire from *Serapis* quickly put most of the other American guns out of service. When the two ships were near one another, Pearson called out, asking whether Jones had surrendered. The American captain is said to have responded "I have not yet begun to fight!"

Jones concluded that close action was his only hope of victory over *Serapis,* which was superior to *Bonhomme Richard* in every respect. Jones grappled with the enemy, while sweeping the British deck clear with musket fire and grenades. Below decks, cannon fire from *Serapis* blasted *Bonhomme Richard's* hull to splinters and the ship began to take on water. The British attempted to board *Bonhomme Richard,* but small arms fire from Americans in the rigging and a counterattack drove them back below. An explosion—perhaps caused by a grenade—set off a series of explosions on the lower gun deck of *Serapis* and sealed its fate. With both vessels on fire, Pearson surrendered. Hundreds of spectators watched the battle from nearby cliffs. The ships moved off together, and the next morning, *Bonhomme Richard* sank. Jones sailed the crippled *Serapis* into a Dutch harbor, where he became an instant celebrity.

The battle was of no great military importance. After the convoy escaped, Pearson might have detached and saved his ship, but rational calculations of that kind did not govern. The contest, though fought with cannons, muskets, pistols, and grenades, was much more like duel between knights than a battle between modern warships. Honor was the prize. Jones won the duel and became the toast of Paris. He was decorated

This British engraving of the savage night battle between HMS *Serapis*, commanded by Richard Pearson, and *Bonhomme Richard*, commanded by John Paul Jones, is one of the few wartime prints to depict a warship of the Continental Navy in action (The Society of the Cincinnati).

by Louis XVI. Jean-Antoine Houdon, the greatest sculptor of the age, carved a marble bust of Jones, whose portrait, like that of Franklin, was suddenly everywhere. Pearson—released in Holland—returned to Britain where he was showered with praise for saving the convoy. Despite losing a valuable warship, he was knighted by George III. "Let me fight him again," Jones said when he heard. "I will make him a Lord!"

The story of Jones and Pearson is a reminder that the Revolutionary War, though it was fought with explosives and spanned the globe, was a premodern conflict, shaped by ideas about personal and national honor and fought by people who idolized courage. To win their independence, Americans needed a great deal of the kind of courage Jones displayed. Such courage made Jones an enduring symbol of daring and determination.

Cooperation between Washington and the comte de Rochambeau, who commanded the French army sent to America in 1780, resulted in the allied victory at Yorktown in October 1781 (Château de Versailles, © RMN-Grand Palais / Art Resource, NY).

Chapter 16 Obstinate and Bloody

The United States was the first nation in modern times to achieve its independence in a war of national liberation. The Revolution was not merely the defining event in the nation's political and constitutional history—a moment in which political theory was harnessed to political practice to establish the first constitutional republic in human history. We remember the political and constitutional achievements of the American Revolution but forget that they were built on a foundation of sacrifice and suffering. We celebrate the Declaration of Independence as if its adoption created our nation, when in fact, our nation was born out of war that went on for eight long years.

Today the Revolutionary War seems small—its battles mere skirmishes compared to the great battles of later wars, its death toll paltry, its suffering minor, its sacrifices modest. We are easily deceived by the war's scale. It was, until the foreign wars of modern times, the longest war in American history. It touched every part of the new nation, from Maine to Florida, and westward to the Mississippi. It touched every community and brought sorrow and loss to many thousands of families. In proportion to the population, it took the lives of more Americans than any other war in our history except the Civil War, a war in which the losses of both sides must be counted. The Revolutionary War was itself a civil war that set brother against brother and degenerated into a partisan war between loyalists and patriots. It was a traumatic event punctuated by episodes of extraordinary courage and of remarkable brutality.

As so often happens in long wars, the suffering and brutality which had been an inherent part of the struggle from the start increased in the war's final phase, driven by frustration and desperation and fueled by simmering resentments, old hatreds, and fresh atrocities. Whatever hope the British had ever had of reconciliation with America had vanished by the spring of 1780. All that was left was

to bleed America white. Whatever inclination the British had ever had to soften the brutality of the war was gone. Their success dependent on loyalist support, they encouraged loyalist excess, which turned the interior of Georgia and the Carolinas into a killing ground where loyalists and patriots vied with one another in a war of ambush, reprisal, and revenge.

Charleston

From the beginning of the war, British leaders believed that support for the American rebellion was weak in Georgia and the Carolinas, and that most southerners were either loyal to Britain or neutral. The conquest of Georgia and the reestablishment of royal government there in 1779 convinced them that royal authority could be restored in the Carolinas as well. General Sir Henry Clinton, the British commander in chief, was so pleased with the success of the British army in Georgia that he left Hessian General Knyphausen in command in New York City and sailed with about 8,500 men to Savannah, where he prepared for an attack on Charleston.

Charleston is built at the end of a peninsula between two tidal rivers and faces a harbor enclosed by islands and surrounded by marshland cut by tidal inlets and channels. The narrow entrance to the harbor passed over a treacherous sandbar and between two islands. In 1776 South Carolina patriots manning a makeshift fort on Sullivan's Island had repulsed a British squadron attempting to force its way into the harbor. Intent on avoiding a similar fate, General Clinton had the navy land his army on a coastal island thirty miles south of Charleston, from which he marched overland and down the Charleston peninsula to lay siege to the city from the land side.

The city was guarded by an army of Con-

The British army trapped Benjamin Lincoln's Continental Army in Charleston, took control of the harbor, and cut off any possible escape across the Cooper River (Library of Congress).

tinental troops and militia under the command of Benjamin Lincoln, who did little to impede Clinton's difficult and circuitous march through the marshy islands southeast of Charleston. Lincoln's army waited in its fortified line stretching across the Charleston peninsula, which was punctuated at intervals by redoubts and protected on its northern side by a flooded ditch that made an assault there impossible. At the center of the line was an imposing fort called the Horn Work, covering ten acres, with an elevated gun platform thirty feet above ground level. The line was too strong for the British to storm without heavy casualties, but it could be taken by the methodical advance of fortified siege lines mounted with artillery, which is what Clinton intended to do.

Lincoln was under pressure from South Carolina authorities to protect the city, but he tried to keep an escape route open by maintaining control of the upstream crossings of the Cooper River, which flows past the Charleston peninsula on the east. Lincoln's options vanished very quickly in early April, when Commodore Abraham Whipple, commanding the Continental Navy flotilla dispatched to guard the harbor, refused to do so, allowing British warships to force their way past the island forts and into the harbor. A few days later Banastre Tarleton, who commanded a mixed force of cavalry and infantry called

the British Legion, attacked American cavalry at Monck's Corner on the Cooper River, cutting Lincoln's escape route. With no hope of rescue, Lincoln defended his lines for as long as possible, then surrendered Charleston and his army on May 12. The British captured over five thousand Americans, most of the American army in the South.

Clinton then dispatched Tarleton to chase down the remaining Continental troops in South Carolina. Tarleton's cavalry caught up with Colonel Abraham Buford's 350 Continentals infantry, which had been marching toward Charleston, at the Waxhaws. Tarleton called on the outnumbered Americans to surrender. When Buford refused Tarleton launched his attack, quickly overpowering the Americans. The fighting was brief but vicious. One of Buford's captains, John Stokes, had his right hand cut off and his head gashed by saber blows. He was stabbed repeatedly with bayonets, sustaining twenty-three separate wounds. Somehow he survived. At least one hundred others were killed on the spot. The charge that Tarleton's men slaughtered soldiers trying to surrender circulated widely.

In response to the charge that he had presided over a massacre, Tarleton later explained that in the confusion at the end of the battle, his horse had been shot and fallen over with him and that his men believed he had been killed. After the war he wrote:

Slaughter was commenced before Lieutenant-colonel Tarleton could remount another horse, the one with which he led his dragoons being overturned by the volley. . . . The loss of officers and men was great on the part of the Americans, owing to the dragoons so effectually breaking the infantry, and to a report amongst the cavalry, that they had lost their commanding officer, which stimulated the soldiers to a vindictive asperity not easily restrained. Upwards of one hundred officers and men were killed on the spot; three colours, two six-pounders, and above two hundred prisoners . . . fell into the possession of the victors.

The reader is left to consider what Tarleton meant by "slaughter was commenced" and "a vindictive asperity not easily restrained." There are often two sides to a story, and determining which one is

Banastre Tarleton rose through skill and daring from a junior officer to lieutenant colonel and commander of the British Legion at the age of twenty-four. He favored stern and often savage treatment of the king's enemies. Leniency and generosity, he wrote, "did not experience in America the merited returns of gratitude and affection." His dashing pose in this detail from a 1782 portrait by Joshua Reynolds disguises the fact that he had lost two fingers on his right hand at the Battle of Guilford Court House (© The National Gallery, London).

true—or closer to the truth—is sometimes difficult. Tarleton was later involved in incidents that added to his reputation for cruelty and seem to support the charge that his men killed Americans trying to surrender at the Waxhaws. Within a few weeks of their victory at Charleston, the British snuffed out most armed resistance in South Carolina. General Clinton sailed back to New York, leaving the army under the command of General Cornwallis.

Treason

As soon as they reached New York City, Clinton and his adjutant, Major John André, were drawn into one of the most bizarre and dramatic incidents of the war. For over a year, Benedict Arnold had been exchanging messages with Clinton, offering his services to the British. Arnold was one of the most accomplished American generals of the war. He had been one of the leaders in the capture of Fort Ticonderoga in 1775 and had commanded troops in the invasion of Canada with great courage. He had fought bravely at Saratoga, where he was badly wounded. He was angry that he had not received as much credit for the victory at Saratoga as his commander, General Gates, and frustrated that Congress did not promote him.

Clinton had referred Arnold's offer to André, who ran the army's intelligence operations. By July 1779, Arnold was providing André with information about American troop positions and supplies, in coded letters and using invisible ink, for which Arnold made it clear he expected ten thousand British pounds and compensation for the American property he would lose if he went over to the British. The stakes went up in the summer of 1780, when Arnold was given command of West Point, the Hudson River fortress that protected the flow of supplies from New England to Washington's army, which was stationed in a broad arc from western Connecticut to central New Jersey.

West Point was the key to Washington's strategic encirclement of New York City and essential to the survival of his army. Arnold secretly offered to facilitate the British capture of the fortress in return for twenty thousand British pounds. On September 21, Arnold and André met behind American lines to finalize the arrangements. Arnold gave André plans of West Point, which André hid in his boot. While making his way back to British lines, André was captured by three American militiamen who searched him and found the plans. Washington examined the documents on September 24 and realized that Arnold had betrayed his country. Arnold managed to evade capture by escaping to a British ship in the Hudson River, but André had been caught in civilian clothes and was hanged as a spy.

A few days later, Arnold published a statement explaining his motives from the safety of British-held New York City. He had gone to war, he wrote, because the British government had abused American rights. "Redress of Grievances," he insisted, "was my only Object and aim." The Carlisle Commission, he argued, had offered to "grant the wished for redress" in ways that "exceeded our wishes and expectations." Thereafter America had no reason to fight and had been taken in by France. Congress had unnecessarily continued the war, sacrificing the interests of the United States "to the Partial Views of a Proud, Antient, and Crafty Foe . . . the Enemy of the Protestant Faith . . . avowing an affection for the liberties of mankind, while she holds her Native Sons in Vassalage and Chains." He concluded that "the Reunion of the British Empire" was "the best and only means to dry up the streams of misery that have deluged this country." Arnold made no mention of his demands. He was paid over six thousand pounds for betraying his country and commissioned a brigadier general in the British army.

No explanation could redeem Arnold, whose name became synonymous with treason and betrayal. He immediately became the American Judas. "Treason of the blackest dye was yesterday discovered," was recorded in the army's orderly books: "Genl. Arnold who commanded at West Point, lost to every sentiment of honor, of private and public obligation, was about to deliver up that important post into the hands of the Enemy."

An enlisted man, Joseph Plumb Martin, had encountered Arnold on the road near the Hudson a few days before his treason was revealed. "I had an acquaintance with Arnold from my childhood," Martin wrote fifty years later, "and never had too good an opinion of him." Martin "thought that he was upon some deviltry" that day:

In exchange for his release, John André offered his captors his expensive watch and a large sum of money. Although poor, they refused and turned their prisoner over to the Continental Army. They were long celebrated as common men of incorruptible virtue. In this depiction by Asher Durand, the central figure is John Paulding, a plainly dressed young man refusing André's bribes (Birmingham Museum of Art, Alabama).

I could not help taking notice of him, and thought
it strange to see him quite alone in such a lone place.
He looked guilty, and well he might, for Satan was
in full possession of him as ever he was of Judas; it
only wanted a musket ball to have driven him out.

Arnold's address "to the inhabitants of America" was a self-serving effort to justify betraying his country, his comrades, and his command, but he probably believed he could persuade nervous Americans that Congress had been taken in by "the Insidious offers of France." The war in the north was at a standstill in the summer of 1780. Washington's army surrounded New York City and attacked British outposts but could not drive the enemy out. The British position was simply too strong. The British army had built fortifications all around New York City and was supported by

the Royal Navy. The American economy was in shambles and it was increasingly difficult to supply Washington's army.

French support had failed to recover Newport and Savannah, but Washington believed that with the support of a French army and a French fleet he could drive the British out of New York and end the war. In 1779 he had dispatched Lafayette to France to plead with the French court to send an army to America. On July 11, 1780, a French army of 5,500 men landed in Newport, Rhode Island, under the command of General Jean-Baptiste de Vimeur, comte de Rochambeau. Seven years older than Washington, Rochambeau was a professional soldier who had served with distinction in the Seven Years' War in Europe. He had never been to America and spoke no English.

Washington rode to Newport in September 1780 to meet with Rochambeau. Washington was impressed by the quality of the soldiers in Rochambeau's army and by Rochambeau himself. Where d'Estaing had been difficult, even imperious, Rochambeau was collegial and even deferential. The two generals agreed that it was too late in the year to start a campaign against the British and that the French army should spend the winter in Newport, where it was supported by the French navy. They planned to combine their efforts in the spring.

Arnold met with André during Washington's absence. Washington unraveled Arnold's treason on the day he returned. Dismayed by Arnold's betrayal, Washington was even more concerned by the threat to West Point. Its loss would have cut his army off from supplies and reinforcements from New England and would have made joint operations with Rochambeau difficult, and perhaps impossible. The loss of West Point, Washington believed, would have been a "fatal stab" to the American cause, which had been wounded by the loss of Charleston.

The Carolina Backcountry

Savannah and Charleston were port cities—commercial centers where the goods produced in the interior were bought and shipped to Britain and the British colonies in the Caribbean. Both cities were surrounded by an extensive region of islands, marsh, slow-moving rivers, swamps, and low-lying plantations where rice was the most important crop. Offensive military operations in this region were extraordinarily difficult. Defenders familiar with its roads, river crossings, and hiding places could tie up an eighteenth-century army almost indefinitely. The British army might march through it, but controlling it was nearly impossible.

This low country, which extended from Florida to the Great Dismal Swamp on the North Carolina-Virginia border, was bounded on the west, above the fall line, by a region of level uplands and low hills, much of it covered by native pine and hardwood forests cut by branching streams extending into the foothills of the Appalachians. Colonists had settled in this upland region in the middle decades of the eighteenth century, pushing the Indians into the mountains, and had established a series of market towns—some little more

than trading posts—along a network of roads that ran from Augusta, Georgia, through Ninety Six and Camden in South Carolina and on to Charlotte and Hillsborough, North Carolina.

The upland region was far from ideal for eighteenth-century armies. It was vast and unevenly populated, with cultivated farms around the market towns but large empty stretches in between where armies could find little to eat. Men and supplies had to move over roads that were little more than paths, cut by streams that could be forded at crossing points easily guarded by the enemy. Occupying this region would be difficult, but the British had to control it in order to restore royal authority in the Carolinas.

After the fall of Charleston, the British installed garrisons at Ninety Six and Camden and prepared to move into North Carolina. In response, Congress sent Horatio Gates, the victor of Saratoga, to take command of a small army of Continental troops and militia on the Deep River, halfway between Hillsborough and Charlotte, North Carolina. Gates immediately marched his army through the summer heat toward Camden. The march took three weeks to cover some 125 miles and passed through a largely barren region where his soldiers could get little other than green corn to eat.

Cornwallis, who had assumed personal command at Camden, marched north on the night of August 15-16, and ran into Gates in the dark. After a skirmish the two armies pulled back a short distance and waited for morning, when Cornwallis attacked. He found the American army in a line of battle running through an open pine forest in which the smoke of battle lingered heavily in the air. The militia on the American left, terrified, ran as soon as the British Regulars appeared through the smoke. Gates fled with them, leaving Maj. Gen. Johann Kalb and his Continentals, mostly Maryland and Delaware veterans, to fight on their own. They were soon surrounded, and most were killed, wounded, or captured. Kalb—a German who had distinguished himself in the French army before volunteering for service in America—was mortally wounded and captured. He died three days later. After the battle, Tarleton's cavalry rode over the countryside, burning the homes of American soldiers and driving their families into hiding.

235

In William Tylee Ranney's 1850 painting of Francis Marion and his men crossing the Pee Dee River in South Carolina, Marion is not the officer mounted on a black horse who appears to be the center of attention. Marion is the mounted officer wrapped in a brown cloak. This was a clever visual tribute to Marion's ability to disguise his plans and hide from his enemies (Amon Carter Museum of American Art, Fort Worth, Texas).

Camden was a catastrophe and convinced pessimists that South Carolina was lost. After the battle, Cornwallis appointed an official to seize and sell the property of the king's enemies, with the proceeds to go to the army paymaster. He then set out for Charlotte, North Carolina, intent on further conquests.

It soon became clear to Cornwallis that his victory at Camden had done little to pacify the region in which he was operating. The remnants of the beaten American army began to reform in North Carolina, and new units, infantry and mounted troops, formed across the Carolina back-country. Small groups of militiamen and other ordinary citizens formed partisan bands to resist the British. Employing hit-and-run tactics, they attacked British outposts, burned British supplies, and barred British and loyalists troops from gathering food and forage. The British and their loyalist allies regarded these partisans as criminals to be hung rather than treated as prisoners of war. They burned the homes and farms of suspected partisans.

These cruel tactics only encouraged more resistance. The partisan bands grew larger and their commanders, including Andrew Pickens and

Thomas Sumter, became folk heroes. Among the most successful partisan leaders was Francis Marion, the legendary "Swamp Fox," who operated mainly in the lowcountry of northeastern South Carolina. Many of Marion's men carried their own guns and rode their own horses. They were experts at attacking British supply wagons and ambushing British and loyalists troops on the march and then disappearing into the woods and swamps. Cornwallis ordered Tarleton to track Marion down and capture or kill him, but Tarleton was never able to find him.

Camden, in hindsight, was the high point of Cornwallis's campaign in the Carolina backcountry. Having won a battle, he would find himself undone by bad roads, summer heat, malaria and other diseases, and the fighting qualities of the Americans who pursued his detachments, raided his supplies, and confronted the main body of his army, only to retreat farther into the interior without risking a major battle. To his disappointment they were more numerous than the loyalists he had been assured would join him.

"Ferguson and his party are no more"

As he marched into North Carolina, Cornwallis ordered Major Patrick Ferguson to lead some thousand loyalist troops north along the foothills of the Blue Ridge Mountains, covering the western flank of the British advance. To discourage Americans who lived west of the mountains from forming partisan bands, Ferguson made the mistake of sending them a message to lay down their arms. If they did not, he threatened to "march his army over the mountains, hang their leaders and lay waste their country with fire and sword."

Most of the over-mountain men had stayed out of the war, but Ferguson's threat made them angry. Over one thousand gathered at a meeting place called Sycamore Shoals in what is now eastern Tennessee. They caught up with Ferguson and his loyalists on October 7, 1780, at Kings Mountain, just south of the border between North and South Carolina. The frontiersmen quietly surrounded the mountain and launched a surprise attack on Fergusson's position on top. Colonel Isaac Shelby, one of their commanders, reported that the enemy

had taken post at that place with the confidence that no force could rout them; the mountain was high, and exceedingly steep, so that their situation gave them greatly the advantage; indeed, it was almost equal to storming a battery. In most places we could not see them till we were within twenty yards of them. They repelled us three times with charged bayonets; but being determined to conquer or die, we came up a fourth time, and fairly got possession of the top of the eminence.

The battle lasted a little more than an hour. Ferguson was killed and everyone in his command was killed, wounded, or captured. The frontiersmen, who fired rifles from behind rocks and trees, suffered few casualties. At the end of the battle they killed several loyalists who were in the act of surrendering and pulled out thirty loyalists suspected of looting and other crimes for a hasty trial. Nine were promptly hanged. William Campbell, the Virginia militia colonel who was the senior officer on the field, wrote with satisfaction to his brother that "Ferguson and his party are no more in circumstances to injure the citizens of America."

Kings Mountain was perhaps the greatest victory achieved by militia and irregulars during the entire war. It played to their strengths: rugged determination, individual initiative, and skilled marksmanship. Militia and irregulars were at a disadvantage in conventional military operations. They lacked the discipline and training to execute the maneuvers necessary to maintain unit cohesion and deliver the kind of concentrated fire required to win a conventional battle. At Camden the militia had run from the redcoats advancing with bayonets and supported by artillery. At Kings Mountain the enemy was trapped in a fixed position on a low mountaintop, unable to maneuver. The situation was perfectly suited to irregular tactics that came naturally to men used to hunting game. Frustrated and furious, Cornwallis complained that rebel tactics threatened to make the war "truly savage," then promptly encouraged the Indians to attack the frontier settlements of the over-mountain men.

At the Battle of Cowpens, Colonel William Washington was leading his dragoons in pursuit of the enemy when three British dragoon officers turned to confront him. In William Tylee Ranney's 1845 painting of the fight, an American sergeant rides to Washington's defense and a young "waiter"—the contemporary term for a personal servant, free or enslaved—fires a pistol, wounding one of Washington's attackers. The painting is faithful to the first-hand account of Col. John Eager Howard of Maryland, who witnessed the incident (State of South Carolina).

Patriots were inspired by the victory. After months of almost unrelieved disaster, they had delivered a crushing blow of their own. Recruiting improved. Militiamen who had given up returned to the field with renewed hope. Partisan ranks swelled. Sir Henry Clinton, reflecting on Kings Mountain after the war, said that it was "the first link of a chain of evils that followed each other in regular succession until they at last ended in the total loss of America."

"We . . . shouted Liberty! Liberty!"

Stunned by the loss and concerned that the Americans might cut his supply line, Cornwallis withdrew into South Carolina. He made his headquarters at Winnsboro, forty-five miles west of Camden, and prepared for another advance into North Carolina. He might have pressed on. The pause gave the Americans time to regroup.

Congress turned to Washington to choose a general to replace Horatio Gates, who had disgraced himself by fleeing the battlefield at Camden. Washington dispatched his most able subordinate, Nathanael Greene, to take command. His prospects did not seem promising. "I arrived here the 2d of this month," he wrote to his wife from Charlotte on December 7, "and have been in search of the Army I am to command, but without much success, having found nothing but a few, half-starved soldiers who are remarkable for nothing but poverty and distress."

It took Greene a few weeks to assemble his command, which soon included, in addition to the half-starved stragglers he had encountered, some of the best soldiers in the Continental Army. He also had some of Washington's best officers, including Daniel Morgan, Thaddeus Kosciuszko, Virginians Henry Lee and William Washington, and Marylanders John Eager Howard and Otho Holland Williams. Greene assumed command at Hillsborough on December 3 and began gathering more men and supplies to resist Cornwallis.

He gave Morgan command of half of the army and sent him south to delay the British advance. Morgan's little army, bolstered by militia, met a British force commanded by Tarleton near the South Carolina-North Carolina border at a

place called the Cowpens on January 17, 1781. Morgan put the militia, commanded by Andrew Pickens, in a line in front of his Continental Army veterans. Morgan knew the militia would be nervous, so he asked them to fire just two volleys at the approaching British and then retreat behind the main line.

Fire from the militia disorganized the attacking British. When the militia retreated as planned, Tarleton charged. The British ran straight into the main American line commanded by Col. John Eager Howard, whose men fired and then charged the British with their bayonets. Pickens rallied the militia and they joined the attack. The surprised British were surrounded. Tarleton escaped, but over seven hundred of his men surrendered. Morgan wrote with pleasure that he had given Tarleton "a devil of a whipping." He reported to Greene:

The Troops I had the Honor to command have been so fortunate as to obtain a compleat Victory over a Detachment from the British Army commanded by Lt Colonel Tarlton. The Action happened on the 17th Instant about Sunrise at the Cowpens. It perhaps would be well to remark, for the Honour of the American Arms, that Altho the Progress of this Corps was marked with Burnings and Devastations and altho' they have waged the most cruel Warfare, not a man was killed, wounded or even insulted after he surrendered.

Cornwallis was furious. He decided to attack Greene as soon as possible and try to bring the war in the Carolinas to an end. Greene, unwilling to give battle, retreated toward the Dan River, near the border between North Carolina and Virginia. Cornwallis pursued him. "In the most barren, inhospitable, unhealthy part of North America," wrote British Brigadier General Charles O'Hara, "opposed by the most savage, inveterate perfidious cruel Enemy, with zeal and with Bayonets only, it was resolv'd to follow Green's Army, to the end of the World." Greene reached the Dan first and crossed to the north side of the river.

After reinforcements arrived, Greene crossed back over the Dan and challenged the British. Cornwallis attacked Greene near Guilford Court

Using the vast, undeveloped southern backcountry to his advantage, Nathanael Greene led the British army on an exhausting chase across North Carolina, then turned to confront Cornwallis and his weary army at Guilford Court House (National Portrait Gallery, Smithsonian Institution).

House on March 15, 1781. Greene, who had time to prepare, organized his men in three lines, instructing the militia in the first line to fire two rounds and then retreat, as Morgan had done at Cowpens. Private Samuel Houston, a Virginia militiaman in the second line, described the chaos of battle in his diary:

> Standing in readiness, we heard the pickets fire; shortly the English fired a cannon, which was answered; and so on alternately . . . Soon the enemy appeared to us; we fired on their flank, and that brought down many of them; at which time Capt. Tedford was killed. We pursued them about forty poles, to the top of a hill where they stood, and we retreated from them back to where we formed. Here we repulsed them again; and they a second time made us retreat back to our first ground, where we were deceived by a reinforcement of Hessians, whom we took for our own, and cried to them to see if they were our friends, and shouted Liberty! Liberty! and advanced up till they let off some guns; then we fired sharply on them, and made them retreat a little. But presently the light horse came on us, and . . . we were obliged to run, and many were sore chased, and some cutdown. We lost our major and one captain then, the battle lasting two hours and twenty-five minutes.

The British pushed through the first two lines but suffered heavy losses. The Virginia militia in the second line punished the Hessians so badly that Tarleton's cavalry attacked them to save the Hessians. The main body of the British marched past to attack Greene's third line, made up of Continental Army veterans. After fierce fighting, Greene withdrew his army from the battlefield. The British were too exhausted to pursue. Cornwallis had lost one-fourth of his army, which was too weak to fight another battle. The loyalist reinforcement he had hoped for never appeared. "I could not get 100 men in all the Regulator's country to stay with us, even as militia."

Cornwallis led his worn-down army to the port of Wilmington, two hundred miles away on the North Carolina coast. He was followed and harassed by militia and partisan rangers who prevented his army from collecting supplies in the countryside. "I have experienced the dangers and distresses of marching some hundreds of miles," Cornwallis complained, "in country chiefly hostile, without one active or useful friend." His army was spent. "North Carolina," he wrote to Clinton "is of all the Provinces in America the most difficult to attack."

Greene left the North Carolina militia and partisan rangers to keep Cornwallis pinned down in Wilmington while he marched south. "I am determined to carry the war immediately into South Carolina," he told Washington. Greene marched south and fought a series of battles in South Carolina. He lost most of them, but pressed the British back toward Charleston. "We fight, get beat, rise, and fight again," he wrote. "The whole country is one continuous scene of blood and slaughter." General Anthony Wayne, sent south by Washington, drove the British out of most of Georgia. By late 1781 Americans had the British pinned down in Charleston and Savannah.

Lafayette and Cornwallis

"What is our plan?" Cornwallis asked after retreating to Wilmington. "Without one, we cannot succeed, and I assure you that I am quite tired of marching about the country in quest of adventures. If we mean an offensive war in America, we must abandon New York and bring our whole force into Virginia; we have then a stake to fight for and a successful battle may give us America."

Cornwallis had a better grasp of the strategic situation than Sir Henry Clinton. After the American victory at Great Bridge in 1775 the war had barely touched Virginia—the largest, wealthiest, and most populous British colony on the North American mainland. Since then, supplies and men had moved from Virginia to the American armies—never in the quantity or number their commanders hoped for, but in sufficient volume to convince Cornwallis that Britain would never recover America without conquering it.

The problem, as Cornwallis would discover, was that Virginia's people and wealth were spread over a vast area. Its economic life was organized around river valleys—the Potomac, Rappahannock, York, James, and their tributaries. Towns

Later formal portraits of Charles, Lord Cornwallis, give the impression of an aging, stout, slow-moving man. In the summer of 1781 he was just forty-two, and the most able, energetic, aggressive, and feared British general of the war. He drove himself and his army to exhaustion pursuing Greene and then Lafayette in an effort to bring the war in the South to an end (©The Trustees of the British Museum).

had under his command. He had, by the spring of 1781, abandoned the idea that loyalists would fill his ranks as soon as he marched into Virginia. This had not happened in the Carolinas, and he had no reason to believe it would happen in Virginia.

Clinton never abandoned the idea that raising loyalist troops was essential to victory if victory was possible at all. In December 1780 he dispatched some 1,600 men to Virginia to destroy arms manufacturing and military supplies and to raise loyalist troops, all under the command of his newly appointed brigadier general, Benedict Arnold, who assured him that Virginia planters would support reconciliation with Britain just as he did. It was a fantasy. Virginia had its share of wealthy planters who preferred stability and would have welcomed reconciliation, but few of them were willing to risk their lives or property by supporting the British army, which, after six years of war, controlled only the ground on which it stood.

Washington responded in March 1781 by sending 1,200 men to oppose (and with luck, capture) Arnold, under the command of the marquis de Lafayette—the American general who most fully embodied the French alliance and whose personal commitment to the American cause contradicted everything Arnold said about the treacherous character of the French. Clinton, in response, sent more men to Virginia, and Washington did the same, dispatching Anthony Wayne and Steuben to Lafayette's aid. In April 1781, Cornwallis left North Carolina and marched into Virginia, where he took command of all British forces. Despite Clinton's blindness to the strategic importance of Virginia, the armies were

were small and however locally important, of negligible military value. Conquering Virginia, if it could be accomplished at all, would require cutting off its trade, which was a job for the Royal Navy, and destroying Virginia's capacity to provide American armies with arms, supplies, and men. This was a job for the army, and Cornwallis was right to think that it would take more men than he drawn into the state. There, as Cornwallis had anticipated, the war would be decided.

Cornwallis spent the summer chasing Lafayette's little army around Virginia. Lafayette had fewer than half as many men as Cornwallis, but he convinced the British that he had thousands more. "Were I to fight a battle," Lafayette wrote to Washington, "I should be cut to pieces." Instead, Lafayette played a game of cat and mouse with Cornwallis, skirmishing with the pursuing British but avoiding a major battle. Cornwallis eventually tired of chasing Lafayette and went into camp at Yorktown, a small town on the York River not far from the Chesapeake Bay. There he expected to receive supplies and reinforcements by sea, or for Clinton to withdraw his troops from Virginia and concentrate the army to repel an attack on New York.

While Cornwallis chased Lafayette around Virginia, Washington and Rochambeau gathered their armies outside New York City. Washington had about five thousand men. Rochambeau had about the same number. To oppose them, Clinton had about fourteen thousand men, protected by fortifications and supported by the guns of the Royal Navy. Washington and Rochambeau realized an attack on New York could not succeed, even with the help of the French navy. The two generals then learned that a large French fleet commanded by Admiral de Grasse was sailing north from the Caribbean to Virginia to support an attack on Cornwallis. Washington and Rochambeau decided to march to Virginia. There, with the help of the French navy, they believed they could force Cornwallis to surrender.

The French fleet, with twenty-four ships of the line, reached the mouth of the Chesapeake Bay on August 30, 1781. A British fleet of nineteen ships of the line, sent from New York to help Cornwallis, arrived on September 5. The British were outnumbered and several of their ships were in poor repair, but surprise was on their side. Admiral de Grasse was expecting Admiral Barras and his squadron from Newport and did not recognize the British ships until they were closing in. Finally recognizing the enemy, the French sailed out of the bay in disorder. The British had a chance to attack the lead French ships and beat them before the rest could form a line of battle. Instead the British commander, Admiral Thomas Graves, carefully maneuvered his fleet into line of battle, giving the French a chance to organize a line of battle of their own.

The resulting Battle of the Chesapeake lasted for nearly three hours, during which the two fleets fired broadsides at each other from short range. About nineteen thousand French sailors and thirteen thousand British sailors participated in the battle, on forty-three ships carrying over three thousand cannons. They maneuvered for two more days without renewing the battle. Admiral de Grasse defended his position with great skill. British Admiral Graves finally concluded he could not force his way into the Chesapeake Bay or drive the French out. Admitting that the French had "so great a naval force in the Chesapeake" that they were "absolute masters of its navigation," Graves sailed away, leaving Cornwallis on his own.

The French fleet carried over three thousand infantry under the command of the marquis de Saint-Simon. They disembarked at Jamestown—the site of the original English settlement in Virginia—and marched across the peninsula between the James and York rivers, through Williamsburg, to join American troops under the command of the marquis de Lafayette. Cornwallis pretended to despise Saint-Simon's troops, saying that they were nothing more than "undisciplined vagabonds collected in the West Indies." In fact, Saint-Simon commanded the regiments of Gâtinais, Agenais, and Touraine, some of the finest troops in the French army. An American reported, "you have not seen troops as universally well-made, so robust, or of such appearance as those General Saint-Simon has brought to our assistance." Together Lafayette and Saint-Simon blocked the roads leading out of Yorktown, pinning the British army in its fortified lines.

Fort Griswold

For much of the Revolutionary War, Washington's army denied the British army the opportunity to collect food and forage. Although the British army successively occupied Boston, New York, and Philadelphia, its control extended no farther than its outposts on the periphery of each city. Foraging parties sent out to gather supplies in

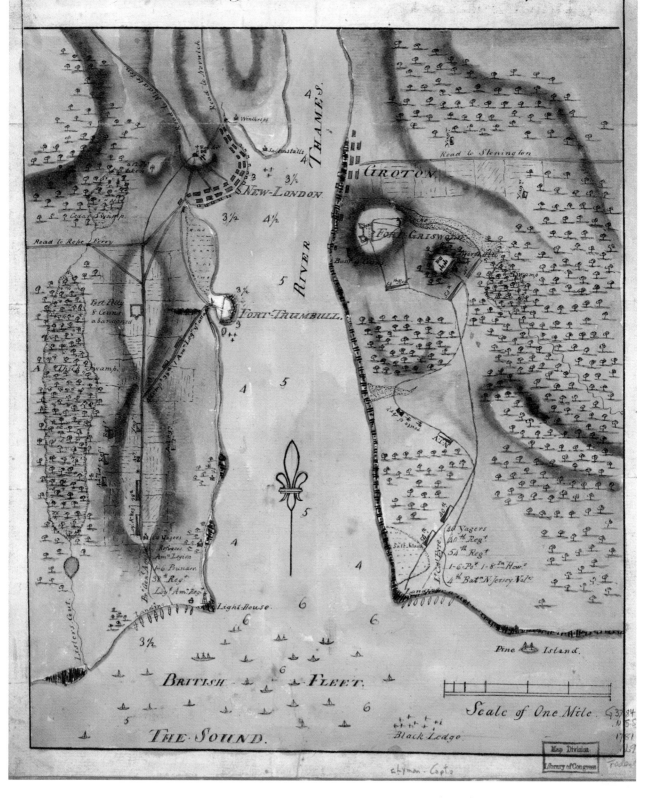

A SKETCH of
NEW LONDON & GROTON
with the Attacks made on
FORTS TRUMBULL & GRISWOLD by the BRITISH TROOPS
under the Command of BRIG. GEN. ARNOLD, Sep. 6th 1781.

the hinterland, encumbered by wagons, were easy targets for American dragoons, light infantry, and militia, and frequently returned to British lines empty handed, if they returned at all. Although Washington's army lost most of the pitched battles in which it fought, it was adept at this aspect of eighteenth-century warfare. The British were forced to rely on supply ships from England, Ireland, and Nova Scotia, which were easy targets for American privateers.

Privateers were merchant vessels, fitted out with cannons and rigged for speed and maneuverability. Most were two-masted schooners and brigantines, capable of running down heavily laden supply ships and forcing them to surrender. Privateers were privately owned and operated for profit. Each one carried a commission, called a letter of marque and reprisal, issued by the Continental Congress, which authorized the captain to capture British vessels and sell the ships and their cargoes. During the war some eight hundred American vessels made privateering cruises and captured some six hundred British ships, costing the British between eighteen and twenty million dollars in losses, an amount equivalent to the costs of maintaining British and Hessian troops in America for a year. Warships of the French, Spanish, and Continental navies preyed on supply ships and added to British losses. Among the most active privateering ports were Boston, Beverly, Salem, and Newburyport in Massachusetts, Newport and Providence in Rhode Island, and New Haven and New London in Connecticut.

Privateers brought an unusual number of captured British merchant vessels in to New London during the summer of 1781, including the brig *Hannah,* bound for New York with a cargo worth eighty thousand British pounds. General Clinton decided to make an example of the town. He dispatched Benedict Arnold, at the head of a force of some 1,700 British Regulars, Hessians, and loyalists, loaded on twenty-four transports, to destroy the *Hannah* and any privateering vessels caught in the harbor and to burn any military supplies they found.

New London occupies the west bank of the Thames River a short distance above Long Island Sound. It was defended by Fort Trumbull—a

waterside battery close to the town—and Fort Griswold, an imposing stone fort on a hill on the opposite side of the river, above the village of Groton. Arnold landed some 850 men under Lt. Col. Edmund Eyre to surround Fort Griswold while he led the attack on New London. After taking Fort Trumbull and a smaller battery, Arnold led his men through the town, which he knew well, and ordered torch parties to burn everything of military value. They burned over 140 buildings, including docks, warehouses, shops, barns, and houses, as many as a dozen ships, and a considerable quantity of military stores. They also set fire to the church, jail, courthouse, and other public buildings. Arnold spared almost nothing, and made no effort to restrain his men from looting and burning private homes. Gunpowder stored in one of the warehouses ignited, spreading fire through the town. Militiamen rushed toward New London from the neighboring towns in ones, twos, and small groups, but were leaderless and disorganized, and hovered ineffectively just beyond the town. They watched, powerless, as New London burned.

It took the troops landed on the opposite bank time to get into position to attack Fort Griswold, by which time around 150 defenders—local militia, including at least two African Americans and one Pequot Indian—had gathered in the fort. Some were armed with pikes. Eyre sent a message demanding surrender, which the commander—a militia colonel named William Ledyard—refused. When the British charged the fort, a privateer captain, Elias Halsey, fired a round of grapeshot from a heavy cannon at close range, killing and wounding dozens of attackers. The defenders repulsed the British twice with heavy losses, including Eyre and his second in command.

On their third attempt, the British went up and over the twelve-foot walls, though they were exposed to musket fire that left dozens of dead and wounded men in the ditch below. Inside the fort, the two sides fired at close range. Fighting was briefly hand-to-hand, with bayonets and muskets turned and used as clubs. William Seymour, Ledyard's nephew—many of the defenders were related—was shot in the knee and stabbed seven

Fort Trumbull and Fort Griswold, on opposite sides of the Thames River, protected New London from attack by water. Benedict Arnold, who was intimately familiar with the area, landed his forces on the beaches at the mouth of the river and marched overland to take the forts from the land side. This British map of the expedition offers no hint of its barbarity (Library of Congress).

times with bayonets. Stephen Hempstead was shot through the elbow, bayoneted in the hip, and had his ribs shattered. Within minutes Ledyard could see that further resistance was hopeless and signaled to his men to surrender.

When a British officer challenged, "Who commands this fort?" Col. Ledyard stepped forward and said, "I did, sir, but you do now," extending the hilt of his sword in surrender. The British officer seized the sword and ran Ledyard through, killing him. Soldiers who rushed to Ledyard's side were cut down with bayonets. Redcoats pouring in through the open gate fired by platoons on Americans, many of whom had thrown down their weapons when Ledyard signaled for surrender. Dozens of Americans were stabbed repeatedly with bayonets. Sixteen-year-old Peter Avery was among the few survivors of the massacre, and remembered it vividly more than fifty-five years later: "the Americans were finally overcome by the superior numbers of the enemy and most inhumanely butchered by British Barbarity." When the massacre began he fled into the barracks, where pursuing British soldiers killed three wounded men. Avery escaped into another room, where he hid until the killing stopped.

Before they were finished the British killed eighty-five Americans. Many were shot, then stabbed with bayonets. The British wounded thirty-nine Americans, many of whom died later. Arnold's men took thirty prisoners, including wounded men, and herded them on to transports. They were confined in a sugar warehouse in New York, where several more died. Other residents of New London—how many is not clear—died in their burning homes or were shot down by roving looters. As the sun went down, the departing redcoats set fire to the village of Groton, then boarded their transports and sailed for New York, leaving the survivors, wives and mothers, to search for their husbands and sons among the dead and dying.

With this senseless slaughter of defenseless men and boys, the last battle of the Revolutionary War in the north ended—a final act of mass brutality, to add to the long list of cruel and vicious acts reaching back to the spring of 1775, when redcoats shot men down on the Lexington Common. Like

the defenders of Lexington, the men and boys executed at Fort Griswold simply wanted to be free.

Yorktown

By the time Arnold returned to New York City, it was clear that the combined armies of Washington and Rochambeau had gone. Washington's army passed through Philadelphia on September 2, followed by the French army the next day. It was too late for Clinton to follow.

From Newport to Yorktown, the French army covered 756 miles in one of the most extraordinary marches in history. The American army marched nearly as far. By late September, Washington had over 16,000 soldiers within a few miles of Yorktown. Half of them were French troops, including the men under Saint-Simon who had arrived with Admiral de Grasse. Cornwallis made no effort to escape. His army had surrounded Yorktown with a powerful defensive line of earthworks. They had sixty-five cannon and some 7,500 officers and men guarding the works. Cornwallis boasted that "there was but one wish throughout the whole army, which was, that the enemy would advance." Washington gave orders for the allied army to surround the British on September 28, but he had no intention of storming the British works. The French fleet made it impossible for the Royal Navy to rescue Cornwallis, so the allies had time to lay siege to Yorktown and force the British to surrender. French engineers took charge of constructing the siege lines, which were built in long parallels—entrenchments angled slightly toward the enemy, punctuated by gun emplacements, each one closer to the British earthworks.

The first parallel was ten feet wide, four feet deep, and two miles long. The digging went on at night, when the British could not see what was happening. The British artillery fired constantly, trying to stop the digging, but with no success. By October 9 the French and Americans had enough artillery in place to maintain a constant bombardment of the British works. A few days and nights of continuous cannon fire made life inside the British lines miserable. Cornwallis moved his headquarters to a shallow cave in the river bank where allied artillery could not reach him. Within the British

American light infantry led by Alexander Hamilton seized British Redoubt Ten on the evening of October 14, while French troops stormed nearby Redoubt Nine. "Nothing could exceed the firmness and bravery of the troops," Washington reported to Congress. "They advanced under the fire of the enemy without returning a shot, and effected the business with the bayonet only" (Courtesy of the Library of Virginia).

lines, food and other supplies started to run low.

The French and Americans began a second parallel even closer to the British lines, but two British fortifications—Redoubt Nine and Redoubt Ten—stood in their way. On the night of October 14, French and American troops led by Guillaume, comte de Deux-Ponts, and Alexander Hamil-ton, overwhelmed the two redoubts in a surprise assault. The captured works were included in the second parallel. Allied cannon fire soon made it impossible for the British to defend their lines. "The whole peninsula," wrote American surgeon James Thacher, "trembles under the incessant thunderings of our infernal machines."

The British march out of their fortified lines to surrender in this miniature painted by French court artist Louis-Nicolas van Blarenberghe in 1785. The artist based the painting on maps and the descriptions of French officers. The defeat broke the will of British officials to continue the war and ensured the independence of the United States (The Colonial Williamsburg Foundation).

Cornwallis realized that no help was coming from New York and that there was no chance he could break through the siege lines and escape with his men. On October 17 he asked the allies for terms and quickly agreed to surrender. On October 19—the morning of the surrender ceremony—Cornwallis claimed to be sick and turned the humiliating task over to his second in command, General Charles O'Hara. Nearly eight thousand British troops—one fourth of all British forces in the United States—filed out of their entrenchments and past the allied army. The French, in their faultless white uniforms, and the Americans, making the best appearance they could in uniforms provided by France, were drawn up on either side of the road.

Washington, Rochambeau, and their senior officers were gathered near the end of the road. O'Hara, anxious to surrender to the French rather than the rebels, approached Rochambeau to surrender his sword. Rochambeau motioned him toward Washington, and Washington—recognizing O'Hara's inferior rank—directed O'Hara to surrender his sword to Benjamin Lincoln, Washington's second in command. Thus Lincoln—a sturdy Massachusetts farmer who had served in the militia before joining the Continental Army and who limped on an ankle shattered by a musket ball at Saratoga—received the surrender. He directed the British troops to an open field where they grounded their arms and turned over their battle flags.

It is yet to be decided whether the Revolution must ultimately be considered as a blessing or a curse: a blessing or a curse, not to the present Age alone, for with our fate will the destiny of unborn Millions be involved.

GEORGE WASHINGTON
JUNE 8, 1783

INDEPENDENT AMERICA

Benjamin West began this painting of the commissioners who negotiated the Treaty of Paris, but the British commissioners refused to pose for him and the painting remains unfinished. The American commissioners (from left to right) were John Jay, John Adams, Benjamin Franklin, and Henry Laurens. Franklin's grandson William Temple Franklin, at far right, served as secretary to the American negotiators (Courtesy of Winterthur Museum).

Chapter 17 War's End

The British war effort in the South collapsed during the fall of 1781, as American troops pressed the British and their loyalist supporters everywhere from Virginia to the Georgia frontier, making the restoration of royal authority in Virginia and the Carolinas all but impossible.

On September 8, 1781, Nathanael Greene attacked the British at Eutaw Springs on the lower Santee River. The British managed to repulse the attack, but afterwards withdrew to Charleston. By the time Cornwallis surrendered in Virginia, the British held no more of South Carolina than they had held when Charleston surrendered in 1780.

In the weeks after Cornwallis surrendered, North Carolina troops defeated loyalists in savage fights along the Cape Fear River, then took up positions on the outskirts of Wilmington, which the British had occupied since January 1781. The British commander, short on supplies and expecting a siege, expelled patriot sympathizers, including women and children, from the town.

There was nothing glamorous about this twilight of the war. It was fought by plain men, most without uniforms, many carrying their own muskets, at places like Raft Swamp and Moore's Plantation and the Brick House—in little battles with twenty or fifty or two hundred men on each side. Men died in these little battles as surely as they died at Bunker Hill and Princeton, with no painter to portray them as heroes and barely any documents recalling their service. Fifty years after the war, when he was living in Tennessee, Private George McLain remembered the North Carolina State Legion fighting loyalists on their way to Wilmington—that they "killed about twenty of them" at Raft Swamp and then marched to the Brick House, a landmark across the Cape Fear from Wilmington, where they "killed about a dozen" more.

George McLain remembered this part of the war as a succession of killings. But it was not aimless. When their enlistments ran out before Wilmington was taken, McLain and seventeen other men in his company decided to stay with the legion. They elected their lieutenant, Philip Null, as their new captain, and kept on fighting. The British boarded transports and evacuated Wilmington, their last post between New York and Charleston, on November 18, 1781. With them went any hope the British had of subduing the South.

The partisan war between patriots and loyalists continued for another year, fueled by hatred and stoked by years of violence. This fighting served no strategic purpose. The worst of the combatants were indistinguishable from criminal gangs, operating in areas where governments and laws no longer functioned and on parts of the western frontier where they had never functioned. The war had been marked by cruelty since the beginning. As long as the outcome of the war remained uncertain, the killing continued.

After the British retired behind the fortified lines of Charleston, Nathanael Greene's army controlled no more of the state than the ground where it stood. Much of the interior was ravaged by partisans who ignored military conventions. They plundered and burned the homes of their enemies—some partisan commanders regarded plunder as a form of pay—and executed men in the act of surrendering.

In November 1781 a loyalist band of some 150 men under William Cunningham cut its way through the South Carolina interior. A South Carolina judge, Aedanus Burke, reported that Cunningham "killed in his rout every person he met with (it is said to the number of 50) whom he suspected to be friends to this Country, and burnt their Habitations." On November 19, Cunningham came to a house occupied by 35 patriot militia under Col. Joseph Hayes, who refused to surrender. "An attack commenced," the judge wrote, *and a hot fire kept up, with some Loss on both*

In this contemporary watercolor of the naval battle for St. Kitts, the British fleet has interposed itself between the attacking French fleet and the town of Bassterre, while French troops attack the British fort on Brimstone Hill at upper left. The image illustrates the conventional eighteenth-century tactic of deploying large warships in line of battle, making fleet actions contests of concentrated firepower. Smaller warships posted behind each line transmitted their admiral's commands to the fleet in code using signal flags (The Society of the Cincinnati).

marked by the same kind of brutality, occurred in many parts of America during the last stages of the war. People on all sides, and many simply hoping to keep out of harm's way, were victims. They included white and black Americans as well as Indians. Fear, greed, revenge, desperation, ethnic hatred, and frustration motivated the perpetrators, many of whom had grown too accustomed to the violence of war.

Freedom cannot endure such conditions for long. Proud declarations about natural and civil rights, republican constitutions limiting the powers of government, and principled statements about liberty, equality, and citizenship have little meaning for people living under constant threat of violence and constant pressure for basic needs. Freedom can only flourish under the rule of law that ensures them safety and the secure possession of property. Without it, fear and want lead people to accept authoritarian rule, and freedom is lost.

News from America

At that moment, the outcome of the war and the future of the United States passed into the hands of American diplomats in Europe. Reports of the allied victory at Yorktown reached Paris before they reached London. Vergennes told Franklin the news on November 20. "History," Vergennes wrote, "offers few examples of a success so complete; but one would be wrong to believe that it means an immediate peace; it is not in the English character to give up so easily."

The British were stubborn and proud, as Vergennes observed, and the war would drag on for a year before they agreed to preliminary articles of peace, but Yorktown made a treaty ending the war and acknowledging American independence

Sides, for about three hours; the British party possessed themselves of the out buildings, and at last set fire to the house in which Colo. Hays was posted. In this distressful Situation . . . reasonable terms were offered; that they should march out, lay down their arms and be treated as prisoners of war until exchanged; and a Capitulation was formally signed and interchanged. The Americans had no sooner marched out and laid down their Arms, but the British seized Colo. Hays, and with the Capitulation in his hand, pleading the terms of it and begging for Mercy, they hanged him to the limb of a tree and then fired a Bullet thro' him. Captn. Williams the second in Command, was treated in the same manner. After which Cuningham, with his Own hands slew some of the prisoners and desired his men to follow his example. A most cruel slaughter of the prisoners ensued.

254 Scenes like this one, varying in the number and nature of the victims and other details, but

inevitable. News of the defeat at Yorktown reached London on November 25. Lord North took it, said a witness, like "a ball in the breast," and moaned, "Oh God! It is all over!"

North understood that the surrender at Yorktown was a catastrophe for Britain, but not because of the loss of men and material. The largest British force in North America, Clinton's army in and around New York City, was still intact, and British troops held Charleston and Savannah. The British had lost seven thousand men, but they still had some thirty thousand men stationed in America, from Nova Scotia to East Florida—far more men than the Continental Army and the French army in America could muster.

Unfortunately for the British, General Clinton did not grasp the broader strategic situation. He was aware during August that Washington and Rochambeau might move south to attack Cornwallis, but he assumed that the Royal Navy would maintain control of the mouth of the Chesapeake Bay and could thus support Cornwallis or evacuate his army if the allies had him at a disadvantage. Clinton acted—or rather, failed to act—based on the assumption that an allied move, either against Cornwallis or against New York, was bound to fail, and that thereafter Washington's unpaid, under-supplied army would finally disintegrate. "Time alone," Clinton wrote, "would soon bring about every success we could wish."

Time was actually a luxury the British did not have. Every day the war continued, the costs of the war to the British government and British merchants mounted. American, French, and Spanish privateers, joined by French and Spanish warships, were preying on British shipping. In August 1780 the Spanish had captured an entire convoy bound for the West Indies, including fifty-five ships carrying eighty thousand muskets, nearly three hundred cannons, a vast quantity of naval stores, and the entire 90th Regiment of Foot. The loss had driven maritime insurance rates, which were already high, to record levels. The insurance crisis deepened in October 1780, when one of the most powerful hurricanes in recorded history hit the Caribbean, devastating Barbados and sinking nearly all of the ships there, then leaving a path of destruction through the islands to the north. Shipping losses and high insurance costs made it difficult for merchants to make money, and they were demanding an end to the war.

Territorial losses were mounting as well. By the time Cornwallis surrendered his army, the British had lost Dominica, St. Vincent, Grenada, and Tobago to the French navy and West Florida to Spanish forces led by Bernardo de Galvez, the governor of Louisiana, who took Pensacola in May 1781. The Spanish were besieging the British fortress at Gibraltar, and a French fleet under Admiral Suffren was on its way to the Indian Ocean, threatening Britain's possessions in India and the business of the British East India Company. Admiral de Grasse returned to the Caribbean after the surrender of Cornwallis, threatened Barbados, and then took the small British colonies of St. Kitts, Nevis, Monserrat, Demerara, and Essequebo. The British braced for an attack on Jamaica. The Royal Navy was hard pressed to defend all of these points at once, and the longer the war went on the more difficult it became, because the navy was running short of new masts, lumber, tar, pitch, and rope, all of which had come from the American colonies before the war.

Time, which General Clinton thought would bring success, was running out. Eighteenth-century wars were fought by limited forces for limited aims, and they continued only so long as governments had the resources to continue them. European governments lacked the ability, which they would develop in the nineteenth century and perfect in the twentieth, of mobilizing their people and the productive capacities of their economies to support wars on a massive scale involving continental conquests and even the enslavement or extermination of their opponents. Despite taxes that seemed at times confiscatory to many of their subjects, eighteenth-century monarchs were never able to harness more than a small fraction of their nations' wealth in wartime. They taxed and spent, or borrowed and spent, until their limited resources were exhausted. Then they made peace.

Britain had an enormously productive economy, but the government's resources were running out at the end of 1781, and remaining popular support for the war in America evaporated with the news of the surrender at Yorktown. George III wanted to fight on, but the country gentry who had loyally supported the war effort were tired of paying taxes to send armies and the vast quantity of supplies they consumed to be wasted in America. Members of the West India lobby, a group that included Caribbean plantation owners who lived in Britain and held seats in Parliament, were afraid that if the war continued Barbados and Jamaica would be lost, and their fortunes ruined. Pessimists warned that Britain might lose Canada, Newfoundland, and Nova Scotia. With support for the war in Parliament gone, Lord North could not secure adoption of a budget to continue the war in America.

"A School of Sharks"

A treaty of peace acknowledging American independence was inevitable, but the terms of that treaty, and their implications for the future of the United States, were far from certain. Americans were as anxious to make peace as the British, but despite the allied victory at Yorktown, they were in no position to dictate terms. Recruiting soldiers for the Continental Army was at a standstill. The arms captured at Yorktown were sufficient to meet the needs of Washington's army for some time, but the army was chronically short of uniforms, shoes, and other basic supplies. The army had no money to pay its soldiers. Congress had no means to finance the war except borrowing, and the French ministry and European bankers were reluctant to lend money to a government that had no power to tax its people to repay the debt.

Nor were the Americans in a position to drive the British out. Washington's army marched back to New York, but it lacked the strength to take New York City. Rochambeau's army spent the winter in Virginia, and in the spring it marched to Boston and departed for the Caribbean. The French navy was occupied in the Caribbean as well. Washington wanted to resume offensive operations against the British in New York or to retake Charleston and Savannah, but without French naval support, he could only watch and wait.

Peace could only be secured through negotiation. The Treaty of Alliance prescribed that the United States and France would make war and peace together, but Vergennes was not quite ready to make peace. He looked forward to completing

a French victory by depriving Britain of Jamaica, while Spain—which was allied with France but not with America—was determined to take Gibraltar. France was pledged to support Spain and would not make peace until the siege of Gibraltar ended. The fate of America was thus entangled with the struggle between the three great imperial powers in the Caribbean and with the fate of Gibraltar, neither of which had any direct bearing on the future of the United States.

None of the imperial powers had an interest in a strong, stable, and free republic in North America. Vergennes wanted the United States to remain a client of France—a trading partner dependent on French naval support, a useful ally in war, and a willing market in peace. Congress nonetheless instructed American diplomats to consult with Vergennes and the French ministry about peace talks with the British, on the naïve assumption that Vergennes was a patron who would protect American interests.

Congress had dispatched John Adams to Paris in 1779 with authority to negotiate a peace treaty. Vergennes, who disliked and distrusted Adams, had employed intermediaries to persuade Congress to appoint additional peace commissioners. Congress named Benjamin Franklin, John Jay, Henry Laurens, and Thomas Jefferson to join Adams. "You are to make the most candid and confidential Communications upon all subjects to the Ministers of our generous Ally the King of France," Congress instructed the commissioners,

> to undertake nothing in the Negotiations for Peace or Truce without their Knowledge and Concurrence; and ultimately to govern yourselves by their Advice and Opinion; endeavouring in your whole Conduct to make them sensible how much we rely upon his Majesty's Influence for effectual support in every thing that may be necessary to the Peace, Security, and future Prosperity of the United States of America.

Vergennes, in fact, relied on the United States to distract Britain while France plundered the British Empire. His concern for the interests of the United States extended no further than the interests of France dictated. The imperial powers

In Spain, John Jay (left) matched wits with José Moñino, conde de Floridablanca, one of the most sophisticated, reform-minded Spanish statesmen of the eighteenth century (National Portrait Gallery, Smithsonian Institution). Floridablanca (right) resisted recognizing American independence because he worried that Spanish colonies would follow their example and rebel against Spanish rule, which they did in the early nineteenth century (Art Institute of Chicago).

were all predatory by nature and they adjusted their policies and shifted their alliances to suit their interests.

Vergennes did not hide his disappointment with American dependence on French arms, supplies, and money, and America's inability to defeat the British on their own, or even to prevent the British from detaching troops for service in the West Indies. When Lafayette returned to Paris in early 1782, Vergennes told him, "I am not marvelously pleased with the country that you have just left. I find it barely active and very demanding." By that point France had loaned the United States twenty-eight million livres, equivalent to at least four hundred million dollars today. Lafayette managed to persuade Vergennes to lend Congress an additional six million livres to keep the American war effort going.

Holland had an interest in the American war effort, too. Britain had declared war on the Dutch in 1780 to stop Dutch trade with the United States and France. Since the beginning of the war, much of America's exports, including naval stores bound for France, had passed through Dutch ports in the West Indies, where they were exchanged for arms bound for Washington's army. The British had agents in the Dutch colonies and were well aware of these transactions, but there was little they could do to stop them short of going to war with the Dutch. With Britain at war with America, France, and Spain, most members of Parliament were reluctant to go to war with Holland as well.

This began to change in 1779, when the Dutch sheltered John Paul Jones and his prize, HMS *Serapis*, from the pursuing Royal Navy. Then in September 1780 a British cruiser, HMS *Vestal*, captured an American vessel, the *Mercury*, off Newfoundland. On board was Henry Laurens, a South Carolina planter who had succeeded John Hancock as president of the Continental Congress. Laurens was on his way to Holland seeking money and arms. He had in his possession the draft of a commercial treaty between the United States and Holland, which the British regarded as grounds for war with the Dutch. They charged Laurens with treason, locked him in the Tower of London—the same treatment Washington, Franklin, and other American leaders would have received if the British had captured them—and declared war on Holland.

With Laurens in the Tower, John Adams left Paris in August 1780 and traveled to Amsterdam to persuade the Dutch government to recognize American independence and Dutch bankers to loan money to the United States. He described his mission as "that of a Man in the midst of the Ocean negotiating for his Life among a School of Sharks."

Everyone Adams met in Amsterdam had a prophesy. "One Says America will give France the Go By," he wrote to Franklin, who remained in Paris.

Another that France and Spain, will abandon America. A Third that Spain will forsake France and America. A Fourth that America, has the Interest of all Europe against her. A Fifth that She will become the greatest manufacturing Country, and thus ruin Europe. A Sixth that She will become a great and an ambitious military and naval Power, and consequently terrible to Europe.

All that mattered to the imperial powers, Adams understood, were their interests: "No Arguments are seriously attended to in Europe but Force." A stubborn realist, Adams distrusted everyone and succeeded admirably, persuading the Dutch government to recognize the independence of the United States and securing a loan of five million guilders from Dutch bankers.

John Jay, the American representative in Spain, had to deal with sharks of his own. Spain was the largest imperial power in the Americas, and had no interest in the success of an American republic, which might encourage its own colonies to rebel. Spanish officials, led by the king's chief minister, Don José Moñino, conde de Floridablanca, recognized that American settlement west of the Appalachians posed a threat to Spain's control of Mississippi River and the Gulf of Mexico. Excluding other nations from the gulf, Floridablanca told

Jay, was "the principal Object to be obtained by the war" and one the king would never relinquish.

Jay tried to sooth Spanish concern about American settlement between the Appalachians and the Mississippi, insisting that "ages will be necessary to settle those extensive regions," but at the rate the American population was growing, Floridablanca knew this was not true. Americans had already settled in Kentucky and what would become Tennessee. They were pushing into the Ohio country and had explored the Alabama and Tombigbee rivers, which flow through what would become Alabama into Mobile Bay. Some had settled on the banks of the Mississippi north of New Orleans.

America, Floridablanca insisted, must relinquish the right to navigate the Mississippi as a condition of Spanish support. Jay was under strict instructions from Congress not to give up the navigation of the Mississippi, and Franklin advised him not to budge. "Poor as we are," Franklin wrote, "yet as I know we shall be rich, I would rather agree with them to buy at a great Price the whole of their right on the Mississippi, than sell a Drop of its Waters. A neighbour might as well ask me to sell my street Door." Although Congress softened its position, Jay left Madrid in May 1782 without giving Spain what it wanted and secured only a token promise of financial support.

Peace Overtures

Negotiations to end the war began in an atmosphere of clashing interests and mutual distrust and were complicated by divisions within the warring governments and antagonism between the men responsible for making peace. The British government, humiliated by defeat at Yorktown, was torn by faction and personal animosities. Lord George Germain, the secretary of state for the American department, wanted to continue the war. If peace had to be made, he proposed to limit the United States to the region east of Appalachians and to keep New York, Charleston, and Savannah as British enclaves from which the Royal Navy could overawe the American states and support the defense of Britain's Caribbean colonies. Under pressure from the opposition in Parliament, he resigned, followed soon thereafter by Lord North, who resigned at the end of March 1782.

With great reluctance, George III asked Charles Watson-Wentworth, Lord Rockingham, the leader of the opposition in Parliament, to succeed North as prime minister. Rockingham had long argued in favor of the rights of the king's American subjects. He took office with the understanding that Britain would make peace on the basis of American independence.

Expecting the Rockingham government to open peace negotiations, Franklin called John Jay to Paris. Shortly thereafter he secured the release of Henry Laurens from the Tower of London by exchanging him for Lord Cornwallis, who had returned to England as a prisoner of war on parole. The British were satisfied with the exchange, but until Congress approved it, Laurens regarded his freedom as uncertain and declined to take part in peace talks. Thomas Jefferson, as events unfolded, never left the United States to join in the negotiations. That left John Adams, who distrusted Franklin nearly as much as he distrusted Vergennes. He remained in Amsterdam negotiating with the Dutch, leaving Franklin and Jay to begin the work.

Rockingham directed the new home secretary, William Fitzmaurice, Earl of Shelburne, to oversee the negotiations on behalf of Britain. Shelburne was one of the most perceptive, intellectually sophisticated British statesmen of the eighteenth century. He surrounded himself with some of the most innovative British thinkers of his generation, including Richard Price and Joseph Priestley, friends of Benjamin Franklin who admired the American Revolution-

aries and promoted political and economic reform in Britain. Priestley, the leading British chemist of his generation, thought Shelburne was "for ability and integrity together, the very first character in

Lord Shelburne, who served as British prime minister during the peace negotiations, had long opposed the war and sympathized with America's passion for liberty (Saltram © National Trust Images).

this kingdom." That view was not widely shared, at least in Parliament, where Shelburne had enemies.

Shelburne was one of the few members of Parliament who embraced the free market ideas of Adam Smith, whose *Inquiry into the Nature and Causes of the Wealth of Nations,* published in 1776, reflected the most advanced thinking in economics.

Charles James Fox, one of Shelburne's many political opponents, said that Smith's book was tedious and incomprehensible. Shelburne shared Smith's view that Britain would benefit from American independence, shedding the expenses of dominion, profiting from selling Americans manufactured goods and providing Americans with credit and a steady market for raw materials and agricultural products. Shelburne preferred to maintain a formal tie between Britain and America, but he saw very clearly that Britain's interests were to ensure that America became a valuable trading partner for England and not a satellite of France.

Shelburne had known Franklin in London before the war. He wrote to Franklin on April 6 that he "should be very glad to talk to you as I did then . . . upon the means of promoting the Happiness of Mankind, a Subject much more agreeable to my Nature, than the best concerted Plans for spreading Misery and Devastation." This message was delivered by Richard Oswald, a wealthy merchant Shelburne employed to conduct the day-to-day negotiations in Paris. Rockingham and Shelburne were anxious to make peace before more defeats compromised the future of the British Empire.

The situation changed dramatically shortly after Oswald arrived in Paris. In the West Indies, the French fleet under Admiral de Grasse, including thirty-five ships of the line, sailed from Martinique on a course to rendezvous with twelve Spanish ships of the line and transports carrying French and Spanish troops for the conquest of Jamaica. The British fleet under Admiral George Rodney, with thirty-six ships of the line, intercepted de Grasse near the Iles de Saintes, a group of small rocky islands south of Guadeloupe. After preliminary maneuvers the two fleets engaged on April 12. Rodney defeated the French in spectacular fashion, capturing de Grasse and his flagship, the massive *Ville de Paris,* which carried 104 guns.

News of the battle reached London and Paris in May. The British celebrated their victory but gave no thought to renewing the war. The victory offered Rockingham and Shelburne an opportunity to make peace at a moment when the balance of naval power in the Caribbean had shifted, perhaps only temporarily, in Britain's favor. Vergennes assured Franklin that France would fight on, but the mounting cost of the war had stretched French finances to their limit. The French had promised the Spanish to fight until the British surrendered Gibraltar, but the British had successfully defended the fortress for three years and showed no sign of wavering.

The Treaty of Paris

From its start, the American Revolution had been shaped by global patterns. As if to remind the negotiators of this fact, a deadly influenza pandemic, which began in China, reached Europe early in 1782. It had passed through India into Russia by way of central Asia. It soon reached Germany, Holland, France, and Britain. Adams caught it in Holland, and John Jay was incapacitated by the illness shortly after he arrived in Paris. In Britain, the fifty-two-year-old prime minister, Lord Rockingham, died from the disease on July 1.

George III promptly appointed Lord Shelburne to succeed Rockingham. Despite his intellectual sophistication and to some extent because of it, Shelburne was distrusted by many in his own Whig party. Shelburne's deep respect for the monarchy distinguished him from many of his party's leaders and his independence—some said unreliability—alienated him from others. Several of the ministers who had accepted office under Rockingham promptly resigned when Shelburne became prime minister. Some of them joined with Lord North and his associates in opposition to Shelburne. With a shallow majority in the House of Commons, Shelburne needed to move quickly to make peace.

John Jay distrusted Shelburne and bristled at the suggestion that American independence was a negotiating point rather than an accomplished fact. Franklin counseled Jay not to press Oswald on the matter, but Jay insisted that Britain acknowledge American independence and negotiate with America's representatives as equals. Shelburne instructed Oswald to concede this point, and the discussions continued.

Jay soon learned to distrust Vergennes as well. Vergennes, Jay told Franklin, would trade America's future to satisfy the Spanish desire to keep Americans out of the trans-Appalachian West. "If we lean on her love of liberty, her affection for America, or her disinterested magnaminity," Jay warned, "we shall lean on a broken reed." Jay's distrust was well justified. Vergennes wanted to ensure that America remained dependent on France, not a rising power with a vast inland empire at its disposal, and even sent an emissary to London to discourage the British from granting the United States fishing rights off Newfoundland.

Circumstances shifted again in September, when the Spanish and French mounted a major attack on Gibraltar intended to overwhelm the British garrison and bring the three-and-a-half-year siege to an end. The allies gathered the largest military force assembled in any one place during the entire war—some thirty-five thousand Spanish infantrymen and over seven thousand French soldiers, supported by heavy artillery and a combined fleet of forty-nine ships of the line, forty gunboats, twenty bomb vessels, and ten elaborate floating batteries—massive timber barges carrying more than one hundred and thirty heavy cannons and manned by over five thousand men. The floating batteries were to take up positions in the bay and demolish the British fortifications in preparation for an infantry assault that would take Gibraltar.

Nothing happened as planned. Shortly after taking up their positions on the morning of September 12, two of the floating batteries caught fire. It was immediately apparent that the allegedly indestructible vessels were deathtraps. The Spanish commander gave orders to scuttle the batteries,

and within hours they were all destroyed by fire and tremendous explosions as their powder stores ignited. The Spanish and French lost thousands of men, while British casualties were light. Gibraltar held. The Spanish and French agreed that mounting another attack was out of the question. The Spanish reluctantly abandoned the siege and prepared to make peace without taking Gibraltar.

Reports of the catastrophe reached Paris within a week and Holland a few days later. Jay recognized that the American commissioners needed to move quickly to complete a peace agreement with Britain before American interests were compromised in a general peace accord in which France might insist on American concessions to Spain. Adams left Amsterdam and arrived in Paris on October 26. He found that he and Jay were of like mind that the commissioners should pursue America's interests and ignore their instructions to consult with Vergennes.

The negotiations began in earnest on October 30, with Oswald joined by Henry Strachey, who had been sent from London with fresh instructions. Jay and Adams were hard-working men by nature, and persuaded Oswald and Strachey to meet for several hours each day. Franklin's health would not permit him to keep up such a pace. He left his younger colleagues to do most of the work. Boundaries, fishing rights, the treatment of loyalists, and the settlement of pre-war debts were the major issues. Shelburne wanted to force the Americans to compensate loyalists for their losses

The dramatic destruction of the floating batteries at Gibraltar was one of the most celebrated events of the war. The British were proud that their sailors rescued hundreds of the enemy from the burning vessels, an act of humanity celebrated in this detail from a design for a printed handkerchief sold in British shops (The Society of the Cincinnati).

and to promise that Americans would pay pre-war debts to British merchants. He directed Oswald and Strachey to insist on excluding much of Maine from American jurisdiction and to deny Americans most of the trans-Appalachian West as leverage.

Jay and Adams insisted that British forces must evacuate New York, Charleston, and Savannah, and acknowledge American sovereignty from the southern frontier of Georgia to the northern frontier of Maine and from the Atlantic Ocean to the Mississippi River. New Englanders also wanted the right to fish the Newfoundland Banks and to come ashore to dry their catch—an essential part of commercial fishing before refrigeration. Thousands of ordinary New Englanders made their living by fishing and would be ruined if they were excluded from these fishing grounds.

The negotiators contested every point. Oswald found Jay "uncommonly stiff" and Strachey complained that Adams and Jay were "the greatest quibblers I ever knew." Adams complained that Strachey "pushes and presses every Point as far as it can possibly go." The four men nonetheless moved quickly, and completed their work by November 5, when Strachey set off for London with a draft

treaty, to which Shelburne gave his approval.

On November 30, 1782, more than a year after the British surrender at Yorktown, Franklin, Adams and Jay, joined by Henry Laurens, went to Oswald's hotel to sign the preliminary treaty of peace. The British formally acknowledged American independence. The boundaries of the new nation were defined and included Maine and extending from the Appalachians to the Mississippi River. The British agreed to withdraw their forces from inside those boundaries "with all convenient speed." The British agreed that Americans could fish in the waters off Canada as they had always done. The Americans agreed not to interfere with loyalists who chose to leave and pledged not to interfere with the collection of pre-war debts Americans still owed to British merchants.

Vergennes was astonished by the generous terms the Americans had secured. "The English buy peace rather than make it," he wrote. Vergennes expressed severe disappointment that the American negotiators had disobeyed the instructions of Congress by not consulting with him. France and Spain agreed to separate peace terms with Britain a few weeks later. Despite bringing the war to an end, Shelburne lost the confidence of Parliament

This French allegorical engraving reflects the French view that American independence was a gift from France. It depicts an Indian, symbolizing America, beside a monument bearing portraits of Franklin, "Waginston," and Louis XVI, with the inscription "America and the seas, O Louis, recognize you as their liberator." The British lion lies defeated at America's feet. The broken trident symbolizes the end of Britain's dominance at sea (The Society of the Cincinnati).

Isaiah Thomas of Worcester, Massachusetts, published this broadside as soon as news of the preliminary articles of peace reached him. He assured his readers that the news was "Sure and Certain" and explained that it had arrived by ship in Philadelphia and passed through New York and Boston on its way to Worcester, adding "Great rejoicing has been manifested wherever the above intelligence came" (Courtesy, American Antiquarian Society).

Important Intelligence of PEACE!
Between America and Great-Britain, and all the European Powers at War.

SURE and CERTAIN.

NEW-YORK, March 26.
A GENERAL PEACE.

LATE on Monday night, arrived an express from New-Jersey, which brought the following account :—That on Sunday last the 23d inst. a vessel arrived at Philadelphia from Cadiz, with dispatches to the Continental Congress, informing them, That on TUESDAY the 21st of JANUARY, the PRELIMINARIES to a GENERAL PEACE, between Great-Britain, France, Spain, Holland, and the United States of America, were signed at Paris, by all the Commissioners from those powers; in consequence of which, hostilities, by sea and land, were to cease in Europe, on Thursday the 20th of February ; and in America, on THURSDAY the 20th of March, in the present year, one thousand seven hundred and eighty-three.

This very important intelligence was on Monday night announced by the firing of cannon, and great rejoicings at Elizabeth-Town.

Late last night arrived Lewis Morris, Esq; express from Philadelphia, who brought a printed paper, from which the following are copied.

PHILADELPHIA, March 24, 1783.

Yesterday arrived after a passage of 32 days from Cadiz, a French sloop of war, commanded by M. du Quesne, with the agreeable intelligence of PEACE.

The particular articles respecting this happy and glorious event are as follows :

The principal ARTICLES of the PRELIMINARIES of PEACE, of the 21st of January 1783.

FRANCE to retain Tobago and Senegal. France to restore to Great-Britain, Grenada, Saint Vincents, Dominica, and Saint Christophers.

St. Eustatia, Demerara, Barbice, and Issequibo, to be restored to the Dutch.

Great-Britain to restore to France, Goree, St. Lucia, St. Pierre, and Miquelon.

The Fishery of France and England, on the Coast of Newfoundland, to remain on the same footing on which they were by the Treaty of 1763, except that part of the Coast of Bonavista, at Cape St. John's, shall belong to the English.

France to be re-established in the East-Indies, as well in Bengal, as on the East and West Coast of the Peninsula, as regulated by the Treaty of 1763.

The Articles of the preceeding Treaties, concerning the demolition of Dunkirk, to be suppressed.

Spain to retain Minorca and West-Florida.

Great-Britain cedes East-Florida to Spain.

An agreement to be entered into between Spain and Great-Britain, about the cutting of wood in the bay of Honduras.

Great-Britain to retain the Dutch settlement of Negapatnam, in the East-Indies.

Great Britain to restore Trinquemale to the Dutch if not retaken.

St. Eustatia, Demarara, and Isequebo, to be restored by the French to the United Provinces.

Great-Britain acknowledges the *Sovereignty* and *Independence* of the *Thirteen United States of America*.

The limits of the United States to be as agreed upon in the Provisional Articles between them and Great Britain; except that they shall not extend further down the river Mississippi than the 32d degree of North latitude from whence a line is to be drawn to the head of the river St. Mary, along the middle of that river down to its mouth.

WORCESTER, April 1, 5 o'Clock, P. M. 1783.

We have this moment received the above truly interesting and pleasing intelligence by a Gentleman directly from Boston. The Intelligence arrived there yesterday in four days from the City of New-York.

Great rejoicing has been manifested wherever the above glorious intelligence came.

The preliminaries with America nearly as published last Thursday.

Copy of a letter from Elias Boudinot, Esq; President of the Continental Congress, to William Livingston, Esq; Governor of New-Jersey.

" An express has just arrived from on board a sloop of war in the river, which left Cadiz February 14.—She announces that the definitive treaty, having been signed by all the belligerent powers, on the 21st of January, all hostilities had ceased in Europe ; and that the same happy event was to take place in this country on the 20th of March instant. The Count d' Estaing, who was ready to sail with sixty ships of the line, a very formidable armament, had given up the attempt, and was dispersing his fleet to the different ports. This ship does not bring us official dispatches, having been sent by the Count d' Estaing, and the Marquis de la Fayette, in hopes that she might by accident (as she has done) be the fortunate medium of the earliest communication.—Although the stage goes to-morrow morning, I could not with satisfaction to my own mind, suffer your Excellency and my friends in Trenton, to be deprived of the knowledge of so happy an event, one moment longer than absolute necessity required.

I have the honor to be, &c. &c.

LAUS DEO.

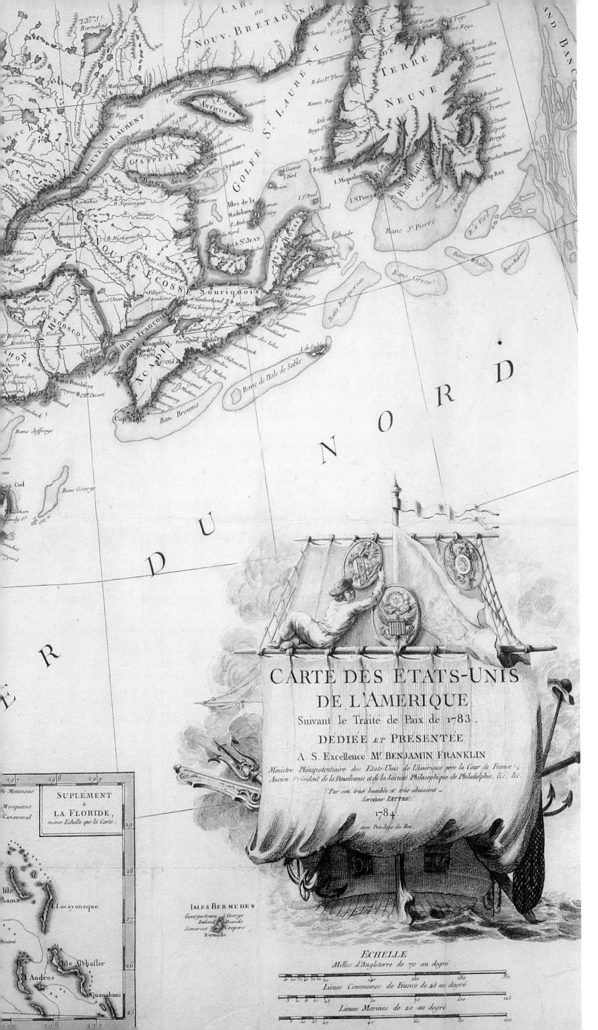

CARTE DES ETATS-UNIS
DE L'AMERIQUE
Suivant le Traité de Paix de 1783.

DÉDIÉE ET PRESENTÉE

A S. Excellence M. BENJAMIN FRANKLIN

Ministre Plénipotentiaire des Etats-Unis de l'Amerique près la Cour de France,
Ancien Président de la Pensilvanie et de la Société Philosophique de Philadelphie, &c. &c.

Par son très humble et très obéissant
Serviteur LATTRÉ.

1784.
avec Privilège du Roi.

SUPLEMENT
a
LA FLORIDE,
même Echelle que la Carte.

ISLES BERMUDES
Georgetown S. George
Ireland S. Davids
Somerset S. Coopers
Bermude

ECHELLE
Milles d'Angleterre de 70 au degré

Lieues Communes de France de 25 au degré

Lieues Marines de 20 au degré

The United States
and Great Britain
exchanged documents
confirming their ratifi-
cation of the Treaty of
Paris in May 1784. The
next month Jean Lattré,
an official engraver to
Louis XVI, published
this large-scale map—
the first map to delin-
eate the full extent of
the new United States
of America after the
ratification of the treaty
(The Society of the
Cincinnati).

265

and was forced to resign in February 1783, about the time news of the treaty reached America. Congress approved the terms and sent word back to the commissioners to sign the treaty. The final Treaty of Paris was signed on September 3, 1783.

The treaty was one of the most remarkable accomplishments of the American Revolution, made possible by twenty years of stubborn resistance and eight years of wartime suffering and struggle by thousands of Americans. Together they broke Britain's will to continue fighting. Benjamin Franklin, with brilliance, charm, and patient skill, had forged the French alliance and secured the arms, supplies, money, and military support America needed. Two determined realists—John Jay and John Adams—had detached the negotiations from the alliance and navigated the predatory diplomacy of the imperial powers, taking advantage of a moment when the British ministry was in the hands of men who recognized that American prosperity was worth much more to Britain than vengeance. They had secured peace on the best possible terms, and with it the future of the United States as a continental republic of almost limitless opportunities.

When it was all over, Jay wrote to Robert Livingston, the secretary for foreign affairs, warning that the French "are interested in separating us from Great Britain, and on that point we may, I believe depend upon them; but it is not their interest that we should become a great and formidable people, and therefore they will not help us to become so." Jay understood that independent America had to make its own way: "I think we have no rational dependence except on God and ourselves."

"Conquerers at last!"

While Jay, Adams, and Franklin negotiated an end to the war, Washington's army remained in its camps on the Hudson, keeping watch of the British army in New York City. In South Carolina, Nathanael Greene's little army camped outside Charleston, sparring occasionally with British foraging parties. In one of these inconsequential

skirmishes, Col. John Laurens, a former aide to George Washington and the son of Henry Laurens, was killed.

News of the preliminary treaty of peace reached Congress in February 1783. With no money to pay the army or keep the soldiers fed or supplied, Congress instructed Washington to send most of the men home on furlough—essentially unpaid leave—rather than discharge them. There was a remote possibility that the British government would refuse to ratify the final treaty and the war would resume. If that happened it would be better to recall men from furlough than to recruit and train a new army. The more immediate reason for the furloughs was that the men might mutiny if they were discharged without being paid what they were owed.

Common soldiers understood this as clearly as any member of Congress. Nearly every man in the army was owed back pay, much of it years overdue. Joseph Plumb Martin, a sergeant who had enlisted in 1777, explained that "to discharge us absolutely in our present pitiful forlorn condition, it was feared, might cause some difficulties, which might be too hard for the government to get easily over."

From the start of the war, recruiting and retaining enlisted men had been a constant challenge. In Europe, labor surpluses and chronic underemployment assured that armies could depend on landless laborers and the urban poor to fill their ranks. In America, labor shortages and low unemployment forced Congress and the states to offer inducements to secure volunteers, including cash bounties at enlistment and promises of land warrants—documents that entitled the holders to have a specified number of acres of public land surveyed and granted to them—and cash bonuses at discharge. Retaining officers was just as difficult. Congress and the states made extravagant promises of post-war land grants and generous pay to attract and keep Continental officers.

At first these promises were made in a spirit of irrational optimism, and later out of desperation. Congress was unable to fulfill them. It promised pay and bonuses without having the power to tax and promised land without controlling a

Maj. James Fairlie, an aide-de-camp to General Steuben, was one of many young Continental Army officers who joined the Society of the Cincinnati. The Society's insignia—a gold eagle suspended from a blue and white ribbon—symbolized his service and his pride in the achievements of the Continental Army (The Society of the Cincinnati).

single acre. The public domain belonged to the states. Writing almost fifty years after the war, Joseph Plumb Martin remembered that when they enlisted, the men of his regiment were promised six dollars and sixty-six cents a month. "How did we fare in particular?" he wrote.

Why, as we did in every other. I received the six dollars and two thirds, till (if I remember rightly) the month of August, 1777, when paying ceased. And what was six dollars and sixty-seven cents of this 'Continental currency' as it was called, worth? it was scarcely enough to procure a man a dinner. Government was wisely ashamed to tantalize the soldiers any longer with such trash, and wisely gave it up for its own credit. I received one month's pay in specie while on the march to Virginia, in the year 1781, and except that, I never received any pay worth the name while I belonged to the army. Had I been paid as I was promised to be at my engaging in the service, I needed not to have suffered as I did . . . there was enough in the country, and money would have procured it.

Martin's last point touched one of Washington's greatest frustrations. The men of the Continental Army had gone hungry in a land of plenty. "It would be well for the troops," Washington wrote to Gouverneur Morris in 1780, "if like Chameleons, they could live upon Air—or like the Bear suck their paws for sustenance." Men had deserted simply to find food to eat. Hungry soldiers mutinied at West Point in January 1780. Two Connecticut regiments prepared to march home that spring after weeks of short rations. "There are certain bounds," Washington told Governor Trumbull of Connecticut, "beyond which it is impossible for Human nature to go. We are arrived at these." Pennsylvania and New Jersey troops, pushed beyond their limits, mutinied in January 1781. They were starving. They had worn their uniforms to rags and their shoes had fallen to pieces. "Our soldiery are not devoid of reasoning faculties," Anthony Wayne warned Pennsylvania officials. "They have now served their country for near five years, poorly clothed, badly fed, and worse paid."

Soldiers had gone hungry because Congress had no power to tax and thus could not supply their basic needs. Congress had appealed to the states for money, which yielded little. It had sold loan office certificates—what we now call government bonds—until the market for them collapsed because the interest was paid in Continental paper money, which lost its value very quickly. Benjamin Franklin said that the depreciation of Continental paper money was the same as a tax that spread the costs of the war over the entire population, but he never starved because the money became worthless. Congress had borrowed from foreign creditors until its credit was exhausted. By the end of the war Congress and the army resorted to paying their bills with interest-bearing certificates of indebtedness called indents. These were essentially promissory notes, payable at some fixed time after the end of the war. By the last years of the war farmers were reluctant to accept these promises as payment. In 1780 Washington admitted in private that the army had been reduced to taking "every ounce of Forage . . . and a good deal of the Provisions . . . at the point of the Bayonet."

Officers struggled to maintain order, but most of them were just as angry and frustrated as their men. Like their soldiers, they had gone without pay. In 1780 Congress had promised the officers half of their yearly pay every year for the rest of their lives if they would serve until the end of the war. In 1783 Congress changed its mind and decided it would give the officers five years of full pay instead. For a young man—most of the officers were under thirty and might live forty or fifty more years—full pay for five years was much less than half pay for life. It seemed like an empty promise either way, because Congress had no money.

Encouraged by a few equally frustrated members of Congress, some of Washington's officers discussed using the army to take control of the government—something that has happened in many countries over the last two hundred years. The details of this conspiracy, and even whether the discussions went far enough to be called a conspiracy, are hazy. Men contemplating the military overthrow of governments are usually careful not to commit too much to paper. What is clear is that the conspirators hoped George Washington would lead them and that Washington learned enough about their plans to be alarmed. At a meeting called by discontented officers in March 1783, Washington appealed to the men he had led for so long not "to overturn the liberties of our Country" and "deluge our rising Empire in Blood." He asked them to put their faith in the justice of Congress. If they would do so, Washington said,

You will give one more distinguished proof of unexampled patriotism and patient virtue, rising superior to the pressure of the most complicated sufferings; And you will, by the dignity of your Conduct, afford occasion for Posterity to say, when speaking of the glorious example you have exhibited to man kind, had this day been wanting, the World had never seen the last stage of perfection to which human nature is capable of attaining.

While he was speaking, Washington pulled a pair of new reading glasses from his pocket. "Gentlemen," he said, "you will permit me to put on my spectacles, for I have not only grown gray, but almost blind, in the service of my country." Few of the officers had ever seen Washington wearing glasses and the sight surprised them. They realized that Washington had sacrificed as much as any of them. The meeting ended with the officers pledging their loyalty to Congress. Nothing more was said about seizing control of the government.

As they prepared to go home, the officers formed an organization they called the Society of the Cincinnati, named after Cincinnatus, a hero of the ancient Roman republic who served his country in wartime with honor and then returned to his farm. The Society would provide the officers with a reason to gather as friends after the war and an organization through which they could help one another. The Society would also remind Congress of the debt owed to the officers. It adopted the eagle as its symbol. George Washington agreed to serve as the first president general, an office he held for the rest of his life. The original members made an additional commitment: they promised to remind Americans to remember and honor the achievements of the Revolution.

The Society was proposed and shaped by two of Washington's generals, Henry Knox and Baron Steuben, but most of its original members were veteran lieutenants and captains. Most were young men who had sacrificed the years of their lives when they might have been developing farms or establishing themselves in business. They had served their country instead and were going home with nothing but consciousness of duty faithfully performed. Membership in the Society of the Cincinnati and the opportunity to wear its gold Eagle insignia were marks of honor for young men who had little else. In the absence of any public commitment to care for veteran officers in need, the original members of the Society pledged "brotherly kindness in all things," including "the most substantial acts of beneficence, according to the ability of the society, towards those officers and their families, who unfortunately may be under the necessity of receiving it." The original members each contributed one month's pay to create a fund dedicated to the relief of fellow veteran officers and their widows.

In place of the back pay they were owed, furloughed soldiers were given certificates promising their pay within a few years. These promises had little value to hungry men in rags, and most soldiers sold these "final settlement certificates" for a few cents on the dollar to men who were willing to gamble that the government might one day have the money to make good on its promises. Joseph Plumb Martin sold his certificate and used the little money he received to buy new clothes to wear home so his family would not see him in rags. "The country was rigorous in exacting my compliance to *my* engagements," he wrote, "but equally careless in performing her contracts with me; and why so? One reason was, because she had all the power in her hands, and I had none. Such things ought not to be."

As his soldiers left camp, Washington had time to reflect on what those remarkable men had accomplished. In the future, he wrote to Nathanael Greene,

it will not be believed that such a force as Great Britain has employed for eight years in this Country could be baffled . . . by numbers infinitely less, composed of men oftentimes half starved, always in Rags, without pay, and experiencing, at times, every species of distress which human nature is capable of undergoing.

They were, he wrote, "veterans who have patiently endured hunger, nakedness and cold, who have suffered and bled without a murmur, and who with perfect good order have retired to their homes, without the settlement of their Accounts or a farthing of Money in their pockets." They were men of honor—ordinary men made extraordinary by their devotion to a great cause. American freedom has been built on their sacrifice.

Enlisted men had won the war, wrote Joseph Plumb Martin, yet in the end they had been "turned adrift like old worn-out horses." Few men wrote about our Revolutionary War with such unsentimental clarity or condemned its corruption and failures more bluntly. Yet for all his cynicism and frustration, Martin was a patriot who confessed he had felt "a secret pride swell my heart" at Yorktown, "when I saw the 'star-spangled banner' waving majestically in the very faces of our implacable adversaries." He was amazed that men "starved, and naked, and suffering every thing short of death . . . should be able to persevere through an eight years' war, and come off conquerers at last!" The American Revolution, for all its vices, astonished him. It should astonish us, too.

The veterans of the Revolutionary War were mostly gone by 1848, when William Tylee Ranney painted *Veterans of 1776 Returning from the War*. Threadbare but happy, Ranney's veterans are ordinary soldiers and the proud survivors of Bunker Hill, Trenton, Princeton, Saratoga, and Yorktown—names they have chalked on the wagon bearing them home (Dallas Museum of Art).

Chapter 18 Novus Ordo Seclorum

Many Americans imagined that the end of the Revolutionary War would mark the beginning of a new era of prosperity and peace in which the United States would flourish. Having freed themselves from the threat of British tyranny and the restrictions and taxes imposed by Parliament, established their independence, and created republican institutions to govern their affairs, they expected to realize the promise of their Revolution.

Aspirations for the new era varied nearly as much as the American people. Some idealists looked forward to a golden age in which the United States would recreate the lost glory of ancient Athens and the Roman Republic. They imagined that their Revolution was a watershed in human history, a sentiment reflected in the seal of the new nation, which bears the Latin motto *Novus Ordo Seclorum*, meaning a new order of the ages.

Others imagined that the people of the United States would fulfill the bright promise of the Enlightenment and create a new society based on ideals of universal equality, natural right, and benevolence, shaped by the insights of modern science and philosophy. Some looked forward to building a new world in which the unrestricted exchange of ideas and goods would break down the barriers that divided peoples and shape a new kind of society in which governments would exist mainly to resolve disputes between their citizens and in which imperial ambitions, war, and taxation would disappear in a global society in which commerce—intellectual and material—would be the defining force.

Americans who knew nothing of Cincinnatus and Cicero, who never read the works of Newton, Locke, or Adam Smith, and whose ideas about commerce extended no further than their account in a storekeeper's ledger and the market price for their crops, looked forward to enjoying greater personal independence than before the war. Landless veterans looked forward to acquiring the bounty land that Congress and the state governments had promised them. Many Americans hoped to live prosperous and happy lives in the communities where they were born, while others planned to move over the Appalachians into the rich valleys of the Ohio, Cumberland, and Tennessee rivers.

Some were less concerned about material prosperity and looked forward to the enjoyment of religious liberty, practicing their faith without interference from government, free from threats, intimidation, and violence. Among them were people who imagined the Revolution as an opportunity for moral reformation, in which Americans

Washington said farewell to his officers at Fraunces Tavern in New York City on December 4, 1783. Col. Benjamin Tallmadge, who was present, wrote that the officers were gathered before Washington entered the room.

His emotion, too strong to be concealed, seemed to be reciprocated by every officer present. After partaking of a slight refreshment in almost breathless silence, the General filled his glass with wine, and turning to the officers, he said "With a heart full of love and gratitude I now take leave of you. I most devoutly wish that your latter days may be as prosperous and happy as your former ones have been glorious and honorable." After the officers had taken a glass of wine, Gen. Washington said: "I cannot come to each of you, but shall feel obliged if each of you will come and take me by the hand." Gen. Knox being nearest to him, turned to the Commander-in-Chief who, suffused in tears, was incapable of utterance, but grasped his hand; when they embraced each other in silence. In the same affectionate manner every officer in the room marched up . . .

Artist Alonzo Chappel, who depicted the event in this painting completed in 1865, relied on Tallmadge's account to imagine the scene (Chicago History Museum).

The reverse of the Great Seal of the United States depicts an incomplete pyramid with thirteen layers topped with a triangle enclosing the eye of God, with the motto "Annuit Cœptis"—"He approves of our undertaking." The pyramid bears the date 1776 and the motto "Novus Ordo Seclorum"—"A New Order of the Ages." This 1786 engraving is the first published version (The John Carter Brown Library).

included more Germans and Irish than English—resumed after the war, but even it was touched by the idealism of the Revolution. The arrival of a shipload of servants in New York in January 1784 seemed to a group of wealthy citizens as "contrary to . . . the idea of liberty this country has so happily established." They collected funds to pay for their passage and free them from bondage. The enslaved understood—whatever their enslavers said—that the Revolutionary claim of universal equality and natural rights applied to them. Some of them imagined a future without chains in which they would labor for their own benefit and the benefit of their families.

A few Americans regarded the new era with caution, their optimism chastened by the difficulties and disappointments of eight years of war. They were realists in a time of passion and enthusiasm. The wisest among them understood that the new nation would struggle at every step in a world resistant to change—a world dominated by empires intent on expanding their power and reach, heedless of the natural rights and fundamental needs of others, a world in which greed and cruelty were more common than generosity and compassion, and in which people used to subjection and subordination did not comprehend the vast potential of free society.

The obstacles to realizing these varied aspirations and ambitions were greater than most Americans imagined. Nearly all, in the short run at least, were disappointed. The war had brought with it an unprecedented upheaval. Parts of the country had been made desolate by the armies or laid waste by partisans. Exports, upon which the national income depended, had been interrupted. The new nation was hemmed in by Britain and Spain, powers hostile to American expansion into the trans-Appalachian West. Congress was deep in debt to domestic and foreign creditors, with no means to pay its debts, including the back pay owed to veterans. Most of them had returned home with no money at all.

The new nation had no institution capable of addressing these issues effectively. Congress had conducted the war in a haphazard way. It was not equipped to govern the nation nor was it intended to do so. It derived its authority from the consent of thirteen sovereign states that were only rarely unan-

and ultimately the world would turn away from materialism and toward Christian brotherhood.

People who worked for wages hoped that the end of the war would lead to more work and better opportunities as fishing, shipbuilding, maritime commerce, construction, and other sources of employment disrupted by the war revived and expanded. Some of them were former indentured servants. The number of indentured servants had declined during the war because the servant trade was disrupted and because thousands of indentured servants—exactly how many is not clear—enlisted in the Continental Army or the militia, and some acquired their freedom as a consequence. The indentured servant trade—the new migrants imous about anything. They had created the Continental Congress in 1774 to address a common emergency that almost immediately degenerated into war. Congress had never possessed the authority it needed to conduct the war effectively. Such authority as it possessed was formalized in Articles of Confederation and Perpetual Union drawn up immediately after Congress declared the former colonies independent of British rule. Congress debated the proposed Articles of Confederation for more than a year before submitting them to the states for ratification. Twelve states ratified them by early 1779, but Maryland withheld ratification until early 1781, when the Articles went into effect.

In the interim Congress had conducted business as if the Articles had been ratified. The powers the Articles defined were no more than the powers Congress had assumed by the implied consent of the colonies—chiefly to manage the war, support the army, and conduct relations with foreign powers. The Articles vested Congress with a few additional powers, including the power to establish uniform weights and measures and manage the post office. The Articles gave Congress the authority to mint coins but made no reference to paper money. Congress issued it anyway, in such abundance that it became worthless. The Articles did not grant Congress authority to levy taxes. A 1781 proposal to amend the Articles to allow Congress to collect a five percent tax on imports, with the revenue dedicated to paying off wartime debts, failed to win unanimous approval from the states. Rhode Island refused its consent. When the war ended, Congress could not meet current expenses, much less pay off its debts. It was essentially bankrupt. What legitimacy it possessed began to fade as soon as the preliminary treaty of peace was announced and the army was disbanded.

American Cincinnatus

The obstacles to creating a new order of things weighed heavily on George Washington, whose responsibilities as commander in chief were coming to an end. At that moment Washington was the most important man in America. His potential influence was enormous and his views, if he expressed them, might shape the future of the nation.

George Washington's views had been shaped by an unconventional life. As the third son of a moderately successful Virginia planter, his prospects were as modest as his inheritance. Whatever success he was to achieve had to be achieved by other means. At an early age Washington learned the importance of patronage and benefitted from it, first from the patronage of his older half-brother Lawrence, who had inherited the largest part of their father's estate, and then from the aristocratic Fairfax family into which Lawrence had married.

As a young man Washington accompanied Lawrence on a journey to Barbados, which, however brief, gave him a broader view of the British Empire than many of his contemporaries. He met some of the island's leading men and military officers responsible for defending it, and took advantage of opportunities to examine its defenses. Then or shortly thereafter he conceived the idea of seeking advancement through military service. This was a conventional path for the younger sons of British aristocrats but rarely followed by colonials, who lacked the powerful patrons they needed to secure their commissions.

In his early twenties, Washington sought to ingratiate himself with a series of potential patrons, including Lord Fairfax, Governor Dinwiddie, and finally General Edward Braddock. Despite achieving some fleeting notoriety in Britain for his exploits at the beginning of the French and Indian War, Washington's ambition to secure a place in the British army eluded him. At the end of his service in the war he abandoned that ambition, married a wealthy young widow, and retired to Mount Vernon, which he acquired from Lawrence's widow. He was then just twenty-seven. He threw himself into making Mount Vernon a model estate, but he never relinquished his interest in military affairs. He did, however, relinquish his attachment to the conventional dependence of Virginia gentlemen of his generation on the networks of patronage and clientage that bound them together and reinforced their provincialism. Patronage had failed him. His success was based on his own merits, which led him to weigh the value of others by their merits rather than their connections. It also encouraged a spirit of self-reliance and independence that sustained him during the extraordinary trials of the Revolutionary War.

The war was the most important experience of Washington's life, but it was not the defining one. The war, desperate and difficult as it was, only confirmed and reinforced views he already held, including some that were in sharp contrast to those held by many of his Revolutionary peers. Washington abhorred debt and was scrupulous about meeting his obligations promptly and in full, a habit that distinguished him from contemporaries who lived beyond their means and were cavalier about discharging their debts. Washington did not regard the military as a threat to liberty and shared none of the traditional fear that standing armies are instruments of tyranny. He knew that armies were expensive and excessive expenses needed to be guarded against, but he was certain that an effective professional army commanded by qualified officers was essential for defense. He was also certain that the United States needed a central government endowed with sufficient authority to protect the nation and advance its economic interests in a world dominated by competitive, predatory empires. Power, in the mind of many of Washington's Revolutionary peers, was the enemy of liberty. To Washington, power was essential to protect liberty. He had no fear of a central government endowed with "energy," by which he meant a government with authority led by men of character.

Washington was convinced that a man's character mattered more than his social connections, powerful patrons, or even his experience. As commander in chief he surrounded himself with men of fine character—honest, dependable, committed, sober, unpretentious, hard-working men others would follow and obey—regardless of their background. He made use of Charles Lee and Horatio Gates, men with regular British army experience, but he regarded them as untrustworthy and avoided them as soon as he was able. Washington's most trusted lieutenants—Nathanael Greene and Henry Knox—were men of no great social distinction and had neither powerful patrons nor much useful experience, but they were remarkably unselfish, dedicated, and able men.

Washington looked for those characteristics he cultivated in himself. In him they were united with two characteristics others admired—courage, which he displayed on the battlefield in a combination of serenity and energy untouched by fear, and personal grace, which he exhibited without effort when he rode and danced and which was evident whenever he walked into a room. His presence was commanding, even when he was not giving commands. Washington's character—carefully cultivated and exhibited continuously through eight years of war—made him the most widely admired person in America.

Washington had served without pay and at no small sacrifice to his private interests and was generally regarded as incorruptible—a living embodiment of the virtues attributed to the ancient Roman hero Cincinnatus. In the summer of 1783 he decided to take advantage of his reputation to draw the attention of Americans to the critical state of national affairs.

"The destiny of unborn Millions"

In June 1783 Washington wrote a long letter addressed to the governors of the states, offering his advice about what needed to be done to ensure the future prosperity, peace, security, and happiness of the American people. The letter was immediately published in pamphlets and newspapers, as Washington expected. He thus made his views known directly to the American people, circumventing Congress.

His purpose, he explained, was

to offer my sentiments respecting some important subjects which appear to me to be intimately connected with the tranquility of the United States, to take my leave . . . as a public Character, and to give my final blessing to that Country, in whose service I have spent the prime of my life, for whose sake I have consumed so many anxious days and watchful

This copy of General Washington's circular letter to the state governors was owned by Capt. Robert Coltman, a veteran of the Continental artillery. Along with Continental soldiers, Coltman and his men had gone unpaid, poorly fed, and badly supplied because Congress lacked the power to tax (The Society of the Cincinnati).

A Circular Letter,

FROM
HIS EXCELLENCY
George Washington,
COMMANDER IN CHIEF
OF THE
ARMIES OF THE
UNITED STATES
OF
AMERICA;

Addressed to the GOVERNORS of
the several STATES, on his
resigning the Command of the
Army, and retiring from public Business,

PHILADELPHIA:
Printed by Robert Smith, jun.
back of the Fountain Inn, between Second and Third streets.

nights, and whose happiness, being extremely dear to me, will always constitute no inconsiderable part of my own.

The United States, he wrote, faced important decisions. Americans had won their independence, but the future of the country depended on what they did with that independence. The nation had almost limitless potential, including "a vast tract of Continent . . . abounding with all the necessaries and conveniences of life" and the "absolute freedom and Independancy" to shape its own destiny.

Americans were fortunate that their Revolution had occurred in the century of the Enlightenment, "when the rights of Mankind were better understood and more clearly defined, than at any former period" and "the researches of the human Mind after social happiness have been carried to a great extent," and "the treasures of knowledge acquired by the labours of Philosophers, Sages and Legislators . . . are laid open for our use." The foundations of free society were to be found in the "cultivation of letters, the unbounded extension of Commerce, the progressive Refinement of manners, the growing liberality of sentiment, and, above all, the pure and benign light of Revelation." With all of these advantages, Washington concluded, the American people should be "completely free and happy." If they were not, he added, "the fault will be entirely their own." The decisions Americans had to make would determine "whether the Revolution must ultimately be considered as a blessing or a curse: a blessing or a curse, not to the present Age alone, for with our fate will the destiny of unborn Millions be involved."

The government of the United States, Washington urged, must be given the authority to "govern the general concerns of the confederated republic, without which the Union cannot be of long duration." Washington was thinking mainly about the power to impose and collect taxes. Because Congress had lacked authority to collect taxes, Washington wrote, the war had taken much longer to win than was necessary.

Second, he insisted, Americans must have "a sacred regard to public Justice." The debts owed by the government had to be paid. These debts included money owed to foreign governments and bankers who had made loans to the American government. The debts also included the pay that was due to officers and men who had served in the army. "It was the price of their blood and of your Independency," Washington wrote, "it is therefore more than a common debt, it is a debt of honor."

Third, Washington recommended "the adoption of a proper Peace Establishment," by which he meant the organization of the military strength of the United States to provide for effective defense. He added that "the formation and discipline of the militia of the continent should be absolutely uniform" and the weapons used should be of the same kind everywhere. This would make it possible to combine the state militias into an effective army to defend the country if an enemy ever threatened the United States.

Washington concluded by asking the states to "forget their local prejudices and policies" and, when necessary, sacrifice their own interests to those of the whole country. He ended his letter with a prayer:

I now make it my earnest prayer, that God would have you, and the State over which you preside, in his holy protection, that he would incline the hearts of the Citizens to cultivate a spirit of subordination and obedience to Government, to entertain a brotherly affection and love for one another, for their fellow Citizens of the United States at large, and particularly for their brethren who have served in the Field, and finally, that he would most graciously be pleased to dispose us all, to do Justice, to love mercy, and to demean ourselves with that Charity, humility and pacific temper of mind, which were the Characteristics of the Divine Author of our blessed Religion, and without an humble imitation of whose example in these things, we can never hope to be a happy Nation.

On November 25, 1783, the last British troops boarded ships and left New York City. As

By personally resigning his commission, Washington reminded Americans that he had acted for eight years with powers delegated by Congress, which needed more extensive authority to address the challenges facing the nation (Yale University Art Gallery).

they departed, George Washington and his officers, along with some of the remaining soldiers of the Continental Army, took possession of the city.

Washington had one more task. When he accepted command of the Continental Army in June 1775, Congress had presented Washington with a commission naming him general and commander in chief, vesting him "with full power and authority to act as you shall think for the good and Welfare of the service." Conscious of the deep symbolic importance of his conduct, Washington was determined to present himself to Congress and return that commission, making his resignation a formal public act acknowledging the authority of Congress. He had served the republic in war for nearly eight and a half years and was going home without any reward beside the applause and gratitude of his country and the consciousness of duty faithfully performed. He expected that returning his commission would be the final act of his public life, and that he would return to his farm, like the Roman hero Cincinnatus, to live the remainder of his life as a private citizen.

Many Europeans expected Washington would assume control of the American government. Since ancient times, many victorious generals had claimed the authority of a king or the power of a dictator. Few Americans thought Washington should be king, but many expected him to become the leader of the new government. In London, King George III asked American-born painter Benjamin West what Washington would do now that he had won the war. West said that he believed Washington "would retire to a private situation." The king paused for a moment, then replied. "If he did that, he would be the greatest man in the world."

George Washington left New York City and rode south to Annapolis, Maryland, where Congress was meeting. On December 23, 1783, he appeared before Congress and made this short speech:

The great events on which my resignation depended having at length taken place; I have now the honor of offering my sincere congratulations to Congress and of presenting myself before them to surrender into their hands the trust committed to me, and to claim the indulgence of retiring from the service

of my country. Happy in the confirmation of our independence and sovereignty, and pleased with the opportunity afforded the United States of becoming a respectable nation, I resign with satisfaction the appointment I accepted with diffidence. A diffidence in my abilities to accomplish so arduous a task, which however was superseded by a confidence in the rectitude of our cause, the support of the supreme power of the union, and the patronage of heaven. The successful termination of the war has verified the most sanguine expectations, and my gratitude for the interposition of Providence, and the assistance I have received from my countrymen, increases with every review of the momentous contest. . . . I consider it an indispensable duty to close this last solemn act of my official life, by commending the interests of our dearest country to the protection of almighty God, and those who have the superintendence of them, to His holy keeping. Having now finished the work assigned me, I retire from the great theatre of action; and bidding an affectionate farewell to this august body under whose orders I have so long acted, I here offer my commission, and take my leave of all the employments of public life.

Having finished the speech, Washington bowed to Congress. The members quietly stood as a gesture of respect. Washington left the chamber and rode home to Mount Vernon. Reports of his resignation spread across the country and around the world. He was recognized as the greatest hero of his time.

Desolation

George Washington reached Mount Vernon on Christmas Eve. Except for a brief stop on the march to Yorktown, he had not been home since he left to take his seat in the Continental Congress in 1775. In his absence Washington had entrusted the management of Mount Vernon to a cousin, but despite his best efforts the war had taken a heavy toll on the estate. Fields had been neglected, buildings were in disrepair, and tools were worn, broken, or lost. The plantation no longer made the profits that had once sustained the hundreds of people, enslaved and free, who lived there. As Washington set to work repairing his estate, he watched to see if the nation's leaders would heed his advice.

George Washington was vastly better off than millions of Americans in the winter of 1783. The worst off lived in regions ravaged by partisan war between patriots and loyalists. Much of the interior of Georgia and South Carolina and parts of North Carolina had been rendered uninhabitable by civil war. Gen. William Moultrie, riding through the backcountry in 1782, was dismayed to find areas once filled with livestock stripped of horses, cattle, hogs, and even deer. Moultrie's scouts found that "no living creature was to be seen" except here and there a few vultures, feasting on the dead. Fences, outbuildings, and houses were burned. Many of the inhabitants had fled. Those who remained lived in extreme poverty and either turned to crime or were victimized by criminals. Government in the region had entirely collapsed.

Nowhere else were conditions quite that bad, but wherever the partisan war had gone on for months or years, farms had been stripped of their livestock, crops had been seized, fields burned, and houses and barns destroyed. Parts of Westchester County, New York—where loyalist troops sparred with Continentals and militia over the livestock needed to feed the armies—were burnt over. So were parts of New Jersey and the Mohawk Valley of New York. Pockets of destruction were scattered across the middle states, including corners of Delaware and the Eastern Shore of Maryland where British troops had never set foot, but where patriot and loyalist militias clashed.

The armies had visited similar destruction on large areas of the country. British and Hessian troops put farms and houses to the torch on their march through New Jersey in the fall of 1776. For many of the Hessians, visiting terror and destruction on civilians was a conventional strategy to break the enemy's will to resist. British officers alternately sought to restrain wanton destruction and licensed it, depending on the circumstances. The British campaign through Virginia in 1781 was marked by looting and destruction. French troops who landed at Jamestown in September found dead civilians, victims of the British army,

scattered through the ruined town. Coastal towns burned by British or loyalist troops or by the Royal Navy stretched from Maine to Georgia. The attack on New London, Connecticut, marked by extraordinary ferocity and wanton indifference to life, was not unusual. On the frontiers, fighting between Americans and Indians allied with the British left death, ruined lives, and property destruction from one end of the country to the other. American Gen. John Sullivan led an army through the Finger Lakes region of New York in 1779, burning Iroquois fields and villages abandoned by the Indians as his army approached, retribution for Indian raids that visited death and destruction in the Wyoming Valley of northern Pennsylvania and village of Cherry Valley, New York, in 1778.

Even areas unscarred by marching armies, partisan vengeance, and the sordid violence of frontier fighting bore the marks of prolonged war: neglected farms, worn and damaged houses, empty barns, and ruined commerce. Retail trade, which had always depended heavily on goods from Britain, had withered. Shops were shuttered or empty.

Everywhere families were missing fathers and sons, and men were crippled and disfigured by wounds or injuries. At the close of the Revolutionary War, Abraham Lincoln wrote in 1837,

nearly every adult male had been a participator in some of its scenes. The consequence was, that of those scenes, in the form of a husband, a father, a son, or a brother, a living history was to be found in every family—a history bearing the indubitable testimonies to its own authenticity in the limbs mangled, in the scars of wounds received in the midst of the very scenes related; a history too that could be read and understood alike by all, the wise and the ignorant, the learned and the unlearned.

Americans had paid a heavy price for their independence.

The Fate of the Loyalists

Loyalists paid an even heavier price for opposing independence and had no expectation that the end of the war would usher in a new era of

The original of this watercolor of the loyalist camp on the St. Lawrence River was executed by James Peachey, one of the surveyors responsible for laying out the townships and farm lots for the loyalists who occupied the camp during the summer of 1784. It is one of the few sympathetic contemporary depictions of loyalist refugees (Archives of Ontario).

prosperity. They faced it with disappointment and dread. Many believed the British had sacrificed their interests in making peace, ignoring their loyalty and rewarding the king's enemies.

John Adams estimated that one third of Americans remained loyal to Britain. How Adams arrived at this conclusion is not clear. If as many as one third of Americans actively opposed the war, it is difficult to imagine how it succeeded and even more difficult to imagine how a stable peace was secured when the war was over. If Americans were so evenly divided, those divisions might have continued, perhaps in new forms, long after the war ended, and been reflected in political partisanship,

open rebellion, or active repression. Sporadic incidents of violence against loyalists occurred, but in general the new United States was spared the continuing partisan rancor and violence that followed many other civil wars in the last two hundred years.

Loyalists were probably not as numerous as Adams thought. The best estimate of their numbers is based on their military service. About 19,000 Americans served in various provincial units with the British army during the war. These men were committed loyalists who took up arms for the Crown for sustained terms of service, much like Continental soldiers. In a study identifying 6,000 loyalists—all adult men—about one in seven

Loyalists nonetheless constituted a very large discontented and potentially disruptive minority. Fortunately for the future of the American republic, many chose to leave. In the preliminary articles of peace concluded in November 1782, the commissioners agreed that all "Loyalists or Refugees as well as all such British Merchants or other Subjects as may be resident in any of the United States at the time of the Evacuation thereof by the Arms and Garrisons of His Britannic Majesty shall be allowed Six Months thereafter to remove to any part of the World." Those whose property had been seized by the Revolutionary state governments or otherwise lost because of their loyalty to Crown were eligible to apply to the British government for compensation for their losses.

served in provincial units. This suggests that the 19,000 provincial soldiers were one seventh of a total population of 126,000 adult male loyalists. Since adult males constituted about one fourth of the population, we can conclude that the total number of loyalists during the war, including women and children, was around 500,000. About 3,000,000 people lived in America during the Revolutionary War, which means that loyalists constituted about one sixth of the total population, or deducting the enslaved population of 500,000, one fifth of the white population. Adams' estimate that one third of Americans were loyal to the Crown seems to have doubled their number.

About 60,000 loyalists left the United States, taking with them at least 15,000 enslaved people. Most of them departed with British troops evacuating New York, Charleston, Savannah, and East Florida. About 30,000, nearly all of whom embarked at New York, made their way to Nova Scotia and New Brunswick. About 6,000 settled on land granted to them along the St. Lawrence River, in what became known as Upper Canada and ultimately the Canadian province of Ontario. Some 13,000 including about 5,000 free blacks, migrated to Britain. Another 3,000 white loyalists fled to the Bahamas, taking 4,000 enslaved people with them. The case of East Florida was more complicated.

Something like 5,000 white and 6,000 to 7,000 blacks, mostly enslaved, arrived in East Florida during the war. Many moved elsewhere after the war, some returning to the United States. Around 3,000 white loyalists went to Jamaica, taking 8,000 enslaved people with them.

Loyalist refugees were no more than fifteen percent of the loyalist population, but they included a disproportionate number of loyalist leaders and the most committed supporters of the Crown. Among them, James DeLancey moved to Nova Scotia, where he became a member of the assembly. William Cunningham took refuge in East Florida, where he led a gang of outlaws. Thomas "Burnfoot" Brown settled on the island of St. Vincent, where he acquired a fine sugar plantation and lived until 1825, more than fifty years after being left for dead by a patriot mob in Georgia.

Former loyalist soldiers left behind were leaderless. Like most Continental Army veterans, many were young men with little or no property. Most went home and eventually made peace, however uneasily, with their neighbors. Some moved to new communities or migrated to the frontier. A minority in most parts of the country, the defeated loyalists never organized.

Efforts to prevent loyalists from resuming their prewar lives were widespread, and incidents of violence were reported. After the British evacuated New York City, at least one loyalist was tarred and feathered. In Charleston, a mob burned the wharf of a loyalist sympathizer and harassed residents who had collaborated with the British during the occupation. A popular assembly resolved against allowing loyalists to return to the city. The North Carolina legislature voted to deny citizenship to former loyalists, and Maryland banned loyalist attorneys from practicing in its courts. A town meeting in Worcester, Massachusetts, voted not to allow loyalists to return, resolving that they were "fixedly opposed to those rights, and to that freedom" Americans had fought to secure. The idea that they could ever become good citizens was "groundless and fallacious."

Vigilante attacks on loyalists reflected the bitterness many patriots felt. The worst incidents occurred in the South Carolina backcountry, where the population was more evenly divided between patriots and loyalists than elsewhere. Wartime atrocities were not quickly forgotten. Returning to his home in the Ninety Six District, a loyalist named Matthew Love was lynched by his neighbors who remembered he had slaughtered wounded rebels after a skirmish. "The people of Ninety Six appear very desirous to forget the injuries of the war," Judge Aedanus Burke assured the governor, "provided those do not return among them who have committed wanton acts of barbarity."

In parts of the North and South Carolina backcountry desolated by wartime house burning, plundering, and wanton destruction, circumstances prefigured the aftermath of civil wars to come. There patriots and loyalists were reduced to grinding poverty. Many turned to crime, which only increased the misery of the inhabitants, while it offered wartime enemies opportunities to settle old scores. In an effort to establish order, courts imposed severe sentences for property crimes. In 1784 the South Carolina legislature changed the punishment for horse theft from whipping to death. Hangings were frequent as long as the disorder continued.

Years passed before peace truly returned to the region. In 1784 a Charleston newspaper reported that twelve loyalists who had reoccupied their former homes on Fishing Creek in the northern part of the state were warned by neighbors to leave within twenty days. When they did not, eight were killed and the rest allowed to escape "to tell the news to their brother Tories." In the most desolate parts of the new nation, the return of peace offered the victors little more than opportunities for revenge.

Religious Freedom

For many Americans, the great promise of the American Revolution was not prosperity, political equality, or the opportunity to participate in civic life. It was the promise of freedom to worship according to the dictates of conscience, without harassment or legal disabilities, and of freedom from taxation to support an established church. Their aspiration was for religious freedom. Like other forms of freedom for which the Revolutionary generation struggled, religious freedom was largely unknown and barely understood, even by those who sought it. The American Revolution made religious freedom a basic principle of free society, one we still struggle to fulfill.

Religious freedom can only exist in a society in which religious faiths are treated with equality by the law and with mutual respect by the people. Religious liberty—the absence of formal legal restraints on religious thought and practice and legal protection of religious thought and practice from interference, threats, intimidation, and violence—is fundamental to religious freedom. So, too, is a culture of mutual respect among people of faith towards one another and toward non-believers, who must likewise respect those whose beliefs they do not share. Establishing and maintaining religious freedom demands compromises in matters about which many people have strong convictions that make compromises difficult. The American Revolution did not secure complete religious freedom for the American people, but it made great strides toward that end and expressed ideals about religious freedom that continue to challenge us.

When the American Revolution began, the English-speaking world had only recently emerged from centuries of religious persecution, in which people suspected of heresy—holding beliefs contrary to the official orthodoxy—were subjected to intimidation and torture, and anyone convicted of heresy faced severe corporal punishment or death. Judicial torture to force suspects to confess, recant, and name other heretics ended in Britain and its colonies by the beginning of the eighteenth century but brutal punishments for religious offenses continued. For blasphemy, a person might have his tongue nailed to a pillory.

By the time of the Revolution such brutal punishments were being replaced by fines and imprisonment, but extralegal violence against dissenters—especially evangelical ministers who sought converts by preaching outdoors—was not unusual and often ignored or encouraged by sheriffs and other officials who regarded nonconformists a threat to the good order of society. Violence and threats of violence were never far from efforts, official and unofficial, to maintain religious order.

Despite efforts to maintain religious orthodoxy, dissent became more common during the eighteenth century, as more and more British Americans insisted on making their own choices about matters of faith. As religious diversity increased, civil and religious authorities retreated from efforts to control religious *thought* to efforts to control religious *practice.* People could believe what they wished, but the law imposed limits on dissenting practice. Dissenters might be required to obtain licenses to conduct religious services, discouraged from recruiting others to share their beliefs, required to pay taxes and tithes to support the established church, and barred from holding public office.

Religious freedom existed almost nowhere in America before the Revolution. At the beginning of the Revolutionary War, nine of the thirteen colonial governments maintained established religions: Congregationalism in New Hampshire, Massachusetts, and Connecticut, and Anglicanism in New York, Maryland, Virginia, the Carolinas, and Georgia. Four colonies—Rhode Island, New Jersey, Pennsylvania, and Delaware—had no established churches and were home to a broad array of Protestant denominations that generally managed to coexist without too much friction, demonstrating the value of mutual forbearance and toleration. Maryland, which had a long tradition of religious toleration, was home to an influential Roman Catholic minority. Georgia was more receptive to religious diversity than other southern colonies. Jewish congregations were found in several seaboard cities.

Yet even in the most peaceable places, the thinly disguised disdain of one sect for another occasionally broke through the veneer of tolerance. Many personal disputes reflected differences of religion or were magnified by them and occasionally degenerated into ugly confrontations and even violence. Political life often divided along religious lines. In Pennsylvania, which was celebrated throughout the English-speaking world as proof of the value of tolerance and benevolence to overcome centuries of religious rancor, social harmony was compromised by doctrinal disagreements and religious intolerance. Many of Pennsylvania's Quakers and Anglicans looked with distaste on their state's growing number of Presbyterians, Lutherans, and other denominations, who clashed with one another in the hinterland counties where they were most numerous.

The American Revolution began as dispute over civil authority, but it inevitably involved religious practice, which was regulated by civil law. By

285

THE
HOLY BIBLE,

Containing the OLD and NEW

TESTAMENTS:

Newly tranflated out of the

ORIGINAL TONGUES;

And with the former

TRANSLATIONS

Diligently compared and revised.

VIRTUE LIBERTY AND INDEPENDENCE

PHILADELPHIA:

Printed and Sold by R. AITKEN, at Pope's
Head, Three Doors above the Coffee
House, in Market Street.
M.DCC.LXXXII.

286

declaring their independence from Britain, Americans also declared their independence from the Church of England. Anglican establishments were abolished quickly in states where the established church was already weak. In North Carolina, backcountry Presbyterians, increasing in number and political influence, pressed for disestablishment. It was accomplished in the state constitution of 1776, which provided that

there shall be no establishment of any one religious church or denomination in this State, in preference to any other; neither shall any person, on any presence whatsoever, be compelled to attend any place of worship contrary to his own faith or judgment, nor be obliged to pay, for the purchase of any glebe, or the building of any house of worship, or for the maintenance of any minister or ministry, contrary to what he believes right, or has voluntarily and personally engaged to perform; but all persons shall be at liberty to exercise their own mode of worship.

The New York constitution adopted in 1777 was even more explicit in rejecting the religious establishment. "We are required," it reads,

by the benevolent principles of rational liberty, not only to expel civil tyranny, but also to guard against that spiritual oppression and intolerance wherewith the bigotry and ambition of weak and wicked priests and princes have scourged mankind, this convention doth further, in the name and by the authority of the good people of this State, ordain, determine, and declare, that the free exercise and enjoyment of religious profession and worship, without discrimination or preference, shall forever hereafter be allowed, within this State, to all mankind.

In declaring religious liberty and abolishing taxation to support a state church, North Caro-

lina and New York affirmed their attachment to Protestantism, requiring officeholders to accept its basic tenets. The North Carolina constitution provided that "no person, who shall deny the being of God or the truth of the Protestant religion, or the divine authority either of the Old or New Testaments . . . shall be capable of holding any office or place of trust" in the state government. Balancing this attachment to Protestant Christianity with their commitment to religious liberty, both states forbid ministers from holding public office—a restriction repeated in other states.

Nowhere in these Revolutionary assertions in favor of freedom of religious thought and practice did a state declare the separation of religion and the state. Most states, indeed, expressed the view that the rights of the people were a gift from God and that they should comport themselves in a manner consistent with the principles of Protestant Christianity. Civil oaths prescribed by law referred to God. State guarantees of "liberty of conscience" and "free exercise" meant that citizens could think and practice as they wished, but did not guarantee that governments would treat all faiths, or even all Christian faiths, as equal before the law. Those guarantees encouraged but could not ensure mutual respect among people of different faiths, without which religious freedom cannot flourish.

"Free to profess, and by argument to maintain"

The most decisive victory for religious freedom took place in Virginia, where dissenters—chiefly Presbyterians and Baptists—had been challenging the Anglican establishment since the 1750s. By 1775 Virginia's Anglican establishment was over 150 years old. In a colony with few towns, parishes were the basic unit of local government and reflected the organization of society. Local gentry served on parish vestries, which oversaw many of the functions of local government. They determined

The Bible was by far the most widely owned and read book in Revolutionary America. Nearly all were imported from Britain. The war halted the shipment of new Bibles, leading Congress to consider underwriting the production of Bibles in America. In 1782 Congress passed a resolution endorsing the publication of the Bible by Philadelphia printer Robert Aitken—the first complete edition of the Bible in English published in the Americas. Aitken included the resolution following the title page, which bears the arms of Pennsylvania, with the motto "Virtue, Liberty and Independence" (Courtesy of the Free Library of Philadelphia).

and collected the parish levy, which was the largest tax most of His Majesty's subjects in Virginia paid. Vestries managed poor relief, directed road construction and maintenance, settled boundary disputes, and hired the minister. On Sundays vestrymen and their families occupied the boxed pews at the front of each parish church, with the middling people and their families seated behind them and the poor at the rear of the church.

Many Virginia Presbyterians accepted licensing requirements, paid their taxes, and conducted themselves in ways that Anglican vestrymen and ministers were grudgingly prepared to accept. Other dissenters, mainly evangelical Baptists, challenged the traditional order of society by defying the authority of the Anglican vestries. They resisted regulation and paid a price for their independence. Sheriffs arrested Baptist ministers for preaching without a license and for marrying couples contrary to law, which required all marriages be conducted by Anglican clergy. Itinerant Baptist ministers who preached in private homes or conducted services outdoors were arrested and charged with vagrancy, unlawful assembly, and disturbing the peace. Several were imprisoned for months at a time, during which some of them preached through their prison windows to crowds gathered outside. Others were pelted with stones or dragged from their makeshift pulpits and beaten. On more than one occasion, mobs dragged Baptist preachers to the nearest water and held them under, mocking the practice of adult baptism.

The persecution of Baptist ministers outraged young James Madison, a planter's son raised in the Anglican church. Madison had attended college at

the Presbyterian College of New Jersey, where the college president, Jonathan Witherspoon, nurtured Madison's commitment to religious freedom. "I have . . . nothing to brag of as to the State and Liberty of my Country," he wrote to a college friend in 1774, adding

That diabolical Hell conceived principle of persecution rages among some and to their eternal Infamy the Clergy can furnish their Quota of Imps for such business. This vexes me the most of any thing whatever. There are at this time in the adjacent County not less than 5 or 6 well meaning men in close Gaol for publishing their religious Sentiments.

Madison later wrote that he "spared no exertion to save them from imprisonment," setting aside "the enthusiasm which contributed to render them obnoxious to sober public opinion, as well as the laws then in force, against Preachers dissenting from the Established Religion."

Evangelicals and orthodox Anglicans were divided by cultural differences that fed their mutual animosity. Baptists, wrote one of their elders, rejoiced at "christians shouting, sinners trembling and fall down convulsed, the devil raging and blaspheming." Many Anglican gentlemen regarded the Baptists' religious enthusiasm as a mental disorder, as John Locke had written, "rising from the conceits of a warmed or overweening brain" that undermined true religion and the good order of society. They were also angered by evangelicals calling on people to abandon graceless Anglican ministers and seek churches where the Holy Spirit could reach them. The Baptists ignored the Anglican churches and gathered their own

The bookish son of a wealthy Virginia planter, James Madison was a committed advocate of religious freedom. Only five feet four inches tall and weighing less than one hundred pounds, Madison was not a great public speaker, but as a political thinker and writer he had few rivals (Library of Congress).

congregations, set their own standards, and policed their own communities, free of the oversight of the gentlemen who occupied the choice pews in the local Anglican church. The evangelicals regarded one another as equals in sight of God, and refused to obey the Anglican gentry.

Independence gave Baptists and other evangelicals their opportunity. In petition after petition, they demanded change—not merely toleration, but religious equality. In his first draft of the Virginia Declaration of Rights, George Mason proposed to an article asserting that "all Men should enjoy the fullest Toleration in the Exercise of Religion, according to the Dictates of Conscience." James Madison, then a twenty-five-year-old delegate to the Virginia Convention, pressed for religious equality. The final version asserted that "all men are equally entitled to the free exercise of religion, according to the dictates of conscience; and that it is the mutual duty of all to practise Christian forbearance, love, and charity toward each other."

Dissenters were finally entitled to the free exercise of their religion, but their ministers were still required to secure licenses to preach and they had to pay fees to Anglican clergy to record their marriages. This disability was finally removed in 1780, when the legislature made it lawful for any minister to conduct a marriage ceremony, but scattered prosecutions for unlicensed preaching, unlawful assembly, and disturbing the peace continued during the war. So did random attacks on Baptist ministers.

The war weakened the Anglican church. Ministers who refused to violate their oaths of loyalty to the king as head of the church left their parishes. By 1777, only a third of Virginia's nearly one hundred Anglican parishes had an ordained minister. The legislature suspended taxes to support the church and the payment of clerical salaries. Scores of Anglican churches ceased to function. In 1779 a group of Anglicans joined with some of the dissenters in support of a new tax, referred to as a general assessment, to be used to support Protestant ministers of any denomination. The bill failed to pass, but support for the idea grew.

The issue was still not resolved in November 1784, when Virginia Baptists presented another petition asserting that the established church was "oppressive and repugnant to the equal rights of religious liberty." Advocates of a general assessment urged their bill to support Protestant churches on an equal basis as a solution. Patrick Henry, who had supported legal rights for dissenters for a generation, championed the bill. James Madison led the opposition. Thomas Jefferson, then in Europe, despaired of stopping Henry. He wrote to Madison that "what we have to do I think is *devoutly* to *pray for his death.*"

Madison had a better idea. On November 17, at Madison's instigation, the legislature elected Henry to a fourth term as governor, removing the great orator from the House of Delegates. Then Madison managed to get a final vote on the assessment bill delayed until the next fall. Madison spent the year building an unlikely alliance of Baptists and enlightened gentlemen skeptical of organized religion. The Baptists hated the Anglican establishment and disapproved of the materialism and Deism so common among the gentry. Many of them were deeply distrustful of any government authority in matters of religion, even a law that prescribed the distribution of tax funds to their churches. They preferred to rely on voluntary support. Madison's circle of enlightened gentlemen opposed religious establishments as an infringement of freedom of thought.

Madison framed his objections to the bill in a carefully written, anonymous *Memorial and Remonstrance Against Religious Assessments,* which was copied and passed from hand to hand in the summer of 1785. Christianity, Madison argued, did not need state support. Echoing Baptist petitions against assessment, he pointed out that Christianity had flourished in adversity. Moreover, he warned, acknowledging the authority of the legislature to support several Christian denominations was the same as acknowledging the authority of the state to support one denomination, and to require citizens to adhere to its doctrines. Established religion, Madison wrote, inevitably led to "pride and indolence in the Clergy, ignorance and servility in the laity," and "superstition, bigotry and persecution."

Baptist petitions against the assessment bill probably reflected the opinions of ordinary Virginians better than Madison's scholarly *Memorial and Remonstrance.* "Faithfulness shall scourge the growing Vices of the Age" a petition from Westmoreland County Baptists confidently predicted.

Let Ministers manifest to the World that they are inwardly moved by the Holy Ghost to take upon them that Office, that they seek the good of Mankind, and not worldly Interest . . . Then shall Religion (if departed) speedily return, and Deism be put to open Shame, and its dreaded Consequences removed.

The assessment, the Westmoreland Baptists warned, would not support the faithful ministers called by God. It would simply "call in many Hirelings." Copies of this petition bearing the signatures of 4,899 Virginians, including eleven women, were presented to the legislature. When the legislature reconvened in the fall, Madison and his allies defeated the assessment bill.

Madison then reintroduced a bill for establishing religious freedom Thomas Jefferson had written in 1777 and that had failed to pass. The operative portion of the statute was at once simple and comprehensive, affirming freedom of religious thought and practice, an end to taxation to support any religious institution, and an end to civil disabilities imposed on account of religion:

no man shall be compelled to frequent or support any religious worship, place, or ministry whatsoever, nor shall be enforced, restrained, molested, or burthened in his body or goods, nor shall otherwise suffer on account of his religious opinions or belief, but that all men shall be free to profess, and by argument to maintain, their opinions in matters of Religion, and that the same shall in no wise diminish, enlarge or affect their civil capacities.

Jefferson included an extended preamble expressing the importance of individual intellectual and spiritual independence to a free society, beyond the immediate issue of freedom of religion. "Truth is great," he wrote,

and will prevail if left to herself, that she is the proper and sufficient antagonist to error, and has nothing to fear from the conflict, unless by human interposition disarmed of her natural weapons free argument and debate, errors ceasing to be dangerous when it is permitted freely to contradict them.

The legislature passed the Virginia Statute for Establishing Religious Freedom on January 16, 1786. Governor Patrick Henry signed it into law three days later. It became, in time, one of the most influential statements about liberty of conscience in American history.

For James Madison the act was a triumph for intellectual and spiritual freedom, not a rejection of faith or the importance of religious instruction for the good of society. In 1825, near the end of a remarkably productive life, Madison wrote that "belief in a God All powerful wise and good, is . . . essential to the moral order of the world and to the happiness of man." He preferred for churches to provide that instruction, without the slightest interference from the state, but he never hinted, in a lifetime of public utterances, that the state should not draw inspiration and moral guidance from the religion of its people. Indeed the statute announced that all people were "free to profess, and by argument to maintain" their religious views, and made no suggestion that those views should have no part in public life.

Thomas Jefferson was immensely proud that the bill had finally became law, and later directed that the monument erected at his grave identify him as its author. The achievement belonged just as much to the many thousands of ordinary Virginians who signed petitions demanding religious freedom and to the brave Baptist ministers who endured beatings and imprisonment for their faith. America is free because they refused to be silenced.

The Virginia Constitution of 1776 required that all bills be published for public consideration before a final vote in the legislature. This broadside of Jefferson's proposed bill for establishing religious freedom was published in 1779, when the measure was first considered and rejected (Boston Public Library).

A BILL *for establishing* RELIGIOUS FREEDOM, *printed for the consideration of the* PEOPLE.

WELL aware that the opinions and belief of men depend not on their own will, but follow involuntarily the evidence proposed to their minds, that Almighty God hath created the mind free, and manifested his Supreme will that free it shall remain, by making it altogether insusceptible of restraint: That all attempts to influence it by temporal punishments or burthens, or by civil incapacitations, tend only to beget habits of hypocrisy and meanness, and are a departure from the plan of the holy author of our religion, who being Lord both of body and mind, yet chose not to propagate it by coercions on either, as was in his Almighty power to do, but to extend it by its influence on reason alone: That the impious presumption of legislators and rulers, civil as well as ecclesiastical, who, being themselves but fallible and uninspired men, have assumed dominion over the faith of others, setting up their own opinions and modes of thinking, as the only true and infallible, and as such, endeavouring to impose them on others, hath established and maintained false religions over the greatest part of the world, and through all time: That to compel a man to furnish contributions of money for the propagation of opinions which he disbelieves and abhors, is sinful and tyrannical: That even the forcing him to support this or that teacher of his own religious persuasion, is depriving him of the comfortable liberty of giving his contributions to the particular pastor whose morals he would make his pattern, and whose powers he feels most persuasive to righteousness, and is withdrawing from the Ministry those temporal rewards which, proceeding from an approbation of their personal conduct, are an additional incitement to earnest and unremitting labour for the instruction of mankind: That our civil rights have no dependance on our religious opinions, any more than on our opinions in physicks or geometry: That therefore the proscribing any citizen as unworthy the publick confidence, by laying upon him an incapacity of being called to offices of trust and emolument, unless he profess or renounce this or that religious opinion, is depriving him injuriously of those privileges and advantages to which, in common with his fellow citizens he has a natural right: That it tends also to corrupt the principles of that very religion it is meant to encourage, by bribing with a monopoly of wordly honours and emoluments, those who will externally profess and conform to it: That though indeed these are criminal who do not withstand such temptation, yet neither are those innocent who lay the bait in their way: That the opinions of men are not the object of civil government, nor under its jurisdiction: That to suffer the civil Magistrate to intrude his powers into the field of opinion, and to restrain the profession or propagation of principles on supposition of their ill tendency, is a dangerous fallacy, which at once destroys all religious liberty; because he being of course Judge of that tendency will make his own opinions the rule of judgment, and approve or condemn the sentiments of others only as they shall square with, or differ from his own: That it is time enough for the rightful purposes of civil government for its officers to interfere when principles break out into overt acts against peace and good order: And finally, that truth is great and will prevail if left to herself; that she is the proper and sufficient antagonist to errour, and has nothing to fear from the conflict, unless by human interposition, disarmed of her natural weapons, free argument and debate; errours ceasing to be dangerous when it is permitted freely to contradict them

WE the General Assembly of *Virginia* do enact, that no man shall be compelled to frequent or support any religous Worship place or Ministry whatsoever, nor shall be enforced, restrained, molested, or burthened in his body or goods, nor shall otherwise suffer on account of his religious opinions or belief, but that all men shall be free to profess, and by argument to maintain their opinions in matters of religion, and that the same shall in no wise diminish, enlarge, or affect their civil capacities.

AND though we well know that this Assembly, elected by the people for the ordinary purposes of legislation only, have no power to restrain the acts of succeeding Assemblies, constituted with powers equal to our own, and that therefore to declare this act irrevocable would be of no effect in law; yet we are free to declare, and do declare, that the rights hereby asserted are of the natural rights of mankind, and that if any act shall be hereafter passed to repeal the present, or to narrow its operation, such act will be an infringement of natural right.

Chapter 19 Crisis

Americans had won their independence, but they had not secured it, nor had they secured the freedoms for which they had fought. For twenty years, Americans had contended with Britons for independence—first to establish their independence within the British Empire and then to establish their independence from the British Empire. By the end of 1783 they had accomplished that goal, at least nominally. They no longer owed allegiance to the British Crown nor were they subject to British dominion. Americans had won their political independence, but it remained to be seen whether the United States could establish its economic independence and avoid being dominated by one or more of the European imperial powers.

The struggle to do so continued for nearly forty years. It included securing access to foreign markets for American products, developing domestic markets and manufacturing to free the United States from dependence on imported goods and exclusive reliance on income from exports, overcoming threats posed by Spain and Britain to the new nation's frontiers and the economy of the trans-Appalachian West, and a prolonged conflict with Britain, France, and Spain to establish and maintain American rights at sea. It involved a series of wars with Indian tribes used as proxies by imperial powers, an undeclared war at sea with France, and a second war with Britain. These conflicts were not merely a consequence of the American Revolution. They were a continuation of it, and American freedom depended on the outcome.

The United States ultimately became a continental nation with the largest, most diverse, and most productive economy in the world—a nation of unprecedented wealth and power with extraordinary influence over the global economy. In hindsight we can identify factors that contributed to American economic dominance, including a rapidly growing population, vast natural resources, technological and entrepreneurial innovation, the development of rich internal markets, competitive success in world markets, a stable constitutional and legal order defined by the rule of law that encouraged and protected economic investment, effective educational institutions, isolation from the debilitating international conflicts that sapped the energy and productivity of other nations, and freedom from the kinds of colonial exploitation that have impoverished subject peoples all over the globe.

Despite the many factors that contributed to it, the economic success of the United States was not inevitable. It was contingent on decisions Americans have made, beginning with decisions made in an effort to resolve the severe economic crisis that followed the Revolutionary War. In his circular letter to the state governors in summer of 1783, Washington urged the new nation to empower its government to address the common concerns of the republic, resolve its debts, honor its obligations, and provide for the common defense in a manner that would command the respect of foreign powers. Until it did so, the United States could not achieve economic independence. European powers would dictate the conditions of American trade, constrain the westward expansion of the republic, and limit the economic opportunities of all Americans.

The Revolution created opportunities for ambitious men like Elijah Boardman. By 1789, when Ralph Earl portrayed the twenty-nine-year-old veteran standing proudly in his New Milford, Connecticut, shop, Boardman had established his business, weathered a depression in trade, and become a successful retailer. He invested wisely in Ohio land and later served in the Connecticut legislature and the United States Senate (Metropolitan Museum of Art).

"The Revolution has robbed us of our trade"

Economic opportunity is fundamental to freedom. Tyranny feeds on poverty and distress by tempting its victims with promises of at least a marginally better life in return for their submission. Everywhere in the world, tyranny relies on desperation and takes hold where people are convinced that wealth is limited, and one person's gain is inevitably another's loss. The tyrant's supporters depend on the tyrant's patronage to ensure that they are among the favored few—the winners in a unjust competition for a share of limited wealth. The rest are victims of an economic and political order defined by injustice.

Freedom, by contrast, flourishes where opportunity and economic success are widely enjoyed. It flourishes most fully where economic growth is consistent over long periods and over broad areas, touching the lives of a large proportion of the people and where material limits pose no obvious constraints. Where these conditions prevail, it is rational to believe that people can become rich without impoverishing others. Under such conditions, traditional social hierarchies in which people are divided between aristocrats, gentry, commoners, and servants break down, because the ambitions of ordinary people can be satisfied without patronage. Economic opportunity frees people from traditional dependencies and builds personal independence, which free societies protect through impartial justice.

Americans had rebelled against British rule, in part, because they believed changes in British government policy threatened their economic freedom and would ultimately deny them the opportunity to prosper. The American people had varying ideas about economic opportunity and often quite different ways in mind to pursue it, but enough felt sufficiently threatened to make war to achieve their independence. Having won, they looked forward to prospering. Experience, in the short term, did not match their expectations.

The American economy was built on the production and export of agricultural staples—chiefly wheat, rice, and tobacco—as well as dried fish. Americans also exported large quantities of lumber and naval stores—mainly tar, pitch, and turpentine—as well as indigo, hides, pig iron, whale oil, corn, and salted beef and pork. At least three-fourths of these products were exported to Britain or Britain's West Indian colonies. During the war exports collapsed. Trade with the British Empire came to a halt. Wartime exports to France, other European nations, and their colonies never equaled more than a small fraction of pre-war exports to Britain and the British West Indies.

Many Americans expected the economy to revive with the return of peace. Trade with Britain and its empire would resume and become more profitable than ever. No longer encumbered by taxes or British trade restrictions, Americans would take advantage of new markets in France other European countries and in the Caribbean. They would repair the ravages of war and prosper with the resumption of exports to Britain and its colonies.

Lord Shelburne's enthusiasm for free trade gave hope that the British would reopen their Caribbean colonies to American exports, but Shelburne's ministry fell in April 1783 and the new ministry promptly banned American-owned vessels from the British West Indies. This was a disaster for American merchants who had long sold rice, wheat, dried fish, lumber, and other American products to Britain's Caribbean colonies. American goods could only enter the ports of the British West Indies in British vessels and were subject to new duties that encouraged West Indian merchants to buy goods from elsewhere. To get their products into the West Indian market, American merchants had to sell to British merchants for less than the competition. Thus the new British duties, though they would be paid by merchants in Jamaica,

Robert Morris served as superintendent of finance for the Confederation from 1781 to 1784 and worked desperately to secure funds to supply the army and pay the interest on the public debt. He advocated a five percent tariff on imported goods, dedicated to paying the debts incurred in the war, including the pay due to soldiers, but Rhode Island refused its assent. "From my Soul I pity the Army," he wrote to Washington in February 1783, "and you my dear Sir in particular, who must see and feel for their Distresses without the Power of relieving them. I did flatter myself that I should have been able to present them that Justice to which they are entitled, and in the mean Time I labored to made their Situation as tolerable as Circumstances would permit" (Courtesy of Independence National Historical Park).

Barbados, and Britain's other island colonies, functioned as taxes on American merchants and ultimately on American farmers. The ban on American-owned vessels was also devastating to New England shipbuilders who built most of the sloops and brigs employed in this trade.

Britain opened the home market to American goods, which led to a spike in American exports to Britain. From 1784 to 1786, American merchants exported 2.5 million British pounds worth of goods to Britain. Over the same three years, American merchants bought 7.6 million British pounds worth of goods to import to the United States in an effort to satisfy the demand for consumer products that had built up during eight years of war.

Americans needed hoes, shovels, and metal tools of all kinds, sturdy cloth, ceramics, paper, and other basic manufactured goods. Domestic manufacturing of most of these goods had increased during the war, but the volume was not sufficient to meet consumer demand. Despite the cost of trans-Atlantic shipping, many British-made goods were cheaper than American-made ones because the British manufacturers produced in greater volume, achieving an economy of scale impossible in the United States, and because British labor was generally cheaper than American labor.

This left a deficit of 5.1 million British pounds owed to British merchants. This was not an entirely new situation. American trade with Britain

New England ports—like the idealized town in this overmantel painting from a home in Exeter, New Hampshire—depended on shipbuilding and maritime trade for their existence. British trade restrictions and tariffs threatened the livelihood of everyone from wealthy merchants to the working men who built, maintained, and manned their ships (Currier Museum of Art, Manchester, New Hampshire).

had been conducted at a deficit before the Revolutionary War, when American bought more from British merchants than it sold to them. But before the war, American trade with the British West Indies had yielded a surplus, since West Indian merchants paid more for American products than American merchants spent for the sugar and molasses they bought from them. American merchants balanced their accounts with British merchants, or came close to doing so, by transferring the credits they accumulated in the West Indies trade to their British creditors. The West Indian merchants, in turn, settled their accounts with British merchants by shipping them large amounts of sugar, as well as molasses and rum.

During the colonial period, this trade rarely worked out evenly. Colonials typically bought more from Britain than they sold there, and consequently wound up owing some money to British merchants, but the balances owed were usually a fraction of the value of the exchange, and the British merchants carried the resulting colonial debts. This trade was nearly all conducted through the exchange of goods and various kinds of promissory notes. Gold and silver rarely changed hands.

After the war this changed. Barred from selling goods in the British West Indies, American merchants had no credits to balance their accounts with British merchants, who wanted Americans to settle their debts with hard money—gold and silver. This led to the constant flow of hard money out of the United States. This might not have posed a serious problem if American merchants had been able to earn large surpluses in other markets, but they were not. The Spanish barred Americans from trading directly with most of their colonies. The French opened their Caribbean colonies to American merchants. St. Domingue, which we now call Haiti, supplied most of the sugar and coffee imported into the United States, but its merchants did not buy enough American products to balance the American trade deficit with Britain.

Nor did trade with France come remotely close to making up the difference. American merchants sold the French tobacco, wheat, rice, whale oil, and other goods, but never enough of any of them to earn what they owed to British merchants. Nor did they profit much by selling French goods in America. French manufacturers did not make the kinds of goods Americans wanted. They excelled at making luxury goods—hosiery, hats, lace, gloves, soap, ribbons, and perfume. Americans had little interest in French cargoes of anchovies, night caps, truffles, and olives. Brandy, wine, vinegar, linen, and salt were among the products Americans bought from the French. To make matters worse, French merchants were reluctant to sell on credit, often demanding gold and silver in payment. Between 1784 and 1790, the value of French imports was no more than five percent of the value of British imports.

The trade deficit with Britain was a disaster. "The Revolution has robbed us of our trade with the West Indies," James Madison lamented, "the only one which yielded us a favorable balance, without opening any other channels to compensate for it. . . . In every point of view, the trade of this country is in a deplorable condition."

The trade deficit drove the country into a depression. The downward spiral began with a glut of British imports in America. British merchant creditors demanded prompt payment, forcing American merchants to sell the imported goods at little or no profit, depressing prices and draining the nation's supply of hard money. Profits on exports did not make up for lost profits on imports. American tobacco, rice, and flour were so plentiful that prices fell. Wages fell and bankruptcies and defaults increased dramatically as merchants and farmers could not obtain currency or credit.

Gross domestic product appears to have fallen by some thirty percent. Per capita income fell by about fifteen percent during the war and perhaps more—a decline comparable to the decline Americans experienced in the Great Depression of the 1930s, though it would have been experienced very differently. In the 1930s the United States was an industrial society in which some fifty-six percent of the population lived in urban areas and nearly eighty percent of workers were engaged in manufacturing, commercial, and service jobs. Those without savings were entirely dependent on paychecks for shelter and food. A major decline in per capita income translated into millions of people in desperate need.

In the 1780s, by contrast, the United States was an overwhelmingly agricultural society. Over ninety-five percent of American lived in rural areas and were engaged in farming. A small percentage of the population was dependent on wages for shelter and food. Unemployment was a severe problem for workers directly involved in commerce—dock workers, sailors, teamsters, and others involved in moving goods, workers in shipbuilding—and manufacturing workers in enterprises closely tied to commerce. Urban craftsmen and other workers who supported the commercial sector, directly or indirectly, were also hit hard by the crisis. The effects of the decline in exports was softened during the war by privateering, which provided employment to thousands of sailors and supported many others, but privateering ended with the return of peace and left many without work. The post-war economic crisis was most deeply felt in the cities and other ports, many of which had sustained severe damage during the war and were hard hit by the collapse of exports.

Adams in London

An effective government responds to foreign trade barriers by regulating the flow of foreign goods to its own market. Often the threat of tariffs and other restrictions is sufficient to persuade foreign governments to lower barriers and open their markets, particularly if their own economic success depends on the sale of manufactured goods. In the 1780s British manufacturers and merchants needed American customers as much as Americans needed British goods, but Congress had no authority to impose tariffs or other restrictions on British products entering the American market. Some of the states imposed tariffs, but these were completely ineffective. British merchants simply landed their goods where no tariffs were charged. The British could thus close their Caribbean colonies to American merchants and impose tariffs on American goods without worrying that the powerless American government would restrict their access to American customers.

The British position was aptly summarized by a member of Parliament, John Baker Holroyd, baron Sheffield, in a pamphlet titled *Observations on the Commerce of the American States with Europe and the Indies,* first published in 1783. Sheffield

argued that it was in Britain's interest to restrict American trade with the British Empire. Having chosen independence, Americans could not expect to enjoy the same privileges as His Majesty's subjects. Congress, Sheffield explained, could not regulate American trade and was otherwise powerless to retaliate. American state governments had opened their ports to British vessels and British products with few restriction to satisfy American consumers, who were eager to buy British manufactured goods. Britain, he concluded, had nothing to gain by making concessions to benefit the United States.

The Americans states, to the delight of Sheffield's British readers, could not agree on a common policy. "By the latest letters from the American States," the London *Gentleman's Magazine* reported, "the restraint laid upon their trade with the British West Indies has thrown them into the utmost perplexity; and by way of retaliation they are passing laws inimical to their own interest; and what is still worse, inconsistent with each other. . . . Hence the dissensions that universally prevail throughout what may be called the thirteen Dis-United States."

John Adams recognized the desperate need for reforming the Confederation. "The Politicks of Europe are such a Labyrinth of profound Mysteries," John Adams wrote to Robert Livingston in July 1783,

that the more one sees of them, the more Causes of Uncertainty and Anxiety we discover. The United States will have Occasion to brace up their Confederation, and act as one Body with one Spirit. If they do not, it is now very obvious that G. Britain will take Advantage of it, in such a manner, as will endanger our Peace, our Safety, and even our very Existence.

Adams suggested a five percent import duty on British goods, which he said "would effectually defeat their Plan," but Congress had no authority to impose such a duty.

In the spring of 1785, Congress appointed Adams ambassador to Great Britain and instructed him to press the ministry to relax restrictions on trade with the British West Indies and to demand,

ew of the **BALL** at St James's *on the celebration of* **HER MAJESTY's BIRTH NIGHT** *Fe which was opened by their Royal Highnesses the prince of Wales & the Princess R*

John Adams disliked the pomp of royal courts like this ball in February 1786 celebrating the queen's birthday. At another ball a few weeks later Adams met Lord Shelburne and the earl of Harcourt, advocates for American rights who had opposed the war in America. "There is conscious Guilt and Shame in their Countenances, when they look at me," Adams wrote in his diary. "They feel that they have behaved ill, and that I am sensible of it" (Royal Collection Trust / © Her Majesty Queen Elizabeth II 2022).

"in a respectful but firm Manner," that the British army relinquish the forts on the Great Lakes it continued to occupy in violation of the Treaty of Paris. His mission demonstrated the hopelessness of depending on Britain to reform its policies as long as the American government lacked the power and will to retaliate.

When he arrived in London, Adams sought out Jonathan Sewall, a Boston lawyer who had been one of his closest friends before the war. A loyalist who had emigrated to London in 1775, Sewall was pleased to see his old friend. "Humane, generous, and open," Sewall called him, but he privately wrote that Adams would be unsuccessful as an ambassador. "He cannot dance, drink, game, flatter, promise, dress, swear with the gentlemen, and small talk and flirt with the ladies," Sewall wrote, and "in short, he has none of those essential arts or ornaments which constitute a courtier. There are thousands who, with a tenth of his understanding and without a spark of his honesty, would distance him infinitely in any court in Europe."

King George III formally received Adams at St. James's Palace on June 1. Escorted into the reception room, Adams approached the king, bowed three times, and assured him that Americans hoped "to cultivate the most friendly and liberal Intercourse, between your Majestys Subjects and their Citizens," adding that "I Shall esteem myself the happiest of Men, if I can be instrumental in recommending my Country, more and more to your Majestys Royal Benevolence and of restoring an entire esteem, Confidence and Affection . . .between People who, tho Seperated by an Ocean and under different Governments have the Same Language, a Similar Religion and kindred Blood."

The king, Adams thought, was moved by these words, and responded:

The Circumstances of this Audience are so extraordinary, the language you have now held is So extreamly proper, and the Feelings you have discovered, So justly adapted to the Occasion, that I must Say, that I not only receive with Pleasure, the Assurances of the friendly Dispositions of the United States, but that I am very glad the Choice has fallen upon you to be their Minister . . . I was the last to consent to the Seperation: but the Seperation having been made, and having become inevitable, I have always Said as I say now, that I would be the first to meet the Friendship of the United States as an independent Power.

"There is an Opinion, among Some People," the king added, "that you are not the most attached of all Your Countrymen, to the manners of France."

"That Opinion sir, is not mistaken," Adams replied, "I must avow to your Majesty, I have no Attachments but to my own Country."

"An honest Man," the king replied, "will never have any other." With that, the interview ended.

Always anxious to get work accomplished, Adams disliked such rituals. "The Essence of Things is lost in Ceremony, in every Country of Europe,"

he wrote to Jay. "We must submit to what We cannot alter. Patience is the only Remedy."

As Adams anticipated, the British ministry had no interest in changing its trade policy. Free trade, unencumbered by restrictions and tariffs, had few supporters in Britain. Shelburne and his circle could see the advantages Britain would gain by strong trade relations with the United States as it grew in population and economic importance, but few Britons considered the long term. "Futurity," Adams wrote, was "less attended to in this Country at present than in any other in the World. Present Advantage is all they aim at."

Adams concluded that American attachment to free trade was a mistake. Free trade would only work if both sides in a trading relationship embraced it. "We have hitherto been the Bubbles of our own Philosophical and equitable Liberality," he wrote, and have simply encouraged the British "to take a Selfish and partial Advantage of Us." Adams advised John Jay, the secretary of foreign affairs, that "nothing but Retaliation, reciprocal Prohibitions, and Imposts and putting ourselves in a Posture of defence will have any Effect." He was convinced that such a response would alter British policy. "Patience will do us no good."

The Internal Market

The depression of the mid-1780s masked changes in the American economy that created new opportunities for ordinary Americans. Many of these changes were related, directly or indirectly, to the war. Some might have happened if the war had never occurred, but they would have happened more slowly.

The most important, in the long term, was the development of a more robust internal market involving increasing trade between states and within them. Most contemporaries failed to recognize the importance of the internal market. Their attention was focused on international trade. They still imagined the accumulation of wealth as a competition between nations, in which the gain of one was the loss of another. They considered internal trade as the mere shuffling of goods from one person to another and did not understand that each profitable transaction added to the wealth of the nation.

A rising demand for consumer goods spread across the English-speaking world in the second half of the eighteenth century. In this British painting a shopkeeper tempts her customer with a set of metal clothing buttons. To her left are conical loaves of sugar wrapped in brown paper and a green tea tin. By the 1780s ordinary Americans were anxious to acquire these and other simple luxuries. The development of a robust internal market provided them with opportunities and choices—two essential characteristics of free societies (© CSG CIC Glasgow Museums and Libraries Collections).

Before the war, intercolonial trade was relatively modest. Merchants were more likely to deal with trading partners in Britain or the West Indies than merchants in another mainland colony. The war disrupted overseas trade but it led to the constant movement of goods between states, in many cases along inland trade routes that had seen little commercial traffic before the war. Inland towns like Lancaster, Pennsylvania, became centers for commerce serving wide areas. People who had never traded outside their local community found themselves engaged in trading networks spanning several states, buying and selling everything from food and horses to wagons, blankets, tents, and tools.

Paper money issued by Congress and the state governments facilitated this domestic trade. The currency depreciated rapidly, but for a few years it circulated freely among people who had never relied much on money. Before the war, most people traded locally with people they knew and operated in a bookkeeping economy in which debts accumulated on ledgers and were often discharged through barter. In September 1777, Henry Laurens wrote with surprise that the demand for paper money was "not confined to the capital towns and cities within a small circle of trading merchants, but spread over a surface of 1,600 miles in length and 300 broad."

The wartime market for agricultural staples spurred farmers to produce larger surpluses. Many were used to living just above the subsistence level, taking part of their harvests to market to earn enough to buy tools, cloth, and other essential manufactured goods. Expanding markets encouraged them to grow and sell more, and to spend their profits to acquire simple luxuries like buttons made of metal or turtle shell to replace their homemade wooden ones, finer cloth to make more stylish clothes or curtains for their windows, or a few Windsor chairs made by skilled craftsmen to replace the rough stools around their tables. Despite non-importation agreements and other protests that disrupted trade, this consumer marketplace had been growing before the war. Regardless of the scarcity of imported goods, the wartime economy encouraged Americans to produce more in order to consume more, creating an unprecedented demand for consumer goods.

Rapid changes in wartime prices during the Revolutionary War tempted ordinary people to become speculators, investing for short-term profits. Alexander Graydon, a paroled Continental Army captain, wrote to a friend in 1779 about his latest investment: "I have been confoundedly bit in a Purchase of Salt, the only Article I believe by which I could have lost, however I expect to retrieve this Loss by a Quantity of Bar Iron which rises to my Wish." Speculating in commodities in this way—buying in order to sell again, without adding value—became a common practice, but until the end of the eighteenth century it was regarded as immoral or at least morally suspect, and in its most flagrant form was a common law crime—forestalling, defined by a 1782 law dictionary as "buying or bargaining" for any products in a market with "the intent to sell the same again, at a higher and dearer price." The revolutionary transformation of the American economy blurred the distinction between speculation and investment and erased the stigma long attached to buying in order to resell at a profit.

Pent up demand led to a dramatic increase in consumer spending after the war. Prices declined, partly because British merchants had a large inventory of unsold goods, partly because rising demand in Britain and America enabled manufacturers to produce goods in larger volume, creating economies of scale, and partly because American merchants, pressed for payment by suppliers, lowered prices to move goods quickly. Lower prices made it possible for ordinary people to buy consumer goods that until recently had been enjoyed mainly by the gentry. Gentility—an idea shaped by the ideals and habits of the gentry—became a charac-

teristic to which ordinary American could aspire. It was signified by genteel behavior, stylish dress, and habits like tea drinking, newspaper reading, and hanging fashionable prints on the wall.

These changes, and many others that would in time define the middle class, were not unique to America. They were happening in Britain and, with local differences, elsewhere in the Atlantic world, but in the United States they touched the lives of an enormous number of people and were associated in their minds with the political and cultural changes of the Revolution. Consumption and gentility were linked to liberty and equality and became defining characteristics of a society in which freedom was associated with choices like where to live, what to do, how to worship, what to wear, and whether to spend or save.

The growth of the internal market for imported and domestic goods encouraged entrepreneurs to open retail shops in country towns that had never had retail shops. Villages grew into towns. Baltimore, Maryland—a modest town before the war—grew at an extraordinary rate, due in part to expanding markets for iron and wheat, much of it brought down the Susquehanna River, which had been an insignificant artery of trade before the war. Iron furnaces and flour mills turned those raw materials into marketable commodities that provided people in Baltimore and its hinterland with money to buy English woolens, Indian cotton cloth, tea, wine, clocks, guns, books, and earthenware dishes. A merchant in Baltimore reported in 1784 that "large quantities of goods are expected this Spring and Summer by the Citizens of this State, from London, many of whom were never in business before. Obviously, even novices expected to cash in on the profits I expected from trade." When the first United States census was taken in 1790, Baltimore had a population of over 18,000 and had passed Charleston to become the country's third largest city.

The depression of the mid-1780s slowed the development of the internal marketplace. Tariffs imposed by the states stifled interstate commerce and the increasing scarcity of hard money and credit posed serious challenges to entrepreneurs, but internal markets continued to grow. The barriers to a full and effective union of the states were increasingly political rather than economic.

Dismantling those barriers by eliminating internal taxes and turning the United States into a single market—one of the most important achievements of the constitutional reformers of the 1780s—would release the productive capacity of the American people and help create one of the most dynamic economies in the world, with rising wealth based on internal trade.

The Trans-Appalachian West

One of the most important consequences of the Revolution was the westward movement of the American people. The opening of the trans-Appalachian West created economic opportunities for thousands and ultimately millions of Americans and fueled the growth of the American economy for generations. The development of roads, canals, steamboats, and ultimately railroads connecting the West with commercial centers in the East employed many thousands of Americans and facilitated a vast internal market that tied the states together in new ways and enriched thousands of merchants, manufacturers, and entrepreneurs, and investors.

Above all, the opening of the trans-Appalachian West made it possible for millions of Americans to become independent property owners. Among them were people from every part of Europe, drawn by the possibility of acquiring farms of their own, something that was increasingly difficult if not impossible in their native lands. The opening of the trans-Appalachian West facilitated one of the greatest movements of people in world history, and by the late nineteenth century it made the United States into a nation of immigrants. Many were refugees from tyranny, religious oppression, or poverty. They were drawn to America by economic opportunity and the promise of freedom.

British-Americans began exploring the vast region between the Appalachians and the Mississippi River in the middle of the eighteenth century. Victory in the French and Indian War confirmed Britain's claim to the region, but after the war the British government tried to prevent colonists from crossing the Appalachians to settle on land to the west. Those restrictions were never particularly effective. The British refused to sanction the acquisition of large tracts of the mountains by

speculative land companies, and did little to prevent individuals, families, and small groups from crossing the mountains and settling in the valleys on their western flanks. The frontier was simply too long to police.

Thousands of Americans crossed the mountains to make new lives for themselves and their families. They cleared their land, built their homes, and fought Indians intent on driving them off. The men who came east to defeat Ferguson at Kings Mountain had settled on the rivers of southern Virginia and what became east Tennessee—the Holston, Clinch, and Powell rivers that rise in Virginia, the Watauga, Nolichucky, and French Broad rivers beginning in North Carolina—and in the creek valleys and hollows around them. They were toughened by life on the frontier and pitiless in battle.

Among them was John Crockett, born in Frederick County, Virginia, around 1753. His family moved south to Tryon County, North Carolina, around 1768, and then after the defeat of the Regulators they moved west of the mountains to the Holston River valley. John's father was killed by Cherokees in 1777. John Crockett fought the Cherokee and then in 1780 fought loyalists at Kings Mountain. Around the end of the Revolutionary War, he moved his growing family south to the Nolichucky River, where his fifth son was born in 1786. Named for his grandfather, Davy Crockett grew to manhood in east Tennessee. He was already one of the most famous frontiersmen of his generation when he fought in the Texas Revolution and died at the Alamo in 1836.

Davy Crockett became a frontier folk hero and the subject of tall tales, but his family's story—of restless movement, back-breaking labor, poverty, petty debts, and Indian fighting, was characteristic of the early frontier. The Crocketts were like thousands of other families who pressed their way across the mountains in the Revolutionary era. Life on the trans-Appalachian frontier was difficult and dangerous but those who headed west took advantage of a kind of freedom offered nowhere else in world.

By the 1770s hunters from Virginia and North Carolina were familiar with the bison trails and Indian paths of Kentucky and had blazed trails of their own. They guided explorers, surveyors, and

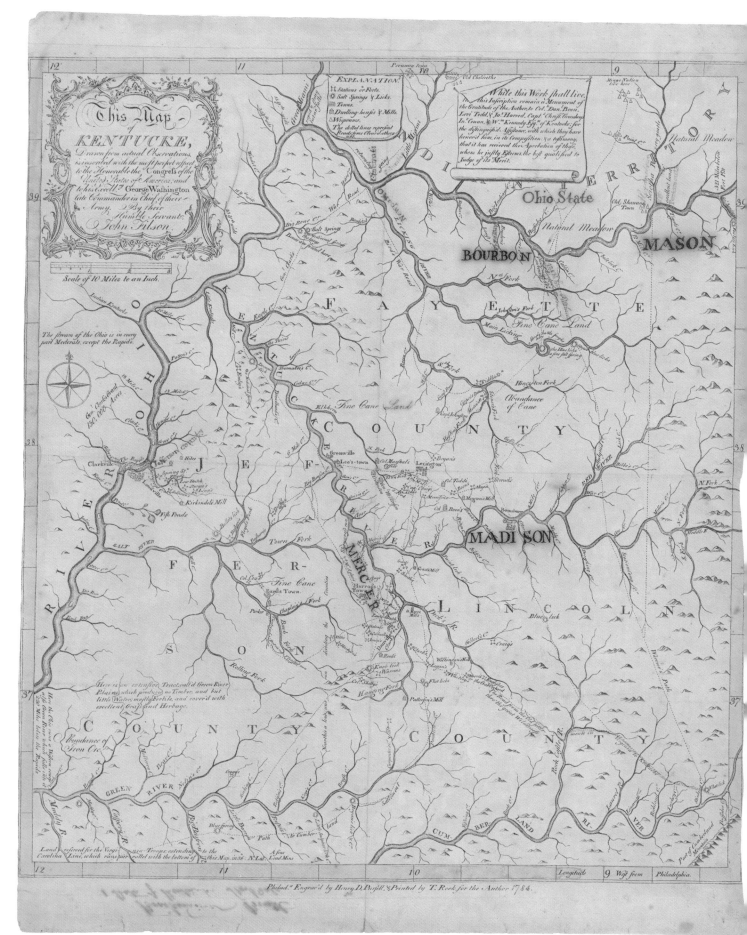

This Map of KENTUCKE, Drawn from actual Observations, is inscribed with the most perfect respect to the Honorable the Congress of the United States of America; and to his Excell.cy George Washington late Commander in Chief of their Army. By their Humble Servant, John Filson.

Scale of 10 Miles to an Inch.

EXPLANATION.
Stations or Forts.
Salt Springs & Licks.
Towns.
Dwelling-houses & Mills.
Wigwams.
The dotted lines represent Rendezvous Roads & others.

While this Work shall live,
May this Inscription remain a Monument of the Gratitude of the Author, to Col. Dan. Boon, Levi Todd, & Jno. Harrod, Capt. Chrstr. Greenhup, Jno. Cowan, & Wm. Kennedy Esqr.s of Kentucke; for the distinguish'd Assistance, with which they have honor'd him, in its Composition, &c. a testimony, that it has received their Approbation of those whom he justly Esteems, the best qualified to judge of its Merit.

Ohio State

BOURBON

MASON

FAYETTE

Fine Cane Land

Fine Cane Land

COUNTY

MADISON

LINCOLN

MERCER

JEFFERSON

COUNTY

COUNTY

The stream of the Ohio is in every part Moderate, except the Rapids.

Gen.l Clarks Grant 150,000 Acres.

Here is an extensive Tract, call'd Green River Plains; which produces no Timber, and but little Water, mostly Fertile, and cover'd with excellent Grass and Herbage.

Abundance of Iron Ore.

GREEN RIVER

OHIO RIVER

CUMBERLAND RIVER

Land reserved for the Virginia Troops; extending to the Carolina Line, which runs parrallel with the bottom of this Map, in 36. N Lat.

A fine Lead Mine.

Here the Ohio runs in a Western course to Green River which falls into it West Mile below the Rapids.

Philad.a Engrav'd by Henry D. Pursell, & Printed by T. Rook for the Author 1784.

Longitude 9 West from Philadelphia.

migrants into the region in the last years before the Revolutionary War. These early migrants were all attracted by the fertility of the soil and the open grasslands, interspersed with stands of mature hardwood trees, found in the region. The grasslands were home to herds of bison and other game, which made Kentucky—the name means grassland or meadow in several Indian languages—an ideal hunting ground.

Many of the Indians living west of the Appalachians were determined to stop white settlement before it destroyed their way of life. They belonged to many different tribes, including the Shawnee, Wyandot, Delaware, and Miami in the Ohio Country, the Shawnee and Cherokee in Kentucky and Tennessee, and the Creek, Cherokee, Choctaw, and Chickasaw from Tennessee southward. Together their warriors were formidable but they rarely acted in unison. Chiefs exerted only limited control over warriors. The Indian tribes spoke different languages—the diversity of American Indian languages and the relatively small number of speakers of each language and dialect is one of the distinctive characteristics of Indian culture—and often used sign language to communicate across the boundaries of spoken language. Despite differences that sometimes led to war between them, the Indians shared a spiritual tie to the land. Indians regarded the land as a gift of a great spirit to their people and whites as invaders whose presence was a kind of spiritual desecration.

During the war, the British provided several Indian tribes with arms and supplies to resist American encroachment. The British hoped that fighting with the Indians would distract Americans and make it easier to suppress the American rebellion. The British had little interest in defending the Indians or their way of life. Indian leaders, among whom were some sophisticated diplomats,

were well aware of this fact, but concluded that the British would restrain settlers, at least temporarily, more effectively than an American government. Indian resistance slowed the rate of westward migration and in some areas rolled it back temporarily, but did not stop it. By one estimate, as many as twenty thousand migrants settled in Kentucky in 1779 and 1780 alone. Independence and liberty were not abstractions on the frontier. Independence meant personal autonomy and the opportunity to acquire land and make a better life. Liberty was the absence of government restraint.

The frontier war, rising and falling in intensity, continued wherever migrants and Indians were in contact. It claimed hundreds of innocent victims. Neither side distinguished between the armed and unarmed. Both slaughtered men, women, children, and the elderly without discrimination. The horror reached its low point in March 1782 when Pennsylvania militia systematically murdered ninety-six unarmed Delawares and Mohicans, all of them pacifist Christians converted by Moravian missionaries, at the village of Gnaddenhutten in what became eastern Ohio. The militia commander accused the Christian Indians of collaborating with hostile Delawares before ordering the execution of every Indian in the village, a pitiless genocidal atrocity in which some men hardened by years of ferocious warfare refused to participate.

The Indian tribes of the trans-Appalachian West were not parties to the treaty ending the war between Britain and America. They continued to resist settlement in a frontier war that continued for more than a decade after the Treaty of Paris. Migrants negotiated treaties and purchases with Indian leaders to secure land. Those agreements were often made with one group of Indians but rejected by others who continued to resist. Migrants often violated the terms of the agreements made on

This 1784 map of Kentucky was published with John Filson's *The Discovery, Settlement, and Present State of Kentucke.* **A schoolteacher and surveyor, Filson included an account of the adventures of Daniel Boone that made the frontiersman famous. Oriented with north to the left, the map depicts the roads, towns, and forts along the rivers flowing into the Ohio (The John Carter Brown Library).**

(Overleaf) Abel Buell of New Haven, Connecticut, published this map—the first complete map of the independent United States designed and printed in America—in 1784. It depicts the western land claims of several states, which were based on their colonial charters or proprietary grants. Vague language, imprecise boundary descriptions, and overlapping claims led to disputes between the states. This map depicts Connecticut's claim to a strip of land extending to the Mississippi River (Courtesy of David M. Rubenstein).

their behalf. Violent attacks gave way to reprisals in a brutal war of revenge. Despite the uncertainty of frontier life, migrants continued to arrive and were ultimately so numerous that it was impossible for Indian warriors to drive them out.

The Western Land Question

The Treaty of Paris conveyed Britain's claim to the entire region west of the Appalachians to the United States. That it would be governed as the common territory of the United States and then organized into separate states admitted to the union on equal terms with the thirteen original states was not inevitable. Few decisions made by the Revolutionary generation have had more enduring importance for the American republic and its citizens than the decision to organize the trans-Appalachian West into states, each a new republic, admitted to the union when their population was large enough to sustain a state government. That process continuously reshaped the United States for nearly two hundred years. It secured the benefits of state and local government, responsive to the people's will, and created a system through which millions of Americans ultimately acquired property and with it, economic opportunities and personal independence.

When the Revolutionary War ended, the West was a patchwork of overlapping claims based on colonial charters and proprietary grants issued by the British government in the seventeenth century, when the interior of North America had not been mapped. Virginia claimed the present states of West Virginia, Kentucky, Ohio, Indiana, Michigan, Illinois, and Wisconsin, as well as part of western Pennsylvania and northeastern Minnesota. Connecticut, with a colonial charter that placed its western boundary at the Pacific Ocean, asserted its right to a slice of land claimed by Virginia, in a band extending across the northern third of Pennsylvania and including the southern shore of Lake Erie, part of what became northern Ohio, southern Michigan, northern Illinois, and southern Wisconsin. Massachusetts claimed part of what become Michigan and Wisconsin. New York asserted a more dubious claim to sovereignty over any land occupied by the Iroquois, on the grounds that a

colonial governor had declared them subjects of the Crown under the protection of New York.

South of the Ohio the disposition of western land was clearer. Virginia's claim to Kentucky was unchallenged except by the Indian tribes that valued it as a hunting ground. North Carolina's western region was comparatively well defined—it extended to the Mississippi, bounded on the north by a generally recognized boundary with Virginia and on the south by the thirty-fifth parallel. Whether South Carolina had a claim to land west of the Appalachians was not clear. Georgia's charter fixed its northern limit at the source of the Savannah River, which flowed out of the mountains near the border of North and South Carolina. Depending on which of its several branches was regarded as the source, South Carolina might own a strip of land twelve miles from north to south and over four hundred miles wide or it might have no western land at all. Georgia claimed land extending to the Mississippi, the limits of which depended on the very uncertain location of the northern border of West Florida, which the British returned to Spain in 1783.

Conflicting claims and disputes over the territory north of the Ohio threatened to permanently cripple or even destroy the tentative union of the states. The Maryland legislature refused to ratify the Articles of Confederation as long as Virginia persisted in its expansive claims in region. Maryland was only one of the states with no western land claim, but it was the state that Virginia's claims most clearly endangered. The sale of land from such an enormous domain, some believed, would fund Virginia's government for generations and would relieve Virginians of state taxation. Maryland, meanwhile, would have to impose taxes to finance its activities, which would inevitably lead Marylanders to move to neighboring Virginia. Maryland leaders feared that their state would be depopulated and impoverished as Virginia grew in population and economic strength. In Maryland and elsewhere, men with an interest in land companies organized to acquire large tracts and sell parcels at a profit were reluctant to acknowledge Virginia's claims. The Virginia legislature had declared their claims, which were based on purchases of dubious legality from various Indians, invalid.

In January 1781, the Virginia legislature

offered to cede to Congress the state's claims north of the Ohio while retaining its claim to Kentucky. Virginia thus offered to settle the controversy over claims in the West in a way that confirmed its sovereignty over an immensely valuable region while ceding land disputed by other states and peopled by hostile Indian tribes that would make occupying the region difficult and dangerous. The offer provided that the land ceded to Congress should be divided into new states and "that the States so formed shall be distinct Republican States and be admitted Members of the Federal Union having the same Rights of Sovereignty Freedom and Independence as the other States." Congress declined the Virginia cession because it included a condition nullifying the claims of land companies organized in other states to large tracts, but the Maryland legislature was sufficiently encouraged by Virginia's offer to ratify the Articles of Confederation, which finally went into operation in the spring of 1781.

George Washington worried that unless effective government was established in the West, the whole region would "be overrun with Land Jobbers—Speculators, and Monopolizers" and with "scatter'd settlers" who would embroil the new nation in "inextricable perplexities, and more than probably in a great deal of Bloodshed." He urged that settlement be managed to prevent speculation, preserve peace with the Indians—for which Washington recommended the establishment of a line beyond which migrants would be forbidden—and to do justice to the soldiers who had been promised land, and "who have fought and bled to obtain it."

New Republics

At war's end, members of Congress were increasingly anxious to acquire a national domain in order to fulfill their promises of land grants to Continental Army veterans and to raise revenue through land sales to pay the nation's mounting debts. When Virginia renewed its offer to cede its claims north of the Ohio in early 1784, Congress accepted. Virginia compromised by relinquishing its demand that Congress formally recognize the state's sovereignty over Kentucky. Congress agreed not to acknowledge land company claims invalidated by Virginia law.

The other states with western claims subsequently relinquished them. Massachusetts ceded its claim without reservation in 1785. Connecticut ceded its claim in 1786, but retained title to over three million acres in what later became northeastern Ohio, which was known as the Connecticut Western Reserve. The state sold much of it to private investors and set aside half a million acres to compensate citizens of Connecticut, including residents of Danbury and New London, whose homes and businesses had been burned by the British during the war.

The task of devising a plan for the new national domain fell to Thomas Jefferson, who had returned to Congress after serving as governor of Virginia. Jefferson imagined an expanding union of self-governing republics and was determined not to allow future territorial disputes to destroy the fragile union and ruin what he called the new nation's "well founded prospects of giving liberty to half the globe." As chairman of a committee to propose a resolution organizing the western territory, Jefferson urged that the entire region west of the Appalachians, whether or not the land had yet been ceded to the Confederation government, be divided into states of comparable size with clearly defined boundaries.

Reflecting his passion for rational order, Jefferson proposed organizing the states in a grid superimposed on a map of the West. Each state was to span two degrees of latitude—138 miles north to south—beginning at the forty-fifth parallel (which passes through northern Michigan). Any territory north of that parallel was attached to the state to south. Jefferson suggested names for ten of the new states, including Sylvania, Michigania, Cherronesus, Assenisipia, Metropotamia, Illinoia, Saratoga, and Washington for the states north of the Ohio, and Polypotamia and Pelisipia for the region south of the Ohio claimed by Virginia and North Carolina. His proposed boundaries and state names were soon discarded, but the idea that the new states carved out of the West would be equal to one another and in most ways equal to the original states, endured.

Each new state would have a republican form of government and would be expected to share in paying the debts of the Confederation and the costs of maintaining the common government.

A MAP of the north west parts of the UNITED STATES of AMERICA

The several divisions on the NW of the Ohio is the form which that Country is to be laid off into States according to an ordinance of Congress of may the 20th 1785

The author presents this to the public as the production of his leisure hours, and flatters himself that altho it is not perfect few capital errors will be found in it. He has not attempted to take the exact meanders of the Waters but only their general course — In forming this Map he acknowledges himself to have been indebted to the ingenious labours of Thomas Hutchins and Willm McMurray Esqrs But from his own Surveys and observations he was led to hope he could make considerable improvements on those and all that have gone before him. How far he has succeeded is now submited to the impartial public. by their very hble servt — John Fitch

To Thos Hutchins, Esqr Geographer to the United States.
Sir It is with the greatest diffidence I beg leave to lay at your feet a very humble attempt to promote a science of which you are so bright an ornament. I wish it were more worthy your patronage—Unaccustomed to the business of engraving I could not render it as pleasing to the eye as I would have wished— But this as I flatter myself will be easily forgiven by a Gentleman who knows how to distinguish between form and Substance, in all things. I have the honr to be Sir your very hble Servt John Fitch

SCALE of MILES
10 20 30 40 50   100   200

LAKE SUPERIOR

Lake of the Woods
Pant L.
Ld Rain L.
Red River L.
Cold R.
St Louis R.
West B.
Strawbery R.
Goddard R.
R. St Francis
Rum R.
Copper ore in great quantity here
Ille Royal
Phillipeaux I.
The Line between the UNITED STATES

The falls of St Anthony exhibit one of the grandest spectacles in nature; the water dashing over tremendous rocks from a height of about forty feet perpendicular

Falls of St Anthony
St Croix R.
the great Cave
Matabountway R.
L. Peppin
Chippeway R.
a great T. of the Sioux
Buck R.
Leon Ore
Yellow R.
Ouisconsing River
a Sauke T.
Turkey R.

Green R.
Winnebago

AMERICA and Canada According to the Definitive

LAKE HURON
Mattatoualin I.
Michilimakinac Fly Str
Thunder B.
Saguinam B.
St Marys
Pauchilino

An High Plain

P.M.
St Nicholas R.
Sable R.
Blanch

LAKE MICHIGAN

Mohcon
LaGrue R.
Rau Raisin
RauBark
R. Murae
R. Noire
St Joseph R.
Wakeguack R.

Milowaques R.
R. au Ceder

The falls of Niagara are at present in the middle of a plane about five miles back from the summit of the Mountain over which the waters once tumbled we may suppose. The action of the water in a long course of time has worn away the solid rock and formed an immense Ditch which no one may approach without horror. After falling perpendicular 150 feet (as some have computed) it continues to descend in a rapid Seven miles further to the Landing place.

PART OF LAKE ONTARIO
Niagara Falls
NiagaraFalls
St Joshuas

Detroit
Laroche R.
Goose C.
Cochran's
Maumi R. to Taway T.

LAKE ERIE
Peace Signed at Paris Septr 3d 1793

PART OF NEW YORK STATE

The lands on this lake are generally flat & Swampy; but will make rich pasture, and Meadow Land.

Venango
Br Boccet
Fort Pitt

PART OF PENNSYLVANIA

From Fort Lawrance and thence to the mouth of Sioto a westerly course to the Illinois is generally a rich level country abounding with living springs and navigable waters.

This Country has once been settled by a people more expert in the Art of war than the present inhabitants. Regular fortifications and some of these incredibly large are frequently to be found Also many graves or Towers like Pyramids of earth

L'Aboche
a la Roche
Ld Meschekh R.
Mine R.
Sagamond R.
Plain R.
Plan R.
Demi Quain R.
Tha R.
Thebila R.
Far R.
Tranquil R.
Vermilion R.
Meadow R.
Sakamma R.
Myssinous R.
Andoni R.

On the M inhabited tis are a number of Indian Towns Shawanoe Delawares Mingos &c

MISSISSIPPI RIVER
ILLINOIS RIVER

Lit. Beaver C.
Yellow C.
White C.
Will C.

OHIO RIVER

Plowkes Wintering ground
Fort C.
Island C.
Kaskaskias
States Bank
Beaver C.
Big Hill C.
Blind C.
R. de Maramec

MISSOURI R.

Wabash River
Tipphicanoe River
Marias R.
Post Vincent
White R.
Indian Kings
Sugar R.

Green River Barrens
Green R.
Coffers R.
Midley R.
Big Barren R.
Cumberland R.

PART OF THE KENTUCKEY

OHIO

Louisville
New York
Salt R.
Boonsburgh
Elkhorn
Lexington
N. Fork
The Blue licks
Kingston Fork

KENTUCKEY

N Fork From the Pennsylvania Line thence a Southwesterly course to the Carolina line is generally very poor & rocks and broken land and very mountainous

The Kentuckey country is not so level as it is generally represented to be there being a range of hilly land running thro it RN

Lit. Miami R.
N. Miami R.
Lickin C.
Adams C.

GREAT RIVER
Sandy R.
Gt Sandy R.
Blue Stone R.
Wolf C.
New R.
Bluestone Mountain

Kanhawa R.
Gaul R.
Green Br.

From the mouth of Sioto thence to Fort Lawrance between that line and the Ohio the soil is extremely good but generally much broken with sharp hills

Ironbanks settled
Waters of Cumberland
Blockhouse
Reed C.
Allegany

When the population of a new state reached twenty thousand free inhabitants the people could hold a convention to adopt a state constitution and create a permanent state government. Once its population equaled the number of free inhabitants of any of the original thirteen states it would be eligible to send delegates to Congress. The plan provided for a substantial degree of autonomy for the new states from the earliest stage of their development.

Under Jefferson's plan, there were two important ways in which the new states would differ from the original states. The first was that they would have no control over public land and were strictly forbidden to interfere with the sale or other disposition of the land by the Confederation government. Control over the distribution of land was one of the most important functions of colonial governments and of the state governments that succeeded them and an important source of revenue. The new states would have to rely on taxation instead.

The second way the new states Jefferson imagined differed from the old states was that slavery would be forbidden in all of them after 1800. The proposed Land Ordinance of 1784 included a provision that "there shall be neither slavery nor involuntary servitude in any of the said states, otherwise than in punishment of crimes whereof the party shall have been convicted to have been personally guilty."

This clause reflected Jefferson's conviction that slavery was a violation of the natural rights of the enslaved and corroded the character of those who enslaved them. Like most of the leaders of Revolutionary Virginia, Jefferson benefited all his life from the labor of people he deliberately enslaved, yet he recognized the inherent inconsistency of slavery with the principles of universal natural rights he expressed so eloquently in the Declaration of Independence. Born into a society in which enslavement was an accepted practice as well as the basis of the economy of Virginia and his own family, Jefferson nonetheless concluded as a young man that slavery

should be abolished. As a young attorney he argued for the enslaved in at least six freedom suits before the Revolutionary War.

In 1783, anticipating a convention to revise Virginia's Revolutionary constitution, he wrote a draft constitution calling for a process of gradual abolition that would free every child born to an enslaved mother after 1800. If adopted, that provision would have ended Virginia's dependence on enslaved labor by the second quarter of the nineteenth century and all but extinguished slavery by 1860. No such convention was called, but a few months after writing his draft constitution Jefferson inserted his more aggressive antislavery provision in the proposed Land Ordinance of 1784, under which slavery would have been tolerated until 1800 and then forbidden absolutely.

As it did for many thoughtful white Virginians of his generation, slavery posed a dilemma for which Jefferson had no immediate solution. Jefferson could imagine a world without slavery, but he had no practical vision of what his native Virginia would be like after slavery ended. Jefferson interacted with many free blacks—their numbers increased dramatically as a consequence of the Revolution—but he doubted that white Virginians could live in harmony with a large population of free black Virginians after slavery was abolished. He could not envision a multiracial society without slavery. The only large-scale solution Jefferson imagined was colonization—moving freed slaves to Africa or an enclave in South or Central America.

The West, in Jefferson's mind, offered the possibility of shaping an ideal republican society of sturdy farmers uncorrupted by slavery. Although a small number of enslaved people already lived north of the Ohio, the region was not dependent on enslaved labor. Jefferson did not intend to allow it to become dependent on slavery. The idea of ending slavery in Virginia and settling freed slaves in the vast Trans-Appalachian West—creating a revolutionary multiracial society of landowners—eluded him. Even if he had conceived such a solution, persuading Virginia slaveholders to accept

The forts occupied by the British at Niagara, Detroit, and the Mackinac Straits controlled the water routes between four of the Great Lakes and dominated the northern frontier of the trans-Appalachian West. This map was produced in 1785 by inventor John Fitch to develop interest among investors in his plans for a steamboat. Steam navigation came to dominate commerce on the Great Lakes as well as the Ohio and Mississippi rivers and their tributaries (Courtesy of Mount Vernon Ladies' Association).

it would have been an extraordinary, and perhaps insurmountable, challenge.

When Congress debated the proposed Land Ordinance, only ten states were represented on the floor. The delegations from the four New England states, New York, and Pennsylvania voted for the clause, leaving one state less than required to adopt it. New Jersey would have joined them, but a delegate was absent due to illness, leaving the state without sufficient representation for its vote to be counted. North Carolina's delegation was evenly divided. The antislavery provision, Jefferson reported to James Madison, "was lost by a single vote." Congress adopted the Land Ordinance of 1784 without it.

If the antislavery clause had been included in the Land Ordinance of 1784, slavery would have been precluded after 1800 in all states formed from the national domain, including the states that became the cotton belt of the South. During the sixteen years before this provision of the ordinance took effect, slave masters would have been reluctant to take their slaves into western territories where slavery would soon be abolished. A political battle to overturn the prohibition might have occurred, forcing the nation to confront the future of slavery during the Revolutionary era. Instead of spreading to what became Alabama, Mississippi, and Tennessee, slavery might have been contained on the eastern seaboard and millions might have been spared the horror of enslavement.

The antislavery clause of the Land Ordinance of 1784 was the first antislavery law ever considered by a national government. Though this first effort to keep slavery out of the West failed, the idea that slavery should be prohibited from the national domain and prevented from spreading through the West persisted and became the central principle of the free soil movement and of the Republican Party of Abraham Lincoln. The language of Jefferson's prohibition echoes through our history—first in the Northwest Ordinance of 1787, which forbid slavery north of the Ohio, and then in the Thirteenth Amendment to the Constitution, adopted by Congress in 1865: "Neither slavery nor invol-

untary servitude, except as a punishment for crime whereof the party shall have been duly convicted, shall exist within the United States, or any place subject to their jurisdiction."

"The touch of a feather"

The Land Ordinance of 1784 did not define how western land would be divided and sold, matters of enormous importance since Congress intended the sale of public land to raise the revenue to pay the nation's war debts. This issue was settled by the Land Ordinance of 1785, which created a system for dividing the public land for sale. Based on the New England township, the system called for the public domain to be surveyed in an orderly grid of townships, each one six miles square. Townships were divided into thirty-six sections, each one mile square and containing 640 acres. Section sixteen, near the center of each township, was reserved for the support of a school. Townships and sections, once laid out by official surveyors, were to be sold at public auction for not less than one dollar an acre.

This checkerboard system of land ownership spread over the region north of the Ohio and ultimately over most of the West. In sections, half sections, and quarter sections, much of the land was occupied by farmers who went west from the long-settled eastern states or who came to the United States for the opportunity to cultivate their own land. "The western world opens an amazing prospect as a national fund," wrote David Howell, "it is equal to our debt. As a source of future population and strength, it is a guaranty to our independence. As its inhabitants will be mostly cultivators of the soil, republicanism looks to them as its guardians."

The potential of the West was vast, but realizing it required overcoming enormous political and diplomatic challenges. Americans west of the Appalachians could not send farm products back across the mountains to sell them because transporting goods across the mountains was too costly. This

The Land Ordinance of 1785 called for laying out the public domain in the West in an orderly grid of townships and sections. This work began with the land bordering the upper Ohio River. This system extended westward across the continent (The John Carter Brown Library).

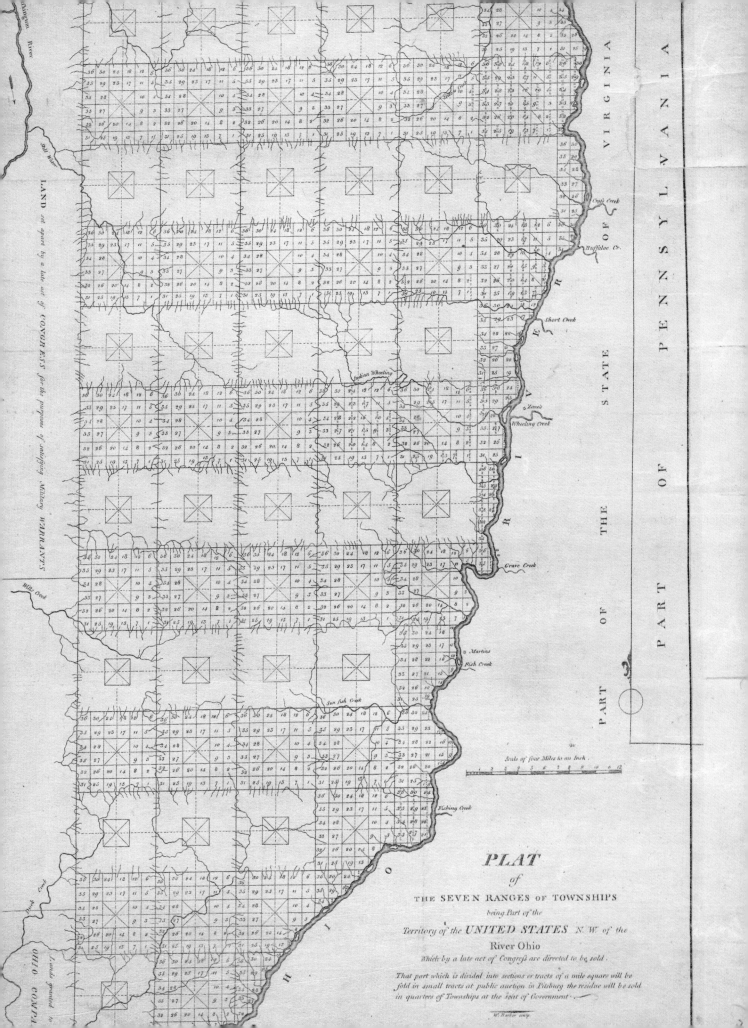

PLAT
of
THE SEVEN RANGES OF TOWNSHIPS
being Part of the
Territory of the UNITED STATES N.W. of the
River Ohio
Which by a late act of Congress are directed to be sold.

That part which is divided into sections or tracts of a mile square will be
sold in small tracts at public auction in Pittsburg the residue will be sold
in quarters of Townships at the seat of Government.

Scale of four Miles to an Inch

W. Barker sculp

LAND set apart by a late act of CONGRESS for the purpose of satisfying Military WARRANTS

OHIO COMPA

PART OF THE STATE OF VIRGINIA

PART OF PENNSYLVANIA

Cross Creek
Buffaloe Cr.
Short Creek
Zane's
Wheeling Creek
Indian Wheeling
Grave Creek
Martins
Fish Creek
Sun fish Creek
Fishing Creek
Wills Creek
Muskingum River

O H I O

was not a major problem for the earliest migrants, who produced no more than they needed to survive, but as farms grew and yields increased farmers would need access to the market. The most obvious one was shipping goods down the Ohio and Mississippi to New Orleans, which was controlled by the Spanish. In 1784 the Spanish announced that no more American goods could be bought or sold there. They intended to discourage American settlement on the Ohio and Mississippi rivers, fearing that Americans would eventually threaten Spanish control of New Orleans and the vast territory extending to the Pacific.

Migrants settling along the Great Lakes might ship their goods through the lakes and down the St. Lawrence River, but this route was dominated by a series of British forts controlling passage between the lakes. These forts were in territory ceded to the United States by the Treaty of Paris, but the British held on to them on the flimsy grounds that Americans had not fulfilled their treaty obligations respecting pre-war debts and the treatment of loyalists. In fact, the British wanted to discourage American settlement between the Ohio and the Great Lakes, maintain control of the Indian trade, and supply Indians with arms and ammunition to resist American expansion.

George Washington worried that economic necessity would push American settlers toward their foreign neighbors. As long as the Mississippi River remained the cheapest way to get their products to market, Washington realized, American migrants in the West would look to Spain, and not the United States. Eventually the western settlements might separate from the United States and ally themselves with Spain or even accept Spanish rule in order to enjoy unrestricted access to the Mississippi. "The Western settlers," Washington wrote, "stand as it were upon a pivot—the touch of a feather would turn them any way."

In 1785 Congress directed John Jay to negotiate an agreement with Spain settling the various issues dividing the two countries, including access to Spanish colonial ports, the northern boundary of West Florida, and the American right to navigate the Mississippi. Despite American claims that the Treaty of Paris had guaranteed them the right to trade on the Mississippi, no such right existed. Goods shipped by river would have to be transferred to ocean-going vessels at New Orleans, which was deep in Spanish territory. The Spanish ambassador, Don Diego de Gardoqui, agreed to open Havana and other Spanish colonial ports to American trade and agreed to a Florida boundary favorable to American interests, but he refused to grant Americans permission to ship goods through New Orleans. Congress rejected the treaty along sectional lines. Northern delegates were pleased to secure access to Spanish ports and indifferent to the navigation of the Mississippi. Southern delegates, led by James Madison and James Monroe, insisted that any treaty with Spain include the right to trade on the Mississippi.

In London, John Adams made no progress persuading the British to evacuate the forts on the Great Lakes. In my private opinion," he wrote to Jay in August 1785, "it is their fixed design to keep Possession of the Posts upon the Frontier." By December Adams was certain. "They rely upon it that We shall not raise An Army, to take the Posts," he wrote to Jay. "The Expence and Difficulty they know will be great, and therefore they think they may play with Us, as long as they please." Adams concluded that his mission would do his country little good. "I am like to be as insignificant here, as you can imagine," he wrote. "I shall be treated as I have been, with all the Civility that is shewn to other foreign Ministers but shall do nothing."

Jay and Adams were unsuccessful because they represented a government incapable of imposing its will. After the Continental Army disbanded, the army was reduced to fewer than two hundred men—too small a force to defend the western frontier, force the British to abandon their forts, or compel the Spanish to open the Mississippi to American commerce. In the predatory world of eighteenth-century empires, diplomacy rarely secured more than a nation was capable of taking by force.

314 **Bitterly disappointed when the British ceded the area between the Great Lakes and the Ohio River to the United States, Indian leaders formed a confederacy to resist American encroachment. Among them was Mohawk chief Thayendanegea, also known as Joseph Brant, who had led Iroquois warriors allied with the British during the war. In 1785 he traveled to Britain seeking arms and assistance. That year, Gilbert Stuart painted this portrait in London (©The Trustees of the British Museum).**

Thayendanegea otherwise Joseph Brant War Chief of the Mohawks

Chapter 20   "House on Fire"

The government established by the Articles of Confederation was barely a government at all. It had no power to tax and thus no way to repay the money Congress had borrowed to conduct the Revolutionary War. It had no money to pay what it owed to thousands of men who had served in the Continental Army. It had no authority to tax commerce and thus defend the American economy from the predatory trading practices of the European imperial powers. And it had no military power with which to defend the interests of the American people in a world where international relations relied on force and threats of force. It was incapable of defending the freedom Americans had won in the Revolutionary War.

Between 1780 and 1786, laws to fulfill the highest ideals of the Revolution, including the Pennsylvania Statute for the Gradual Abolition of Slavery and the Virginia Statute for Establishing Religious Freedom, were adopted by state governments. Congress, which had no authority to protect the natural and civil rights of the people, had no role in those achievements. In the years after the war, enterprising Americans created new businesses, cleared new farms, and moved west, regardless of the impotence of the Confederation.

Despite all of this restless, creative energy, by 1786 the nation was in crisis. With no government capable of protecting its interests, the United States had fallen into a commercial depression that threatened the economic independence of the nation and the personal independence of the American people. Western migrants depended on the militia, on one another, and ultimately on themselves to defend their lives and farms, but could do nothing

to secure the British posts dominating the Great Lakes, compel the Spanish to open the Mississippi River to American commerce, or prevent either of those imperial powers from supplying Indians with arms and ammunition to make war on them. As George Washington anticipated, a few Americans in the West entered into secret discussions with the Spanish about separating western settlements from the United States and becoming clients of the Spanish Empire.

Congress was bankrupt. It was entirely dependent on money requisitioned from the states, which the states constantly ignored. In October 1781 Congress requested eight million dollars from the states to cover the anticipated expenses for 1782. By January 1783 it had received only $420,000. Congress made additional requests in 1784, 1785, and 1786. By early 1787 the states had paid two-thirds of the 1781 and 1784 requisitions, about one fifth of the 1785 requisition, and almost nothing in response the 1786 requisition. "Requisitions are actually little better than a jest," Washington wrote, because "thirteen sovereign, independent disunited States are in the habit of discussing and refusing compliance with them at their option." Without a reliable source of revenue, Congress could not even pay its own operating expenses and considered disbanding.

"I think often of our Situation," Washington wrote to John Jay in May 1786, "and view it with concern. From the high ground on which we stood—from the plain path which invited our footsteps, to be so fallen!"

"Our affairs seem to lead to some Crisis," Jay responded, "some Revolution—something that I

By May 1785, when Robert Edge Pine visited Mount Vernon to paint his portrait, George Washington was increasingly frustrated by the weakness of the Confederation. "It is one of the most extraordinary things in nature," he wrote a few months later, "that we should Confederate for National purposes, and yet be afraid to give the rulers thereof who are the Creatures of our own making—appointed for a limited and short duration—who are amenable for every action—recallable at any moment—and subject to all the evils they may be instrumental in producing, sufficient powers to order and direct the affairs of that Nation" (National Portrait Gallery, Smithsonian Institution).

cannot foresee, or conjecture." The Revolutionary War had been difficult, Jay wrote, but he was convinced of the nation's ultimate success. "The Case is now altered—we are going and doing wrong, and therefore I look forward to Evils and Calamities." Jay worried that "People who are orderly and industrious, who are content with their Situations and not uneasy in their Circumstances" would grow disgusted with the incompetence of Confederation and come to regard "the Charms of Liberty as imaginary and delusive." Jay feared they would abandon republican government for some more authoritarian system that secured their interests.

The problem, Washington replied, was the weakness of the Confederation. When he resigned his commission as commander in chief of the Continental Army, he advised the nation to vest Congress with more authority but "my Sentiments . . . have been neglected, tho' given as a last legacy in the most solemn manner." Fear of vesting Congress with that authority, Washington wrote, was "the very climax of popular absurdity and madness," concluding "I do not conceive we can exist long as a Nation, without having lodged somewhere a power which will pervade the whole Union."

The nation—if indeed the people of such a loose Confederation can be called a nation—faced a choice. It was not a choice between the weak government established by the Articles of Confederation and a strong central government. It was a choice between establishing a common government or having no common government at all.

"Combustibles in every State"

The crisis Washington and Jay anticipated might have come in one of many forms. It came in the form of civil unrest over private debts and burdensome taxes, rooted in the inability of the Confederation to pay its debts, regulate international trade to protect American interests, and provide a stable money supply. These are fundamental aspects of government. Failure to address them limits economic opportunity and leads to distress.

Much of the economic activity of the postwar years, particularly consumer spending, was based on credit, which was tied to international credit networks. British merchants extended credit to American merchants in Boston, Providence, New York, Philadelphia, Baltimore, Charleston, Savannah, and other ports. American merchant importers shipped goods on credit to local merchants in smaller ports and inland market towns, who in turn extended credit to retailers who sold the goods to consumers who bought on credit.

This elaborate system functioned well, with very little hard money changing hands, as long as the British export merchants in the middle of the web of credit and debt periodically renewed the notes of the American importers to whom they sold. If they declined to do so and called in their notes or limited credit by demanding quick payment for goods sent to America, their American trading partners had to resolve their debts, either by finding new creditors or by paying off their debts in hard money—gold or silver. In a general contraction—that is, when credit tightened across the British economy—an American merchant might not be able to secure credit and would have to call in his own notes. At that point the web of credit and debt would disintegrate, as each creditor in the network pressed his borrowers for payment in hard money.

A general contraction could be precipitated by an event on the other side of the world. A severe drought in India that caused British East India Company revenue to sag, a bad harvest in Europe, the outbreak of a war that upset the sale of British goods somewhere, or even a short term depletion of gold or silver held by the Bank of England could cause the fragile network to shudder or even collapse. At the end of the eighteenth century markets were already global. An economic shift in East Asia could reach around the world and leave its mark in the account books of a storekeeper in rural Massachusetts and lead him to call on his customers to pay their accounts in gold or silver, and to take the debtors to court for nonpayment if they did not. No one in the courtroom would understand why the contraction had occurred or even how widespread it might be, none of which mattered to a farmer faced with losing his farm or being imprisoned for debt. Unable to grasp a global market for commodities and credit, he could see only the storekeeper and the judge, and blame them, along with Boston merchants and the state legislature, for his predicament.

Writing to Thomas Jefferson from London, Abigail Adams attributed the disorder in Massachusetts to "Luxery and extravagance both in furniture and dress" that had been adopted by "all orders of our Countrymen and women" and was leading them into debt (Fenimore Art Museum, Cooperstown, New York).

Such a crisis occurred in the middle of 1780s and was felt severely in New England, where the rural marketplace of small-scale commercial farmers and retail shopkeepers was more fully developed than in most other parts of the country. Creditors, faced with their own ruin, demanded payment for goods they had sold on credit so they could pay the British merchants who had sold them the goods. The British would only accept gold and silver, so American storekeepers and other retail creditors demanded payment in gold or silver. With agricultural prices falling—a consequence of overproduction, limited export demand, and the falling money supply—farmers who had incurred debt, in many cases to invest in land, tools, and livestock, were hard pressed to pay.

The crisis was not confined to New England. "There are combustibles in every State," George Washington commented, "which a spark might set fire to." Debtors resisted tax collectors and court proceedings and demanded debt relief in the form of paper money from Maine to South Carolina. When a South Carolina sheriff tried to serve Col. Hezekiah Mayham a writ for debt, the veteran of Nathanael Greene's army forced the sheriff to chew and swallow it. In Port Tobacco, Maryland, rioters shut down a court with a docket of debt cases, and the local "Liberty Boys" threatened to break into the home of a merchant in nearby Piscataway and burn all his account books to destroy evidence of debts. Some two hundred armed citizens descended on the meetinghouse in Exeter, New Hampshire, where the legislature was in session and demanded the members approve the emission of paper money. The governor called out the militia, which drove off the protestors and arrested thirty-nine. Virginians in frontier Greenbrier County signed a remonstrance against the unpopular state tax and threatened to prevent courts from sitting. Virginia legislators bent with the storm and looked for ways to accommodate debtors. Most were planters and understood the challenges that their farming neighbors faced.

Legislators were not so accommodating in Massachusetts, where debt was compounded by heavy taxes, including a poll tax levied on every able-bodied man sixteen or older, part of which had to be paid in gold or silver. Ironically Massachusetts imposed the tax, in part, to fulfill a requisition from Congress, which most of the states routinely ignored. Sheriffs pursued landowners for nonpayment of taxes while creditors, including storekeepers who had sold goods on credit, turned to the courts to help them collect what they were owed.

Massachusetts farmers and tradesmen who were unable to pay their debts or taxes protested. They formed local committees, adopted resolves expressing their views, sent petitions to the state legislature, and published essays in newspapers seeking debt relief—state emissions of paper money, which would probably produce inflation, and stay acts to halt prosecutions. When these tactics failed, they turned to armed resistance. In August 1786, armed men prevented the county court from meeting in Northampton. A few weeks later another group of armed men forced the county court at Worcester to close. In Concord, men led by a Revolutionary War veteran named Job Shattuck prevented the court from sitting. County sheriffs could not keep order alone. The governor and local judges called for help from the militia, but in some places militiamen refused to help keep order.

The protestors called themselves regulators, an allusion to the North Carolina Regulators of the 1760s. Their aim was not to overturn the government. By stopping the courts they appear to have intended to stop prosecutions for debt and nonpayment of taxes while the legislature considered their appeals. Hundreds of them had already been prosecuted for debt or had watched while relatives and neighbors had been called into court. Many feared prosecution.

People unacquainted with the practical economics of farming attributed the indebtedness of farmers to wasteful spending on imported luxuries. Nineteen-year-old John Quincy Adams wrote that the protestors should look "to their Idleness, their dissipation and extravagance, for their grievances; these have led them to contract debts, and at the same time, have rendered them incapable of paying them." Young Adams blamed the unrest on "fondness for foreign frippery" that had led the rioters into debt, and called their complaints "imaginary grievances." He wrote to his mother that "the insurrections are not immediately dangerous, but our government has not sufficient vigor and energy to suppress them at once." Writing to Thomas Jefferson from London, Abigail Adams attributed the disorder to "Luxury and extravagance both in furniture and dress" that had been adopted by "all orders of our Countrymen and women" and was leading them into debt.

Jefferson saw the more substantial causes, explaining that the people "are not entirely without excuses." The distressed condition of American trade and "a tax too heavy to be paid" were, in his view, the real reasons for the distress. Rufus King, a Massachusetts delegate to Congress, had reached the same conclusion, writing to John Adams that Massachusetts was imposing taxes "beyond what prudence would authorize."

Shays' Rebellion

The unrest of summer turned to open rebellion in the fall. In late September several hundred armed men led by a veteran Continental Army captain named Daniel Shays gathered in Springfield to prevent the supreme court from meeting. Shays had been prosecuted for debt on at least two occasions in the years immediately before the rebellion. Like Shays, many of the protestors had served in the army and been paid with certificates of debt that they had sold for pennies on the dollar. They were justifiably furious that the government was taxing them—the soldiers who had earned those certificates—to pay the interest due to the speculators who had bought them. "A man who sells a note for a fifth of its value and then is taxed to pay the full sum to the purchaser," Noah Webster wrote to Governor Bowdoin, is "a wickedness peculiar to the present case." Militiamen were on hand to defend the court, but the judges decided to adjourn without hearing any cases. James Warren of Plymouth reported to John Adams: "We are now in a State of Anarchy and Confusion bordering on a Civil War."

Many of the men who rioted and took up arms in Massachusetts in 1786 were property owners of limited means caught in a credit crisis, not propertyless workers rising up against capitalist exploitation. They were the participants in an emerging capitalist system that was driving the development of the American middle class and which became one of the defining features of free society. They were unfortunate victims of economic and political circumstances neither they nor the state government understood or were able to control. A few of the protestors were probably shiftless or profligate and some of the state officials who stubbornly insisted on imposing heavy taxes stood to profit from the use of proceeds to pay off debt certificates they held, but the crisis was not the result of wastefulness or greed. It was a result of

Daniel Shays of Pelham and Job Shattuck of Groton, depicted here in a woodcut in *Bickerstaff's Genuine Boston Almanack for 1787*, were Revolutionary War veterans, as were many of the protestors who followed them. Shattuck was captured and tried for "most wickedly and traitorously devising and conspiring to levy war against this Commonwealth." He was found guilty and sentenced to death but was pardoned by the new governor, John Hancock (National Portrait Gallery, Smithsonian Institution).

the impotence of the Confederation. Congress had accumulated debts, including debts to the soldiers who won American independence, without the authority to impose a rational system of taxation to raise the revenue to pay those debts and without the authority to regulate foreign trade in a way that would protect American farmers and maritime commerce. Congress could not effectively manage the money supply and stood by helplessly as deflation, driven in part by the lack of money in circulation, magnified debts and amplified the misery of ordinary Americans.

Having been the victims of the arbitrary power of the British government, Americans had tried to insulate themselves from tyranny by creating a government so impotent than it could not protect their economic interests. The nation desperately needed a comprehensive approach to trade, public revenue, and taxation, which could only be provided by a central government endowed with sufficient authority to manage public affairs. Without such a government, the nation was destined to stumble into repeated crises, sacrifice the attachment of the people, and expose itself to domination by the imperial powers waiting for the American republic to degenerate into chaos.

Shays' Rebellion illustrates the liminal state of public life in the 1780s. Americans were not yet accustomed to seeking and accepting political resolutions through a competitive electoral system. The protestors turned to the strategies of pre-war protest: meetings, county conventions, petitions, threats, and coercion to stop the functions of government and the execution of the laws, even though those laws had been adopted by a duly constituted republican legislature in which they had full representation. Government officials, after briefly ignoring the protests, decided to end them by force, just as colonial governments had done, and to punish as many of the protestors as possible. They did not grasp that a republic is best governed by building consensus and often by compromise—by finding resolutions to disputes no one likes but most accept.

The Massachusetts government, wholly unprepared to deal with the crisis and oblivious to the underlying economic conditions driving it, pressed on toward a violent confrontation with the protestors, abetted by Boston merchants unaccustomed to wielding public influence. The merchant community that dominated pre-war Boston, at least half of whom had fled as loyalists, had been replaced by new men. James Bowdoin wrote to a friend in 1783 that when he came to Boston, he would "scarcely see any other than new faces," adding that "the change which in that respect has happened in the few years since the revolution is as remarkable as the revolution itself."

The result was a confrontation in which the parties were polarized and each side demonized the other. Belazeel Howard, a young minister in Springfield, observed the rebellion with more detachment than most. The protestors, he thought, were irrational. "Like the dogs in a village: if one bark all bark." Town meetings to instruct members of the legislature, he thought, would have succeeded "and secured our Liberties more Effectually." Unfortunately government lacked the spirit of conciliation. It was vindictive when it ought to have been magnanimous. Public distress, Howard wrote, "Called for amendment and redress, but Guns and Bayonets and Hostile appearances was far from being the proper way to accomplish the design."

In January 1787, Shays and a force of over one thousand men marched on the arsenal at Springfield. Militiamen defending the armory fired two cannons, killing four of the insurgents and wounding about twenty others. The rebels retreated. To restore order, a militia army commanded by General Benjamin Lincoln marched west from Boston and surprised the armed protestors in their camp on the morning of February 4. Over one hundred rebels were captured. The rest fled. Shays and other rebel leaders escaped and went in hiding in Vermont. In late February, a party of about 120 rebels raided stores and homes in Stockbridge, Massachusetts, before fighting a skirmish with local militia. About thirty rebels were wounded and dozens were taken prisoner. This brought Shays' Rebellion to an end.

Over four thousand citizens confessed that they had participated in the rebellion and were pardoned. Eighteen leaders were tried, convicted and sentenced to death, but most of these eventually went free. Two men were executed. Daniel Shays was pardoned in 1788 and returned from hiding in Vermont. The Massachusetts legislature passed a law preventing any leader of the rebellion from ever holding office, but it also lowered taxes and slowed the collection of debts, providing some of the relief the protestors had wanted.

James Madison wrote that Shays' Rebellion was "distressing beyond measure," but he found that the uprising "furnish new proofs of the necessity of such a vigour in the Genl. Govt. as will be able to restore health to any diseased part of the federal body. An attempt to bring about such an amendment of the Federal Constitution is on the Anvil. The Meeting of deputies for that purpose is to be held in May next in Philadelphia."

"Our case is desperate"

The movement for fundamental constitutional reform began before Shays' Rebellion, but it drew strength from the violence in Massachusetts. The Articles of Confederation had barely gone into operation before Alexander Hamilton, a newly elected delegate from New York, drew up a resolution called for a convention to revise them. In 1785 delegates meeting at Mount Vernon, called to discuss the improvement of Potomac River navigation, recommended a more general meeting of delegates from all thirteen states to consider measures to improve trade and commerce. That meeting, held in Annapolis in September 1786, attracted delegates from Virginia, New Jersey, New York, Delaware, and Pennsylvania. The legislatures in North Carolina, Massachusetts, Rhode Island, and New Hampshire appointed delegates but they failed to arrive on time. The delegates in attendance, including James Madison, Alexander Hamilton, John Dickinson, and Edmund Randolph, soon to be governor of Virginia, agreed that improving trade was inextricably tied to broader reforms. They proposed a convention to consider amending the Articles of Confederation.

At Madison's urging, the Virginia legislature adopted an act in November 1786 authorizing the appointment of delegates to meet in Philadelphia in May 1787 to propose remedies for the defects of the Confederation. Reports of the unrest in Massachusetts, including one from Henry Lee that the rebellion was a portent of an "extensive national calamity." Madison wrote to Washington that "our case is desperate."

"The crisis is arrived," the Virginia act declared,

at which the good people of America are to decide the solemn question, whether they will by wise and magnanimous efforts reap the just fruits of that independence which they have so gloriously acquired, and of that Union which they have cemented with so much of their common blood; or whether, by giving way to unmanly jealousies and prejudices, or to partial and transitory interests, they will renounce the auspicious blessings prepared for them by the Revolution, and furnish its enemies an eventual triumph over those, by whose virtue and valour, it has been accomplished.

Madison immediately advised Washington that he would be appointed to the Virginia delegation, leaving Washington to decide whether to accept the appointment. While Washington was pleased to learn that the legislature had embraced a plan "so interesting to the well-being of the confederacy," he immediately expressed reluctance to serve. Madison asked him to reconsider, writing "your name could not be spared."

The importance of Washington's participation in the proposed convention could not be overestimated. Washington had devoted a large part of his life to ensuring the prosperity and success of an independent American republic. He was convinced, as he had written in 1783 and many times since, that the nation's future depended on enlarging the powers of Congress. He was universally respected and extraordinarily well connected. He entertained people from all parts of the country almost continuously—his house, he wrote to his mother "may be compared to a well resorted tavern"—and corresponded regularly with other advocates of reform. Without leaving Mount Vernon or holding public office, he was the most influential person in America.

While Madison persuaded the Virginia legislature to appoint delegates to meet in Philadelphia, Washington advised Congressman Henry Lee about the proper response to the uprising in Massachusetts. "Know precisely what the Insurgents aim at," he wrote. "If they have real grievances, redress them, *if possible,* or acknowledge the justice of their complaints and your inability of doing it, in the present moment." If their grievances were without merit, Washington advised employing "the force of government against them." It would not

AN ACT

FOR APPOINTING DEPUTIES FROM THIS COMMONWEALTH TO A CONVENTION PROPOSED TO BE HELD IN THE CITY OF PHILADELPHIA IN MAY NEXT, FOR THE PURPOSE OF REVISING THE FŒDERAL CONSTITUTION.

WHEREAS the Commissioners who assembled at Annapolis, on the fourteenth of September last, for the purpose of devising and reporting the means of enabling Congress to provide effectually for the Commercial Interest of the United States, have represented the necessity of extending the revision of the fœderal system to all its defects; and have recommended, that Deputies for that purpose be appointed by the several Legislatures to meet in convention in the city of Philadelphia, on the second day of May next; a provision which seems preferable to a discussion of the subject in Congress, where it might be too much interrupted by the ordinary business before them; and where it would besides, be deprived of the valuable councils of sundry individuals, who are disqualified by the constitution or laws of particular states, or restrained by peculiar circumstances from a seat in that Assembly:

AND WHEREAS, the General Assembly of this Commonwealth, taking into view the actual situation of the Confederacy, as well as reflecting on the alarming representations made from time to time, by the United States in Congress, particularly in their act of the fifteenth day of February last, can no longer doubt that the crisis is arrived at which the good people of America are to decide the solemn question, whether they will by wise and magnanimous efforts reap the just fruits of that independance which they have so gloriously acquired, and of that Union which they have cemented with so much of their common blood; or whether, by giving way to unmanly jealousies and prejudices, or to partial and transitory interests, they will renounce the auspicious blessings prepared for them by the Revolution, and furnish to its enemies an eventual triumph over those, by whose virtue and valour, it has been accomplished:

AND WHEREAS, the same noble and extended Policy, and the same fraternal and affectionate sentiments, which originally determined the Citizens of this Commonwealth, to unite with their Brethren of the other States, in establishing a fœderal Government, cannot but be felt with equal force now as the motives to lay aside every inferior consideration, and to concur in such farther concessions and provisions, as may be necessary to secure the great objects for which that Government was instituted, and to render the United States as happy in Peace, as they have been glorious in war.

Be it therefore enacted, by the General Assembly of the Commonwealth of Virginia, That seven Commissioners be appointed by joint ballot of both Houses of Assembly, who, or any three of them, are hereby authorized as Deputies from this Commonwealth to meet such Deputies as may be appointed and authorized by other states, to assemble in Convention at Philadelphia, as above recommended, and to join with them in devising and discussing all such alterations and farther provisions, as may be necessary to render the fœderal Constitution, adequate to the exigencies of the Union, and in reporting such an act for that purpose, to the United States in Congress, as when agreed to by them, and duly confirmed by the several states, will effectually provide for the same.

And be it further enacted, That in case of the death of any of the said Deputies, or of their declining their appointments, the Executive are hereby authorized to supply such vacancies; and the Governor is requested to transmit forthwith a copy of this Act, to the United States in Congress, and to the Executives of each of the states in the Union.

November 9, 1786, read the third time and passed the House of Delegates.

JOHN BECKLEY, C. H. D.

November 23, 1786, passed the Senate.

H. BROOKE, C. S.

do to delay. "To be more exposed in the eyes of the world and more contemptible than we already are, is hardly possible."

Advocates of reform were as deeply disturbed by the actions of the state legislatures as they were by the threat of domestic insurrection. Stay laws halting prosecution for debt and paper money emissions satisfied the demands of indebted farmers but were unjust to creditors. Paper money acts provided much needed currency but depreciated rapidly. Paper money issued by Rhode Island had fallen to one-fifteenth its face value. These kinds of debtor relief laws were popular, but they only exacerbated the economic crisis, which called for national solutions that would open markets, provide a reliable money supply, and secure stable credit, all of which were prerequisites to sustained economic growth and national prosperity.

Despite the increasingly desperate condition of the Confederation, Washington was reluctant to risk his reputation for disinterested patriotism on a convention that might not succeed. He was concerned that the proposed meeting would not be committed to the kind of broad-ranging reforms he knew were necessary, and so withheld his consent to attend until he was confident such reforms might be achieved. With Henry Knox, Washington worried that the convention "might devise some expedients to brace up the present defective confederation so as just to keep us together . . . assisting us to creep on in our present miserable condition."

The rebellion in Massachusetts underscored the urgent need for reform. "If three years ago," Washington wrote to Knox in February 1787, "any person had told me that at this day, I should see such a formidable rebellion against the laws and constitutions of our own making as now appears I should have thought him a bedlamite—a fit subject for a mad house." The time for debate about the most proper mode for amending the Articles, Washington concluded, had passed. "That which takes the shortest course to obtain them, will, in my opinion, under present circumstances, be found best. Otherwise, like a house on fire, whilst the most regular mode of extinguishing it is contending for, the building is reduced to ashes."

New Jersey, Pennsylvania, North Carolina, Delaware, and Georgia followed Virginia's lead and committed to send delegates to Philadelphia, despite critics who charged that the proposed meeting had not been authorized by Congress and thus had no legal standing. When Congress convened in February 1787 it resolved that problem by authorizing the meeting, "for the sole and express purpose of revising the Articles of Confederation and reporting to Congress and the several Legislatures such alterations and provisions therein as shall when agreed to in Congress and confirmed by the States render the federal Constitution adequate to the exigencies of Government and the preservation of the Union."

Washington finally decided to attend the convention. Knox assured him that his reputation for disinterested patriotism would benefit and popular confidence in his wisdom would ensure the adoption of any important measures the convention might propose.

The Professor and Plowman

Thomas Jefferson, viewing American affairs from his post in Paris, was not deeply concerned by Shays' Rebellion. He agreed with Madison that the insurgents had committed "absolutely unjustifiable" acts, but he attributed them to misunderstanding. "They were founded in ignorance, not in wickedness." The insurgents did not understand that their distress was the result of economic conditions the government was incapable of addressing.

Although the people were sovereign, Jefferson wrote, they would not always be right. "The people can not be all," he wrote, "and always, well informed." In a government in which the people have a just degree of influence a certain amount of "turbulence" was inevitable. Indeed, Jefferson thought, public indifference to distress blamed, improperly or not, on the government was "the forerunner of death to the public liberty."

Protest, on the other hand, could be useful. "It prevents the degeneracy of government, and nourishes a general attention to the public affairs.

Governor Edmund Randolph sent copies of the Virginia act for appointing delegates to meet in Philadelphia to consider reforming the "federal system" to the governors of the other states, leading all but Rhode Island to appoint delegates of their own (Library of Congress).

I hold it that a little rebellion now and then is a good thing, and as necessary in the political world as a storm is in the physical." He urged that "honest republican governors" should be "so mild in their punishments of rebellions, as not to discourage them too much."

Jefferson recognized that the United States faced serious problems and he shared much of Madison's conviction that the weakness of the Confederation and the inability of the states to address the issues facing the new nation compounded those problems, but he was concerned that Shays' Rebellion might lead reformers to conclude "that nature has formed man insusceptible of any other government but that of force, a conclusion not founded in truth, nor experience." A government based on force—including monarchy in all its forms—was inherently unjust. "It is a government of wolves over sheep."

The best alternative was government based on the sovereignty of the people, accepting the risks and occasional turbulence inherent in popular government. The people would not always be right, but optimistic leaders, including Jefferson, thought they could be depended on to make good decisions. Jefferson was persuaded that people have a "moral sense" that guides them and allows them to make judgments quickly and intuitively, without close study or the application of acquired learning. This idea had been most fully developed by Scottish thinkers, including Frances Hutcheson and David Hume. In the summer of 1787, Jefferson explained the moral sense in a letter to his nephew Peter Carr, a student at the College of William and Mary, advising him to skip lectures on moral philosophy:

I think it lost time to attend lectures in this branch. He who made us would have been a pitiful bungler if he had made the rules of our moral conduct a matter of science. For one man of science, there are thousands who are not. What would have become of them? Man was destined for society. His morality therefore was to be formed to this object. He was endowed with a sense of right and wrong merely relative to this. This sense is as much a part of his

nature as the sense of hearing, seeing, feeling; it is the true foundation of morality . . . The moral sense, or conscience, is as much a part of man as his leg or arm. It is given to all human beings in a stronger or weaker degree, as force of members is given them in a greater or less degree. It may be strengthened by exercise, as may any particular limb of the body. This sense is submitted indeed in some degree to the guidance of reason; but it is a small stock which is required for this: even a less one than what we call Common sense. State a moral case to a ploughman and a professor. The former will decide it as well, and often better than the latter, because he has not been led astray by artificial rules.

Jefferson was in Paris when he wrote this letter and unable to participate in the Federal Convention, but the two most active delegates in the convention, James Madison and James Wilson, were trained in the moral philosophy of the Scottish Enlightenment and as fully persuaded as Jefferson that ordinary people possess an intuitive moral sense. This optimistic view of the capacity of ordinary people to make good moral and ethical judgments is an important justification of popular sovereignty—the defining ideal of the Federal Constitution—and is the ultimate foundation of American democracy.

Jefferson's comment that the plowman will decide as well as the professor is often quoted, but his admonition that the moral sense "may be strengthened by exercise" is usually overlooked. "Above all things," Jefferson concluded,

lose no occasion of exercising your dispositions to be grateful, to be generous, to be charitable, to be humane, to be true, just, firm, orderly, courageous etc. Consider every act of this kind as an exercise which will strengthen your moral faculties, and increase your worth.

No better advice can be offered to people yearning to breathe free nor to those determined to preserve their freedom.

Thomas Jefferson was not worried that the United States was descending into anarchy. "We have had 13 states independant 11 years," he calculated in November 1787. "There has been one rebellion. That comes to one rebellion in a century and a half for each state. What country before ever existed a century and half without a rebellion? And what country can preserve its liberties if their rulers are not warned from time to time that their people preserve the spirit of resistance? Let them take arms. The remedy is to set them right as to facts, pardon and pacify them. What signify a few lives lost in a century or two? The tree of liberty must be refreshed from time to time with the blood of patriots and tyrants. It is its natural manure" (Metropolitan Museum of Art).

We the People

of the United States, in order to insure domestic Tranquility, provide for the common defence, promote the general Welfare, and and our Posterity, do ordain and establish this Constitution for the United States of America.

Article. I.

Section. 1. All legislative Powers herein granted shall be vested in a Congress of the United States, which shall consist of a Senate and House of Representatives.

Section. 2. The House of Representatives shall be composed of Members chosen every second Year by the People of the several States, and the Electors in each State shall have the Qualifications requisite for Electors of the most numerous Branch of the State Legislature.

No Person shall be a Representative who shall not have attained to the Age of twenty five Years, and been seven Years a Citizen of the United States, and who shall not, when elected, be an Inhabitant of that State in which he shall be chosen.

Representatives and direct Taxes shall be apportioned among the several States which may be included within this Union, according to their respective Numbers, which shall be determined by adding to the whole Number of free Persons, including those bound to Service for a Term of Years, and excluding Indians not taxed, three fifths of all other Persons. The actual Enumeration shall be made within three Years after the first Meeting of the Congress of the United States, and within every subsequent Term of ten Years, in such Manner as they shall by Law direct. The Number of Representatives shall not exceed one for every thirty Thousand, but each State shall have at Least one Representative; and until such enumeration shall be made, the State of New Hampshire shall be entitled to chuse three, Massachusetts eight, Rhode-Island and Providence Plantations one, Connecticut five, New-York six, New Jersey four, Pennsylvania eight, Delaware one, Maryland six, Virginia ten, North Carolina five, South Carolina five, and Georgia three.

When vacancies happen in the Representation from any State, the Executive Authority thereof shall issue Writs of Election to fill such Vacancies.

The House of Representatives shall chuse their Speaker and other Officers; and shall have the sole Power of Impeachment.

Section. 3. The Senate of the United States shall be composed of two Senators from each State, chosen by the Legislature thereof, for six Years; and each Senator shall have one Vote.

Immediately after they shall be assembled in Consequence of the first Election, they shall be divided as equally as may be into three Classes. The Seats of the Senators of the first Class shall be vacated at the Expiration of the second Year, of the second Class at the Expiration of the fourth Year, and of the third Class at the Expiration of the sixth Year, so that one third may be chosen every second Year; and if Vacancies happen by Resignation, or otherwise, during the Recess of the Legislature of any State, the Executive thereof may make temporary Appointments until the next Meeting of the Legislature, which shall then fill such Vacancies.

No Person shall be a Senator who shall not have attained to the Age of thirty Years, and been nine Years a Citizen of the United States, and who shall not, when elected, be an Inhabitant of that State for which he shall be chosen.

The Vice President of the United States shall be President of the Senate, but shall have no Vote, unless they be equally divided.

The Senate shall chuse their other Officers, and also a President pro tempore, in the Absence of the Vice President, or when he shall exercise the Office of President of the United States.

The Senate shall have the sole Power to try all Impeachments. When sitting for that Purpose, they shall be on Oath or Affirmation. When the President of the United States is tried, the Chief Justice shall preside: And no Person shall be convicted without the Concurrence of two thirds of the Members present.

Judgment in Cases of Impeachment shall not extend further than to removal from Office, and disqualification to hold and enjoy any Office of honor, Trust or Profit under the United States: but the Party convicted shall nevertheless be liable and subject to Indictment, Trial, Judgment and Punishment, according to Law.

Section. 4. The Times, Places and Manner of holding Elections for Senators and Representatives, shall be prescribed in each State by the Legislature thereof; but the Congress may at any time by Law make or alter such Regulations, except as to the Places of chusing Senators.

The Congress shall assemble at least once in every Year, and such Meeting shall be on the first Monday in December, unless they shall by Law appoint a different Day.

Section. 5. Each House shall be the Judge of the Elections, Returns and Qualifications of its own Members, and a Majority of each shall constitute a Quorum to do Business; but a smaller Number may adjourn from day to day, and may be authorized to compel the Attendance of absent Members, in such Manner, and under such Penalties as each House may provide.

Each House may determine the Rules of its Proceedings, punish its Members for disorderly

Chapter 21   A More Perfect Union

Delegates began gathering in Philadelphia at the beginning of May. Some arrived late and a few, dissatisfied, left the convention early. In all, fifty-five delegates from twelve states—Rhode Island did not send delegates—served in the convention. Their average age was just forty-two, but they had considerable experience in public life. Thirty-nine had served in Congress and seven as state governors. Many had served in the Continental Army and commanded men who had gone unpaid, poorly supplied, and unfed because Congress lacked the authority to tax.

The delegates included some remarkably talented men, but the convention was also distinguished by the men who were not present. Patrick Henry, the most influential political leader in Virginia, refused to attend, suspecting the convention would challenge the autonomy of the states. Richard Henry Lee also refused to serve. He thought the Articles of Confederation were sufficient and that all would be well if the states honored the requisitions made by Congress. Beyond that Lee would not go. "The first maxim of a man who loves liberty," he wrote to Samuel Adams, "should be, never to grant to Rulers an atom of power that is not most clearly and indispensably necessary for the safety and well being of Society." Samuel Adams and John Hancock did not attend.

The absence of these men and others committed to state sovereignty and suspicious of enlarging the powers of Congress was fortunate for the reformers. Patrick Henry and Richard Henry Lee were two of the nation's most gifted public speakers—"the Demosthenes and Cicero of America," an admiring congressman had called them—and Adams and Hancock were skilled at making alliances and building coalitions behind the scenes. In concert these men might have steered the conven-

tion in a different direction.

John Adams, a profound constitutional thinker and draftsman of the widely admired Massachusetts Constitution of 1780, was missing as well—wasting his time in London, where he had concluded that his mission as ambassador was futile. To fill his time he was at work on a three-volume treatise titled *A Defense of the Constitutions of the United States of America*. Thomas Jefferson, his effectiveness as ambassador to France also hobbled by the inability of Congress to regulate international trade, visited Adams in London during the summer of 1787. Both men would have been far more useful in Philadelphia.

Although he said little in the meetings, the most important delegate was George Washington, whose presence ensured that the convention's work would be given a respectful hearing. Benjamin Franklin, whose international fame rivaled that of Washington, attended but contributed little to the daily give and take. His mind was sharp but he was slowed by age. He played the vital role of conciliator. Heavy rain and ill health kept Franklin at home on May 25, the convention's first day, when he was to have proposed Washington as president. The whole Pennsylvania delegation nominated Washington instead, which James Madison thought was an act of grace, "as Doctor Franklin alone could have been thought of as a competitor."

The delegates met six days a weeks, generally at ten o'clock, and usually worked until four o'clock. They agreed to keep their deliberations secret so they could speak their minds freely, though this meant keeping the windows and doors closed in the heat and humidity of a Philadelphia summer, which meant the room was often stifling. They adopted rules. The delegates were to rise to speak, and address the president. No delegate was

The Federal Constitution created a government in which the authority of the legislative, executive, and judicial branches depend on the sovereignty of the people "to form a more perfect Union, establish Justice, insure domestic Tranquility, provide for the common defense, promote the general Welfare, and secure the Blessings of Liberty to ourselves and our Posterity" (National Archives).

to speak more than twice on a single question and was not to speak a second time until every other delegate who wanted to be heard had had a chance to speak. This led, inevitably, to the delegates who had a lot to say holding the floor for a long time, which could try the patience of the others, but no one was to read or talk while someone was speaking. Considering the heat, the long sessions, and the complex questions before them, the delegates maintained an extraordinary degree of civility. If there was a momentary lapse, the silent, disapproving glare of George Washington was enough to restore order. When the convention began no one knew that it would consume nearly four months. Through it all, James Madison kept detailed notes on whatever was said. Without those notes, first published in 1840—four years after Madison's death—we would know little about what happened in the convention.

Madison and Wilson

James Madison took the lead and became the convention's most important contributor. He went to Philadelphia with a plan for a thorough, systemic overhaul of government. Not content with revising the Articles of Confederation, he wanted to establish a national republic with a bicameral legislature, a powerful executive, and an independent judiciary. He arrived early from New York, where he had been attending a meeting of Congress, and devoted several days to discussing the work of the convention and building alliances with delegates from Virginia and Pennsylvania, so that when the delegates convened his plan became the basis for their deliberations.

The Pennsylvania delegation included two of the most prominent advocates of financial reforms: Robert and Gouverneur Morris. The two were not related, but they had worked together as superintendent and assistant superintendent of finance and each was charming in his way. Robert Morris was the orphaned son of a Liverpool shipping agent and made his fortune as a Philadelphia merchant before the Revolutionary War. He was amiable in private but did not make much of an impression in debate. Gouverneur Morris more than made up for his partner's silence. Handsome, urbane, and

sophisticated, the younger Morris was a member of one of New York's wealthiest family. He entered King's College at twelve, completed a master's degree at nineteen, and was admitted to the bar at twenty-two. He served in the New York legislature and in Congress before moving to Philadelphia. In debate, wrote William Pierce of Georgia, Morris "charms, captivates, and leads away the senses of all who hear him."

The most useful of Madison's Pennsylvania allies proved to be James Wilson. He had none of Gouverneur Morris's easy grace, but he had as deep an understanding of legal and political thought as any man in the convention. Wilson subscribed to the idea that governments derive their power from the consent of the governed and followed the logic of that idea to the conclusion that a just government can only be constructed on democratic principles at a time when the word democracy was widely regarded as a synonym for chaos. Despite his democratic views Wilson opposed the Pennsylvania Constitution of 1776 because he feared that vesting all legislative authority in a single house would lead to political instability, disorder, and ultimately tyranny. He sympathized with Philadelphians who rioted when runaway inflation drove prices so high they could barely feed their families, but he also sympathized with ordinary shopkeepers and artisans, caught in the same inflationary spiral, who would have been ruined by the price controls the rioters demanded.

Wilson was convinced that a national government with the power to tax and regulate trade was essential to create the economic stability that would make it possible for ordinary Americans to prosper. An entirely self-made man from a struggling farm family, Wilson understood that popular demands for paper money and easy credit reflected the desire of ordinary people to participate in the marketplace—to buy and sell land, expand and improve their farms, and profit from retail trade. Wilson shared this desire, investing all he could earn or borrow, mostly in land. By the time the Federal Convention met, Wilson had acquired thousands of undeveloped acres in Pennsylvania, New York, and Virginia. He was also a leading member of the Illinois-Wabash Company, one of the land companies that claimed title to land north of the Ohio River based on private purchases from Indians—a claim Virginia refused to validate.

The Federal Constitution Madison and Wilson worked to create has been described as a counter-revolutionary document, shaped by anxieties about the excesses of democratically elected state legislatures and the frustrations of public creditors with a congress unable to fulfill its obligations. The correspondence of George Washington, John Jay, Henry Knox, and many other leaders were indeed filled with such anxieties and frustrations, which many other Americans felt.

But the wisest of those leaders understood that the problems facing the nation were not caused by the abuse of power. The conduct of the democratically elected state legislatures was a symptom of an underlying problem, which was the lack of power where it was most needed.

In the summer of 1787 James Madison, James Wilson, and their reform-minded allies sought to fulfill the promise of the Revolution by creating a government with the power necessary to resolve the problems facing the new nation—the

Left: A Scotsman with a reputation as the most bookish member of the Philadelphia bar, James Wilson had graduated from the University of St. Andrews before emigrating to Philadelphia in 1765. He studied law under John Dickinson at the height of Dickinson's fame. Wilson came to public notice in 1774 when he published a pamphlet titled *Considerations on the Nature and Extent of the Legislative Authority of the British Parliament*, which asserted that the colonies were tied to the British Empire only by their allegiance to the king. Elected to Congress, he devoted much of his life thereafter to public service. George Washington appointed him one of the first associate justices of the United States Supreme Court (Smithsonian American Art Museum).

Right: At thirty-six James Madison had no profession except public service. He was not a lawyer, though he understood the principles of law better than most practitioners. Profoundly well read in ancient and modern political thought, he can best be described as a public intellectual. Soft spoken and shy, he was nonetheless determined and confident in his ideas (Gilcrease Museum, Tulsa, OK).

power to pay its debts, establish its credit, provide a stable money supply, and create the conditions for sustained economic growth that would benefit prosperous and poor Americans alike. Such a government would possess the means to raise and pay an army to defend its borders and the leverage to compel foreign nations to trade on terms that benefitted Americans. The Confederation government had never possessed such powers and neither had governments of any of the thirteen independent, sovereign states. The aim of the reformers was not to strip the states of their authority, though they believed some of the state governments had acted irresponsibly. Their aim was to create a national government capable of fulfilling the promise of the Revolution.

They relied on a theory of government shaped by the rich and varied political, social, and economic thought of the Enlightenment and the practical experience of statecraft in a generation of revolutionary debate and constitution making. In their theory of government, power was derived from sovereign people rather than a sovereign state. Beyond the philosophical musings of political theorists, sovereign power resided in government, and in most of the world in the unlimited, or barely limited, sovereign power of monarchs.

The practical implementation of a theory of popular sovereignty on a national scale was so new that it baffled many of the delegates who gathered in Philadelphia for the Federal Convention, and their anxieties about the critical circumstances of the Confederation obscured their ability to imagine the future of democratic government. Ambitious reformers, including James Madison, were wracked by doubts about the future of the republic and the government they created. None approached that future with as much confidence as James Wilson, who imagined, he said, "the influence which the Government we are to form will have, not only on our people and their multiplied posterity, but on the whole Globe." He was, Wilson admitted, "lost in the magnitude of the object."

"We the People"

In the days before the delegates convened, Madison and Wilson agreed on what became

known as the Virginia Plan. Madison persuaded his fellow delegate Edmund Randolph, the sitting governor of Virginia, to present the plan, in which the states would become administrative districts related to the nation in the same way counties relate to state governments. Randolph laid the plan in front of the convention on the third day, after all the preliminaries had been completed. He praised the authors of the Articles of Confederation "as having done all that patriots could do, in the . . . infancy of the science of constitution and of confederacies." He reviewed the defects of the Confederation and then outlined the remedy Madison had devised.

The Virginia Plan set the agenda for the convention. The next day, the delegates made the first crucial decision, agreeing to a resolution offered by George Read of Delaware that in order to carry out "the design of the States in forming this convention . . . a more effective government consisting of a Legislative, Judiciary, and Executive ought to be established." With that the delegates discarded their charge from Congress to propose amendments to the Articles of Confederation and set out to design an entirely new government. For the next two months the delegates discussed and debated its general principles, modifying and elaborating the Virginia Plan as they went.

At the heart of the Virginia Plan was a bicameral legislature consisting of a larger lower house and a smaller upper house. Together these two parts of the legislature—later the convention decided to call them the House of Representatives and the Senate—would have the power to tax, regulate commerce, impose tariffs, coin money, and make laws governing all matters not delegated to the states. Members of the lower house would be elected by the people in direct proportion to the population, each member representing an equal number of citizens. This proposal, which gave substance to the abstract principle of popular sovereignty, was extraordinary. It has since become commonplace, but at the end of the eighteenth century no national legislature had ever been constituted in this way. The British House of Commons, in which members were elected to represent constituencies that varied in size from a few people to thousands and in which many thousands of people went unrepresented, was archaic by comparison.

Hard as it may now be to imagine, eighteenth-century governments did not know with any degree of certainty how many people they governed or where they lived. To the extent they felt any need to know, they relied on estimates and guesswork. To elect a national legislature based on population required counting every American and repeating the process periodically to keep representation in balance with a growing and moving population. Embedded in the Constitution is a mandate to count the entire population of the United States every ten years. The first census of the United States, conducted in 1790, was the first systematic national census conducted in modern times.

The decennial census became the foundation of American democratic government. It reflects the confidence of the Enlightenment in the potential of governments based on rational principles to serve their people rather than subjugate them and the faith of the Enlightenment in the fundamental equality of people. A government that aims at the public good must begin by finding out the people's numbers and where they live. Once it institutionalized the census, the federal government used it to collect all sort of additional information about the people—their occupations, living conditions, national origins, and other information that has made it possible to serve them more effectively.

In his notes, Madison credited James Wilson with making the strongest case "for drawing the most numerous branch of the Legislature immediately from the people. He was for raising the federal pyramid to a considerable altitude, and for that reason wished to give it as broad a basis as possible. No government," Wilson said, "could long subsist without the confidence of the people. In a republican Government this confidence was peculiarly essential." Confidence would come, Wilson contended, from a legislature that was "the most exact transcript of the whole Society." George Mason seconded Wilson, agreeing that representatives "should sympathize with their constituents" and "think as they think, and feel as they feel."

Here James Madison interjected a powerful argument of his own. He acknowledged that people tend to be selfish and impulsive and form local factions to advance their interests. But in a continental republic the people would be divided into many parties and interests and no local faction

would be able to command a legislative majority. The solution to the dangers inherent in democracy, said Madison, was to "enlarge the sphere" of government, and thus divide the people "in so great a number of interests and parties" that they would be unable to establish a common interest separate from the good of the whole. Madison thus turned the traditional view that democracy was only suited to small, homogeneous societies on its head. Democracy, he had concluded, was best suited to large, diverse societies.

The idea of a national government founded on popular sovereignty was far from the mind of delegates disgusted by the stay laws and paper money acts adopted by democratically elected state legislatures. "The people," Roger Sherman said, "should have as little to do as may be about the government" because "they want information and are constantly liable to be misled." Elbridge Gerry agreed. "The evils we experience flow from the excess of democracy," he said, pointing to popular opposition to the government in Massachusetts. Madison's argument that a multiplicity of selfish, impulsive interests would cancel one another out in the continental nation does not seem to have won over many skeptics.

According to the Virginia Plan, members of the smaller, upper house were to be elected by the lower house, from nominees chosen by the state legislatures. This was Madison's modest concession to the states. The number of members from each state would be proportioned to population. Virginia, with a population ten times that of Rhode Island, would have been entitled to ten times the number of members from Rhode Island. Wilson departed from the Virginia Plan by objecting to involving the state legislatures in the process. Wilson "thought it wrong," Madison wrote, "to increase the weight of the State Legislatures by making them the electors of the national Legislature. All interference between the general and local Governments should be obviated as much as possible." Wilson would have preferred the upper house represented by the people. "If we depart from the principle of representation in proportion to the numbers," Wilson said, "we will lose the object of our meeting."

Most of the delegates were intent on vesting the national government with more power, but the

Oliver Ellsworth of Connecticut, portrayed here with his wife, Abigail, introduced the Connecticut Compromise, providing for direct representation of the people in the House of Representatives and equal representation of the states in the Senate. He wrote *Letters of a Landholder* to promote the ratification of the Constitution in Connecticut. Adopting the pose of a prosperous farmer, he advised Connecticut farmers that foreign restrictions on American trade would ruin them. "A federal government of energy is the only means which will deliver us, and now or never is your opportunity to establish it, on such basis as will preserve your liberty and riches" (Wadsworth Atheneum Museum of Art).

idea of a bicameral legislature elected solely on the basis of population was simply too radical a departure from a confederation of sovereign states for most of them to accept. Many were anxious that Virginia—vast, wealthy, and populous—would dominate the other states. By mid-June they were alarmed enough to offer an alternative. Delegates from New Jersey, New York, Connecticut, and Delaware proposed a plan, introduced by William Paterson of New Jersey. Their New Jersey Plan called for amendments to the Articles of Confederation to give Congress the taxing power it needed, but otherwise leaving the sovereignty of the states intact. Voting in Congress would continue to be by state.

The New Jersey Plan was consistent with the charge to propose revisions to the Articles of Confederation that had brought the delegates together. This advantage was offset by the intellectual and political talent of the advocates of the

Virginia Plan, including Gouverneur Morris and George Mason in addition to Madison and Wilson. Together they dominated the debate, speaking more often, and often at greater length, than their opponents.

The New Jersey Plan threw the convention into brief disorder and provided Alexander Hamilton with an opportunity to lay his own plan before the delegates. It was unlike all the others. Hamilton called for a bicameral legislature, with a popularly elected lower house, but he proposed vesting most of the powers of government in an elected upper house and a single executive, both of which would serve during good behavior, or essentially for life. State governors would be appointed by the national government, which would also enjoy sole authority over the militia. When Hamilton finished, no delegate expressed support for his ideas.

Madison and Wilson then led the debate that convinced the majority to reject the New Jersey Plan. "Mr. Wilson ranks among the foremost in legal and political knowledge," noted William Pierce. "No man is more clear, copious, and comprehensive than Mr. Wilson, yet he is no great Orator. He draws the attention not by the charm of his eloquence, but by the force of his reasoning." During the convention. Pierce described Madison as "a Gentleman of great modesty, with a remarkable sweet temper," adding that "every Person seems to acknowledge his greatness." Madison "cannot be called an Orator," Pierce wrote, but "he is a most agreable, eloquent, and convincing Speaker" and "always comes forward the best informed Man of any point in debate."

Despite their gifts, Madison and Wilson had to compromise in order to win over a majority. Instead of a reducing the states to mere administrative units of a sovereign national government, they agreed to a national government of specific or enumerated powers—most particularly the power to tax, borrow and coin money, and regulate commerce. In return, the states were barred from conducting foreign relations, imposing tariffs on foreign goods, coining money, emitting bills of credit, or passing laws compromising contracts.

This was not all Madison had proposed and that he thought essential. He regretted that he could not secure the power to veto state laws, which he believed was critical to the stability of the new nation. But the compromise secured for the national government the power to address British tariffs and trade regulations and at least some of the leverage it needed to negotiate effectively with Spain about the navigation of the Mississippi. The compromise also deprived the states of the power to accommodate debtors by passing stay laws and issuing inflationary paper money that compromised the interests of creditors and thus threatened future prosperity. Prohibiting the states from collecting tariffs on imported goods, the most common and effective form of taxation in the eighteenth century, was by itself a revolutionary change in the way the United States was governed.

The compromise that broke the impasse over representation in the new national legislature was proposed by Oliver Ellsworth of Connecticut, who agreed to support a popularly-elected lower house with representation on the basis of population, but proposed that the members of upper house should be elected by the state legislatures, and that the states should elect the same number of members. Wilson said that this plan would result in the minority ruling the majority. In fact, Ellsworth said, "the power is given to the few to save them from being destroyed by the many." The populous states objected to this Connecticut Compromise, but Franklin, again the conciliator, urged compromise.

The debates over the nature of the Senate continued for weeks, with the proponents of representation based on population and those who favored equal representation of the states repeating their arguments and growing weary and frustrated in the process. Wilson insisted that equal representation of unequal states was "a fundamental and perpetual error" that would ultimately destroy the union. Caleb Strong of Massachusetts responded, "If no Accommodation takes place . . . the Union itself must soon be dissolved." The delegates finally adopted Ellsworth's proposal by a margin of one vote. Without equal representation in what became the United States Senate, delegates from the less populous states would almost certainly have refused to support the work of the Convention.

The Presidency

Debates about the executive branch occupied nearly as much time as debates about the legislature. The Virginia Plan called for an independent national executive with "general authority to execute the National laws" along with "the Executive rights vested in Congress by the Confederation," to be elected periodically by the legislature. When the delegates took up executive powers on June 1, James Wilson immediately proposed vesting the executive powers in a single person.

Madison noted that "a considerable pause" followed Wilson's proposal. The delegates understood that a more effective executive was essential but they were not immune to anxieties about executive power, especially when it was held by one person. The Revolution had been fueled by real

and perceived abuses of executive authority by customs officials, tax collectors, colonial governors, the distant colonial bureaucracy in London, the king's ministers, and ultimately, the king himself. In creating their state governments Americans had gone to great lengths to prevent the abuse of executive power, vesting executive authority in committees, limiting the power of governors, holding frequent elections, and shifting executive authority to local officials, where citizens could keep watch for signs of corruption.

Sensing that delegates believed he was proposing a kind of elective monarch, Wilson assured the convention that he had no such thought. The British monarch, Wilson said, wielded executive, judicial, and legislative powers, including the power to make war without legislative restraint. This concentration of these different powers was why monarchs

George Washington presides over the delegates in one of the earliest depictions of the Federal Convention, published in 1823. Georgia delegate William Pierce said that Washington, "like Cincinnatus . . . returned to his farm perfectly contented with being only a plain Citizen, after enjoying the highest honor of the Confederacy, and now only seeks for the approbation of his Countrymen by being virtuous and useful" (The Society of the Cincinnati).

degenerated into tyrants. Wilson explained that "the only powers he conceived strictly Executive were those of executing the laws." A single executive would be a safeguard against tyranny.

Madison suggested that the delegates consider the powers of the executive before deciding whether to vest those powers in one or more people. The delegates agreed that the function of the executive was to execute the laws and fill appointive offices before considering how the executive should be chosen. Wilson took the floor on this question and proposed direct election by the people. George Mason liked the idea but thought a national election was impractical. Roger Sherman was for election by the legislature, being convinced that an independent executive was "the very essence of tyranny." John Rutledge preferred to entrust the choice to the Senate.

Time and experience have justified Wilson's confidence in the people, but the convention was not prepared to join him. As an alternative Wilson proposed that the people choose independent electors, who would in turn choose the executive. Few of the delegates liked that idea any better than direct election by the people, so the question was set aside. The delegates voted against successive versions of the electoral system with no one suggesting a practical alternative. Wilson "remained unshaken" in his determination to rely on the people, either directly or through electors. The delegates ultimately accepted the electoral system as the convention drew to a close as the least objectionable alternative available.

Debates over the nature and powers of the executive and the proper way to fill executive office continued through the summer. The delegates finally decided to vest executive authority in a single person. George Washington's presence—no one imagined anyone else as the nation's first chief executive—gave the delegates confidence in this decision. Pierce Butler of South Carolina wrote that "many of the members cast their eyes towards General Washington as President; and shaped their Ideas of the Powers to be given to a President, by their opinions of his Virtue."

"The mere distinction of colour"

The delegates met for nearly four months, discussing, debating, compromising, composing, and revising as they went. In debate they divided along the fault lines of the Confederation—between large and small states, between commercial and agricultural interests, between those with more or less at stake in the West, and between the states that had abolished or were committed to abolishing slavery and those where slavery was fundamental to the economy and slaveowners were determined to defend it.

The convention faced the challenge of devising a national government that would unite states where slavery was sanctioned by law and those where legislators had either abolished slavery or set it on the path to extinction. Unlike the other issues that divided the delegates, slavery was an ethical and moral dilemma as well as a practical political problem. The convention has been criticized for failing to abolish slavery, but if the delegates had tried to do so the Constitution would surely have been rejected by the states where planters were dependent on enslaved labor and where enslaved people constituted a large share of the wealth.

The criticism fails to comprehend the magnitude of the challenge facing the Revolutionary generation. Slavery was a global injustice. Before the American Revolution, slavery was practiced in every European colony in the Americas, from Canada south to Chile and Argentina. The wealth of the European empires was built on forced labor as was the wealth and power of states throughout the Eastern Hemisphere. In the Caribbean enslaved people constituted something like ninety percent of the population. Enslaved Africans arrived in the Americas as early as 1501, more than a century before the first enslaved people were landed in British America. By 1820 some 10 million Africans had been transported in chains to the Western Hemisphere. During the same period only 2.6 million white Europeans migrated to the Americas, many of them indentured servants or convicted criminals. The colonial Americas were peopled by men and women in bondage.

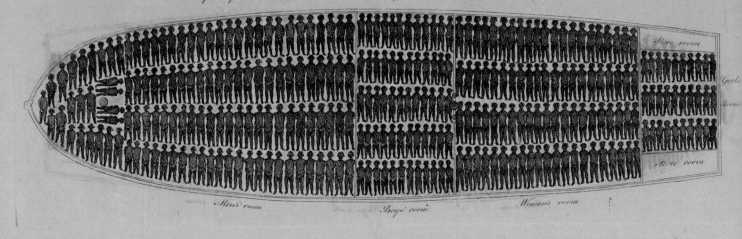

REMARKS on the SLAVE TRADE,

Extracted from the AMERICAN MUSEUM, for May, 1789.

And published by order of the Pennsylvania society for promoting the ABOLITION of slavery, &c.

IT must afford great pleasure to every true friend to liberty, to find the case of the unhappy Africans engrosses the general attention of the humane, in many parts of Europe; but we do not recollect to have met with a more striking illustration of the barbarity of the slave trade, than in a small pamphlet lately published by a society at Plymouth, in Great Britain; from which the Pennsylvania society for promoting the abolition of slavery have taken the following extracts, and have added a copy of the plate, which accompanied it. Perhaps a more powerful mode of conviction could not have been adopted, than is displayed in this small piece. Here is presented to our view, one of the most horrid spectacles—a number of human creatures, packed, side by side, almost like herrings in a barrel, and reduced nearly to the state of being buried alive, with just air enough to preserve a degree of life, sufficient to make them sensible of all the horrors of their situation. To every person, who has ever been at sea, it must present a scene of wretchedness in the extreme; for, with every comfort, which room, air, variety of nourishment, and careful cleanliness can yield, it is still a wearisome and irksome state. What then must it be to those, who are not only deprived of the necessaries of life, but confined down, the greater part of the voyage, to the same posture, with scarcely the privilege of turning from one painful side to the other, and subjected to all the nauseous consequences arising from sea-sickness, and other disorders, unavoidable amongst such a number of forlorn wretches? Where is the human being, that can picture to himself this scene of woe, without at the same time execrating a trade, which spreads misery and desolation wherever it appears? Where is the man of real benevolence, who will not join heart and hand, in opposing this barbarous, this iniquitous traffic?

Philadelphia, May 29, 1789.

" THE above plate represents the lower deck of an African ship, of two hundred and ninety-seven tons burden, with the slaves stowed on it, in the proportion of not quite one to a ton.

" In the men's apartment, the space, allowed to each, is six feet in length, by sixteen inches in breadth. The boys are each allowed five feet, by fourteen inches. The women, five feet ten inches, by sixteen inches; and the girls, four feet by one foot, each. The perpendicular height, between the decks, is five feet eight inches.

" The men are fastened together, two and two, by handcuffs on their wrists, and by irons rivetted on their legs—they are brought up on the main deck every day, about eight o'clock, and as each pair ascend, a strong chain, fastened by ringbolts to the deck, is passed through their shackles; a precaution absolutely necessary, to prevent insurrections. In this state, if the weather is favourable, they are permitted to remain about one third part of the twenty-four hours, and during this interval they are fed, and their apartment below is cleaned; but when the weather is bad, even these indulgences cannot be granted them, and they are only permitted to come up in small companies, of about ten at a time, to be fed, where, after remaining a quarter of an hour, each mess is obliged to give place to the next, in rotation.

" It may perhaps be conceived, from the crouded state, in which the slaves appear in the plate, that an unusual and exaggerated instance has been produced; this, however, is so far from being the case, that no ship, if her intended cargo can be procured, ever carries a less number than one to a ton, and the usual practice has been, to carry nearly double that number. The bill, which was passed the last session of parliament, only restricts the carriage to five slaves for three tons: and the Brooks, of Liverpool, a capital ship, from which the above sketch was proportioned, did, in one voyage, actually carry six hundred and nine slaves, which is more than double the number that appear in the plate. The mode of stowing them was as follows: platforms, or wide shelves, were erected between the decks, extending so far from the sides towards the middle of the vessel, as to be capable of containing four additional rows of slaves, by which means the perpendicular height above each tier, after allowing for the beams and platforms, was reduced to two feet six inches, so that they could not even sit in an erect posture; besides which, in the men's apartment, instead of four rows, five were stowed, by placing the heads of one between the thighs of another. All the horrors of this situation are still multiplied in the smaller vessels. The Kitty, of one hundred and thirty-seven tons, had only one foot ten inches; and the Venus, of one hundred and forty-six tons, only one foot nine inches perpendicular height, above each layer.

" The above mode of carrying the slaves, however, is only one, among a thousand other miseries, which those unhappy and devoted creatures suffer, from this disgraceful traffic of the human species, which, in every part of its progress, exhibits scenes, that strike us with horror and indignation. If we regard the first stage of it, on the continent of Africa, we find, that a hundred thousand slaves are annually produced there for exportation, the greatest part of whom consists of innocent persons, torn from their dearest friends and connexions, sometimes by force, and sometimes by treachery. Of these, experience has shewn, that forty five thousand perish, either in the dreadful mode of conveyance before described, or within two years after their arrival at the plantations, before they are seasoned to the climate. Those who unhappily survive these hardships, are destined, like beasts of burden, to exhaust their lives in the unremitting labours of slavery, without recompense, and without hope.

" It is said by the well-wishers to this trade, that the suppression of it will destroy a great nursery for seamen, and annihilate a very considerable source of commercial profit. In answer to these objections, mr. Clarkson, in his admirable treatise on the impolicy of the trade, lays down two positions, which he has proved from the most incontestable authority—First, that so far from being a nursery, it has been constantly and regularly a grave for our seamen; for that in this traffic only, more men perish in one year, than in all the other trades of Great Britain, in two years:

" And, secondly, that the balance of the trade, from its extreme precariousness and uncertainty, is so notoriously against the merchants, that if all the vessels, employed in it, were the property of one man, he would infallibly, at the end of their voyages, find himself a loser.

" As then the cruelty and inhumanity of this trade must be universally admitted and lamented, and as the policy or impolicy of its abolition is a question, which the wisdom of the legislature must ultimately decide upon, and which it can only be enabled to form a just estimate of, by the most thorough investigation of all its relations and dependencies; it becomes the indispensable duty of every friend to humanity, however his speculations may have led him to conclude on the political tendency of the measure, to stand forward, and to assist the committees, either by producing such facts as he may himself be acquainted with, or by subscribing, to enable them to procure and transmit to the legislature, such evidence as will tend to throw the necessary lights on the subject. And people would do well to consider, that it does not often fall to the lot of individuals, to have an opportunity of performing so important a moral and religious duty, as that of endeavouring to put an end to a practice, which may, without exaggeration, be stiled one of the greatest evils at this day existing upon the earth.

" By the Plymouth committee,

" W. ELFORD, chairman."

The American Revolution increased awareness of the inhumanity of enslavement and demands for the abolition of the trans-Atlantic slave trade. This depiction of a Liverpool slave ship, the *Brooke*, on which more than six hundred men, women, and children were packed so tightly that they "were reduced nearly to the state of being buried alive," was published by order of the Pennsylvania Society for Promoting the Abolition of Slavery and the Relief of Free Negroes Unlawfully Held in Bondage (Library Company of Philadelphia).

Dismantling the legal, cultural, and social foundations of enslavement was an enormous task that could not be accomplished in a single generation, much less a single frame of government. When the delegates gathered in Philadelphia, the American Revolutionaries had already set slavery on the path to extinction in much of the United States in the first successful assault on the practice of enslavement in modern history. Abolitionist ideas, which were barely expressed in the middle of the eighteenth century, were rising from the American Revolutionaries' bold assertion of universal equality. The Federal Convention created a framework in which enslavement was contained and ultimately dismantled in the United States, an extraordinary accomplishment considering the resistance of slavery's defenders and the uncertainty of its opponents about a world without slavery.

The convention revealed the ambivalence of many of the delegates about slavery. Enslavement was so deeply woven into the economy that few were free from some connection, direct or indirect, with it. Many of the delegates had concluded that slavery was ethically and morally reprehensible and utterly at odds with the principles of natural rights on which the Revolution was based. "We have seen the mere distinction of colour," James Madison said near the beginning of the convention, "made in the most enlightened period of time, a ground of the most oppressive dominion ever exercised by man over man." Yet Madison, like many of the delegates, owned slaves. He lamented the injustice of slavery but for all his creativity he could not imagine a just, peaceful, and productive multi-racial society.

The literature of the Enlightenment in which Madison, Jefferson, Wilson, Hamilton, and other educated leaders of the Revolutionary generation were schooled offered no clear solution to this dilemma. Despite their confidence in the capacity of reason to overcome injustice, the thinkers of the Enlightenment were divided about racial equality. Voltaire, David Hume, and Immanuel Kant argued that sub-Saharan Africans were by nature intellectually inferior to Europeans, while Condorcet, Montesquieu, and Frances Hutcheson argued for the universal equality of mankind.

Philosophy suggested no practical means to achieve that equality where the economy was dependent on enslaved labor. Some form of gradual abolition seemed to many thoughtful people to be the only solution. "I never mean (unless some particular circumstances should compel me to it) to possess another slave by purchase" Washington wrote in September 1786, "it being among my first wishes to see some plan adopted, by the legislature by which slavery in this Country may be abolished by slow, sure, and imperceptable degrees."

In the meantime Washington remained, however reluctantly, the master of hundreds of enslaved people. He held many of them in trust for the heirs of Martha Washington's first husband. Those men and women Washington had no lawful right to emancipate, but he began making plans to free the rest of the people he enslaved in his will. He had no wish to see people in slavery, Washington wrote to Robert Morris. "There is not a man living who wishes more sincerely than I do, to see a plan adopted for the abolition of it."

Washington expressed this laudable sentiment while asking Morris to assist Philip Dalby, an Alexandria, Virginia, storekeeper, to recover Frank, a seventeen-year-old Dalby enslaved, after Frank had been persuaded by Philadelphia abolitionists to seek his freedom under the Pennsylvania Statute for the Gradual Abolition of Slavery. Dalby managed to recover Frank, but in the spring of 1787, shortly before the Federal Convention met, Frank made his escape, the chance to claim his freedom outweighing the risk of punishment or a life of poverty. Plans for gradual emancipation did little to satisfy the aspirations of enslaved men and women to be free.

The progress of gradual abolition, however slow, gave hope to many of the convention delegates. When the convention met, five northern states and the independent republic of Vermont were in the process of abolishing slavery within their borders. Antislavery agitation was pushing two other northern states toward gradual abolition. Roger Sherman of Connecticut optimistically observed "that the abolition of slavery seemed to be going on in the United States, and that the good sense of the several States would probably by degrees complete it." A practical politician, he urged that the delegates avoid antagonizing slaveholders in order to create "as few objections as possible to the proposed scheme of government." Even Gouverneur Morris, the most outspoken opponent of slavery among the delegates and far less confident than Sherman that it was on its way to extinction, was under no illusion that the convention could propose a new frame of government abolishing slavery and expect it to be ratified by the states below the Potomac.

Most opponents of slavery in the convention rested their hopes for the eventual extinction of slavery on the abolition of the trans-Atlantic slave trade. By the 1770s that trade had been exposed as a violent, degrading, and dehumanizing nightmare for its victims and its abolition had become a major cause for antislavery advocates in America and Britain. Anthony Benezet focused attention on the brutality of the slave trade and inspired the development of principled opposition to it on both sides of the Atlantic. Opposition to the slave trade in Britain, inspired by American abolitionists, was growing.

Many opponents of the slave trade believed that its abolition would lead to the gradual extinction of slavery because they thought the enslaved population would dwindle if it was cut off from its source in Africa. They discounted natural increase, not recognizing that enslaved populations in most parts of the United States were growing regardless of the number of slaves being imported. The mortality of enslaved people, which remained appallingly high in the Caribbean, was dropping in the United States.

Some pinned their hopes to the idea that slavery would wither as farmers shifted to crops better suited to free labor. Washington, who abandoned growing tobacco before the Revolutionary War, found enslaved labor less practical for growing and harvesting wheat. Still others expected that slavery would fade as the population pressed west into regions they wrongly believed were unsuited to enslaved labor. Rice cultivation, which made extensive use of enslaved labor, was limited to coastal regions where it was already established and had no prospect of moving west. So was long staple cotton, a minor crop grown close to the sea. Short staple cotton could be grown in the southern interior, but very little was, because removing the seeds from the fibers by hand took too much labor to be profitable. No one in or out of the convention could have foreseen that within a decade a Connecticut inventor named Eli Whitney would perfect the cotton gin, a machine for removing the seeds. The cotton gin made short staple cotton a profitable crop and led to a dramatic expansion in the plantation slavery at the very time Washington and others apparently expected the institution to go into decline.

Others believed that white laborers would replace enslaved people as the population grew. Oliver Ellsworth recognized that "slaves multiply so fast in Virginia and Maryland that it is cheaper to raise than import them" while in "the sickly rice swamps foreign supplies are necessary," but he concluded that in the long term, slavery was doomed.

"As population increases, poor laborers will be so plenty as to render slaves useless. Slavery in time will not be a speck in our Country."

The abolition of the slave trade came before the convention because the Virginia Plan shifted the regulation of international trade from the states to the national government. Delegates anxious to keep the slave trade open wanted assurances that Congress would not interfere with the trade or try to stop it altogether. The issue was susceptible to compromise, because planters in the Maryland and Virginia tidewater were in no great need of additional labor. As Ellsworth pointed out, the enslaved population of the region was growing without the importation of enslaved people from Africa or the Caribbean. The shift from tobacco to wheat on some plantations was reducing the need for enslaved labor. Ending the slave trade would enhance the market value of the people enslaved in the region by limiting the supply. A similar situation prevailed in some parts of the Carolina low country, where well established planters expected to gain from halting the importation of enslaved people, but most planters in the Carolinas and Georgia were anxious to keep the slave trade open.

The debate was fierce. Luther Martin, the attorney general of Maryland, enslaved six people, yet argued that slave trade was "inconsistent with the principles of the revolution and dishonorable to the American character." John Rutledge and Charles Pinckney, both from South Carolina, warned that any effort to limit the slave trade would alienate the lower South and endanger the union. Rutledge pointed out that the New England states profited from the trade, an argument that was not lost on some of the New England delegates. George Mason, who enslaved some three hundred people at his plantation in Virginia, condemned both the slave trade and slavery itself. "Every master of slaves is born a petty tyrant," Mason said. "They bring the judgment of heaven on a Country. As nations cannot be rewarded or punished in the next world, they must be in this. By an inevitable chain of causes and effects providence punishes national sins, by national calamities." Charles Pinckney responded sharply that "if slavery be wrong, it is justified by the example of the whole world."

The delegates agreed, finally, to a compromise that defied the example of the whole world.

The convention agreed that Congress would not interfere in the slave trade for twenty years, after which it might prohibit the trade altogether. The compromise entangled delegates opposed to slavery in its most odious and widely condemned practice, but facilitated the end of the legal importation of enslaved people, which many Americans believed would lead inevitably to the extinction of slavery. In 1800, Congress made it a crime for Americans to engage in the international slave trade, and effective January 1, 1808—the earliest date allowed by the compromise struck in the Federal Convention—the importation of enslaved people was forbidden by law.

The Three-Fifths Compromise

Enslaved people constituted such a large part of the population in the states dependent on them for forced labor that the question of how they should be counted for the purposes of representation was unavoidable. Once the convention agreed to make population the basis of representation in the House of Representatives, delegates from the Carolinas and Georgia insisted that the people they enslaved be counted for the purpose of representation. The enslaved, they argued, were dependent people like women and children, who were all counted for the purposes of representation despite not being eligible to vote or hold public office. Most northern delegates objected to the idea that enslaved people, "who were property in the South," said Elbridge Gerry, should "be in the rule of representation any more than the cattle and horses of the North."

James Wilson proposed a compromise that would base representation on the number of "white and other free Citizens," including women, children, and indentured servants and "three-fifths of all other persons," excluding Indians who did not pay taxes. Wilson took the three-fifths ratio from agreement reached in the Continental Congress in 1783, when the issue was how to calculate the value of property as the basis of taxation. At the time, southern congressman had contended that the labor of an enslaved person was worth only three-fifths of value of the labor of a free worker, and should be taxed accordingly. The delegates

readily embraced Wilson's compromise by a vote of nine states to two. Once the matter was settled, some of the southern delegates had misgivings. Charles Pinckney and Pierce Butler pressed for reconsideration, Pinckney insisting that "blacks ought to stand on an equality with whites" for the purposes of representation. Pinckney's appeal moved no votes.

Gouverneur Morris continued to resist the compromise on the grounds that that it would encourage the slave trade. He made a motion on July 17 to reconsider the matter, but the motion died without a second. On August 12 he rose again to attack the immorality of enslavement, arguing that "the inhabitant of Georgia and South Carolina who goes to the Coast of Africa, and in defiance of the most sacred laws of humanity tears away his fellow creatures from their dearest connections and damns them to the most cruel bondages, shall have more votes in a government instituted for the protection of the rights of mankind, than the citizen of Pennsylvania or New Jersey who views with a laudable horror so nefarious a practice." Morris said that slavery called down "the curse of heaven on the states where it prevailed," repeating what had become a common sentiment in the northern states where slavery had been abolished or was under attack. "The rights of human nature and the principles of our holy religion loudly call on us to dispense the blessing of freedom to all mankind." Eloquent as he was, Morris failed to move the other delegates, who were satisfied with the compromise.

The three-fifths compromise is now frequently cited as evidence that the delegates regarded enslaved Americans as lesser beings, but the alternative was to count the enslaved as full persons for the purposes of apportioning representation in Congress, an outcome that would have dramatically increased the number of congressional representatives from the southern states and made future restrictions on slavery harder to pass. The compromise was a defeat for defenders of slavery, who would have preferred to have counted the enslaved as full persons. Frederick Douglass and other abolitionists saw the compromise as a defeat for slaveholders. "It is a downright disability laid upon the slaveholding States," Douglass argued, "one which deprives those States of two-fifths of

Liberty Displaying the Arts and Sciences, commissioned for the reading room of the Library Company of Philadelphia and completed in 1792, is one of the first works of art dedicated to the abolition of slavery. Richly symbolic, it depicts the liberating power of knowledge (Library Company of Philadelphia).

their natural basis of representation. . . . So much for the three-fifths clause; at its worst, it still leans to freedom, not slavery."

The language of the compromise did not refer to slaves or slavery. Instead it employed the euphemism "three-fifths of all other persons." The compromise over the slave trade employed similar language, referring to the "Migration or Importation of such Persons as any of the States now existing shall think proper to admit." John Dickinson, a Delaware slaveowner who had freed the people he enslaved during the war, wrote in his notes that "omitting the WORD will be regarded as

an Endeavour to conceal a principle of which we are ashamed." Many modern commentators have described it in that way, but by refusing to treat slavery as an institution clearly and unambiguously recognized by the Constitution, the delegates rendered slavery an institution recognized solely by state laws.

The decision to exclude the words slave and slavery from the Constitution was supported by the majority of the delegates, who agreed with Elbridge Gerry that they "ought to be careful not to give any sanction to it." The Constitution held slavery at arm's length, excluding what Madison called "the idea that there could be property in men." While individual delegates defended enslavement and the right of slaveowners to their property, the convention refused to acknowledge enslaved people as property, and thus declined to validate the slaveholders' defense that a man's right to human property is either legitimate or inviolable. This left open the possibility that the national government might halt slavery's expansion into the West or provide for its gradual abolition as Pennsylvania and other states had done.

Congress, meeting in New York, was in the process of doing just that by adopting an ordinance to organize a government in the territory north of the Ohio River. The Northwest Ordinance specified that "there shall be neither slavery nor involuntary servitude in the said territory, otherwise than in the punishment of crimes whereof the party shall have been duly convicted," thus fulfilling, for the states to be carved out of the Northwest Territory, the antislavery provision of the Land Ordinance of 1784.

The idea that refusing to acknowledge slavery openly was a dishonorable evasion that implicated the convention in the horrors of enslavement misses the ultimate importance of refusing to acknowledge slavery as a legitimate institution and enslaved people as property at a time when slavery was the norm throughout the Americas. As the antislavery movement grew in strength in the early nineteenth century, the silence of the Constitution on slavery provided abolitionists with grounds to hinder slavery's expansion and argue for its abolition as acts consistent with the Constitution.

There would be radical abolitionists—William Lloyd Garrison is the most famous—who would denounce the Constitution as an "agreement with hell," but most abolitionists embraced the Constitution. Frederick Douglass spoke for them: "Does the United States Constitution guarantee to any class or description of people in that country the right to enslave, or hold as property, any other class or description of people in that country?" Garrison and his followers, Douglass granted, thought that it did. "I, on the other hand, deny that the Constitution guarantees the right to hold property in man, and believe that the way to abolish slavery in America is to vote such men into power as will use their powers for the abolition of slavery."

"A republic if you can keep it"

The Federal Constitution was a classic compromise. It completely satisfied none of the delegates, but it made most of them unhappy in about equal measure. Washington wrote to Henry Knox that he hoped the people would accept the constitution. "I am fully persuaded it is the best that can be obtained at the present moment, under such diversity of ideas as prevail." The absence of a national veto over state legislation was particularly disappointing to Madison, who wrote to Jefferson that the plan "will neither effectually answer its national object nor prevent the local mischiefs which every where excite disgusts against the state governments." He did not understand that the Federal Constitution would turn out to be both effective and enduring.

Of the fifty-five men who served in the convention, only forty-two were there at the end. Several had left during the summer for personal reasons and others because they disagreed with the direction the other delegates were taking. During the final week, three of the remaining delegates decided they could not support the Constitution the convention had worked so hard to complete.

On September 10, Edmund Randolph explained that he was uncomfortable with impeachment trials being conducted in the Senate, about the small size of the legislature, the provisions that gave the national government the means to maintain a standing army at will, the power to impose export duties, and with the ill-defined nature of the clause that gave Congress the power to make whatever laws seemed "necessary and proper" for national purposes. He said he believed the plan "would end in Tyranny." He suggested that the plan be submitted to Congress and state conventions, followed by a second general convention to prepare a constitution based on the guidance it received. If this was not done, he announced, he would not "put his name to the instrument."

George Mason joined Randolph in dissent. On September 12 he had made a final effort to persuade the Convention to add a bill of rights to the Constitution, which he said "would give great quiet to the people" and "might be prepared in a few hours." Elbridge Gerry moved for a committee to prepare a bill of rights, but no state delegation voted in favor of the motion. On September 15 Mason said he thought the government outlined in the Constitution "would end either in monarchy, or a tyrannical aristocracy." He supported Randolph's idea of calling a second general convention. Without it, he would not sign. Elbridge Gerry, agreeing with Randolph and Mason, announced that he would withhold his signature as well.

The delegates' final disagreements were put to rest by the evening of Saturday, September 15, and their secretary turned the finished document over to Jacob Shallus, the thirty-seven-year-old assistant clerk of the Pennsylvania legislature, to engross the Constitution on four pages of parchment. Shallus was a first generation American, the son of German migrants, and a veteran of the Revolutionary War who marched to Quebec in early 1776. When his regiment marched from Philadelphia the men's clothing, their commander wrote, was "very scanty." They suffered through a winter campaign without enough blankets or tents and they lacked bayonets and other basic equipment. At the end of the year their colonel reported "the men almost naked" and worn out from exposure. Jacob Shallus and thousands like him had suffered because Congress was never able to provide for American soldiers. The men who spent the summer of 1787 creating the Federal Constitution, including men who had commanded those soldiers, were determined it should never happen again.

Shallus completed his work in less than forty hours, in time for the delegates to gather on Monday, September 17, to sign the Constitution. Benjamin Franklin prepared a speech for the occasion, but he was too weak to present it himself. He sat quietly while James Wilson read it to the other delegates.

I confess that there are several parts of this constitution which I do not at present approve, but I am not sure I shall never approve them: For having lived long, I have experienced many instances of being obliged by better information, or fuller consideration, to change opinions even on important subjects, which I once thought right, but found to be otherwise. It is therefore that the older I grow, the more apt I am to doubt my own judgment, and to pay more respect to the judgment of others. . . .

In these sentiments, sir, I agree to this Constitution with all its faults—if they are such—because I think a general government necessary for us, and there is no form of government but what may be a blessing to the people if well administered; and I believe, further, that this is likely to be well administered for a course of years, and can only end in despotism, as other forms have done before it, when the people shall become so corrupted as to need despotic government, being incapable of any other. I doubt, too, whether any other convention we can obtain may be able to make a better Constitution; for, when you assemble a number of men, to have the advantage of their joint wisdom, you inevitably assemble with those men all their prejudices, their passions, their errors of opinion, their local interests, and their selfish views. . . . Thus I consent, Sir, to this Constitution because I expect no better, and because I am not sure, that it is not the best.

Franklin asked the other delegates to keep their doubts about the constitution to themselves and to express their unreserved support for the document in public.

At the last moment, Nathaniel Gorham suggested, "if it was not too late," that the number of members of the House of Representatives should not exceed one for every thirty thousand rather than one for every forty thousand. If the delegates hesitated to make the change, George Washington persuaded them. Making his view on a matter of substance known for the first time, he urged the delegates to accept Gorham's proposal "The smallness of the proportion of Representatives had been considered by many members of the convention, an insufficient security for the rights and interests of the people." Washington "acknowledged that it had always appeared to himself among the exceptionable parts of the plan; and . . . he thought this of so much consequence that it would give much satisfaction to see it adopted." The delegates agreed unanimously to make this change. With that final change, the Federal Constitution was complete.

Thirty-nine of the forty-two remaining delegates signed the Constitution and then all the delegates adjourned to the nearby City Tavern for a farewell dinner. Afterwards George Washington returned to his lodgings, wrote letters, and in the evening took possession of the journal and papers of the convention. Then, as he recorded in his diary, Washington "retired to meditate on the momentous work which had been executed."

Washington could look on that work with satisfaction. The Federal Constitution provided for a government capable of addressing what he had called the "general concerns" of the nation. The new government would be authorized to regulate commerce and collect taxes, including import duties on foreign goods, which would provide the United States with leverage in addressing the trade practices of foreign powers. The authority to tax would also make it possible for the government to discharge its debts, including money owed to foreign governments and bankers, to the many Americans who held government securities, and to officers and men of the Continental Army." The Federal Constitution would also make it possible for the United States to organize its military strength for effective defense of American interests, which was essential for the survival of the United States in a world of predatory powers.

The Federal Constitution, in short, would establish what Washington had called "a power which will pervade the whole Union." The question that evening, as Washington reflected on the work of the convention, was whether the states and the American people would, as he had urged, "forget their local prejudices and policies" and commit themselves to the interests of the nation.

A gracious hostess who could "animate and give a brilliancy to the whole Conversation," Elizabeth Willing Powel frequently entertained the delegates at her Philadelphia home. In his diary for September 18, 1787, Maryland delegate James McHenry recorded that she asked Benjamin Franklin, "Well Doctor what have we got a republic or a monarchy?" Franklin replied, "A republic if you can keep it." In 1814 she wrote that "I have no recollection of any such conversations . . . Yet I cannot venture to deny after so many Years have elapsed that such conversations had passed. I well remember to have frequently associated with the most respectable, influential Members of the Convention that framed the Constitution, and that the all-important Subject was frequently discussed at our House" (Pennsylvania Academy of the Fine Arts).

To Yale College Library, as a specimen of New Haven antiquities.

The
UNITED STATES
were first declar'd —
Free and Independent
July 4th 1776

The Present
CONSTITUTIO
was form'd by the —
Grand Convention
held at Philadelphia Sep.t 17
1787

ARMES of the UNITED STATES

NEW HAMPSHIRE 2 SENATORS 3 REPRESENTATIVES

MASSACHUSETTS 2 SENAT. 8 REPR

RHOD.

President of the UNITED STATES of AMERICA. The Protector of his COUNTRY. and the Supporter of the rights of MANKIND.

GEORGE WASHINGTON

Born 11th Feb 1732 O.S.

The number of Inhabitants in the several States is according as they were returned in the Grand Convention held at Philadelphia in 1787

The number of Senators and Representatives is what the Constitution allowed each State at Congress

A DISPLAY of the UNITED STATES of AMERICA

To the Patrons of Arts and Sciences, in all parts of the World, this Plate

is most respectfully Dedicated, by their most obedient humble Servants

Amos Doolittle & Ebn.r Porter

Printed & Sold by A. Doolittle New Haven where Engraving & Roling Press Printing is performed

Epilogue   The People's Debate

George Mason was injured when his carriage overturned on his way home from Philadelphia, but that did not slow him from sharing his objections to the Constitution. As soon as he reached Gunston Hall he began sending his thoughts, laboriously written out by hand, in letters addressed to political leaders in all parts of the country.

This was how politics had been conducted on a continental scale a decade earlier. In the last years before the Revolutionary War, like-minded gentlemen like Richard Henry Lee and Samuel Adams had written to one another to exchange views and make plans, which then they then shared with their respective circles. They called this composing the business. They considered national politics the business of gentleman like themselves. Only a few of them grasped how profoundly the Revolution had changed public life and would continue to change it.

The battle over the ratification of the Federal Constitution was conducted in newspapers, pamphlets that were published and republished with extraordinary speed across the country, and in town meetings, public assemblies, and even in a few riots and tavern brawls. Gentlemen discussed the Constitution in parlors and exchanged views in private letters, but the Revolution had made politics the business of the sovereign people. Gentlemen like Mason might hope that the sovereign people would defer to educated leaders like themselves, but in most cases they were sorely disappointed. Public life had changed. The rich, well born, and able still enjoyed a disproportionate share of political influence, but they could no longer afford to ignore the people. The deference of ordinary Americans to the gentry was eroding, worn away by the idea of popular sovereignty,

frequent elections, large-scale market forces that diminished the influence of local gentlemen in the lives of their neighbors, the decline of established churches traditionally dominated by local gentlemen, and a flood of newspapers and pamphlets that was transforming the way people exchanged ideas and learned about public issues.

Advocates of ratification, who called themselves Federalists and labelled their opponents Antifederalists, recognized the way politics and public life was changing more clearly than men like Mason. The most active Federalists were young men who had entered public life during the Revolution. James Madison, Alexander Hamilton, John Jay, and many other active Federalists were too young to have participated in the political culture of the mid-eighteenth century. For them, politics was a public endeavor. The strategized in private but staked out their positions in public. They quickly secured the support of newspaper printers and dominated the duel for public support through the press. The most enduring work in support of ratification, a series of eighty-five newspaper essays signed "Publius," published to secure ratification in New York, was written by Hamilton, Madison, and Jay. Since known collectively as the Federalist Papers, the essays explained the Constitution in astonishing breadth and learned detail. The Antifederalists produced nothing half as rich. They were overwhelmed.

In the genteel political fashion of the passing age, Mason sent Washington a copy of his objections, which he grumpily noted might have been removed by "a little Moderation and Temper, in the latter End of the Convention." As if to underscore the way politics had changed, George Washington's private secretary, a twenty-five-year-old Harvard graduate named Tobias Lear, sent

Amos Doolittle, who published the first views of the fighting at Lexington and Concord in 1775, engraved this print celebrating the union created by the ratification of the Federal Constitution and the election of George Washington as first president of the United States. The thirteen interlocking rings represent the states of the union (Yale University Art Gallery).

Mason's objections to the local newspaper, the *Virginia Journal, and Alexandria Advertiser,* which published them, followed by Lear's answers to Mason's arguments, which Lear signed "Brutus," gleefully writing that "it is not known, even to the General, by whom it is done."

When a twenty-five-year-old private secretary dared to take on a sixty-two-year-old statesman in the press to expose what he called the "futility" of his elder's objections, it was clear that politics was becoming a popular enterprise, dependent on winning the support of people whose views traditional gentry leaders had once barely considered. "The people," Madison wrote in his notes near the end of the Federal Convention, "were in fact, the fountain of all power, and by resorting to them, all difficulties were got over."

As their last act, the delegates to the Federal Convention had referred their draft Constitution to Congress, which passed it on to the states for ratification by the people, through conventions to be called exclusively for the purpose of considering the Constitution. This approach to establishing the authority of constitutions as fundamental law, superior to the act of any legislature, was one of the most important contributions of the American Revolution to constitutional practice. The first revolutionary state constitutions, like the Virginia Constitution of 1776, were fashioned by state legislatures and had no more legal authority than ordinary statutes. The idea of establishing constitutions as superior to statutes led John Adams, the author of the Massachusetts Constitution of 1780, to provide for the ratification of that constitution by the popular vote of freeholders assembled in their town meetings. The provision of the Federal Constitution calling for ratification by conventions in each state employed this strategy on a continental scale.

The debate over the ratification of the Federal Constitution was the greatest exercise in democratic governance that had ever been undertaken. Ratification was the central issue in American public life for some ten months and was the occasion for hundreds of newspaper essays, pamphlets, speeches, and public debates in state legislatures, town meetings, and anywhere else people gathered—in taverns, private homes, and in carriages jolting their way from town to town.

In each state the climactic debates took place in the state ratifying convention. Some 1,650 men served in these conventions. The delegates included state and local office holders but most were simply private citizens. They included lawyers, planters, and merchants, along with hundreds of plain farmers and other ordinary people respected for their judgment in the town or county where they lived. Many of the delegates were veterans of the Continental Army or had served in the militia during the Revolutionary War. Among the delegates were some of the most learned men in the new nation. In the conventions they sat down with men who owned taverns, made saddles, kept stores, milled grain, and many who plowed, planted, and harvested crops with their own hands. Men who could read Latin and Greek and quote Locke and Montesquieu exchanged views with men who could barely spell and whose speech was as plain as the simple clothes they wore.

Federalists and Antifederalists

Support for ratification came from Americans of widely varying backgrounds who believed a national government endowed with sufficient power could resolve the crisis into which the Confederation had fallen. Merchants looked to the new government to secure them greater access to foreign markets. Urban artisans expected the new government to protect and encourage domestic manufacturing by imposing tariffs on foreign goods. Sailors expected the government would secure access to foreign ports where American shipping was forbidden. Farmers imagined new markets and higher prices for their crops. With remarkable unity, Federalist spokesmen assured Americans that a government empowered by the Federal Constitution would establish stability at home and respectability abroad, protect national independence, and defend the rights and liberties for which Americans had fought and so many had died.

The Antifederalists were unified by little more than opposition to unconditional ratification. Many were concerned by the absence of a bill of rights. Among them were people who earnestly believed that political power should remain at the state and local level. Some were concerned mainly

tended that the small size of the proposed national legislature would deprive the people of substantive participation in governance. Some argued for a larger and thus, they believed, more representative national legislature. Others argued that maintaining the authority of state governments was the only way to facilitate popular engagement.

These two groups of Antifederalists differed considerably in their social and economic outlook. Those who argued for the primacy of state and local government tended to be drawn from traditional gentry or their Revolutionary successors, and included George Mason, Richard Henry Lee, and Elbridge Gerry. They valued deference to established leaders like themselves and

Federalists dominated the debate over ratification in the press. The three authors of *The Federalist*—Alexander Hamilton, James Madison, and John Jay—turned out eighty-five essays in six months. Hamilton wrote fifty-one of them (The Society of the Cincinnati).

by the fact that shifting power to a national government would deprive them of influence but many were convinced that state and local governments were more responsive to the will of the people and better at guarding popular liberty.

A second group of Antifederalists were less concerned about preserving state and local authority than they were with defending and nurturing democratic engagement in public life. Some of them did not object in principle to shifting some authority to a national government, but they con-

many were suspicious of democratic politics.

Antifederalists who emphasized democratic values were mostly rising men, resistant to gentry dominance and interested in commercial prosperity. Their opposition to the Constitution was fueled by the expectation that the gentry would monopolize federal offices. For these Antifederalists, maintaining political authority at the state and local level increased their chances to compete with the more established gentry for political influence. Many were middling merchants or commercial

130

AGAINST the New Federal Constitution.

From the VIRGINIA GAZETTE.

The following are the so much talked of Objections against the New Federal Constitution, of the Hon. GEORGE MASON, Esq; one of the Delegates to the late Federal Convention from the State of Virginia.

" THERE is no declaration of rights; and the laws of the general government being paramount to the laws and constitutions of the several States, the declarations of rights in the separate States are no security. Nor are the people secured even in the enjoyment of the benefits of the common law, which stands here upon no other foundation than its having been adopted by the respective acts forming the constitutions of the several States.

" In the House of Representatives there is not the substance, but the shadow only of representation; which can never produce proper information in the Legislature, or inspire confidence in the people; the laws will therefore be generally made by men little concerned in, and unacquainted with their effects and consequences *.

" The Senate have the power of altering all money bills, and of originating appropriations of money, and the salaries of the officers of their own appointment in conjunction with the President of the United States; although they are not the representatives of the people, or amenable to them.

" These with their other great powers (viz. their power in the appointment of ambassadours and other publick officers, in making treaties, and in trying all impeachments) their influence upon and connexion with the supreme executive from these causes, their duration of office, and their being a constant existing body almost continually sitting, joined with their being one complete branch of the Legislature, will destroy any balance in the government, and enable them to accomplish what usurpations they please upon the rights and liberties of the people.

" The judiciary of the United States is so constructed and extended as to absorb and destroy the judiciaries of the several States; thereby rendering law as tedious, intricate and expensive, and justice as unattainable by a great part of the community, as in England, enabling the rich to oppress and ruin the poor.

" The President of the United States has no constitutional council (a thing unknown in any safe and regular government) he will therefore be unsupported by proper information and advice; and will be generally directed by minions and favourites—or he will become a tool to the Senate—or a Council of State will grow out of the principal officers of the great departments; the worst and most dangerous of all ingredients for such a council in a free country; for they may be induced to join in any dangerous or oppressive measures, to shelter themselves, and prevent an inquiry into their own misconduct in office; whereas had a constitutional council been formed (as was proposed) of six members, viz, two from the eastern, two from the middle, and two from the southern States, to be appointed by vote of the States in the House of Representatives, with the same duration and rotation in office as the Senate, the Executive would always have had safe and proper information and advice; the President of such a council might have acted, as Vicepresident of the United States *pro tempore*, upon any vacancy or disability of the chief Magistrate; and long continued ses-

* Col. Mason acknowledges that this objection was lessened by inserting the word *thirty* instead of *forty*, as it was at first determined, in the 3d clause of the 2d section of the 1st article.

ions of the Senate would in a great meafure have been prevented.——

"From this fatal defect of a conftitutional council has arifen the improper power of the Senate, in the appointment of publick officers, and the alarming dependence and connexion between that branch of the Legiflature and the fupreme Executive.——

"Hence alfo fprung that unneceffary and dangerous officer the Vicepreſident; who for want of other employment is made Preſident of the Senate; thereby dangeroufly blending the executive and legiſlative powers; befides always giving to fome of the States an unneceffary and unjuft preeminence over the others.——

"The Prefident of the United States has the unreftrained power of granting pardons for treafon; which may be fometimes exercifed to fcreen from punifhment thofe whom he had fecretly inftigated to commit the crime, and thereby prevent a difcovery of his own guilt.——

"By declaring all treaties fupreme laws of the land, the Executive and the Senate have, in many cafes, an exclufive power of legiflation; which might have been avoided by proper diftinctions with refpect to treaties, and requiring the affent of the Houfe of Reprefentatives, where it could be done with fafety.——

"By requiring only a majority to make all commercial and navigation laws, the five fouthern States (whofe produce and circumftances are totally different from that of the eight northern and eaftern States) will be ruined; for fuch rigid and premature regulations may be made as will enable the merchants of the northern and eaftern States not only to demand an exorbitant freight, but to monopolize the purchafe of the commodities at their own price, for many years; to the great injury of the landed intereft, and impoverifhment of the people: And the danger is the greater, as the gain on one fide will be in proportion to the

lofs on the other. Whereas requiring two thirds of the members prefent in both houfes would have produced mutual moderation, promoted the general intereft, and removed an infuperable objection to the adoption of the government.

"Under their own conftruction of the general claufe at the end of the enumerated powers, the Congrefs may grant monopolies in trade and commerce, conftitute new crimes, inflict unufual and fevere punifhments, and extend their power as far as they fhall think proper; fo that the State Legiflatures have no fecurity for the powers now prefumed to remain to them; or the people for their rights.

"There is no declaration of any kind for preferving the liberty of the prefs, the trial by jury in civil caufes; nor againft the danger of ftanding armies in time of peace.

"The State Legiflatures are reftrained from laying export duties on their own produce.

"The general Legiflature is reftrained from prohibiting the further importation of flaves for twenty odd years; though fuch importations render the United States weaker, and more vulnerable, and lefs capable of defence.

"Both the general Legiflature and the State Legiflatures are exprefsly prohibited making *ex poſt facto* laws; though there never was nor can be a Legiflature but muft and will make fuch laws, when neceffity and the publick fafety require them, which will hereafter be a breach of all the conftitutions in the Union, and afford precedents for other innovations.

"This government will commence in a moderate ariftocracy; it is at prefent impoffible to forefee whether it will, in its operation, produce a monarchy, or a corrupt oppreffive ariftocracy; it will moft probably vibrate fome years between the two, and then terminate between the one and the other."——

Many of the foregoing objections, and the reafonings upon them, ap-

Isaiah Thomas reprinted George Mason's objections to the Federal Constitution for his Massachusetts readers in December 1787. The ratification of the Federal Constitution was the first truly national political contest in which Americans had opportunities to consider views from all parts of the country (Image courtesy of Seth Kaller, Inc.).

351

farmers interested in creating a new social order based on merit, usually measured by success in the marketplace. Some of their spokesmen, including Samuel Bryan of Pennsylvania and Melancton Smith of New York, charged the Federalists with seeking to impose an aristocracy. In a series of essays signed "Centinel," Bryan warned that "aspiring despots" were "prostituting the name of a Washington to cloak their designs upon your liberties."

That two such mutually antagonistic groups were allied, even briefly, was the consequence of the sudden pressure to take a position on ratification. They could not cohere for long and in fact did not. Many genteel Antifederalists made their peace with the new federal government as soon as the Bill of Rights, which restrained federal authority, was adopted. Some became active Federalist politicians in the early years of the new government. Middling Antifederalists later adhered to the Jeffersonian Republican opposition to Federalist policies. Distrust of national government and preference for state sovereignty, views with deep roots in the Revolutionary experience, have recurred through our national history. Antifederalism, to the extent that it ever had a coherent message beyond opposition to ratification and demands for a bill of rights, quickly dissolved.

The vast majority of Antifederalists were neither anxious state or local gentry nor democratically-inclined commercial men. They were ordinary farmers and tradesmen afraid that a powerful, distant national government would ignore their interests or tax them into poverty. Amos Singletary spoke for many of these ordinary Antifederalists in the Massachusetts ratifying convention. "We contended with Great Britain," he argued,

some said for a three-penny duty on tea, but it was not that. It was because they claimed a right to tax us and bind us in all cases whatever. And does not this Constitution do the same? Does it not take away all we have—all our property? Does it not lay all taxes, duties, imposts, and excises? And what more have we to give?

Assurances that Congress would collect all the revenue it needed through import duties were

not to be trusted, Singletary added. Import duties would never be enough. The new Congress would inevitably impose what Singletary called "dry taxes"—excise taxes, stamp duties, land taxes, and other fees.

These lawyers, and men of learning, and moneyed men, that talk so finely, and gloss over matters so smoothly, make us poor illiterate people swallow down the pill, expect to get into Congress themselves . . . and get all the power and all the money into their own hands. And they will swallow up all us little folks.

Singletary may have called himself one of the "poor illiterate people," but he was neither poor nor illiterate. He operated a Worcester County gristmill and had served repeatedly in the Massachusetts legislature.

Jonathan Smith, a representative from Lanesborough, rose in opposition to Singletary, giving voice to views shared by many ordinary farmers and tradesmen who supported the ratification of the Constitution.

I am a plain man and get my living by the plough. I am not used to speak in publick, but I beg your leave to say a few words to my brother plough-joggers in this house. I have lived in a part of the country where I have known the worth of good government by the want of it. There was a black cloud that rose in the east last winter, and spread over the west. . . . It brought on a state of anarchy, and that leads to tyranny. I say it brought anarchy. People that used to live peaceably, and were before good neighbours, got distracted and took up arms against government. . . . People, I say took up arms, and then if you went to speak to them, you had the musket of death presented to your breast. . . . Our distress was so great that we should have been glad to catch at any thing that looked like a government for protection. Had any person, that was able to protect us, come and set up his standard we should all have flocked to it, even if it had been a monarch, and that monarch might have proved a tyrant, so that you see that anarchy

States—like the gen'rous vine fupported live,
The ftrength they gain is from th'embrace they giv
THE FEDERAL PILLARS.

UNITED THEY STAND—DIVIDED FALL.

A veffel arrived at Cape-Ann, after a fhort paf-
fage from Georgia, confirms the pleafing intelligence announced in our laft, that that State has u-
nanimoufly ratified the Federal Conftitution. Thus
is a FIFTH PILLAR added to the glorious fabrick.
May Maffachufetts rear the SIXTH.

In December 1787 the *Massachusetts Gazette* described "the *disunited* states of America" as "thirteen distinct, separate, independent, unsupported columns." Benjamin Russell, publisher of the *Massachusetts Centinel*, employed this metaphor in this woodcut
published while the Massachusetts ratifying convention was meeting. It depicts the sixth pillar of the new union, Massachusetts,
being raised into place by the hand of God (Center for the Study of the American Constitution).

leads to tyranny, and better have one tyrant than so many at once.

Now, Mr. President, when I saw this Constitution, I found that it was a cure for these disorders. It was just such a thing as we wanted. I got a copy of it and read it over and over. I had been a member of the Convention to form our own state Constitution, and had learnt something of the checks and balances of power, and I found them all here. I did not go to any lawyer, to ask his opinion, we have no lawyer in our town, and we do well enough without. I formed my own opinion, and was pleased with this Constitution. . . . I don't think the worse of the Constitution because lawyers, and men of learning and monied men, are fond of it. I don't suspect that they want to get into Congress and abuse their power.

Smith, like many other ordinary Federalists, wanted the government to provide stability and order. Like George Washington, he did not worry that a government endowed with sufficient power to provide stability and order would degenerate into tyranny. From his perspective, anarchy was more likely to lead to tyranny, while an energetic government with checks and balances would protect liberty and property, creating conditions in which freedom could flourish.

"A leap in the dark"

Exchanges like this occurred in every state ratifying convention, with scarcely anyone noticing that a debate about the merits of a national constitution between men like Singletary and Smith, a mill owner and a farmer, reflected a degree of popular participation in public life that would have been unimaginable a generation earlier. The American Revolution had begun, in the early 1760s, as a movement to preserve traditional rights and liberties. Over a generation of constitutional debate and statecraft, punctuated by war and a profound crisis in the economy, Americans had concluded that popular sovereignty could only be realized through an unprecedented degree of democratic participation in politics.

"Some gentlemen say, don't be in a hurry," Jonathan Smith concluded,

take time to consider, and don't take a leap in the dark. I say take things in time—gather fruit when it is ripe. There is a time to sow and a time to reap; we sowed our seed when we sent men to the federal convention, now is the harvest, now is the time to reap the fruit of our labour, and if we don't do it now I am afraid we never shall have another opportunity.

Smith and many other were ready to take "a leap in the dark." His fear that the opportunity for reform was passing was widely shared and created an urgency that gave the Federalists a decisive advantage. They were proposing reforms to resolve the crisis into which the Confederation had descended. The Antifederalists opposed the Federalist reform program but had no program of their own. Some called for a second constitutional convention but that proposal attracted little support and actually underscored the Federalist contention that the Confederation had failed. Others insisted that the pervasive sense of crisis was, as Richard Henry Lee wrote, "a temporary Insanity" and the rush to ratify the Constitution was "certainly the most rash and violent proceeding in the world to cram thus suddenly into men a business of such infinite moment to the happiness of millions."

The Federalists were more determined, better organized, and more effective at making their case to the people than the opposition. They secured ratification in Delaware on December 7, 1787. Pennsylvania Federalists, with a clear majority in their state convention, resisted efforts by backcountry delegates to qualify ratification with conditions or recommended amendments, including a bill of rights. The Pennsylvania convention ratified on December 12 by a vote of 46 to 23. Within a month, New Jersey, Georgia and Connecticut ratified the Constitution. Like Delaware, those three states were tied economically to larger neighbors and suffered as a consequence of their neighbors' commercial regulations. They were all anxious to join a stronger union. The vote in Delaware, New Jersey, and Georgia was unanimous. In Connecticut the Federalists prevailed by a vote of 128 to 40.

Thereafter the process slowed. Massachusetts was predictably divided between the commercial seacoast, devastated by the depression and predictably Federalist, and the backcountry counties where debt and taxes had fueled Shays' Rebellion and many citizens were suspicious of government power. People in central and western Massachusetts who had opposed the uprising tended to support ratification but delegates from the region were mostly Antifederalist. Urban tradesmen, storekeepers, and people dependent on maritime trade were anxious for a government capable of protecting their economic interests. Most of them were Federalist. Paul Revere and other tradesmen gathered at the Green Dragon Tavern in Boston to express their unqualified support for ratification. Samuel Adams, who had been waiting to see which way his constituency of urban working men would lean, thereafter softened his Antifederalist rhetoric. Governor John Hancock, absent for much of the convention, returned to propose ratification along with recommendations for amendments. On that basis Massachusetts became the sixth state to ratify on February 6 by a vote of 187 to 168.

The Maryland convention ratified the Constitution on April 28 by a vote of 63 to 11, followed by South Carolina on May 23 by 149 to 73, and New Hampshire became the ninth state to ratify on June 21 by the narrower margin of 57 to 47. Nine states were sufficient to launch the new government, but an effective union without Virginia and New York was inconceivable. The future of the United States turned on those conventions.

The Virginia Convention, which met in Richmond from June 2 to June 25, was dominated by Patrick Henry, who argued that a government empowered by the Federal Constitution would end in a monstrous tyranny that would deprive Virginians of their most cherished rights. The burden of contending with Henry fell mainly on the soft-spoken James Madison. The Federalists won by a vote of 89 to 79. The New York ratifying convention met on June 17 and sat for more than a month. The Federalists prevailed by a vote of 30 to 27.

The Federalist triumph was not complete. The North Carolina convention met in Hillsborough and rejected the Constitution by a vote of 184 to 84 on August 2. The first federal elections were held and the new government launched before

North Carolina called a second ratifying convention that met in Fayetteville in November 1789. It reversed the earlier decision and ratified by a vote of 194 to 77.

Even then Rhode Island remained outside the union, its legislature determined to pay off the state debt in depreciated Rhode Island paper money. The legislators refused to call a convention. Only when the new Congress threatened to discriminate against Rhode Island trade did the legislature relent and call a convention, but it adjourned without a decision. In May 1790 Congress adopted economic sanctions against Rhode Island, forbidding trade between the state and any part of the United States. The convention promptly reconvened and ratified the Constitution by a vote of 34 to 32.

Each of the men who voted to ratify the Constitution, except those burdened by instructions, did so for reasons that satisfied themselves. Many probably arrived at their conventions with their minds made up, but some—more than enough to swing some of the conventions—were prepared to be persuaded by reasoned debate. There is no reason to believe that men like Jonathan Smith who voted for ratification were the tools of those Amos Singletary scornfully called "lawyers, and men of learning, and moneyed men" who "talk so finely." Smith explained as much. He had been a delegate to the convention that framed the Massachusetts Constitution of 1780 and had learned about checks and balances and other principles of Revolutionary constitutionalism. The experience of living through the American Revolution had empowered him, and many thousands of other ordinary Americans, to make their own judgments about constitutional principles.

For all of their flaws, nothing quite like these conventions had ever happened before and because they succeeded, nothing quite like them has happened since. The nation had been led to this moment by a group of men who engaged in public service, not as a profession, but from a sense of duty. Many of them had neglected their private affairs to serve the public. They relished honor and the most ambitious and far-sighted of them—Washington, John Adams, Franklin, Jefferson, Madison, Hamilton, and Wilson among them—recognized that they were living through a fleeting moment in history in which they had an opportunity to distinguish themselves as founders of a new kind of nation, established on rational principles articulated by the great thinkers of antiquity and the greatest minds of their own century of Enlightenment and based on principles of personal independence, liberty, universal equality, natural right, and responsible citizenship, all resting on the sovereignty of the people.

Even the most far-sighted of them could not imagine where these principles would lead the nation they shaped. They had all been born and grown to manhood in a society characterized by grotesque injustice, ruled by monarchs and dominated by aristocrats and the fortunate, wealthy few, governed by institutions perpetuated by them for their benefit. The society in which they had spent most of their lives was built on the coarsest forms of exploitation—of people enslaved, indentured servants bought and sold, and women denied personal independence and opportunities for individual fulfillment. Most of the wider world was the same or worse—a dark and dreary world of cruelty and violence in which the vast potential of humanity was stifled by arrogance and greed.

They had talents and opportunities to rise in a society built on inequality and then led a struggle in favor of popular sovereignty. Their success assured the development of a democratic society unlike any the world had ever known—a society in which gentlemen like themselves would no longer dominate public life and in which public office would be monopolized by men for whom politics was a profession. America will never have another generation of leaders like George Washington and John Adams, but because of them and the famous and forgotten Revolutionaries at their sides, we have benefitted from the wisdom and imagination

of Abraham Lincoln, who was born in poverty and taught himself reading borrowed books by firelight.

A man like Lincoln would have lived and died in obscurity in the eighteenth century, but because the generation of Washington and Adams committed the nation to popular sovereignty and created a stable government founded on that ideal, Lincoln could rise to the highest office in the land. Because the generation of Washington and Adams committed the nation to ideals of natural right and universal equality, future generations would be inspired by Frederick Douglass, born in slavery, and Susan B. Anthony, born to a middling family, her father a cotton mill manager who lost everything when she was a teenager. Democratic society, imperfect as it was, provided them and thousands more with opportunities to match their talents. The Revolution made possible the society that gave us Thoreau, Melville, and Whitman. It made possible a society in which men and women of energy and principle fight for the freedom of the marginalized and oppressed.

The men and women who shaped our democratic society and culture knew the debt they owed to the men and women, famous and forgotten, of the Revolutionary generation. So have millions of Americans since, including millions of immigrants fleeing oppression and seeking opportunity and millions who have marched, petitioned, campaigned, and protested to secure for themselves and others the liberty, natural rights, and personal independence the Revolutionaries insisted were the common rights of humanity. The idealism of the Revolution is the foundation of our freedom and the hope of people who long for freedom in every part of the world.

The youthful goddess of Liberty lifts a cup to feed an eagle, symbol of the new republic, in this 1796 print by Edward Savage celebrating the overthrow of monarchy and the establishment of the independent United States (Gilcrease Museum, Tulsa, OK).

A Note on Names

One of the challenges of writing about the American Revolution involves the names we use to refer to people and groups in circumstances that were continuously changing. In this book, the names we use reflect interpretive decisions. Each name is the result of deliberation and thought. Others may think differently and make different decisions, but we hope they will understand and respect the choices we have made in this book.

We refer to the thirteen colonies that formed the American union as British America, though we recognize that the first of these colonies were properly English rather than British. The terms Britain and British, though very old, were only firmly associated with the state and its empire in the early eighteenth century. When Jamestown was settled, it was an English colony, but by the middle of the eighteenth century it was universally understood to be a British colony, and since our focus is on the Revolution, we have referred to the thirteen colonies as British America. They were only part of British America, which included Britain's small but extraordinary lucrative colonies in the West Indies, as well as other colonies, including Nova Scotia, that did not join in the American Revolution.

Before the imperial crisis began in the 1760s, the people of British America, with the exception of the Indians, were all colonists. Some, like the enslaved, were unwilling colonists, and others, including many indentured servants, were reluctant ones, but they were all colonists. We have used the word migrants to describe many of the people who came to British America and the phrase religious refugees to refer to those who migrated to British America in order to escape religious disability or persecution. These terms are not commonly used in discussing colonial America, but they should be. We use these terms to refer to people who enter the United States today, and they apply with equal justice to many people who came to British America in the seventeenth and eighteenth centuries.

We have termed people held in perpetual bondage as enslaved people rather than slaves. We have used slave and slavery to refer to legal status and to the institution, but we draw the line at referring to people as slaves, a term that subordinates their individual identities and defines them solely in relation to their oppressors. The American Revolution challenged the idea that enslavement was morally or ethically just and led to its ultimate demise. A work aimed at encouraging understanding and appreciation of the constructive accomplishments of the Revolution should embrace one of its most important: the insistence that all men are created equal and possess the same natural rights. Those rights belong to all of us, men and women, as individuals, and the way we refer to one another, living and dead, should reflect that fact.

We have not, however, referred to indentured servants as indentured people. Perhaps we should. The idea that a person should be defined by his or her servile status, while not as repugnant as defining a person as a slave, is similarly dehumanizing. Indentured servitude was not an occupation, nor was it a status many people willingly chose for themselves. It was a status imposed on people by cruel economic necessity or, as it was in many cases, a punishment. It was part of the fundamentally dehumanizing social conditions of the seventeenth and eighteenth century against which the American Revolution was, in part, a rebellion. We have not adopted the term indentured people only because indentured servitude, as an institution, is now so unfamiliar that the old term, including the word servitude, still has considerable value in defining the status. Indentured servitude is, of course, part of the abhorrent complex of practices, called by various names, involved in the modern system of human trafficking. We are morally bound to eradicate those practices because they violate the universal natural rights claimed for all mankind by the American Revolution.

We have referred to Americans as white and black when those descriptive terms are useful. We have not adopted the new treatment of black as a proper noun, with a capital letter. There are reasons to imagine African Americans as a single ethnic group, but abundant reasons to resist doing so when thinking about the seventeenth and eighteenth centuries. Some enslaved people cherished memories of their African tribal or ethnic identity, and it was one of the tactics of enslavers to deprive them of those memories—to make them simply black, depriving them of the culture that shaped their individual identities. Jeffrey Brace, whose story we tell, was from what we call Mali, and his cultural heritage was important to him. His oppressors looked on him as simply black. We should not. We have referred to some as enslaved Africans when they could not yet be imagined to have developed an American identity, and African Americans when they can be imagined to have done so.

We have referred to indigenous peoples, when we can, by tribal names. Often the documentation does not identify them in this way, however, and we have referred to them as Indians—a collective term imposed on them, erroneously, by Europeans, but for which in many cases no better alternative is available. Native American, while descriptive, is confusing. Migrants from other parts of the world have lived in North America for nearly five hundred years, and their descendants are native to America. Using tribal names respects the cultural variety and richness of the peoples whose ancestors have lived in the Americas for many thousands of years.

What to call Americans who supported and opposed the Revolution through its shifting phases from protest to resistance to rebellion to open war against Britain and its empire is a more complicated challenge. From the beginning of the imperial crisis, the colonists divided between those who supported resistance to greater imperial regulation and taxation and those who accepted those innovations and opposed resistance. At first these groups were ill-defined and the labels we might apply tend to obscure more than they clarify the various positions.

Modern political labels—left and right, liberal and conservative—have no value in describing them. In some respects, those who supported resistance to imperial innovations, at least at the beginning of the imperial controversy, were more attached to the status quo than the innovators they opposed. The latter claimed to support the sovereignty of the Crown and the authority of Parliament, while the former supported traditions of local government. In this sense, they all began as conservatives, differing mainly in what they valued most, and hence wanted to conserve.

Liberal is equally unhelpful. Although it would emerge in the nineteenth century as a label for defenders of individual liberty and free markets, it had no political application in Revolutionary America. The word was used for most of the eighteenth century to refer to people of broad interests, whose thoughts were not restrained by unwavering attachment to conventions. We still use the term in this way when we refer to a liberal education. Liberal would, in time, be attached to the ideas of John Locke and others about individual liberty and individual rights. Today, in American public life, it is commonly used to refer to people and ideas concerned with group rights, a use of the term that would confuse eighteenth-century thinkers, who devoted much of their intellectual energy to establishing that individual people, despite superficial differences of appearance and culture, are fundamentally the same, and thus possess the same natural rights. The idea of group rights was the very thing they opposed, beginning with the right of a royal family to rule, and of aristocrats to hereditary privileges protected by law.

We have referred to the wealthiest Americans as gentry, a term widely used in the eighteenth century, and avoided terms derived by the social sciences, like elites, that are often ill-defined. Nor have we used the language of social class. Eighteenth-century Americans lived in a highly stratified society, but it was one in which people identified themselves vertically, in relation to those above and below them in the social hierarchy, rather than horizontally, recognizing their common interests with others of similar income or property or relationship to the means of economic production. There were working people in eighteenth-century America, but no working class, if class describes groups that recognize shared economic interests and organize themselves accordingly. Likewise, there were middling people in eighteenth-century America—shopkeepers, successful craftsmen and tradesmen, ship's captains, millers, and farmers with comfortable homes who employed laborers and servants—but no middle class. The ship's captain defined his place in society in relation to the merchant who employed him and the sailors he commanded, not by his common interest with shopkeepers and tradesmen. Pre-Revolutionary Americans tended to identify themselves by occupation, region, or religion. One of the long-term consequences of the American Revolution was to encourage Americans to recognize their common interests with people in other occupations, or who lived in other regions, or who belonged to other religions. The idea of equality and the increased opportunities to participate in public life helped shape class consciousness in the decades after the Revolutionary War.

The gentry was the only class in eighteenth-century America. Its members were aware of common interests with gentlemen in other regions. Wealthy farmers, successful lawyers, and prosperous merchants shared many cultural practices—they read similar books, danced the same dances, dressed in the same fashions, and had similar attitudes about the people below them in the social hierarchy. Most of all, they were bound together by the view that they were society's natural leaders.

Few colonists were enthusiastic about more energetic imperial regulation or increased taxes, but those who accepted them, or at least acknowledged the authority of the British government to impose them, gravitated toward loyalism. We have used the terms loyalist and loyalism to refer to those Americans and their ideas. Contemporaries referred to them as loyalists, but more often as Tories—connecting them to the British party more supportive of royal prerogatives than their Whig opponents, who were more attached to Parliamentary rule. They were also referred to in more descriptive ways, like "the king's friends." Many

histories refer to them as Loyalists and their ideas as Loyalism, using capital letters, making these terms proper nouns. We do not. Loyalists were never a clearly defined group, and they certainly weren't an organized political party, like modern Democrats and Republicans. Loyalism embraced a wide spectrum of views, ranging from the views of Americans who favored independence and even republican government, but who doubted their partisans could win, all the way to the views of Americans, probably relatively few in number, who were convinced that kings rule by divine right. Calling them loyalists rather than Loyalists suggests that the Americans who opposed the Revolution had a wide range of views. In short, it respects their individuality.

We have termed those who resisted and protested against imperial regulation and taxation, as they came together as a self-conscious group, as patriots. This is a term they used for themselves, along with others—liberty men and whigs among them. Patriot is a bit of a misnomer. It is an imprecise term that originally combined attachment to the state and love of country, which are not always compatible. The American Revolution ultimately reshaped the very idea of patriotism, which became less about the state and place and more about ideas—the ideas articulated by the Revolution about independence, equality, natural and civil rights, and citizenship, as well as ideas about American national identity related to history, traditions, and symbols. We have used patriot sparingly, to refer to those engaged in the last years of resistance and the first year of the Revolutionary War. We have used patriot beyond that point when contrasting patriots and loyalists. As with loyalist, we have not treated patriot as a proper noun.

We have, without hesitation, referred to supporters of the American Revolution, from the start of the Revolutionary War, and particularly after the Declaration of Independence, as Americans. We recognize that loyalists were Americans as well, but the adoption of the Declaration of Independence was a watershed, at which the colonies became states and together claimed a place among "the powers of the Earth." The Declaration ended the subjection of the colonies and the colonists. Subjects became citizens, and collectively the only way to refer to them is as Americans. Loyalists made a different choice. As long as they rejected citizenship and held on to their subjection to the king, they were British Americans, perhaps, but they were no longer properly described as Americans. Many left the United States at the end of the war. Those who remained gradually made their peace with their neighbors and became Americans—reluctant ones, perhaps, but Americans nonetheless.

How we refer to people is fundamental to how we imagine them. Our preference is to regard people as individuals. Histories that deal with large themes and long periods do not usually commit much space to individuals, and when they do, the individuals tend to be famous political and military leaders. Ordinary people often disappear. We have resisted that tendency and looked for opportunities to introduce ordinary people of the Revolution—Thomas "Burnfoot" Brown, Margaret Corbin, and Jeffrey Brace among them. These individuals are not presented as representatives of a group, though they can be imagined that way. They are presented as actors who, through individual acts of daring, protest, desperation, or imagination, helped shape the American Revolution.

Nowhere in this book have we used the phrase Founding Fathers or its modern variant, the Founders. These terms are used by many writers to refer to the leading political figures of the American Revolution, implying that these men were responsible for the American Revolution and its creative accomplishments. Every generation has leaders, but in most generations, including the Revolutionary generation, leaders reflect the views of the people they lead as much as they direct and shape those views. If they don't, they find themselves without followers. We have had a great deal to say in this book about George Washington, John Adams, Thomas Jefferson, Benjamin Franklin, Patrick Henry, and other leaders of the Revolution, but we never lose sight of the fact that for each of those men, whose letters and papers we can read today, there were thousands of other Revolutionaries—men and women—whose conduct was shaped by ideas and aspirations of their own. They, and not a group of patriarchs, made the American Revolution one of the most important, and most deeply consequential, popular movements in modern history.

Acknowledgments

The central argument of this book—that the Revolutionary generation secured our independence, established our republic, created our national identity, and committed the new nation to ideals of liberty, equality, natural and civil rights, and responsible citizenship that we have been working out ever since—is the product of decades of reading, reflection, conversation, and debate about the enduring importance of the American Revolution.

I owe a great deal to the people who helped me arrive at this understanding. My first debt is to Audrey Warren, who would buy me any history book I wanted, and Jack Warren, Sr., who would take me to any battlefield as long as I wrote him a paper about the battle before we went. Lessons learned from teachers and mentors are scattered through this book. At the University of Mississippi, Bob Haws taught me about eighteenth-century law and constitutionalism and Sheila Skemp nurtured my interest in the Revolution and taught me about the wily merchants of eighteenth-century Rhode Island, the sort of men who burned the *Gaspée*. Winthrop Jordan sharpened my thinking about race and Willie Morris about storytelling. At Brown University my ideas about the Revolution were shaped by Gordon Wood and my thinking about eighteenth-century scholarship by Norman Fiering, director of the indispensable John Carter Brown Library. Peers at Brown University, especially Joyce Botelho, John Wills, Lauren Butler, and Brad Thompson, listened, discussed, and debated with me. Libertarian scholars at the Institute for Humane Studies helped me refine my work on the political ideas of the Revolutionary generation. Russell Kirk corresponded with me about the relationship between the Revolution

and the conservatism of Edmund Burke. Edmund Morgan gave generously of his time and ideas. Fellowships at the Philadelphia Center for Early American Studies (now the McNeil Center for Early American Studies), the Historical Society of Pennsylvania, and the Library Company of Philadelphia shaped my ideas about the cultural and political life of eighteenth-century Pennsylvania, for which I am particularly grateful to Richard Dunn and John Van Horne. Colleagues at the University of Virginia, where I was an editor of *The Papers of George Washington*, shaped my approach to the political and military history of the Revolution and sharpened my understanding of the documentary record, especially Dorothy Twohig and Mark Mastromarino. A brief glance at the notes will demonstrate the debt I owe to historical documentary editors, whose work will endure long after today's monographs are forgotten. I am grateful to all of these people and institutions. None is likely to agree with everything I have written, but their influence is reflected in this book.

I have tried out parts of this book on audiences at George Washington's Mount Vernon, George Mason's Gunston Hall, and the North Carolina Museum of History, at a lecture sponsored by the North Carolina Society of the Cincinnati. David Rubenstein invited me to discuss George Washington with him at an event at the Library of Congress for members of the U.S. Congress. Members from both sides of the aisle proved to be an attentive and perceptive audience, alive to the fact that we are heirs to an extraordinary Revolutionary tradition. Rayne Guilford and Will Hearst have welcomed me to address the extraordinary young people the Hearst Foundation's United States Senate Youth Program brings to Washington

363

each spring, and Lewis Larson, president of the James Madison Memorial Fellowship Foundation, has invited me to lecture to the Madison Fellows, a group of remarkable teachers, each summer. Smarter, better prepared audiences would be hard to find. They each helped me refine my thinking and choose the right stories to illustrate my points. The young people ask the best questions.

I walked many of the battlefields of the Revolutionary War while working on this book, ending with a visit to Lexington and Concord and the Battle Road between them with my colleague Andrew Outten. When I got home I made a final adjustment to this book based on something I had just learned. Visiting battlefields builds an understanding of our shared history reading alone cannot convey. It brings us closer to the ordinary people of the past. It gives us a chance to imagine their fears and aspirations. I am indebted to the fine people of the National Park Service and the state agencies who care for our battlefields. I am inspired by the extraordinary staff of the American Battlefield Trust, especially David Duncan, Jim Campi, Garry Adelman, and the trust's president emeritus, Jim Lighthizer. My account of the Battle of Princeton was shaped during their successful campaign to save a crucial part of that battlefield. If this book leads readers to visit Princeton, Saratoga, or Fort Griswold, I will be pleased. If they walk a few miles on the Battle Road at Minuteman National Historical Park or hike up Kings Mountain, they will be richly rewarded.

I wrote this book while I was executive director of the Society of the Cincinnati and the founding director of the Society's American Revolution Institute. It reflects my twenty years of involvement with the Society and its members. Many of those members cherish the memory of ancestors who fought in the Revolutionary War and have done considerable research to recover their stories. Through them I learned about young men like David Dorrance, who served at the Siege of Boston and fought in most of the battles of Washington's army. In 1781 Captain Dorrance was shot in the groin during a raid in what is now the Bronx. It took him seventeen months to recover, but as soon as he was able he returned to his company and served until the army was discharged in the summer of 1783. He walked with a limp for the rest of his life. David Dorrance gave eight years and nearly lost his life to secure the independence of the United States. For Ross Perry, his great-great-great-great-grandson, his sacrifice is not a distant abstraction. He feels Dorrance's hand on his shoulder. So do I. Heroes of the American Revolution like David Dorrance—there were thousands of them, men and women, white and black, rich and poor alike—belong to all Americans.

At the Society of the Cincinnati, Rob Norfleet was my sponsor, friend, and mentor. Jay Jackson persuaded me of the importance of the tragedy at Fort Griswold. Forrest Pragoff worked closely with me to create and launch the American Revolution Institute, dedicated to promoting understanding and appreciation of the constructive achievements of the American Revolutionaries. Forrest also introduced me to Frenchmen—especially Raynald, duc de Choiseul, and Ambassador Bernard, marquis de Montferrand—who helped me understand our war for independence from a French point of view (attending a formal banquet at Versailles with them offered a special perspective on the dazzling social world in which Franklin, Adams, and Jay found themselves). Ross Perry and Jonathan Woods have been friends and patient, constant champions of this book. Cliff and Christine Lewis read an early draft and commented on every part. Chip Bragg, Mark Williams, and Joel Daves read a later draft and made useful suggestions. Bill and Renee Marshall made sure I appreciated the importance of Revolutionary Charleston by showing it to me. Preston Russell did the same in Savannah, where Ty Butler has offered friendly encouragement. My understanding of the Revolution in Massachusetts was enriched by Renny Little, Woody Goss, Arch O'Reilly, and Herb Motley; in New Hampshire by Ed Woods, Hollis Merrick, and Stephen Jeffries; in New Jersey by Bob Harper and Jim Burke; in Connecticut by Stephen Shaw; in Delaware by Scott Johnson and Keith Peoples; in Maryland by Philip Roulette and Tripp Onnen. Members of the New York State Society have welcomed me to discuss this project on several occasions and offered their warmest support. Members who care deeply about the future of American Revolution education—George Rich, Jack London, Fred Graham, Bill Savage, John Douglass, and Herb Berg, among them—have been champions of this work.

This project also reflects the efforts of the very fine staff of the Society of the Cincinnati with whom I was privileged to work for a generation, especially Ellen Clark, the library director, who delighted in exploring the insights offered by the Society's rich and growing collection of rare printed and manuscript materials on the art of war in the Revolutionary era, and Emily Parsons, deputy director and curator, with whom I worked on a succession of exhibitions and who was chiefly responsible for building the Society's collections of portraits, armaments, and other artifacts of the Revolutionary War and crafting the website of the American Revolution Institute, on which I have aired many of the ideas in this book. Eleesha Tucker, the Society's first director of education, challenged me to devise a summary statement on the achievements of the Revolution to help her shape educational programs. My response is the central argument of this book. Her successor Stacia Smith has used drafts as the basis for lesson plans and other educational tools. The handsome design is the work of Glenn Hennessey, a gifted visual stylist who has made my work look extraordinary (even when my prose was pedestrian). And while I was writing, the Society was sustained by the dedicated work of other members of the staff: Susan Benjamin, Zaheera Ramjag, Joseph Wong, Jason Hoffman, Andy Morse, E.K. Hong, Rachel Nellis, Diane Crespy, Paul Newman, Andrew Outten, Kathleen Higgins, Denise Austin, Clara Rubio, and Digna Vasquez. None of these fine people is responsible for what I've written, but each of them, in his or her way, helped me do it, for which I thank them.

This book and its author have benefited most from the counsel of two extraordinary and very different men. Frank Price, the founding chairman of the American Revolution Institute, is the wisest man I know. As the head of two major Hollywood studios, he oversaw the creation of some of the most successful motion pictures of all time. Few people know more about effective storytelling. Chuck Coltman is the stubborn smart older brother I never had. He has walked through every chapter with me, scowled at too much of this and pressed for more of that. His counsel is always thoughtful and his support unwavering. Both men know that how this generation of Americans understands the legacy of our Revolution will shape the future of our republic.

That leaves me to thank the people closest to this project, who happen to be the people closest to me. Emily Rose Warren, a very fine historian of early Japan, commiserates with me about the challenges of constructing historical narratives, while Audrey Louise Warren and Jack D. Warren III, both scientists, offer healthy challenges to the conclusions I've drawn from my evidence. My children are tough critics. They take after their mother. Janet is an engineer, but she prefers storytelling to analysis. I've worked hard to balance the two, but I never cease to be moved by stories of ordinary Americans whose lives were transformed by our Revolution.

List of Illustrations

The visual record of the American Revolution is astonishingly rich and remarkably varied. It is represented in this book by 172 images drawn from the collections of 71 libraries, museums, historical societies, and other institutions, as well as images provided by private collectors and dealers in rare materials and two by living artists who graciously granted permission to reproduce their work. The illustrations include photographs of paintings, artifacts, sculptures, prints, maps, broadsides, manuscripts, newspapers, pamphlets, magazines, and books. Most are from the late eighteenth century and a few from the seventeenth century. Among the works illustrated are thirty-one from the collections of the Society of the Cincinnati, for which we are grateful to the donors who made their acquisition possible. We are also grateful to the repositories, collectors, and artists that have made their collections and works available for all of us to learn from and enjoy.

Paintings are the most important images presented. The problem of relying on paintings from the period is that most of them were created for customers able to pay for them. Thus the subjects tend to be people of means. Ordinary Americans are uncommon in American art of the period, but nineteenth-century artists, working in the democratic society shaped by the Revolution, focused more attention on them, as have historical artists working in the last century. We have included photographs of historical paintings from the nineteenth century by Alonzo Chappel, Auguste Couder, Asher Durand, Eugene-Louis Lami, Emanuel Leutze, William Tylee Ranney, P.F. Rothermel, Christian Schussele, Thomas Sully, John Trumbull, and William Walcutt. Some of these paintings sacrifice the literal accuracy we are conditioned by photography to expect but express important ideas about the scenes they depict and include many more ordinary Americans than appear in eighteenth-century American art.

To these we have added turn-of-the-twentieth-century sculptures by Paul Bartlett and Samuel Murray and a very recent, scrupulously researched portrayal of an African American soldier of the Sixth Regiment of the Connecticut Continental Line by Don Troiani, the dean of modern American military artists, as well as a new sculpture of Margaret Corbin by Tracy H. Sugg, a gifted sculptor whose work reflects the courage of her subject without the sentimentality of older representations of women in the Revolutionary War.

All of the paintings listed are in oil on canvas unless otherwise indicated.

Chapter 5: Protest

Chapter 6: Resistance

Chapter 7: Americans Unite

Though the engraving is not signed by Paul Revere, he made a note in his account book on October 15, 1773, of the receipt of eighteen shillings from Isaiah Thomas for "Engraving a plate for Almanack." On the reverse page the almanac includes this text: "how wretched, how intolerable, are the last Moments of one who has made it his Business to sacrifice Mankind to accumulate a little Pelf! Look at the Engraving on the first Page, and endeavor to form some faint Idea of the Horrors that Man must endure, who owes his Greatness to his Country's Ruin, when he is about taking Leave of this World, to receive a just and proper Punishment for his Crimes. Let the Destroyers of Mankind behold and Tremble!"

Chapter 8: Intolerable Acts

Chapter 9: Colonists at War

Notes

The Revolutionary generation left us with a rich and varied documentary record of their thoughts and activities. Thanks to them, the liberation of the American people from colonial rule and the establishment of the United States is more clearly documented than the founding of any other important nation in the world. Some of the leaders of the Revolution, including George Washington, John Adams, and Thomas Jefferson, were acutely aware that they were participants in one of the great events in history and carefully preserved their papers for subsequent generations to read. Others, including Samuel Adams, Patrick Henry, and James Wilson, were indifferent record keepers, but we nonetheless can know a remarkable amount about them. Thousands of ordinary Americans were equally conscious that they were participants in important events and left us with diaries, letters, and other records of their thoughts and actions.

We also owe thanks to the many historians and antiquarians of the nineteenth century who collected and in many cases edited and published documents from the Revolutionary generation that might otherwise have been scattered and lost. We can know as much as we do about the early western frontier because of the extraordinary industry of Lyman Draper, about the political and constitutional history of the Revolution thanks to Peter Force, and about scores of other topics, large and small, thanks to the people who gathered documents and interviewed people who participated in the Revolution, including many hundreds of ordinary people, before their stories died with them.

We are also indebted to the documentary editors who have labored for the last century to collect, transcribe, annotate, and publish the papers of the leading Revolutionaries. Our ability to understand them and appreciate their achievements is based on the work of Lyman Butterfield and his successors in bringing us the Adams family papers; Julian Boyd and the editors who followed him in bringing us *The Papers of Thomas Jefferson*; W.W. Abbot, Dorothy Twohig, Philander Chase, and their colleagues at *The Papers of George Washington*; and all of their peers who have brought us modern scholarly editions of the papers of Benjamin Franklin, James Madison, Alexander Hamilton, Henry Laurens, and Nathanael Greene, as well as more modest editions of the papers of George Mason, the correspondence of Benjamin Rush, letters of delegates to Congress, and other documentary editions that smooth the way for new scholarship and offer general access to materials that were once accessible only to specialists able to travel to the repositories where the originals are held.

Some of the notes below are presented as examples of the critical analysis of sources. Attentive readers should always be prepared to ask how a historian knows something, especially when that something is a quotation from someone from the period. The answer in such cases is often a reference to a surviving document written by the person quoted, but sometimes the answer is much more complicated, especially when it involves something a person quoted is alleged to have said. How do we know what Captain John Parker said to the militia assembled on the Lexington Green on the morning of April 19, 1775? Did he say, "Stand your ground. Don't fire unless fired upon, but if they mean to have a war, let it begin here"? That's what's carved on the boulder on the green marking the spot where the militia assembled to face the British Regulars. Did an American officer tell the men on Bunker Hill not to fire on the approaching Regulars until they could see the whites of their eyes? Did the Hessian commander at Trenton really respond to advice to prepare for an attack by saying, "Fiddlesticks! These clodhoppers will not attack us"? Would a native speaker of German have used words like "fiddlesticks" and "clodhoppers"? Quotations like these get repeated in our history books, often by one historian citing another historian, neither of whom traced the quotation to its source and weighed its reliability. Respecting the scholarship of the past doesn't mean accepting it uncritically.

In many cases critical analysis is inconclusive. Absolute certainty is elusive, but it almost always gets us closer to understanding and it sharpens our critical faculties. Explore what Parker said on Lexington Green and you will learn a tremendous amount about who was there that morning, what they saw, what they heard, and what they remembered. The sources you'll encounter will lead you to ask and answer questions you would not have thought of otherwise. You'll end with a deeper understanding of the event and a greater appreciation for the ordinary people who participated in it.

Epigraph

Posterity! You will never know, how much it cost the present Generation . . . John Adams to Abigail Adams, April 26, 1777, Lyman H. Butterfield, ed., *Adams Family Correspondence,* vol. 2: June 1776–March 1778 (Cambridge, MA: Harvard University Press, 1963), 223–24.

Preface: Why Is America Free?

"As he had been a brave soldier . . ." [caption] *Maryland Gazette,* November 10, 1825.

I: British America

Numerous as the people are in the several old provinces, they cost you nothing . . . Benjamin Franklin, Examination Before the Committee of the Whole of the House of Commons, February 13, 1766, Leonard W. Labaree, ed., *The Papers of Benjamin Franklin,* vol. 13: January 1–December 31, 1766 (New Haven: Yale University Press, 1969), 124–62.

Chapter 1: The People of British America

Opening

The story of the American Revolution begins in the sixteenth and seventeenth centuries . . . J.H. Parry, *The Establishment of European Hegemony, 1415–1715: Trade and Exploration in the Age of the Renaissance* (New York: Harper & Row, 1961) is a superb, concise introduction to European expansion in the early modern era. *See also* G.V. Scammell, *The First Imperial Age: European Overseas Expansion, c. 1400–1715* (London: Routledge, 1992).

Their first settlement on the North American mainland was on Roanoke Island . . . On the abortive efforts to establish an English settlement on Roanoke Island, *see* David Beers Quinn, *Set Fair for Roanoke: Voyages and Colonies, 1584–1606* (Chapel Hill: University of North Carolina Press, 1985), and Karen Ordahl Kupperman, *Roanoke: The Abandoned Colony* (2nd revised edition, Lanham, MD: Rowman & Littlefield, 2007).

The English and the Indians

The English were not sure what to make of these Indians. Nor were the Indians sure what to make of the new arrivals. Bernard Bailyn, *The Barbarous Years: The Peopling of British North America—the Conflict of Civilizations, 1600–1675* (New York: Alfred A. Knopf, 2012) is a highly original treatment of the conflicted and often violent involvement of European migrants with Indians, written with sensitivity to the rich cultural and spiritual traditions of the Indians that were challenged by the presence of Europeans who did not share in their ways.

When the weather was bad or crops failed for some other reason, people in Europe sometimes starved. *See* Andrew Appleby, *Famine in Tudor and Stuart England* (Stanford: Stanford University Press, 1978).

Eastern Woodland Indian farming produced much less food per acre . . . Indian agriculture was not, however, as primitive or inefficient as might be imagined. Their staple crop, corn or maize, has more calories than wheat and the other small grains Europeans grew per unit volume, and Indians practiced mixed culture and allowed fields to lie fallow, both of which are better for maintaining soil fertility than European practices, though the evidence of these Indian practices is sparse and largely anecdotal. That European migrants soon adopted corn, beans, and other Indian staples is not a surprise. For a comparison of Indian and English agriculture in the early seventeenth century, *see* Edmund S. Morgan, *American Slavery, American Freedom: The Ordeal of Colonial Virginia* (New York: W.W. Norton, 1975), 52–58, 64. On the productivity of Indian agriculture in Virginia, *see* Alan Taylor, *American Colonies: The Settling of North America* (New York: Penguin Books, 2001), 126, 189. Taylor's work is a

remarkable synthesis of more than a generation of scholarship on colonial America.

That distrust frequently led to violence and often to war . . . On the violent relationship between migrants and Indians, *see* Taylor, *American Colonies,* esp. 131–33, 194–202. On early Virginia, *see* Frederick Gleach, *Powhatan's World and Colonial Virginia: A Conflict of Cultures* (Lincoln: University of Nebraska Press, 1997).

The Disorderly Empire

A new group of English settlers arrived in America in 1607. Morgan, *American Slavery, American Freedom* sets the peopling of early Virginia against the background of poverty and chronic underemployment in England, which provided a reservoir of cheap indentured labor for the early Chesapeake, and traces the social and economic changes that ultimately made enslaved Africans a cheaper alternative and created a division between poor whites and enslaved Africans that fostered the development of racism. Some of Morgan's conclusions are subject to debate, but the logic of his argument remains compelling.

It was a disorderly empire, created without a plan. Nick Bunker, *Empire on the Edge: How Britain Came to Fight America* (New York: Alfred A. Knopf, 2014), contends that the old colonial regime historians call the first British Empire "never really amounted to an empire at all, in the way a Russian tsar or Queen Victoria might understand" (p. 28). He points to the varied aims and private or corporate nature of British colonial ventures in the seventeenth century as a source of the disorder imperial reformers of the 1760s were intent on eliminating.

Migrants

Today we would call them migrants, because the most striking thing about them was that they left Britain and other European countries and risked their lives to move thousands of miles . . . The circumstances that led people to migrate—the push of poverty and even hopelessness, the pull of making some kind of better life—is hard to discern for most individuals beyond small and well-documented groups like the first settlers of Plymouth. Bernard Bailyn, *Voyagers to the West: A Passage in the Peopling of British North America on the Eve of the Revolution* (New York: Vintage Books, 1986) is based on an extraordinary register of every emigrant known to have left Britain for America between December 1773 and March 1776. Of those thousands, some hundreds of stories of ordinary people, with varied needs and ambitions, come into focus—where they came from, the pressures that led them to emigrate, and their ultimate destinations in British America. This group was part of a larger surge of migrants who came to British America after the French and Indian War, many of whom wound up in the backcountry and compounded the rising challenges to the British Empire on the American frontier. *See also* Nicholas Canny, "English Migration into and across the Atlantic During the Seventeenth and Eighteenth Centuries," in Nicholas Canny, ed., *Europeans on the Move: Studies in European Migration, 1500–1800* (Oxford: Clarendon Press, 1994), 39–75.

Most were fleeing oppression, whether it was religious discrimination or simply the oppression of poverty, unem-

ployment, hunger, and hopelessness. The rural peasants who made up most of the English population were sliding into distress in the latter part of the sixteenth century and the first half of the seventeenth, a period of depressed prices and underemployment punctuated by occasional famines. Economic growth failed to keep pace with the population, which grew from four to five million between 1600 and 1650. *See* Keith Wrightson, *English Society, 1580–1680* (London: Hutchinson, 1982). Conditions in England were relatively better in the eighteenth century, but in some areas only marginally. Elsewhere famine killed 400,000 people in Ireland in 1739–1741.

They had little voice in the decisions of government, and few of them expected to share in making those decisions. Ordinary people might participate in popular politics—riots and mob actions and various kinds of rituals expressing support for the institutions of public life. *See,* e.g., David Underdown, *Revel, Riot & Rebellion: Popular Politics and Culture in England, 1603–1660* (New York: Oxford University Press, 1985). Mob action, rioting, and other forms of popular politics played an important role in public life in Britain in the 1760s and 1770s. *See* John Brewer, *Party Ideology and Popular Politics at the Accession of George III* (New York: Cambridge University Press, 1976).

Ordinary people were nowhere free to speak their minds . . . David Colclough, *Freedom of Speech in Early Stuart England* (Cambridge: Cambridge University Press, 2005) illustrates the severe limitations on the very concept of free speech, much less its acknowledgment as a natural right.

Religious Refugees

Many of the early colonists were refugees from religious oppression. Alan Taylor (*American Colonies,* 339) cautions against assuming seventeenth-century English men and women fled religious persecution to secure religious freedom in America. Most of the dissenters—Quakers and some smaller sects who understood their minority status excepted—looked forward to imposing their own kind of orthodoxy.

By the middle of the eighteenth century, British America was home to people from more religious traditions . . . *See* Jon Butler, *New World Faiths: Religion in Colonial America* (New York: Oxford University Press, 2007).

Servants and Freeholders

To earn their passage, many poor people agreed to work as servants without pay . . . Abbot Emerson Smith, *Colonists in Bondage: White Servitude and Convict Labor in America, 1607–1776* (Chapel Hill: University of North Carolina Press, 1947), despite many more recent works involving indentured servitude, remains a useful starting point.

"many Hundreds are sterving for want of employment . . ." Edward M. Riley, ed., *The Journal of John Harrower, an Indentured Servant in the Colony of Virginia, 1773–1776* (Williamsburg: Colonial Williamsburg, 1963), 14–18 (January 24, 1774). *See also* Bailyn, *Voyagers to the West,* 276–78.

Some never did and lived out their lives as farm laborers or tenant farmers. Despite the abundance of undeveloped land, tenancy was on the rise through much of eighteenth-century British America. *See* Lucy Simler, "Tenancy in Colonial Pennsylvania: The Case of Chester County," *William and Mary Quarterly,* 3rd ser., vol. 43, no. 4 (1986): 542–69; Sung

Bok Kim, *Landlord and Tenant in Colonial New York: Manorial Society, 1664–1775* (Chapel Hill: University of North Carolina Press, 1978).

Those who became freeholders achieved a kind of personal independence . . . On the social and cultural dynamics of the farm economy, including the evolving distinction between regions and the pressures exerted by eighteenth-century population growth and the demand for new land to farm, *see* Alan Kulikoff, *From British Peasants to Colonial American Farmers* (Chapel Hill: University of North Carolina Press, 2000), and Richard Lyman Bushman, *The American Farmer in the Eighteenth Century: A Social and Cultural History* (New Haven: Yale University Press, 2018). *See also* James T. Lemon, *The Best Poor Man's Country: A Geographical Study of Early Southeastern Pennsylvania* (Baltimore: Johns Hopkins University Press, 1972).

The Gentry

They were not aristocrats. They were mostly the sons, grandsons . . . Darrett B. Rutman and Anita H. Rutman, *A Place in Time: Middlesex County, Virginia, 1650–1750* (W.W. Norton, 1984) examines the social evolution of a single county in tidewater Virginia (for which the documentation is unusually good) over a century, charting the decline of a scattered community of farms worked by indentured servants and the growth of larger plantations worked by large numbers of enslaved people (the black population went from seven percent to more than fifty over that time) presided over by established gentry families. With regional and local variations and accounting for contingent circumstances, this sort of pattern was repeated all over British America as families favored with success over a few generations came to dominate local government, church affairs, and economic activity.

Members of this American gentry lived in gracious country homes . . . Hunter Dickinson Farish, ed., *The Journal and Letters of Philip Vickers Fithian: A Plantation Tutor in the Old Dominion* (Williamsburg: Colonial Williamsburg, 1943) is the insightful diary, supplemented by some personal letters, of a young Princeton graduate who served as tutor on the plantation of Robert Carter on the eve of the Revolutionary War. Fithian had never before been to Virginia, and his diary is distinguished by the kinds of reflections about the plantation gentry, which constituted a clearly defined social class, only a newcomer would have offered.

The Enslaved

On the opposite end of the social scale from the gentry were enslaved Africans . . . The literature on and related to the African-American experience in the seventeenth and eighteenth centuries is now so rich that we have to organize it thematically. A large body of work deals with slavery as an institution, and involves the legal and political conditions under which enslavement spread, was maintained, and ultimately dismantled. Although of enormous importance to the lives of African Americans, much of this institutional history of slavery is about the white people who made the laws and managed the institutions. Studies of abolition and emancipation are an important exception. Formerly, such studies focused mainly on white actors, but the agency of enslaved and free blacks in securing emancipation is the focus of much recent work. On the painfully slow end of slavery, Ira Berlin, *The Long Emancipation: The Demise of Slavery in the United States* (Cambridge, MA: Harvard University Press, 2015) is an excellent place to begin.

A second body of work deals with the history of racism. This work, too, is mostly about white people. While several important books address this theme, including Edmund S. Morgan, *American Slavery, American Freedom,* the most important remains Winthrop Jordan, *White Over Black: American Attitudes toward the Negro, 1550–1812* (Chapel Hill: University of North Carolina Press, 1968), a sprawling intellectual history that lays bare the social and psychological circumstances that led whites to classify blacks as inferior and suited only for exploitation and manual labor.

Another body of work deals with the experience of enslaved people. Among the most important for this period are Ira Berlin, *Many Thousands Gone: The First Two Centuries of Slavery in North America* (Cambridge, MA: Harvard University Press, 1998), and Philip Morgan, *Slave Counterpoint: Black Culture in the Eighteenth-Century Chesapeake and Low Country* (Chapel Hill: University of North Carolina Press, 1998).

The experience of free blacks is the focus of James Oliver Horton and Lois M. Horton, *In Hope of Liberty: Culture, Community, and Protest among Northern Free Blacks, 1700–1860* (New York: Oxford University Press, 1997), and Gary B. Nash, *Forging Freedom: The Formation of Philadelphia's Black Community, 1720–1840* (Cambridge, MA: Harvard University Press, 1998).

These categories are not rigid. Many studies contribute to more than one line of inquiry. This scholarly literature is now so rich that it constitutes a large and important part of American history. David Brion Davis, *Inhuman Bondage: The Rise and Fall of Slavery in the New World* (New York: Oxford University Press, 2006) is an extraordinary synthesis of the work done up to that point, achieving originality even as it draws on the work of others.

Chapter 2: The Limits of Freedom
King and Parliament

The House of Commons . . . did not, in fact, represent the common people. Parliament dramatically increased its power at the expense of the monarchy in the seventeenth century. Nineteenth- and twentieth-century historians celebrated this as a major step in the development of free institutions, but it remains far from clear how ordinary English men and women benefited from this change, since their influence in Parliament was no greater than their influence with the Crown, and neither sought to improve their lot. For many British subjects, such freedoms as they enjoyed seem to have been eroding in the seventeenth and eighteenth centuries. On the organization and functioning of the British government in the middle of the eighteenth century, *see* Lewis Namier, *The Structure of Politics at the Ascension of George III* (London: Macmillan, 1957). Startling when it was published, Namier's meticulous portrait of the political world dismissed the importance of lofty principles and focused on personal relationships, patronage and clientage, logrolling and corrupt dealing among country oligarchs and the king's ministers.

There was nothing remotely democratic about the distribution of the seats or the way elections were conducted.

The wholly unrepresentative way the House of Commons was organized, the archaic nature of the franchise, and the oligarchic control of the seats is documented in rich detail in Edward Porritt, *The Unreformed House of Commons: Parliamentary Representative before 1832* (2 vols., Cambridge: Cambridge University Press, 1909).

In truth the British government was an oligarchy . . . Peter Jupp, *The Governing of Britain, 1688–1848: The Executive, Parliament and the People* (New York: Routledge, 2006) effectively describes the administrative machinery responsible for managing the state and its empire.

The Rulers and the Ruled

"an odious title" Horace Walpole, *Memoirs of the Reign of King George the Third,* vol. 1 (London: Richard Bentley, 1845), 113. Reporting on a 1761 debate in the House of Commons, Walpole quoted Grenville: "He had heard with surprise that *one* man ought to direct. What had been the constant charge against Sir Robert Walpole, but his acting as sole minister? Yet his modesty had declined the appellation. Prime Minister was an odious title: he was sorry it was now thought an essential part of the constitution."

Life was held cheap. On crime and punishment, *see,* e.g., Douglas Hay, Peter Linebaugh, et al., *Albion's Fatal Tree: Crime and Society in Eighteenth Century England* (New York: Pantheon Books, 1975). For good measure, read John Langbein, "Albion's Fatal Flaws," *Past & Present,* no. 98 (February 1983): 96–120, a response seeking to refute the Marxist interpretation presented in the lead essay, "Property, Authority and the Criminal Law." Nicholas Rogers, *Mayhem: Post-War Crime and Violence in Britain, 1748–1753* (New Haven: Yale University Press, 2013) illustrates how instability and violence wracked British society in the middle of the eighteenth century and how authorities tried to deal with these challenges to the social order with harsher laws, increasingly invasive regulation, surveillance, penal transportation, and public executions.

Penal transportation to Britain's American colonies was employed . . . *See* A. Roger Ekirch, *Bound for America: The Transportation of British Convicts to the Colonies, 1718–1775* (Oxford: Clarendon Press, 1987). On colonial Australia's beginning as a penal colony to replace British America as a dumping ground for the "criminal class," *see* Robert Hughes, *The Fatal Shore: The Epic of Australia's Founding* (New York: Alfred A. Knopf, 1986). The story offers grim insight into the imperial vision of the authoritarian reformers against whom Americans fought.

Their appearance . . . religious practices, inability to speak English, and African customs made them . . . *See* Jordan, *White Over Black,* 3–43.

Governing the Colonies

To the people of British America, the government that presided over the empire was both distant and almost incomprehensible. On the other side, British administrators fumed about the irrationality of an American empire, including the West Indies, composed of thirty separate colonies, twenty-five with their own legislature, local laws, and claims to charter, proprietary, or some other kind of special privileges. *See* Nick Bunker, *Empire on the Edge: How Britain Came to Fight America* (New York: Alfred A. Knopf, 2014), 106–8.

"**the governor, representing the King . . .**" William Douglass, *A Summary, Historical and Political, of the First Planting, Progressive Improvements, and Present State of the British Settlements in North-America* (London: reprinted for A. Baldwin, 1755), 214.

The analogy was commonly advanced, but colonial government actually bore little resemblance to the British government. The colonists, moreover, were aware of this fact, and it caused many of them considerable anxiety. If Britain's success and the preservation of its celebrated liberty were due to the genius of its balanced constitution, the excessive authority of colonial governors, and executive power in general, seemed like a threat to liberty. This anxiety about the threat that power poses to liberty is the central theme of Bernard Bailyn, *The Origins of American Politics* (New York: Alfred A. Knopf, 1968).

Through the first half of the eighteenth century, the Crown and Parliament devoted little attention to the affairs of their North American colonies. James Henretta, *Salutary Neglect: Colonial Administration under the Duke of Newcastle* (Princeton: Princeton University Press, 1972) follows the tenure of Thomas Pelham-Holles, duke of Newcastle, who was appointed secretary of state for the southern department, charged with most aspects of executive administration in British America, in 1724. Newcastle held that post until 1748 and thereafter moved to the northern department before becoming first lord of the treasury. He exerted enormous influence over British American affairs. Bureaucratic inertia, indolence, and a succession of political distractions shaped his long tenure, and ensured that the fundamental constitutional, political, and increasingly economic issues that ultimately divided Britain and the colonies went unaddressed.

Jack P. Greene, *The Constitutional Origins of the American Revolution* (New York: Cambridge University Press, 2010) contends that the failure of British ministers and the king's American subjects to reach an understanding about the constitutional arrangements defining the governance of the colonies in the second quarter of the eighteenth century was a fundamental precondition of the constitutional crisis that preceded the Revolutionary War. Each colony had its own constitutional relationship to Britain, Greene explains, including those defined by proprietary privileges and corporate charters. The imperial crisis of the 1760s and 1770s was shaped by British intransigence—a refusal to accept the sanctity of colonial charters and the colonists' understanding of their relationship to the empire. Greene's work, including *The Quest for Power: The Lower Houses of Assembly in the Southern Royal Colonies, 1689–1776* (1963) and *Peripheries and Center: Constitutional Development in the Extended Polities of the British Empire and the United States, 1607–1789* (1986), locates the origins of the American Revolution in the constitutional and political development of the colonies, which was intertwined with, but distinct from, their economic, social, and cultural development and the intellectual and ideological preoccupations of Revolutionary leaders.

Under the circumstances, local government had more influence in the lives of ordinary colonists than the governors or assemblies. On the role of county gentry in public life in Virginia, the largest and most populous colony, *see* Charles S. Sydnor, *Gentlemen Freeholders: Political Practices in Washington's Virginia* (Chapel Hill: University of North Carolina

Press, 1952, published in 1965 as *American Revolutionaries in the Making*.

Among the institutions of local government, Douglas Edward Leach, *Arms for Empire: A Military History of the British Colonies in North America, 1607–1763* (New York: Macmillan, 1973) makes it clear that the militia was a vital part of life in British America in the eighteenth century, at the same time it was declining in importance in Britain. For most of the colonial era the British government expected the colonists to take care of their own military needs and they generally did. In the wars of the eighteenth century, the appearance of British Regulars in the colonies led to mutual antagonism that prefigured the resentment of the Regulars in Boston during the last years before the Revolutionary War.

The Rule of Law

More important was the English Bill of Rights of 1689 . . . Lois G. Schwoerer, *The Declaration of Rights, 1689* (Baltimore: Johns Hopkins University Press, 1981) provides a historical and constitutional overview of the English Bill of Rights.

Possession of these rights was one of many ways eighteenth-century Britons distinguished their country . . . By the eve of the American Revolution, it was clear to serious political thinkers that the rule of law was essential to the promotion and preservation of liberty. Adam Smith, the Scottish writer who defined the free market economics that form the basis of the modern liberal order, contended that liberty requires the regular administration of justice and ultimately the rule of law as a means of checking the power of monarchs and aristocrats. Smith argued that "upon the impartial administration of justice depends the liberty of every individual, the sense which he has of his own security." Adam Smith, *An Inquiry into the Nature and Causes of the Wealth of Nations*, vol. 2 (2nd ed., London: Printed for W. Strahan and T. Cadell, 1778), 331.

The Conditions of Freedom

Literacy was more widespread in Britain's American colonies than almost anywhere else. On this theme, *see* Kenneth Lockridge, *Literacy in Colonial New England* (New York: W.W. Norton, 1974), and more recently, E. Jennifer Monaghan, *Learning to Read and Write in Colonial America* (Amherst: University of Massachusetts Press, 2007), which addresses all parts of the British American mainland and includes Indians and African Americans.

"**several renowned generals but three feet high**" John Adams, March 15, 1756, in Lyman H. Butterfield, ed., *Diary and Autobiography of John Adams*, vol. 1: 1755–1770 (Cambridge, MA: Harvard University Press, 1961), 13–14.

"**who cannot read or write . . . is as rare as a comet . . .**" John Adams, "A Dissertation on the Canon and the Feudal Law," Number 3, September 30, 1765, in Robert J. Taylor, ed., *Papers of John Adams*, vol. 1: September 1755–October 1773 (Cambridge, MA: Harvard University Press, 1977), 118–23.

Degrees of Freedom

Freedom was fragmented and limited along social lines. Society in British America was stratified in the same way as British society—organized along vertical line of patronage, clientage, and dependence rather than horizontally along lines of social class. The chief difference was that no British American possessed the kind of wealth, prestige, or influence enjoyed by the British aristocracy. America also lacked a chronically poor white underclass, although the presence of the enslaved more than made up for this difference. For an able description of the social hierarchy in eighteenth-century Britain, see Roy Porter, *English Society in the Eighteenth Century* (New York: Penguin Books, 1982), 63–112.

Women of all ages and social ranks were the largest group of unfree people in British America. *See* Carol Berkin, *First Generations: Women in Colonial America* (New York: Hill and Wang, 1996), an able synthesis of a remarkably diffuse but important subject—half of the people of British America, white, black, and Indian, free and enslaved, rich and poor.

Chapter 3: A World of Ideas
Opening

Britain's American colonies grew and prospered during a time of enormous intellectual and practical creativity . . . The literature on the Enlightenment is vast. Students of the Enlightenment should all be acquainted with Peter Gay's two-volume history of the movement: *The Enlightenment: An Interpretation—The Rise of Modern Paganism* (New York: Alfred A. Knopf, 1966) and *The Enlightenment: An Interpretation—The Science of Freedom* (New York: Alfred A. Knopf, 1969). Neither of these volumes is light reading. A sprightly introduction that draws the connection between the scientific outlook of the Enlightenment and the American Revolution is found in Timothy Ferris, *The Science of Liberty: Democracy, Reason, and the Laws of Nature* (New York: HarperCollins, 2010), 57–88.

Natural Rights

Philosophers called these *natural rights*, because they are the result of our natural condition. On Locke and natural rights, and ultimately on his influence on the Revolutionary generation, see Michael P. Zuckert, *Natural Rights and the New Republicanism* (Princeton: Princeton University Press, 1994).

The idea that all people possess certain fundamental rights . . . was, as late as 1770, a theoretical construct. On the rise of natural rights as an ethical concept involving inescapable imperatives rather than a philosophical abstraction, *see* Lynn Hunt, *Inventing Human Rights: A History* (New York: W.W. Norton, 2007). See, in particular, her chapter on the abolition of torture, 79–112.

The Science of Government

The development of natural rights theory was only one of many intellectual accomplishments of the Enlightenment. Never before had philosophy comprehended so many fields of intellectual endeavor and bridged the divide between them, particularly the divide between science, morality, and political thought, facilitating the emergence of an ambitious science of politics. "The interpenetration of philosophy with science and mathematics in the early modern period," writes

Scott Soames, "was matched by its interpenetration with emerging descriptive and normative investigations of politics, economics, morality and the relationship between the individual and the state." Scott Soames, *The World Philosophy Made: From Plato to the Digital Age* (Princeton: Princeton University Press, 1997), 73–91. The result was the theoretical foundation of limited government and its corollaries, free markets and free people.

"wise enough to govern themselves" and **"their statesmen are patriots"** [caption] William Barton, *Memoirs of the Life of David Rittenhouse* (Philadelphia: Edward Parker, 1813), 543–577. The quoted passages are on pp. 520 and 566.

"the constant and universal principles of human nature" David Hume, "An Enquiry Concerning Human Understanding," in David Hume, *Essays and Treatises on Several Subjects* (2 vols., London: Printed for T. Cadell, 1777), 2:83. Hume tinkered with his work throughout life. This was the first edition of the essay published after his death in 1776, and includes his final revisions. The key passage for understanding Hume's project to create a science of human nature asserts that people are fundamentally the same regardless of the time and place in which they live and that their actions have common aims. Based on this insight, Hume believed that politics—the proper organization of public life—could be reduced to a science:

"It is universally acknowledged that there is a great uniformity among the actions of men, in all nations and ages, and that human nature remains still the same, in its principles and operations. The same motives always produce the same actions: the same events follow from the same causes. Ambition, avarice, self-love, vanity, friendship, generosity, public spirit: these passions, mixed in various degrees, and distributed through society, have been, from the beginning of the world, and still are, the source of all the actions and enterprises, which have ever been observed among mankind. Would you know the sentiments, inclinations, and course of life of the Greeks and Romans? Study well the temper and actions of the French and English: You cannot be much mistaken in transferring to the former most of the observations which you have made with regard to the latter. Mankind are so much the same, in all times and places, that history informs us of nothing new or strange in this particular. Its chief use is only to discover the constant and universal principles of human nature, by showing men in all varieties of circumstances and situations, and furnishing us with materials from which we may form our observations and become acquainted with the regular springs of human action and behaviour. These records of wars, intrigues, factions, and revolutions, are so many collections of experiments, by which the politician or moral philosopher fixes the principles of his science, in the same manner as the physician or natural philosopher becomes acquainted with the nature of plants, minerals, and other external objects, by the experiments which he forms concerning them. Nor are the earth, water, and other elements, examined by Aristotle, and Hippocrates, more like to those which at present lie under our observation than the men described by Polybius and Tacitus are to those who now govern the world."

The anticlerical ideas of the Enlightenment had little relevance in America . . . On the distinctive character of the Enlightenment in British America, *see* Henry May, *The*

Enlightenment in America (New York: Oxford University Press, 1976). See also Henry Steele Commager, The Empire of Reason: How Europe Imagined and America Realized the Enlightenment (Garden City, NY: Doubleday, 1977), and Gertrude Himmelfarb, The Roads to Modernity: The British, French, and American Enlightenments (New York: Random House, 2008).

The Humanitarian Impulse

This humanitarian impulse went beyond the kinds of charity encouraged for centuries by the church. See Sidney James, A People among Peoples: Quaker Benevolence in Eighteenth-Century America (Cambridge, MA: Harvard University Press, 1963), and Thomas Haskell, "Capitalism and the Origins of the Humanitarian Sensibility," American Historical Review 90 (April–June 1985). While there are many fine specialized and local studies, the complexity and diffuse nature of humanitarian activity in eighteenth-century America has so far defied synthesis.

Those who embraced this new humanitarian spirit were confident that many kinds of suffering and want could be eliminated. Few people exemplify the idealism of eighteenth-century humanitarianism in America better than Benjamin Rush, whose interests included public health, criminal justice reform, the elimination of poverty, and other causes. See George W. Corner, ed., The Autobiography of Benjamin Rush: His "Travels Through Life," Together with His Commonplace Book for 1789–1813 (Princeton: Published by Princeton University Press for the American Philosophical Society, 1948).

"agreeable and wholesome variety of food" and **"the strongest men and the most beautiful women."** Adam Smith, An Inquiry into the Nature and Causes of the Wealth of Nations, vol. 1 (London: Printed for W. Strahan and T. Cadell, 1776), 95, 201.

"Men would multiply, and poverty . . . would be unknown." William Buchan, Domestic Medicine . . . to which are added Observation on the Diet of the Common People; Recommending a Method of Living Less Expensive, and more Conducive to Health, than the Present (Leominster, MA: Printed by Adam & Wilder for Isaiah Thomas, 1804), 404.

"More than half the habitable world . . . is still populated by two-footed animals . . ." Voltaire, The Works of Voltaire: A Contemporary Version with notes by Tobias Smollett . . . new translations by William F. Fleming, vol. 11 (Paris: E.R. DuMont, 1901), 186.

The Beginning of Abolitionism

The humanitarian impulse led many people to indignant opposition to slavery. Early antislavery thought drew heavily on the spirit and language of humanitarianism. See especially Margaret Abruzzo, Polemical Pain: Slavery, Cruelty, and the Rise of Humanitarianism (Baltimore: Johns Hopkins University Press, 2011). Ultimately, she demonstrates that humanitarian ideals became so ubiquitous that pro-slavery polemicists of the early nineteenth century argued that emancipation was unacceptable because they alleged it was cruel and that enslavement was a benefit to the enslaved. Abruzzo regards such ambiguous uses of humanitarian rhetoric as evidence of humanitarianism's intellectual instability. Rising repugnance to slavery's cruelty, especially after 1830, demonstrates its importance.

"the Quakers of Pennsylvania, are the first body of men . . ." James Millar, The Origin of the Distinction of Ranks: or, An Enquiry into the Circumstances which Give Rise to Influence and Authority, in the Different Members of Society (Edinburgh: Printed for William Blackwood, 1806), 273.

No one embodied the principles of Quaker benevolence . . . more fully than Anthony Benezet . . . See Maurice Jackson, Let This Voice Be Heard: Anthony Benezet, Father of Atlantic Abolitionism (Philadelphia: University of Pennsylvania Press, 2009).

"I have found amongst the negroes as great a variety of talents, as amongst a like number of whites . . ." Roberts Vaux, Memoirs of the Life of Anthony Benezet (Philadelphia: Published by James F. Parke, 1817), 22.

Benjamin Franklin

Among the people Anthony Benezet convinced of the evils of slavery was Benjamin Franklin . . . Edmund S. Morgan, Benjamin Franklin (New Haven: Yale University Press, 2002), a graceful, insightful, and compact biography, stands out among the many books on Franklin.

Although Franklin delighted in the world of ideas, he turned continuously to their practical application . . . See Alan Rogers, Benjamin Franklin and the Politics of Improvement (New Haven: Yale University Press, 2008).

He retired from business in 1748 and thereafter devoted himself completely to public service. That Franklin considered retiring from trade a prerequisite to active public service, especially holding elective office, is explored in Gordon S. Wood, The Americanization of Benjamin Franklin (New York: Penguin Press, 2005).

"I would rather have it said, He lived usefully, than, He died rich." Leonard W. Labaree, ed., The Papers of Benjamin Franklin, vol. 3: January 1, 1745–June 30, 1750 (New Haven: Yale University Press, 1961), 474–75.

"I am very sorry, that you intend soon to leave our Hemisphere . . ." David Hume to Benjamin Franklin, May 10, 1762, in Leonard W. Labaree, ed., The Papers of Benjamin Franklin, vol. 10: January 1, 1762–December 31, 1763 (New Haven: Yale University Press, 1959), 80–82.

"against their own nation, which protects and encourages them . . ." Benjamin Franklin, The Interest of Great Britain Considered, With Regard to her Colonies, And the Acquisitions of Canada and Guadaloupe. To which are added, Observations concerning the Increase of Mankind, Peopling of Countries, &c. (London: Printed for T. Becket, 1760), reprinted in Leonard W. Labaree, ed., The Papers of Benjamin Franklin, vol. 9: January 1, 1760–December 31, 1761 (New Haven: Yale University Press, 1966), 47–100.

American Revival

By the middle of the eighteenth century, Britain's mainland colonies were home to an extraordinarily diverse array of Protestant denominations. See Butler, New World Faiths.

"old, rotten, and stinking routine religion" This charge was made by John Henry Goetschius, a New Light Dutch Reformed Church minister who preached in barns and open fields in the manner of George Whitfield; quoted in Randall H. Balmer, A Perfect Babel of Confusion: Dutch Religion and

English Culture in the Middle Colonies (New York: Oxford University Press, 1989), 127. I am grateful to Alan Taylor for pointing to this source.

"multitudes were seriously, soberly and solemnly out of their wits." Ezra Stiles (1761), quoted in Sydney E. Ahlstrom, *A Religious History of the American People* (2nd ed., New Haven: Yale University Press, 2004), 404.

This approach to matters of faith was shared, with important variations, by many of the men who led the American Revolution. On George Washington and religion, see Mary V. Thompson, *"In the Hands of a Good Providence": Religion in the Life of George Washington* (Charlottesville: University of Virginia Press, 2008). Washington's many references to Providence make it clear that he was not a Deist.

The revivals weakened the hold of traditional churches on many communities and led many colonists to assert greater personal independence in matters of religion. On the connection between the revivals and the American Revolution, see Alan Heimert, *Religion and the American Mind: From the Great Awakening to the Revolution* (Cambridge, MA: Harvard University Press, 1966), and Nathan Hatch, *The Sacred Cause of Liberty: Republican Thought and the Millennium in Revolutionary New England* (New Haven: Yale University Press, 1977).

Chapter 4: The Frontiers of Empire

American Empires

By far the largest and most populous of the European empires in the Western Hemisphere . . . J.H. Parry, *Trade and Dominion: The European Overseas Empires in the Eighteenth Century* (New York: Praeger, 1971)defines the large-scale economic, social, political, and technological dynamics that shaped the European maritime empires in the eighteenth century without losing sight of the contingent decisions that shaped each of them.

The Spanish empire reached across the future states of Texas, New Mexico, and Arizona to southern California . . . Alan Taylor, *American Colonies*, 396–477, recognizing that the early modern history of what would become the United States is not limited to British America but includes the peoples living west of the Mississippi and on the Pacific.

The Ohio Country

By 1750 the prospect of occupying land to the west of the Appalachians was beginning to stir the imagination of colonists . . . On the Indians of the region, *see* Michael McConnell, *A Country Between: The Upper Ohio Valley and Its People, 1724–1774* (Lincoln: University of Nebraska Press, 1992), which addresses conflict along the frontier between Indians and British Americans from an Indian perspective. For those unfamiliar with the Indians of the region, Paul R. Misencik and Sally E. Misencik, *American Indians of the Ohio Country in the Eighteenth Century* (Jefferson, NC: McFarland, 2020) is a useful introduction. The Miami, Wyandot (or Huron), Delaware (or Lenape), and Shawnee migrated to the Ohio Country in the eighteenth century as a consequence of pressure from whites and changing patterns of trade or to escape hostile Indian neighbors. For the Great Lakes region, where interaction between Indians and Europeans was even

more complex, *see* Richard White, *The Middle Ground: Indians, Empires, and Republics in the Great Lakes Region, 1650–1815* (Cambridge: Cambridge University Press, 1991).

By the 1740s the British and the French were aware of the potential value of the Ohio Country . . . For the frontier as a boundary to be defended rather than a land of unfulfilled promise, *see* Patrick Spero, *Frontier Country: The Politics of War in Early Pennsylvania* (Philadelphia: University of Pennsylvania Press, 2016).

Young Man Washington

Washington was then almost wholly unknown. Among the hundreds of books about Washington, the most authoritative remains Douglas Southall Freeman, *George Washington: A Biography* (7 vols., New York: Charles Scribner's Sons, 1948–1954, with the seventh completed by Freeman's assistants, John A. Carroll and Mary Wells Ashworth, 1957). This monumental work was built on the foundation laid by John C. Fitzpatrick, editor of *The Writings of George Washington* (39 vols., Washington, DC: Government Printing Office, 1931–1944), which included all of Washington's outgoing correspondence then known. Since 1976 Fitzpatrick's work has been almost entirely replaced by the more comprehensive, annotated documentary edition, *The Papers of George Washington*, which includes incoming correspondence as well as many Washington documents unknown to Fitzpatrick. Published in series—colonial, Revolutionary War, Confederation, presidential, and retirement, and a separate edition of Washington's diaries—*The Papers of George Washington* is the fundamental source for modern Washington scholarship. I have cited *The Papers of George Washington* in these notes, citing Fitzpatrick's *Writings of Washington* for documents from the last stages of the Revolutionary War not yet published in the new edition. Freeman's account of young Washington's expedition to Fort LeBoeuf is in vol. 1: 274–326.

"to restrain all such Offenders, and in Case of resistance . . . destroy them." Editorial Note, Expedition to the Ohio, 1754, Donald Jackson and Dorothy Twohig, eds., *The Diaries of George Washington,* vol. 1: March 11, 1748–November 13, 1765 (Charlottesville: University Press of Virginia, 1976), 162–73.

"to exert our Noble Courage with Spirit." George Washington to John Augustine Washington, May 31, 1754, in W.W. Abbot, ed., *The Papers of George Washington,* Colonial Series, vol. 1: July 7, 1748–August 14, 1755 (Charlottesville: University Press of Virginia, 1983), 118–19. Washington wrote about hearing bullets whistle in a postscript.

"He would not say so, if he had been used to hear many." Horace Walpole, *Memoirs of the Reign of King George the Second,* vol. 1 (London: Henry Colburn, Publisher, 1847), 400. "In August came news of the defeat of Major Washington in the Great Meadows on the western borders of Virginia: a trifling action, but remarkable for giving date to the war. The encroachments of the French have been already mentioned; but in May they had proceeded to open hostilities. Major Washington with about fifty men attacked one of their parties, and slew the commanding Officer. In this skirmish he was supported by an Indian half king and *twelve* of his subjects, who in the Virginian accounts, is called a very considerable Monarch. On the third of July, the French being reinforced to the number of nine hundred, fell on Washington in a small fort, which they took, but dismissed the Commander with military honours, being willing, as they expressed it in the capitulation, to show that they treated them like friends! In the express which Major Washington dispatched on his preceding little victory, he concluded with these words; 'I heard the bullets whistle, and believe me, there is something charming in the sound.' On hearing of this letter, the King said sensibly, 'He would not say so, if he had been used to hear many.' However, this brave braggart learned to blush for his rodomontade, and desiring to serve General Braddock as Aide-de-camp, acquitted himself nobly."

Braddock's March

The British sent a small army under General Edward Braddock to take Fort Duquesne . . . Two studies of Braddock's campaign offer important insights. Paul Kopperman, *Braddock at the Monongahela* (Pittsburgh: University of Pittsburgh Press, 1977) was the first modern study to draw together the sources, particularly on the British and America side, and assess them with a critical eye. More recently, David Preston, *Braddock's Defeat: The Battle of the Monongahela and the Road to Revolution* (New York: Oxford University Press, 2015) offers a more comprehensive account, drawing heavily on French sources as well as cultural studies of Indian participants.

The Great War for Empire

The disastrous outcome of Braddock's campaign overshadowed the others. The standard modern treatment of the French and Indian War is Fred Anderson, *Crucible of War: The Seven Years' War and the Fate of Empire in British North America, 1754–1766* (New York: Alfred A. Knopf, 2000). Anderson understands the Indians to have been a third power in the competition for dominance and argues that the postwar imperial controversy should be understood as an effort to redefine the relationship between Britain and its colonies in the wake of what he describes as the most important war of the eighteenth century rather as a movement toward revolution. It was, in fact, both at once. Anderson's treatment of the war and indeed that of nearly all scholars of the conflict owes a considerable debt to Lawrence Henry Gipson, *The Great War for Empire: The Years of Defeat, 1754–1757* (New York: Alfred A. Knopf, 1948) and *The Great War for Empire: The Victorious Years, 1758–1760* (New York: Alfred A. Knopf, 1950), two volumes in Gipson's magisterial work *The British Empire before the American Revolution*, a fifteen-volume political history of the British Empire in America from 1748 to the beginning of the Revolutionary War. Gipson summarized his view of the relationship between the war and the American Revolution in "The American Revolution as an Aftermath of the Great War for Empire, 1754–1763," *Political Science Quarterly* 65 (March 1950): 86–104.

II: The Shaping of the Revolution

"Our country is in danger, but not to be despaired of . . ." Joseph Warren, *An Oration; delivered March Sixth, 1775. At the Request of the Inhabitants of the Town of Boston; to Commemorate the bloody Tragedy of the fifth of March, 1770* (Boston: Edes and Gill, 1776), 21.

Chapter 5: Protest
The Proclamation Line of 1763

From the perspective of many American colonists, the war had been fought to secure the land beyond the mountains . . . Jack M. Sosin, *The Revolutionary Frontier, 1763–1783* (New York: Holt, Rinehart and Winston, 1967) is an able introduction to this phase of frontier history.

Amherst managed to provoke the Indians on his own . . . On Pontiac's War, *see* David Dixon, *Never Come to Peace Again: Pontiac's Uprising and the Fate of the British Empire in North America* (Norman: University of Oklahoma Press, 2014), which draws on studies of Indian cultural history as well as richer documentation than older works on this subject.

In the fall of 1763 . . . George III issued a proclamation forbidding settlement beyond the Appalachians. For a creative modern examination of the Proclamation Line of 1763 and other efforts to regulate colonial boundaries from London, *see* S. Max Edelson, *The New Map of Empire: How Britain Imagined America before Independence* (Cambridge, MA: Harvard University Press, 2017).

Regulating the Empire

The case against the writs was presented by James Otis, Jr. . . . M.H. Smith, *The Writs of Assistance Case* (Berkeley: University of California Press, 1978) is a comprehensive treatment of the legal case that also illuminates the broader challenges and implications of regulating imperial trade.

"Otis was a flame of fire! . . ." John Adams to William Tudor, Sr., March 29, 1817, quoted in Horatio Nelson Otis, "Genealogical and Historical Memoir of the Otis Family," *New England Historical and Genealogical Register* 2 (July 1848): 290.

Taxation Without Representation

"If our trade may be taxed, why not our lands? . . ." Samuel Adams, Instruction to Boston's Representative, May 24, 1764, quoted in John Adams to William Wirt, March 7, 1818, in John P. Kennedy, *Memoirs of the Life of William Wirt, Attorney-General of the United States,* vol. 2, (revised edition, New York: G.P. Putnam and Sons, 1872), 48–49. On the British side, *see* John L. Bullion, *A Great and Necessary Measure: George Grenville and the Genesis of the Stamp Act, 1763–1765* (Columbia: University of Missouri Press, 1982).

"The very act of taxing, exercised over those who are not represented . . ." The most useful and readily accessible edition of Dickinson's *Farmer's Letters* is in Gordon S. Wood, ed., *The American Revolution: Writings from the Pamphlet Debate*, vol. 1: 1764–1772 (New York: Library of America, 2015).

American colonists protested immediately. On the Stamp Act protests, *see* Edmund S. Morgan and Helen M. Morgan, *The Stamp Act Crisis: Prologue to Revolution* (Chapel Hill: University of North Carolina Press, 1953). *See also* Edmund S. Morgan, *Prologue to Revolution: Sources and Documents on the Stamp Act Crisis, 1764–1766* (Chapel Hill: University of North Carolina Press, 1959), which makes a fine companion to the earlier work.

"enormous Engine . . . for battering down all the Rights and Liberties of America." John Adams, in Butterfield, ed., *Diary and Autobiography of John Adams,* 1:263 (December 18, 1765).

"I did not know whether I should have escaped from this mob . . ." George Meserve to Secretary Conway, July 31, 1766, quoted in John C. Miller, *Origins of the American Revolution* (Boston: Little, Brown, 1943), 133. The original MS is held by the British National Archives in Kew, England, where it is cataloged as C.O. 5/934.

"Protection and obedience are reciprocal. . . ." George Grenville, Speech in the House of Commons, January 14, 1766, in T.C. Hansard, comp., *The Parliamentary History of England, from the Earliest Period to the Year 1803,* vol. 16: 1765–1771 (London: Printed for T.C. Hansard, 1813), 101–3. The assertion quoted is on 102.

The Empire Divided

In 1767 Parliament adopted . . . the Townshend Acts . . . Patrick Griffin, *The Townshend Moment: The Making of Revolution and Empire in the Eighteenth Century* (New Haven: Yale University Press, 2017) combines the story of Charles Townshend's effort to impose a new system of imperial taxation and regulation on British America with his brother George Townshend's effort to bring order to Ireland, offering an unusual view of imperial reorganization at its peak.

"late unconstitutional Act, imposing Duties on Tea, Paper, Glass . . ." Virginia Nonimportation Resolutions, May 17, 1769, in Julian P. Boyd, ed., *The Papers of Thomas Jefferson,* vol. 1: 1760–1776 (Princeton: Princeton University Press, 1950), 27–31.

"Be united with one spirit, in one cause"

"for the common good of all." The most useful and readily accessible edition of John Dickinson's *Farmer's Letters* is in Wood, ed., *American Revolution,* 1:405–89.

"I am a farmer" [caption] Wood, ed., *American Revolution,* 1:409.

Chapter 6: Resistance

Opening

"We are to be governed by the absolute command of others . . ." [caption] Joseph Warren, *An Oration Delivered March 5th, 1772. At the Request of the Inhabitants of the Town of Boston; to Commemorate the Bloody Tragedy of the Fifth of March, 1770* (Boston: Edes and Gill, 1772), 15. For a readily accessible version, *see* Wood, ed., *American Revolution,* 1:743–57.

"They will shrink on the day of trial . . ." [caption] Thomas Gage to Lord Barrington, September 26, 1768, in Clarence E. Carter, ed., *The Correspondence of General Thomas Gage* (2 vols., New Haven: Yale University Press, 1931), 2:488.

Christopher Seider

On February 22, 1770 . . . a ten-year-old boy named Christopher Seider . . . The role of Christopher Seider's killing and funeral in fueling popular resentment of the army's occupation of Boston in the days before the Boston Massacre has not received the attention it deserves until recently. A most illuminating treatment of the story is presented by J.L. Bell in

a series of short online essays in his long-running blog *Boston 1775:* "The Life and Death of Christopher Seider," February 24, 2020, https://boston1775.blogspot.com/2020/02/the-life-and-death-of-christopher-seider.html; "'A Grand Funeral' for Christopher Seider," February 26, 2020, https://boston1775.blogspot.com/2020/02/a-grand-funeral-for-christopher-seider.html; "'My Eyes Never Beheld Such a Funeral'" February 26, 2020 , https://boston1775.blogspot.com/2020/02/my-eyes-never-beheld-such-funeral.html; and "The Trial of Ebenezer Richardson," April 20, 2020, https://boston1775.blogspot.com/2020/04/the-trial-of-ebenezer-richardson.html.

"How well the cry for Liberty . . ." [caption] Phillis Wheatley to Samson Occum, published in the *Connecticut Gazette,* March 11, 1774.

"as sure as there was a God in heaven, he'd blow a Lane thro 'em." Robert Treat Paine, Minutes of the Trial, *Rev. v Richardson,* 1770–1772, Suffolk Superior Court, April 1770, in L. Kinvin Wroth and Hiller B. Zobel, eds., *Legal Papers of John Adams,* vol. 2: Cases 31–62 (Cambridge, MA: Harvard University Press, 1965), 416–25. I am indebted to Professor Robert J. Haws of the University of Mississippi for introducing me to this and related documents.

"the friends of Liberty may have an opportunity of paying their last respects . . ." *Boston Evening-Post,* March 5, 1770.

"a vast number of boys walked before the coffin . . ." Butterfield, ed., *Diary and Autobiography of John Adams,* 1:349–50. The *Boston-Gazette,* March 5, 1770, reported on the funeral, reminding readers that "in the gayest Season of Life . . . we are continually expos'd to the *unseen* Arrows of Death."

Sixteen-year-old Phillis Wheatley witnessed the funeral procession . . . Phillis Wheatley's poem, "On the Death of Mr. Snider Murder'd by Richardson," was not included in her *Poems on Various Subject, Religious and Moral* (London: Printed for A. Bell, 1773), perhaps because it was too politically charged. Wheatley wrote a different version of the poem discovered in manuscript by Robert Kuncio. *See* his "Some Unpublished Poems of Phillis Wheatley," *New England Quarterly* 43, no. 2 (June 1970): 287–97. The latter version is in John C. Shields, ed., *The Collected Works of Phillis Wheatley* (New York: Oxford University Press, 1988), 136–37. The version quoted is found in Julian D. Mason, ed., *The Poems of Phillis Wheatley* (revised and enlarged edition of a work first published in 1966; Chapel Hill: University of North Carolina Press, 1989), as well as Vincent Carretta, ed., *Phillis Wheatley: Complete Writings* (New York: Penguin Books, 2001).

The "hated brood" Phillis had in mind was the British army. Wheatley's story—her enslavement, her personal struggle, her desire to be heard, the questions raised and answers sought about the authenticity of her work, the derivative nature of that work (like so much in that insecure cultural periphery of the Atlantic world)—lies at the center of the American Revolution. Of the growing literature on her, *see* Henry Louis Gates, *The Trials of Phillis Wheatley: America's First Black Poet and Her Encounters with the Founding Fathers* (New York: Basic Civitas Books, 2003). *See also* Gary B. Nash, *The Unknown American Revolution: The Unruly Birth of Democracy and the Struggle to Create America* (New York: Viking Penguin, 2005), 137–41.

The Boston Massacre

White called for help. Captain Thomas Preston appeared with six armed soldiers. Hiller B, Zobel, *The Boston Massacre* (New York: W.W. Norton, 1970) is the pioneering modern, dispassionate treatment of the event. A lawyer and judge, Zobel offers a superb reconstruction of the three Boston Massacre trials. He acknowledges that "no one yet knows what really happened" and that the "fog surrounding the Massacre and its sequels has never been dispelled" (p. 303). Eric Hinderaker, *Boston's Massacre* (Cambridge, MA: Harvard University Press, 2017) is a fine modern treatment of the massacre, although the author is more cautious than Zobel about the details of what happened that night, which he says are forever lost in the conflicting testimony of witnesses. Professor Hinderaker attaches great importance to the ways later generations have viewed the event. Far less persuasive is Serena Zabin, *The Boston Massacre: A Family History* (Boston: Houghton Mifflin Harcourt, 2020), which offers an original and illuminating treatment of the lives of British soldiers and the wives they brought with them to Boston and of the interaction between soldiers and civilians, but attaches little importance to the seething resentment of the occupation by Bostonians, which Zobel argued made an armed confrontation inevitable. Richard Archer, *As If an Enemy's Country: The British Occupation of Boston and the Origins of Revolution* (New York: Oxford University Press, 2010) captures that resentment and places the massacre in the broader context of the military occupation, focusing on the way the occupation drew Bostonians together and shaped the ways in which they imagined their connection to the British Empire.

"For God's sake, take care of your men. If they fire, you must die." Knox's counsel to Preston is in the records of the trial of the soldiers. For those who wish to explore this primary evidence in detail, the third volume of L. Kinvin Wroth and Hiller B. Zobel, eds., *Legal Papers of John Adams* (3 vols., Cambridge, MA: Harvard University Press, 1965) is indispensable. Their reconstruction of the evidence presented at trial makes it clear that Adams and his associate, Josiah Quincy, managed to secure acquittals by persuading a Boston jury that the violent hostility of drifters, seamen, and other transients in the crowd gave the soldiers a legitimate reason to fear for their lives, a defense strategy that exonerated Bostonians and soldiers alike and continues to shape assessments of the massacre.

"foundation of American independence was laid" John Adams to Matthew Robinson-Morris, March 2, 1786, in Gregg L. Lint et al., eds., *Papers of John Adams,* vol. 18: December 1785–January 1787 (Cambridge, MA: Harvard University Press, 2016), 192–95. Adams made this comment in a wide-ranging correspondence with Robinson-Morris, an elderly, eccentric, and wealthy former member of Parliament, about politics and commercial relations. Adams was reacting to reports of a confrontation between colonists and British troops in Bridgetown, Barbados, in which solders had fired into a crowd protesting the seizure of goods illegally sold by an American merchant captain. The *Morning Chronicle and London Advertiser,* March 1, 1786, reported that "upwards of twenty" people had been killed or wounded. His allusion to the Boston Massacre was offered as a warning that British policies were "Sowing the seeds of disquiet and discontent in your Colonies that will alienate them all if persisted in."

"the Promoters of the Effigies and the Exhibitions . . ." Thomas Hutchinson to Lord Hillsborough, April 21, 1770, in John W. Tyler and Margaret Hogan, eds., *The Correspondence of Thomas Hutchinson,* vol. 3: January–October 1770 (Boston: Colonial Society of Massachusetts, 2021), 179–80. Hutchinson was reporting on the trial to Hillsborough and commented on the injustice of the jury's verdict that Richardson was guilty of murder, Oliver having instructed the jury that Richardson could be guilty of nothing worse than manslaughter because the evidence presented demonstrated that he had reason to fear for his life. The prosecution argued that Richardson's use of deadly force was not justified because Seider was neither armed nor threatening Richardson with deadly violence. Hutchinson explained: "I trouble your Lordship with this Narrative to confirm what I have so often observed, that in all matters which relate to the Controversy between the Kingdom and the Colonies, popular error and prejudice prevail against Law and Justice in spight of the Efforts of the few who have firmness to with stand the former and to attempt maintaining the latter."

Frontier Discontent

Often their grievances involved securing ownership of land. As people moved into the backcountry in unprecedented numbers, conflict over land titles and political disputes over boundaries, land companies, treaties, and purchases from Indian tribes dominated colonial politics. For an effort to deal with these political conflicts in a comprehensive way, *see* Lawrence Henry Gipson, *The Triumphant Empire: Rumblings of the Coming Storm, 1766–1770* (New York: Alfred A. Knopf, 1967), 305–550.

Protests . . . flared along the colonial frontier from Vermont . . . Michael A. Bellesiles, *Revolutionary Outlaws: Ethan Allen and the Struggle for Independence on the Early American Frontier* (Charlottesville: University of Virginia Press, 1993) analyzes the grievances of settlers in the borderland between New Hampshire and New York who resisted the efforts of New York speculators to deprive them of their land and whose struggle became part of the wider popular Revolutionary effort to achieve personal independence and autonomy.

The most serious of these protests occurred in North Carolina. For a detailed analysis of discontent over representation and land policy in North Carolina and the resulting rebellion, *see* Gipson, *Triumphant Empire,* 498–540.

The Regulators

The situation became so bad that in April 1768, settlers in Orange County . . . Marjoleine Kars, *Breaking Loose Together: The Regulator Rebellion in Pre-Revolutionary North Carolina* (Chapel Hill: University of North Carolina Press, 2002) is an outstanding narrative and interpretive history of the Regulator movement, placing it in the context of agrarian populist discontent that manifested itself in the South, in different ways, into the twentieth century. Bushman, *American Farmer in the Eighteenth Century,* 22–76, places the Regulators within the context of eighteenth-century frontier violence.

"an absolute Insurrection" Minutes of the North Carolina Governor's Council, April 27, 1768, in William L. Saunders, ed., *Colonial Records of North Carolina* (10 vols., Raleigh: P.M. Hale, State Printer, 1886–1890), 7:720–22.

This state preceded the governor's proclamation of the same date, "strictly commanding and requiring all persons any ways concerned in such Insurrections immediately to disperse and retire to their Respective habitations" (p. 721).

"we . . . have too long yielded ourselves slaves to remorseless oppression." The "Petition of the Inhabitants of Anson County being part of the Remonstrance of the Province of North Carolina," October 9, 1769, in Saunders, ed., *Colonial Records of North Carolina*, 8:75–80.

"rejected the Terms offer'd with disdain . . ." Journal of the Expedition Against the Insurgents in the Western Frontier of North Carolina, Begun the 20th April, 1771, State Records of North Carolina, in Walter Clark, ed., *The State Records of North Carolina* (26 vols., Winston, NC: M.I. & J.C. Stewart, 1895–1907), 19:837–854 (April 21–June 21, 1777), quotation on p. 843 (May 16).

"The enemy took to tree fighting and much annoyed the men . . ." William Tryon to Lord Hillsborough, May 18, 1771, in Clark, ed., *State Records of North Carolina*, 8:609–10.

"separate state" and **"set a dangerous example to the people of America."** John Murray, earl of Dunmore, to William Legge, earl of Dartmouth, May 16, 1774, in Dunmore Correspondence 343, John D. Rockefeller, Jr., Library, Colonial Williamsburg. (The Rockefeller Library holds typescripts of Lord Dunmore's correspondence, many, like this one, based on the original held by the British National Archives in Kew, England, where this manuscript is cataloged as C.O. 5/1352/71-75.) I am grateful to James Corbett David, author of *Dunmore's New World: The Extraordinary Life of a Royal Governor in Revolutionary America—with Jacobites, Counterfeiters, Land Schemes, Shipwrecks, Scalping, Indian Politics, Runaway Slaves, and Two Illegal Royal Weddings* (Charlottesville: University of Virginia Press, 2013), for this lead.

"I now see most clearly that they have been provoked . . ." Josiah Martin to Wills Hill, Lord Hillsborough, August 30, 1772, in Saunders, ed., *Colonial Records of North Carolina*, 9:329–33.

"a sacrifice—like a slaughter of defenceless, deluded sheep . . ." [caption] Josiah Martin to Samuel Martin, Jr., June 27, 1771, quoted in Vernon O. Stumpf, "Josiah Martin and His Search for Success: The Road to North Carolina," *North Carolina Historical Review* 53, no. 1 (January 1976): 55–79 (quotation on p. 75).

Chapter 7: Americans Unite

Opening

"genuine good-natured wit . . ." [caption] Francis Bickley, ed., *The Diaries of Sylvester Douglas, Lord Glenbervie* (2 vols., London: Constable & Co., 1928), 1:326.

"so preposterous a law . . ." and **"to insult our authority, to dispute our rights, and to aim at independent government."** Hansard, comp., *Parliamentary History of England*, 16:852–55. The phrase "so preposterous a law" was omitted from the report of the speech in an earlier description in *A View of the History of Great-Britain during the Administration of Lord North, to the Second Session of the Fifteenth Parliament* (London: Printed for G. Wilkie, 1782), 7.

"Drank Green Tea, from Holland I hope." Lyman H. Butterfield, ed., *Diary and Autobiography of John Adams*, vol.

2: 1771–1781 (Cambridge, MA: Harvard University Press, 1961), 6 (February 14, 1771).

The Conspiracy Against Liberty

"every Day with some one Member of Parliament . . . It is surprising how ignorant some of them are of *Trade* and *America*." Henry Cruger, Jr., to Henry Cruger, February 14, 1766, in [Worthington C. Ford, ed.] *Commerce in Rhode Island, 1726–1800* (2 vols., Boston: Massachusetts Historical Society, 1914–1915), 1:139. These volumes were published in the Massachusetts Historical Society Collections, series 7, vols. 9–10. Ford was the editor of the Society.

"a notion it was upon the coast of Sumatra . . ." William Samuel Johnson's London journal, November 27, 1769, Johnson Manuscripts, Connecticut Historical Society. Johnson was agent for the colony of Connecticut. I owe this reference and the preceding one to Michael Kammen, "The Colonial Agents, English Politics and the American Revolution," *William and Mary Quarterly* 22, no. 2 (April 1965): 244–63.

"The great Defect here is, in all sorts of People, a want of attention . . ." Benjamin Franklin to Samuel Cooper, July 7, 1773, in William B. Willcox, ed., *The Papers of Benjamin Franklin*, vol. 20: January 1, 1773–December 31, 1773 (New Haven: Yale University Press, 1976), 268–71.

The leaders of the American resistance were prepared to believe . . . The idea that Americans were convinced that they were confronted by a conspiracy to deprive them of liberty is the central theme of Bernard Bailyn, *The Ideological Origins of the American Revolution* (Cambridge, MA: Harvard University Press, 1967). Bailyn's aim was to explain the intellectual and rhetorical sources of the ideas that shaped the Revolution, not to dismiss them as irrational. The idea that American anxieties were irrational occurred to many of Bailyn's readers because *The Ideological Origins of American History* had followed quickly on the heels of Richard Hofstadter's widely read essay "The Paranoid Style in American Politics," first published in *Harper's Magazine* in November 1964 and then in Hofstadter's *The Paranoid Style in American Politics and Other Essays* (New York: Alfred A. Knopf, 1965), in which Hofstadter traced a thread of irrationality through American political history. Gordon S. Wood explore this theme in an important essay, "Conspiracy and the Paranoid Style: Causality and Deceit in the Eighteenth Century," *William and Mary Quarterly*, 3rd ser., vol. 39, no. 3 (July 1982), 401–44, in which he explains that eighteenth-century people, lacking the intellectual tools to discern other patterns, conventionally turned to human agency, including conspiracies, to explain complex circumstances. None of this insightful analysis demonstrates that British policy did not, in fact, undermine American liberties, whether as the result of a deliberate conspiracy or, more likely, unthinking decisions made in London by men concerned with imperial administration who had little knowledge or concern about American circumstances and who were largely or wholly indifferent to American rights.

Pauline Maier, *From Resistance to Revolution: Colonial Radicals and the Development of American Opposition to Britain, 1765–1776* (New York: Alfred A. Knopf, 1972) works through the implications of Bailyn's *Ideological Origins* for the imperial controversy. She follows the disillusionment of colonial radicals step by step from the Stamp Act crisis to the beginning of the war, as events mount up, demonstrating that the British ministry is engaged in a conspiracy to subvert American liberties.

HMS *Gaspée*

"beast of prey" and **"brutal, hoggish manners . . ."** Butterfield, ed., *Diary and Autobiography of John Adams,* 2:72–73 (December 28, 1772).

One of Montagu's ships was HMS *Gaspée* . . . Bunker, *Empire on the Edge* is among the few books on the development of American resistance to place the *Gaspée* incident in its proper place at the center of events. *See* pp. 50–69.

"the King and Parliament had no more Right to make Laws . . ." Deposition of Samuel Peabody, September 15, 1758, Rhode Island Manuscripts, 12: 21, Rhode Island Historical Society, cited in Jack P. Greene, *The Constitutional Origins of the American Revolution* (New York: Cambridge University Press, 2010), 40.

"the power exercised by the Parliament of Great Britain . . ." Joseph Wanton to Hillsborough, May 5, 1769, in John Russell Bartlett, ed., *Records of the Colony of Rhode Island and Providence Plantations, in New England,* vol. 6: 1757–1769 (Providence: Knowles, Anthony & Co., State Printers, 1861), 584–85.

"I have devoted almost the whole of my time in devising measures for punishing the offender." Nathanael Greene to Samuel Ward, [April?] 1772, in Richard Showman et al., eds., *The Papers of General Nathanael Greene* (13 vols., Chapel Hill: University of North Carolina Press, 1976–2005), 1:26.

Late that night a party of about sixty armed men rowed down from Providence. Like the Boston Massacre, many of the facts involved in the burning of the *Gaspée* are difficult to discern through the conflicting testimony of contemporaries and the evident determination of authorities to shield the perpetrators. Steven Park, *The Burning of His Majesty's Schooner Gaspee: An Attack on Crown Rule before the American Revolution* (Yardley, PA: Westholme, 2016) does a fine job sifting through the evidence.

Much of what we know about the *Gaspée* affair rests on three documentary sources. The first is William R. Staples, *The Documentary History of the Destruction of the Gaspee* (Providence: Knowles, Vose, and Anthony, 1845), the pioneering effort to collect the pertinent documentation on the event. The event is ably summarized in Samuel Greene Arnold, *History of the State of Rhode Island and Providence Plantations* (2 vols., New York: D. Appleton & Company, 1859–1860), 2:309–20; further documentation is presented in John Russell Bartlett, *A History of the Destruction of His Britannic Majesty's Schooner Gaspee in Narragansett Bay on the 10th June, 1772* (Providence: A. Crawford Greene, Printer to the State, 1861), which includes the correspondence between Wanton, Dudingston, Montagu, and others, as well as Ephraim Bowen's account of the destruction of the *Gaspée.* Bartlett knew Bowen personally and had heard the latter's recollections at first hand.

"Ephe, reach me your gun, and I can kill that fellow." Ephraim Bowen, Jr. (1752–1842), a member of the party that attacked and burned the *Gaspée,* made a detailed statement about the event on August 29, 1839. He had served in the Continental Army, rising to deputy quartermaster general of the Continental Army with the rank of colonel. After the war he was a successful distiller. In 1839 he was the last known survivor of the raid. His is the most detailed account of the event. It was first published in Staples, *Documentary History of the Destruction of the Gaspee,* 8–9, and was republished by Samuel Greene Arnold and John Russell Bartlett. I am grateful to Sheila Skemp for sharing her insights on the wily ways of colonial Rhode Island merchants.

"A powerful cause of union"

"repugnant to every dictate of reason, liberty, and justice." *Providence Gazette,* December 19, 1772.

"a pack of worse than Egyptian tyrants . . ." *Providence Gazette,* December 26, 1772. This piece was signed by "Americanus," who added: "My countrymen, it behooves you, it is your indispensable duty to stand forth in the glorious cause of freedom, the dearest of all your earthly enjoyments; and, with a truly Roman spirit of liberty, either prevent the fastening of the infernal chains now forging for you, and your posterity, or nobly perish in the attempt. To live a life of rational beings is to live free; to live a life of slaves is to die by inches."

"To be firmly attached to the cause of liberty on virtuous principles . . ." Richard Henry Lee to Samuel Adams, February 4, 1773, in James Curtis Ballagh, *The Letters of Richard Henry Lee,* vol. 1: 1762–1778 (New York: Macmillan, 1911), 82–83. For Adams' reply, *see* the work of his grandson, also Richard Henry Lee, *Memoir of the Life of Richard Henry Lee, and his Correspondence . . .* (2 vols., Philadelphia: Carey and I. Lea, 1825), 1:87–90. Insightful interpretations of Lee and Adams are found in Pauline Maier, *The Old Revolutionaries: Political Lives in the Age of Samuel Adams* (New York: Vintage Books, 1981). Professor Maier interprets both men as concerned chiefly with the preservation and promotion of moral order, common ground that was the basis of an otherwise unlikely political partnership between a Virginia grandee and a Boston agitator.

"the most urgent of all measures . . ." Paul L. Ford, ed., *Autobiography of Thomas Jefferson, 1743–1790* (New York: G.P. Putnam's Sons, 1914), 10.

The East India Company

"The East India Company will leave no Stone unturned to become your Masters . . ." [caption] *Pennsylvania Gazette,* December 8, 1773.

Most troubling was the precarious condition of the British East India Company. The British East India Company, which Adam Smith called "a strange absurdity" and Edmund Burke denounced as "a state in the guise of a merchant" has been the subject of many books. John Keay, *The Honourable Company: A History of the English East India Company* (New York: Macmillan, 1994) is a light introduction. More recently, William Dalrymple, *The Anarchy: The East India Company, Corporate Violence, and the Pillage of an Empire* (London: Bloomsbury, 2019) explores the ruthless manner in which the company exploited, and to a degree fomented, the internal decay of native rule in India, imposed its will with a vast private army, and extracted heavy taxes in 1769–1770 while one in five people in Bengal starved. Most important for the light it casts on the American Revolution is James M. Vaughn, *The Politics of Empire at the Accession of George III: The East India Company and the Crisis and*

Transformation of Britain's Imperial State (New Haven: Yale University Press, 2019). Vaughn illuminates the emergence of a second British empire based on exploitation, authoritarian rule, and wealth extraction, *predating* the collapse of the first British empire based on maritime trade, chiefly with British colonies peopled by British migrants who enjoyed a considerable degree of liberty. Vaughn compels us to reflect on the fate of British America, and indeed of liberal ideals, if the American Revolution had not intervened.

On October 25, 1774, fifty-one women in Edenton, North Carolina . . . [caption] *See* Maggie Hartley Mitchell, "Treasonous Tea: The Edenton Tea Party of 1774," in Jeff Broadwater and Troy L. Kickler, eds., *North Carolina's Revolutionary Founders* (Chapel Hill: University of North Carolina Press, 2019), 25–42.

Tea consumption in Britain and the colonies had been increasing for decades . . . Tea had been a rare commodity in Britain in the middle of the seventeenth century and it remained a scarce status symbol until the second quarter of the eighteenth century, when the price fell enough for middling people in Britain and America to afford it. The main variety was a Bohea (pronounced boo-hee), a somewhat haphazard blend of tea that smelled like burnt grass. It was the lowest grade of tea produced in China. On the tea trade, *see* Jane T. Merritt, *The Trouble with Tea: The Politics of Consumption in the Eighteenth-Century Global Economy* (Baltimore: Johns Hopkins University Press, 2017).

Tea Parties

"You are sent out on a diabolical Service . . ." Broadside, *To the Delaware Pilots* [and] *To Capt. Ayres, Of the Ship Polly, on a Voyage from London to Philadelphia,* Philadelphia, November 27, 1773, signed by the "Committee of Taring and Feathering," Printed Ephemera Collection (Portfolio 142, Number 31), Library of Congress. For further documentation on Philadelphia opposition to the landing of the tea, *see* Thomas B. Taylor, "The Philadelphia Counterpart of the Boston Tea Party," *Bulletin of Friends' Historical Society of Pennsylvania* 3, no. 1 (Second Month [February], 1909): 21–49.

"under the protection of the point of a bayonet, and muzzle of the cannon." The secretary of state for the colonies, Lord Dartmouth, wrote to Tryon on March 2, 1774: "I must lament that the Body of the People within your Province should have been so influenced by the audacious Insult offer'd to the Authority of this Kingdom at Boston, that in your Opinion the landing those Teas at New York could be effected only under Protection of the Point of the Bayonet, and Muzzle of the Cannon." Cadwallader Colden Papers, New-York Historical Society. *See also* Richard M. Ketcham, *Divided Loyalties: How the American Revolution Came to New York* (New York: Henry Holt, 2002), 335. Colden was lieutenant governor and assumed authority when Tryon left for Britain in April 1774. Colden wrote separate letters to Dartmouth and Tryon on May 4, 1774, regarding resistance to the Tea Act. *See* Colden to Dartmouth, May 4, 1774, and Colden to Tryon, May 4, 1774, in *Collections of the New-York Historical Society for the Year 1877* (New York: Printed for the Society, 1878), 334–35 and 335–38.

On the evening of December 16, 1773, Boston patriots took action. Benjamin Woods Labaree, *The Boston Tea Party* (New York: Oxford University Press, 1964) remains the authoritative account of the destruction of the tea in Boston and resistance to the Tea Act in Charleston, Philadelphia, New York, and elsewhere. Benjamin L. Carp, *Defiance of the Patriots: The Boston Tea Party and the Making of America* (New Haven: Yale University Press, 2011) sets the destruction of the tea in its global context, addressing the spread of tea drinking in the Atlantic world and the commercial network that tied American tea drinkers to Chinese producers.

Professors Labaree and Carp each benefited from Francis Samuel Drake, *Tea Leaves: Being a Collection of Letters and Documents Relating to the Shipment of Tea to the American Colonies in the Year 1773, by the East India Company* (Boston: A.O. Crane, 1884), an invaluable compilation of documents relating to the sale of tea in Boston in the early 1770s, deliberations in the summer of 1773 about the East India Company's decision to ship tea to America, correspondence from American merchants anxious to profit from the sale, details of each shipment, anxiety about opposition to the sale of the tea, the formal proceedings of the opponents, the depositions of the masters of the tea ships regarding the destruction of the cargo at Boston, and the fate of the shipments sent to New York and Philadelphia. The lengthy introduction, a sketch history of the fate of the tea in Boston, includes documentation on the destruction of the tea. The book also includes short biographical sketches of the men known or thought to have participated in the act.

"I could easily have prevented the Execution of this Plan . . ." quoted in Labaree, *Boston Tea Party,* 145.

"Well, boys, you've had a fine pleasant evening for your Indian caper . . ." The account of the first mate of the *Beaver* handing over keys and providing candles is in [Benjamin Bussey Thatcher,] *Traits of the Tea Party; Being a Memoir of George R.T. Hewes, one of the last of its survivors; with a history of that transaction; reminiscences of the massacre, and the siege, and other stories of old times* (New York: Harper & Brothers, 1835), 181–82. The exchange between Admiral Montagu and the crowd is on p. 185. George Robert Twelves Hewes, a shoemaker, participated in the Boston Tea Party and was a central figure in the tarring and feathering of John Malcolm (see pp. 99–101) as well as other events of the Revolution. For a perceptive interpretation of Hewes, see Alfred Young, *The Shoemaker and the Tea Party: Memory and the American Revolution* (Boston: Beacon Press, 2000). *Traits of the Tea Party* was probably the first publication to refer to the destruction of the tea as the Boston Tea Party. That name was not used at the time, although a Bostonian is reported to have yelled, "Boston harbor a tea-pot to-night!" at the public meeting immediately before the tea was thrown overboard (Drake, *Tea Leaves,* lxxii).

Chapter 8: Intolerable Acts

Opening

"I wish this cursed place was burned" [caption] Thomas Gage to Lord Barrington, June 25, 1775, in Carter, ed., *Correspondence of General Thomas Gage,* 1:687.

By the beginning of 1774, the surprise and dismay the colonists had expressed a decade earlier had hardened into distrust and anger. In 1774 the logic of their resistance led them into revolution, even before the fighting started at Lexington and Concord. Mary Beth Norton, *1774: The Long Year of Revolution* (New York: Alfred A. Knopf, 2020) presents the events of 1774 from the perspective of many actors—loyalists, moderates, and radicals—and carefully avoids looking ahead, allowing her narrative of revolution to unfold as it did for participants, each step contingent on the one before.

Tar and Feathers

On the night of January 25, 1774, an angry mob dragged John Malcolm . . . Malcolm's story is reviewed in Frank W. C. Hersey, "Tar and Feathers: The Adventures of Captain John Malcom," *Publications of the Colonial Society of Massachusetts* 34 (April 1941): 429–73. *See also* Norton, *1774: The Long Year of Revolution,* 72–73, which places the event in broader context.

"attacked a lad in the street, and cut his head with a cutlass . . ." John Adams described the Malcolm affair in the fifth of his letters of Novanglus, published in the *Boston Gazette* on February 20, 1775. *See* Robert J. Taylor, ed., *Papers of John Adams,* vol. 2: December 1773–April 1775 (Cambridge, MA: Harvard University Press, 1977), 284–85. Contrary to Adams' report, the *Boston Gazette* reported on January 21, 1774, that Malcolm threatened the boy rather than struck him and that Malcolm struck Hewes with his cane.

"was occasioned by his beating a Boy in the Street . . ." Three years after the affair, Malcolm made various charges against his former superior in Falmouth, Collector of Customs Francis Waldo, addressed to the Lords of the Treasury. Waldo answered those changes in a letter to the Lords of the Treasury dated November 21, 1776, reproducing each of Malcolm's charges and refuting them point by point. Malcolm blamed Waldo for exposing him to the anger of the mob in Falmouth, which Waldo denied, pointing out that Malcolm had thereafter gone "to Boston and brought upon himself a second Taring & Feathering—he has not however assigned the true Cause of this last Misfortune, which happened some time after the India Companys Teas were destroyed, & was occasioned by his beating a Boy in the Street in such a manner as to raise a Mob." The manuscript of Waldo's memorandum is in the British National Archives, Kew, cataloged as T1 [Treasury Board Papers and In-Letters], Subseries 525/117-120. Waldo's memorandum is reproduced in full in Hersey, "Tar and Feathers," 440–44. I am grateful to Jon Brown and Amberly Dyer for their assistance on these points.

"cursing, damning, threatening and shaking a very large cane . . ." *Massachusetts Spy,* January 27, 1774.

"Nothing else could have saved you." Hewes' account of his encounter with Malcolm, his subsequent treatment by Dr. Joseph Warren, including Warren's comment about Hewes' skull, and the tarring and feathering of Malcolm is in [Benjamin Bussey Thatcher,] *Traits of the Tea Party,* 126–34.

"had joined in the murders at North-Carolina . . ." *Massachusetts Spy,* January 27, 1774.

They put Malcolm in a cart, stripped him, and coated him with pine tar and feathers. Many historians—it seems like most—misunderstand the tar used to tar and feather people in the Revolutionary era. Tar is a liquid extracted from pine by heating it in a dense pile deprived of oxygen to prevent the wood from catching fire. Under these controlled conditions the pine resin melts and runs off as a viscous, strong-smelling, sticky liquid with the consistency of motor oil or light syrup. Tar production was a major industry in the pine forests of North Carolina. Tar was used on boats of all kinds as a water repellent and wood preservative. Ropes used on ships were also treated with tar to repel water and extend their useful life. Barrels of tar were common on wharves, shipyards, and sailing vessels, and sailors were commonly referred to as "tars" because they handled the stuff so much and must have smelled like it. Tar is liquid at room temperature. It dries like varnish when applied and does not need to be heated for use. People subjected to tarring and feathering were coated with tar just as it came from the barrel, at whatever the ambient temperature was at the time, most often using a bucket and mop of the sort used to coat decks with tar, one of tar's most common uses. In the print of the tarring and feathering of John Malcolm on page 100, a tar bucket and mop are in the left foreground. When tar is heated to a sustained boil it thickens and becomes pitch, which hardens to a waterproof solid when it cools. Pitch was used to seal the joints between planks and other ships' timbers. Boiling tar to make pitch was a common activity in shipyards because pitch has to be used immediately or it hardens in the pot. Pitch made by boiling tar and cooling it was sold in solid chunks that had to be reheated to near boiling for use. People who were tarred and feathered were coated with tar, not pitch. Anyone coated with pitch would have sustained very serious and probably fatal burns. The popular error—that people were tarred with a boiling hot liquid—is probably perpetuated because the word tar is now commonly, though improperly, used to refer to asphalt used to pave roads. Asphalt is a petroleum byproduct that must be heated for use, and anyone coated with hot asphalt would suffer life-threatening burns, but asphalt and tar are entirely different products. Victims of tarring and feathering were not burned, but they were typically injured in others ways. They were often beaten and sustained cuts and broken bones. Tar and feathers were applied to humiliate rather than injure them.

Franklin in London

The official reason for the hearing was to ask Franklin . . . The publication of the correspondence of Thomas Hutchinson and Andrew Oliver and the resulting controversy is ably addressed in Bernard Bailyn, *The Ordeal of Thomas Hutchinson* (Cambridge, MA: Harvard University Press, 1974).

"abridgement of what are called English liberties." The letters were published as *Copy of Letters Sent to Great-Britain, by his Excellency Thomas Hutchinson, the Hon. Andrew Oliver, and several other Persons, born and educated among us. Which original Letters have been returned to America, and laid before the honorable House of Representatives of this Province* (Boston: Edes and Gill, 1773) and thereafter reprinted in America and Britain. On the title page, Edes and Gill asserted that "the judicious Reader" of the letters "will discover the fatal Source of the Confusion and Bloodshed in which this Province especially has been involved, and which threatned [*sic*] total Destruction to the Liberties of all America."

"perpetually offering every kind of insult to the English nation . . ." This and the subsequent quotations of Wedderburn in this subchapter are from "The Final Hearing before the Privy Council Committee for Plantation Affairs on the Petition from the Massachusetts House of Representatives for the Removal of Hutchinson and Oliver," January 29, 1774, in William B. Willcox, ed., *The Papers of Benjamin Franklin,* vol. 21: January 1, 1774–March 22, 1775 (New Haven: Yale University Press, 1978), 37–70. Having listened to Wedderburn denounce Franklin, the Privy Council dismissed the petition to remove Hutchinson and Oliver. The petitioners had asserted that the two men had lost the confidence and support of the people of Massachusetts. Their appointments, the privy counselors knew, did not depend on the consent of the governed. They had been appointed by the king and acknowledging that the people they governed had anything to say about their appointments or conduct would only undermine the king's prerogatives.

"**indecency**" [caption] William Petty, earl of Shelburne, to William Pitt, earl of Chatham, February 3, 1774, in William Stanhope Taylor and John Henry Pringle, eds., *Correspondence of William Pitt, Earl of Chatham* (4 vols., London: J. Murray, 1838–1840), 4:322–26.

"War with all America"

"**considered as two independent states.**" North made this assertion in his speech to the House of Commons on March 14, 1774, when he proposed the closing of the port of Boston. *The History, Debates, and Proceedings of Both Houses of Parliament of Great Britain, from the Year 1743 to the Year 1774* (7 vols., London: Printed for J. Debrett, 1792), 7:69–72. For a perceptive analysis of the official British response to the destruction of the tea, *see* Jack M. Sosin, "The Massachusetts Acts of 1774: Coercive or Preventive?," *Huntington Library Quarterly* 26, no. 3 (May 1963): 235–52.

"**create that association of the Americans which you have so much wished to annihilate**" *History, Debates, and Proceedings of Both Houses of Parliament,* 7:90–91.

"**that you wish to go to war with all America.**" In response to Lord North's proposal to close the port of Boston, Edmund Burke gave a speech on March 14, 1774, concluding: "There are but two ways to govern America; either to make it subservient to all your laws, or let it govern itself by its own internal policy. I abhor the measure of taxation where it is only for a quarrel, and not for a revenue; a measure that is teizing and irritating without any good effect; but a revision of this question will one day or other come, wherein I hope to give my opinion. But this is the day that you wish to go to war with all America; in order to conciliate that country to this; and to say that America shall be obedient to all the laws of this country. I wish to see a new regulation and plan of a new legislation in that country, not founded upon your laws and statutes here, but grounded upon the vital principles of English liberty" (*History, Debates, and Proceedings of Both Houses of Parliament,* 7:97–99).

"**to decide the matter by tarring and feathering.**" This remark was made by Henry Herbert, a member of the House of Commons from Wilton, in a short speech on March 25, 1774, in which he said that "the Americans were a strange set of people" from whom it was vain to expect reasoned argument (*History, Debates, and Proceedings of Both Houses of Parliament,* 7:86–87).

John Adams called this the "Murder Act" John Adams to Joseph Palmer, September 26, 1774, in Taylor, ed., *Papers*

of John Adams, 2:173–74. I am indebted to J.L. Bell for his research on the use of the phrase "Murder Act," which is wrongly attributed to George Washington in some modern works. Samuel Adams used the phrase and others undoubtedly did as well, but there is no evidence Washington used it. See "The Murder Act as It Is Commonly Called,'" *Boston 1775,* August 28, 2013, https://boston1775.blogspot.com/2013/08/the-murder-act-as-it-is-commonly-called.html.

"**I would burn and set fire to all their woods . . .**" Charles Van, member of the House of Commons from Brecon in Wales, made this threat in a speech on April 14, 1774 (*History, Debates, and Proceedings of Both Houses of Parliament,* 7:123).

"**a race of convicts, and ought to be thankful for any thing . . .**" James Boswell, *The Life of Samuel Johnson* (2 vols., London: Printed by H. Baldwin for C. Dilly, 1791), 2:458.

"**voluntarily resigned the power of voting**" Samuel Johnson, *Taxation no Tyranny; An Answer to the Resolutions and Address of the American Congress* (London: Printed for T. Cadell, 1775), 50.

"**Democracy is too prevalent in America . . .**" Thomas Gage to Lord Barrington, August 5, 1772, in Carter, ed., *Correspondence of General Thomas Gage,* 2:615–16.

The Common Cause

"**though made immediately upon us, is doubtless designed for every other colony . . .**" "The Committee of Correspondence of Boston to the Committee of Correspondence of Philadelphia," May 13, 1774, in Harry Alonzo Cushing, ed., *The Writings of Samuel Adams* (New York: G.P. Putnam's Sons, 1904–1908), 109–11.

"**pimps and parasites**" The residents of Farmington, Connecticut, adopted the Farmington Resolves on May 19, 1774, condemning British authorities and resolving "That those pimps and parasites who dared to advise their master to such detestable measures be held in utter abhorrence by us and every American, and their names loaded with the curses of all succeeding generations." *See* Peter Force, *American Archives: consisting of a collection of authentick records, state papers, debates, and letters and other notices of publick affairs, the whole forming a documentary history of the origin and progress of the North American colonies; of the causes and accomplishments of the American Revolution; and of the constitution of government for the United States, to the final ratification thereof* [hereafter *American Archives*], series 4, vol. 1 (Washington, DC: M. St. Clair Clarke and Peter Force, 1837), 336.

"**a day of Fasting, Humiliation, and Prayer . . .**" Resolution of the House of Burgesses Designating a Day of Fasting and Prayer, in Boyd, ed., *Papers of Thomas Jefferson,* 1:105–7.

"**totally incompatible with the Privileges of a free People . . .**" Fairfax County Resolves, July 18, 1774, in W.W. Abbot et al., eds., *The Papers of George Washington,* Colonial Series, vol. 10: March 21, 1774–June 1775 (Charlottesville: University Press of Virginia, 1995), 119–28.

The Continental Congress

"**the celebrated Pennsylvania farmer**" Silas Deane described John Dickinson in this way in his letter to his wife, Elizabeth Deane, of September 23, 1774, in Paul H. Smith, ed., *Letters of Delegates to Congress, 1774–1789,* vol. 1: August

1774–August 1775 (Washington, DC: Library of Congress, 1976), 91–93. Deane described many of the delegates he met in letters home, which are among the most valuable documentation on personal dynamics in the First Continental Congress.

"the oddest looking Man in the World . . ." Butterfield, ed., *Diary and Autobiography of John Adams*, 2:120–22.

"Shall we supinely sit, and see one Provence after another fall a Sacrafice to Despotism?" George Washington to Bryan Fairfax, July 20, 1774, in W.W. Abbot et al., eds., *The Papers of George Washington*, Colonial Series, vol. 10: March 21, 1774–June 1775 (Charlottesville: University Press of Virginia, 1995), 128–31.

"double vengeance . . ." John Adams to Josiah Quincy III, December 23, 1808, Adams Family Papers, Massachusetts Historical Society.

"The distinction between Virginians, Pennsylvanians, New Yorkers and New Englanders . . ." Patrick Henry made this assertion in remarks to Congress on September 6, 1774. *See* William Wirt Henry, *Patrick Henry: Life, Correspondence and Speeches* (3 vols., New York: Charles Scribner's Sons, 1891), 1:221–22.

"life, liberty and property." Congress adopted Declaration and Resolves, also known as the Declaration of Rights and Grievances, and sometimes simply as the Declaration of Rights, on October 14, 1775, asserting their right to "life, liberty and property" and other enumerated rights founded on "the immutable laws of nature, the principles of the English constitution, and the several charters or compacts." *See* Worthington C. Ford, ed., *Journals of the Continental Congress*, vol. 1: 1774 (Washington, DC: Government Printing Office, 1904), 63–73. That document may have been further altered before Congress adjourned on October 26. For a perceptive, detailed analysis of the uncertainties involved in the formulation of the Declaration and Resolves, see Neil L. York, "The First Continental Congress and the Problem of American Rights," *Pennsylvania Magazine of History and Biography* 122, no. 4 (October 1998): 353–83.

On October 25, Congress adopted a petition to the king, listing the grievances of the colonies, asking the king to intervene with Parliament on their behalf, and concluding with expressions of loyalty: "We ask but for Peace, Liberty, and Safety. We wish not a diminution of the prerogative, nor do we solicit the grant of any new right in our favour. Your Royal authority over us, and our connection with Great Britain, we shall always carefully and zealously endeavour to support and maintain." *See* Ford, ed., *Journals of the Continental Congress*, 1:115–22. The petition was sent to London and presented to the House of Commons on January 19, 1775. Benjamin Franklin reported that it was laid before Parliament at the same time as other documents, newspapers, pamphlets, and other materials recently arrived from America and was barely given any notice. The king never replied.

"no coercive or legislative Authority . . ." John Rutledge, Notes of Debates in the Continental Congress, 6 September 6, 1774, in Butterfield, ed., *Diary and Autobiography of John Adams*, 2:125.

"I never met, nor scarcely had an Idea of Meeting . . ." Silas Deane to Elizabeth Deane [September 6, 1774], in Smith, ed., *Letters of Delegates to Congress*, 1:29–30.

"the compleatest Speaker I ever heard . . ." Silas Deane to Elizabeth Deane [September 10–11, 1774], in Smith, ed., *Letters of Delegates to Congress*, 1:60–63, describes the Virginia delegates, including Patrick Henry, Richard Henry Lee, and George Washington.

"Col. Washington . . . a very young Look, & an Easy Soldierlike Air . . ." Silas Deane to Elizabeth Deane [September 10–11, 1774], in Smith, ed., *Letters of Delegates to Congress*, 1:60–63.

The Country in Arms

"If you think ten Thousand Men sufficient . . ." Gage wrote to Lord Barrington on November 2, 1774: "If you think ten Thousand Men sufficient, send Twenty, if one Million is thought enough, give two; you will save both Blood and Treasure in the end. A large Force will terrify and engage many to join you, a middling one will encourage Resistance, and gain no Friends." The reference to one or two million is to pounds to support military operations (Carter, ed., *Correspondence of General Thomas Gage*, 2:659). In December Gage wrote Lord Barrington again: "I hope you will be firm, and send me a sufficient Force to command the Country, by marching into it, and sending off large Detachments to secure obedience thro' every part of it; affairs are at a Crisis, and if you give way it is for ever" (Carter, ed., *Correspondence of General Thomas Gage*, 2:663).

"Go home, and tell your master he sent you on a fool's errand . . ." Charles M. Endicott, *Account of Leslie's Retreat at the North Bridge, in Salem, on Sunday, Feb'y 26, 1775* (Salem: Wm. Ives and Geo. W. Pease Printers, 1856), 29.

"We observed to her that it was a very fine country . . ." Documentation of the British officers' encounter with the African-American serving woman survived by chance. On February 22, 1775, General Gage ordered Captain John Brown and Ensign Henry De Berniere to sketch the roads between Boston and Worcester and gather intelligence on the situation in the interior. Gage's written instructions, De Berniere's report on their expedition, his report on a subsequent expedition to Concord, and a report on the events of April 19, with an account of British casualties, was found in Boston after the British evacuation in 1776 and was published as *General Gage's Instructions of 22d February, 1775 to Captain Brown and Ensign D'Bernicre (of the army under his command) whom he ordered to take a sketch of the roads, passes, heights, &c. from Boston to Worcester, and to make other observations: With a curious Narrative of Occurrences during their mission, Wrote by the Ensign* (Boston: J. Gill, 1779).

"a tumultuous and riotous rabble" Lord George Germain characterized the opposition in Massachusetts in this way in a short speech to Parliament on March 14, 1775. *History, Debates, and Proceedings of Both Houses of Parliament*, 7:106–8.

"It is to no purpose to attempt to destroy the opposition . . ." *American Archives*, series 4, vol. 1, pp. 1066–67, where it is labeled "Extract of a letter from a gentleman of Philadelphia, to a member of the British Parliament dated December 26, 1774." The ministry had concluded by January 1775 that the colonies were in rebellion and that opposition leaders should be arrested and military force employed to prevent the colonists from preparing for war. *See* Allan J. McCurry, "The North Government and the Outbreak of the

American Revolution," *Huntington Library Quarterly* 34, no. 2 (February 1971): 141–57.

Liberty or Death

"captivated all with his bold and splendid eloquence." [caption] Thomas Jefferson to William Wirt, August 4, 1805, enclosing a memorandum of recollection of Patrick Henry, Thomas Jefferson's Notes on Patrick Henry [before April 12, 1812], in J. Jefferson Looney, ed., *The Papers of Thomas Jefferson,* Retirement Series, vol. 4: June 18, 1811–April 30, 1812 (Princeton: Princeton University Press, 2007), 598–605 and Editorial Note, 595–96.

The southern planters, Gage wrote, "can do nothing . . ." Thomas Gage to William Legge, earl of Dartmouth, August 27, 1774, in Carter, ed., *Correspondence of General Thomas Gage,* 1:367.

"this colony be immediately put into a posture of defense." Proceedings of the Second Virginia Convention, March 23, 1775, in William J. Van Schreeven, comp., and Robert L. Scribner and Brent Tarter, eds., *Revolutionary Virginia: The Road to Independence* (7 vols., Charlottesville: University Press of Virginia, 1973–83), 2:366–70.

"If we wish to be free . . ." Patrick Henry devoted little attention to his papers. No contemporary manuscript of Henry's "Liberty or Death" speech survives (if Henry ever wrote it down). Nor is there a transcript of the speech taken down at the time or a detailed contemporary report. Henry died in 1799. His first biographer, William Wirt, working in the early nineteenth century, reconstructed the conclusion of the speech from the recollections of men who were present, some of whom remembered the speech quite vividly. The results were published in *Sketches of the Life and Character of Patrick Henry* (Philadelphia: James Webster, 1817), 120–23. Commentators have been wary of endorsing Wirt's reconstruction, and some have suggested that it is more Wirt than Henry, even though Wirt insisted that he could not possibly imitate Henry's distinctive oratorical style. Wirt admitted that the research for the book was "up-hill all the way." *See* William Wirt to Dabney Carr, August 20, 1815, in John P. Kennedy, *Memoirs of the Life of William Wirt* (2 vols., Philadelphia: Lea and Blanchard, 1849), 1:387–93. For a balanced modern biography, *see* Jon Kukla, *Patrick Henry: Champion of Liberty* (New York: Simon & Schuster, 2017).

"greatly absurd for us to plead for liberty . . ." This sentiment was expressed in the reply of the town meeting of Medfield, Massachusetts, to a letter from a committee of correspondence. The reply is not dated, but the committee to prepare it was appointed on December 14, 1774. William S. Tilden, ed., *History of the Town of Medfield, Massachusetts, 1650–1886* (Boston: George H. Ellis, 1887), 160–62.

"The colonists are by the law of nature free born, as indeed all men are, white or black." James Otis, *The Rights of the British Colonies Asserted and Proved* (Boston: Edes and Gill, 1764), 29.

"freedom is unquestionably the birth-right of all mankind . . ." *Virginia Gazette,* March 19, 1767.

"We expect great things . . ." Petition of Peter Bestes, Sambo Freeman, Felix Holbook, and Chester Doie, Boston, April 20, 1773, Broadside, Printed Ephemera Collection (Portfolio 37, Number 16), Library of Congress.

III: The Glorious Cause

Tyranny, like hell, is not easily conquered . . . Thomas Paine, *The American Crisis No. 1,* December 19, 1776, in Philip Foner, ed., *The Complete Writings of Thomas Paine* (2 vols., New York: Citadel Press, 1945), 2:50.

Chapter 9: Colonists at War
Opening

Late on the evening of April 18, 1775, nine hundred British Regulars set out . . . J.L. Bell, *The Road to Concord: How Four Stolen Cannon Ignited the Revolutionary War* (Yardley, PA: Westholme, 2016) is a meticulously researched, gracefully written account that explains, in scrupulous detail, precisely what the British were after on April 19, 1775.

A dog barked as they passed. The killing of the barking dog and the march on Concord are documented in the diary of Lt. Frederick Mackenzie, 23rd Regiment of Foot, published as *Diary of Frederick Mackenzie: Giving a Daily Narrative of His Military Service as an Officer of the Regiment of Royal Welch Fusiliers during the Years 1775–1781 in Massachusetts, Rhode Island, and New York* (2 vols., Cambridge, MA: Harvard University Press, 1930), 1:18 (April 18, 1775).

Thanks to Revere and the other riders . . . The most complete and authoritative treatment of Paul Revere's role in the events of April 18–19, 1775, is David Hackett Fischer, *Paul Revere's Ride* (New York: Oxford University Press, 1994). Professor Fischer places Revere in the broader context of New England culture and stresses his participation in a complex network of overlapping groups engaged in resistance to imperial regulation and military occupation. The result is a history of the beginning of the Revolutionary War in which events are shaped by decisions made by Revere and other British and colonial actors. The book includes an authoritative treatment of the fighting on the war's first day. Robert Gross, *The Minutemen and Their World* (New York: Farrar, Straus & Giroux, 1976), in which Professor Gross reconstructs the social networks that bound together the people who shaped the war's first day, is a work of enduring importance.

"There are so few of us it is folly to stand here . . ." In 1827, when he was sixty-eight, Robert Douglass gave a deposition documenting what he remembered about the events at Lexington on the morning of April 19, 1775. A young resident of nearby Woburn, he arrived in Lexington shortly before the British arrived and mustered with the Lexington militia on the green. He recalled that someone said, "There are so few us, it would be folly to stand here," and that Parker replied that "the first man who offers to run shall be shot down."

Douglass's deposition was collected by Rev. Ezra Ripley of Concord and published with other documents in *A History of Fight at Concord, on the 19th of April, 1775 . . . showing that then and there the first regular and forcible resistance was made to the British soldiery, and the first British blood was shed by armed Americans, and the Revolution War thus commenced* (Concord: Allen & Atwill, 1827), 52. The book was a response to Elias Phinney, *History of the Battle at Lexington, on the Morning of the 19th April 1775* (Boston: Phelps and Farnham, 1825), a compilation of old men's recollections of the events at Lexington. Phinney and residents of Lexington claimed that first fighting of the war had taken place at Lexington. Ripley and residents of Concord claimed that Lexington militia did not return fire and that Lexington was simply the scene of "blood and massacre" (*History of Fight at Concord,* 37) not properly described as a battle at all. In his deposition, Douglass testified that he did not witness any of the Lexington militia returning fire.

The depositions compiled by Elias Phinney made the opposite claim. According to the deposition of John Munroe, a corporal in the Lexington militia on April 19, 1775, Captain Parker "gave orders for every man to stand his ground" as the British approached. After the British fired, he remembered returning fire and witnessed a British soldier killing Jonas Parker with a bayonet (Deposition of John Munroe, December 28, 1824, in *History of the Battle at Lexington,* 35–26). William Munroe likewise remembered the last moments of Jonas Parker, firing his musket with his musket balls in his hat at his feet (Deposition of William Munroe, March 7, 1825, in ibid., 33–35). Both John and Ebenezer Munroe and others remembered a British officer ordering them to lay down their arms and disperse. Both testified that after the first British shots, smoke made it difficult to see much of what was happening; we can safely assume it was equally difficult to hear as well, but they were certain Lexington militiamen returned fire (Deposition of Ebenezer Munroe, April 2, 1825, in ibid., 26–27).

With respect to Captain Parker's orders to his men, Ebenezer Munroe remembered that Parker said to "stand their ground, and not to molest the regulars, unless they meddled with us." None of the eyewitnesses recalled Captain Parker saying, "Don't fire unless fired upon, but if they want to have a war, let it begin here," the version inscribed on a boulder on Lexington Green marking the approximate position of the Lexington militia during the encounter. That version of Parker's injunction to his men was attributed to him by his grandson, the Reverend Theodore Parker, in 1855, when the Unitarian minister was on trial in Boston for having incited a riot against the Fugitive Slave Act. In closing remarks offered in his own defense, Parker explained that his actions were inspired by faith and commitment to the high ideals of the Revolution, inherited from a grandfather who defied the armed might of Britain and invited a war of liberation. The sentiment "if they want to have war, let it begin here" was an implicit challenge to the "Slave Power" of the South Parker denounced, and is in *The Trial of Theodore Parker, for the "Misdemeanor" of a Speech in Faneuil Hall against Kidnapping, before the Circuit Court of the United States, at Boston, April 3, 1855* (New York: D. Appleton and Company, 1864), 220 (an earlier edition of this work was privately printed for Parker in 1855). On September 10, 1858, Theodore Parker wrote to George Bancroft, thanking the historian for his new book on the Revolution, giving his grandfather's words as "Don't fire unless fired upon; but if they mean to have a war, *let it begin here!"* The letter is printed in John Weiss, *Life and Correspondence of Theodore Parker* (2 vols., London: Longman, Green, Longman, Roberts and Green, 1863), 1:11–12. Theodore Parker was born in 1810, thirty-five years after Captain Parker's death. He claimed the stirring words were handed down to him as a family tradition and that he remembered them being uttered at a commemoration of the battle by William Munroe, a veteran of the battle. That commemoration took place in 1822, when Theodore Parker was twelve. William Munroe made no allusion to the words in the deposition he gave in 1825.

"Let the troops pass by, and don't molest them, without they begin first." Paul Revere recorded these as Parker's words in an undated memorandum presented to the Massachusetts Provincial Congress, now in the manuscript collections of the Massachusetts Historical Society. Revere appears to have composed it in 1775 to document his activities on April 18–19. He explained that he was assisting Samuel Adams and John Hancock in making their escape from the approaching British troops and had returned with a second man to Buckman's Tavern to retrieve a trunk of papers. They were passing by the militia assembled on the green when Revere heard Parker give this order. Recording within months (and perhaps days or weeks) of the event, this is the most reliable surviving account of Parker's orders before the firing began.

Stone walls "were all lined with people who kept up an incessant fire . . ." "The Diary of Lieutenant John Barker, Fourth (or The King's Own) Regiment of Foot, from November, 1774, to May, 1776," *Journal of the Society for Army Historical Research* 7, no. 28 (April 1928): 81–109. Barker participated in the march on Concord and provides a vivid and detailed account of the day's fighting, concluding that the expedition "from beginning to end was as ill plan'd and ill executed as it was possible to be." He blamed delays in setting off for Concord for giving the country people time to spread the alarm and contest their march. As a consequence, he concluded, for a "few trifling Stores" the army had nearly lost all of its grenadiers and light infantry. By the time the rescue column arrived, "there were very few Men had any ammunition left, and so fatigued that we cou'd not keep flanking parties out, so that we must soon have laid down our Arms, or been picked off by the Rebels at their pleasure" (p. 101). Barker's diary was previous published in Elizabeth Ellery Dana, *The British in Boston* (Cambridge, MA: Harvard University Press, 1924), but the print run was small and that version is not readily accessible. Both Lieutenant Barker and Lieutenant Mackenzie report that colonists fired from cover, including houses. Mackenzie wrote that "the Soldiers were so enraged at suffering from an unseen Enemy, that they forced open many of the houses which the fire proceeded, and put to death all those found in them." This passage can be found in the two-volume edition of Mackenzie's diary or the shorter edited version, Allen French, ed., *A British Fusilier in Revolutionary Boston: Being the Diary of Lieutenant Frederick Mackenzie, Adjutant of the Royal Welch Fusiliers, January 5–April 30, 1775, with a Letter Describing His Voyage to America* (Cambridge, MA: Harvard University Press, 1926), 56.

"We were totally surrounded with such an incessant fire . . ." "Diary of Lieutenant John Barker," 100. I am indebted to Robert Morris (president of Friends of Minute Man National Historical Park), archaeologist Meg Watters, and historian Andrew Outten for their insights on the fighting on April 19.

"The frenzy that has been so long growing"

"false patriotism or democratic zeal" Josiah Martin to William Legge, earl of Dartmouth, April 20, 1775, in Clark, ed., *State Records of North Carolina,* 9:1223–28.

"the frenzy that has been so long growing among the People of these Colonies . . ." Josiah Martin to William Legge, earl of Dartmouth, May 18, 1775, in Clark, ed., *State Records of North Carolina,* 9:1255.

In late May the people of Mecklenburg County, in the North Carolina piedmont, adopted resolutions . . . The Mecklenburg Resolves were adopted by residents of Mecklenburg County who met in Charlotte in May 1775. They were first published in the *North-Carolina Gazette* on June 6 and subsequently published in the *South Carolina Gazette* on June 13. No contemporary manuscript of the resolves is known, but their publication in the newspapers leaves no reason to doubt their authenticity. The resolves asserted the authority of the provincial government while leaving open the possibility of reconciliation with Britain if Parliament relinquished its claims to legislate for the colonies. After the war the resolves were forgotten until 1838.

The resolves should not be conflated with the so-called Mecklenburg Declaration of Independence, a document first published in the *Raleigh Register and North Carolina Gazette* on April 30, 1819. The author of the newspaper article, Joseph M. Alexander, asserted that residents of Mecklenburg County adopted the declaration in May 1775, more than a year before the Continental Congress declared American independence. No contemporary copy of this declaration has ever been found. Alexander claimed that the original document had been destroyed by fire in 1800 but that he had a manuscript copy that had belonged to his father.

The authenticity of the declaration has been much debated. Critics argue that no such declaration was adopted, and that the text of the Mecklenburg Declaration of Independence presented by Alexander was an attempt to reconstruct the text of the Mecklenburg Resolves. The case of the critics rests on the fact that no contemporary copy of the declaration has ever been found, that the alleged declaration is inconsistent with the resolves, which leave open the possibility of reconciliation with Britain, and that it includes phrases that seem to have been drawn from the Declaration of Independence adopted by the Continental Congress on July 4, 1776, suggesting that the text of the alleged declaration was written after the Revolutionary War by someone, perhaps Alexander's father, attempting to reconstruct the resolves from memory. Thomas Jefferson regarded the document as a fraud because, if genuine, it exposed him to the charge that he had plagiarized the Mecklenburg Declaration of Independence in writing the Declaration of Independence adopted by the Continental Congress more than a year later. The case for the authenticity of the declaration was made by George W. Graham, *The Mecklenburg Declaration of Independence, May 20, 1775, and Lives of Its Signers* (New York: Neale, 1905). The case of the critics was framed by William Henry Hoyt, *The Mecklenburg Declaration of Independence: A Study of Evidence Showing That the Alleged Declaration of Independence by Mecklenburg County, North Carolina, on May 20th, 1775, Is Spurious* (New York: G.P. Putnam's Sons, 1907). The critics' case has been made more recently by Pauline Maier, *American Scripture: Making the Declaration of Independence* (New York: Alfred A. Knopf, 1997), 172–74.

"declare Freedom to the Slaves, and reduce the City of Williamsburg to Ashes." Governor Dunmore's threat was made to Dr. William Pasteur, a Williamsburg apothecary, who visited the Governor's Palace on April 23, 1775, and encountered Dunmore, who "seemed greatly exasperated" by the events of the previous day. Pasteur's statement regarding the matter was laid before the House of Burgesses on June 14. *See* John Pendleton Kennedy, ed., *Journals of the House of Burgesses of Virginia, 1773–1776 Including the record of the Committee of Correspondence* (Richmond, VA: Colonial Press, 1905), 231.

News of the fighting in Massachusetts prompted patriots on the northern frontier . . . For Ethan Allen's own account of the capture of Fort Ticonderoga, *see* [Ethan Allen,] *A Narrative of Col. Ethan Allen's Captivity* (Walpole, NH: Thomas & Thomas, from the press of Charter & Hale, 1807), 13–21. For a modern account that places Allen and his Green Mountain Boys in the broader context of conflict on the Revolutionary frontier, *see* Michael Bellesiles, *Revolutionary Outlaws: Ethan Allen and the Struggle for Independence on the Early American Frontier* (Charlottesville: University Press of Virginia, 1995).

"Uniforms and Regimentals are as thick as Bees . . ." John Adams to James Warren, May 21, 1775, in Robert J. Taylor, ed., *Papers of John Adams,* vol. 3: May 1775–January 1776 (Cambridge, MA: Harvard University Press, 1979), 11.

"set up governments of their own . . ." Lyman H. Butterfield, ed., *The Diary and Autobiography of John Adams,* vol. 3: Diary, 1782–1804, Autobiography, Part One to October 1776 (Cambridge, MA: Harvard University Press, 1961), 351–52 (June 2, 1775).

"excepting only from the benefit of such pardon . . ." General Gage's proclamation of June 12, 1775, was printed as a broadside by Margaret Draper of Boston and Hugh Gaines of New York. Patriot printer Benjamin Edes published a copy mocking the proclamation. Two other broadside versions were issued by printers whose identities are unknown. While Gage issued his proclamation nearly two months after the march on Concord resulted in armed conflict, Lord Dartmouth directed Gage to arrest the most active opponents of the king's government and to use his authority to pardon acts of treason and rebellion in a letter of April 15 (Dartmouth to Gage, April 15, 1775, *American Archives,* series 4, vol. 2, p. 336).

Bunker Hill

General Ward ordered General Israel Putnam and Colonel William Prescott to fortify Bunker Hill . . . The Battle of Bunker Hill is the most famous battle of the Revolutionary War and has generated an enormous literature, not least because it was fought within sight of Boston. Rich contemporary documentation and recollections of participants provide abundant evidence for historians, who have been writing about the battle since the Revolutionary generation. For many years the standard narrative history of the battle was Richard Ketchum, *Decisive Day: The Battle of Bunker Hill* (New York: Doubleday, 1962). Nathaniel Philbrick, *Bunker Hill: A City, a Siege, a Revolution* (New York: Viking, 2013) is much better documented than Ketchum's treatment but not as tightly focused on the battle. Philbrick presents the battle as the pivotal event at beginning of the war and makes Dr. Joseph Warren the tragic hero of the story. A better short account than the one in Rick Atkinson, *The British Are Coming: The War for America, Lexington to Princeton, 1775–1777* (New York: Henry Holt, 2019), 90–126, is hard to imagine.

"until you see the whites of their eyes." That American soldiers at Bunker Hill were ordered not to fire until they could see the whites in the eyes of approaching British infantry was a conventional part of nineteenth-century accounts of the battle, in which the command was attributed to Israel Putnam. For most of the last century historians have treated it with skepticism. Allen French, *The First Year of the American Revolution* (Boston: Houghton Mifflin, 1934), a scholarly treatment of the beginning of the war, rejected it as a tradition without basis in evidence (p. 230). Richard Ketchum mentioned the order but did not attribute it to a particular officer. Paul Lockhart, in a book titled *The Whites of Their Eyes,* wrote that William Prescott *may* have given such an order. "The phrase has been attributed to Stark and Putnam, too," he adds, "but it makes little difference who said it or even if it was said at all. It was common sense, and all the veteran commanders in the American lines would have said the very same thing in different ways." Paul Lockhart, *The Whites of Their Eyes: Bunker Hill, the First American Army, and the Emergence of George Washington* (New York: HarperCollins, 2011), 280. Nathaniel Philbrick kept his distance from "the whites of their eyes" by banishing it to a note (Philbrick, *Bunker Hill,* 341–42).

In fact, the authority for the order is Israel Putnam himself, who described Bunker Hill to his minister, Rev. Josiah Whitney of Brooklyn, Connecticut, who preached a sermon on the death of Putnam in 1790. Ten years later, Rev. Elijah Parish of Byfield, Massachusetts, published a sermon on the death of Washington in which he alluded to Bunker Hill, writing that "Putnam was the commanding officer of the party, who went upon the hill the evening before the action: he commanded in the action: he harangued his men as the British first advanced, charged them to reserve their fire, till they were near, '*till they could see the white of their eyes,*' were his words. . . . These things he related to the Reverend Mr. Whitney, his Minister, by whose permission they are now published." *See* Josiah Whitney, *Sermon on the Death of Putnam* (Windham, CT: John Byrne, 1790). Parish repeated the story in a textbook he coauthored with Jedidiah Morse, *A Compendious History of New England Designed for Schools and Private Families* (Charlestown, MA: Printed and Sold by Samuel Etheridge, 1804), describing Putnam at Bunker Hill: "He charged them 'to be cool, and reserve their fire till the enemy were near; till they could see the whites of their eyes.' They obeyed." (p. 342). Later editions of the book, a favorite in New England schools, were published in Newburyport in 1809 and Charlestown in 1820. *See* William Gribbin, "A Mirror to New England: The *Compendious History* of Jedidiah Morse and Elijah Parish," *New England Quarterly* 45, no. 3 (September 1972): 340–54. The skepticism of later historians is probably rooted in the fact that Mason Locke Weems included "the whites of their eyes" in his account of Bunker Hill in his popular *Life of George Washington.* Weems is known to have fabricated anecdotes, but in this case he almost certainly borrowed from Parish and Morse. Weems added "the whites of their eyes" in the 1808 edition of his *Life of George Washington,* having had ample time to read their *Compendious History.* I am indebted to J.L Bell for his research on these points. *See* "A Solid Source for the 'Whites of Their Eyes' Tradition," *Boston 1775,* February 15, 2014, https://boston1775.blogspot.com/2014/02/a-solid-source-for-whites-of-their-eyes.htmlb. Bell argues that the

phrase was not original to Putnam and hypothesizes that it was used by eighteenth-century Royal Navy officers to encourage their men to hold fire until their ships closed with the enemy, and that Putnam and possibly others on the field at Bunker Hill were repeating a common injunction.

"I wish we could sell them another hill at the same price." Nathanael Greene to Jacob Greene, June 28, 1775, in Showman et al., eds., *Papers of General Nathanael Greene,* 1:92–93.

Washington Takes Command

The success of the New England militia around Boston led many Americans to believe that the war could be won with part-time volunteer soldiers. The gallant conduct of the militia at Lexington, Concord, and Bunker Hill, in combination with traditional suspicions about standing armies and frustration at the cost of maintaining the Continental Army, encouraged Americans to exaggerate the capacity of the militia and, after the war, to credit the militia with securing American victory. Persisting for decades, this view discouraged providing pensions to Continental Army veterans. For a veteran's passionate response to the idea that "the Militia were competent for all that the crisis required" and "that the Revolutionary army was needless," *see* Joseph Plumb Martin, *Narrative of Some of the Adventures, Dangers and Sufferings of a Revolutionary Soldier; Interspersed with Anecdotes of Incidents that Occurred within His Own Observation* (Hallowell, ME: Printed by Glazier, Masters & Co., 1830), 210.

Congress appointed George Washington to lead the new Continental Army. Atkinson, *The British Are Coming,* 116–26, tells the familiar story of Washington's arrival in Cambridge to take command of the army in a properly understated way.

"the best horseman of his age" Thomas Jefferson to Walter Jones, January 2, 1814, J. Jefferson Looney, ed., *The Papers of Thomas Jefferson,* Retirement Series, vol. 7: November 28, 1813–September 30, 1814 (Princeton: Princeton University Press, 2010), 100–104. This is sometimes misquoted as "the best horseman of the age," which is unambiguous high praise, but Jefferson's use of "his age" leaves open the possibility that he meant that Washington was a better rider than men of his chronological age, not the best of his time.

"It has been determined in Congress that the whole Army . . ." George Washington to Martha Washington, June 18, 1775, in Philander D. Chase, ed., *The Papers of George Washington,* Revolutionary War Series, vol. 1: June 1–September 15, 1775 (Charlottesville: University Press of Virginia, 1985), 3–6.

Creating the Continental Army

"Confusion and Discord reigned in every Department" George Washington to Philip Schuyler, July 28, 1775, in Chase, ed., *Papers of George Washington,* Revolutionary War Series, 1:188–90.

"generally speaking are the most indifferent kind of People I ever saw." George Washington to Lund Washington, August 20, 1775, in Chase, ed., *Papers of George Washington,* Revolutionary War Series, 1:334–40.

It would take time, but Washington began to form these men into a true army. The standard treatment of the administrative and organizational history of the Continental Army is Robert K. Wright, Jr., *The Continental Army* (Washington, DC: U.S. Army Center for Military History, 1983).

A few weeks later the first men from outside New England arrived. On the challenge Washington faced in dealing with the riflemen who joined the army in the summer of 1775, *see* David Hackett Fischer, *Washington's Crossing* (New York: Oxford University Press, 2004), 22–25.

"It is among the most difficult tasks I ever undertook . . ." George Washington to Richard Henry Lee, August 29, 1775, in Chase, ed., *Papers of George Washington*, Revolutionary War Series, 1:372–76.

Supplying the army was another constant challenge. George Washington to Jonathan Trumbull, Sr., August 4, 1775, in Chase, ed., *Papers of George Washington*, Revolutionary War Series, 1:244–45; George Washington to Nicholas Cooke, in ibid., 1:221–23. Washington complained that he had only 184 barrels of gunpowder in his letter to Richard Henry Lee of August 29, 1775, in ibid., 1:372–76. I am grateful to Frank Price for focusing my attention on the problem of securing and manufacturing gunpowder and the efforts of Americans to free themselves from reliance on foreign, mainly French, supplies.

"Could I have foreseen what I have, and am likely to experience . . ." George Washington to Joseph Reed, November 28, 1775, in Philander D. Chase, ed., *The Papers of George Washington*, Revolutionary War Series, vol. 2: September 16, 1775–December 31, 1775 (Charlottesville: University Press of Virginia, 1987), 448–51.

"I have often thought how much happier I should have been . . ." George Washington to Joseph Reed, January 14, 1776, in Philander D. Chase, ed., *The Papers of George Washington*, Revolutionary War Series, vol. 3: January 1, 1776–March 31, 1776 (Charlottesville: University Press of Virginia, 1988), 87–92.

The Invasion of Canada

Congress chose two promising leaders to command the invasion—Benedict Arnold, who had helped capture Fort Ticonderoga, and a New Yorker named Richard Montgomery. Considering his central role in the Canadian expedition (and later at Saratoga), trying to understand Benedict Arnold is important to understanding the invasion and its ultimate failure. No one has worked harder to evaluate Arnold than James Kirby Martin, whose *Benedict Arnold, Revolutionary Hero: An American Warrior Reconsidered* (New York: New York University Press, 1997) explores Arnold's obsessive drive for honor and his ideological opposition to arbitrary power. These may not be enough to explain Arnold's subsequent treason, but it informs the justification he offered for it, particularly his disenchantment with the French alliance. Arnold has been the subject of several biographies in recent decades. Martin's is thorough and challenging. On Montgomery, *see* Hal T. Shelton, *General Richard Montgomery and the American Revolution: From Redcoat to Rebel* (New York: New York University Press, 1994), a fine scholarly biography of an important figure, long remembered with Joseph Warren and James Mercer as a martyred hero of the war. For a broader treatment of the invasion, *see* Mark R. Anderson, *The Battle for the Fourteenth Colony: America's War of Liberation in Canada, 1774–1776* (Lebanon, NH: University Press of New England, 2013).

"The Noble Train of Artillery"

In the fall of 1775, twenty-five-year-old Henry Knox suggested a solution. For a modern scholarly biography of Knox, *see* Mark Puls, *Henry Knox: Visionary General of the American Revolution* (New York: St. Martin's Press, 2008).

"Noble Train of Artillery" For Knox's account of his progress and plans for transporting the artillery, *see* Henry Knox to George Washington, December 17, 1775, in Chase, ed., *Papers of George Washington*, Revolutionary War Series, 2:563–65.

John P. Becker, a twelve-year-old boy from Saratoga, New York, was one of the drivers. For his account of Knox's train of artillery written several decades later, *see* John P. Becker, *The Sexagenary: or, Reminiscences of the American Revolution* (Albany, NY: J. Munsell, 1866), 23–35.

Howe agreed and loaded the British army on the ships and sailed away. Four Boston selectmen wrote to George Washington that Howe had given assurances "that he has no intention of destroying the Town Unless the Troops under his Command are molested during their Embarkation, or at their departure by the Armed force without." The American artillery on Dorchester Heights held its fire while the British sailed away. *See* Boston Selectmen to George Washington, March 8, 1776, in Chase, ed., *Papers of George Washington*, Revolutionary War Series, 3:434–35. For an assessment of Washington's generalship at the end of this first phase of the war, *see* "The Siege of Boston in Review," Freeman, *George Washington*, 4:60–76.

Chapter 10: Separation

Opening

"John Adams was our Colossus on the floor . . ." [caption] Jefferson described Adams in this way to Daniel Webster when the latter visited Monticello in 1824. For Webster's memorandum on the conversation, *see* Fletcher Webster, ed., *The Private Correspondence of Daniel Webster* (2 vols., Boston: Little, Brown, 1857), 1:370–71.

"such statutes as more immediately distress any of your Majesty's colonies." Second Petition from Congress to the King, July 8, 1775, in Boyd, ed., *Papers of Thomas Jefferson*, 1:219–23. More commonly called the Olive Branch Petition, this petition to the king was met with the same disregard as earlier appeals. The British government was determined to crush the American rebellion by force.

"as a foreign war." Lord North to George III, July 26, 1775, in John Fortescue, *The Correspondence of King George III*, vol. 3: July 1773–December 1777 (London: Macmillan, 1928), 234. The king responded: "We must persist and not be dismayed by any difficulties" (p. 235). Despite giving the king this advice, North still hoped for reconciliation and a negotiated peace on British terms. On July 31, 1775, he wrote to General John Burgoyne: "Our wish is not to impose on our fellow subjects in America any terms inconsistent with the most perfect liberty. I cannot help thinking that many of the principal persons in North America will, in the calmness of the winter, be disposed to bring forward a reconciliation." In this view can be detected the persistent delusion of the North government that colonists loyal to the Crown would lead the colonies away from the very foreign war North proposed to wage. *See* Peter Whiteley, *Lord North: The Prime Minister Who Lost America* (London: Hambleton Press, 1996), 157. The king was more sanguine. "I am of the opinion that when once these rebels have felt a smart blow," the king had written to Lord Sandwich on July 1, "they will submit." *See* Andrew Roberts, *The Last King of America: The Misunderstood Reign of George III* (New York: Viking, 2021), 268, 270.

"to take up the hatchet against his Majesty's rebellious subjects" Lord Dartmouth to Guy Johnson, July 24, 1775, in E.B. Callaghan, ed., *Documents Relative to the Colonial History of the State of New-York; Procured in Holland, England and France by John Romeyn Broadhead,* vol. 8 (Albany, NY: Weed, Parsons and Company, 1857), 596. Guy Johnson was superintendent of Indian affairs for the northern department. Dartmouth used the same incendiary language in his instructions to John Stuart, superintendent of Indian affairs for the southern department.

"the rebellious war . . . is manifestly carried on for the purpose of establishing an independent empire." The royal proclamation of August 23, 1775, "for Suppressing Rebellion and Sedition" was published as a broadside. It declared that many of the king's North American subjects, having been "misled by dangerous and ill-designing Men," were in "an open and avowed Rebellion . . . promoted and encouraged by the traitorous Correspondence, Counsels, and Comfort of divers wicked and desperate Persons within this Realm" and commanded the king's subjects to assist in bringing "to condign Punishment the Authors, Perpetrators, and Abettors of such traitorous Designs" (London: Printed by Charles Eyre and William Strahan, Printers to the King's most Excellent Majesty, 1775). When news of the proclamation reached America, it undermined the fiction that the colonists were in conflict with Parliament rather than the king. That view became untenable as soon as the text of the king's speech to Parliament of October 26, 1775, reached America, where it was widely reprinted. For a sympathetic view, *see* Roberts, *Last King of America,* 278–80.

"open enemies." The American Prohibitory Act, also referred to as the Trade Prohibition Act, was signed by George III on December 22, 1775, and printed separately as *An Act to prohibit all Trade and Intercourse with the Colonies of New Hampshire, Massachuset's Bay, Rhode Island, Connecticut, New York, New Jersey, Pensylvania, the Three Lower Counties on Delaware, Maryland, Virginia, North Carolina, South Carolina, and Georgia, during the Continuance of the present Rebellion within the said Colonies respectively* (London: Charles Eyre and William Strahan, Printers to the King's most Excellent Majesty, 1776).

"Independency is an Hobgoblin"

"or piratical act, or plundering act . . ." and **"Independency is an Hobgoblin"** John Adams to Horatio Gates, March 23, 1776, in Robert J. Taylor, ed., *Papers of John Adams,* vol. 4: February–August 1776 (Cambridge, MA: Harvard University Press, 1979), 58–60.

Although it lacked the authority to levy taxes, Congress had become, in most other respects, the government of an independent nation. For a perceptive analysis of how the Continental Congress sought to define sovereign authority through symbols, rituals, and public ceremonies and how those efforts ultimately failed to shape, or at least to occupy a central place in, American national identity, see Benjamin H. Irvin, *Clad in the Robes of Sovereignty: The Continental Congress and the People Out of Doors* (New York: Oxford University Press, 2011).

"call a full and free representation of the people . . ." Lyman H. Butterfield, ed., *Diary and Autobiography of John Adams,* vol. 3: Diary, 1782–1804; Autobiography, Part One to October 1776 (Cambridge, MA: Harvard University Press, 1961), 356–57 (Autobiography, October 26, 1775).

"that may cause or lead to a Separation from our Mother Country . . ." "The Pennsylvania Assembly: Instructions to Its Delegates in Congress," November 9, 1775, in William B. Willcox, ed., *The Papers of Benjamin Franklin,* vol. 22: March 23, 1776–October 27, 1776 (New Haven: Yale University Press, 1982), 251–252. John Dickinson, who was a member of the Pennsylvania Assembly as well as a member of the Pennsylvania delegation to the Continental Congress, had a role in drafting these instructions. *See* John Ferling, *Independence: The Struggle to Set America Free* (New York: Bloomsbury Press, 2011), 196.

"being thoroughly convinced that to be free subjects of the king . . ." The Maryland Convention adopted this resolution on January 18, 1776. *See Proceedings of the Conventions of the Province of Maryland held at the City of Annapolis, in 1774, 1775, & 1776* (Baltimore: James Lucas & E.K. Deaver [and] Annapolis: Jonas Green, 1836), 119.

Loyalists

War dissolved the uncertainties and varieties of opinion and divided Americans between two warring camps. Mary Beth Norton, a lifelong student of the loyalists, identifies Jonathan Sewall's letter to Thomas Hutchinson, December 11, 1774, as the earliest reference to American loyalists by that name that she has found: "Temporizing Measures will be fatal to all American Loyalists immediately, and to all Americans finally." Norton, *1774: The Long Year of Revolution,* 447. This timing is consistent with the logic of events. Before 1774 nearly all Americans were loyal subjects, in the sense that they acknowledged the sovereignty of the king and the authority of Parliament (within limits). By the end of 1774 that shared outlook was vanishing.

Loyalists had as many reasons for their loyalism as patriots had for supporting the Revolution. The most perplexed were men like Thomas Hutchinson, whose attachment to Parliamentary supremacy, in their minds, made them true whigs, while colonial radicals who denied the authority of Parliament while insisting on their loyalty to the king seemed to have adopted the position of old English tories. *See* Bailyn, *Ordeal of Thomas Hutchinson* and, along similar lines, Carol Berkin, *Jonathan Sewall: Odyssey of an American Loyalist* (New York: Columbia University Press, 1974). For a general treatment, *see* Robert M. Calhoon, *The Loyalists in Revolutionary America, 1760–1781* (New York: Harcourt Brace Jovanovich, 1973).

"no connection or concern" On the ordeal of Thomas Brown and his subsequent career as a loyalist officer, *see* Gary D. Olson, "Loyalists and the American Revolution: Thomas Brown and the South Carolina Backcountry, 1775–1776," *South Carolina Historical Magazine* 68, no. 4 (October 1967): 201–19; Edward J. Cashin, *The King's Ranger: Thomas Brown* *and the American Revolution on the Southern Frontier* (New York: Fordham University Press, 1999); and Maya Jasanoff, *Liberty's Exiles: American Loyalists in the Revolutionary World* (New York: Alfred A. Knopf, 2011), 21–23.

Civil War

Armed conflict spread throughout the colonies in the fall of 1775. On the path to war in Virginia, the Carolinas, and Georgia, *see* John R. Alden, *The South in the Revolution, 1763–1789* (Baton Rouge: Louisiana State University Press, 1957), 188–206.

"to a proper sense of their duty." *By his Exeecllency the Right Honourable John Earl of Dunmore, his Majesty's Lieutenant and Governour-General of the Colony and Dominion of Virginia, and Vice-admiral of the same. A Proclamation* [Norfolk, 1775], Broadside, Printed Ephemera Collection (Portfolio 178, Folder 18b), Library of Congress. The proclamation was published in Dickson and Hunter's *Virginia Gazette* on November 25, 1775.

Backcountry leaders in South Carolina gathered their neighbors to form loyalist militias . . . Philip G. Swan, "'The Present Defenceless State of the Country': Gunpowder Plots in Revolutionary South Carolina," *South Carolina Historical Magazine* 108, no. 4 (October 2007): 297–315.

Common Sense

"the sacred cause of liberty" For the contemporary use of this phrase, *see*, e.g., Samuel West, *A sermon preached before the Honorable Council, and the Honorable House of representatives, of the colony of Massachusetts-Bay, in New-England. May 29th, 1776* (Boston: John Gill, 1776): "It is an indispensable duty, my brethren, which we owe to God and our country, to rouse and bestir ourselves, and being animated with a noble zeal for the sacred cause of liberty, to defend our lives and fortunes." *See* Harry Stout, *The New England Soul: Preaching and Religious Culture in Colonial New England* (New York: Oxford University Press, 1986), 298.

The most powerful answer to this question came from a most unlikely person. Philip Foner's introduction, "Thomas Paine—World Citizen and Democrat," in his *Complete Writings of Thomas Paine* (pp. ix–xlvi) is a fine basic biography, as is Eric Foner, *Tom Paine and Revolutionary America* (New York: Oxford University Press, 1976), which places Paine (for whom biographical details, particularly about his life in Britain, are scarce) in the Revolutionary context he navigated with such skill. For a definitive text of *Common Sense*, see Foner, *Complete Writings of Thomas Paine*, 1:3–46.

Thousands of copies were sold within weeks. The number of copies of *Common Sense* printed in 1776 has been the subject of considerable exaggeration. In April 1776, Paine claimed that 120,000 copies had been printed, but that figure is baseless. Paine had no way of knowing how many had been printed. Published estimates with no more basis in evidence now range from 100,000 to 500,000. Printers' records for this period are sketchy, and the actual number of copies will never be known. Examples of twenty-five pamphlet editions survive. A print run of 2,000 copies of a pamphlet was extraordinary for most printers, which makes 50,000 a high estimate for the total. The actual number may have been less. *Common Sense*

nonetheless reached more Americans than any published work of the Revolution.

Independent States

"Hope fear, joy, sorrow, love, hatred, malice, envy, revenge . . ." John Adams to Abigail Adams, April 28, 1776, in Lyman H. Butterfield, ed., *Adams Family Correspondence,* vol. 1: December 1761–May 1776 (Cambridge, MA: Harvard University Press, 1963), 398–401.

"So eccentric a Colony . . . sometimes so hot, sometimes so cold" John Adams to James Warren, May 20, 1776, in Taylor, ed., *Papers of John Adams,* 4:195–97.

"That these United Colonies are, and of right ought to be, Free and Independent States . . ." Worthington C. Ford, ed., *Journals of the Continental Congress,* vol. 5: 1776 (Washington, DC: Government Printing Office, 1906), 425–26 (June 7, 1776).

"a Virginian ought to appear at the head of this business" and **"I am obnoxious, suspected, and unpopular . . ."** John Adams to Timothy Pickering, August 6, 1822, in Charles Francis Adams, ed., *The Works of John Adams, Second President of the United States: with a Life of the Author,* vol. 2 (Boston: Charles C. Little and James Brown, 1850), 2:512–17.

"the man to whom the country is most indebted for the great measure of independency is Mr. John Adams . . ." Richard Stockton to John Adams, September 12, 1821, quoted in Charles Francis Adams, ed., *The Works of John Adams, Second President of the United States: with a Life of the Author,* vol. 3 (Boston: Charles C. Little and James Brown, 1851), 56. The manuscript of this letter is in the Massachusetts Historical Society, and the full text will be published in due course by the Adams Papers. The letter writer quoted, Richard Stockton (1764–1828), was a son of Richard Stockton (1730–1781), the delegate to the Continental Congress. The younger Stockton quoted his father's tribute to Adams from memory. For Adams' role in the struggle, *see* David McCullough, *John Adams* (New York: Simon & Schuster, 2001), 96–136.

"Yesterday the greatest Question was debated which ever was debated in America . . ." John Adams to Abigail Adams, July 3, 1776, in Butterfield, ed., *Adams Family Correspondence,* 2:27–29.

Chapter 11: The Declaration of Independence
Opening

"a reputation for literature, science . . ." [caption] John Adams to Timothy Pickering, August 6, 1822, in Adams, ed., *Works of John Adams,* 2:512–17.

John Adams expected Americans would forever celebrate the second of July . . . John Adams to Abigail Adams, July 3, 1776, in Butterfield, ed., *Adams Family Correspondence,* 2:29–33. John Adams wrote: "The Second Day of July 1776, will be the most memorable Epocha, in the History of America.—I am apt to believe that it will be celebrated, by succeeding Generations, as the great anniversary Festival. It ought to be commemorated, as the Day of Deliverance by solemn Acts of Devotion to God Almighty. It ought to be solemnized with Pomp and Parade, with Shews, Games, Sports, Guns, Bells, Bonfires and Illuminations from one End of this Continent to the other from this Time forward forever more."

"not to find out new principles, or new arguments never before thought of . . ." Thomas Jefferson to Henry Lee, May 8, 1825, in Paul L. Ford, ed., *The Writings of Thomas Jefferson,* vol. 10 (New York: G.P. Putnam's Sons, 1899), 343.

Debating the Declaration

Thomas Jefferson wrote the Declaration in the quiet of a rented room over the last three weeks of June 1776. On Jefferson's service in Congress and the drafting of the Declaration, *see* Dumas Malone, *Jefferson and His Time,* vol. 1: *Jefferson the Virginian* (Boston: Little, Brown, 1948), 197–231, and Julian Boyd, *The Declaration of Independence: The Evolution of the Text as Shown in Facsimiles of Various Drafts by its Author, Thomas Jefferson* (Princeton: Princeton University Press, 1945).

"a pretty good one. I hope it will not be spoiled by canvassing in Congress." Josiah Bartlett to John Langdon, July 1, 1776, in Paul H. Smith, ed., *Letters of Delegates to Congress, 1774–1789,* vol. 4: May 16–August 15, 1776 (Washington, DC: Library of Congress, 1979), 350–51.

Congress took up consideration of the Declaration on July 2 . . . Maier, *American Scripture,* 97–153, reviews the revision of Jefferson's draft by the committee and the other delegates.

Shortly thereafter New Yorkers pulled down the gilded equestrian statue of George III . . . The statue weighed four thousand pounds. On this and many other points, *see* Brendan McConville, *The King's Three Faces: The Rise and Fall of Royal America, 1688–1776* (Chapel Hill: University of North Carolina Press, 2006), 309.

"It is hoped that the Emanations of the Leaden George will make as deep an impression . . ." Edward Bangs, ed., *Journal of Isaac Bangs, April 1 to July 29, 1776* (Cambridge, MA: J. Wilson and Son, 1890), 57 (July 10, 1776).

One People

In time the Declaration of Independence itself would become a part of that shared national identity . . . On the symbolic role of Jefferson and the Declaration in American culture, *see* Merrill D. Petersen, *The Jefferson Image in the American Mind* (New York: Oxford University Press, 1960). On the Declaration as a visual symbol of national identity, *see* David Hackett Fischer, *Liberty and Freedom: A Visual History of America's Founding Ideas* (New York: Oxford University Press, 2005), 190–91, 207–8, 211–12. On the Declaration as a definition of the nation's first principles, *see* Harry V. Jaffa, *Crisis of the House Divided: An Interpretation of the Issues in the Lincoln-Douglas Debates* (Chicago: University of Chicago Press, 1959).

The Powers of the Earth

The world that they knew was dominated by a small group of great powers . . . On the international importance of the Declaration of Independence, *see* David Armitage, *The Declaration of Independence: A Global History* (Cambridge, MA: Harvard University Press, 2007). On American ambitions and their fulfillment, *see* Eliga H. Gould, *Among the Powers of the Earth: The American Revolution and the Making of a New World Empire* (Cambridge, MA: Harvard University Press, 2012).

"Every nation which governs itself, without dependency on any foreign country, is a sovereign state . . ." Emerich de Vattel, *The Law of Nations; or Principals of the Law of Nature Applied to the Conduct and Affairs of Nations and Sovereigns* (2 vols., London: Printed for J. Newbery et al., 1760) was the first English edition. It has been continuously in print since. *See* Armitage, *Declaration of Independence: A Global History,* 38–41.

"has been continually in the hands of the members of our congress." Franklin to Charles-Guillaume-Frédéric Dumas, December 9, 1775, in Willcox, ed., *Papers of Benjamin Franklin,* 22:287–91.

Popular Sovereignty

"liberty of man, in society, is to be under no other legislative power, but that established, by consent . . ." John Locke, *Two Treatises of Government: A Critical Edition with an Introduction and Apparatus Criticus by Peter Laslett* (2nd ed., Cambridge: Cambridge University Press, 1980), 301. On the influence of Locke's moral and political ideas in the American Revolution, *see* Thomas L. Spangle, *The Spirit of Modern Republicanism: The Moral Vision of the American Founders and the Philosophy of Locke* (Chicago: University of Chicago Press, 1988), and Michael P. Zuckert, *Natural Rights and the New Republicanism* (Princeton: Princeton University Press, 1994).

Today we take it for granted that the authority of government is based on the consent of the people . . . For an intriguing argument that uncertainty about the meaning and application of popular sovereignty was left unresolved by the Revolutionary generation and shaped subsequent American political and constitutional development, *see* Christian G. Fritz, *American Sovereigns: The People and America's Constitutional Tradition before the Civil War* (New York: Cambridge University Press, 2007).

Original Meanings

"every paper I had in the world, and almost every book." Thomas Jefferson to John Page, February 21, 1771, in Boyd, ed., *Papers of Thomas Jefferson,* 1:34–37. The consequences of the catastrophe for historians seeking to understand the shaping of Jefferson's political ideas is discussed in Garry Wills, *Inventing America: Jefferson's Declaration of Independence* (New York: Houghton Mifflin, 1978), 167–68.

This kind of study can bring us closer to understanding the original meaning of the Declaration of Independence . . . No modern historian has challenged us to take the ideas of the Declaration more seriously than C. Bradley Thompson, whose *America's Revolutionary Mind: A Moral History of the American Revolution and the Declaration That Defined It* (New York: Encounter Books, 2019) seeks to reconstruct the common philosophy he argues shaped the Declaration and the way it was understood, which he calls a "near-unified system of thought." Professor Thompson is puzzled that the interpretation of Revolution political thought that emerged from the work of Bernard Bailyn, J.G.A. Pocock, Gordon Wood, and their contemporaries in the 1960s and 1970s, focused on republican ideas drawn from antiquity and filtered through Renaissance civic humanists, has remained so dominant for so long. In fact it has not. Historians of the last generation are simply not focused on formal political thought or political ideology. They are far more interested in reconstructing the experiences of ordinary people for whom formal political thought had little meaning. Those who are interested in political ideas have whittled away at the republican synthesis by exploring the wide-ranging political ideas of people other than Adams, Jefferson, Hamilton, Madison, and James Wilson. The republic synthesis has not been replaced by a new unified interpretation because today's historians are more interested in other themes and in exploring diversity. But that hasn't stopped Professor Thompson, who seeks, with brilliant erudition, to replace republicanism with Lockean liberalism as the way to understand the Declaration and ourselves.

"Life, Liberty and the Pursuit of Happiness"

Jefferson may have based his ideas about the unalienable right to liberty of conscience and judgment on the work of Scottish philosopher Frances Hutcheson . . . On the influence of Hutcheson on Jefferson, *see* Wills, *Inventing America.* No study of the Declaration has been more effusively praised or more fiercely condemned. Critics found Wills' claim that Hutcheson was more important to Jefferson's thinking than Locke subversive as well as wrong. The debate is a splendid place to begin exploring the varied historical interpretations of the Declaration, which all the participants agree is vital to understanding our republic—hence the remarkable passion with which they approach what may seem, to laymen, like esoteric points about eighteenth-century political philosophy. To begin, *see* Ralph Luker, "Garry Wills and the New Debate over the Declaration of Independence," *Virginia Quarterly Review* 56, no. 2 (Spring 1980), published online at http://www.vqronline.org/essay/garry-wills-and-new-debate-over-declaration-independence.

"no man can really change his sentiments, judgments, and inward affections, at the pleasure of another . . ." Frances Hutcheson, *A System of Moral Philosophy* (3 vols., Glasgow: Printed and Sold by R[obert] and A[ndrew] Foulis, 1755), 1:261–62. The Declaration seems to echo Hutcheson's description of unalienable rights, but in discussing the violation of those rights, Hutcheson writes: "In general, rights are the more sacred the greater their importance is to the public good." This assertion, consistent with much else in Hutcheson's conception of rights, conflicts with the idea that the Declaration was inspired by a Lockean view of individual rights.

The right to pursue happiness was thus a right to seek fulfillment by doing good for others, or what people in the eighteenth century called benevolence. For an alternative reading—these are indeed matters about which serious people disagree—see Thompson, *America's Revolutionary Mind,* 206–10, in which Professor Thompson contends that Jefferson drew "pursuits of happiness" from Locke's *Essay Concerning Human Understanding* and that happiness for Locke is an individual pursuit, constrained only by our ability to recognize the difference between real and imaginary or ephemeral happiness.

Created Equal

"pensive and awful silence . . ." [caption] Benjamin Rush to John Adams, July 20, 1811, in Lyman H. Butterfield, ed., *Letters of Benjamin Rush,* vol. 2: 1793–1813 (Princeton University Press, 1951), 1089–90.

The natural rights of enslaved Americans were ignored. Ira Berlin, *The Long Emancipation: The Demise of Slavery in the United States* (Cambridge, MA: Harvard University Press, 2015), 47–106.

"apt to suspect the Negroes, and in general all other species of men . . ." "Of National Characters," in David Hume, *Essays: Moral, Political, and Literary,* ed. Eugene F. Miller, Thomas Hill Green, and Thomas Hodge Grose (Indianapolis: Liberty Fund, 1987), 629. Hume seems to have been at least somewhat more conflicted about race than this blunt passage suggests. In his essay "On the Populousness of Ancient Nations," written about the same time, Hume wrote, "As far . . . as observation reaches, there is no universal difference discernible in the human species." Ibid., 378.

"right to assume power over others, without their consent." Hutcheson, *System of Moral Philosophy,* 1:299–300.

Among those who insisted that Africans and their descendants possessed natural rights were Africans themselves . . . Sancho's correspondence, published as *Letters of the Late Ignatius Sancho, An African. In Two Volumes. To which are prefixed, Memoirs of his Life* (2 vols., London: Printed for J. Nichols, 1782), reveals a witty, determined man of high principle. Sancho abhorred American war but wrote with anticipation about the future of American society: "When it shall please the Almighty that things shall take a better turn in America—when the conviction of their madness shall make them court peace—and the same conviction of our cruelty and injustice induce us to settle all points in equity—when that time arrives, my friend, America will be the grand patron of genius—trade and arts will flourish—and if it shall please God to spare us till that period—we will either go and try our fortunes there—or stay in Old England and talk about it" (p. 1:170).

The controversy between the colonies and Britain . . . fed the early development of the antislavery movement in America and in Britain. For an authoritative treatment of the development of British antislavery thought in the wake of the American Revolution, *see* Christopher Leslie Brown, *Moral Capital: Foundations of British Abolitionism* (Chapel Hill: University of North Carolina Press, 2006).

While other Americans considered the meaning of the Declaration of Independence . . . These estimates of African-American participation in the armed forces are from Gary B. Nash, *The Forgotten Fifth: African Americans in the Age of Revolution* (Cambridge, MA: Harvard University Press, 2006). These figures may underestimate African-American participation in the armed forces since black soldiers and sailors are not easily distinguished from their white counterparts; most estimates are based on the identification of common and distinctively African-American names and on muster rolls and other contemporary documents that explicitly identify soldiers and sailors as African American. Estimates based on these methods and records inevitably vary.

"Posterity will triumph"

"I am well aware of the toil and blood and treasure, that it will cost us to maintain this Declaration . . ." John Adams to Abigail Adams, July 3, 1776, in Butterfield, ed., *Adams Family Correspondence,* 2:29–33.

"Yet through all the gloom, I can see the rays of ravishing light and glory . . ." John Adams to Abigail Adams,

July 3, 1776, in Butterfield, ed., *Adams Family Correspondence*, 2:29–33.

Chapter 12: An Army of Free Men

Opening

"which had taught him to rebuke and punish insolence" [caption] Osmond Tiffany, *A Sketch of the Life and Services of Gen. Otho H. Williams* (Baltimore: John Murphy & Co., 1851), 8.

"A Bloody Conflict We are destined to endure. This has been my opinion, from the Beginning." John Adams to Samuel Chase, July 1, 1776, in Taylor, ed., *Papers of John Adams*, 4:353–54.

The Challenges of Command

Washington marched the Continental Army from Boston to New York in the spring of 1776 . . . On the nature of Washington's army, *see* Fischer, *Washington's Crossing*, 7–30. On the challenges Washington faced in preparing to defend New York City, *see* "The Problem of Defending New York," Freeman, *George Washington*, 4:77–114. The exuberance many Americans felt in the first half of the year, before the British fleet arrived, is ably captured in David McCullough, *1776* (New York: Simon & Schuster, 2005), 116–38.

One of them was John Glover, a merchant seaman from Marblehead, Massachusetts . . . On Glover, *see* George A. Billias, *General John Glover and His Marblehead Mariners* (New York: Henry Holt & Co., 1960). Glover's regiment reflected the diversity of American sailors and fishermen, and included many African Americans.

"proper discipline and Subordination . . ." George Washington to John Hancock, February 9, 1776, in Chase, ed., *Papers of George Washington*, Revolutionary War Series, 3:274–77.

"all London was in afloat." Daniel McCurtin, a Maryland rifleman, maintained a diary of his experiences in the Siege of Boston and was with the army when it marched to New York, where he arrived on March 28, 1776. On June 29 he wrote: "This morning as I was up stairs in an out house I spied, as I peeped out the Bay, something resembling a Wood of pine trees trimed. I declare at my noticing this that I could not believe my eyes, but keeping my eyes fixed at the very spot, judge you of my surprise, when in about 10 minutes, the whole Bay was as full of shipping as ever it could be. I do declare that I thought all London was in afloat. Just about 5 minutes before I see this sight I got my discharge" (p. 40). The journal, beginning with the unit's departure from Frederick, Maryland, on July 18, 1775, and ending in New York City on June 29, 1776, is published in Thomas Balch, ed., *Papers Relating to the Maryland Line during the Revolution* (Philadelphia: Printed for the Seventy-Six Society, T.K. and P.G. Collins, Printers, 1857), 11–41. At the time the diary was owned by Lemuel Clarke Davis, a newspaper editor.

General Howe's Army

The British government had directed the Howe brothers . . . Ira Gruber, *The Howe Brothers and the American Revolution* (New York: Atheneum, 1972) traces the military careers of the Howes and the difficulties involved in trying to make peace while waging war. On the nature of the British army and the Hessian troops sent to New York, *see* Fischer, *Washington's Crossing*, 33–65.

"George Washington, Esquire . . ." For documentation and details on the failed overture of Lord Howe, *see* Lord Howe to George Washington, July 13, 1776, in Philander D. Chase, ed., *The Papers of George Washington*, Revolutionary War Series, vol. 5: June 16, 1776–August 12, 1776 (Charlottesville: University Press of Virginia, 1993), 296–97.

"a little paltry colonel of militia at the head of banditti or rebels." This was the assessment of General Howe's secretary, Ambrose Serle. See Edward H. Tatum, Jr., ed., *The American Journal of Ambrose Serle, 1776–1778* (San Marino, CA: Huntington Library, 1940), 33 (July 14, 1776). For a perceptive overview of Serle, who regarded the Revolutionaries and their cause with much greater disdain than Howe, see Edward H. Tatum, Jr., "Ambrose Serle, Secretary to Lord Howe, 1776-1778," *Huntington Library Quarterly* 2, no. 3 (April 1939): 265–84.

"awe-struck as if before something supernatural" Henry Knox to Lucy Knox, July 22, 1776, Henry Knox Papers, Gilder Lehrman Collection: "On Saturday I wrote you we had a capital flag of Truce no less than the adjutant general of General Howes army—he had an Interview with General Washington at our House the purport of his Message was in very elegant polite strains to endever to persuade General W. to receive a letter directed to George Washington Eqr &c &c In the course of his talk every other word was may please your Excellency if your Excellency [&c] pleases in short no [person] could pay more respect than the said Adj Genl whose name is Colo Patterson a person we do not know—he said the &c &c implied every thing—it does so says the General and any thing—he said Lord & General Howe lamented exceedingly that any error in the direction [should] interrupt that [frequent] intercourse between both armies which might be necessary in the course of the Service—that Lord Howe had come out with great [power] the General said he had heard that Lord Howe had come out with very great powers to pardon but he had come to the [wrong] place the americans had not offended therefore they needed no pardon—this confus'd him—after a considerable deal of talk about the good disposition of Lord & General Howe, he ask'd has your Excellency no particular commands with which you would please to honor me with the Lord & General Howe—nothing sir but my particular compliments to both—a good answer—General W. was very handsomely dress'd and made a most elegant appearance. Colo Patterson appear'd awe struck as if he was before something supernatural Indeed I wonder at it—he was before a very great man Indeed."

"This to me was what the French call Spitting in the Soup." Benjamin Franklin to William Franklin: Journal of Negotiations in London, March, 22, 1775, in Willcox, ed., *Papers of Benjamin Franklin*, 21:540–99.

"is even now bringing foreign mercenaries to deluge our settlements with blood." Benjamin Franklin to Lord Howe, July 20, 1776, in Willcox, ed., *Papers of Benjamin Franklin*, 22:518–21.

The "foreign mercenaries" Franklin mentioned . . . Historians commonly assert that the British possessed the most powerful military in the world. It did not. The British army was a fraction of the size of the French army and smaller than the armies of several European nations. British artillery was no more powerful or sophisticated than that of France, Prussia, and other Continental powers. The Royal Navy was, indeed, the largest and most powerful in the world, but French warships were superior in many respects to their British counterparts. If Britain had possessed the most powerful military in the world it would have had no need to hire foreign troops. On the Hessians, *see* Rodney Atwood, *The Hessians: Mercenaries from Hessen-Kassel in the American Revolution* (New York: Cambridge University Press, 1980); Brady Crytzer, *Hessians: Mercenaries, Rebels, and the War for British North America* (Yardley, PA: Westholme, 2015); and most recently, Friederike Baer, *Hessians: German Soldiers in the American Revolutionary War* (New York: Oxford University Press, 2022).

The Contest for New York City

On August 22, Admiral Howe's fleet ferried thousands of British and Hessian troops . . . Barnet Schecter, *The Battle for New York: The City at the Heart of the American Revolution* (New York: Walker Books, 2002) documents the American defense of New York City in meticulous detail.

"I only regret that I have but one life to lose for my country." Nathan Hale died in the hands of the British on September 22, 1776, with no American—at least that we know of—present as a witness. The only known eyewitness account written by the witness is in the diary of Frederick MacKenzie, a British army captain. In his diary for September 22, MacKenzie wrote: "A person named Nathaniel Hales, a Lieutenant in the Rebel Army, and a native of Connecticut, was apprehended as a Spy, last night upon Long Island; and having this day made a full and free confession to the Commander in Chief of his being employed by Mr. Washington in that capacity, he was hanged at 11 o'clock in front of the Park of Artillery. He was about 24 years of age, and had been educated at the College of Newhaven in Connecticut. He behaved with great composure and resolution, saying he thought it the duty of every good Officer, to obey any orders given him by his Commander in Chief; and desired the Spectators to be at all times prepared to meet death in whatever shape it might appear." Allen French, ed., *Diary of Frederick Mackenzie Giving a Daily Narrative of His Military Service as an Officer of the Regiment of Royal Welch Fusiliers during the Years 1775–1781 in Massachusetts, Rhode Island and New York* (2 vols., Cambridge, MA: Harvard University Press, 1930), 1:61–62.

During the war reports of Hale's death appeared in two newspapers. The Newburyport, Massachusetts, *Essex Journal* reported on February 13, 1777, that Hale said that "if he had ten thousand lives, he would lay them all down, if called to it, in defence of his injured, bleeding country." On May 17, 1781, the Boston *Independent Chronicle* reported that Hale had said, "I am so satisfied with the cause in which I have engaged, that my only regret is, that I have not more lives than one to offer in its service." The account took familiar shape in Hannah Adams, *Summary History of New-England, from the First Settlement at Plymouth, to the acceptance of the Federal Constitution. Comprehending a General Sketch of the American War* (Dedham, MA: H. Mann and J.H. Adams, 1799), 358–61, in which Adams contrasted Hale with British Major John André, who was hanged as a spy for his involvement in

Benedict Arnold's treason, commenting that many writers had extolled the virtues of André, but "Hale has remained unnoticed, and it is scarcely known that such a character ever existed" (p. 360). At the moment of his execution, Adams wrote, "Unknown to all around him, without a single friend to offer him the least consolation, thus fell as amiable and worthy a young man as America could boast, with this as his dying declaration, 'that he only lamented, that he had but one life to lose for his country'" (p. 359).

Thus far the evidence seems to document the development of a pious fabrication, but Adams included footnotes in her book and noted that she was "indebted to Major-General Hull, of Newton, for the interesting account of captain Hale" (p. 361). This was William Hull, a 1772 graduate of Yale who rose to the rank of lieutenant colonel in the Continental Army and served as a general in the War of 1812. He was a friend of Hale, who was a year behind him at Yale. That he knew Hale was an incontestable fact, but he had not witnessed Hale's execution, so how could he have known his friend's last words? This question was answered, in part, in Maria Hull Campbell, *Revolutionary Services and Civil Life of General William Hull, prepared from his manuscripts . . .* (New York: D. Appleton & Co., 1848), a biography written by his daughter, based on the manuscript left by her father. She quoted her father's recollections of Hale's mission and death at length (pp. 33–38). Hull wrote that a few days after Hale set out on his mission, "an officer came to our camp under a flag of truce" who informed them of Hale's execution. "I learned the melancholy particulars from this officer, who was present at the execution" (p. 37). The officer told Hull that

"the morning his execution . . . my station was near the fatal spot, and I requested the Provost Marshal to permit the prisoner to sit in my marquee [an officer's tent], while making the necessary preparations. Captain Hale entered: he was calm, and bore himself with gentle dignity, in consciousness of rectitude and high intentions. He asked for writing materials, which I furnished him: he wrote two letters, one to his mother and one to a brother officer." He was shortly after summoned to the gallows. But a few persons were around him, yet his characteristic dying words were remembered. He said "I only regret, that I have but one life to lose for my country." (p. 38)

The unnamed officer who came under a flag of truce to report Hale's execution is identified in the diary of Nathan Hale's brother Enoch, who reported on September 26 that he had reached the camp of Webb's Connecticut regiment and learned there that Nathan "went to Stanford & crossed over the sound to Long Island. The next account of him by Col. Motezure with a flag. That one Nathaniel Hale was hanged for a Spy September 22d." This excerpt from Enoch Hale's diary was published in George Dudley Seymour, *Documentary Life of Nathan Hale* (New Haven: Privately Printed for the Author, 1941), 297. Seymour collected every known document related to Hale he could find and carefully transcribed them, producing a work of extraordinary value. "Col. Montezure" was unquestionably Captain John Montresor, a British army engineer. The question that hangs over the documentation is whether Maria Hull Campbell took liberties with her father's manuscript and wrote "I only regret that I have but one life to lose for my country" herself. That seems unlikely. Hannah Adams had used very nearly the same words in 1799, crediting her account to Hull, and the two Massachusetts news-paper accounts—the first published just four months after Hale's death—reported very similar final words. The latter demonstrates that something like the famous last words were in circulation shortly after Hale's execution, as Montresor's report circulated in and beyond the Continental Army. The quotation as it appears here may be a paraphrase of Hale's last words, but the quotation seems to capture the sentiment Nathan Hale expressed in his final moments.

The last position on Manhattan Island held by the Continental Army was Fort Washington . . . For Washington's description of the catastrophe, *see* George Washington to John Augustine Washington, November 6–19, 1776, in Philander D. Chase, ed., *The Papers of George Washington,* Revolutionary War Series, vol. 7: October 21, 1776–January 5, 1777 (Charlottesville: University Press of Virginia, 1997), 102–6. For an assessment of the confused state of affairs and of Washington's frustration and exhaustion, which clouded his judgment in the days before the loss of Fort Washington, *see* "He Who Hesitates Is . . ." in Freeman, *George Washington,* 4:232–70.

His wife, Margaret, was nearby. She was one of hundreds of women who traveled with the army . . . *See* Holly Mayer, *Belonging to the Army: Camp Followers and Community during the American Revolution* (Columbia: University of South Carolina Press, 1986).

Congress later awarded her a soldier's pension . . . On July 6, 1779, Congress resolved to award Margaret Corbin a complete outfit of clothing and one-half of the monthly pay of a private soldier for the rest of her life. By this act Congress formally recognized a female combat veteran for the first time in American history. *See* Worthington C. Ford, ed., *Journals of the Continental Congress,* vol. 14: April 23, 1779–September 1, 1779 (Washington, DC: Government Printing Office, 1909), 805. In 1780, she moved with the Invalid Corps to West Point, where she remained a disabled pensioner in the charge of William Price, commissary of military stores, long after the war was over. On January 31, 1786, Price complained to Henry Knox, who was then secretary of war. "I am at loss what to do with Capt Molly," he wrote. "She is first an offensive person that people are unwilling to take her in charge . . . and I cannot find any that is willing to keep her" (William Price to Henry Knox, January 31, 1786, Letterbook No. 1, West Point 1784–86, Special Collections, United States Military Academy). She was, we can only imagine, in constant pain from her wounds. If she was offensive, we can readily understand why. Margaret Corbin never left West Point. She died there in 1800, just forty-eight, and was buried in a grave that has been lost to memory.

The Crisis

"I think the game will be pretty well up." George Washington to Samuel Washington, December 18, 1776, in Chase, ed., *Papers of George Washington,* Revolutionary War Series, 7:369–72.

"These are the times that try men's souls . . ." Thomas Paine, *The American Crisis,* in Foner, *Complete Writings of Thomas Paine,* 1:47–239. Paine wrote sixteen essays in his *Crisis* series, all of which he signed "Common Sense." The first, *Crisis I,* was written while Paine was with the army on

its retreat across New Jersey after the fall of Fort Washington. "These are the times that try men's souls" is the opening line (p. 50).

Washington Crosses the Delaware

Washington decided to cross the Delaware River and mount a surprise attack. The extraordinary reversal of fortune occasioned by the American victories at Trenton and Princeton is the subject of a rich literature. Fischer, *Washington's Crossing* is a graceful, perceptive, and comprehensive treatment of these events, placing them in their proper social and cultural context while underscoring the vital role of contingency—the decisions made by individuals—in their outcome. His bibliography is a reservoir of sources on the early stages of the war. Two older works of enduring value are William S. Stryker, *The Battles of Trenton and Princeton* (Boston: Houghton Mifflin and Co., 1898), which includes an invaluable array of documents, and William M. Dwyer, *The Day Is Ours! November 1776–January 1777: An Inside View of the Battles of Trenton and Princeton* (New York: Viking Press, 1983), which gathers additional American accounts of the campaign.

"you need not be troubled about that, General, as his boys could manage it." William P. Upham, "A Memoir of Gen. John Glover," *Historical Collections of the Essex Institute* 5, no. 2 (April 1863): 69. Upham offers no documentary source for this quotation, so it may be apocryphal, but its plainspoken quality is certainly consistent with Mercer's character.

"Fiddlesticks . . . these clodhoppers will not attack us." On the evening before the American attack and following an attack on Hessian pickets, Major Friedrich von Dechow, the ranking officer of the Regiment von Knyphausen, interrupted Colonel Rall to advise sending away the baggage, which drew Rall's retort. The exchange is documented in the record of the court martial held in January 1782 for the surviving officers surrendered at Trenton. In a decision dated April 15 the court martial exonerated them all and placed blame for the defeat on Rall and von Dechow, both of whom were mortally wounded in the battle. The court found that on December 25 "the main picket on the Pennington road was attacked and six men were wounded. Major von Dechow, prompted by this, advised Col. Rall to send the baggage to the Grenadiers. Col. Rall answered 'Fudge! these country clowns shall not beat us.' Still he sent Lieutenant Wiederholdt to strengthen the before mentioned pickets, and placed troops over night at the alarm-posts." [William S. Stryker,] "Report of the Court-Martial for the Trial of the Hessian Officers Captured by Washington at Trenton, December 26, 1776," *Pennsylvania Magazine of History and Biography* 7, no. 1 (1883): 45–49. Stryker had acquired a transcript of the court martial decision from Friedrich Kapp (1824–1884), a German-American lawyer and scholar, who was probably responsible for this translation. "Fudge" and "Fiddlesticks" are rough translations of a colloquial German word for nonsense and "country clowns" and "clodhoppers" are rough translations of a German epithet for country people, for which "bumpkins" and "rubes" would be similarly apt. In his later book, *The Battles of Trenton and Princeton,* Stryker published a slightly different translation of the court martial decision, rendering Rall's retort as "Fudge! These country clowns cannot whip us!" (p. 420). For "Fiddlesticks" and "clodhoppers" *see* Bruce E. Burgoyne, *Enemy Views: The American Revolutionary War as Recorded by the Hessian Participants* (Lanham, MD: Heritage Books, 1996), 346.

Rall expressed the same sentiment to Lieutenant (later Captain) Andreas Wiederholdt of the Regiment von Knyphausen. Wiederholdt compiled a record of his experiences in the war called a *tagebuch,* or journal, but it seems to be a post-war memoir, perhaps based on a wartime diary. Similar examples of European manuscript journals are known, clearly written after the war when the writer had the opportunity to copy and revise earlier work and often add comments based on knowledge that could not have been had on the date of the journal entry. Wiederholdt's *tagebuch* includes references to orders given to Americans and foreshadows events, demonstrating that it was composed after the events. Wiederholdt regarded Rall as a commander whose arrogant confidence in his unit and contempt for the enemy resulted in his defeat. He reported that von Dechow had proposed digging some earthworks as a precaution. "'Let them come,' was the Colonel's answer. 'What earth-works! With the bayonet we will go for them.'" Rall assigned Wiederholdt to manage building the earthworks and "repeated his former words, laughed at us for our pains and went his way." This appears to be a record of the same conversation described by the court martial. For the relevant extract from Wiederholdt's *tagebuch,* see "Colonel Rall at Trenton," *Pennsylvania Magazine of History and Biography* 22 (1899): 462–67.

"Here succeeded a scene of war of which I had often conceived . . ." Henry Knox to Lucy Knox, December 28, 1776, in Stryker, *Battles of Trenton and Princeton,* 371–72. For Washington's description of the battle, *see* George Washington to John Hancock, December 27, 1776, in Chase, ed., *Papers of George Washington,* Revolutionary War Series, 7:454–61.

General Howe rushed troops under Cornwallis to the river, but Washington had gone. On reactions to the surrender of the Hessians, *see* Fischer, *Washington's Crossing,* 260–61.

"The day is ours!"

"The day is ours!" This exclamation is attributed to Brigadier General James Mercer, who was mortally wounded in the early stages of the Battle of Princeton. In his 1832 pension application, John Hendy submitted a declaration describing his service as an ensign in the Northampton County, Pennsylvania, militia, which he testified "was annexed to the Brigade under the Command of Gen. Mifflin" at the Battle of Princeton, adding, "From Trenton to Princeton there was what was called an 18 Mile Road and a 12 Mile Road. On the Night of the second our whole Corps took up the line of march for Princeton on the 18 mile Route the enemy having taken the other one—we reached Princeton early on the morning of the third and immediately prepared for Battle—In this engagement Gen. Mercer fell dangerously wounded and was conveyed directly by this deponent to a private house—this brave officer exclaimed as he was carried along 'Cheer up my boys the day is ours.'" Pension File of John Hendy, S.13381, Revolutionary War Pension and Bounty-Land Warrant Application Files, Record Group 15: Records of the Veterans Administration, National Archives.

"We've got the old fox safe now . . ." The source of this boast attributed to Cornwallis is not known, but it is consistent with the circumstances and the orders Cornwallis gave on the night of January 2. Despite the urging of William Erskine, one of his senior commanders, Cornwallis was reluctant to make a night attack. According to American James Wilkinson, Cornwallis told his senior officers that "he had the enemy safe enough, and could dispose of them the next morning," which expresses the same idea as the more colorful allusion to bagging the old fox. *See* James Wilkinson, *Memoirs of My Own Times* (3 vols., Philadelphia: Printed by Abraham Small, 1816), 1:139. Wilkinson's description of the battle (pp. 140–48) is among the most important first-hand accounts, although it is not clear how he learned about the exchange in the British council of war on January 2. Historians of the Battle of Princeton generally repeat the "old fox" quotation, including Fischer (*Washington's Crossing,* 313 and 530, note 22) and most recently, Richard Middleton, in his biography *Cornwallis: Soldier and Statesman in a Revolutionary World* (New Haven: Yale University Press, 2022); he uses the council of war on January 2, 1777, to frame his preface.

Washington's army marched north through the night . . . For Washington's own account of the march from Assunpink Creek to Princeton, the ensuring battle, and the march that followed, with extensive notes on other contemporary documentation, *see* George Washington to John Hancock, January 5, 1777, in Chase, ed., *Papers of George Washington,* Revolutionary War Series, 7:519–30. For the issues he weighed in making the decision to slip away in the night, see Freeman, *George Washington,* 4:343–48.

"I shall never forget what I felt . . . when I saw him brave all the dangers . . ." James Read, who served with the Philadelphia Associators at Princeton, wrote to his wife, Susan, when the army reached Morristown after its march north from Princeton. When it was published in 1892 the date was not supplied, although the headnote indicates it was "dated from Morristown." From context it seems to have been written within a few weeks of the battle: "O my Susan! it was a glorious day and I would not have been absent from it for all the money I ever expect to be worth. I happened to be amongst those who were in the first and hottest of the fire and I flatter myself that our superiors have approved of our conduct. . . . I would wish to say a few words respecting the actions of that truly great man Gen. Washington, but it is not in the power of language to convey any just idea of him. His greatness is far beyond my description. I shall never forget what I felt at Princeton on his account, when I saw him brave all the dangers of the field, and his important life hanging as it were by a single hair with a thousand deaths flying around him. Believe me I thought not of myself. He is surely America's better Genius and Heaven's peculiar care." "Letter of James Read, of Philadelphia, 1777," *Pennsylvania Magazine of History and Biography* 16 (1892): 465–66. I am grateful to Jim Lighthizer, Jim Campi, and their colleagues at the American Battlefield Trust for securing the land over which Washington's charge occurred and focusing fresh attention on the battle.

"a heavy platoon fire on the march." Caesar A. Rodney, ed., *Diary of Captain Thomas Rodney, 1776–1777* (Wilmington: Historical Society of Delaware, 1888), 36 (January 3, 1777).

"It's a fine fox chase, my boys!" James Wilkinson is the authority for Washington's exclamation, citing a 1796 conversation with Captain David Harris of Baltimore, who served at Princeton. *See* Wilkinson, *Memoirs of My Own Times,* 1:145.

"It may be doubted whether so small a number of men . . ." George Otto Trevelyan, *The American Revolution,* part 2, vol. 2 (New York: Longmans, Green, and Co., 1903), 113. Trevelyan offered this assessment at the conclusion of his account of the Battle of Trenton, but it is consistent with his interpretation of the operations along the Delaware ending with the American victory at Princeton, which he regarded as the turning point in the war. "The permanent and paramount consequence of those masterly operations was the establishment of Washington's military reputation, and the increased weight of his political and administrative authority throughout every State of the Confederacy, and up to the latest hour of the war" (p. 142).

"You cannot Conceive the Joy and Raptures . . ." John Chester to Samuel B. Webb, January 17, 1777, in *Reminiscences of Gen'l Samuel B. Webb of the Revolutionary Army* (New York: Globe Stationery and Printing, 1882), 30–31.

IV: Republics at War

Almost every one has heard of the soldiers of the Revolution being tracked by the blood of their feet on the frozen ground . . . Martin, *Narrative,* 206.

Chapter 13: American Republics

Opening

"air is the reverse of grace" [caption] John Adams, September 15, 1775, in Butterfield, ed., *Diary and Autobiography of John Adams,* 2:172–73.

"one of the soundest and strongest pillars of the Revolution" [caption] John Adams to Robert Waln, Jr., November 19, 1822, Adams Family Papers, Massachusetts Historical Society.

The Idea of a Republic

Inspired by the republics of classical antiquity . . . Paul H. Rahe, *Republics Ancient and Modern* (Chapel Hill: University of North Carolina Press, 1992) is a comprehensive treatment of the influence of ancient republicanism on modern republican thought. *See also* Carl Richard, *The Founders and the Classics: Greece, Rome, and the American Enlightenment* (Cambridge, MA: Harvard University Press, 1994).

"It is dangerous to our liberties and destructive to our trade . . ." William Pitt, Speech against appropriating money to support Hanoverian troops to operate in Flanders on January 17, 1744. Pitt insisted, "We ought to maintain as few regular soldiers as possible, both at home and abroad; we ought never to retain them long in the service; knowing that very few, afterwards, will turn for their support to honest and industrious employments." Francis Thackeray, *A History of the Right Honorable William Pitt, Earl of Chatham: Containing his Speeches in Parliament . . .* (2 vols., London: C. and J. Rivington, 1827), 1:127.

Republics were held together by public virtue . . . J.G.A. Pocock, *The Machiavellian Moment: Florentine Political Thought and the Atlantic Republican Tradition* (Princeton: Princeton University Press, 1975). *See also* Albert O. Hirschman, *The Passions and the Interests: Political Arguments*

for Capitalism before Its Triumph (Princeton: Princeton University Press, 1977).

The enthusiasm of educated Americans for republican ideals led them to employ symbols drawn from classical antiquity . . . *See* Garry Wills, *Cincinnatus: George Washington and the Enlightenment* (Garden City, NY: Doubleday, 1984).

Written Constitutions

American constitutionalism was shaped by the British constitutional and legal tradition and the experience of the imperial crisis . . . The work that defines this transformation and continues to shape our understanding of the political and constitutional achievement of the Revolutionary generation is Gordon S. Wood, *The Creation of the American Republic, 1776–1787* (Chapel Hill: University of North Carolina Press, 1969). For a short overview of a few of the main themes, *see* Gordon S. Wood, *Power and Liberty: Constitutionalism in the American Revolution* (New York: Oxford University Press, 2021).

Thoughts on Government

In November 1775, Richard Henry Lee asked Adams . . . Lee visited Adams at his lodgings on November 14, and the two men discussed the best form of government for republican states. Lee apparently asked Adams to write down his thoughts. The next day Adams did so in the form of a letter: John Adams to Richard Henry Lee, November 15, 1776, in Taylor, ed., *Papers of John Adams,* 3:307–8.

"providentially thrown in his Way . . ." John Adams to James Warren, April 20, 1776, in Taylor, ed., *Papers of John Adams,* 4:130–33. Adams enclosed a copy of the pamphlet version of *Thoughts on Government.* In the letter he refers to the author in the third person in order to maintain the pretense that *Thoughts on Government* was the work of an anonymous author, though Warren surely understood that the pamphlet was the work of Adams.

Other delegates heard about the document . . . George Wythe of Virginia asked for a copy, which Adams provided. Then Jonathan Dickson Sergeant of New Jersey asked for one, which Adams prepared, revising and expanding his thoughts. When Lee asked Adams for a copy of his revised thoughts, Adams reclaimed Wythe's copy and asked Lee to have it printed. Lee turned to Philadelphia printer John Dunlap, who completed *Thoughts on Government: Applicable to the Present State of the American Colonies. In a Letter from a Gentleman to his Friend* (Philadelphia: Printed by John Dunlap, 1776) on April 20, 1776. The number of copies Dunlap printed is not known, but it seems likely that most were distributed personally by Adams and Lee, who placed copies in the hands of men who would shape the constitutions of the independent states.

"mark out a Path, and putt Men upon thinking . . ." John Adams to James Warren, April 20, 1776, in Taylor, ed., *Papers of John Adams,* 4:130–33.

"feel, reason, and act" John Adams to John Penn [before March 27, 1776], in Taylor, ed., *Papers of John Adams,* 4:78–86.

"is liable to all the vices, follies, and frailties of an individual . . ." John Adams, *Thoughts on Government* [April 1776], in Taylor, ed., *Papers of John Adams,* 4:86–93. The remaining quotations in this subchapter are from this source.

Like many political thinkers, Adams worried . . . As C. Bradley Thompson has persuasively argued, Adams was an original political thinker who "attempted to synthesize ancient and modern thought in a way that brings into question the views of those scholars who see the founding period from the perspective of either classical republicanism or Lockean liberalism." C. Bradley Thompson, *John Adams and the Spirit of Liberty* (Lawrence: University of Kansas Press, 1998), 308–9.

The Virginia Declaration of Rights

"an Honour and an Happiness . . ." and **"The Dons, the Bashaws, the Grandees, the Patricians, the Sachems, the Nabobs . . ."** John Adams to Patrick Henry, June 3, 1776, in Taylor, ed., *Papers of John Adams,* 4:234–35.

"I am not without hopes it may produce good here . . ." and **"many and powerfull Enemys"** Patrick Henry to John Adams, May 20, 1776, in Taylor, ed., *Papers of John Adams,* 4:200–202. By the time Henry received his copy of *Thoughts on Government,* Richard Henry Lee had arranged for the printing of a handbill version titled "Government Scheme" to be distributed to members of the Virginia Convention as well as for the publication of the same text as "A Government Scheme" in Dixon and Hunter's *Virginia Gazette* on May 10. For the responsibility of Lee for both these publications, *see* John E. Selby, "Richard Henry Lee, John Adams, and The Virginia Constitution of 1776," *Virginia Magazine of History and Biography* 84, no. 4 (October 1976): 387–400. The surviving copy of the handbill (in the Chapin Library, Williams College) bears no date or printer's attribution. Lee had written to John Page on February 15 asking him to have it printed in Williamsburg. That letter does not seem to be extant, but Page replied from Williamsburg on February 20 explaining that he had been prevented from getting to it by the press of business and his own and his wife's illness. *See* John Page to Richard Henry Lee, February 20, 1776, in *American Archives,* series 4, vol. 4, 1208. Whether the handbill was printed in Williamsburg at Page's request between February 20 and April 20 or in Philadelphia after Lee returned there on March 11 is not clear. Lee alluded to the handbill in his letter to Patrick Henry on April 20, in which he sent a copy of the pamphlet version of *Thoughts on Government,* but it is not clear that he enclosed a copy of the handbill. Perhaps Henry had alluded to it in a previous letter not now known, prompting Lee to mention the handbill. *See* Richard Henry Lee to Patrick Henry, April 20, 1776, in Ballagh, ed., *Letters of Richard Henry Lee,* 1:176–80. It seems most likely that Page had the handbill printed in Virginia where it could be readily distributed. The absence of any known letter from Lee transmitting the handbill argues strongly for this to have been the case. However these things were accomplished, they reflect Lee's determination to disseminate Adams' ideas to members of the Virginia Convention, which he plainly accomplished.

"The systems recommended . . . are fraught with all the tumult and riot incident to simple democracy . . ." Braxton wrote an anonymous response to *Thoughts on Government,* published in pamphlet form as *An Address to the Convention of the Colony and Ancient Dominion of Virginia; on the Subject of Government in general, and recommending a particular Form to their Consideration. By a Native of that Colony* (Philadelphia: Printed by John Dunlap, 1776). The text

was republished in Dixon and Hunter's *Virginia Gazette* on June 8 and 15. Henry called Braxton's pamphlet "a silly thing" (Henry to Adams, May 20, 1776, in Taylor, ed., *Papers of John Adams,* 4:200–202).

The leading role in the Virginia Convention . . . On George Mason, *see* Robert A. Rutland, ed., *The Papers of George Mason, 1725–1792* (3 vols., Chapel Hill: University of North Carolina Press, 1970), and Robert Rutland, *George Mason: Reluctant Statesman* (Williamsburg, VA: Colonial Williamsburg, 1961).

"as an oppressive and unjust Invasion of my personal Liberty." George Mason to Martin Cockburn, April 18, 1784, in Rutland, ed., *Papers of George Mason,* 2:799.

"All men are born equally free and independent . . ." Virginia Declaration of Rights [ca. May 20–June 12, 1776], in Rutland, ed., *Papers of George Mason,* 1:274–91.

"A certain set of aristocrats—for we have such monsters here . . ." Thomas Ludwell Lee to Richard Henry Lee, June 1, 1776, in Henry, *Patrick Henry: Life, Correspondence and Speeches,* 1:424–25.

The Pennsylvania Constitution of 1776

The work of the Virginia Convention was widely admired and imitated in the flurry of constitution-making that followed American independence. Willi Paul Adams, *The First American Constitutions: Republican Ideology and the Making of the State Constitutions in the Revolutionary Era* (Chapel Hill: University of North Carolina Press, 1980), the work of a German scholar, remains a major work on Revolutionary constitutionalism. For a succinct discussion of the achievement of the states, *see* Wood, *Power and Liberty,* 32–53.

"Not a sixth part . . . ever read a word on the subject . . ." Thomas Smith to Arthur St. Clair, August 3, 1776, in William Henry Smith, ed., *The St. Clair Papers. The Life and Public Services of Arthur St. Clair Soldier of the Revolutionary War; President of the Continental Congress; and Governor of the North-western Territory with Correspondence and other Papers* (2 vols., Cincinnati: Robert Clarke & Co., 1882), 1:370–72.

"All elections, whether by the people or in general assembly, shall be by ballot . . ." How Pennsylvania's government, which had long been governed by cautious Quakers and their allies, was taken over by men who secured the adoption of the most democratic state constitution of the Revolutionary era has occupied the attention of historians for more than a century. The progress of their work illustrates how historical understanding changes as historians ask new questions, explore new sources, and are influenced by broader work in American history. In *The Revolutionary Movement in Pennsylvania* (Philadelphia: Published for the University [of Pennsylvania], 1901), Charles H. Lincoln argued that in 1776 the disfranchised western and urban population of the state wrested control of government from the "ruling aristocracy." J. Paul Selsam, *The Pennsylvania Constitution of 1776: A Study in Revolutionary Democracy* (Philadelphia: University of Pennsylvania Press, 1936) revised and extended Lincoln's interpretation into a regional- and class-oriented one that fit neatly into the contemporary paradigms of Frederick Jackson Turner and Charles Beard, with additions to account for Pennsylvania's unusual degree of religious and ethnic diversity. Other works along the same lines by Robert Brunhouse, Theodore Thayer, and Elisha Douglass followed in the 1940s and 1950s. David Freeman Hawke, *In the Midst of a Revolution* (Philadelphia: University of Pennsylvania Press, 1961) attributed the change to a determined minority in Philadelphia who controlled a web of Revolutionary committees and who managed to subvert the authority of the assembly and called for a constitutional convention dominated by their allies but didn't explain how. Richard A. Ryerson, *The Revolution Is Now Begun: The Radical Committee of Philadelphia, 1765–1776* (Philadelphia: University of Pennsylvania Press, 1978) explains how it happened—how the committees offered men who had not previously been involved in public life, including artisans, mechanics, shopkeepers, and others traditionally excluded from political office, an opportunity to be engaged in politics. Ryerson turned Hawke's determined minority into a broad movement of middling men.

"No country ever will be long happy . . . which is thus governed." John Adams to Francis Dana, August 16, 1776, in Taylor, ed., *Papers of John Adams,* 4:465–67. Dana, a Boston attorney, had written to Adams on July 28 about the need to form a constitution for Massachusetts, and commented on *Thoughts on Government:* "We want much your aid in this great business. I have seen your little pamphlet. I lament its littleness. I mean that you have not enlarged upon it in the manner you told me you intended to do, if you cou'd spare the time" (p. 4:465–67). In his reply of August 16 Adams explained that "The little Pamphlet you mention was printed, by Coll. Lee, who insisted upon it So much that it could not be decently refused. Instead of wondering that it was not enlarged, the Wonder ought to be that it was ever written. It is a poor Scrap." He added that "The Thoughts on Government were callculated for Southern Latitudes, not northern. But if the House should establish a single Assembly as a Legislature, I confess it would grieve me to the very Soul. And however others may be, I shall certainly never be happy under such a Government. However, the Right of the People to establish such a Government, as they please, will ever be defended by me, whether they choose wisely or foolishly."

"we live in an Age of political Experiments . . ." John Adams to Abigail Adams, October 4, 1776, in Butterfield, ed., *Adams Family Correspondence,* 2:137–38.

Citizens

The creation of republics . . . changed subjects into citizens. On the basis of American citizenship in natural law, *see* Douglas Bradburn, *The Citizenship Revolution: Politics & the Creation of the American Union, 1774–1804* (Charlottesville: University of Virginia Press, 2009), 22–42.

"the liberties of mankind" Petition of a Baptist Church at "Occagon" [May 19, 1776], Religious Petitions, 1774–1802, Library of Virginia. Bradburn, *Citizenship Revolution* (p. 315, note 52) correctly dates this petition to May 19; it is cataloged under June 20, 1776.

"declaration of the Honourable House with regard to equal liberty." Miscellaneous Petition [the Ten-Thousand Name Petition], October 16, 1776, Religious Petitions, Library of Virginia; for further discussion, see Bradburn, *Citizenship Revolution,* 36.

"a Broad base of Civil and religious Liberty . . ." The Petition, Remonstrance and Address of the Town of Pittsfield, quoted in Bradburn, *Citizenship Revolution,* 39.

"a poor man has rarely the honor of speaking to a gentleman on any terms . . ." *Pennsylvania Evening Post,* April 27, 1776.

"Everyone who has the least pretensions to be a gentleman . . ." Samuel Johnston to James Iredell, December 9, 1776, in Griffith J. McRee, ed., *Life and Correspondence of James Iredell* (2 vols., New York: D. Appleton and Co., 1857–58), 1:338–39.

The new men who sought and secured seats in the independent state legislatures . . . The social transformation of public life is a central theme of Gordon S. Wood, *The Radicalism of the American Revolution* (New York: Alfred A. Knopf, 1992).

"We are convinced of our right to be free"

The status of Indians in the new nation was complicated. Douglas Bradburn notes that "one of the most immediate consequences of the citizenship revolution was the bright line drawn between American citizens and American Indians" (Bradburn, *Citizenship Revolution,* 55). More than a generation of almost constant war between colonists and Indians, spanning the French and Indian War, Pontiac's Rebellion, the Cherokee War, and the Revolutionary War, increased the cultural divide between Indians and white Americans and hardened white animosity toward Indians, usually with little or no distinction between tribes. On this theme, *see* Jane T. Merritt, *At the Crossroads: Indians and Empires on a Mid-Atlantic Frontier* (Chapel Hill: University of North Carolina Press, 2003); Peter Silver, *Our Savage Neighbors: How Indian War Transformed Early America* (New York: W.W. Norton, 2008) is about the Pennsylvania frontier, 1750–1780, and argues that Indian conflict unified diverse peoples of European background; Patrick Griffin, *American Leviathan: Empire, Nation, and Revolutionary Frontier* (New York: Hill and Wang, 2007) argues that the sustained violence of incessant frontier warfare engendered a virulent hatred of Indians that ensured their exclusion from the new republic. The Revolution left them on the outside, as Bradburn writes, "to be treated with, bargained with, and bribed, and when those means failed, to be removed by force" (Bradburn, *Citizenship Revolution,* 57). Daniel R. Mandell, *Behind the Frontier: Indians in Eighteenth-Century Eastern Massachusetts* (Lincoln: University of Nebraska Press, 1996) documents the cultural marginalization of Indians who remained in regions along the coast settled by Europeans. These are just a few of the many books and articles about Indians and Indian-white relations in the eighteenth century published in the last thirty years that have collectively enriched our understanding of the period.

Emancipation began, writes Ira Berlin, "in the flames of the American Revolution." Berlin, *Long Emancipation,* 9, 47–106.

In 1781, an enslaved woman who later called herself Elizabeth Freeman brought suit . . . Arthur Zilversmit, "Quok Walker, Mumbet, and the Abolition of Slavery in Massachusetts," *William and Mary Quarterly* 25, no. 4 (October 1968): 614–24.

"born in this country, or brought from over sea" Francis Newton Thorpe, ed., *The Federal and State Constitutions, Colonial Charters, and Other Organic Laws of the States, Territories, and Colonies Now or Heretofore Forming the United States* of America (7 vols. Washington, D.C.: Government Printing Office, 1909), 6:3739–40. On the slow death of slavery in Vermont and continuing racial oppression in the state during its early years, *see* Harvey Amani Whitfield, *The Problem of Slavery in Early Vermont, 1777–1810* (Barre: Vermont Historical Society, 2014), which consists of an essay by Professor Whitfield and a selection of useful documents.

"private or public tyranny and slavery are alike detestable . . ." Mark Sammons and Valerie Cunningham, *Black Portsmouth: Three Centuries of African-American Heritage* (Durham: University of New Hampshire Press, 2004), 66. The New Hampshire legislature determined that the time "was not ripe and further consideration be postponed until a more convenient opportunity." The legislature took up the petition 234 years later and passed SB187, "An Act posthumously emancipating enslaved Africans in New Hampshire," on July 9, 2013. The legislature found that six of the twenty petitioners—Peter Warner, Pharaoh Shores, Jack Odiorne, Prince Whipple, Cesar Gerrish, and Romeo Rindge—had secured their freedom by 1800. The act declared the other fourteen petitioners—Samuel Wentworth, Winsor Moffatt, Cato Warner, Garrett Colton, Kittindge Tuckerman, Peter Frost, Seneca Hall, Nero Brewster, Pharaoh Rogers, Quam Sherburne, Cato Newmarch, Will Clarkson, Zebulon Gardner, and Cipio Hubbard—to be "emancipated freed men."

"all men are born equally free and independent . . ." Thorpe, ed., *Federal and State Constitutions*, 4:2453.

"the common blessings" to which they were "entitled . . . by nature." An Act for the gradual abolition of slavery, March 1, 1780, *Laws of the Commonwealth of Pennsylvania, from the fourteenth day of October, one thousand seven hundred, to the sixth day of April, one thousand eight hundred and two,* vol. 2 (Philadelphia: Published by J. Bioren . . . for Matthew Carey and self, 1803), 246–51. For the consequences of the act, *see* Gary B. Nash and Jean Soderlund, *Freedom by Degrees: Emancipation in Pennsylvania and Its Aftermath* (New York: Oxford University Press, 1991).

Chapter 14: A People's War

Opening

The captured men had been herded into makeshift prisons in and around New York City. On the experience of American prisoners in British hands, *see* Edwin G. Burrows, *Forgotten Patriots: The Untold Story of American Prisoners during the Revolutionary War* (New York: Basic Books, 2008). William Russell, an American sailor, was imprisoned at Mill Prison in Plymouth, England, and then moved to New York, where he was imprisoned on the hulk *Jersey,* from which he wrote to his mother, Mary Russell, on November 25, 1782: "I'm now in the worst of places," he wrote, adding that food "is so scant that it is not enough to keep Soul and Body together" (Robert Charles Lawrence Fergusson Collection, The Society of the Cincinnati). For a published first-hand account, see [Andrew Sherburne,] *Memoirs of Andrew Sherburne: A Pensioner of the Navy of the Revolution* (Utica, NY: William Williams, 1828). A Continental Navy seaman, Sherburne was captured when Charleston fell in 1780. Released, he returned to New Hampshire, where at sixteen he put to sea aboard the privateer *Greyhound.* He was subsequently captured, shipwrecked, recaptured, and then impressed to serve on the

Royal Navy sloop *Fairy,* bound for Plymouth, England. When they reached Plymouth, Sherburne chose to be confined in Mill Prison rather than serve in the Royal Navy. After several months he was taken with other prisoners to New York, where he was imprisoned on the hulk *Jersey,* which he described as "extreme filthy, and abounded with vermin," for the remainder of the war. His memoir offers one of the most important accounts of prison life on the *Jersey.* He wrote his memoirs, he explained, so "Americans may properly appreciate the freedom which they enjoy, while they learn the price of its purchase."

"My brave fellows, you have done all I asked you to do . . . but your country is at stake . . ." This account of Washington's appeal to his men to remain with the army was first published on March 24, 1832, in *The Phenix,* an obscure weekly newspaper published from 1827 to 1832 in Wellsboro, a small town in Tioga County in northwest Pennsylvania. The article was published at a moment of heightened interest in the Revolution stirred by the passage of the Pension Act of 1832, the first comprehensive veteran's pension legislation in U.S. history. It was reprinted under the title "The Battle of Princeton" in *Pennsylvania Magazine of History and Biography* 20 (1896): 515–19.

The text is a first-hand account of events leading to the American victory at Princeton written by a participant identified only as "Sergeant R." In his account of the battle, "Sergeant R" refers to "a comrade of ours whose name was Loomis from Lebanon, Ct." who was killed in the battle and describes having "the end of my forefinger" shot away. The reference to a Connecticut "comrade" indicates that "Sergeant R" was probably a Connecticut soldier. Nathaniel Root (1757–1840) of Coventry, Connecticut, a sergeant in Durkee's Regiment, which was raised in Connecticut, fits the facts. The regiment served with Mercer's Brigade at the Battle of Princeton and thus participated in the first stage of the battle when Mercer fell, all of which "Sergeant R" described in his narrative. Root's pension declaration, which he submitted in support of his application for a pension, resolves the mystery. In it, Root asserted that "the term for which he enlisted having expired the first of January, he continued in the service a volunteer and went with the army to Princeton: he marched with the front guard commanded by General Mercer into Princeton battle, was with him when wounded, and heard his order to retreat. The declarant had also a part of one of his fingures [*sic*] shot off in the battle." Pension Declaration of Nathaniel Root, August 2, 1832, Pension File of Nathaniel Root, S.18574, Revolutionary War Pension and Bounty-Land Warrant Application Files, Record Group 15: Records of the Veterans Administration, National Archives. How Root's narrative came to be published in *The Phenix* in March 1832 remains a mystery. He was then living in Coventry, Connecticut (his handsome Federal-style house is still standing) and was for many years one of the proprietors of a successful glassworks nearby. Tioga County was settled by post-war migrants from Connecticut, so there may have been some connection between Nathaniel Root and people in Wellsboro. None of his several adult children seem to have lived in Tioga County, but there were several Roots living there who may have been related to him.

For Washington's report that "the Continental Regiments from the Eastern Governments have to a Man agreed to stay Six Weeks beyond their Term of Inlistment which was to have expired the last day of this Month," *see* George Washington to the Commanding Officer at Morristown, December 30, 1776, in Chase, ed., *Papers of George Washington,* Revolutionary War Series, 7:490–91.

Amphitrite

On April 20, 1777 . . . *Amphitrite,* **arrived in Portsmouth, New Hampshire.** On *Amphitrite* and her cargo, *see* William Heath to George Washington, April 23, 1777, in Philander D. Chase, ed., *The Papers of George Washington,* Revolutionary War Series, vol. 9: March 28, 1777–June 10, 1777 (Charlottesville: University Press of Virginia, 1999), 244–46.

King George III and his ministers were well aware that the French were equipping the rebels . . . For examples of a British intelligence report on *Amphitrite* and other French efforts to supply the Americans, *see* the letters of David Murray, Lord Stormont, British ambassador to France, to Thomas Thynne, Lord Weymouth, British secretary of state for the southern department, of June 19, July 2, and July 9, 1777, in William James Morgan, ed., *Naval Documents of the American Revolution,* vol. 9: June 1, 1777–September 31, 1777 (Washington, DC: Naval Historical Center, 1986), 411–14, 452–53, 478–81. Stormont knew what was in the cargo hold of *Amphitrite* long before Washington because Edward Bancroft, secretary to American diplomats Silas Deane and Benjamin Franklin, was a British spy who copied confidential documents and passed them to Stormont by slipping them into a bottle hidden in a certain hollow tree on the south terrace of the Tuileries every Tuesday. The documents were copied in an invisible ink for which Stormont had the developing wash. Toward the end of 1777, Lord North sent Admiral Richard Howe an accounting of the arms and military stores secured by the American diplomats in France, making it clear that the British ministry knew the contents of these shipments, in some cases down to the last musket ball and bayonet. *See* Samuel Flagg Bemis, "Secret Intelligence, 1777: Two Documents," *Huntington Library Quarterly* 24, no. 3 (May 1961): 233–49.

Danbury

In April, Howe sent a force of some 1,900 men to destroy the supplies stored in Danbury. The chief source for the British side of the Danbury raid is Harry M. Lydenberg, ed., *Archibald Robertson: His Diaries and Sketches in America, 1762–1780* (New York: New York Public Library, 1930). For a narrative of the expedition, *see* Christopher Ward, *The War of the Revolution* (2 vols., New York: Macmillan, 1952), 2:492–503.

According to a local tradition, Ludington sent his sixteen-year-old daughter, Sybil . . . The earliest known reference to the ride of Sybil Ludington (1761–1839) is a letter from her nephew Charles H. Ludington (1825–1910) to Henry Deming, a Connecticut lawyer and legislator, of April 22, 1854, in which Ludington wrote: "I have been grievd at the neglect and injustice done to the memory of my Grandfather Henry Ludington who bore an important part in the engagement which succeeded the burning of Danbury. He held his commission from Washington and his regiment was made up of the hardy militia of the town of Kent in the then County of Dutchess and vicinity and he was a terror to the Tories and Cowboys who infested that district. On the eve-

ning of the 25th of April 1777, a messenger arrived his home with the intelligence that the British under Gen. Tryon had landed at Old Well and were marching toward Danbury. After dressing himself, he put my Aunt Sybil, a young girl of about fourteen on horseback in the dead of night dispatched her to Cold Spring a distance of some 25 miles through a country infested with Cowboys and Skinners to inform Gen'l Putnam who was stationed there. He then sounded the alarm and by daybreak was on the march toward Danbury" (Ludington Family Papers, New-York Historical Society). The rest of the letter provides details about Colonel Ludington's service in repulsing the raiders.

Deming was scheduled to give an oration on April 27, 1854, at the dedication of a monument to General Wooster, who was mortally wounded leading an attack on the raiders, and Charles H. Ludington apparently hoped he would mention Col. Henry Ludington in the oration. He did not, but decades later Charles H. Ludington shared his family's traditions about Colonel Ludington with Martha J. Lamb, who mentioned the colonel very briefly in her *History of the City of New York: its origins, rise and progress,* vol. 2 (New York: A.S. Barnes and Co., 1880). Lamb found Sybil's story more interesting, and wrote that since no one was at hand to alert the colonel's men, "his daughter Sibyl Ludington, a spirited young girl of sixteen, mounted her horse in the dead of night and performed this service, and by breakfast-time the next morning the whole regiment was on its rapid march to Danbury" (pp. 159–60). According to this new version, rather than a ride to alert Israel Putnam (who was actually stationed at Princeton, New Jersey, at the time), Sybil had ridden like Paul Revere to rouse the militia in her father's command. Substantially the same brief account was repeated, with some literary flourishes, in Willis Fletcher Johnson, *Colonel Henry Ludington: A Memoir* (privately printed, 1907), 89–90, to which the copyright was held by Charles H. Ludington and another grandchild of the colonel, Lavinia Elizabeth Ludington, who clearly sponsored the work.

The only serious scholarly examination of this family tradition is Paula D. Hunt, "Sybil Ludington, the Female Paul Revere: The Making of a Revolutionary War Heroine," *New England Quarterly* 88, no. 2 (June 2015): 187–222. Hunt connects Sybil's story to the various cultural forces historians associate with the development of American historical consciousness in the late nineteenth century, including anxiety about foreign immigration and broader economic and social changes, and notes that historical consciousness continues to be shaped today "away from the influence of the academy." She starts with the assumption that the Ludington family tradition that Sybil made some sort of nighttime ride to spread an alarm is false because no contemporary documentary evidence is known, but never marshals evidence tying Charles H. Ludington to the xenophobia and nostalgia she suggests motivated him and seems to have overlooked his 1854 letter mentioning Sybil's ride. Charles H. Ludington was born in 1825. The woman he calls his "Aunt Sybil" lived until 1839. She was not an imaginary person or someone conjured out of the distant past. The idea that she might have ridden out to spread an alarm, and that he heard the story from her or someone close to her, is not at all preposterous. A sixteen-year-old was not a child in 1777. Margaret Corbin and many other women who followed the army and shared in its privations were not much older. In the absence of better evidence, Sybil's ride remains an unsubstantiated family tradition, but a perfectly plausible one.

"the town had been laid in ashes . . ." Martin, *Narrative,* 46.

The British never attempted another inland raid of the kind. Alexander Hamilton recognized that the fierce American response to the raid made a success out of what could have been a complete disaster. He wrote to the New York Committee of Safety: "I congratulate you . . . on the Danbury expedition. The stores destroyed there have been purchased at a pretty high price to the enemy. The spirit of the people on the occasion does them great honor—is a pleasing proof that they have lost nothing of that primitive zeal, with which they begun the Contest, and will be a galling discouragement to the enemy from repeating attempts of the kind. Such an opposition under such circumstances was not to be expected. By every account both from our friends, and from themselves, they cannot have sustained a loss of less than 500 killed, wounded and taken. An honest intelligent lad, a prisoner with them, who made his escape two or three days ago, informs that he saw three vessels loaded with wounded. He was permitted to look into the hold of two of them, and affirms there could not be fewer than forty in each. He attempted to inspect the contents of the third but was hindered by the Sentries. He also informs, that there were loud wailings and lamentations among the soldiers' women on the occasion, and that the people of New York considered the affair in the light of a defeat to the British troops." Hamilton to the New York Committee of Correspondence, May 7, 1777, in Harold C. Syrett, ed., *The Papers of Alexander Hamilton,* vol. 1: 1768–1778 (New York: Columbia University Press, 1961), 248–50.

Among the American dead was twenty-five-year-old Samuel Elmer, Jr. I am indebted to Paul B. Elmore, a lineal descendant of Lieutenant Elmer and his father (the spelling of the family name has changed), for sharing his research on the two men, of whom he is properly very proud.

"Thus was I, a slave . . . fighting for liberty"

Among the soldiers in action that day was Jeffrey Brace . . . Jeffrey Brace, *The Blind African Slave, or Memoirs of Boyrereau Brinch, Nicknamed Jeffrey Brace,* ed., with an introduction by Kari J. Winters (Madison: University of Wisconsin Press, 2004), is a modern edition of the same title published by Harry Whitney in St. Albans, Vermont, in 1810. The original edition was undoubtedly very small, perhaps no more than a few hundred copies, and is now one of the rarest books dealing with the Revolutionary era. Brace was nearing seventy when he told his story to an idealistic young lawyer named Benjamin Prentiss, who wrote the book. Prentiss was plainly motivated by the ideals of the American Revolution and determined to see the nation fulfill their promise. "In America," Prentiss wrote, "that spirit of liberty, which stimulated us to shake off a foreign yoke and become an independent nation, has caused the New-England states to emancipate their slaves, and there is but one blot to tarnish the lustre of the American name, which is permitting slavery under a constitution, which declares that 'all mankind are naturally and of right ought to be free.' Whoever wishes to preserve the constitution of our general government, to keep sacred the enviable and ines-

timable principles, by which we are governed, and to enjoy the natural liberty of man, must embark in the great work of eliminating slavery and promoting general emancipation." *The Blind African Slave* was shocking in 1810 and it remains so today. It is a story worth grappling with—a raw account of the inhumane brutality of enslavement, of a fight for personal independence, and of endurance despite the crushing weight of racial injustice, recorded by a white man who challenged his generation to live up to the ideals of the Revolution.

"I believe all mankind should be free." In October 1777 the Connecticut legislature passed "An Act concerning Indians, Mulatto, and Negro Servants and Slaves," asserting that "sound Policy requires that the Abolition of Slavery should be effected as soon as may be, consistent with the Rights of Individuals, and the public Safety and Welfare." The law forbid the introduction of enslaved people into the state and provided that any enslaved person born after March 1, 1784, would be free at age twenty-five (in 1784 this was lowered to twenty-one). The law did not forbid the sale of enslaved people in Connecticut nor transporting them out of the state. The law also provided that enslavers could "apply to the Select-Men of the Town to which he belongs, for Liberty or License to emancipate or make free any such Servant or Slave," and that in such cases "it shall be the Duty of such Select-Men to Enquire into the Age, Abilities, Circumstances and Character of such Servant or Slave, and if they or the major Part of them shall be of Opinion that it is likely to be consistent with the real Advantage of such Servant or Slave, and that it is probable that the Servant or Slave will be able to support his or her own Person, and he or she is of good and peaceable Life and Conversation; such Select-Men or the major Part of them, shall give to the Owner or Master of such Servant or Slave, Certificate under their Hands, of their Opinion in the Premises, and that the Master or Owner of such Servant or Slave, hath Liberty to emancipate and set at Liberty such Servant or Slave." *Acts and Laws of the State of Connecticut, in America* (Hartford: Printed by Hudson and Goodwin, 1796), 396–99. The town records of Wallingford document that Rachel Johnson availed herself of this provision and pledged to emancipate an eight-year-old named Dolly when she reached the age of eighteen: "I Rachel Johnson for divers good reasons and causes but more especially because I believe all mankind should be free I do hereby manumit my servant maid Dolly who is about 8 years of age, that is I do make her free from all bonds that she is under to me when she shall be 18 years of age." The Wallingford record book records the emancipation of several other enslaved people, one or two at a time. Presumably the selectmen determined in 1788 that Dolly would be able to support herself. See C. Bancroft Gillespie, comp., *A Century of Meriden: An Historic Record and Pictorial Description of the Town of Meriden Connecticut and Men Who Have Made It* (Meriden, CT: Journal Publishing Co., 1906), 252.

"all mankind by nature are entitled to equal liberty and freedom" Manumissions under the act of 1777 continued for many years. Abijah Holbrook, a miller who settled in Torrington after the war, freed Jacob and Ginna Prince in 1798, when they were about twenty-eight. Holbrook was a miller who settled in Torrington after the war. Lemuel Hayes, the first ordained African-American minister in the Congregational Church, was pastor in Torrington when Holbrook arrived. Whether Hayes, an eloquent spokesman for the liberty of African Americans, influenced Holbrook's views on slavery is more than we know. Coincidentally, abolitionist John Brown was born in Torrington in 1800. Holbrook's declaration read: "Know all men by these presents that I, Abijah Holbrook of Torrington, in the county of Litchfield and state of Connecticut, being influenced by motives of humanity and benevolence, believing that all mankind by nature are entitled to equal liberty and freedom; and whereas I the said Holbrook agreeable to the laws and customs of this state and the owner and possessor of two certain negroes which are of that class that are called slaves for life: viz, Jacob Prince a male negro, and Ginne a female, wife of said Jacob; and whereas the said negroes to this time have served me with faithfulness and fidelity, and they being now in the prime and vigor of life, and appear to be well qualified as to understanding and economy to maintain and support themselves by their own industry, and they manifesting a great desire to be delivered from slavery and bondage: I therefore the said Abijah Holbrook, do by these presents freely and absolutely emancipate the said Jacob and Ginne, and they are hereby discharged from all authority, title, claim, control and demand that I the said Holbrook now have or ever had in or unto the persons or services of them the said Jacob and Ginne, and they from and after the date hereof shall be entitled to their liberty and freedom, and to transact business for themselves, in their own names and for their own benefit and use. To witness whereof I have hereunto set my hand and seal this 18th day of August A.D. 1798." Samuel Orcutt, *History of Torrington, Connecticut, from its first settlement in 1737, with biographies and genealogies* (Albany, NY: J. Munsell, Printer, 1878), 212.

Even on the New England frontier, he could not escape bigotry and exploitation. On the challenges black settlers faced in early Vermont, *see* Whitfield, *Problem of Slavery in Early Vermont.* Brace's experience in Vermont was not unusual. For the story of another African-American veteran who moved to Vermont, Peter Hunter, and his widow's struggled to secure the pension due to her, *see* Jack D. Warren, Jr., *America's First Veterans* (Washington, DC: American Revolution Institute, 2020), 146–48.

Burgoyne

John Burgoyne . . . devised a plan he believed would end the war. For an excellent sketch of Burgoyne, *see* Andrew Jackson O'Shaughnessy, *The Men Who Lost America: British Leadership, the American Revolution, and the Fate of the Empire* (New Haven: Yale University Press, 2013), 123–64. Burgoyne's account of his campaign, including a narrative, transcripts of parliamentary hearings, and documents he assembled to defend his conduct, is collected in [John Burgoyne,] *A State of the Expedition from Canada, as laid before the House of Commons, by Lieutenant-General Burgoyne, and verified by evidence; with a collection of authentic documents, and an addition of many circumstances which were prevented from appearing before the House by the prorogation of Parliament* (London: Printed for J. Almon, 1780).

"By what we herd they will not trouble us here . . ." Aquila Cleaveland to Mercy Cleaveland, June 8–10, 1777, Pension File of Aquila Cleaveland, R.2036, p. 25, Revolutionary War Pension and Bounty-Land Warrant Application Files,

Record Group 15: Records of the Veterans Administration, National Archives.

"the Messengers of Justice and of Wrath await them . . ." Burgoyne issued his proclamation on June 23. It was published in *The Gentleman's Magazine,* August 1777 (London: Printed for D. Henry, 1777), 359–60. Lord Germain had advised Burgoyne as early as August 1776, "I hope every precaution has been taken to secure the Indians to our interest. . . . The dread the people of New England etc. have of a war with the savages, proves the expediency of our holding that scourge over them." Germain to Burgoyne, August 23, 1776, in W.O. Hewlett, ed., *Report on the Manuscripts of Mrs. Stopford-Sackville, Of Drayton House, Northamptonshire* (2 vols., Hereford: Printed for His Majesty's Stationery Office, 1904–1910), 2:39–40. Lafayette, who had just joined Washington's army, wrote that Burgoyne "issued a pompous and ridiculous proclamation for which he has since paid dearly." Lafayette to the duc d'Ayen, December 16, 1777, in Stanley J. Idzerda, ed., *Lafayette in the Age of the American Revolution: Selected Letters and Papers, 1776–1790,* vol. 1: December 7, 1776–March 30, 1778 (Ithaca, NY: Cornell University Press, 1977), 188–95.

"friends of Government . . . will be found so numerous . . ." William Howe to Guy Carleton, April 5, 1777, in Hewlett, ed., *Report on the Manuscripts of Mrs. Stopford-Sackville,* 2:65–66.

"Warriors, you are free . . . strike at the common enemies of Great-Britain and America . . ." "Substance of the Speech of Lieutenant-General Burgoyne to the Indians . . . June 21, 1777," in Burgoyne, *State of the Expedition,* xii–xiii (pages in the appendix are numbered in Roman).

Facing Burgoyne was the army of Major General Philip Schuyler . . . Historians have had mixed views about Schuyler. Benson Lossing, *The Life and Times of Philip Schuyler* (2 vols., New York: Sheldon & Co., 1860), one of the carefully documented biographies of a Revolutionary War general, is laudatory. Martin H. Bush, *Revolutionary Enigma; A Re-Appraisal of General Philip Schuyler of New York* (Port Washington, NY: Ira J. Friedman, 1969) describes Schuyler as a lukewarm patriot, more concerned about his honor than the cause, an interpretation disputed by Don Gerlach, *Proud Patriot: Philip Schuyler and the War of Independence, 1775–1783* (Syracuse: Syracuse University Press, 1987), a thoroughly documented study, credits Schuyler with delaying Burgoyne and making the subsequent victory at Saratoga possible. Don Higginbotham, a leading military historian of the Revolution, thought Gerlach overreached in giving Schuyler more credit for that victory than Gates.

"A wild and unknown country . . ."

"a wild and unknown country." August Wilhelm Du Roi, *Journal of Du Roi the Elder, In the Service of the Duke of Brunswick, 1776–1777,* translated by Charlotte S.J. Epping (New York: D. Appleton & Co., 1911), 105.

The army used the lake to move south . . . For historical and archaeological details about the kinds of bateaux Burgoyne used, *see* Nathan A. Gallagher, "The Lake George Bateaux: British Colonial Utility Craft in the French and Indian War," M.A. thesis, Texas A&M University, 2015.

"No finer or more beautiful sight can be imagined . . ." Du Roi, *Journal of Du Roi the Elder,* 90.

"Such perseverance is seldom found in history, except in a republic . . ." Du Roi, *Journal of Du Roi the Elder,* 98.

"the worst and most disagreeable swampy road that ever was." "Journal of Lieutenant Ebenezer Elmer of the Third Regiment of New Jersey Troops in the Continental Service," [continued from vol. 2,] *Proceedings of the New Jersey Historical Society,* vol. 3: 1848–1849 (Newark: Printed at the Office of the Daily Advertiser, 1849), 21–90; Elmer had traversed this road on October 30, 1776 (p. 39).

"The woods here are immense . . ." Du Roi, *Journal of Du Roi the Elder,* 107–8.

"They came over to fight the rebels, and the rebels can always select the best places . . ." Du Roi, *Journal of Du Roi the Elder,* 108.

"Burgoyne's Army will meet, sooner or later an effectual Check . . ." George Washington to Philip Schuyler, July 22, 1777, in Frank E. Grizzard, Jr., ed., *The Papers of George Washington,* Revolutionary War Series, vol. 10: June 11, 1777–August 18, 1777 (Charlottesville: University Press of Virginia, 2000), 363–65.

"There are your enemies . . . we must have them in half an hour, or my wife sleeps a widow this night." There seem to be as many versions of John Stark's words to his men just before the Battle of Bennington as there are accounts of the battle. All involve pointing out the enemy and insisting that they would defeat them or he would die in the attempt, leaving his wife a widow. In some versions it's "Molly Stark sleeps a widow," or some variant using her name. John Stark died in 1822 at the age of ninety-three. The earliest known version of what he said before the battle was written by Caleb Stark, the general's son, and appeared in an 1831 book combining a reprinting of Robert Rogers' reminiscences of the frontier fighting in the French and Indian War (John Stark served under Rogers) with the younger Stark's memoir of his father: *Reminiscences of the French War; Containing Rogers' Expeditions with the New-England Rangers Under His Command, as Published in London in 1765 . . . to Which is Added an Account of the Life and Military Services of Maj. Gen. John Stark; with notice and anecdotes of other officers distinguished in the French and Revolutionary War* (Concord, NH: Luther Roby, 1831). Caleb Stark, who was born in 1759, served with his father from the Siege of Boston to the Battle of Princeton and remained in the army after his father resigned after being passed over for promotion to brigadier general. Caleb was not present at Bennington but was granted leave and visited his father within weeks of the battle. Shortly thereafter John Stark was commissioned brigadier general in the Continental Army. Caleb served with him for the remainder of the war. He had abundant opportunities to hear accounts of Bennington from his father and others. In his account, which there is no reason to dispute, he writes: "General Stark . . . addressed his yeomanry as follows. 'There are your enemies the red coats, and Tories—we must have them in half an hour, or my wife sleeps a widow this night'" (p. 250). There is no sound documentary evidence for any other version. Caleb's son, also named Caleb, expanded his father's work and included a sketch of his father in a new book: Caleb Stark, *Memoir and Official Correspondence of Gen. John Stark, with notices of several other officers of the Revolution* (Concord, NH: Published by G. Parker Lyon, 1860). The younger Caleb included a sketch of his father and

a different version of his grandfather's words at Bennington: "'There are the enemies, boys, the red coats and tories; you must beat them, or Betty Stark sleeps a widow to-night'" (p. 100). He offered no explanation for the difference.

"I believe that the English have counted too much . . ." Du Roi, *Journal of Du Roi the Elder,* 116.

"marauding and cruelties . . ." Du Roi, *Journal of Du Roi the Elder,* 99.

Saratoga

"if we by any Means could be put in a Situation of attacking the Enemy . . ." Philip Schuyler to George Washington, August 4, 1777, in Grizzard, ed., *Papers of George Washington,* Revolutionary War Series, 10:506.

"We shall never defend a Post, until We shoot a General" John Adams to Abigail Adams, August 19, 1777, in Butterfield, ed., *Adams Family Correspondence,* 2:319–20.

"not one . . . was properly uniformed . . ." [caption] From a letter published in Ray Waldron Pettengill, *Letters from America, 1776–1779: Being Letters of Brunswick, Hessian, and Waldeck Officers with the British Armies during the Revolution* (Boston: Houghton Mifflin, 1924), 110. Pettengill translated letters originally published in August Ludwig Schlözer, *Briefwechsel meist historischen und politischen Inhalts,* published in Gottingen from 1776 to 1782. An important German historian, Schlözer published letters in his *Briefwechsel* from mercenaries serving with the British army in America, most of them apparently addressed to him and discussing topics it seems Schlözer asked the men to write to him about. The writers, unfortunately, are not identified.

The armies fought at a place called Freeman's Farm on September 19. Kevin J. Weddle, *The Compleat Victory: Saratoga and the American Revolution* (New York: Oxford University Press, 2021) focuses tightly and well on the strategic and tactical decisions of generals but gives scant attention to ordinary soldiers and the social dynamics, involving settlers and Indians, that shaped warfare along the Lake Champlain–Hudson River corridor in the eighteenth century. Richard M. Ketchum, *Saratoga: Turning Point of America's Revolutionary War* (New York: Henry Holt, 1997) takes effective advantage of varied sources and the drama of the campaign.

"behaved more like a madman than a cool and discreet officer." Samuel Woodruff to William Leete Stone, October 31, 1827, published as an appendix to William Leete Stone, *Life of Joseph Brant—Thayedanegea, including the Border Wars of the American Revolution, and Sketches of the Indian Campaigns of Generals Harmar, St. Clair, and Wayne* (2 vols., Cooperstown, New York: H. & E. Phinney, 1844), 1:xlix–lvi (pages in the appendix are numbered in Roman).

Lafayette

"composed entirely of Virginians" Lafayette to the duc d'Ayen, December 16, 1777, in Idzerda, ed., *Lafayette in the Age of the American Revolution,* 1:188–95. The best way to begin to understand and appreciate Lafayette is reading his letters like this one, written from Valley Forge to his skeptical father-in-law, which is brimming full of youthful enthusiasm: "I have had the happiness of gaining the friendship of everyone and I flatter myself that it is impossible to desire to be better off than I am here. No occasion is lost to give me proofs of it. You know my intention was to command a division, yet I went the whole summer without such a command. All that time I spent in General Washington's household, just as though I were in the home of a friend of twenty years. After my return from Jersey, he asked me to choose from several brigades the division that would suit me best. I have taken one composed entirely of Virginians. It is undermanned at the present, even in proportion to the weakness of the whole army; it is almost entirely naked, but I have been led to believe that I shall get some cloth with which I shall make some clothing, and some recruits, of whom I must then make soldiers at about the same time."

"a people who are entirely free." Lafayette to Marie Adrienne Françoise de Noailles, marquise de Lafayette, January 6, 1778, Arthur H. and Mary Marden Dean Lafayette Collection, Cornell University Library. Lafayette wrote to his wife, explaining why he must remain in America: "I have a great desire to see this revolution succeed. The humiliation of insolent England, the advantage to my country, the welfare of humanity, for which it is important that there be in the world a people who are entirely free, and the sacrifices that I and my friends have already made for this cause."

"as pure a son of liberty as I have ever known." Thomas Jefferson to Horatio Gates, February 21, 1798, in Barbara B. Oberg, ed., *The Papers of Thomas Jefferson,* vol. 30: January 1, 1798–January 31, 1799 (Princeton: Princeton University Press, 2003), 123–24.

Brandywine and Germantown

Washington moved south and barred Howe's way . . . For the strategic challenge Washington faced when Howe sailed from New York, *see* "Maneuver Wears Out Men and Shoes," Freeman, *George Washington,* 4:443–70. On the Battle of Brandywine, the largest since Brooklyn, *see* Ward, *War of the Revolution,* 1:334–54. The most comprehensive treatment of the battle is Michael C. Beattie, *Brandywine: A Military History of the Battle That Lost Philadelphia but Saved America, September 11, 1777* (El Dorado Hills, CA: Savas Beatie, 2014).

Washington's winter camp at Valley Forge, in a hilly region west of Philadelphia, was easily defended . . . On the winter encampment, *see* the creative work of Steven Elliott, *Surviving the Winters: Housing Washington's Army during the Revolutionary War* (Norman: University of Oklahoma Press, 2021). He explains that building hundreds of huts to make a winter encampment was an innovation. European armies typically spent winters in barracks or billeted in towns, occupying houses and outbuildings, as the British did in Boston, New York, and Philadelphia. Having neither a town to occupy nor barracks, Washington's army built its own winter quarters, which became, in effect, some of the most populous if ephemeral towns in America. *See also* Charles Royster, *A Revolutionary People at War: The Continental Army and American Character, 1775–1783* (Chapel Hill: University of North Carolina Press, 1979), 190–254. When the army arrived at Valley Forge, Lafayette wrote to his father-in-law: "Here the American army will attempt to clothe itself, because it is practically naked, to improve itself, because it is great need of training, and to rebuild itself, because it is very deficient in numbers." Lafayette to the duc d'Ayen, December 16, 1777, in Idzerda, ed., *Lafayette in the Age of the American Revolution,* 1:188–95.

"appears to be a man profound in the Science of war . . ." John Laurens to Henry Laurens, February 28, 1778, in David R. Chesnutt and C. James Taylor, eds., *The Papers of Henry Laurens,* vol. 12: November 1, 1777–March 15, 1778 (Columbia: University of South Carolina Press, 1990), 483–84.

Chapter 15: The French Alliance

Opening

Callet and his assistants painted twelve copies . . . [caption] On the Callet portrait of Louis XVI, *see* Sarah Medlam, "Callet's Portrait of Louis XVI: A Picture Frame as a Diplomatic Tool," *Furniture History* 43 (2007): 143–54.

The outcome of the campaigns of 1777 might have led the British government to conclude that persisting in the war was folly. The king would have nothing of it. *See* Roberts, *Last King of America,* 331–33.

"I am very melancholy notwithstanding our victory . . ." Lord North to William Eden, November 4, 1777, in Charles R. Ritcheson, *British Politics and the American Revolution* (Norman: University of Oklahoma Press, 1954). Eden was undersecretary of state for the northern department and a confidant of North. He directed the gathering of intelligence in Europe and went to America with the Carlisle Commission in 1778. *See also* Whiteley, *Lord North,* 171.

Empire and Revolution

The British Empire in North America had always been chaotic and disorganized . . . Bunker, *Empire on the Edge* describes the British Empire on the eve of the war as "an empire whose time had passed: an odd and fragile empire no one had designed and very few people could claim to understand" (p. 12).

"Numerous as the people are in the several old provinces . . ." Benjamin Franklin, Examination before the Committee of the Whole of the House of Commons, February 13, 1766, in Labaree, ed., *Papers of Benjamin Franklin,* 13:124–62.

the price of dominion included the growing costs of the military establishment required to preserve and extend the royal domain . . . By the end of what Lawrence Henry Gipson aptly termed the Great War for Empire, Britain was a fiscal-military state dependent on rising taxation to pay the mounting costs of the Royal Navy and the much smaller army and to service its debts. The campaign of authoritarian reformers to extract tax revenue from British America seemed essential to maintain the empire. *See* John Brewer, *The Sinews of Power: War, Money, and the English State, 1688–1783* (New York: Alfred A. Knopf, 1989). On the dramatic increases in the cost of making war in the eighteenth century, *see* Geoffrey Parker, *The Military Revolution: Military Innovation and the Rise of the West, 1500–1800* (Cambridge: Cambridge University Press, 1988).

The American Revolution, with its demands for local independence and autonomy, popular sovereignty, and universal liberty, challenged the European imperial system. The Revolution defied British imperial reformers intent on imposing a more orderly but also dramatically more authoritarian system for governing the empire. What Americans perceived as a conspiracy against liberty was actually a program of authoritarian reform against which Americans successfully rebelled. *See* Justin du Rivage, *Revolution Against Empire: Taxes, Politics, and the Origins of American Independence* (New Haven: Yale University Press, 2017), one of the most important books on the Revolution of the last decade.

"Without a decisive naval force we can do nothing definite . . ." George Washington to the marquis de Lafayette, November 15, 1781, in Fitzpatrick, ed., *Writings of George Washington,* 23:340–42.

"the maddest idea in the world" John Adams, Notes of Debates, October 7, 1775, in Butterfield, ed., *Diary and Autobiography of John Adams,* 2:198–202.

Franklin in Paris

King Louis XVI of France and his ministers were imperialists . . . To secure an alliance with France, American emissaries had to navigate the complex web of European diplomacy. The best modern overview is Jonathan R. Dull, *A Diplomatic History of the American Revolution* (New Haven: Yale University Press, 1985), which is deeply informed by modern scholarship and an intimate knowledge of American diplomatic correspondence. It differs in emphasis from the earlier classic work of Samuel Flagg Bemis, *The Diplomacy of the American Revolution* (New York: D. Appleton-Century Co., 1935), which devotes more attention to the boundaries of the new nation, neutral shipping, and fishing rights.

Persuading the king's government was the task of Benjamin Franklin . . . Franklin's mission to France has been the subject of many works. The authors of the best have had erudite volumes of *The Papers of Benjamin Franklin* at their disposal. Jonathan R. Dull, *Benjamin Franklin and the American Revolution* (Lincoln: University of Nebraska Press, 2010), the work of one of the editors, is an excellent starting point. Dull explodes the older view of Franklin, which Franklin cultivated, of a gentle conciliator, insisting that Franklin was a committed, passionate revolutionary who disguised his radicalism under a veneer of genial affability. *See also* Wood, *Americanization of Benjamin Franklin.*

The French foreign minister, the comte de Vergennes . . . supported an alliance with the United States . . . On Vergennes, *see* especially Bernard de Montferrand, *Vergennes, La gloire de Louis XVI* (Tallandier: Paris, 2017), a perceptive interpretation of Vergennes by a seasoned modern diplomat alive to the possibilities and limitations under which Vergennes labored and the imagination and dedication Vergennes brought to his work. I am grateful to Ambassador Montferrand for his assistance on these points.

"A little revenge"

That moment came on December 4, 1777, when a detailed report of Burgoyne's surrender and of the Battle of Germantown reached Paris. The arrival of news of the victory at Saratoga and the Battle of Germantown is recorded in the diplomatic journal of Arthur Lee, September 26, 1777–May 10, 1778, in Richard Henry Lee, *Life of Arthur Lee* (2 vols., Boston: Wells and Lilly, 1829), 1:333–413. Lee's report of the news of December 4 is on p. 357.

"more Influence upon the European Mind than that of Saratoga . . ." John Adams to James Lovell, July 26, 1778,

in Robert J. Taylor, ed., *Papers of John Adams,* vol. 6: March–August 1778 (Cambridge, MA: Harvard University Press, 1983), 318–20. The influence of the victory at Saratoga on French calculations has been overemphasized in the historical literature. The French had been preparing for a naval war with Britain for a long time, and the failure of the British to end the war in 1777 provided the opening. *See* Jonathan R. Dull, *The French Navy and American Independence: A Study in Arms and Diplomacy, 1774–1787* (Princeton: Princeton University Press, 1975).

"former proposition of an alliance" On December 6 Arthur Lee recorded in his diplomatic journal that Gérard met with them at Franklin's house in Passy: "He said that as there now appeared no doubt of the ability and resolution of the states to maintain their independency, he could assure them it was wished they would resume their former proposition of an alliance, or any new one they might have, and that it could not be done too soon" (Lee, *Life of Arthur Lee,* 1:357).

"a little revenge . . . I wore this coat on the day Widderburn abused me . . ." Franklin's comment was recorded by Benjamin Rush, who made notes on his "Conversations with Dr Franklin" beginning in 1785. In the final entry for June 12, 1789, Rush recorded this exchange between Silas Deane and Franklin: "'Why do you wear that old coat to day,' said Mr Dean to Dr F on their way to sign the treaty with the United States. 'To give it a little revenge. I wore this Coat on the day Widderburn abused me at Whitehall,' said the Doctor." "Excerpts from the Papers of Dr. Benjamin Rush," *Pennsylvania Magazine of History and Biography* 29 (1905): 15–30. The exchange between Deane and Franklin is on p. 28.

That the coat was made of reddish-brown or rusty red colored velvet (and not blue, as is reported in some modern accounts of the treaty signing) is attested to by Marie Anne de Vichy-Chamrond, marquise du Deffand, a famous French hostess and indefatigable letter writer. Madame du Deffand described Franklin's appearance in her letter to Horace Walpole of March 22, 1778: "Le Franklin avait un habit de velours mordoré, des bas blanc, des cheveux étalés, ses lunettes sur le nez et un chapeau blanc sous le bras. Ce chapeau blanc est-il un symbole de la liberté?" [Franklin wore a coat of reddish-brown velvet, white stockings, his hair flowing down, his spectacles on his nose and a white hat under his arm. Is this white hat a symbol of liberty?]. W.S. Lewis, ed., *The Yale Edition of the Correspondence of Horace Walpole,* vol. 7: Walpole's Correspondence with Madame du Deffand and Wiart [vol. 5 of this correspondence, edited by W.S. Lewis and Warren Hunting Smith] (New Haven: Yale University Press, 1939), 33–35. Madame du Deffand could not have seen Franklin on the day of the signing; she had been blind since 1754. She was undoubtedly told what Franklin was wearing by a spectator. It seems that it was the report that Franklin wore a white hat that caught her interest, and that she described the rest to fill out the picture. *See also* Richard Meade Bache, "Franklin's Ceremonial Coat," *Pennsylvania Magazine of History and Biography* 23 (1899): 444–52. The Franklin Institute owns three small pieces of brown fabric said by the donors—descendants of Franklin's daughter, Sarah Franklin Bache—to have been taken from this suit, the largest just 1.25 by 2.25 inches, with wales about .25 inches wide. They are what would now be called cotton corduroy, but which in eighteenth-century Britain and America was called Manchester velvet.

This was probably the same suit in which Joseph Siffred Duplessis depicted Franklin in his 1778 portrait, now in the Metropolitan Museum of Art. The choice of the reddish-brown color for the suit in the portrait cannot be a coincidence. In the artist's pastel sketch, also in the Metropolitan Museum of Art, the suit is gray. Nor is the addition of the fur collar a random one: X-ray analysis by the museum demonstrates it was added after the rest of the painting was complete. The addition of the fur collar to the coat Franklin wore at Whitehall is an elaborate visual pun at Wedderburn's expense, undoubtedly devised by Franklin himself. In his denunciation of Franklin, Wedderburn mocked Franklin's reputation as a man of letters, saying that Franklin was actually "homo trium literatum"—a man of three letters, *fur*, the Latin word for thief. The Duplessis portrait is displayed in an elaborate carved frame bearing, in place of Franklin's name, the three letters *vir*, the Latin word for a man of virtue, an assertion about Franklin underscored by the addition of the fur collar, which had appeared on many French representations of Franklin as a symbol of the rustic simplicity of America. On the portrait as a visual response to Wedderburn, *see* Keith Arbour, "One Last Word: Benjamin Franklin and the Duplessis Portrait of 1778," *Pennsylvania Magazine of History and Biography* 118, no. 3 (July 1994): 183–208. Arbour makes the connection between the fur collar in the portrait and Wedderburn's denunciation but does not note that the reddish-brown coat in the portrait is the *habit de velours mordoré* described by Madame du Deffand. *See also* "The Presentation of the American Commissioners at Versailles: Two Accounts," March 20, 1778, in William B. Willcox, ed., *The Papers of Benjamin Franklin,* vol. 26: March 1, 1778–June 30, 1778 (New Haven: Yale University Press, 1987), 138–41.

The Carlisle Commission

George III met with James Hutton, one of Franklin's many British friends . . . Georges Grand (often referred to as George Grand by British and Americans correspondents), a Dutch banker, wrote to the comte de Vergennes on January 1, 1778, that Hutton had gone to Paris "to see his old and intimate friend Dr. Franklin" and that Hutton had told him that his meeting with Franklin "was both cordial and affectionate, and their conversation very animated for two hours. This man sees the King and Queen a good deal, by whom he is esteemed, as he is by all who know him, in consequence of his recognized virtues and probity. If he is a fresh emissary, I regard him as more dangerous than any other, because of his merits, of the confidence he inspires, and of his old ties. He told me plainly during the conversation, that he had had a tête-a-tête conference of an hour with the King; that that Prince, whom he adores, breathed nothing but peace; that he had given a proof thereof by putting an end to the last war as soon as he could, and that, in order to finish this one, he was disposed to grant to the Americans everything they might ask, except the word *independence*. He added to me that, if the House of Bourbon had sacrificed twenty millions sterling to cause English heads to be broken by Englishmen, the Ministry could not have served it better; that it was time to put an end to this butchery, and to prevent the total ruin of the two people." Georges Grand to Vergennes, in John W. Jordan, "Some Account of James Hutton's Visit to Franklin, in France, in

December of 1777," *Pennsylvania Magazine of History and Biography* 32, no. 2 (1908): 223–32.

"short of absolute Independency . . ." James Hutton to Benjamin Franklin, January 27, 1778, in William B. Willcox, ed., *The Papers of Benjamin Franklin,* vol. 25: October 1, 1777–February 28, 1778 (New Haven: Yale University Press, 1986), 529–30.

"You have lost this mad War . . ." Benjamin Franklin to James Hutton, February 1, 1778, in Willcox, ed., *Papers of Benjamin Franklin,* 25:562–63.

"admit of any claim or title to independency" Instructions by King George III to his Commissioners to treat with the North American Colonies, April 12, 1778 [Historical Manuscripts Commission], *The Manuscripts of the Earl of Carlisle, Preserved at Castle Howard* (London: Printed for Her Majesty's Stationery Office, by Eyre and Spottiswoode, 1897), 322–33. This publication includes most of the important British documents relating to the Carlisle Commission, including some not found elsewhere.

"decently tarred and feathered." Henry Laurens to James Duane, April 17, 1778, in Paul H. Smith, ed., *Letters of Delegates to Congress, 1774–1789,* vol. 9: February 1, 1778–May 31, 1778 (Washington, DC: Library of Congress, 1982), 429–31.

"The injuries we have received from the British Nation . . ." George Washington to John Banister, April 21, 1778, in David R. Hoth, ed., *The Papers of George Washington,* Revolutionary War Series, vol. 14: March 1, 1778–April 30, 1778 (Charlottesville: University of Virginia Press, 2004), 573–79.

"baffled, defeated . . . disgraced . . ." Patrick Henry to Richard Henry Lee, June 18, 1778, in Henry, *Patrick Henry,* 2:564–65.

"The common people hate us in their hearts . . ." Francis Howard, Earl of Carlisle, to Margaret Caroline Howard, Countess of Carlisle, July 21, 1778, in *Manuscripts of the Earl of Carlisle,* 356–57.

"I have nothing very interesting to do here . . ." Lafayette to Admiral d'Estaing, September 13, 1778, in Stanley J. Idzerda, ed., *Lafayette in the Age of the American Revolution: Selected Letters and Papers, 1776–1790,* vol. 2: April 10, 1778–March 20, 1780 (Ithaca, NY: Cornell University Press, 1979), 182, note 2. For Lafayette's written challenge to Carlisle, October 5, 1778, *see Manuscripts of the Earl of Carlisle,* 374. The original is in French, of which this is a translation: "I had thought up to now, my lord, that I would never have any business except with your generals, and I hoped for the honor of seeing them only at the head of the troops which are respectively entrusted to us. Your letter of August 26 to the Congress of the United States, and the insulting reference to my country which you wrote there, could only give me something to settle with you. I do not deign to refute it, my lord, but I desire to punish it. It is you, as head of the Commission, whom I summon to give me satisfaction for it, as public as the offense was, and as the refutation which follows it will be; it would not have been so late if the letter had reached me sooner. Forced to be away for a few days, I hope to find your answer when I return. M. de Gimat, a French officer, will make arrangements for me at your convenience. I have no doubt that for the honor of his compatriot General Clinton will agree to do so [for you]. As for me, my lord, all are good to me, provided that to the glorious advantage of being French, he adds that of proving to a man of your nation that mine will never be attacked with impunity." The challenge is also in Idzerda, ed., *Lafayette in the Age of the American Revolution,* 2:187–89. *See also* Lafayette to Washington, September 24, 1778, in Philander D. Chase, ed., *The Papers of George Washington,* Revolutionary War Series, vol. 17: September 15, 1778–October 31, 1778 (Charlottesville: University of Virginia Press, 2008), 118–19. For an early account of the affair, *see* Ebenezer Mack, *The Life of Gilbert Motier de Lafayette* (Ithaca, NY: Andrus, Woodruff, & Gauntlett, 1843), 105–6.

Monmouth

"Farther concession is a joke." George III to Lord North, August 12, 1778, in W. Bodham Donne, ed., *The Correspondence of King George III with Lord North From 1768 to 1783* (2 vols., London: John Murray), 2:207–8.

The greatest threat was to Britain's colonies in the West Indies . . . The military alliance between France and the United States forced the British government to shift its military priorities to the defense of the West Indies and a naval war with its most powerful imperial rival. On British war plans, *see* Piers Mackesy, *The War for America* (Cambridge, MA: Harvard University Press, 1964), 190–234.

Clinton decided to return to New York by land . . . On the brief Monmouth campaign, *see* Freeman, *George Washington,* 5:1–36, which benefits from Freeman's method of not disclosing more than Washington knew at the moment he was forced to make decisions. Mark Edward Lender and Gary Wheeler Stone, *Fatal Sunday: George Washington, the Monmouth Campaign, and the Politics of Battle* (Norman: University of Oklahoma Press, 2016) is a strong modern treatment.

"in a great passion . . ." Martin, *Narrative,* 93.

"had never known or conceived the value of military discipline . . ." The source of this statement by Hamilton is William North, "Biographical Sketch of the Late Baron Steuben," *American Magazine: A Monthly Miscellany* 1, no. 5 (October 1815): 177–183, in which North wrote, "On the 17th of June, the battle of Monmouth was fought. Colonel Hamilton said he had never known, or conceived the value of discipline, till that day" (p. 182). The *American Magazine* was a short-lived periodical edited by Horatio Gates Spafford and printed for the editor by E. & E. Hosford of Albany, New York. North's "Biographical Sketch" was published in two parts. The second is in vol. 1, no. 6 (November 1815): 209–16. North was a close friend of Hamilton and an aide to Steuben, and his report is thus reliable. His "Biographical Sketch" was a source for Frederich Kapp, *The Life of Frederick William von Steuben, Major General in the Revolutionary Army* (New York: Mason Brothers, 1859), who altered North's version to read: "Alexander Hamilton . . . was afterwards heard to say that he had never known or conceived the value of military discipline till that day" (p. 161). The difference is subtle, but subsequent historians have improperly quoted Kapp, or someone quoting Kapp, rather than North.

"a woman whose husband belonged to the Artillery . . ." Martin, *Narrative,* 96–97. The literature on the Molly Pitcher legend is extensive but inconclusive about her identity. By the middle of the nineteenth century, recollections of women on the battlefield had faded, their place taken in popular culture by the legendary Molly Pitcher, who may have been based on one or another of the real women who served with the artillery in battle or a convergence of recollections of more than one. "The memory of the Revolutionary women," pioneering women's historian Elizabeth Ellet wrote in 1848, "has passed from remembrance with the generation that witnessed it." Elizabeth F. Ellet, *The Women of the Revolution* (3 vols., New York: Baker and Scribner, 1848 [vols. 1 and 2] and 1850 [vol. 3]), 1:2–22.

"The french . . . left us in a most Rascally manner"

After conferring with Washington, d'Estaing sailed for Newport . . . Christian M. McBurney, *The Rhode Island Campaign: The First French and American Operation of the Revolutionary War* (Yardley, PA: Westholme, 2011) offers a thorough treatment of this neglected campaign based on extensive and careful documentation.

"the french . . . left us in a most Rascally manner." Edward Fields, ed., *Diary of Colonel Israel Angell Commanding the Second Rhode Island Continental Regiment during the American Revolution, 1778–1781* (Providence: Preston and Rounds Company, 1899), 4 (August 23, 1778).

"lamenting the sudden unexpected departure of the French fleet . . ." John Sullivan's general orders for August 24, 1778, are recorded in William P. Upham, "A Memoir of Gen. John Glover," published in two parts in *Historical Collections of the Essex Institute* 5, no. 2 (April 1863): 49–72, and no. 3 (June 1863): 97–132. The "Memoir" consists mostly of documents copied from seven manuscript books presented to the Essex Institute by the grandson and great-grandson of General John Glover, including Glover's letterbook and six orderly books for Glover's regiment from the beginning of the war to February 21, 1777, when Glover was promoted to brigadier general. Sullivan's general orders of August 24, 1778, are in the fourth orderly book (pp. 123–24), which covers October 19–November 24, 1776, and June 28–October 14, 1778.

"a people old in war, very strict in military etiquette . . ." Washington to John Sullivan, September 1, 1778, in David R. Hoth, ed., *The Papers of George Washington,* Revolutionary War Series, vol. 16: July 1, 1778–September 14, 1778 (Charlottesville: University of Virginia Press, 2006), 464–65. Washington had cautioned Sullivan to "put the best face upon the matter and, to the World, attribute the removal to Boston, to necessity. The Reasons are too obvious to need explaining. The principal one is, that our British and internal enemies would be glad to improve the least matter of complaint and disgust against and between us and our new Allies into a serious rupture." Hoth, ed., *Papers of George Washington,* Revolutionary War Series, 16:406–7.

a large cargo of uniforms arrived from France . . . At the beginning of 1778 Washington struggled to address the clothing shortage by specifying that the limited supply of cloth for coats be used to make short jackets rather than full-length coats. *See* Washington to James Mease, January 21, 1778, in Edward G. Lengel, ed., *The Papers of George Washington,* Revolutionary War Series, vol. 13: December 26, 1777–February 28, 1778 (Charlottesville: University of Virginia Press, 2003), 305–7. The arrival of the shipment from France eased the clothing shortage. Washington wrote on November 23 that he had just learned "that 20,011 suits of Uniforms" had arrived from France and that there was "a sufficiency of the French Cloaths for the whole Army." *See* George Washington to Richard Peters, November 23, 1778, in Edward G. Lengel, ed., *The Papers of George Washington,* Revolutionary War Series, vol. 18: November 1, 1778–January 14, 1779 (Charlottesville: University of Virginia Press, 2008), 272–73.

Savannah

The attack was set for four o'clock on the morning of October 9. Archaeological investigation of the site of the Spring Hill Redoubt in 2005 uncovered the remains of the earthwork, including an intact section of the palisade trench, and considerable evidence of the battle despite the fact that the area was built over long ago and was for many years covered by railroad tracks and rail-related construction. The report on the excavation is an outstanding source for primary-source documents on the battle. Rita Folse Elliot, *"The Greatest Event That Has Happened the Whole War—Archaeological Discovery of the 1779 Spring Hill Redoubt, Savannah, Georgia* (Savannah: Coastal Heritage Society, 2011). I am grateful to the late Preston Russell for introducing me to this archaeological project.

"I think that this is the greatest event that has happened the whole war." Henry Clinton to Henry Pelham-Clinton, 2nd Duke of Newcastle-under-Lyne, November 19, 1779, item Ne C 2640, Sub-Group Ne C [items 2230-4495, correspondence of Henry Pelham-Clinton], Correspondence and Political Papers of the Dukes of Newcastle under Lyne, 1608–1945, in the Newcastle (Clumber) Collection, University of Nottingham Manuscripts and Special Collections. The recipient, Henry Pelham-Clinton, 2nd Duke of Newcastle-under-Lyne, was the nephew and heir to the 1st Duke of Newcastle-under-Lyne, who served as prime minister, as did his brother Henry Pelham. Newcastle and Pelham secured valuable sinecures for Pelham-Clinton, including appointment as controller of customs for London. When he succeeded his uncle as duke in 1768, he became one of the wealthiest and most powerful aristocrats in Britain. He was General Sir Henry Clinton's first cousin and chief patron. He supported Clinton's promotion to commander-in-chief in America, and his son served as Clinton's aide. Clinton's letter of November 19 reads:

My last told you that Destaign with 22 sail of the line & 4 frigates &c., &c., and 6 or 8000 men was on the coast of Georgia & had probably landed. I have now the pleasure to inform you that an express is this moment arrived from thence with an account of Destaign's and Lincoln's having made general assault upon Savannah on the 9th of October, were repulsed with great loss since which the Rebels retired into Carolina and the French on board their Fleet. For further particulars I must refer you to Capt Loyd. 'Tis certainly the greatest event since the beginning of the War. We have likewise taken W[ashington's] dispatches to Destaign by which it appears that R Island and this place were their next objects. The French embarked the 22d and there was a violent gale of wind from 25th to 27th. 'Tis probable they suffered. I think they cannot remain on this coast, and when they quit it we may possibly begin. Lord Thos is very well & of course wishes to your Lordship. I refer you to Mr. Eden to whom I write more at large. I have written a short letter to the Duke giving

him the above particulars. I have the honor to be faithfully & affectionately your Lordships humble sert H. Clinton

Equally delighted, George III ordered cannons fired . . . Richard C. Cole, "The Siege of Savannah and the British Press, 1779–1780," *Georgia Historical Quarterly* 65, no. 3 (Fall 1981): 189–202.

"I have not yet begun to fight!"

The battle was joined as night fell. The classic treatment of John Paul Jones' career is Samuel Eliot Morison, *John Paul Jones: A Sailor's Biography* (Boston: Little, Brown, 1959). For the battle between the *Bonhomme Richard* and *Serapis, see* chapter 13, "The Battle Off Flamborough Head," pp. 265–92. Morison was a skilled sailor and so understood and appreciated Jones' seamanship in a way no landsman can.

"I have not yet begun to fight!" The authority for this famous reply is Henry Sherburne, *Life and Character of Chevalier John Paul Jones, a captain in the navy of the United States during their Revolutionary War* (New York: Vanderpool & Cole, Printers, 1825). The book consists mainly of letters and documents from the war, to which Sherburne added an account of the battle secured from Richard Dale (pp. 126–29), titled "Particulars of the engagement between the Bon homme Richard and the Serapis, furnished by First Lieutenant Richard Dale, of the Bon homme Richard, for this work." In it, Dale explained that early in the battle, Captain Pearson of *Serapis* sought to pass *Bonhomme Richard* and then turn to cross in front of her bow, raking *Richard* with a broadside as he passed. As soon as Pearson put over, he realized that he did not have sufficient clearance and that *Richard* would collide with *Serapis* amidships. Pearson promptly turned *Serapis* on to the same line as *Richard,* but *Serapis* slowed in turning and *Richard'*s bow ran into the stern of *Serapis.* "We had remained in this situation but a few minutes when we were again hailed by the Serapis, 'Has your ship struck?' To which Captain Jones answered, 'I have not yet begun to fight'" (pp. 126–27). A slightly different account is recorded in the autobiography of Benjamin Rush, who described a dinner party at which Jones told the story of the battle: "It was delivered with great apparent modesty and commanded the most respectful attention. Towards the close of the battle, while his deck was swimming in blood, that captain of the Seraphis [*sic*] called him to strike. 'No, Sir,' said he, 'I will not, we have had but a small fight as yet.'" George W. Corner, *The Autobiography of Benjamin Rush: His "Travels Through Life" together with his Commonplace Book for 1789–1813* (Princeton: Published for the American Philosophical Society by Princeton University Press, 1948), 157. "I have not yet begun to fight" and "We have had but a small fight as yet" are similar sentiments. Rush wrote his account of the dinner party years after the event and can be forgiven if he paraphrased Jones. Dale was a participant, and even though he wrote his account for Sherburne more than forty years after the battle, he seems like a much more reliable source than Rush. Of course it is entirely plausible that Dale did not hear what Jones said over the noise of battle. What Rush's account suggests is that "I have not yet begun to fight," or some version of it, was part of the story of the battle as Jones told and retold it. Whether or not Dale actually heard Jones say it in battle, he had abundant opportunities afterwards to hear Jones tell his version of the story. It is also possible that Rush reported accurately, and that Jones had recounted a second exchange late in the battle.

Chapter 16: Obstinate and Bloody
Opening

"Obstinate and bloody" The phrase was widely used in the second half of the eighteenth century to describe the most severe fighting. Nathanael Greene described the Battle of Guilford Court House as "long, obstinate and bloody" in a letter to Joseph Reed, March 18, 1781, in Showman et al., eds., *Papers of General Nathanael Greene,* 7:448–51; Peter Muhlenberg repeated Greene's use of the phrase in a letter to Col. Taverner Beale, written from the siege lines at Yorktown on October 2, 1781, in "Letters of General Daniel Morgan and Peter Muhlenberg" [to Taverner Beale], *Pennsylvania Magazine of History and Biography* 21 (1897): 490; Alexander Hamilton used the phrase "obstinate and bloody" to describe the Battle of Eutaw Springs in his Eulogy on Nathanael Greene [4 July 1789], in Harold C. Syrett, ed., *The Papers of Alexander Hamilton,* vol. 5: June 1788–November 1789 (New York: Columbia University Press, 1962), 345–59.

As so often happens in long wars, the suffering and brutality . . . Walter Edgar, *Partisans and Redcoats: The Southern Conflict That Turned the Tide of the American Revolution* (New York: William Morrow, 2001) surveys the war in the South with skill and grace and captures much of its savage nature.

Charleston

The city was guarded by an army of Continental troops and militia . . . The authoritative modern account of the Siege of Charleston is Carl P. Borick, *A Gallant Defense: The Siege of Charleston, 1780* (Columbia: University of South Carolina Press, 2003). I am indebted to Dr. Borick for sharing his intimate knowledge of the visible remains of the siege, apparent to his trained eye beneath modern city streets.

One of Buford's captains, John Stokes, had his right hand cut off and his head gashed by saber blows. The wounding of Capt. John Stokes is described in William Dobein James, *A Sketch of the Life of Brigadier General Francis Marion and a History of his Brigade From Its Rise in June 1780 until Disbanded in December 1782* (Charleston: Gould and Miles, 1821), in which James reprinted a letter describing the attack. The extent to which Tarleton's men were guilty of unusual savagery, and of killing men trying to surrender, is a subject of some modern debate.

"Slaughter was commenced before Lieutenant-colonel Tarleton could remount . . ." Banastre Tarleton, *A History of the Campaigns of 1780 and 1781, in the Southern Provinces of North America* (London: T. Cadell, 1787), 30–31.

"did not experience in America the merited returns of gratitude and affection." [caption] Tarleton, *History of the Campaigns of 1780 and 1781,* 90.

Treason

As soon as they reached New York City, Clinton and his adjutant, Major John André, were drawn into one of the most bizarre and dramatic incidents of the war. Benedict Arnold's treason has fascinated Americans since it happened

and has been the subject of more books and articles than almost any other event of war. Nineteenth-century writers treated Arnold as courageous, ambitious, and proud, as well as rash, quarrelsome, selfish, and corrupt. Jared Sparks, *The Life and Treason of Benedict Arnold* (New York: Harper and Brothers, 1851) acknowledged Arnold's "deliberate courage and gallantry" (p. 79) and expressed empathy for Arnold's frustration over not being promoted to major general in early 1777 (p. 87). Sparks reconstructed Arnold's treason with scholarly skill before concluding that he had abandoned himself to his passions, confounded "duty with selfishness and honor with revenge," and sunk to the lowest level of depravity (p. 326). The first serious effort to examine Arnold's wartime career as a whole and to give Arnold credit for his service before his treason was written by a distant relative, Isaac Newton Arnold, *Benedict Arnold; His Patriotism and His Treason* (Chicago: Jansen, McClurg & Co., 1880). Modern historians have tried to balance Arnold's treason with his prior accomplishments, particularly his conduct in the invasion of Canada, his subsequent ingenious defense of Lake Champlain, which delayed a British advance until 1777, and his heroics at Saratoga. Among the most recent are Stephen Brumwell, *Turncoat: Benedict Arnold and the Crisis of American Liberty* (New Haven: Yale University Press, 2018), Joyce Lee Malcolm, *The Tragedy of Benedict Arnold: An American Life* (New York: Pegasus Book, 2019), and Nathaniel Philbrick, *Valiant Ambition: George Washington, Benedict Arnold, and the Fate of the American Revolution* (New York: Viking, 2016).

"Redress of Grievances was my only Object and aim . . ." Arnold's effort to justify his betrayal of the American cause addressed "To the Inhabitants of America" was published in occupied New York City in a loyalist newspaper, *The Royal Gazette,* on October 11, 1780, and widely reprinted. It was printed in the *London Chronicle* on November 14, 1780.

"Treason of the blackest dye was yesterday discovered . . ." Among them was the Orderly Book of Lord Stirling's Division, August 1–October 7, 1780, Robert Charles Lawrence Fergusson Collection, The Society of the Cincinnati, in which "Treason" is written in large letters and heavily underlined (September 26, 1780). I am grateful to my colleague Ellen McCallister Clark for pointing out this example in the outstanding collection of orderly books in the Fergusson Collection.

The words are from Washington's General Orders, September 26, 1780: "Treason of the blackest dye was yesterday discovered! General Arnold who commanded at Westpoint, lost to every sentiment of honor—of public and private obligation—was about to deliver up that important Post into the hands of the enemy. Such an event must have given the American cause a deadly wound if not a fatal stab. Happily the treason has been timely discovered to prevent the fatal misfortune. The providential train of circumstances which led to it affords the most convincing proof that the Liberties of America are the object of divine Protection. At the same time that the Treason is to be regretted the General cannot help congratulating the Army on the happy discovery. Our Enemies despairing of carrying their point by force are practising every base art to effect by bribery and Corruption what they cannot accomplish in a manly way. Great honor is due to the American Army that this is the first instance of Treason of the kind where many were to be expected from the nature of the dispute—and nothing is so bright an ornament in the character of the American soldiers as their having been proof against all the arts and seduction of an insidious enemy. Arnold has made his escape to the Enemy but Mr André the Adjutant General to the British Army who came out as a spy to negotiate the Business is our Prisoner. His Excellency the commander in Chief has arrived at Westpoint from Harford and is no double taking the proper measures to unravel fully, so hellish a plot." Fitzpatrick, ed., *Writings of George Washington*, 20:94–95.

"I had an acquaintance with Arnold from my childhood . . ." Martin, *Narrative*, 148.

On July 11, 1780, a French army of 5,500 men landed in Newport, Rhode Island . . . Rochambeau's army awaits the historian who will tell its story from the perspective of its own soldiers rather than as a part of the story of the Yorktown campaign. The potential for such work is growing. One of the major accomplishments of the last several decades of American Revolution scholarship is the discovery, transcription, translation, and publication of correspondence and first-hand accounts of service in America by French participants, including officers of Rochambeau's army. Much of this work might have happened in the first half of the twentieth century but was slowed and disrupted by two world wars and the reluctance of some private owners to permit the publication of their ancestor's journals and papers. Among the material made available is the journal of Baron Ludwig von Closen, a young aide to Rochambeau. The von Closen journal, fortunately, was transcribed by American scholars before the original manuscript was destroyed in a fire that consumed the family castle in Bavaria. *See* Evelyn M. Acomb, "The Journal of Baron Von Closen," *William and Mary Quarterly* 10, no. 2 (April 1953): 196–236. Formally he was Hans Christoph Friedrick Ignatz Ludwid Von Closen-Haydenburg. His father was an officer in the Dutch army, and an uncle was colonel of the French army's Royal Deux-Ponts Regiment, which was composed chiefly of German-speaking soldiers. The massive French army included soldiers from many European nations, including thousands of men from the Catholic provinces of Germany. As many as one-third of the soldiers in Rochambeau's army were German or Swiss. Closen's journal, like some of the others kept by French army officers, says little about military operations. It is filled with descriptions of the country, towns, houses, and manners and appearances of the people he met. Closen also commented on slavery, noting that "the whites believe that they debase themselves if they engage in the work they say is fit only for these wretched beings. I should observe that in new England there are almost no negro *slaves* any longer, whereas in the *southern* provinces all the negroes are still enslaved" (p. 223).

The most impressive documentary publication of this sort is Howard C. Rice, Jr., and Anne S.K. Brown, eds., *The American Campaigns of Rochambeau's Army, 1780, 1781, 1782, 1783* (2 vols., Princeton and Providence: Princeton University Press and Brown University Press, 1972). The first volume contains the translated and edited journals of three of Rochambeau's officers—Louis-Alexandre Berthier, Jean-François-Louis, comte de Clement-Crèvecoeur, and Jean-Baptiste-Antoine de Verger—the second volume contains dozens of colored maps prepared by French engineers wherever the army went

or camped in America. Verger caught the enthusiasm many Americans felt for the cause: "We have seen parties of militia in this country perform feats that veteran units would have gloried in accomplishing" (1:152).

These sources join others published in the Revolutionary generation, including Abbé Robin, *New Travels through North-America: In a Series of Letters; Exhibiting the History of the Victorious Campaign of the Allied Armies, under his Excellency General Washington, and the Count de Rochambeau, in the Year 1782* (Philadelphia: Robert Bell, 1783).

Of similar character are the unpublished journal and letters of François-Ignace Ervoil d'Oyré, a French army engineer, now in the Robert Charles Lawrence Fergusson Collection, The Society of the Cincinnati. *See also* Norman Desmarais, ed., *The Road to Yorktown: The French Campaigns in the American Revolution, 1780–1783 by Louis-François-Bertrand, comte de Lauberdière* (El Dorado Hills, CA: Savas Beatie, 2021), and Robert A. Selig, "A German Soldier in America, 1780–1783: The Journal of Georg Daniel Flohr," *William and Mary Quarterly* 50, no. 3 (July 1993): 575–90. I am grateful to Dr. Selig for sharing his many insights on the composition and campaigns of Rochambeau's army. His work documenting the march of Rochambeau's army to and from Yorktown is some of the most important work now being done on the military history of the Revolutionary War.

The Carolina Backcountry

Cornwallis, who had assumed personal command at Camden, marched north . . . For a fine collection of documentation on the Battle of Camden from British and American participants and observers, *see* Jim Piecuch, *The Battle of Camden: A Documentary History* (Charleston, SC: History Press, 2006).

The remnants of the beaten America army began to reform in North Carolina . . . On this phase of the war in the South, in addition to Edgar, *Partisans and Redcoats, see* John Buchanan, *The Road to Guilford Court House: The American Revolution in the Carolinas* (New York: John Wiley and Sons, 1997).

"Ferguson and his party are no more"

"march his army over the mountains . . . and lay waste their country . . ." No contemporary manuscript of Ferguson's threat is known. The threat was reported by several participants whose recollections were collected by Lyman C. Draper and published in his *King's Mountain and Its Heroes: History of the Battle of King's Mountain, October 7th, 1780, and the events which led to it* (Cincinnati: Peter G. Thomson, 1881), one of the monumental works of nineteenth-century scholarship on the Revolutionary War. The source of this quotation is a pamphlet, Isaac Shelby, *Battle of King's Mountain: Address to the Public Relating to William C. Preston's Article Entitled, "Colonel Campbell and Governor Shelby"* [Lexington, KY: T. Smith, 1823], which Draper republished as an appendix to *King's Mountain and Its Heroes*, pp. 560–73. Shelby wrote the pamphlet (which is now very rare) to substantiate his claim that William Campbell had received undo credit for his role in the battle and that in fact Campbell had gone to the rear and avoided the fighting. Campbell's champions responded in his defense. Much like the dispute about whether

Lexington or Concord was the scene of the first fighting in which American militia returned British fire, the Shelby-Campbell controversy produced several valuable statements from participants. In his pamphlet, Shelby wrote that Ferguson had camped "at Gilbert Town. At that place he paroled a prisoner (one Samuel Philips, a distant connection of mine) and instructed him to inform the officers on the Western waters, that if they did not desist from their opposition to the British arms, and take protection under his standard, he would march his army over the mountains, and lay their country waste with fire and sword. Philips lived near my residence, and came directly to me with this intelligence. I then commanded the militia of Sullivan County, North Carolina. In a few days I went fifty or sixty miles to see Col. Sevier, who was the efficient commander of Washington County, North Carolina, to inform him of the message I had received, and to concert with him measures for our defence" (Draper, *King's Mountain and Its Heroes*, 562). Shelby's aim in the pamphlet was to claim credit for himself and Sevier for the march against Ferguson. Regardless of the accuracy of what he wrote about Campbell's conduct in the battle, there is no reason to doubt the accuracy of his claim about Ferguson's threat. We cannot be certain Ferguson told Philips to say "lay waste their country with fire and sword," but such dramatic language came easily to Ferguson.

"had taken post at that place with the confidence that no force could rout them . . ." Isaac Shelby to Evan Shelby, November 4, 1780, in Draper, *King's Mountain and Its Heroes*, 524–25. Ferguson's unfounded confidence in the strength of his position was reflected in a short letter he wrote to loyalist Maj. Robert Tenpenny, an officer in the Third Battalion of New Jersey Volunteers, who had been ordered to reinforce Ferguson, shortly after arriving at Kings Mountain on October 6: "Between you and I, there has been an inundation of Barbarians, rather larger than expected, joind (by repeated intelligence) to Sumpter, Macdowal, Hampton, Cleveland, Brevard & Graham. they give themselves out for 3800 men. In fact they are not above half that number, at least without Sumpter. We are inferior in number but as to quality—but we must not praise ourselves. I did not think it necessary to stake our young Militia to an over match without Orders—but with the advantage of Arms, our People and four Officers from Cruger. I should have thought myself justifiable in committing myself, had I not expected reinforcements." In a postscript he wrote, "Here we are Kings of King Mountain." This letter demonstrates that Ferguson was well aware of the forces arrayed against him. This letter was not known to Draper. It was apparently forwarded to British army headquarters in New York and is among the Henry Clinton Papers at the Clements Library, University of Michigan, and is published in Randolph G. Adams, "Two Documents of the Battle of Kings Mountain," *North Carolina Historical Review* 8, no. 3 (July 1931): 348–52.

"Ferguson and his party are no more in circumstances to injure the citizens of America." William Campbell to Arthur Campbell, October 20, 1780, in Draper, *King's Mountain and Its Heroes*, 526.

"truly savage" Cornwallis to Sir Henry Clinton, December 4, 1780, in Charles Ross, ed., *Correspondence of Charles, First Marquis Cornwallis* (3 vols., London: John Murray, 1859), 1:72–73.

At the Battle of Cowpens, Colonel William Washington was leading his dragoons . . . [caption] Maryland Col. John Eager Howard witnessed this encounter and described it to William Johnson, who published an account of it in his *Sketches of the Life and Correspondence of Nathanael Greene, Major General of the Armies of the United States, in the War of the Revolution* (2 vols., Charleston, SC: Printed for the author, by A.E. Miller, 1822): "In the eagerness of pursuit, Washington advanced near thirty yards in front of his regiment. Three British officers, observing this, wheeled about, and made a charge upon him. The officer on his right aimed a blow to cut him down as an American sergeant came up, who intercepted the blow by disabling his sword arm. The officer on his left was about to make a stroke at him at the same instant, when a waiter, too small to wield a sword, saved him by wounding the officer with a ball from a pistol. At this moment, the officer in the centre, who was believed to be Tarlton, made a thrust at him which he parried; upon which the officer retreated a few paces, and then discharged a pistol at him, which wounded his horse" (pp. 382–83). The same account appears in the 1832 edition of John Marshall, *The Life of George Washington* (2 vols., Philadelphia: James Crissy, 1832), 1:404.

"the first link of a chain of evils that . . . ended in the total loss of America." After the Revolutionary War Sir Henry Clinton devoted much of his time to defending his conduct in America and engaged in published exchanges with Cornwallis and others about the campaign that ended with the British defeat at Yorktown. Clinton drafted, but left unpublished, a more comprehensive manuscript he titled "An Historical Detail of Seven Years Campaigns in North America from 1775 to 1782," which was among the Clinton manuscripts acquired by the William L. Clements Library at the University of Michigan in 1926. In the manuscript, Clinton described Kings Mountain as "an Event which was immediately productive of the worst Consequences to the Kings Affairs in South Carolina, and unhappily proved the first Link of a Chain of Evils that followed each other in regular Succession until they at last ended in the total Loss of America." Clinton regarded Cornwallis' decision to detach Ferguson's command to operate independently as the mistake that led to the disaster, which he compared to Lexington and Concord, Trenton, Danbury, and Bennington—engagements in which detachments had been mauled. In Clinton's view Cornwallis compounded the defeat by retreating rapidly into South Carolina and abandoning loyalists who were turning out to support him, throwing away "for ever after all their *Confident of support from the Kings Army."* For an overview of Clinton's papers, *see* Randolph G. Adams, *The Headquarters Papers of the British Army in North America During the War of the American Revolution: A Brief Description of Sir Henry Clinton's Papers in the William L. Clements Library* (Ann Arbor, MI: William L. Clements Library, 1926). The definitive scholarly edition of Clinton's "Historical Detail" is William B. Willcox, ed., *The American Rebellion: Sir Henry Clinton's Narrative of His Campaigns, 1775–1782* (New Haven: Yale University Press, 1954), which includes references to the Clinton papers at the Clements Library and a very fine introductory essay in which Professor Willcox concludes that Clinton was weak-willed, vacillating, and lacking in initiative. He elaborated on these conclusions in his *Por-*

trait of a General: Sir Henry Clinton in the War for Independence (New York: Alfred A. Knopf, 1964).

"We . . . shouted Liberty! Liberty!"

"I arrived here . . . and have been in search of the Army I am to command . . ." Nathanael Greene to Catharine Littlefield Greene, December 7, 1780, in Richard K. Showman et al., eds., *Papers of General Nathanael Greene,* 6:542.

"a devil of a whiping . . ." Daniel Morgan to Nathanael Greene, January 19, 1781, in Showman et al., eds., *Papers of General Nathanael Greene,* 7:152–61. The editor's notes to Morgan's report cover the documentation on a wide range of tactical details. Lawrence E. Babits, *A Devil of a Whipping: The Battle of Cowpens* (Chapel Hill: University of North Carolina Press, 1998) is a carefully constructed narrative of the battle based on careful examination of a richer array of sources than earlier accounts. Don Higginbotham, *Daniel Morgan: Revolutionary Rifleman* (Chapel Hill: University of North Carolina Press, 1961) presents Morgan as a man of extraordinary courage, deeply loyal, confident in himself and his men, but also temperamental and occasionally rash.

"In the most barren, inhospitable, unhealthy part of North America . . ." Charles O'Hara to the Augustus Henry FitzRoy, 3rd Duke of Grafton, April 20, 1781, in George C. Rogers, Jr., ed., "Letters of Charles O'Hara to the Duke of Grafton," *South Carolina Historical Magazine* 65 (July 1964): 158–80; Andrew Waters, *To the End of the World: Nathanael Greene, Charles Cornwallis, and the Race to the Dan* (Yardley, PA: Westholme, 2020) addresses Greene's strategic retreat to the Virginia border—in which he averted disaster more than once—in illuminating detail.

Cornwallis attacked Greene near Guilford Court House . . . Lawrence E. Babits and Joshua B. Howard, *Long, Obstinate, and Bloody: The Battle of Guilford Courthouse* (Chapel Hill: University of North Carolina Press, 2009) is a fine modern study of the battle.

"Standing in readiness, we heard the pickets fire . . ." The diary of Samuel Houston is published in William Henry Foote, *Sketches of Virginia: Historical and Biographical* (Philadelphia: J. B. Lippincott & Co., 1855), 141–49.

"I could not get 100 men in all the Regulator's country . . ." Cornwallis to Sir Henry Clinton, April 10, 1781, in Clark, ed., *State Records of North Carolina,* 17:1010–12.

"I have experienced the dangers and distresses of marching . . ." Cornwallis to Sir Henry Clinton, April 23, 1781, in Ross, ed., *Correspondence of Charles, First Marquis Cornwallis,* 1:92–93.

"North Carolina is . . . the most difficult to attack." Cornwallis to Sir Henry Clinton, Wilmington, April 10, 1781, in Ross, *Correspondence of Charles, First Marquis Cornwallis,* 1:87–88.

"I am determined to carry the war immediately into South Carolina" John Buchanan, *The Road to Charleston: Nathanael Greene and the American Revolution* (Charlottesville: University of Virginia Press, 2019) offers a rich account of Greene's campaign to recover South Carolina.

"We fight, get beat, rise, and fight again . . ." Nathanael Greene to Anne-César de La Luzerne, April 28, 1781, in Showman et al., eds., *Papers of General Nathanael Greene,* 8:167.

Lafayette and Cornwallis

"What is our plan?" Cornwallis to Major General Phillips, April 10, 1781, in Ross, ed., *Correspondence of Charles, First Marquis Cornwallis,* 1:87–88.

Clinton never abandoned the idea that raising loyalist troops was essential to victory . . ." Mark Lender and James Kirby Martin, "A Traitor's Epiphany: Benedict Arnold in Virginia and His Quest for Reconciliation," *Virginia Magazine of History and Biography* 125, no. 4 (2017): 314–57, argues that Arnold expected to rally planters to the loyalist banner.

"Were I to fight a battle I should be cut to pieces." Lafayette to George Washington, May 24, 1781, in Stanley J. Idzerda, ed., *Lafayette in the Age of the American Revolution: Selected Letters and Papers, 1776–1790,* vol. 4: April 1, 1781–December 23, 1781 (Ithaca, NY: Cornell University Press, 1981), 124.

"so great a naval force in the Chesapeake . . ." Admiral Thomas Graves to Sir Henry Clinton, September 9, 1781, quoted on pp. 27–28 of William B. Willcox, "The British Road to Yorktown: A Study in Divided Command," *American Historical Review* 52, no. 1 (October 1946): 1–35, an extremely valuable assessment of the failures of the British army and navy commanders. Graves' letter is in the Henry Clinton Papers at the Clements Library, University of Michigan. Cornwallis, Willcox argues, was undone by his own failure to understand that the fate of his operations in Virginia ultimately depended on naval power: "His mind did not project itself to sea, and out of the sea came the force which destroyed him" (p. 35).

"undisciplined vagabonds, collected in the West Indies." Robin, *New Travels through North-America,* 57. That Cornwallis used these precise words is subject to dispute. Abbé Robin placed them in quotation marks, but no other contemporary source is known and he could not have heard Cornwallis cast this aspersion. If Cornwallis said something like this, Robin might have heard of it after the British surrender. The contempt expressed is consistent with Cornwallis' boast to Clinton that his army welcomed the advance of the enemy (Cornwallis to Clinton, September 29, 1781, in Ross, *Correspondence of Charles, First Marquis Cornwallis,* 1:120–21), yet when Saint-Simon landed Cornwallis had redoubled his effort to fortify his lines (Cornwallis to Clinton, September 8, 1781, in ibid., 1:117–18). On Saint-Simon, *see* Harold A. Larrabee, "A Neglected French Collaborator in the Victory of Yorktown: Claude Anne, Marquis de Saint-Simon (1740–1819)," *Journal de la Société des Américanistes* 24, no. 2 (1932): 245–57.

"you have not seen troops as universally well-made . . ." Frank Moore, ed., *Diary of the American Revolution from Newspapers and Original Documents* (2 vols., New York: Charles Scribner, 1860), 2:485, citing the *Pennsylvania Packet,* September 18, 1781.

Fort Griswold

Privateers were merchant vessels, fitted out with cannons and rigged for speed . . . For a recent general account, *see* Kylie A. Hulburt, *The Untold War at Sea: America's Revolutionary Privateers* (Athens: University of Georgia Press, 2022). Robert H. Patton, *Patriot Pirates: The Privateer War for Freedom and Fortune in the American Revolution* (New York:

Pantheon Books, 2008) is aimed at a popular audience and weaves engaging stories of individual privateers, including one from New London, into a broader narrative that claims an important role for privateering in the war.

William Seymour . . . was shot in the knee and stabbed seven times with bayonets. Henry Seymour to Lemuel Whitman, March 6, 1824, Pension File of William Seymour, S. 20,951, p. 30; on the wounding of Stephen Hempstead: Affidavit of Dr. Bernard Gaines Farrar [Sr.], St. Louis, Missouri, June 11, 1828, Pension File of Stephen Hempstead, S. 24,612, p. 9, Revolutionary War Pension and Bounty-Land Warrant Application Files, Record Group 15: Records of the Veterans Administration, National Archives.

"Who commands this fort? . . ." The Fort Griswold massacre was overshadowed by the victory at Yorktown and did not receive as much attention as it deserved. Aside from contemporary newspaper accounts and official reports, the earliest important account of the affair was a narrative written by Stephen Hempstead (1754–1831), a veteran of the massacre, who had moved to St. Louis (where his son Edward was a prominent attorney) in 1811. His account was published in two parts in the St. Louis *Missouri Republican* on February 23, 1826 (page 1, column 1), and March 2, 1826 (page 3, column 3). It was reprinted in the Jackson, Missouri, *Independent Patriot* on May 13, 1826 (page 1, column 3), and published as a broadside: *The following narrative of the battle of Fort Griswold, on Groton Heights, on the 6th of September, 1781, was communicated to the Missouri Republican* [St. Louis, Missouri, 1826]. Jonathan Sizer, a New London printer, issued a broadside version of Hempstead's narrative in 1840.

Hempstead's pioneering effort was followed by Jonathan Rathbun, *Narrative of Jonathan Rathbun, with accurate accounts of the capture of Groton Fort, the massacre that followed, and the sacking and burning of New London, September 6, 1781, by the British Forces under the command of the traitor Benedict Arnold, By Rufus Avery and Stephen Hempstead, Eye witnesses of the same. Together with an interesting appendix* ([New London, CT?]: s.n., 1840), 27. Rathbun was a sixteen-year-old militiaman from Colchester, Connecticut (about twenty miles northeast of New London), who answered the alarm on September 6. Arnold was gone when the Colchester militia arrived at the burning remains of the town, which Rathbun described as "a scene of suffering and horror which surpasses description" (p. 9). He assisted in burying the dead. Rathbun's little book, which includes narratives by two survivors of the massacre, is dated 1840, but the publisher and place of publication are not identified. It may have been published in New London, although Rathbun lived in or near Colchester all his life.

The massacre figured in Sparks' *Life and Treason of Benedict Arnold* (1851), pp. 324–26, but Sparks added nothing new. The next substantial publication was by William W. Harris, *The Battle of Groton Heights: a collection of narratives, official reports, records, &c., of the storming of Fort Griswold, and the burning of New London by British troops, under the command of Brig. Gen. Benedict Arnold, on the sixth of September, 1781* (New London, CT: Privately published, 1870), which was limited to only 100 copies. A second edition, "revised and enlarged, with additional notes," was written and published by Charles Allyn in 1882, who owned a bookstore and small publishing operation in New London. Though published under the same title, it should be understood as a separate and much more substantial work. It is the foundation for subsequent work on the events of September 6. Allyn included contemporary newspaper accounts, a revised version of Rufus Avery's narrative based on Avery's manuscript, with which Rathbun had taken liberties (duplicated by Harris), Stephen Hempstead's narrative (including his account of Ledyard's death, p. 52), the narrative of John Hempsted (preserving in his irregular spelling hints of the plain speech of his time), as well as the narratives of participants and witnesses Thomas Hertell, Jonathan Brooks, Avery Downer, and George Middleton. He also included Arnold's report to Clinton, September 8, 1781, and dozens of official documents. The vest and shirt Ledyard was wearing, pieced by the blade that killed him, are preserved in the collections of the Connecticut Historical Society.

Sixteen-year-old Peter Avery was among the few survivors of the massacre . . . Pension Declaration of Peter Avery, January 8, 1837, Revolutionary War Pension and Bounty-Land Warrant Application Files, Record Group 15: Records of the Veterans Administration, National Archives.

Yorktown

"there was but one wish . . ." Cornwallis to Sir Henry Clinton, Yorktown, September 29, 1781, in Ross, *Correspondence of Charles, First Marquis Cornwallis*, 1:120.

Washington gave orders for the allied army to surround the British . . . Freeman, *George Washington*, 5:297–394, presents the Yorktown campaign from Washington's perspective in authoritative detail.

"Nothing could exceed the firmness and bravery of the troops . . ." [caption] George Washington to the President of Congress [Thomas McKean], October 16, 1781, in Fitzpatrick, ed., *Writings of Washington*, 23:227–29.

"The whole peninsula trembles under the incessant thunderings of our infernal machines." James Thacher, *Military Journal of the American Revolution, From the commencement to the disbanding of the American army, Comprising a detailed account of the principal events and battles of the Revolution, with their exact dates, and A Biographical Sketch of the most Prominent Generals* (Hartford: Hurlburt, Williams & Co., 1862), 286 (October 17, 1781).

V: Independent America

It is yet to be decided whether the Revolution must ultimately be considered . . . George Washington, Circular to the States, June 8, 1783, in Fitzpatrick, ed., *Writings of Washington*, 26:483–496.

Chapter 17: War's End

Opening

"killed about twenty of them . . ." Pension application of George McLain (McLean), W21793, Bedford County, Tennessee, November 7, 1832, Revolutionary War Pension and Bounty-Land Warrant Application Files, Record Group 15: Records of the Veterans Administration, National Archives.

"killed in his rout every person he met . . ." Aedanus Burke to Benjamin Guerard, December 14, 1784, Records of the General Assembly, Governor's Messages, No. 313, South Carolina Archives.

News from America

"**History offers few examples of a success so complete . . .**" quoted in George Bancroft, *History of the United States of America, from the discovery of the continent,* vol. 5 (New York: D. Appleton and Co., 1885), 523. This edition included Bancroft's final revisions. Bancroft's *History* is the earliest use of this quotation I have found. I have not located Bancroft's source.

"**a ball in the breast . . .**" This anecdote is recorded in N. William Wraxhall, *Historical Memoirs of My Own Time* (London: Printed for T. Cadell and W. Davies, 1815). In November 1781 Wraxhall was a thirty-year-old member of Parliament. According to Wraxhall, Lord George Germain received an official dispatch informing him of the surrender around noon on November 25. He went immediately to the homes of Lord Stormont, secretary of state for the northern department, and Baron Thurlow, the lord high chancellor, and the three of them went on to North's residence on Downing Street: "He had not received an intimation of the event, when they arrived at his door, in Downing-street, between one and two o'clock. The First Minister's firmness, and even his presence of mind, gave way for a short time, under this awful disaster. I asked Lord George afterwards, how he took the communication, when made to him? 'As he would have taken a ball in his breast,' replied Lord George. For he opened his arms, exclaiming wildly, as he paced up and down the apartment during a few minutes, 'Oh, God! it is all over!' Words which he repeated many times, under emotions of the deepest Consternation and distress" (pp. 102–3). Wraxhall dined with Germain and several others that evening a Germain's home. Germain told the group that Cornwallis had surrendered (pp. 104–8). Given Wraxhall's account of the dinner, it does not appear that Germain told his guests about North's reaction to the news. Wraxhall probably learned about that later. Charles Ross points out that Clinton's official dispatch did not reach London until midnight and surmises that Wraxhall may have been referring to unofficial news just arrived from France. Ross, ed., *Correspondence of Charles, First Marquis Cornwallis,* 1:135–36.

"**Time alone would soon bring about every success we could wish.**" Quoted in Lord Mahon, *History of England from the Peace of Utrecht to the Peace of Versailles, 1713–1783,* vol. 7. (London: John Murray, 1854), 165; *see also* Willcox, *Portrait of a General,* 394.

"A School of Sharks"

"**You are to make the most candid and confidential Communications . . .**" Continental Congress to the American Peace Commissioners: Instructions [15 June 1781], Barbara B. Oberg, ed., *The Papers of Benjamin Franklin,* vol. 35: May 1–October 31, 1781 (New Haven: Yale University Press, 1999), 166–67.

"**I am not marvelously pleased with the country . . .**" Vergennes to Lafayette, January 23, 1782, quoted in Louis Gottschalk, *Lafayette and the Close of the American Revolution* (Chicago: University of Chicago Press, 1942), 353.

"**that of a Man in the midst of the Ocean . . .**" John Adams to Robert R. Livingston, May 16, 1782, in Gregg L. Lint et al., eds., *Papers of John Adams,* vol. 13: May–October 1782 (Cambridge, MA: Harvard University Press, 2006), 48–52.

"**One Says America, will give France the Go By . . .**" John Adams to Benjamin Franklin, August 17, 1780, in Gregg L. Lint and Richard Alan Ryerson, eds., *Papers of John Adams,* vol. 10: July 1780–December 1780, (Cambridge, MA: Harvard University Press, 1996), 76–78.

"**the principal Object to be obtained by the war**" Notes of a Conference between his Excellency the Count de Florida Blanca and Mr Jay, at St Ildefonso, on Saturday Evening, September 23d, 1780, in Jared Sparks, ed., *The Diplomatic Correspondence of the American Revolution,* vol. 7 (Boston: Nathan Hale and Gray and Gray & Bowen, 1830), 371–94. Floridablanca's assertion about the Gulf of Mexico is on p. 379.

"**ages will be necessary to settle those extensive regions**" John Jay, Instructions to William Carmichael, January 27, 1780, in Francis Wharton, ed., *Revolutionary Diplomatic Correspondence of the United States,* vol. 3 (Washington, DC: Government Printing Office, 1889), 472–74.

"**Poor as we are, yet as I know we shall be rich . . .**" Benjamin Franklin to John Jay, October 2, 1780, in Barbara B. Oberg, ed., *The Papers of Benjamin Franklin,* vol. 33: July 1–November 15, 1780 (New Haven: Yale University Press, 1997), 355–58.

Peace Overtures

Negotiations to end the war began in an atmosphere of clashing interests and mutual distrust . . . On the end of the North ministry, *see* Mackesy, *War for America,* 460–70.

"**for ability and integrity together, the very first character in this kingdom.**" Joseph Priestley to Richard Price, July 21, 1772, in Robert E. Schofield, ed., *A Scientific Autobiography of Joseph Priestley (1733–1804): Selected Scientific Correspondence* (Cambridge: Massachusetts Institute of Technology, 1966), 105–8.

"**should be very glad to talk to you as I did then . . .**" Lord Shelburne to Benjamin Franklin, April 6, 1782, in Ellen R. Cohn, ed., *The Papers of Benjamin Franklin,* vol. 37: March 16–August 15, 1782 (New Haven: Yale University Press, 2003), 102–4.

After preliminary maneuvers . . . Rodney defeated the French in spectacular fashion . . . On the Battle of the Saintes, *see* Peter Thew, *Rodney and the Breaking of the Line* (Barnsley, UK: Pen & Sword Military, 2006).

The Treaty of Paris

From its start, the American Revolution had been shaped by global patterns. On contemporary understanding of the influenza pandemic, *see* Margaret DeLacy, "The Conceptualization of Influenza in Eighteenth-Century Britain: Specificity and Contagion," *Bulletin of the History of Medicine* 67, no. 1 (Spring 1993): 74–118. Contemporary discussions of the pandemic are unusually rich. *See,* e.g., Donald Munro, *A Short Account of the Present Epidemical Disorder, commonly called Influenza* (London: s.n., 1782).

The negotiations began in earnest on October 30 . . . For a summary of the negotiations from the British point of view, *see* Mackesy, *War for America,* 505–10.

The negotiators contested every point. For the comments of the negotiators about one another, *see* Preliminary Articles of Peace: Second Draft Treaty [4–7 November 1782], in Ellen R. Cohn, ed., *The Papers of Benjamin Franklin,* vol. 38: August 16, 1782–January 20, 1783 (New Haven: Yale University Press, 2006), 263–75.

"pushes and presses every Point as far as it can possibly go." John Adams' Diary, November 4, 1782, in Lyman H. Butterfield, ed., *The Adams Papers,* Diary and Autobiography of John Adams, vol. 3 [Diary 1782–1804; Autobiography Part One to October 1776] (Cambridge, MA: Harvard University Press, 1962), 45–46.

Vergennes was astonished by the generous terms the Americans had secured. Andrew Stockely, *Britain and France at the Birth of America: The European Powers and the Peace Negotiations of 1782–1783* (Exeter, UK: University of Exeter Press, 2001) examines the negotiations between all of the belligerents from a European point of view. Vergennes and Shelburne each recognized benefits in dealing generously with the Americans, but they were less concerned with America than with the balance of power in Europe.

"The English buy peace rather than make it" Vergennes to Gérard de Rayneval, December 4, 1782, in Henri Doniol, *Histoire de la Participation de la France à l'Établissement des Etats Unis d'Amérique,* vol. 5 (Paris: Imprimerie Nationale, 1892), 187–88. Rayneval, undersecretary of state for foreign affairs, was in London when Vergennes sent this letter, enclosing a translation of the preliminary articles of peace agreed to by the British and Americans: "La traduction de ces mêmes préliminaires l'ont ete le meme jou par M. Oswald d'une part et par les quatre plenipotentiaires americains de l'autre. La traduction de ces mêmes préliminaires que je joins ici, M., me dispense d'entrér dan aucun détail sur leur contenû; vous y remarquerés que les Anglais achètent la paix plutot qu'ils ne la font: leurs concessions en effet tant por les limites pour les pècheries et les loyalistes excedent tout ce que j'avois crû possible; quel est le motif qui a pû amenér une facilité que l'on pourroit interpretér pour une espèce d'abandon, vous ètes plus en état que moi de la découvrir" [The translation of these same preliminaries was done the same day by Mr. Oswald on the one hand and by the four American plenipotentiaries on the other. The translation of these same preliminaries which I enclose, M[onsieur], saves me from entering into any detail on their content; you will notice there that the English buy peace rather than make it; their concessions indeed as much for the limits for the fisheries and the loyalists exceed all that I had believed possible; what is the reason that could have brought about an ease that could be interpreted as a kind of abandonment, you are in a better position than I to discover].

"are interested in separating us from Great Britain . . ." John Jay to Robert Livingston, November 17, 1782, in Henry P. Johnston, ed., *The Correspondence and Public Papers of John Jay,* vol. 2: 1781–1782 (New York: G.P. Putnam's Sons, 1891), 366–452. The quoted passage is on p. 450. Jay wrote this very long letter—his report on the peace negotiations—when those negotiations were complete. The last pages contain his advice to trust neither the British nor the French.

He acknowledged that he had "written many disagreeable things in this letter, but I thought it my duty" (p. 452).

"Conquerers at last!"

Col. John Laurens . . . was killed. On John Laurens, *see* Gregory D. Massey, *John Laurens and the American Revolution* (Columbia: University of South Carolina Press, 2000). Laurens was one of the most interesting officers of the Continental Army. The son of a South Carolina planter, he advocated the enlistment of black soldiers in return for their emancipation. An intimate friend of Alexander Hamilton and the marquis de Lafayette, Laurens exceeded them both for reckless courage.

"to discharge us absolutely . . ." Martin, *Narrative,* 202.

"How did we fare in particular? . . ." Martin, *Narrative,* 208.

"It would be well for the troops . . ." George Washington to Gouverneur Morris, December 10, 1780. The recipient's copy in Washington's hand is in the William L. Clements Library at the University of Michigan. Washington's draft is in the George Washington Papers at the Library of Congress. I am indebted to William D. Ferraro, senior associate editor of the *Papers of George Washington,* for this transcription of the recipient's copy. The full text of the letter will be published in volume 29 of *The Papers of George Washington,* Revolutionary War Series, forthcoming.

"There are certain bounds . . ." George Washington to Jonathan Trumbull, May 26, 1780, in Fitzpatrick, ed., *Writings of George Washington,* 18:425–26.

"Our soldiery are not devoid of reasoning faculties . . ." Anthony Wayne to Joseph Reed, December 16, 1780, in William B. Reed, ed., *Life and Correspondence of Joseph Reed* (2 vols., Philadelphia: Lindsay and Blakiston, 1847), 2:315–17.

"every ounce of Forage . . ." George Washington to Gouverneur Morris, December 10, 1780, cited above.

In 1780 Congress had promised the officers half of their yearly pay every year for the rest of their lives . . . On the fate of the promise of half pay for life, *see* Warren, *America's First Veterans,* 35–36, 45–49, 100–103.

"to overturn the liberties of our country . . ." George Washington to Officers of the Army, March 15, 1783, in Fitzpatrick, ed., *Writings of Washington,* 26:222–226. Washington's response to the officers was recognized in the Revolutionary generation as one of the most important acts of his career and was widely published and reprinted for decades. *See,* e.g., *The Patriot's Monitor, or Speeches and Addresses of the Late George Washington, Commander in Chief of the American Armies, and First President of the United States* (New York: G. Bunce for Evert Duyckinck, 1809), 140–44, in which it is published together with his 1783 circular letter to the states, his 1783 farewell orders to the army, his 1789 response to the congressional reply to his first inaugural address, his seven annual messages to Congress (what we now call the State of the Union addresses), and his 1796 Farewell Address (there titled "President Washington's Resignation").

Most were young men who had sacrificed . . . On the meaning of military service for the young officers of the Continental Army as well as the dilemmas they faced at the end of the war, *see* John A. Ruddiman, *Becoming Men of Some Consequence: Youth and Military Service in the Revolutionary War* (Charlottesville: University of Virginia Press, 2014).

"brotherly kindness in all things . . ." Institution of The Society of the Cincinnati, May 13, 1783, Society of the Cincinnati Archives, Washington, DC. The Institution was widely reprinted. *See, e.g., The Institution of the Society of the Cincinnati. Formed by the Officers of the Army of the United States, for the laudable Purposes therein mentioned* (New York: Printed by Samuel Loudon, 1784). The Society of the Cincinnati library holds Henry Knox's personal copy of this edition.

"The country was rigorous in exacting my compliance to *my* engagements . . ." Martin, *Narrative,* 208.

"it will not be believed that such a force as Great Britain has . . . could be baffled . . ." George Washington to Nathanael Greene, February 6, 1783, in Fitzpatrick, ed., *Writings of Washington,* 26:103–5.

"turned adrift like old worn-out horses." Martin, *Narrative,* 205.

"a secret pride swell my heart . . ." Martin, *Narrative,* 168.

"starved, and naked, and suffering every thing short of death . . ." Martin, *Narrative,* iv.

Chapter 18: Novus Ordo Seclorum
Opening

"His emotion, too strong to be concealed . . ." [caption] [F.A. Tallmadge, ed.,] *Memoir of Col. Benjamin Tallmadge, Prepared by Himself, at the Request of his Children* (New York: Thomas Holman, 1858), 63.

"contrary to . . . the idea of liberty this country has so happily established." On the freeing of a shipload of indentured servants, *see* [New York] *Independent Gazette,* January 24, 1784; *see also* David W. Galenson, "The Rise and Fall of Indentured Servitude in the Americas: An Economic Analysis," *Journal of Economic History* 44 (March 1984): 1–26.

The new nation had no institution capable of addressing these issues effectively. Progressive historians, inclined to view American history through the lens of social and economic conflict, chiefly between the wealthy and everyone else, argued that the government under the Articles of Confederation reflected the interests of ordinary Americans and was adequate, with perhaps some modest reforms, to the challenges of the post-war years. They interpreted the Federal Constitution as a counterrevolution that subverted the democratic thrust of the Revolution by shifting political authority from the state legislatures to the new Federal Congress and from state governors to the president, all in the interest of the rich and well-born. This school of thought is most closely associated with Charles Beard, the author of an early twentieth-century study of the origins of the Constitution, but its most able proponent was Merrill Jensen, author of *The Articles of Confederation: An Interpretation of the Social-Constitutional History of the American Revolution, 1774–1781* (Madison: University of Wisconsin Press, 1940) and the considerably more important *The New Nation: A History of the United States during the Confederation, 1781–1789* (New York: Alfred A. Knopf, 1950). The former is a study of how the Articles were framed and adopted. The latter is a history of the year during which the Articles were in force. Jensen argues that the Confederation was a period of extraordinary economic, social, and cultural vitality. The country recovered rapidly from the post-war economic downturn, Jensen writes, and the states were addressing the issues of veterans, loyalists, wartime debts, trade regulation, and the money supply. There was, in Jensen's view, no cause for alarm. More recent research on the economy and on the various issues Jensen claimed were being effectively addressed has demonstrated that the economic crisis was, in fact, deep and prolonged. The bankrupt and impotent Confederation was incapable of addressing it, as were the states. The creative energy of the period had nothing to do with the Articles. The 1780s was a time of considerable conflict, but it was not simply conflict between the people and the interests, or populists and capitalists. The decade was shaped by conflicts between factions in state and national leadership, between regions and states, between religious denominations and ethnic groups. It was shaped by the clashing ambitions of people empowered or inspired by the Revolution.

American Cincinnatus

George Washington's views had been shaped by an unconventional life. On Washington's early life, *see* especially "The Young Man Washington," in Samuel Eliot Morison, *By Land and Sea: Essays and Addresses* (New York: Alfred A. Knopf, 1954); *see also* Jack D. Warren, Jr., "The Childhood of George Washington," *Northern Neck of Virginia Historical Magazine* 49 (1999): 5785–5809.

As a young man Washington accompanied Lawrence on a journey to Barbados . . . For further information, *see* Jack D. Warren, Jr., "The Significance of George Washington's Journey to Barbados," *Journal of the Barbados Museum and Historical Society* 47 (November 2001).

The war . . . only confirmed and reinforced views he already held . . . Washington's abhorrence of debt, his lack of concern about a standing army, and his conviction that a government endowed with "energy" was essential to the future of the United States were among the principles that shaped his conduct as president. *See* Jack D. Warren, Jr., *The Presidency of George Washington* (Mount Vernon, VA: Mount Vernon Ladies Association, 2000). Washington's views about power—power in government was a source of anxiety to many Americans—are interpreted in Edmund S. Morgan, *The Genius of George Washington* (New York: W.W. Norton, 1980).

Washington's character—carefully cultivated and exhibited continuously through eight years of war—made him the most widely admired person in America. For reflections on Washington's embodiment of his generation's ideals of public virtue, *see* Gordon S. Wood, "The Greatness of George Washington," *Virginia Quarterly Review* 68, no. 2 (Spring 1992): 189–207. The essay also appears in Gordon S. Wood, *Revolutionary Characters: What Made the Founders Different* (New York: Penguin Press, 2006).

"The destiny of unborn Millions"

"to offer my sentiments respecting some important subjects . . ." George Washington, Circular to the States, June 8, 1783, in Fitzpatrick, ed., *Writings of Washington,* 26:483–496.

"with full power and authority to act . . ." Commission from the Continental Congress, June 19, 1775, in Chase, ed., *Papers of George Washington*, Revolutionary War Series, 1:6–8.

"would retire to a private situation" and **"If he did that he would be the greatest man in the world."** James

Greig, ed., *The Farington Diary by Joseph Farington, R.A.,* vol. 1: July 13, 1793–August 24, 1802 (London: Hutchinson & Co. [1922]), 278. Joseph Farington was an English landscape painter who knew Benjamin West well. Farington is barely remembered as a painter, but he was a member of the Royal Academy and very active among British artists. He was also well known in London society. His diary is an invaluable source on contemporary artists and other people Farington met and the events of his time. In his diary entry for December 28, 1799, Farington recorded a conversation with West, presumably that day, in which West told him:

> After the defeat of Lord Cornwallis, a report was circulated here that the Royal Standard was raised in Philadelphia. West was one day with the King when He came from Court to Dinner, & His Majesty mentioned the circumstances & asked West if he corresponded with any persons in America & had heard of it. West told his Majesty that a Quaker was here lately arrived from Philadelphia and was with him the day before, and He asked the King when the Standard was raised. The said the day mentioned was June 25th. West observed that the Quaker left Philadelphia July 1st—and knew nothing of such a circumstance. The Queen was present at this conversation.

> The next day West had occasion to go to the Queens Palace to transact some business for the Queen, which when He had do it, she asked him if He was engaged that morning. He said not. She then told him to go into Her Closet with Her which He did & found the King sitting there. The King began to talk abt. America. He asked West what would Washington do were America to be declared independant. West said He believed He would retire to a private situation. The King said if He did He would be the greatest man in the world. He asked West how He thought the Americans would act towards this country if they became independant. West said the war made much ill blood but that would subside, & the dispositions of many of the Chiefs, Washington, Lawrence [Laurens], Adams, Franklin, Jay were favorable to this country which would so have a preference to any other European Nation. During the conversation the Queen was much affected, & shed tears. The next day Lord Shelburne was appointed Minister.

West's reference to Shelburne's appointment as prime minister, which occurred on July 1, 1782, gives us the date of this conversation—June 30, 1782. This is consistent with the king's questions about what would happen if America was independent. Peace negotiation with the American commissioners in Paris were only then beginning.

George III apparently expressed a very similar sentiment about Washington to West after Washington relinquished the presidency in 1797. In a memorandum by Rufus King, then in London as ambassador to Britain, dated May 3, 1797, King recorded:

> Mr. West called on me—we entered into politics after speaking of the Dinner at the Royal Academy and of the Annual exhibition; Mr. West said things respecting Amer. had changed very much; that people would cd. not formerly find words of unkindness eno' now talked in a different language; that the King had lately spoken in the most explicit manner of the wisdom of the American Gov. and of the abilities and great worth of the characters she produced and employed. He said the King had lately used very handsome expressions respecting Mr. Jay and _____ and that he also spoke in a very pleasing manner about Mr. Gore.

> But that in regard to Genl. Washington, he told him since his resignation that in his opinion "that act closing and finishing what had gone before and viewed in connection with it, placed him in a light the most distinguished of any man living, and he thought him the greatest character of the age."

Charles R. King, ed., *The Life and Correspondence of Rufus King comprising his letters, private and official[,] his public documents and his speeches,* vol. 3: 1799–1803 (New York: G.P. Putnam's Sons, 1896), 3:545. The memorandum, which is published out of its natural sequence in the volumes, is in an appendix to volume 3.

Most writers relating the anecdote about West's exchange with George III are content to cite the work of an earlier writer and don't pursue the anecdote to its source. Some are skeptical but don't do the research and cast doubts on the story even while repeating it. In *George Washington: The Wonder of the Age* (New Haven: Yale University Press, 2017), John Rhodehamel repeats the anecdote but writes "the story may be apocryphal" (p. 192). The sources are actually clear enough to anyone who reads them. Neither Farington nor King had reason to fabricate or embroider their accounts of West's stories, so an assessment of the accuracy of West's stories rests ultimately on a judgment about West's credibility. While West might have tried to flatter Rufus King, an American diplomat who knew Washington well, by telling him that the king admired Washington, he had no reason to fabricate the story he told to Farington, who was English. Coincidentally, the conversation between West and Farington took place two weeks after Washington's death, but the news had not yet reached London.

"The great events on which my resignation depended having at length taken place . . ." George Washington, Address to Congress on Resigning His Commission, December 23, 1783, in Fitzpatrick, ed., *Writings of Washington,* 27:284–85.

Desolation

"no living creature was to be seen" William Moultrie, *Memoirs of the American Revolution, so far as it relates to the states of North and South Carolina, and Georgia,* vol. 1 (New York: David Longworth, 1802), 354–55. *See also* C.L. Bragg, *Crescent Moon over Carolina: William Moultrie and American Liberty* (Columbia: University of South Carolina Press, 2013).

French troops who landed at Jamestown in September found dead civilians . . . Jean-Charles-François Aved de Magnac to [his father or mother], October 21, 1781, photocopy of original on file, Society of the Cincinnati library, Washington, DC. Aved de Magnac was a French naval officer in command of one of the launches that landed French troops under the marquis de Saint-Simon at Jamestown at the end of August 1781. He reported seeing "dead bodies on the ground" and gruesome evidence of British atrocities.

"nearly every adult male had been a participator in some of its scenes . . ." Abraham, Lincoln, "The Perpetuation of Our Political Institutions," Address before the Young Men's Lyceum of Springfield, Illinois, January 27, 1837, in Roy P. Basler, ed., *The Collected Works of Abraham Lincoln,* vol. 1: 1824–1828 (New Brunswick, NJ: Rutgers University Press, 1953), 108–15.

The Fate of the Loyalists

John Adams estimated that one third of Americans remained loyal to Britain. John Adams wrote to Thomas McKean on August 31, 1813: "Upon the whole, if we allow two thirds of the people to have been with us in the revolution, is not the allowance ample?" (Thomas McKean Papers, Historical Society of Pennsylvania). On the number of loyalists, *see especially* Paul H. Smith, "The American Loyalists: Notes on Their Organization and Numerical Strength," *William and Mary Quarterly,* 3rd ser., vol. 25 (April 1968): 259–77.

Fortunately for the future of the American republic, many chose to leave. On the experience of loyalists who left the United States at the end of the war, *see* Mary Beth Norton, *The British-Americans: The Loyalists Exiles in England: 1774–1789* (Boston: Little, Brown, 1972), and Maya Jasanoff, *Liberty's Exiles: American Loyalists in the Revolutionary World* (New York: Alfred A. Knopf, 2011).

About 60,000 loyalists left the United States . . . For estimates of the number of loyalists who left the United States for various destinations, *see* Jasanoff, *Liberty's Exiles,* 351–68. The best estimate for the number of runaway slaves who managed to leave the United States is eight to ten thousand. On this point, see Cassandra Pybus, "Jefferson's Faulty Math," *William and Mary Quarterly,* 3rd ser., vol. 62 (April 2005): 243–64. On ordinary loyalists, most of whom did not leave, *see* Joseph Tiedemann, Eugene Fingerhut, and Robert Venables, eds., *The Other Loyalists: Ordinary People, Royalism, and the Revolution in the Middle Colonies, 1763–1787* (Albany: State University of New York Press, 2009).

"fixedly opposed to those rights . . ." "A Meeting of the Freeholders and Other Inhabitants of the Town of Worchester May 22, 1783," *Pennsylvania Packet,* June 19, 1783.

"The people of Ninety Six appear very desirous to forget the injuries of the war . . ." Aedanus Burke to Gov. Benjamin Guerard, December 14, 1784, Aedanus Burke Papers, South Caroliniana Library, University of South Carolina, describing the lynching of Matthew Love.

In parts of the North and South Carolina backcountry desolated . . . *See* Jerome Nadelhaft, "The 'Havoc of War' and Its Aftermath in South Carolina," *Histoire Sociale/Social History* 12, no. 23 (May 1979): 97–121.

"to tell the news to their brother Tories." *Gazette of the State of South Carolina,* May 6, 1784.

Religious Freedom

When the American Revolution began, the English-speaking world had only recently emerged . . . While British America was a refuge for religious refugees, Europeans brought their confessional disputes and religious animosities with them, along with conventions for employing violence to impose religious norms and punish dissent. What happened in the New World was not really new. It was an extension of the Old World's religious conflicts sharpened by contact with pagan Indians and Africans. For an insightful treatment of this theme, *see* Susan Juster, *Sacred Violence in Early America* (New York: Oxford University Press, 2006).

Religious freedom existed almost nowhere in America before the Revolution. On the extent—and limits—of religious toleration in mid-eighteenth-century British America, and the Revolutionary shift toward religious freedom, *see* Chris Beneke, *Beyond Toleration: The Religious Origins of American Pluralism* (New York: Oxford University Press, 2006).

Georgia was more receptive to religious diversity than other southern colonies. On religious liberty in Georgia, *see* Joel A. Nichols, "Religious Liberty in the Thirteenth Colony: Church-State Relations in Colonial and Early National Georgia," *New York University Law Review* 80 (December 2005): 1693–1772.

"there shall be no establishment of any one religious church or denomination in this State . . ." North Carolina Constitution of 1776, Article 34, in Thorpe, ed., *Federal and State Constitutions,* 5:2793.

"We are required by the benevolent principles of rational liberty . . ." New York Constitution of 1777, in Thorpe, ed., *Federal and State Constitutions,* 5:2636–37.

"Free to Profess, and by argument to maintain"

Other dissenters, mainly evangelical Baptists, challenged the traditional order . . . On the persecution of Baptist ministers, *see* Lewis Peyton Little, *Imprisoned Preachers and Religious Liberty in Virginia: A Narrative Drawn from the Official Records of Virginia Counties, Unpublished Manuscripts, Letters, and Other Original Sources* (Lynchburg, VA: J.P. Bell Co., 1938).

"I have . . . nothing to brag of . . ." James Madison to William Bradford, January 24, 1774, in William T. Hutchinson and William M. E. Rachal, eds., *The Papers of James Madison,* vol. 1: March 16, 1751–December 16, 1779 (Chicago: University of Chicago Press, 1962), 104–8.

"spared no exertion to save them from imprisonment . . ." Madison made this assertion in a brief autobiographical statement he sent to James K. Paulding in 1832. See Madison to Bradford, January 24, 1774, note. 9. On Madison's commitment to religious liberty, *see* Adrienne Koch, *Madison's "Advice to My Country"* (Princeton: Princeton University Press, 1966).

"christians shouting, sinners trembling and fall down convulsed, the devil raging and blaspheming." Journal of Elder John Williams, 1771, Virginia Baptist Historical Society, Richmond. I owe this reference to Richard R. Beeman and Rhys Isaac, "Cultural Conflict and Social Change in the Revolutionary South: Lunenburg County, Virginia," *Journal of Southern History* 46, no. 4 (November 1980): 525–50. The quotation is on p. 534. According to Robert Semple, writing after 1800, Baptist preachers in Virginia employed "strong gestures and a singular tone of voice. Being deeply affected themselves while preaching, corresponding affections were felt by their pious hearers which were frequently expressed by tears, tremblings, screams, shouts, and exclamations." Robert Semple, *A History of the Rise and Progress of Baptists in Virginia* (Richmond, VA: Published by the author, 1810), 4.

"rising from the conceits of a warmed or overweening brain" Peter H. Nidditch, ed., *The Clarendon Edition of the Works of John Locke: An Essay Concerning Human Understanding* (New York: Oxford University Press, 1975), book 4, chapter 19.

"all Men should enjoy the fullest Toleration in the Exercise of Religion . . ." George Mason, Committee Draft of the Virginia Declaration of Rights [May 27, 1776], in Rutland, ed., *Papers of George Mason*, 1:282–86.

"all men are equally entitled to the free exercise of religion . . ." Virginia Declaration of Rights, in Thorpe, ed., *Federal and State Constitutions*, 7:3812–14.

In 1779 a group of Anglicans joined with some of the dissenters . . . The idea of a tax for the support of Protestant churches generally was not unique to Virginia. A very similar law was adopted in Georgia in 1785, which set a tax of four pence per hundred pounds' valuation of real estate and was to be paid to one minister in each county chosen by the taxpayers. Any twenty taxpayers could form a new parish and petition to receive its share of the tax money. The law does not ever seem to have been enforced and was superseded by Georgia's 1798 constitution, which provided that no person would "ever be obliged to pay tithes, taxes, or any other rate" to support any religious activity (*see* Nichols, "Religious Liberty in the Thirteenth Colony").

"oppressive and repugnant to the equal rights of religious liberty." A "memorial of a committee of sundry Baptist associations" was laid before the House of Delegates on November 11, 1784; *see* Charles F. James, *Documentary History of the Struggle for Religious Liberty in Virginia* (Lynchburg, VA: J.P. Bell Co., 1900), 126.

"what we have to do I think is *devoutly* to pray for his death." Thomas Jefferson to James Madison, December 8, 1784, in Julian P. Boyd, ed., *The Papers of Thomas Jefferson*, vol. 7: March 2, 1784–February 25, 1785 (Princeton: Princeton University Press, 1953), 557–60.

"pride and indolence in the Clergy . . ." and **"superstition, bigotry and persecution."** James Madison, Memorial and Remonstrance against Religious Assessments [ca. June 20, 1785], in Rutland, ed., *Papers of James Madison*, 8:295–306.

"Faithfulness shall scourge the growing Vices of the Age . . ." On the number of signers of the Westmoreland petition, *see* Memorial and Remonstrance against Religious Assessments [ca. June 20, 1785], editorial note, in Rutland, ed., *Papers of James Madison*, 8:295–98.

"no man shall be compelled to frequent or support any religious worship, place, or ministry whatsoever . . ." William Waller Hening, ed., *The Statutes at Large; Being a Collection of all the Laws of Virginia, from the First Session of the Legislature in the year 1619*, vol. 12 (Richmond, VA: Printed for the Editor, by George Cochran, 1823), 84–86. This language was embodied in Article 3, Section 11 of the Virginia Constitution of 1830. Some modern scholars have argued that some Virginians did not regard the general assessment bill as incompatible with the bill for establishing religious freedom, but the plain language of the latter precludes taxation to support any church. Anyone who thought otherwise was mistaken. For an opposing view, in an otherwise extremely valuable interpretation of the context in which the Act for Establishing Religious Freedom became law, *see* Daniel Dreisbach, "Thomas Jefferson and Bills Number 82–86 of the Revision of the Laws of Virginia 1776–1786: New Light on the Jeffersonian Model of Church-State Relations," *North Carolina Law Review* 69 (1990): 159–211.

"belief in a God All powerful wise and good . . ." James Madison to Frederick Beasley, November 20, 1825,

in David B. Mattern et al., eds., *The Papers of James Madison*, Retirement Series, vol. 3: March 1, 1823–February 24, 1826 (Charlottesville: University of Virginia Press, 2016), 636–37.

The achievement belonged just as much to the many thousands of ordinary Virginians . . . Federal court decisions on the application of the Establishment Clause of the First Amendment to state laws, particularly those involving prayer in schools and other invocations of religious faith by the states, have relied since 1947 on interpretations of Jefferson's understanding of the meaning of First Amendment and the Virginia Statute for Establishing Religious Freedom and to a lesser extent on Madison's *Memorial and Remonstrance*, despite the fact that Jefferson was not a member of the legislatures responsible for either, and that the document often cited to elucidate Jefferson's understanding is his letter to the Danbury Baptist Association of January 1, 1802, in which he wrote that the Establishment Clause was responsible for "building a wall of separation between Church & State." What Jefferson meant by this metaphor is worthy of discussion, as is the question of whether his views regarding the First Amendment, or even the Virginia Statute, have any special relevance for understanding the intent of the legislators who voted for either one. When he was an associate justice of the United States Supreme Court, former chief justice William Rehnquist argued that "there is simply no historical foundation for the proposition that the Framers intended to build the 'wall of separation.'" For Rehnquist's dissenting opinion as well as those of the majority, *see Wallace v. Jaffree*, 472 U.S. 38 (1985).

Chapter 19: Crisis

"The Revolution has robbed us of our trade"

"From my Soul I pity the Army . . ." [caption] Robert Morris to George Washington, February 27, 1783, in John Catanzariti, ed., *The Papers of Robert Morris, 1781–1784*, vol. 7: November 1, 1782–May 4, 1783 (Pittsburgh: University of Pittsburgh Press, 1988), 475–76.

"The Revolution has robbed us of our trade . . ." James Madison to Richard Henry Lee (draft), July 7, 1785, in Robert A. Rutland and William M. E. Rachal, eds., *The Papers of James Madison*, vol. 8: March 10, 1784–March 28, 1786 (Chicago: University of Chicago Press, 1973), 314–16. In the recipient's copy, Madison wrote, "We have lost by the Revolution our trade with the West Indies, the only one which yielded us a favorable balance, without having gained new channels to compensate it."

The trade deficit drove the country into a depression. On the debt-deflation spiral that led to the depression of the mid-1780s, *see* Scott C. Miller, "A Merchant's Republic: Crisis, Opportunity, and the Development of American Capitalism, 1765–1807," Ph.D. diss., University of Virginia, October 2018, especially chapter 2, "Crisis: Uncertainty and Growth," 63–122.

Per capita income fell by about fifteen percent during the war and perhaps more . . . On the decline in income during and after the Revolution, *see* Peter H. Lindert and Jeffrey G. Williamson, "American Incomes Before and After the Revolution," NBER Working Papers Series, Working Paper 17211 (Cambridge, MA: National Bureau of Economic

Research, July 2011), an accessible introduction to the problem of assessing income during this period. *See also* Peter H. Lindert and Jeffrey G. Williamson, *Unequal Gains: American Growth and Inequality since 1700* (Princeton: Princeton University Press, 2016); the estimate of a thirty percent drop in GDP is from Lindert and Williamson, p. 85. *See also* John J. McCusker and Russell Menard, *The Economy of British America, 1607–1789* (Chapel Hill: University of North Carolina Press, 1985), 374.

The post-war economic crisis was most deeply felt in the cities . . . On the extent of the post-war depression, *see* Thomas K. McCraw, *The Founders and Finance: How Hamilton, Gallatin, and Other Immigrants Forged a New Economy* (Cambridge, MA: Harvard University Press, 2012), 47. On wartime economic destruction and post-war disruption, *see* Peter C. Mancall, *Valley of Opportunity: Economic Culture along the Upper Susquehanna, 1700–1800* (Ithaca, NY: Cornell University Press, 1991), esp. 130–59, and Kulikoff, *From British Peasants to Colonial American Farmers,* esp. 256–80.

Adams in London

"By the latest letters from the American States . . ." [London] *Gentleman's Magazine,* 55 (September 1785), 740.

"The Politicks of Europe are such a Labyrinth . . ." John Adams to Robert R. Livingston, July 16, 1783, in Gregg L. Lint et al., eds., *Papers of John Adams,* vol. 15: June 1783–January 1784 (Cambridge, MA: Harvard University Press, 2010), 122–26.

"in a respectful but firm Manner . . ." John Adams' Instructions as Minister to Great Britain, March 7, 1785, in Gregg L. Lint et al., eds., *Papers of John Adams,* vol. 16: February–March 1785 (Cambridge, MA: Harvard University Press, 2012), 548–49.

"There is conscious Guilt and Shame in the Countenances . . ." [caption] Butterfield, ed., *Diary and Autobiography of John Adams,* 3:184 (March 30, 1783).

"Humane, generous, and open . . ." Jonathan Sewall to Joseph Lee, September 21, 1787; for the portion of this letter describing John Adams, *see* John Adams to Abigail Adams, July 9, 1774, in Butterfield, ed., *Adams Family Correspondence,* 1:134–37, note 5.

"to cultivate the most friendly and liberal Intercourse . . ." John Adams to John Jay, June 2, 1785, in Gregg L. Lint et al., eds., *Papers of John Adams,* vol. 17: April–November 1785 (Cambridge, MA: Harvard University Press, 2014), 134–45.

"Futurity . . . less attended to in this Country . . ." John Adams to John Jay, December 3, 1785, in Lint et al., eds., *Papers of John Adams,* 18:5–12.

"We have hitherto been the Bubbles . . ." John Adams to John Jay, August 10, 1785, in Lint et al., eds., *Papers of John Adams,* 17:321–23.

"nothing but Retaliation . . ." John Adams to John Jay, August 30, 1785, in Lint et al., eds., *Papers of John Adams,* 17:374–78.

The Internal Market

Inland towns like Lancaster, Pennsylvania, became centers for commerce serving wide areas. *See,* e.g., Jerome H. Wood, Jr., *Conestoga Crossroads: Lancaster, Pennsylvania,* *1730–1790* (Harrisburg: Pennsylvania Historical and Museum Commission, 1979).

"not confined to the capital towns and cities . . ." "Extract of a Letter to the President [of South Carolina John Rutledge] from H[enry] Laurens," September 10, 1777, in Robert Wilson Gibbes, *Documentary History of the American Revolution, 1776–1782* (New York: D. Appleton & Co., 1857), 88–91. Note that the chief executive in South Carolina was referred to as the president until 1778, when the title was changed to governor. In modern scholarly works this letter is widely misdated as having been written in 1778. Laurens wrote this letter from Philadelphia on the eve of the nearby Battle of Brandywine.

Despite . . . protests that disrupted trade, this consumer marketplace had been growing . . . Much has been written about the so-called consumer revolution of the eighteenth century, although historians differ about when this revolution began and how long it lasted. The latter is certainly important to understanding whether the growth of consumption and development of consumer culture was indeed a revolution—a major change that took place over a limited period. It appears that demand for consumer goods—everything from books and prints to curtains, upholstered furniture, matching dishes, and luxury food and drink—grew from the end of the seventeenth century in urban areas of Britain and spread in the eighteenth century to provincial towns and the countryside in Britain and that demand (and production to meet that demand) grew rapidly during the second half of the eighteenth century. This development occurred in Britain's American colonies about the same time it occurred in provincial parts of Britain, and so was happening in the middle of the century and accelerated in the third quarter, when it became intertwined with colonial resistance to British import duties and commercial regulations. On the latter, *see* Timothy Breen, *The Marketplace of Revolution: How Consumer Politics Shaped American Independence* (New York: Oxford University Press, 2004).

"I have been confoundedly bit in a Purchase of Salt . . ." Alexander Graydon to John Lardner, January 15, 1779, Lardner Family Papers, Historical Society of Pennsylvania.

"buying or bargaining" with **"the intent to sell the same again . . ."** Giles Jacob, comp., *A New Law-Dictionary,* 10th ed., "corrected and greatly enlarged by J. Morgan" (London: Strahan and W. Woodfall, 1782).

Gentility . . . became a characteristic to which ordinary American could aspire. On the spread of gentility and its relationship to consumption, *see* Richard L. Bushman, *The Refinement of America: Persons, Houses, Cities* (New York: Vintage Books, 1993).

The growth of the internal market for imported and domestic goods encouraged entrepreneurs to open retail shops . . . On the growth of rural shops and the spread of consumer culture, *see* Winifred Barr Rothenberg, *From Market-Places to a Market Economy: The Transformation of Rural Massachusetts, 1750–1850* (Chicago: University of Chicago Press, 1992), and Ann Smart Martin, *Buying into the World of Goods: Early Consumers in Backcountry Virginia* (Baltimore: Johns Hopkins University Press, 2008).

"large quantities of goods are expected . . ." Richard K. MacMaster and David C. Skaggs, eds., "Post-Revolutionary

Letters of Alexander Hamilton, Piscataway Merchant," *Maryland Historical Magazine* 63 (Spring 1970): 18–35.

The Trans-Appalachian West

Thousands of Americans crossed the mountains to make new lives for themselves and their families. *See* Malcolm J. Rohrbaugh, *The Trans-Appalachian Frontier: People, Societies, and Institutions, 1775–1850* (New York: Oxford University Press, 1978), 15–63.

Among them was John Crockett, born in Frederick County, Virginia, around 1753. James Atkins Shackford, "David Crockett and North Carolina," *North Carolina Historical Review* 28 (July 1951): 298–315.

Indian resistance slowed the rate of westward migration and in some areas rolled it back temporarily but did not stop it. For Washington's views on restraining settlement and maintaining peace with the Indians, *see* George Washington to James Duane, September 7, 1783, in Fitzpatrick, ed., *Writings of Washington,* 27:133–40.

The horror reached its low point in March 1782 ... Eric Sterner, *Anatomy of a Massacre: The Destruction of Gnadenhutten, 1782* (Yardley, PA: Westholme, 2020) does an excellent job placing the massacre in context.

The Western Land Question

That it would be governed as the common territory ... and then organized into separate states ... was not inevitable. The future of the trans-Appalachian West was one of the most divisive issues facing the new nation, involving the interests of the states, investors and speculators, veterans, and many thousands of ordinary Americans, in addition to the Indians whose lives were disrupted by migrants. On the western land disputes that divided the states and their resolution, *see* Peter Onuf, *Origins of the Federal Republic: Jurisdictional Controversies in the United States, 1775–1787* (Philadelphia: University of Pennsylvania Press, 1983), and Peter Onuf, *Statehood and Union: A History of the Northwest Ordinance* (Bloomington: Indiana University Press, 1987).

Whether South Carolina had a claim to land west of the Appalachians was not clear. On South Carolina's claim to a strip of western land twelve miles wide and some four hundred miles long, see William R. Garrett, *History of the South Carolina Cession and the Northern Boundary of Tennessee* (Nashville: Southern Methodist Publishing House, 1884).

The Maryland legislature refused to ratify the Articles of Confederation ... For the fear of Maryland leaders that their state would be depopulated, *see* the instructions to the Maryland delegates presented to Congress on May 21, 1779, in Worthington C. Ford et al., eds., *Journal of the Continental Congress* (Washington, DC: Government Printing Office, 1904–1937), 14:619–22.

"that the States so formed shall be distinct Republic States ..." Thomas Jefferson to Samuel Huntington, January 17, 1781, enclosing a Resolution of Assembly concerning the Cession of Lands, January 2, 1781, in Julian P. Boyd, ed., *The Papers of Thomas Jefferson,* vol. 4: October 1, 1780–February 24, 1781 (Princeton: Princeton University Press, 1951), 386–91. For a concise analysis of Virginia's decision to cede its claim north of the Ohio, *see* Peter Onuf, "Toward Federalism:

Virginia, Congress, and the Western Lands," *William and Mary Quarterly,* 3rd ser., vol. 34 (July 1977): 353–74.

"be overrun with Land Jobbers—Speculators, and Monopolizers ..." George Washington to James Duane, September 7, 1783, in Fitzpatrick, ed., *Writings of Washington,* 27:133–40.

New Republics

"well founded prospects of giving liberty to half the globe." Thomas Jefferson to Samuel Huntington, February 9, 1780, in Julian P. Boyd, ed., *The Papers of Thomas Jefferson,* vol. 3: June 18, 1779–September 30, 1780 (Princeton: Princeton University Press, 1951), 286–89. Jefferson's enthusiasm was matched by others in Congress.

Reflecting his passion for rational order, Jefferson proposed ... For an authoritative treatment of the Land Ordinance of 1784 and related documents, *see* the editorial note, "Plan for Government of the Western Territory," and the six associated documents, including the draft report of Jefferson's committee, which called for the abolition of slavery in the West and proposed names for ten of the new states, the report as revised by Congress, deleting those provisions, and the final ordinance adopted by Congress on April 23, 1784, *see* Julian P. Boyd, ed., *The Papers of Thomas Jefferson,* vol. 6: May 21 1781–March 1, 1784 (Princeton: Princeton University Press, 1952), 613–16.

"was lost by a single vote." Thomas Jefferson to James Madison, April 25, 1784, in Boyd, ed., *Papers of Thomas Jefferson,* 7:118–21.

If the antislavery clause had been included in the Land Ordinance of 1784, slavery would have been precluded after 1800 ... Historians debate the possibility that the antislavery clause of the proposed Land Ordinance of 1784 would have kept slavery out of the future states of Alabama, Mississippi, and Tennessee. Paul Finkelman, one of Jefferson's sternest critics, argues that North Carolina and Georgia would not have ceded their western claims if the clause applied to the region south of the Ohio. Even if they had ceded their claims, large numbers of enslaved people might have been settled there by 1800 and slaveholders would have been successful in repealing the prohibition. The latter ignores the disincentive the law would have posed to moving enslaved people to the region. For a summary of Finkelman's position, *see* Paul Finkelman, "Jefferson and Slavery: Treason against the Hopes of the World," in Peter Onuf, ed., *Jeffersonian Legacies* (Charlottesville: University of Virginia Press, 1993), 181–221. For an able summary of the debate by a scholar who disputes Finkelman's conclusions, with references to the relevant scholarly literature, *see* William G. Merkel, "Jefferson's Failed Anti-Slavery Proviso of 1784 and the Nascence of Free Soil Constitutionalism," *Seton Hall Law Review* 32 (2008): 555–603.

Illustrating a fundamental weakness of the Articles of Confederation, Richard P. McCormick has made a persuasive argument that the Land Ordinance of 1784 was not an ordinance—a rule ordained by Congress—but was, instead, a resolution that had governing force only because the final clause defined its provisions, collectively, as a charter imposed on the citizens of a new state seeking to advance through the stages leading to full participation in the common government. This distinction is a useful illustration of the limits of congressional authority under the Articles of Confederation, which did not specifically include legislating for a public domain, and confusion about how the Confederation Congress should carry out its work without clear authorization to do so. *See* Richard P. McCormick, "The Ordinance of 1784," *William and Mary Quarterly,* 3rd ser., vol. 50 (January 1993): 112–22.

"The touch of a feather"

This issue was settled by the Land Ordinance of 1785 . . . For a useful summary of the operation of the Land Ordinance of 1785, *see* George W. Geib, "The Land Ordinance of 1785: A Bicentennial Review," *Indiana Magazine of History* 81 (March 1985): 1–13.

"The western world opens an amazing prospect as a national fund . . ." David Howell to William Greene, February 1, 1784, in William R. Staples, *Rhode Island in the Continental Congress, with the Journal of the Convention that adopted the Constitution* (Providence: Providence Press Company, 1870), 478–82.

"The Western settlers stand as it were upon a pivot—the touch of a feather . . ." George Washington to Benjamin Harrison, October 10, 1784, in W.W. Abbot, ed., *The Papers of George Washington,* Confederation Series, vol. 2: July 18, 1784–May 18, 1785 (Charlottesville: University Press of Virginia, 1992), 86–98.

"it is their fixed design to keep Possession of the Posts upon the Frontier." John Adams to John Jay, August 30, 1785, in Lint et al., eds., *Papers of John Adams,* 17:374–78.

"They rely upon it that We shall not raise An Army . . ." John Adams to John Jay, December 3, 1785, in Lint et al., eds., *Papers of John Adams,* 18:5–12.

Chapter 20: "House on Fire"
Opening

"it is one of the most extraordinary things in nature . . ." [caption], George Washington to James Warren, October 7, 1785, in W.W. Abbot, ed., *The Papers of George Washington,* Confederation Series, vol. 3: May 19, 1785–March 31, 1786 (Charlottesville: University Press of Virginia, 1994), 298–301.

"Requisitions are actually little better than a jest . . ." George Washington to John Jay, August 15, 1786, in W.W. Abbot, ed., *The Papers of George Washington,* Confederation Series, vol. 4: April 2, 1786–January 31, 1787 (Charlottesville: University Press of Virginia, 1995), 212–13.

"I think often of our Situation . . ." George Washington to John Jay, May 18, 1786, in Abbot, ed., *Papers of George Washington,* Confederation Series, 4:55–56.

"Our affairs seem to lead to some Crisis . . ." John Jay to George Washington, June 27, 1786, in Abbot, ed., *Papers of George Washington,* Confederation Series, 4:130–32.

"my Sentiments . . . have been neglected . . ." George Washington to John Jay, August 15, 1786, in Abbot, ed., *Papers of George Washington,* Confederation Series, 4:212–13.

"Combustibles in every State"

With agricultural prices falling . . . farmers who had incurred debt . . . were hard pressed to pay. On the role of debt in the farm economy, *see* Richard L. Bushman, *The American Farmer in the Eighteenth Century* (New Haven: Yale University Press, 2018), 132–57.

"There are combustibles in every State . . ." George Washington to Henry Knox, December 26, 1786, in Abbot, ed., *Papers of George Washington,* Confederation Series, 4:481–84.

When a South Carolina sheriff tried to serve Col. Hezekiah Mayham . . . *See* Joseph W. Barnwell, ed., "Diary of Timothy Ford, 1785–1786" (continued from the previous issue), *South Carolina Historical and Genealogical Magazine* 13 (October 1912): 193.

In Port Tobacco, Maryland, rioters shut down a court . . . On the disturbances in Charles County, Maryland, *see* Jean B. Lee, "Maryland's 'Dangerous Insurrection' of 1786," *Maryland Historical Magazine* 85 (Winter 1990): 329–43. The Piscataway merchant (Piscataway is just across the line in Prince Georges County) was Alexander Hamilton, a Scottish tobacco factor and storekeeper, not to be confused with the more famous Alexander Hamilton.

Some two hundred armed citizens descended on the meetinghouse in Exeter, New Hampshire . . . On unrest in New Hampshire, Virginia, and elsewhere, *see* Woody Holton, *Unruly Americans and the Origins of the Constitution* (New York: Hill and Wang, 2007), esp. 10–12 and 145–61; *see also* Ronald P. Formisano, *For the People: American Populist Movements from the Revolution to the 1850s* (Chapel Hill: University of North Carolina Press, 2008).

Virginians in frontier Greenbrier County signed a remonstrance . . . On events in Greenbrier County, Virginia (now West Virginia), *see* James McClurg to James Madison, August 22, 1787, in Robert A. Rutland et al., eds., *The Papers of James Madison,* vol. 10: May 27, 1787–March 3, 1788 (Chicago: University of Chicago Press, 1977), 154–56.

Legislators were not so accommodating in Massachusetts . . . On the sources of the uprising in the state's ill-considered tax policies, *see* Roger H. Brown, *Redeeming the Republic: Federalists, Taxation, and the Origins of the Constitution* (Baltimore: Johns Hopkins University Press, 1993), 97–121.

Massachusetts farmers and tradesmen who were unable to pay their debts or taxes protested. On prosecution and fear of prosecution for debt and the importance of kinship and community among the protestors, *see* David P. Szatmary, *Shays' Rebellion: The Making of an Agrarian Insurrection* (Amherst: University of Massachusetts Press, 1980), 56–69.

"to their Idleness, their dissipation and extravagance . . ." David Grayson Allen et al., eds., *Diary of John Quincy Adams,* vol. 2: March 1786–December 1788 (Cambridge, MA: Harvard University Press, 1981), 91–92 (September 7, 1786).

"fondness for foreign frippery . . . imaginary grievances." Allen et al., eds., *Diary of John Quincy Adams,* 2:129–32 (November 26, 1786).

"the insurrections are not immediately dangerous . . ." John Quincy Adams to Abigail Adams, December 30, 1786, in Worthington C. Ford., ed., *Writings of John Quincy Adams,* vol. 1 (New York: Macmillan, 1913), 28–29.

"Luxury and extravagance both in furniture and dress . . ." Abigail Adams to Thomas Jefferson, January 29, 1787, in Julian P. Boyd, ed., *The Papers of Thomas Jefferson,* vol. 11: January 1–August 6, 1787 (Princeton: Princeton University Press, 1955), 86–87.

"are not entirely without excuses . . ." Thomas Jefferson to William Carmichael, December 26, 1786, in Julian P. Boyd, ed., *The Papers of Thomas Jefferson,* vol. 10: June 22–December 31, 1786 (Princeton: Princeton University Press, 1954), 632–34.

"beyond what prudence would authorize." Rufus King to John Adams, in King, ed., *Life and Correspondence of Rufus King,* 1:190–91.

Shays' Rebellion

The unrest of summer turned to open rebellion in the fall. The literature on Shays' Rebellion is rich, but much of it is partisan. The first effort to tell the story was by George Richard Minot, a young attorney, whose *The History of the Insurrections, in Massachusetts, in the Year MDCCLXXXVI, and the Rebellion Consequent Thereon,* was published by Isaiah Thomas in Worcester, Massachusetts, in 1788. Minot wrote to George Washington on August 8, 1788, that his efforts were "dictated by a love of truth, and a wish to preserve the reputation of the country." *See* W.W. Abbot, ed., *Papers of George Washington,* Confederation Series, vol. 6: January 1, 1788–September 23, 1788 (Charlottesville: University Press of Virginia, 1997), 432–33. Minot seems to have been concerned chiefly with persuading British readers that the rebels, though deluded, had some grievances that a wise republican government had pacified. He excoriated neither the rebels nor the government, and recognized that the discontent that led to the insurrection was shaped by economic conditions. Descriptions of Minot's history as hostile to the rebels or intensely partisan are misguided. *See* Robert A. Feer, "George Richard Minot's *History of the Insurrections:* History, Propaganda, and Autobiography," *New England Quarterly* 35 (June 1962): 203–28. Rather than maintain scholarly objectivity, most recent writers have chosen sides, usually that of the protestors.

"A man who sells a note for a fifth of its value . . ." Noah Webster to James Bowdoin, March 15, 1787, in "The Bowdoin and Temple Papers, Part 2," *Collections of the Massachusetts Historical Society,* ser. 7, vol. 6 (Boston: Published by the Society, 1907), 173–83.

"We are now in a State of Anarchy and Confusion . . ." James Warren to John Adams, October 22, 1786, in *Warren-Adams Letters: Being Chiefly a Correspondence among John Adams, Samuel Adams, and James Warren,* vol. 2: 1778–1814 [Massachusetts Historical Society *Collections,* vol. 73] (Boston: Massachusetts Historical Society, 1925), 278–80.

Shays' Rebellion illustrates the liminal state of public life in the 1780s. The liminality of public life was mirrored in cultural life. On this point, *see* the provocative study of Kariann Akemi Yokota, *Unbecoming British: How Revolutionary America Became a Postcolonial Nation* (New York: Oxford University Press, 2011).

"scarcely see any other than new faces . . ." James Bowdoin to Thomas Pownall, November 20, 1783, in "Bowdoin and Temple Papers, Part 2," 21–23.

"Like the dogs in a village . . ." For the narrative of Shays' Rebellion by Rev. Bezaleel Howard, *see* Richard D. Brown, "Shays's Rebellion and Its Aftermath: A View from

Springfield, Massachusetts, 1787," *William and Mary Quarterly,* 3rd ser., vol. 40 (October 1983): 598–615.

"distressing beyond measure . . ." James Madison to George Muter, January 7, 1787, in Robert A. Rutland et al., eds., *The Papers of James Madison,* vol. 9: April 9, 1786–May 24, 1787 and supplement 1781–1784 (Chicago: University of Chicago Press, 1975), 230–31.

"Our case is desperate"

"extensive national calamity." Henry Lee to James Madison, October 25, 1786, in Rutland et al., eds., *Papers of James Madison,* 9:145–46. Lee was in New York serving in Congress, and his agitation may reflect the general mood in that body;

"our case is desperate." James Madison to George Washington, November 8, 1786, in Rutland et al., eds., *Papers of James Madison,* 9:166–67.

"The crisis is arrived at which the good people of America . . ." Bill Providing for Delegates to the Convention of 1787 [November 6, 1786], in Rutland et al., eds., *Papers of James Madison,* 9:163–64.

"so interesting to the well-being of the confederacy" George Washington to James Madison, November 18, 1786, in Abbot, ed., *Papers of George Washington,* Confederation Series, 4:382–83.

"your name could not be spared." James Madison to George Washington, December 7, 1786, in Rutland et al., eds., *Papers of James Madison,* 9:199–200.

On Washington's role in public life between his resignation as commander-in-chief and the Philadelphia Convention, *see* Stanley Elkins and Eric McKitrick, *The Age of Federalism* (New York, Oxford University Press, 1993), 42–44. Elkins and McKitrick describe Washington as "a kind of moral executive" during this period.

"Know precisely what the Insurgents aim at . . ." George Washington to Henry Lee, October 31, 1786, in Abbot, ed., *Papers of George Washington,* Confederation Series, 4:318–20.

"might devise some expedients to brace up . . ." Henry Knox to George Washington, January 14, 1787, in Abbot, ed., *Papers of George Washington,* Confederation Series, 4:7–9. Knox expressed the same concern that the Convention might propose ways "for bracing up the present radically defective thing" in order "to drag on with pain and labor, for a few years." Henry Knox to George Washington, March 19, 1787, in W.W. Abbot, ed., *The Papers of George Washington,* Confederation Series, vol. 5: February 1, 1787–December 31, 1787 (Charlottesville: University Press of Virginia, 1997), 95–98.

"if three years ago, any person had told me . . ." George Washington to Henry Knox, February 3, 1787, in Abbot, ed., *Papers of George Washington,* Confederation Series, 5:7–9.

"for the sole and express purpose of revising the Articles of Confederation . . ." Report of Proceedings in Congress, Wednesday, February 21, 1787, in Charles C. Tansill, comp., *Documents Illustrative of the Formation of the Union of the American States* (Washington, DC: Government Printing Office, 1927), 44–46.

Washington finally decided to attend the convention. For Knox's final encouragement to Washington to attend the

Convention, *see* Henry Knox to George Washington, April 9, 1787, in Abbot, ed., *Papers of George Washington,* Confederation Series, 5:133–35.

The Professor and Plowman

"absolutely unjustifiable" Thomas Jefferson to James Madison, January 30, 1787, in Boyd, ed., *Papers of Thomas Jefferson,* 11:92–97.

"They were founded in ignorance, not in wickedness." Thomas Jefferson to William Stephens Smith, November 13, 1787, in Julian P. Boyd, ed., *The Papers of Thomas Jefferson,* vol. 12: August 7, 1787–March 31, 1788 (Princeton: Princeton University Press, 1955), 355–57.

"The people can not be all, and always, well informed . . ." Thomas Jefferson to William Stephens Smith, November 13, 1787, in Boyd, ed., *Papers of Thomas Jefferson,* 12:355–57.

"It prevents the degeneracy of government . . ." Thomas Jefferson to James Madison, January 30, 1787, in Boyd, ed., *Papers of Thomas Jefferson,* 11:92–97.

"that nature has formed man insusceptible of any other government but that of force . . ." Thomas Jefferson to James Madison, January 30, 1787, in Boyd, ed., *Papers of Thomas Jefferson,* 11:92–97.

"I think it lost time to attend lectures in this branch . . ." Thomas Jefferson to Peter Carr, August 10, 1787, in Boyd, ed., *Papers of Thomas Jefferson,* 12:14–19.

James Madison and James Wilson, were trained in the moral philosophy of the Scottish Enlightenment . . . Wilson's attachment to the moral sense was particularly clear in his later law lectures, in which he said that the "science of morals . . . is founded on truths, that cannot be discovered or proved through reasoning." *See* Thompson, *America's Revolutionary Mind,* 395.

"Above all things, lose no occasion of exercising your dispositions to be grateful . . ." Thomas Jefferson to Peter Carr, August 10, 1787, in Boyd, ed., *Papers of Thomas Jefferson,* 12:14–19.

"We have had 13 states independant 11 years . . ." [caption] Thomas Jefferson to William Stephens Smith, November 13, 1787, in Boyd, ed., *Papers of Thomas Jefferson,* 12:355–57.

Chapter 21: A More Perfect Union
Opening

"The first maxim of a man who loves liberty . . ." Richard Henry Lee to Samuel Adams, in James Curtis Ballagh, ed., *The Letters of Richard Henry Lee,* vol. 2: 1779–1794 (New York: Macmillan, 1914), 343–44.

"the Demosthenes, and Cicero of America" Silas Deane to Elizabeth Deane, [September 10–11, 1774], in Smith, ed., *Letters of Delegates to Congress,* 1:60–63.

John Adams . . . was missing as well . . . On the constitutional thought of the absent John Adams, the indispensable work is C. Bradley Thompson, *John Adams and the Spirit of Liberty* (Lawrence: University Press of Kansas, 1998).

"as Doctor Franklin alone could have been thought of as a competitor." Max Farrand, ed., *The Records of the Federal Convention of 1787* (3 vols., New Haven: Yale University Press, 1911), 1:4 (May 25). On Franklin's role in the Convention, *see* Wood, *Americanization of Benjamin Franklin,* 215–21.

Through it all, James Madison kept detailed notes on whatever was said. Madison was reluctant to publish his notes during his lifetime. Madison died in 1836. His notes were first published in Henry D. Gilpin, ed., *The Papers of James Madison* (3 vols., Washington, DC: Langtree and O'Sullivan, 1840). The notes and Madison's correspondence related to the Constitution make up most of these volumes. The standard scholarly edition of Madison's notes is found in Farrand, ed., *Records of the Federal Convention of 1787.*

Madison revised and elaborated his notes off and on for years after the Convention. While much of their contents remained as he wrote them in the summer of 1787, the notes are not a simple contemporary account of the proceedings. They were recorded by the Convention's most active member who, even if he aimed at complete objectivity in his record, was bound to record at least some of the debates through the lens of his own concerns, though imputing political bias to Madison's notes will not withstand close scrutiny.

The most recent effort to undermine the credibility of the notes is *Madison's Hand: Revising the Constitutional Convention* (Cambridge, MA: Harvard University Press, 2017) by Mary Sarah Bilder, a Boston University law professor. Like many issues relating to the shaping of the Constitution and its meaning for contemporaries, the reliability of the notes has modern relevance. Undermining the objectivity of the notes undermines most constitutional arguments that rely on the notes as a source for understanding the original intent of the authors of the Constitution. The purpose of those who seek to discredit Madison—going so far as to charge him with willful distortion and conscious misrepresentation of what occurred in the Convention—is to persuade scholars and judges that originalist interpretations of the Constitution that rest in whole or part on the notes are unreliable. That those who attack Madison's integrity also oppose originalist jurisprudence is not a coincidence. As Madison pointed out in Federalist No. 49, "even the most rational method of constitutional interpretation will not find it a superfluous advantage to have the prejudices of the community on its side."

All narrative histories of the Federal Convention, of which there are now several, are based on Farrand's *Records of the Federal Convention.* I read my way through a paperback set of Farrand before I read the narrative histories, which made the experience of reading them like watching several movies in succession, all based on a good book I had already read. The one I recommend is Carol Berkin, *A Brilliant Solution: Inventing the American Constitution* (New York: HarperCollins, 2003). Her prose moves, which is not easy when the focus of the story is a long business meeting conducted in secret. She is mindful of the present in which her readers live, but she writes about the convention without looking ahead to what the federal government would become. The men she writes about are neither demigods nor villains. She is mindful of the sense of crisis that brought them together and does not dismiss their anxieties as imagined or founded in selfishness. And best of all, she writes to teach people who read to learn, not to confirm their preconceptions or pick a fight.

Madison and Wilson

"charms, captivates, and leads away the senses . . ."
William Pierce, Character Sketches of Delegates to the Federal
Convention, in Farrand, ed., *Records of the Federal Convention*,
3:92. Pierce's brief, insightful comments on his fellow delegates are not dated but seem to have been composed during or
shortly after his service in the convention.

**The most useful of Madison's Pennsylvania allies
proved to be James Wilson.** James Wilson did not leave
behind a substantial body of correspondence and other papers,
so the scholarly literature on him will never be as rich as it is
on Madison, Jefferson, and other intellectually sophisticated
Revolutionaries. Page Smith, *James Wilson, Founding Father,
1742–1798* (Chapel Hill: University of North Carolina Press,
1956) is the first scholarly biography. It was followed by
Geoffrey Seed, *James Wilson: Scottish Intellectual and American
Statesman* (Milwood, NY: KTO Press, 1978), the first serious
effort to establish Wilson as an important political and constitutional thinker—more narrative than analytical. More recent,
but essentially descriptive, is Mark David Hall, *The Political
and Legal Philosophy of James Wilson, 1742–1798* (Columbia:
University of Missouri Press, 1997). Michael H. Taylor, *James
Wilson: Anxious Founder* (Lanham, MD: Lexington Books,
2021) adds some biographical detail and addresses Wilson's
memory. Robert Green McCloskey, ed., *The Works of James
Wilson* (2 vols., Cambridge, MA: Harvard University Press,
1967) is the first modern edition—extremely useful but far
from comprehensive—of Wilson's writings. It was followed
by Kermit Hall and Mark David Hall, eds., *Collected Works
of James Wilson* (2 vols., Indianapolis: Liberty Fund, 2007),
which is actually a somewhat updated version of Bird Wilson,
The Works of the Honourable James Wilson (3 vols., Philadelphia: Printed for Bronson and Chauncey, 1804), the collection
compiled by Wilson's son, rather than a modern documentary
edition. The Hall and Hall edition adds little to what is available. An insightful treatment of Wilson's thought—perhaps
the first whose author did not feel the need to introduce Wilson to readers—is John Fabian Witt, "The Pyramid and the
Machine: Founding Visions in the Life of James Wilson," in
Witt's *Patriots and Cosmopolitans: Hidden Histories of American Law* (Cambridge, MA: Harvard University Press, 2007),
15–82. He interprets Wilson as an advocate for a unified
nation-state based on popular sovereignty rather than a pluralist republic of balanced, competing interests.

**"the influence which the Government we are to form
. . ."** Farrand, ed., *Records of the Federal Convention*, 1:405–
406 (June 2).

"We the People"

"as having done all that patriots could do . . ." Farrand, ed., *Records of the Federal Convention*, 1:18–19 (May 29).

**"the design of the States in forming this convention
. . ."** Farrand, ed., *Records of the Federal Convention*, 1:30,
33–35 (May 30).

The decennial census became the foundation of American democratic government. On the history of the U.S.
census, *see* Margo J. Anderson, *The American Census: A Social
History* (2nd ed., New Haven: Yale University Press, 2015).
Efforts to enumerate populations are as old as civilization,

but until modern times they were nearly all mandated by
monarchs as a tool to extract revenue or military service from
their subjects. A systematic census of Iceland commissioned by
the king of Denmark conducted in 1702–1703 enumerated
50,358 people with remarkable accuracy and was the first census in the modern sense of the term.

"for drawing the most numerous branch of the Legislature . . ." Farrand, ed., *Records of the Federal Convention*,
1:49 (May 31).

"the most exact transcript of the whole Society." Farrand, ed., *Records of the Federal Convention*, 1:132 (June 6).

"should sympathize with their constituents . . ." Farrand, ed., *Records of the Federal Convention*, 1:133–134 (June
6).

"enlarge the sphere . . ." Farrand, ed., *Records of the Federal Convention*, 1:135–136 (June 6). Madison elaborated on
this argument in Federalist No. 10.

"The people should have as little to do as may be . . ."
Farrand, ed., *Records of the Federal Convention*, 1:48 (May 31).

**"The evils we experience flow from the excess of
democracy"** Farrand, ed., *Records of the Federal Convention*,
1:48 (May 31).

"thought it wrong to increase the weight . . ." Farrand,
ed., *Records of the Federal Convention*, 49 (May 31).

"If we depart from the principle of representation . . ."
Farrand, ed., *Records of the Federal Convention*, 1:183 (June 9).
Wilson first argued for democratic election of senators on May
31; ibid., 1:52.

**"A federal government of energy is the only means
. . ."** [caption] Letters of a Landholder I, *Connecticut Courant*,
November 5, 1787. For an easily accessible modern edition,
see John P. Kaminski and Richard Leffler, eds., *Federalists and
Antifederalists: The Debate over the Ratification of the Constitution* (Madison, WI: Madison House, 1998), 203–5.

**The New Jersey Plan was consistent with the charge to
propose revisions . . .** For the New Jersey Plan, *see* Farrand,
ed., *Records of the Federal Convention*, 1:249–256 (June 16).

The New Jersey Plan . . . provided Alexander Hamilton with an opportunity . . . Madison's record of the long
speech in which Alexander Hamilton presented his astonishingly aristocratic plan is in Farrand, ed., *Records of the Federal
Convention*, 1:282–293 (June 18).

**"Mr. Wilson ranks among the foremost in legal and
political knowledge . . ."** Pierce, Character Sketches of Delegates to the Federal Convention, in Farrand, ed., *Records of the
Federal Convention*, 3:91–92; Wilson spoke in the convention
168 times, second only to Gouverneur Morris, who spoke 173
times. Wilson generally spoke at greater length than Morris,
and thus was the most active speaker in the convention.

**"a Gentleman of great modesty, with a remarkable
sweet temper . . ."** Pierce, Character Sketches of Delegates to
the Federal Convention, in Farrand, ed., *Records of the Federal
Convention*, 3:94–95.

"the power is given to the few to save them . . ." Farrand, ed., *Records of the Federal Convention*, 1:484 (June 30).
For Franklin's homely analogy in support of the Connecticut
Compromise about a cabinetmaker taking a little from each of
two boards to make them fit, *see* ibid., 1:488–489 (June 30).

"a fundamental and perpetual error" Farrand, ed.,
Records of the Federal Convention, 2:10 (July 14).

"**If no Accommodation takes place . . .**" Farrand, ed., *Records of the Federal Convention,* 2:7 (July 14).

The Presidency

"**general authority to execute the National laws . . .**" For the text of the Virginia Plan and the editors' comments on the text, *see* The Virginia Plan, May 29, 1787, Rutland et al., eds., *Papers of James Madison,* 10:12–18.

"**a considerable pause**" Farrand, ed., *Records of the Federal Convention,* 1:65 (June 1).

"**like Cincinnatus . . . returned to his farm . . .**" [caption] Pierce, Character Sketches of Delegates to the Federal Convention, in Farrand, ed., *Records of the Federal Convention,* 3:94.

"**the only powers he conceived strictly Executive . . .**" Farrand, ed., *Records of the Federal Convention,* 1:65–55 (June 1).

"**the very essence of tyranny.**" Farrand, ed., *Records of the Federal Convention,* 1:68 (June 1).

"**remained unshaken**" Farrand, ed., *Records of the Federal Convention,* 2:106 (July 24).

"**many of the members cast their eyes towards General Washington . . .**" Pierce Butler to Weedon Butler, May 5, 1788, in Farrand, ed., *Records of the Federal Convention,* 3:301–4. Butler did not think it wise to depend on Washington's successors being so dependable, and completed this thought by suggesting that Washington, "by his Patriotism and Virtue, Contributed largely to the Emancipation of his Country, may be the Innocent means of its being, when He is lay'd low, oppress'd."

"The mere distinction of colour"

"**The convention faced the challenge of devising a national government that would unite states where slavery was sanctioned by law and those where legislators had either abolished slavery or set it on the path to extinction.**" For a general treatment of the antislavery tenor of the Federal Convention, *see* Sean Wilentz, *No Property in Man: Slavery and Antislavery at the Nation's Founding* (Cambridge, MA: Harvard University Press, 2018).

"**Slavery was a global injustice.**" For an overview of the history of slavery in the Americas and its eventual overthrow, *see* Davis, *Inhuman Bondage.*

"**We have seen the mere distinction of colour . . .**" Farrand, ed., *Records of the Federal Convention,* 1:135 (June 6).

"**I never mean . . . to possess another slave by purchase . . .**" George Washington to John Francis Mercer, September 9, 1786, in Abbot, ed., *Papers of George Washington,* 4:243–44.

"**There is not a man living who wishes . . .**" George Washington to Robert Morris, April 12, 1786, in Abbot, ed., *Papers of George Washington,* Confederation Series, 4:15–17.

"**that the abolition of slavery seemed to be going on . . .**" Farrand, ed., *Records of the Federal Convention,* 2:369–70 (August 22).

"**slaves multiply so fast in Virginia and Maryland . . .**" Farrand, ed., *Records of the Federal Convention,* 2:370–71 (August 22).

"**inconsistent with the principles of the revolution . . .**" Farrand, ed., *Records of the Federal Convention,* 2:364 (August 21).

"**Every master of slaves is born a petty tyrant . . .**" Farrand, ed., *Records of the Federal Convention,* 2:370 (August 22).

"**if slavery be wrong, it is justified . . .**" Farrand, ed., *Records of the Federal Convention,* 2:371 (August 22).

The Three-Fifths Compromise

"**Enslaved people constituted such a large part of the population in the states dependent on them for forced labor . . .**" On origins of the three-fifths compromise and the interpretation of the compromise as a defeat for slaveholders, *see* Don Fehrenbacher, *The Slaveholding Republic: An Account of the United States Government's Relations to Slavery* (New York: Oxford University Press, 2001), 24–32.

"**who were property in the South. . .**" Farrand, ed., *Records of the Federal Convention,* 1:201 (June 11).

"**white and other free Citizens . . .**" Farrand, ed., *Records of the Federal Convention,* 1:193 (June 11).

"**blacks ought to stand on an equality with whites**" Farrand, ed., *Records of the Federal Convention,* 1:542 (July 6).

"**the inhabitant of Georgia and South Carolina . . .**" Farrand, ed., *Records of the Federal Convention,* 2:211–23 (August 12).

"**It is a downright disability laid upon the slaveholding States . . .**" Frederick Douglass, "The Constitution of the United States: Is It Pro-Slavery or Anti-Slavery?" Speech to the Glasgow, Scotland, Anti-Slavery Society, March 26, 1860, in Philip S. Foner, ed., *Frederick Douglass: Select Speeches and Writings,* abridged and adapted by Yuval Taylor (Chicago: Lawrence Hill Books, 1999), 379–89. The edition cited is a convenient one-volume selection based on Philip S. Foner's five-volume *The Life and Writings of Frederick Douglass* (4 vols., New York: International Publishers, 1950–1955, with a supplementary volume published in 1975).

"**omitting the WORD will be regarded as an Endeavour to conceal . . .**" Notes for a Speech by John Dickinson (II), in James H. Hutson, ed., *Supplement to Max Farrand's The Records of the Federal Convention of 1787* (New Haven: Yale University Press, 1987), 158–59 (July 9).

"**ought to be careful not to give any sanction to it.**" Farrand, ed., *Records of the Federal Convention,* 2:372 (August 22).

"**the idea that there could be property in men.**" Farrand, ed., *Records of the Federal Convention,* 2:417 (August 25).

"**there shall be neither slavery nor involuntary servitude in the said territory . . .**" Tansill, comp., *Documents Illustrative of the Formation of the Union of the American States,* 47–54.

"**agreement with hell**" Garrison used this phrase in a resolution he introduced before the Massachusetts Antislavery Society in 1843: "That the compact which exists between the North and South is 'a covenant with death, and an agreement with hell'—involving both parties in atrocious criminality; and should be immediately annulled." *See* Walter M. Merrill, *Against Wind and Tide: A Biography of Wm. Lloyd Garrison* (Cambridge, MA: Harvard University Press, 1963), and John L. Thomas, *The Liberator: William Lloyd Garrison—a Biography* (Boston: Little, Brown, 1963). The phrase is frequently rendered, improperly, as "pact with hell" though I can find no evidence that Garrison ever said or wrote it that way. In a book published by Oxford University Press, an academic author recently wrote that Garrison condemned the Constitution as a "covenant with death and a pact with hell," using quotation marks but not citing a source.

"**Does the United States Constitution guarantee . . .**" Douglass, "The Constitution of the United States: Is It Pro-Slavery or Anti-Slavery?," 379–89.

"A republic if you can keep it"

"**I am fully persuaded it is the best that can be obtained . . .**" George Washington to Henry Knox, August 19, 1787, in Abbot, ed., *Papers of George Washington*, Confederation Series, 5:297.

"**will neither effectually answer its national object . . .**" James Madison to Thomas Jefferson, September 6, 1787, in Rutland et al., eds., *Papers of James Madison*, 10:163–65.

"**would end in Tyranny. . .**" Farrand, ed., *Records of the Federal Convention*, 2:563–64 (September 10) and 631 (September 15).

"**would give great quiet to the people . . .**" Farrand, ed., *Records of the Federal Convention*, 2:587–88 (September 12) and 632–633 (September 15). Mason wrote his objections on a copy of the version of the Constitution distribute to delegates on September 12; for those objections, *see* ibid., 2:637–40.

The delegates' final disagreements were put to rest . . . On Jacob Shallus, see Arthur Plotnik, *The Man Behind the Quill: Jacob Shallus, Calligrapher of the United States Constitution* (Washington, DC: National Archives and Records Administration, 1987); *see also* Arthur Plotnik, "The Search for Jacob Shallus," *Pennsylvania Heritage* 13 (Fall 1987): 24–31.

"**very scanty**" and "**the men almost naked**" Statement of Col. John Philip De Haas, presumably written from Ticonderoga, ca. October 20, 1776, in Thomas Lynch Montgomery, ed., *Pennsylvania Archives*, 5th ser. (Harrisburg: Harrisburg Publishing Company, 1906), 2:64–65.

"**I confess that there are several parts of this constitution . . .**" Farrand, ed., *Records of the Federal Convention*, 2:641–43 (September 17).

"**if it was not too late . . .**" Farrand, ed., *Records of the Federal Convention*, 2:643–44 (September 17).

"**retired to meditate on the momentous work which had been executed.**" Donald Jackson and Dorothy Twohig, eds., *The Diaries of George Washington* (6 vols., Charlottesville: University of Virginia Press, 1976–1979), 5:185 (September 17, 1787).

"**a power which will pervade the whole Union.**" George Washington to John Jay, August 15, 1786, in Abbot, ed., *Papers of George Washington*, Confederation Series, 4:212–13.

"**forget their local prejudices and policies**" George Washington, Circular to the States, June 8, 1783, in Fitzpatrick, ed., *Writings of Washington*, 26:483–96.

"**animate and give a brilliancy to the whole Conversation . . .**" [caption] Ann Willing Francis to Mary Willing Byrd, March 19, 1808, in Everard Kidder Meade, "The Papers of Richard Evelyn Byrd, I, of Frederick County, Virginia," *Virginia Magazine of History and Biography* 54 (April 1946): 106–18.

"**Well Doctor what have we got . . .**" [caption] Diary of James McHenry, James McHenry Papers, Library of Congress.

The full text of the entry reads: "A lady asked Dr. Franklin Well Doctor what have we got a republic or a monarchy. A republic replied the Doctor if you can keep it." A footnote marked with a plus sign reads: "The lady here aluded to was Mrs. Powel of Philadelphia" (September 18, 1787). This anecdote appears in many histories of the Federal Convention, sometimes described as having occurred outside the State House on September 17. In many cases the woman is not identified. Some authors refer to the exchange as apocryphal, but there is no reason to doubt its authenticity. Mrs. Powel was the city's most well-known hostess and the exchange is most likely to have taken place in her home, possibly within McHenry's hearing.

"**I have no recollection of any such conversations . . .**" [caption] Elizabeth Willing Powel to Martha Hare, April 25, 1814, Powel Family Papers, Historical Society of Pennsylvania.

Epilogue: The People's Debate
Opening

George Mason was injured when his carriage overturned . . . *See* George Mason to George Washington, October 7, 1787, in Rutland, ed., *Papers of George Mason*, 3:1001–4. On October 28, 1787, Daniel Carroll wrote to James Madison: "Col. Mason had not sett off for the Assembly when I heard last: I overtook him & the Majr. [James McHenry] on the road: By the time they had reachd within 9 Miles of Baltimore, they had exhausted all the stories of their youth &ca. and had enterd into a discusn. of the rights to the Western World. You know they are champions on opposite sides of this question. The Majr. having pushd the Col. hard on the Charters of Virginia the latter had just wax'd warm, when his Char[i]oteer put an end to the dispute, by jumbling their Honors together by an oversett. I came up soon after. They were both hurt—the Col. most so—he lost blood at Baltimore, & is well." Carroll to Madison, October 27, 1787, in Rutland et al., eds., *Papers of James Madison*, 10:226–27. Carroll, a Marylander, opposed the claims of the western land companies in which Mason and other Virginians had invested.

This was how politics had been conducted on a continental scale a decade earlier. The transformation of public life described by Wood, *Radicalism of the American Revolution* included a revolutionary shift in the way political information and ideas circulated, from what he calls "the personal structure of eighteenth-century politics" (p. 87), in which political business was largely confined to personal letters and pamphlets printed in small numbers and circulated like letters (John Adams' *Thoughts on Government* was disseminated in this way), to one in which a vastly increased number of newspapers, pamphlets, and broadsides were employed to win popular support.

The battle over the ratification of the Federal Constitution . . . For a general review of the ratification of the Constitution, *see* Robert A. Rutland, *The Ordeal of the Constitution: The Antifederalists and the Ratification Struggle of 1787–1788* (Norman: University of Oklahoma Press, 1965). More recent historians have benefited from an extraordinary scholarly work *The Documentary History of the Ratification of the Constitution*, launched at the University of Wisconsin by Merrill Jensen and carried on by John P. Kaminski and a team of documentary editors including Gaspare J. Saladino, Richard Leffler, Charles

H. Schoenleber, and Margaret A. Hogan. The project has collected copies of over sixty thousand documents, including convention and legislative records, private papers, newspaper pieces, broadsides, and pamphlets from well over one thousand libraries. The work of the project is vital to historians and used by judges, lawyers, and legislators in shaping law and public policy. The project published thirty-four volumes between 1976 and 2020, with eight more expected in the coming years. Among the works that makes rich use of *The Documentary History of the Ratification of the Constitution* is Pauline Maier, *Ratification: The People Debate the Constitution* (New York: Simon & Schuster, 2011), the best book on ratification to date. Kaminski and Richard Leffler, eds., *Federalists and Antifederalists* is a useful one-volume collection of documents drawn from those published by the project. *See also* Robert Allison and Bernard Bailyn, *The Essential Debate on the Constitution: Federal and Antifederalist Speeches and Writings* (New York: Penguin Random House, 2018).

. . . a flood of newspapers and pamphlets that was transforming the way people exchanged ideas and learned about public ideas. *See* Joseph M. Adelman, *Revolutionary Networks: The Business and Politics of Printing the News, 1763–1789* (Baltimore: Johns Hopkins University Press, 2019). Newspaper circulation grew during and after the Revolutionary War despite economic dislocation and shortages of paper, ink, type, and other supplies. On circulation, William A. Dill, "Growth of Newspapers in the United States," M.A. thesis, University of Oregon, 1908, esp. pp. 10–33, offers a pioneering account of the growth of newspapers in number, circulation, and numbers issued. Some of his data has been qualified by later specialized studies, but he isolated the basic problems in counting newspapers and calculating their circulation and volume and defined the basic patterns in a way that still holds much value. On the changing cost of printing equipment, paper, and other printers' supplies, *see* John Bidwell, "Printers' Supplies and Capitalization," in Hugh Amory and David D. Hall, eds., *The Colonial Book in the Atlantic World* (New York: Cambridge University Press, 2000), 163–83. On the paper shortage, *see* Roger Mellen, "The Press, Paper Shortages, and Revolution in Early America," *Media History* 21 (2015): 23–41.

The most enduring work in support of ratification . . . signed "Publius" . . . The essays were first published in three New York newspapers—the *Independent Journal,* the *New-York Packet,* and the *Daily Advertiser*—and subsequently reprinted elsewhere. They were printed and bound together as [Alexander Hamilton, James Madison, and John Jay], *The Federalist: A Collection of Essays, Written in Favour of the New Constitution, as agreed upon by the Federal Convention, September 17, 1787* (2 vols., New York: Printed and Sold by John and Andrew M'Lean, 1788). Other editions quickly followed. The standard scholarly edition is Jacob Cooke, ed. *The Federalist* (Middletown, CT: Wesleyan University Press, 1961). Cooke's introduction and the editorial notes and essays in John P. Kaminski, Gaspare J. Saladino, Richard Leffler, Charles H. Schoenleber, and Margaret A. Hogan, eds., *The Documentary History of the Ratification of the Constitution,* vol. 13: Commentaries on the Constitution [one of six volumes of commentaries, vols. 13–18] (Madison: State Historical Society of Wisconsin, 2009), document the history and importance of

The Federalist. The practice of calling the essays "The Federalist Papers" developed in the twentieth century.

"a little Moderation and Temper, in the latter End of the Convention." George Mason to George Washington, October 7, 1787, in Abbot, *Papers of George Washington,* Confederation Series, 5:355–56. Lear described how he sent Mason's objections to the newspaper and then followed it up with his refutation of them in a letter to John Langdon of December 3, 1787; *see* note 3 to Mason's letter to Washington of October 7, 1787. Mason's opposition to the Federal Constitution caused a breach in the relationship between Washington and Mason, who lived only a few miles apart and had known one another for many years. *See* Peter R. Henriques, "An Uneven Friendship: The Relationship between George Washington and George Mason," *Virginia Magazine of History and Biography* 97, no. 2 (April 1989): 185–204. To Professor Henrique's argument I make a friendly addition. In the first months of his presidency, Washington learned that Mason was critical of Washington's formal levees and that guests at Gunston Hall had mocked Vice President Adams. These attacks on the new government went beyond disagreements about policy to the character of Washington and the men around him, which Washington was not inclined to forgive. Washington made peace with many former opponents of the Constitution, including Patrick Henry. Mason's affront was personal. *See* Jack D. Warren, "In the Shadow of Washington: John Adams as Vice President," in Richard A. Ryerson, ed., *John Adams and the Founding of the Republic* (Boston: Northeastern University Press, 2001), 117–41.

"it is not known, even to the General, by whom it is done." Tobias Lear to John Langdon, December 3, 1787, in John P. Kaminski, Gaspare J. Saladino, and Richard Leffler, eds., *The Documentary History of the Ratification of the Constitution,* vol. 8: Ratification of the Constitution by the States: Virginia [the first of three volumes on ratification in Virginia] (Madison: State Historical Society of Wisconsin, 1988), 196–98. Lear wrote: "I now, for once, feel proud of being a native of that part of America which discovers the wisdom of its inhabitants & a just idea of its true interest by receiving the proposed national constitution in so favourable a manner. I think Colo. Mason must, by this time, wish that he had not handed forth his objections at so early a period, or at least that he had considered the matter a little more deliberately—he gave them in manuscript to persons in all parts of the country where he supposed they would make an impression, but avoided publishing them. I waited for a long time in expectation that they would appear in the publick papers, but finding they did not, I conveyed a copy of them & am now answering the rest, but as it is under an assumed signature, it is not known, even to the General, by whom it is done. I do not flatter myself that I am able to cope with a man of Colo. Mason's abilities, on a subject which has been the chief business & study of his life, but my situation here gives me so good an opportunity of gaining information in all matters of publick & governmental concern, that, joined to the knowledge which I have acquired from reading will, I think enable me to accomplish the task which I have undertaken."

"The people, were in fact, the fountain of all power . . ." Farrand, ed., *Records of the Federal Convention,* 2:476 (August 31).

The provision of the Federal Constitution calling for ratification by conventions in each state employed this strategy on a continental scale. On the development of ratifying conventions as a means to establish the superiority of constitutions to statutory law, *see* Wood, *Creation of the American Republic.*

Federalists and Antifederalists

The Antifederalists were unified by little more than opposition to unconditional ratification. On the variety of Antifederalist thought, *see* especially Saul Cornell, *The Other Founders: Anti-Federalism and the Dissenting Tradition in America, 1788–1828* (Chapel Hill: University of North Carolina Press, 1999). Cornell argues that distrust of national government and other Antifederalist principles endured in the Jeffersonian Republican party of the early nineteenth century. *The Other Founders* is a useful antidote to the work of political theorists who tend to interpret Antifederalism as a coherent set of ideas based on philosophical premises rather than the political, economic, and social contexts in which the debate over the Constitution unfolded. *See,* e.g., Herbert J. Storing, *What the Anti-Federalists Were For: The Political Thought of the Opponents of the Constitution* (Chicago: University of Chicago Press, 1981). This short monograph was published as the first volume to Herbert J. Storing, ed., *The Complete Anti-Federalist* (7 vols., Chicago: University of Chicago Press, 1981). *See also* Cecelia M. Kenyon, "Men of Little Faith: The Anti-Federalists on the Nature of Representative Government," *William and Mary Quarterly,* 3rd ser., vol. 12 (January 1955): 3–43.

"aspiring despots" were **"prostituting the name of a Washington . . ."** "Centinel" [Samuel Bryan], Number IV, in *Observations on the proposed Constitution for the United States of America, clearly shewing it to be a complete system of aristocracy and tyranny, and destructive of the rights and liberties of the people* (New York, 1788), 82–89.

"We contended with Great Britain . . ." Amos Singletary, Massachusetts Ratifying Convention, January 25, 1788, in John P. Kaminski et al., eds., *The Documentary History of the Ratification of the Constitution,* vol. 6: Ratification of the Constitution by the States: Massachusetts [one of four vols. on ratification in Massachusetts, vols. 4–7] (Madison: State Historical Society of Wisconsin, 2000), 1345–46.

"I am a plain man and get my living by the plough" Jonathan Smith, Massachusetts Ratifying Convention, January 25, 1788, in Kaminski et al., eds., *Documentary History of the Ratification of the Constitution,* 6:1346–47. Citizens could read the speeches of Amos Singletary and Jonathan Smith within a short time of the convention in *Debates, Resolution and other Proceedings of the Convention of the Commonwealth of Massa-* *chusetts, Convened at Boston, on the 9th of January 1788, and continued until the 7th of February following, for the purpose of assenting to and ratifying the Constitution recommended by the Grand Federal Convention. Together with The Yeas and Nays on the decision of the Grand Question. To which the Federal Constitution is prefixed* (Boston: Printed and Sold Adams and Nourse, and Benjamin Russell, and Edmund Freeman, 1788), 130–31 (Singletary, January 24), 131–32 (Singletary, January 25), 132–34 (Smith, January 25).

"the *disunited* states of America . . ." [caption] *Massachusetts Gazette,* December 7, 1787.

"A leap in the dark"

"Some gentlemen say, don't be in a hurry . . ." Jonathan Smith, Massachusetts Ratifying Convention, January 25, 1788, in Kaminski et al., eds., *Documentary History of the Ratification of the Constitution,* 6:1346–47.

"a temporary Insanity" Richard Henry Lee to William Shippen, Jr., October 2, 1787, in Ballagh, ed., *Letters of Richard Henry Lee,* 2:440–44.

"certainly the most rash and violent proceeding in the world . . ." Richard Henry Lee to George Mason, October 1, 1787, in Ballagh, ed., *Letters of Richard Henry Lee,* 2:438–40.

Each of the men who voted to ratify the Constitution . . . Modern legal scholars John O. McGinnis and Michael Rappaport claim that "the people decided whether to ratify the Constitution based on an explanation of its meaning by those with legal knowledge." John O. McGinnis and Michael Rappaport, "Original Methods Originalism: A New Theory of Interpretation and the Case against Construction," *Northwestern University Law Review* 193 (2009): 771. This allegedly new theory is simply a strategy to sidestep the rich documentation on the extraordinary variety of perspectives that led the members of the ratifying conventions to vote for ratification and impose the tired position that the meaning of the Federal Constitution can be deduced from the contemporary writings of Alexander Hamilton, James Madison, and John Jay, the collaborative authors of *The Federalist,* along with James Wilson and a few others. It cannot. The meaning of the Federal Constitution can only be deduced from the ideas of the hundreds of ordinary Americans who voted to ratify it, just as the meaning of the American Revolution can only be deduced from the ideas and actions of the many thousands of people who secured our independence, established our republic, created our national identity, and committed their new nation to ideals of liberty, equality, natural and civil rights, and responsible citizenship. The outcome of the Revolution was contingent on the choices they made. The future of the republic they founded is contingent on the choices we make.

Index

Americans are generally identified in this index by the state with which they were most closely associated. A few, like Isaac Shelby, who moved between Virginia, North Carolina, Kentucky, and Tennessee, defy this kind of categorization and are described simply as "Frontier" figures. German mercenaries are referred to as Hessians regardless of their origin. Departing from conventional practice, this index groups forts under that term, rather than alphabetizing them by given names. Thus Fort Ticonderoga will be found under that phrase rather than under "Ticonderoga, Fort." References to images are in **bold**.